Essentials of Marketing Management

The overall success of an organization is dependent on how marketing is able to inform strategy and maintain an operational focus on market needs.

With an array of examples and case studies from around the world, Lancaster and Massingham offer an alternative to the traditional American focused teaching materials currently available. Providing a comprehensive overview of the principles and practice of marketing management, topics covered include:

- consumer and organizational buyer behaviour
- product and innovation strategies
- direct marketing
- e-marketing
- a companion website provides additional material for lecturers and students alike: www. routledge.com/textbooks/9780415553476.

Designed and written for business and management studies undergraduates, postgraduates and professional marketing management candidates, *Essentials of Marketing Management* builds on successful earlier editions to provide a solid foundation to understanding this core topic. End-of-chapter cases and an extensive companion website containing longer strategic cases and solutions provide additional support to students, making this an essential companion.

Geoff Lancaster is Dean of Academic Studies at London School of Commerce, UK. He is also Chairman of the Durham Associates Group Ltd.

Lester Massingham is Chairman of CMC Group, a management development and consulting company with businesses in South East Asia, the Middle East and Europe.

Essentials of Marketing Management

Geoff Lancaster and
Lester Massingham

Routledge
Taylor & Francis Group

LONDON AND NEW YORK

First published 2011
by Routledge
2 Park Square, Milton Park, Abingdon, Oxon OX14 4RN

Simultaneously published in the USA and Canada
by Routledge
270 Madison Ave, New York, NY 10016

Routledge is an imprint of the Taylor & Francis Group, an Informa business

© 2011 Geoff Lancaster and Lester Massingham

Typeset in Berling and Futura by
Florence Production Ltd, Stoodleigh, Devon
Printed and bound in India by
Replika Press Pvt, Ltd

British Library Cataloguing in Publication Data
A catalogue record for this book is available from the British Library

Library of Congress Cataloguing in Publication Data
Lancaster, Geoffrey, 1938–.
   Essentials of marketing management/Geoff Lancaster and
   Lester Massingham.
      p. cm.
   Includes bibliographical references and index.
   1. Marketing – Management.   I. Massingham, Lester.   II. Title.
   HF5415.13.L335 2010
   658.8 – dc22   2010002512

ISBN: 978–0–415–55346–9 (hbk)
ISBN: 978–0–415–55347–6 (pbk)
ISBN: 978–0–203–84720–6 (ebk)

Contents

5 Pricing strategies 159

6 Channels of distribution and logistics 190

7 Communications strategy   234

8 Sales management   272

Case studies

Boxes

Figures

Tables

Preface

This textbook covers both the fundamental and strategic elements of marketing. No prior knowledge of the subject is assumed. It is an easy to assimilate text, written in an intelligent, yet comprehensible manner. It was written for those who are studying marketing, either as part of a broader business management type curriculum, or as a specialism in its own rights. Therefore, the book is aimed at diploma, degree and postgraduate candidates in business management as well as candidates on specialist marketing programmes.

It is divided into seventeen chapters and starts by introducing readers to the tenets of the marketing concept and the importance of adopting a strategic approach to the subject. The first chapter is intended to give readers a comprehensive overview of what is to follow, and to allay any apprehensions about what the subject contains.

Case studies at the end of each chapter allow readers to test their understanding of marketing in a practical manner by first tackling these cases and then referring to solutions to these cases on the accompanying website. A comprehensive section on how to handle both small tactical and longer strategic cases is included on the website. A number of more strategic cases are also included together with suggested solutions. Multiple choice tests complement the website as well as typical examinations questions. Each chapter ends with a number of key concepts which students should find useful when revising for examinations.

The text then examines business customers and end consumers, in terms of their purchasing behaviour and this is principally linked to sociological and psychological factors. Segmentation, targeting and positioning are then considered as the logical adjunct to purchasing motives, and practical suggestions are proffered as to how to conduct such an exercise in practice.

The important area of product decisions is then considered, including the three important concepts of new product development, diffusion of innovations and the product life cycle. Service products are particularly singled out for specific consideration in view of their contemporary importance. Technological forecasting and the Internet are specifically considered in the context of how they are now so critical when making product decisions.

Pricing is considered from an economic, an accounting and a marketing perspective and appropriate theories and constructs are explained and examined.

Channels of distribution and logistics are typically areas of marketing that have received scant consideration in the past, but with the development of 'Just-in-Time' or 'lean' manufacturing, delivery of precisely correct components and materials is critical to customers who work with minimal stocks and demand delivery within a precise time window, typically four hours. These implications are considered in the context of reverse marketing, the value chain and more specifically the supply chain.

The broad subject of communications is discussed from a strategic marketing planning viewpoint, and then advertising, sales promotion public relations and sponsorship are dealt with individually. Selling and sales management is also part of the communications mix and this is covered in a separate chapter that deals with recruitment, training, remuneration territory management as well as tactical aspects of the sales sequence. Developments in selling and sales management, including the notion of relationship marketing has meant that the role of salespersons has now changed, and in this context the implications for selling are examined. In fact, relationship marketing and customer care are now so important that this subject warrants a separate chapter. Pointers are given in relation to the establishment of a practical customer care programme. Issues like branding are also considered in the context of relationship marketing.

Direct marketing comprises an increasingly important part of the communications mix and this is dealt with separately. It covers issues like business and consumer direct mail, direct response advertising, mail order, database marketing, multi-level marketing. More specifically, the implications of information technology and its applications are examined in the context of direct marketing.

Information from the marketplace is gathered through marketing research. Practical aspects of marketing research techniques are considered along with strategic elements of the marketing information system including marketing intelligence and the internal accounting system and how these are utilized in the overall corporate planning process. Sales forecasting is the responsibility of marketing and this is the starting point for business planning as well as marketing planning. This important subject is dealt with in a separate chapter that looks at a variety of 'bottom-up' and 'top-down' techniques and discusses these in terms of their applicability to the particular forecasting situation.

The text is as much about strategic marketing planning as it is about basic marketing, so candidates who intend to study the subject of marketing in greater depth should find three chapters very useful as they are devoted to strategic marketing planning issues. Analysing the environment and appraising resources are what is referred to as the SWOT analysis (strengths, weaknesses, opportunities and threats) and these are covered along with environmental scanning, strategic group analysis, value chains and profiling systems. Having appraised the environment, the next step is to evaluate and control strategic marketing and here issues like the internal and external environment and 'noise' are considered. A chapter on the tools of strategic marketing planning includes the work of Porter, Arthur D. Little's industry maturity/competitive position matrix, experience curves effects in strategic planning, the Boston Consulting Group growth/share matrix, the McKinsey/General Electric business screen, the Shell directional policy matrix, profit impact on marketing strategy (PIMS analysis) and Green portfolio analysis.

Chapter 16 examines global issues in marketing including levels of involvement, cultural and social forces, methods of market entry and international marketing research and information systems.

The final chapter considers the marketing of services. Special characteristics like intangibility and non-ownership are considered in terms of inseparability, perishability and variability along with the extra '3Ps' of service marketing i.e. people, process and physical evidence. A particular growth area for the application of marketing concepts and techniques has been the area of not-for-profit organizations. The view is taken that applying marketing to not-for-profit organizations is made easier by regarding their marketing structures first, as one would regard that of any commercial enterprise.

Professor Dr. Geoff Lancaster,
Dean of Academic Studies at the London School of Commerce and
Chairman of the Durham Associates Group of companies

Professor Dr. Lester Massingham,
Chief Executive of CMC International,
Singapore

Chapter 1

Development of a strategic approach to marketing

Its culture; internal macro- and external micro-environmental issues

LEARNING OBJECTIVES

After reading this chapter you will:

- understand the meaning, importance and the evolution of the marketing concept
- appreciate the factors which have given rise to the need for a more strategic approach to marketing management
- be familiar with the steps in strategic marketing planning
- appreciate contemporary developments in understanding and applying marketing ideas and their implications for strategic marketing

INTRODUCTION

Over the past 50 years we have witnessed at first a gradual and then an increasingly rapid recognition that effective marketing is the keystone of organizational success. Having said this, for some companies this recognition came too late. For others its meaning and implications have not been adequately understood or accepted. More important is the fact that at the same time as some companies struggle to come to terms with the basic concepts and meaning of marketing (i.e. the **marketing concept**), markets (and marketing itself) are evolving and changing. With respect to the practice of marketing, the most significant of these changes is that, increasingly, marketing has become more strategic in nature. The significance and implication of this shift, along with the concepts, tools and frameworks needed to achieve such an approach, are the focus of this text.

We start by tracing the **origins**, development and meaning of marketing as this is essential to understanding the second part of the chapter; namely, factors that have given rise to the growth of **strategic marketing**.

THE ORIGIN AND DEVELOPMENT OF MARKETING

As might be expected from a function that has attracted so much research, critical comment and time and effort from those charged with the responsibility of managing it, we now have a substantial body of knowledge relating to the theory and practice of marketing.

Attempting to pinpoint the exact origins of marketing as a business function is challenging, as there is no single, universally agreed **definition**. The confusion over its exact meaning is demonstrated in a passage written by American marketing scholars.

> It has been described as a business activity; as a group of related business activities; as a trade phenomenon; as a frame of mind; as a co-ordinating integrative function in policy making; as a sense of business purpose; as an economic process; as a structure of institutions; as the process of exchanging or transferring ownership of products; as a process of concentration equalization and dispersion; as the creation of time, place and possession utilities; as a process of demand-supply adjustment; and many other things.[1]

Marketing tends to mean whatever the user wants it to mean and has, over the years, been the subject of numerous attempts at definition, including the very succinct:

The function of marketing is the establishment of contact.[2]

Marketing is the delivery of a standard of living to society.[3]

. . . selling goods that don't come back to the people who do (sell them).[4]

A widely accepted definition is the one used by the UK Chartered Institute of Marketing (CIM): 'Marketing is the management process, responsible for identifying, anticipating and satisfying customer requirements profitably.' The American Marketing Association's (AMA) latest definition of marketing was produced in January 2008: 'Marketing is the activity, set of institutions, and processes for creating, communicating, delivering, and exchanging offerings that have value for customers, clients, partners and society at large.' It is our opinion that the AMA definition is more accurate that that of the CIM, as the CIM definition infers satisfying customer requirements profitably: in fact public services like the police and fire service are not-for-profit and in a modern context they undoubtedly apply marketing principles as we discuss in Chapter 17.

This plethora of meanings makes it difficult to say where and when marketing first began. In its most basic form, i.e. people exchanging goods or services in a reciprocal manner, it has existed for centuries. The rudiments of contemporary marketing were discussed as far back as the eighteenth and nineteenth centuries by theorists such as Adam Smith,[5] the father of modern economics, who wrote: 'Consumption is the sole end and purpose of all production and the interests of the producer ought to be attended to only so far as it may be necessary for promoting that of the consumer.' This statement is close to the basis of the modern marketing concept, which postulates that needs and wants of consumers should be a manufacturer's main concern and they should only produce what can be sold. Marketing can be said to have developed in an evolutionary rather than revolutionary manner, alongside, and keeping pace with, our economy.

When economies were agrarian, people were mostly self-sufficient. As time passed, it became evident that some people excelled at certain activities and the concept of the *division of labour* began to emerge. Individuals concentrated on products they were best at producing which inevitably resulted in them making more than they needed for themselves and their families. This laid the foundation for trade. Exchange then began to develop on a simple basis; usually one-to-one trading of products. Trade is at the very heart of marketing. Adam Smith postulated that from the division of labour stem the benefits of specialization and the need for more effective means of exchange.

The next step sees small producers making relatively large amounts of goods in anticipation of future demand. This development produces another type of business person, the 'middleman' or agent, who acts as an intermediary between producer and consumer. This go-between is of utmost importance in a commercial society, as without this the right goods cannot be sold to the right people in the right place at the right time. Torrens[6] was an influential economist of his day whose writing and opinions have only recently been rediscovered: he anticipated this philosophy by more than a century when he wrote

Activities designed to make commodities available at either times or places where they are more in demand than at times and places at which they are available at the outset creates wealth or utility just as much as activities designed to change their physical composition.

This was economic justification for the existence of marketing intermediaries. McCullough,[7] developing this argument, explained:

> Merchants, or dealers collect goods in different places in the least expensive manner, and by carrying them in large quantities at a time, they can afford to supply their respective customers at a cheaper rate than they can supply themselves. . . . They also promote the convenience of everyone, and reduce the cost of merchandising to the lowest limit.

The parties involved, i.e. manufacturers, intermediaries and buyers, gathered together geographically, and trading centres of the world evolved; indeed, such evolution is a continuous process.

As an economy becomes more advanced and sophisticated, so too does marketing. It can be said that marketing is adopted by a country's business and non-business organizations, depending upon the stage of development of its economy. It is generally accepted that modern marketing began in the USA and Stanton[8] maintains that it began with the Industrial Revolution (in Europe as well as the USA) and consequently, migration to urban centres. As the number of factory workers grew, so too did the service industries to meet their growing needs and those of their families. Marketing was a very basic business activity in the USA (and Europe) until the late 1920s, when emphasis was on the growth of manufacturing firms because demand typically far exceeded supply. Modern marketing in the USA began after the First World War when 'over-production' and 'surplus' became commonplace words. Since the late 1920s (with the exception of the Second World War and the immediate post-war period) a strong buyer's market has existed in America. There was no difficulty in producing goods; the problem lay in marketing them.

In tracing the development of marketing within the framework of business practice there are four distinct stages that can be identified:

- production orientation;
- product orientation;
- sales orientation;
- marketing orientation.

Production orientation

This is a philosophy that:

1   concentrates on increasing production;
2   controls and reduces costs;
3   makes profit through sales volume.

The era of **production orientation** occurred in the USA from the mid nineteenth century up to the 1940s and was characterized by focusing efforts on producing goods or services. Management efforts were devoted to achieving high production efficiency (mostly by mass production of standard items) thus denying the customer much choice.

The production department was the central core of the business, with other functions (such as finance, personnel and sales) being secondary. The main philosophy by which production-oriented firms operated was that customers would buy whatever goods were available if the price was reasonable. This era is best epitomized by Henry Ford's classic statement that his customers could have any colour ('Model T' Ford) they wanted as long as it was black. This mass production mentality meant producing one car and attempting to adjust everyone's desires and tastes toward wanting this car. Henry Ford saw the objective as changing consumer attitudes rather than making what the public wanted. Absurd though it may seem, at the time (1913 in the USA) Henry Ford was correct: there was a demand for cheap private transport and his cars sold well. Production orientation in business was suited to an economic climate where demand exceeded supply.

Product orientation

1   good quality products 'sell themselves';
2   companies concentrate on improving and controlling quality;
3   there is greater profit through increased sales due to 'quality products'.

With its emphasis on quality, engineering was predominant in both the USA and Western Europe through the 1950s and 1960s. In the United Kingdom, in particular, during this period, the predominant attitude amongst many manufacturing companies was that designing and engineering the 'best' products was all that mattered and 'sensible' customers would buy products that were best engineered. A popular statement was: 'Build a better mousetrap, and the world will beat a path to your door.' This attitude that underpinned **product orientation** proved for many companies and industries to be their downfall.

In the late 1950s and early 1960s the once dominant UK motor cycle industry began to lose its share of home and export markets. The challengers were Japanese companies such as Honda and Suzuki. A major reason for UK marquees losing out to these new challengers was that Japanese products were not taken seriously by UK producers. Japanese machines were considered to be inferior in terms of basic engineering and design. In fact early Japanese machines were of poorer quality and design than their British counterparts. However, partly because of this 'inferior' specification, Japanese machines were cheaper to buy and run. In addition, they were easier to maintain and came with back-up services. Japanese products also came with features such as electric, rather than kick starting, fairings for protecting the rider from weather and dirt and innovations such as panniers for carrying shopping; features that were scorned by British motor cycle designers.

Hindsight suggests that from a marketing standpoint the Japanese were right. Combinations of a lower engineering specification with its attendant decrease in costs and prices, together with customer-friendly product design and features meant that customers quickly warmed to the new machines. Within a few years the UK motor cycle was decimated. Quite simply, UK manufacturers suffered from being product oriented.

In using the example of motor cycles we are not denying the importance of good design and product engineering backed up by stringent quality assurance and control procedures. In fact, if anything, today's customers are even more interested in quality. However, a problem with a product-oriented approach is that not all customers want, or can afford, the best quality. More importantly, this orientation leads to a myopic view of business with a concentration on product engineering rather than customers' real needs and the benefits they are seeking.

Sales orientation

This philosophy suggests:

1   emphasis on stock clearance;
2   aggressive sales and promotion;
3   profit through quick sales of high volumes.

Mass production started in the USA in 1913 when Henry Ford introduced flow-line production to the Model T Ford production line and was able to reduce unit prices substantially; this car had previously been manufactured on a more expensive batch production basis from 1908. Mass production techniques emerged on a large scale in the USA at first, followed by Western Europe. In the USA, the late 1920s and 1930s saw a shortage of customers rather than of goods. In Western Europe, this phenomenon occurred after the Second World War. This fall-off in demand led to increased competition and to many firms adopting sales orientation by concentrating on advertising and personal selling.

A key issue for management was high levels of output. Here, the underlying philosophy assumed that customers were inherently reluctant to purchase and needed to be coerced into buying. However, even if consumers were willing to buy there were so many potential suppliers that firms had problems of stiff competition to overcome.

This was the situation in the USA in the 1930s and in most developed economies in the late 1950s: over-capacity accompanied by a fall in demand due to the Depression in the USA in the 1930s and in Western Europe due to Second World War shortages being fulfilled in the late 1950s. It was during these periods that many of the 'hard sell' techniques were practised in the USA in the 1930s and in Western Europe in the late 1950s, a great number of which were dishonest and unethical, and contributed to the tainted image of salespeople that still exists in the minds of many people today.

Although a small number of firms still practise **sales orientation**, the consumer is now protected by law from more dubious selling techniques, largely due to the consumer movement.

Consumers International (CI), the global federation of consumer organizations, set out its solutions to the financial fix calling for effective, affirmative, preventative consumer protection as an essential foundation for moving beyond the economic crisis. Following worldwide consultation with its membership, CI submitted its position to the UN Conference on the World Financial Crisis, 24–26 June 2009.

Joost Martens, Director General of Consumers International, said:

> While CI research has shown most consumers manage their finances responsibly, they have been unfairly blamed by governments, media and industry for creating this crisis through irresponsible borrowing, and then prolonging it through insufficient spending. It is high time the so-called experts start listening to consumers, rather than blaming them for the mess the bankers and governments have created.

Driving a Hard Bargain

Despite sophisticated uses of marketing tools and techniques some argue that many of the world's marketers of cars are still sales oriented when dealing with customers in car showrooms. In particular the approach to customers taken by the car salesperson is often based on a 'hard sell' that uses pressure to make a sale. The customer is in essence manipulated into a position where they feel they have to make the purchase. Lots of different sales techniques can be used to hard sell and pressurize the customer into a purchase. For example the salesperson can use the 'time pressure' technique '. . . This is the last one at the old price; prices go up by 5 per cent at the end of the week.' Another example is the 'play off' technique whereby the salesperson plays off one person against another. '. . . I'm sure your partner would appreciate the extra safety features on this model and the park assist system –after all you wouldn't want her to drive something that wasn't one hundred per cent safe would you sir?' Even apparently rational appeals which appear to be based on identifying and satisfying a customer's real needs and wants can be hard sell techniques masked as something else. '. . . I'm sure the change to a four door model will be invaluable when your new baby arrives'. Hard selling is still a feature of the car salesroom experience for many customers. Car salespersons are often still trained in these techniques. Furthermore car sales people are often incentivised by their companies on the basis of sales figures alone rather than more customer oriented bases such as customer satisfaction or customer loyalty.

Perhaps even worse is the fact that often the car salesperson views the sales process as a win/lose process with every unit of extra profit gained from the sale being a victory and every unit of profit lost as a failure. This confrontational attitude to negotiations with customers is that it often results in dissatisfied and ultimately lost customers. Understandably the customer who subsequently feels they have been pressurised into a purchase or who feels they were outmanoeuvred on the terms of the sale is unlikely to purchase again and will often pass on this dissatisfaction to friends and family.

Certainly there is a case for purposeful selling and the effective salesperson should know how to overcome objections and close the sale but hard selling is now recognized as ineffective and inappropriate in the contemporary business environment. Unfortunately, driving hard bargains is still prevalent in many car salesrooms.

CI argues that the financial crisis began with a failure to protect consumers from bad loans in the USA and other mortgage markets. A viable fix for the global economy must include greater regulatory oversight of a far more transparent banking industry. However, while transparency is important, more information for consumers is not enough. The system is simply too complex at present and needs regulatory intervention to remove incomprehensible financial products and services. Robin Simpson, Senior Policy Advisor at Consumers International, said:

> Consumer education is a right, but avoiding financial ruin in the current climate takes more than access to information. No doubt the clients of Bernie Madoff thought their money was in good hands, but the billions he embezzled shows we are all susceptible to the faults in the financial system. Better law, as well as better understanding, is needed.

The meltdown of the financial industry has also led to bank mergers being hurried through by competition authorities. CI is concerned that the banking monopolies emerging from this crisis pose a danger to consumer choice and protection and calls for strict monitoring and reporting requirements to be established to ensure the new financial services landscape works for the consumer. There must also be a clear distinction between retail and investment banking activities. Only then can consumer deposits be protected from the irresponsible behaviour and risky speculation of investment bankers.

CI is worried that the seizure of bank activity is denying customers access to basic bank account services and starving critical public utility developments of investment. This is of particular concern in the developing world where the flow of funds is a vital means of achieving improved consumer access to electricity, water, sanitation and financial services. CI is demanding that taxpayer bailouts come with mandatory obligations to provide basic consumer banking services and investment in major social infrastructure projects. Robin Simpson said:

> The banking sector has elbowed its way to the front of the public expenditure queue as a result of the threat of collapse, effectively holding a gun to the head of government. They cannot simply swallow taxpayer money and carry on as before; firm commitments to provide for basic consumer needs and services must accompany these bailouts.

> http://www.consumersinternational.org/
> Templates/Internal.asp?NodeID=99643
> 24 June 2009

Consumerism

The transition from sales to marketing orientation was brought about partly by the advent of consumerism, which forced companies to become more aware of the needs and wants of their customers. **Consumerism** involves efforts of the public, government and organizational bodies to protect consumers from unscrupulous business practices as epitomized by sales orientation. A disenchantment with the hard sell, together with an increasing disillusionment with some of the problems associated with growing consumption were to give rise to the emergence of the consumer movement which first began in the late 1950s in the USA when writers such as Vance Packard challenged the advertising industry, Rachel Carson criticized the business community for its pollution of the environment and Ralph Nader famously attacked General Motors, whose dubious practices shocked the public at large when they were uncovered.

The role of the US government in consumerism was first set forth in President John F. **Kennedy's** famous '**rights**' speech:[9]

> Additional legislative and administrative action is required if the federal government is to meet its responsibility to consumers in the exercise of their rights. These rights include:
>
> 1   the right to safety;
> 2   the right to be informed;
> 3   the right to choose;
> 4   the right to be heard.

To these rights can now be added:

1   The right to privacy, brought about largely as a result of advances in IT that have developed since Kennedy's speech, and the fact that organizations keep personal records like credit details on databases. Legislation now allows individuals to access information contained on such databases, so it can be challenged if necessary.
2   The right to a clean and healthy environment, brought about largely as a result of 'green' issues and the notion of 'global warming' being universally accepted by governments.

The consumer movement gained popularity more slowly in the United Kingdom than it had in America. The publication of *Which?* Magazine first brought consumerism to the attention of the British public, with a completely new way of thinking; the consumer did not necessarily have to accept whatever manufacturers produced without question. In the past 30 years or so many governments have shown an increasing concern for consumer affairs which is reflected in the number of statutes introduced to protect consumers.

It is no coincidence that at consumerism's most powerful and popular time, a growing number of companies began to adopt the marketing concept as a way of orientating their businesses.

MARKETING ORIENTATION

In the marketing-oriented company, planning and decision making centre on customer needs having due regard to competitors and distributors. It is vital to satisfy customer needs through a co-ordinated set of activities including the actions and functions of all employees of the organization, irrespective of the area of the business in which they work. In other words, a **marketing orientation** requires everyone in an organization to become customer oriented and not just people who work in marketing. An increasing awareness of this need to co-ordinate and integrate all the various functional areas of a business in delivering customer satisfaction has led to the growth of **internal marketing**. We consider the nature and importance of internal marketing later in this chapter and again in Chapter 9 when we consider **customer care** and relationship marketing.

Lancaster and Massingham[10] identify the marketing-oriented firm as follows: 'A marketing oriented firm produces goods and services that consumers want to buy rather than what the firm wants to make.' When a company moves from a sales to a marketing oriented approach it is not just a case of changing the job title of Sales Director to Marketing Director; it requires a revolution in how a company practises its business activities. When shown in diagrammatic form, as in Figure 1.1 from Jobber and Lancaster,[11] this fact is clarified. This also illustrates the importance of the consumer movement during transition from a sales to a marketing based approach, in that marketing orientation stems from customer needs.

For a business to be successful, consumers and their needs must be placed at the very centre of business planning.

There is some confusion as to the difference between selling and marketing and they are sometimes thought to be similar. This is a fallacy. Theodore Levitt,[12] in his classic article 'Marketing Myopia', sums up this distinction between selling and marketing orientation: 'Selling focuses on the

Sales orientation

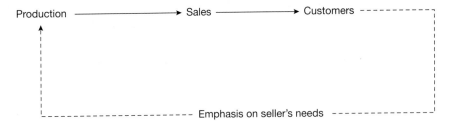

Marketing orientation

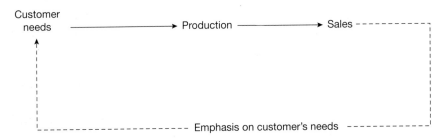

FIGURE 1.1 The distinction between sales and market orientations

Source: Jobber, D. and Lancaster, G. (2009), *Selling and Sales Management*, 8th edn, FT Prentice Hall, p. 17.

needs of the seller, marketing on the needs of the buyer. Selling is preoccupied with the seller's need to convert his product into cash; marketing with the idea of satisfying the needs of the customer. . . .' A philosophy of marketing, even as an important first step, is not the same as putting the philosophy into practice. Once the framework of the marketing concept has been established, the organization must implement it. Doubt has been expressed as to the extent to which the philosophy has been implemented. The practical manifestations of this philosophy are not well known, and this prompts the question: how can marketing orientation be recognized?

The following constitutes a list of requirements that must be met if a move towards marketing orientation within an organization is to be effective:

- Is there good understanding of needs, wants and behavioural patterns of targeted customers?
- Is the enterprise profit directed rather than volume driven?
- Does the chief executive see him/herself as the marketing strategist or marketing champion?
- Does the enterprise have a market driven mission?
- Do strategies reflect realities of the marketplace (including the competitive situation)?
- Is marketing seen as more important by managers than other functions and orientations?
- Is the enterprise organized in such a way that it can be more responsive to marketing opportunities and threats than its competitors?
- Does it have a well designed marketing information system?

- Do managers make full use of marketing research inputs in their decision making?
- Are marketing costs and revenues systematically analysed in relation to marketing activities to ensure the latter are being carried out effectively?
- Is there a strong link between the marketing function and the development of new products and services?
- Does the enterprise employ marketing staff who are professionals (rather than being, say, sales-oriented in their approach)?
- Is it understood that marketing is the responsibility of the entire organization?
- Are decisions with marketing implications made in a co-ordinated way and executed in an integrated manner?

Developing marketing orientation is a long-term process and needs to be thought of as a form of investment that can change the organization's culture, so common values relating to the need to highlight service to customers and a concern for quality in all activities are shared throughout the organization. This cannot be provided by a 'quick fix'; it must permeate the entire culture of the organization.

A variety of steps can be taken to enhance the degree of marketing orientation of an enterprise:

- The first step is to secure top management support. A bottom-up approach would be doomed from the outset, given the company-wide implications of marketing orientation.
- There needs to be a specified mission relating to the development of marketing orientation. This should have a plan associated with it, and the necessary allocation of resources to enable it to be executed.
- A task force should be set up as part of the plan to bring together managers from across the company (possibly assisted by consultants) to carry out tasks such as identifying the current orientation of the company; carrying out a needs analysis as a basis for a management development programme to change the company's culture in a desired way; advising on structural change within the company to support marketing activities; and ensuring commitment to change via a system of rewards (such as bonuses and promotion) that will apply to facilitate change.
- The momentum of change can be maintained by continuously monitoring marketing performance to ensure inertia does not set in. Progress towards improved marketing orientation can be measured by regularly asking questions like: 'Are we easy to do business with?' 'Do we keep our promises?' 'Do we meet the standards we set?' and 'Do we all work together towards a common goal?'
- Developing marketing orientation requires a focus on customers, competitors, the changing environment and company culture. Achieving it is expensive and time consuming. However, companies that make the effort are likely to have a higher level of marketing effectiveness and greater organizational effectiveness. The results may be extremely important amid uncertainties following the worldwide economic downturn and greater competitiveness in modern day commerce.

On 22 February 2008 Northern Rock, for nearly twenty years one of the UK's fastest growing and apparently most successful building societies, which became a bank in 1997, was taken into public ownership. The cause was a major liquidity crisis prompted by the world wide credit crunch. As if this was not bad enough for Northern Rock customers, by March 2009 over 17,000 mortgage accounts were in arrears; an increase of nearly 400 per cent in just over 12 months (Source: Times on Line, 3 March 2009.) Some of these arrears were due to borrowers losing their jobs as a result of the recession. Others were due to illness or changed family circumstances. In other words, reasons that could be considered a normal part of the mortgage business or at least outside of the control of Northern Rock. However, the major reason for default was borrowers who had borrowed more than was prudent.

During the good times Northern Rock developed a mortgage product which allowed customers to take out a personal loan on top of their mortgage loan, in some cases enabling borrowing of upwards of five times earnings. In a period when house prices were rocketing this product had tremendous appeal to borrowers who otherwise were not able to get on the housing ladder. As a result sales of this product soared and Northern Rock expanded its sales and market share quicker than virtually than other company in the industry. At first glance it might appear that Northern Rock was being customer oriented in developing this product; after all, if sales were anything to go by there was a real customer need. However, with the benefit of hindsight, for many customers this was an inappropriate mortgage product.

Far from being market oriented, Northern Rock was very much sales driven. Certainly there was a strong demand, but for many customers the product was unsuitable. Marketing this product to these customers was not in the spirit of the marketing concept.

Standard Life, a major financial services organization in the UK, has been the target of an attempt to demutualize the company. After a long and at times bitter campaign, the management of the company secured victory in their attempt to persuade policyholders to reject the demutualization proposal. In the course of fighting this campaign, Standard Life realized that one of the reasons many investors were considering voting for demutualization was that over time the company had, through sheer inertia, begun to lose contact with its customers e.g. often only communicating with members when policies matured.

The challenge of demutualizers alerted an otherwise excellent company to the need to pay more attention to the needs of its customers and for this to be a company-wide effort backed by senior management commitment and resources.

MARKETING MANAGEMENT

Developing marketing orientation is only part of the equation of improving marketing effectiveness. Marketing management skills must be developed, as it is a management function that involves analysis, planning, implementation and control. Other management functions also have planning structures that link to the corporate plan. In terms of the company organization chart, a typical structure is shown in Figure 1.2. In this organization chart we see the place of marketing alongside major functions of line management.

The board of directors are responsible for strategic direction. Board members are not necessarily full-time employees and in larger companies they are often from outside the organization because

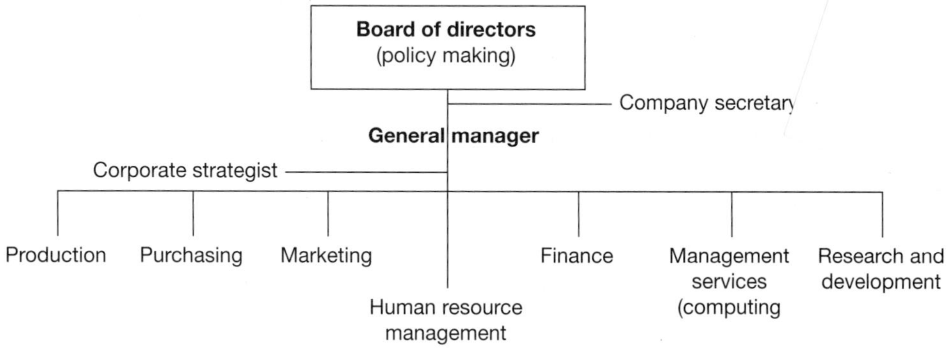

FIGURE 1.2 Traditional organization chart

of the expertise they lend to the board. Such people might be strategy experts, financial experts, people who lend distinction to an organization or they might be on the board of other companies and can bring a cross-fertilization of ideas, financial linkages and potential inter-firm dealings.

The general manager is the person who translates policy into tactics and is responsible for day-to-day operations. When the general manager is a member of the board the title is then managing director.

The company secretary is responsible for legal and administrative matters as well as serving as secretary to the board. This person ensures that board meetings take place at intervals stipulated in the company's articles of association, and produces minutes that sum up board meeting decisions ensuring they are implemented. For this reason, the role of company secretary is a lateral relationship. This relationship similarly applies to the modern function of corporate strategy which may be carried out by general management, but is often a separate, relatively small, function whose role is to ensure that all subdivisions in the organization have a plan (e.g. a marketing plan) and that each of these plans meshes with the five separate elements in the overall corporate plan i.e. operations (or production), human resource, finance, logistics and marketing. The corporate strategist ensures there are no mismatches (e.g. marketing might plan to sell more than the firm can produce).

The major line functions are responsible for translating strategy into tactics in terms of the organization's everyday operations and this includes matters like manufacturing, training and recruitment, design and selling. In many smaller organizations, heads of these line functions are members of the board of directors in which case they would then have 'director' behind their title whose responsibilities would then cover both strategic matters (being a member of the board of directors) and tactical matters (being a functional head of department).

Marketing is but one function within business. Arguably it is the most critical because it interprets customers' needs and requirements into products and services and repeat business without which a business cannot continue. A modern view puts customers in the centre and marketing as the interpretative function surrounding the customer with other major functions of business around this as shown in Figure 1.3. The idea is that all functions of business should be geared towards the satisfactions of customers' requirements and this has led to the notion of customer care.

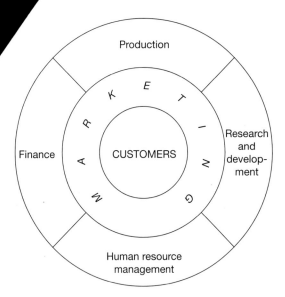

FIGURE 1.3 The place of marketing in the modern organization

Analysis

Effective marketing management requires analysis of factors that affect success and failure. It is the prelude to planning and decision making and includes analysis of the following:

- Market analysis – market size and trends;
- Competitor analysis;
- Customer analysis;
- Company analysis – market share, portfolio analysis and profitability analysis.

Analysis presupposes effective marketing research and intelligence, control of information and forecasting systems. Because of its importance, later chapters centre on tools of analysis.

Planning

Analysis is only a means to an end. It forms the basis of marketing plans that in turn denote decision making. Later chapters centre on the elements of marketing decision making.

Amongst the major marketing decisions to be made by marketing managers are:

- Marketing objectives;
- Product/market scope, segments and targets;
- Company targets;

- Marketing strategies;
- **Marketing mix** decisions – product, price, place and promotion.

At this stage many of these terms and their meanings are unfamiliar. We shall address these and other planning decisions in later chapters.

Implementation

Having made marketing plans, the next step is to ensure they are implemented. This requires that staff and financial resources be allocated together with time-scales for action, allocation of responsibilities and authority. In addition, the organizational structure may need to be changed to enable effective implementation to take place. Again, issues of implementation form the focus of subsequent chapters.

Control

The final element of the management tasks of marketing is monitoring and controlling marketing activities. Control is the subject of Chapter 14, but in essence it completes the cycle of management tasks as control and measurement feed back into the analysis and planning stages of marketing management to restart the cycle.

In summary, the following are seen as capturing the essence of what marketing incorporates i.e. the basic principles:

- The marketing concept is founded on the belief that profitable sales and satisfactory returns on investment can best be achieved by identifying, anticipating and satisfying customer needs and wants;
- Marketing is a philosophy of business (an orientation) and a management function;
- As a business philosophy, it involves the adoption of the marketing concept;
- A company adopting the concept places customers at the centre of all business decisions, i.e. the customers' needs permeate all levels and functions in the organization;
- As a management function, marketing involves analysis, planning, implementation and control.

These are the basic principles of marketing, but as companies accept and implement them, so marketing itself is changing; perhaps not the basic concept or philosophy as outlined here, but rather the perspective and operation of marketing management. Earlier we suggested that the essence of this changing face of marketing is the shift towards a more strategic approach to marketing; hence the focus of this book. So what does this more strategic approach consist of and what forces and factors have contributed to this change?

THE NEED FOR A STRATEGIC APPROACH TO MARKETING

Companies traditionally follow a planning framework. However, this is sometimes short-term, ad hoc and based on intuition. The need is for a more strategic approach, but before we consider its implications, we should consider why it is required. The key reasons are:

The pace of change and environmental complexity

Kotler and Keller[13] suggest that the pace of environmental change is not only increasingly rapid, but these changes are often discontinuous in nature. We shall be examining these environmental factors in strategic marketing planning in Chapter 15, but let us consider a sample of environmental changes with which organizations have had to cope in recent years.

- As we have noted, consumers and legislative bodies have become increasingly concerned about the natural environment and about the ecological and/or health risks associated with some products;
- The last decade of the twentieth century witnessed the birth of a host of new products based on new technology. Developments in information technology, cryogenics and biotechnology are just some examples of these facilitating technologies;
- Divorce rates, crime rates and (in some countries) birth rates have continued to surge ahead;
- There have been substantial changes in patterns of world trade including the emergence of new trading relationships and regulations;
- The worldwide economic 'meltdown' in 2008 and its aftermath took people by surprise.

Healthy and particularly organic foods have been amongst the fastest growing markets in the UK. Once a minority market, appealing to relatively few health food 'fanatics', this sector now represents a huge and growing market. More and more consumers are looking for a healthier diet and avoiding products and brands which may harm their health. Research indicates that nearly 500 food products were launched under the 'healthy' label in the UK in 2009. In addition, sales of organic foods in the UK during 2009 topped £3 billion. ASDA's 'Healthy Choice', the Aviva range from Novatis and Johnson & Johnson's Benecol are all examples of brands that have flourished with the trend towards healthy eating. Changes in attitude towards health and healthy eating will continue to give rise to marketing opportunities and challenges for marketers in the future. The significance of this all of this environmental change is its increased magnitude and pace and this has added to the complexity facing organizations.

Increasing organization size and complexity

A more strategic approach is required as organizations themselves have become increasingly large and complex. The need for strategic market planning has gone hand in hand with the move from functionally organized companies, with relatively narrow product lines, to large diversified companies producing many different products for disparate markets. In turn, this has meant that planning processes that were appropriate for the 1990s are no longer so. Increasingly complex organizations require sophisticated planning tools.

A significant feature of environmental change is its increased magnitude and pace. Technological, social/cultural and political and regulatory change are now rapid and this has added to the complexity facing organizations and the marketer in particular.

Unilever, one of the world's largest companies, currently employ more than 170,000 people producing and marketing in over 150 countries worldwide. Their products and brands encompass personal care products, home products and food products. Thirteen of their brands turn over in excess of $1 billion and there are twenty different nationalities in the top tier of management. They spend an annual total of nearly $1billion on R&D and are involved in supporting a number of good causes throughout the world (see http://www.unilever.com). Marketing planning in a company this large and diverse is complex and requires sophisticated systems and procedures to develop effective strategic marketing plans.

As we can see with Unilever, increasingly, the contemporary organization is often large and complex, encompassing potentially many product lines sold in diverse markets to different customer groups. The different parts of a business each need a strategic marketing plan reflecting different requirements of each product market.

An example of the strategic planning implications of increased organizational size and complexity is the concept of viewing the multi-product, multi-market, organization as a number of sub-units or **'strategic business units'** (SBUs), which need to be viewed and managed as a portfolio of businesses that may each contribute, in different ways and to a different extent, to overall corporate objectives. Lynch[14] has suggested that particularly in larger organizations the strategic business unit is very often the basic organizational unit for the development of strategic marketing plans. Certainly, organizing around SBUs is very prevalent in today's multi-product/multi-market organization and this is now explored.

THE CONCEPT OF STRATEGIC BUSINESS UNITS

The focus is on strategic analysis and the ensuing strategic marketing plans within the business are for individual SBUs. Having said this, it means that at corporate planning level, decisions must be made regarding the balance between different individual SBUs in the business, and in particular, the allocation of resources between them. However, strategic marketing plans in a multi-product/multi-market business can only be developed at the level of each SBU. The SBU concept is thus crucial to the strategic marketing planner, so it is essential to organize the business into identifiable SBUs.

Increasingly, the contemporary organization is large and complex, encompassing potentially many product lines sold in diverse markets to different customer groups. Different parts of a business each need a strategic marketing plan reflecting different requirements of each product market. The American company General Electric is generally acknowledged to be the first company to have dealt with this requirement for individual strategic marketing plans in its large diversified company by organizing business in separate SBUs.

In practice, identifying and delineating a business into SBUs is a complex task and the precise ways in which this will be achieved will depend on several factors which are individual to each organization. For example, the size of each product market in the business and the extent of commonalities between the different product markets. Ideally, however, an SBU should meet the following criteria:

- It should have its own customers and competitors;
- It should, in theory, be able to be operated as a separate individual business;
- It should have its own resources and its own identifiable costs and revenues;
- It should have a manager who is responsible for profitability of the business.

The Swiss multi-national Nestlé organizes its worldwide operations around a series of SBUs. Each SBU has full responsibility for the development of its own strategic marketing plans. SBUs are based on the different product areas within Nestlé. For example, there is an SBU covering confectionery and ice cream products throughout the world, another one for milk products, and so on.

Although increased organizational size and complexity has served as a distinct spur to strategic approaches to marketing, it is not suggested that such an approach is only appropriate for large diversified companies. Small companies also need a strategic approach, as they are often faced with a less certain external or macro-environment than large companies.

Increased competition

Apart from a small number of exceptions such as state-protected or 'natural' monopolies, most organizations throughout the history of commerce and trade have faced competition, both existing and potential. However, as with environmental change, recent years have witnessed an intensifying of competition in many markets. Successful marketing in a competitive economy is about competitive success and positioning and customer focus. Many factors have contributed to this but amongst some of the more significant are the following:

- a growth of global competition as barriers to trade have been lowered and global communications improved;
- linked to the above, the role of the multinational conglomerate which ignores geographical and other boundaries and looks for opportunities on a global scale;
- in most economies, legislation and political ideologies which have aimed at fostering 'free market' entrepreneurial values;
- continual technological innovation, giving rise to new sources of competition for established products and markets.

Successful marketing in a competitive economy is about competitive success and positioning and customer focus.

HMV, the music store chain, was one of the first music retailers to introduce new systems of display and merchandizing in the UK. Recognizing the growing threat from new technology, it launched a transactional website in the UK. Unlike many competitors who shunned internet marketing, HMV supported its use to promote music and stay ahead of competition. From the early days of a few individuals beginning to exchange music on the Internet, downloading music is now big business. There are estimated to be currently over 500 websites, both legal and illegal, where music can be downloaded. This is in addition to music swapping between private individuals. Many in the music industry initially fought against this development, particularly the record companies, but as demand increased and technology such as MP3 and broadband speeds improved they were no longer able to resist. The launch of iTunes was significant in this respect and gave the boost for music downloading to go mainstream. Now the music industry is replete with artists, record companies, electronic product companies and music retailers looking for new ways to find a competitive edge in the music downloading market. Music downloading is here to stay. From an initial fear of this development in the industry most of the industry is now distinctly upbeat about it.

These are the key reasons why a strategic perspective on marketing is so important. What is meant by a strategic approach and what elements does this contain? It is to this issue that we now turn our attention by examining the nature of strategy and strategic management.

STRATEGIC MARKETING PLANNING

When it comes to defining strategic management, we encounter a plethora of different definitions. Below are three definitions which move us from the concept of strategic planning and to the focus of this text, i.e. strategic marketing. Baker[15] proposes this definition of strategy, illustrating both its directional nature and its military antecedents: 'A strategy is the achievement of a stated purpose through the utilization of available resources.' Strategies, then, are the outcome of the strategic planning process that Kotler and Keller[16] define thus:

> Market-oriented strategic planning is the managerial process of developing and maintaining a viable fit between the organization's objectives, skills and resources and its changing market opportunities. The aim of strategic planning is to shape and re-shape the company's businesses and products so that they yield target profits and growth.

Strategic marketing is defined by Cravens[17] as:

> A process of strategically analyzing environmental, competitive and business factors affecting business units and forecasting future trends in business areas of interest to the enterprise; participating in setting objectives and formulating corporate and business unit strategy; selecting target market strategies for product markets in each business unit; establishing marketing objectives and developing, implementing and managing program positioning strategies for meeting target market needs.

Craven's definition encapsulates the key elements in strategic marketing. We now expand key steps as a prelude to examining these in more detail.

The setting for marketing plans: key considerations

Marketing plans take a variety of forms, ranging from verbal intentions or a set of budgets for achievement, to formalized structures and procedures used as part of the corporate planning process. We now provide a framework through which we can structure the key steps and inputs to a strategic marketing plan. In this way marketing becomes a better organized function and makes a substantial contribution to organizational performance in areas in which marketing orientation is needed.

As in any planning system, the providers must be clear on the intended use and the contribution desired from them. Therefore, certain key questions must be asked:

1   Do we have the ability to match our ambitions? Often the ambition to achieve a marketing planning system reaches beyond the realities of ability.
2   Have we considered the planning horizons in terms of time?
3   Have we defined the boundaries of the system clearly?
4   What purposes are to be served by the marketing planning system? (This will help later to determine objectives.)
5   What structure should exist to enable the plan to be implemented, planned and achieved?
6   What do we require to achieve the purpose we have now identified?
7   What constraints currently limit our ability, and can these be overcome?
8   What contributions are we seeking to organizational and financial performance from the plan?

Like all planning, marketing planning concerns the future, which depends on a clear understanding of organizational and market needs. This approach is important as it involves a time dimension which needs to be clearly specified.

A planned approach depends on an ability to predict, anticipate and adapt. Marketing planning means change. It is a process that involves deciding currently what to do in the future with a full appreciation of the resource position; the need to set clear, communicable, measurable objectives; the development of alternative courses of action and a means of assessing the best route towards achievement of specified objectives. Marketing planning is designed to assist the marketing decision-making process under conditions of uncertainty.

Above all, the process of marketing planning has a number of benefits:

■   motivates staff;
■   secures participation and involvement;
■   achieves commitment;
■   leads ultimately to better decision making;
■   requires management staff collectively to make clear judgemental statements about assumptions – the very basis upon which the future depends;
■   ensures a systematic approach to the future has been taken;
■   prevents 'short-termism' i.e. the tendency to place all effort on the 'here and now';
■   creates a climate in which change can be made, and in which standards for performance can be established;

■ enables a control system to be designed and established whereby performance can be assessed against predetermined criteria.

Marketing plans can be both strategic and tactical, the latter operating within the framework imposed by the former. It is this strategic framework that now concerns us. Whether they are tactical or strategic, marketing planning requires the laying down of policies for the acquisition, use and disposal of resources.

Marketing planning as a functional activity can only work within a corporate planning framework. The marketing planner must consider the need to achieve corporate level objectives by means of exploiting product and market combinations. There is an underlying requirement for any organization to set a clearly defined business mission as the basis from which the organizational direction can develop.

STEPS AND INPUTS TO DEVELOPING A STRATEGIC MARKETING PLAN

The final part of this chapter provides an overview of the key steps and considerations in developing a **strategic marketing plan**. It is important to become familiar with this framework, as in the following chapters we look at these steps in more detail. It is easy to lose sight of how individual steps fit together, so from time to time you will need to return to this framework.

1 The corporate plan remit

The **corporate mission statement** needs detailed consideration by top management to establish the business the company is really in and to relate this consideration to future business intentions. It is a general statement that provides an integrating function for the business, from which a clear sense of business definition and direction can be achieved. This stage, which is the starting point for overall corporate planning (elements of which are: human resource, marketing, operations, financial and logistics) is often overlooked in marketing planning; yet without it, the plan will lack a sense of contribution to the development of the total business. By deriving a clear mission statement, boundaries for the 'corporate entity' can be conceived in the context of environmental trends that influence the business.

It is helpful to establish areas of distinctive competence and in so doing, focus upon what customers are buying rather than upon what the company is selling. This will assist in the development of a more marketing-oriented mission statement; it therefore takes into account trends in market consumption patterns. A clear mission statement should include customer groups to be served, customer needs to be served and the technologies to be utilized.

Corporate objectives of the organization are time dependent, designed to achieve shareholder expectations. These should be derived from the mission statement to ensure integration within a corporate and marketing planning system. The time horizon to achieve corporate objectives will vary between organizations, from market to market and from country to country, with time-scales stretching from one to five, or even to 20 or more years.

From a practical viewpoint, both quantitative and qualitative objectives are required to provide the foundation upon which measurable marketing activities can be planned. In particular, quantitative corporate objectives are concerned with rates of return on capital employed and invested, return on shareholder funds etc., and these are inextricably linked to the company's financial year where these key ratios are used as indicators of annual financial performance. Qualitative corporate objectives may relate to image, stance, positioning, projection, appeal, identity and recognition and it is possible to apply quantitative criteria to each of these to make their analysis to make them more objective, techniques of which are discussed in Chapter 12.

Objectives are statements of what is to be achieved and hence provide the stimulus for strategy, i.e. the means by which the objectives will be achieved. Because these objectives are corporate and have company-wide parameters, balance is needed for the attainment of integration in the organization as a whole. Areas to consider when setting up corporate level objectives include: market standing; innovation; productivity; physical and financial resources; staff performance, development and attitude; public responsibility and profitability/financial health.

Corporate constraints are an important consideration. It is the matching of ambition to the ability to maximize performance that is a perennial task which besets senior management. Corporate constraints are the limiting factors that govern corporate capability. As the process of planning is iterative, a clearer understanding of these constraints may arise at subsequent stages in the planning process.

A full appreciation of corporate capability at this stage will affect more realistic resource deployment at later stages in the marketing plan and will assist cross-functional plans which collectively are designed to achieve corporate level objectives.

2 The marketing audit

In most business enterprises, periodic financial reviews are mandatory and systems are established to ensure that these occur within the deadlines set. This should be the case with marketing, but rarely is it so formalized. Essentially the **marketing audit** is a systematic internal and external environmental review of the company's marketing performance for a given period of time. This review provides the basis for subsequent **SWOT** analysis (i.e. a review of company Strengths, Weaknesses, Opportunities and Threats). The purpose of auditing the external internal environment of the organization is to separate controllable from uncontrollable variables that have an impact on corporate performance. Companies should develop a customized checklist of factors for examination that can then be reviewed systematically and periodically.

The external audit will examine '**PEST**' factors – Political, Economic, Socio-cultural and Technological – in the general business environment. Later consideration added the legal impact of these on company operations and the definition was broadened to '**SLEPT**'. Later thinking adds Environmental to this classification which makes the acronym '**PESTLE**' and the word Ecological has now made the acronym '**STEEPLE**'. In addition, a comprehensive market profile is required with a detailed understanding of market movements so that forecasts can be developed for market performance and changes thereto. To support this market profile, the company must place itself in the context of a competitive market environment and a comprehensive profile of competition must be obtained, together with an examination of competitive product offerings.

Internally, a thorough examination of the company's marketing performance is vital. Detailed sales analysis, market shares and profit contribution analysis must be undertaken, together with an assessment of the efficiency of the company's marketing mix and marketing control plans and procedures.

The process of auditing raises a series of questions and produces a series of discoveries. These will need to be compiled into an acceptable format for presentation, a format from which later stages of the plan can be developed. This format is known as the 'SWOT' analysis. The PEST analysis is effectively the antecedent to the SWOT analysis.

3 SWOT analysis

This acronym classifies results of the audit into internal current strengths and weaknesses that largely concern controllable variables, and external future opportunities and threats that largely concern uncontrollable variables. The SWOT analysis used for presentation should be a succinct summary of the audit which concentrates upon main issues for resolution, and for which objectives, strategies and tactics could be set if required. In effect this is a series of bullet points under each of the SWOT elements rather than a dialogue.

4 Assumptions

To move forward from analysis to planning, a conceptual transition is required because something has to be achieved by that which has been assessed, discovered and recorded.

A potential drawback of planning is that if not careful it can become and end in itself. What this means is that in some organizations, particularly those where planning is done centrally using specialist planning staff, extensive and sophisticated analysis is carried out, but little of this feeds into and affects actual marketing plans and activities at divisional or individual brand level. There are various reasons for this, but a frequent one is simply a lack of communication between planners and implementers. Surprisingly, in many organizations brand managers are unaware of the organization's mission and vision statements or have not been informed about market developments and forecasts which may have significant implications for their brands. Another reason is a possible clash of cultures when two previously independent organizations come together. Initially, when the UK supermarket group Morrisons first acquired their competitor, Safeway, in 2003 there were problems bringing together the marketing plans and strategies of each group into one coherent whole. However the senior management of both companies were eventually able to do this and the new combined company has made significant inroads into the market ever since.

Environmental scanning of the market and analysis of competitive and market situations leads to the statement of assumptions for a future planning time horizon. To avoid the need for assumptions, we would have to have perfect knowledge, which is rare. It is upon the statement of assumptions that progress can be made to the planning stage. Assumptions can be classified as internal and external, quantitative and qualitative, in the same format as prescribed for corporate constraints.

5 Time-scales

It is normal practice to design at least an annual marketing plan that co-ordinates with the fiscal year of the organization and hence integrates with the budgetary control and associated management information and control systems. Some companies then extend the planning horizon to a separate plan for around five years, or incrementally on a rolling planning basis. A rolling planning principle ensures plans are at least one year ahead and revised and updated quarterly.

6 Marketing objectives

Objectives are statements of what is to be achieved and strategies are means of achieving objectives.

It is important to realize that marketing objectives should be derived directly from corporate level objectives and, in turn, reflect both quantitative and qualitative criteria. Concentration should be focused on setting objectives for products and markets, because corporate level objectives reflect product/market combinations. Marketing mix objectives, that relate to price, product, place and promotion (each dealt with as individual chapters) can be separated out at a later stage. This simplifies the process of setting marketing objectives, but they must be actionable, achievable and measurable, otherwise the accomplishment of marketing strategies cannot be accurately assessed in the time-scale of the plan.

7 Marketing strategies

Strategy is the means by which objectives are achieved. If objectives specify what is to be done, strategy lays down how it is to be done. A predetermined strategy leads to a series of action statements which are a clear set of steps to be followed to achieve the determined strategy. These actions are known as tactics. Effective marketing strategy is critical to the success of the plan. It must exploit the strengths and opportunities, overcome weaknesses and avoid threats identified in the SWOT analysis.

A strategic marketing programme depends upon an incisive SWOT analysis arising from a clear definition of planned marketing activity as company success is governed by marketing strategy. A company's marketing strategy is the basis upon which operational decisions are made and corporate and marketing objectives achieved within the time periods specified for the plan. The time period for the **tactical** plan is usually one year i.e. the current operating year. It is through the tactical plan that marketing strategy is achieved in practice.

The strategic element of the marketing plan concentrates on the selection of target markets, positioning strategies and the planning and implementation of the elements of the marketing mix, which includes product, price, place and promotion, and in the case of service products/markets, the extended marketing mix elements of people, process and physical evidence.

Marketing research at this stage should provide a vital strategic contribution to the plan.

A key part of the strategic elements of the marketing plan that is often overlooked is the policy statement, which provides the guidelines by which the marketing strategy can be accomplished within determined time planning horizons.

As part of strategic determination, it is common practice to identify alternative means by which specified marketing objectives can be achieved. Criteria for evaluation are then set and applied to the stated alternatives, and the best course of action selected.

The intention of a marketing mix strategy is to achieve marketing positioning for product/market combinations specified in the corporate and marketing objectives sectors. Therefore, market definition, market segmentation and market targeting are prerequisites within which positioning must be achieved.

An idea first put forward by Weihrich[18] in 1982 provides a useful means of applying SWOT analysis principles to form marketing strategies. This is termed the **TOWS matrix** which brings together company strengths and weaknesses and links them with external opportunities and threats to form specific strategies by using elements from the SWOT analysis. For example, consider a small regional bakery where the following SWOT has been produced:

STRENGTHS
1   well established brand
2   in business since 1922
3   good reviews relating to quality
4   reasonable prices
5   family firm with contented workforce
6   no debts or borrowings and good reserves
7   premises can easily be expanded to at least double capacity

WEAKNESSES
1   production semi-automated
2   only sold in one region of the country
3   promotion tends to be word-of-mouth
4   no representatives
5   only a limited range of breads

OPPORTUNITIES
1   local transport company has offered organize deliveries to a wider area
2   to produce a wider range of products
3   capitalize on strong brand position

THREATS
1   large national bakeries are expanding to into the region
2   large supermarkets entering into including cakes strategic alliances with national bakeries
3   recession means that many households are now baking more at home

Suggested marketing strategies using TOWS are:

■   Strengths 1 and 2; Weakness 3; Opportunity 2 produces: 'Use long established brand name and "word of mouth" promotion to develop and retail products other than bread';
■   Strength 7; Weakness 2; Opportunity 1 produces: 'Expand production to enter larger market in other regions using alliance with local transport company';
■   Weakness 1; Strength 6; Threats 1 and 2 produces: 'Use spare capital to update production facilities to counter expansion plans from national bakeries.'

8 Detailed marketing programmes

The level of marketing strategy will vary from plan to plan and company to company, but the final intention is to put the plan into action. It is now time to construct a set of detailed action programmes to achieve the previously stated marketing strategy. This part of the plan is concerned with who should do what, where, when, how and why. In this way responsibility, accountability and action over a specified time-scale can be planned, scheduled, implemented and reviewed.

9 Sales forecast

In many companies, the sales plan will be separated from the marketing plan or even replace the marketing plan in a sales-oriented situation. However, if we adopt marketing as a business philosophy then sales must be included within the marketing plan – it is the means by which many of the plan's objectives will be achieved. Sales forecasts and budgets will provide the means for quantitative achievement and control.

Selling and sales management strategy and tactics should be designed to complement, support and integrate with the marketing mix, components of marketing strategy – in particular promotion and distribution.

10 Staffing the plan

Objectives and strategy can only be achieved through people, structures, systems and methods. In the tactical section of the plan, responsibility and authority for operations should be designated to appropriate individuals. This requires company-wide consideration for organizational and staff development, to bring about any changes required to meet the objectives of the plan. Training and career development programmes, remuneration systems, numbers of staff required, etc., are important considerations, and this will require liaison with the human resource function.

11 Contingency measures

Despite planning ahead for change, environmental factors sometimes force us to change a course of action – often these factors are unforeseeable and frustrating. The time taken to adjust may be less than we would like because of a desire by management to avoid higher costs and incurring losses. Under such conditions, response to contingency situations becomes reactive. To minimize the impact of changed environmental circumstances, companies can be proactive by using **contingency thinking** to anticipate likely events that may occur, and then make plans to reconcile the changed position in which the company might then be placed.

For each element of marketing mix and sales strategy, the marketing planner should ask the question: 'What if?' In so doing, a change scenario will be formulated; a scenario to which the company can choose to respond. By planning ahead, the impact of changes will be reduced. Such thinking, when used in marketing planning, encourages control and may avoid expensive mistakes. Ironically, if the international banking sector had applied such thinking before the late 2008 'financial meltdown' then costly blunders might have been anticipated and appropriate contingency planning applied in good time.

The marketing planner should refer back to the assumptions set previously and consider the impact on the plan if these are not fulfilled.

12 Budgets, reviews and controls

A marketing plan cannot be operated without some element of control to monitor and measure progress.

A system of controls should be laid down whereby the plan is reviewed on a systematic basis, and updated to extend the horizon to the prescribed time-scale. Controls are needed to assess tactics and strategy in the progress towards the achievement of quantitative and qualitative objectives. These controls should be both quantitative and qualitative in design.

The **marketing information system**, and in turn the **management information system**, provide essential inputs to the control system, but the organization depends on people to work the system through regular appraisal. Comparison of performance against target and the coincident variance analysis will enable corrective action to be taken to further exploit marketing and market opportunities and threats. Contingency planning is a form of control that can and should be used, particularly where markets are volatile.

For companies using a formal system of marketing planning, the budget is the means by which the entire plan is co-ordinated financially. Each area of marketing activity should be costed and allocated to centres of responsibility. As a key functional area the marketing budget is one of the key budgets to contribute towards the total budgetary control system. Budgeting is the transitional step between planning and implementation, because the budget, and allocated centres within it, will project the cost of each activity over the specified period of time, and also act as a guide for implementation and control.

This overview of the strategic marketing planning framework is brief. In practice developing strategic marketing plans is complex and multifaceted. This complexity is heightened by the fact that the process is essentially an iterative one, with the planner constantly having to return to earlier stages in the analysis and planning as final plans begin to emerge. In addition, the various elements of the marketing plan need to be consistent, one with another. Marketing mix elements of product, price, place and promotion need to blend into one coherent package. The mix elements must be consistent with overall corporate and marketing objectives, in particular with segmentation, targeting and positioning strategies. The whole process is one of constant checking and re-checking, not only in the preparation of the plan, but throughout its operation.

Figure 1.4 sets out the steps in marketing planning in this wider framework, together with the key elements of analysis that feed into the decision-making steps. In addition, the interrelationships and iterative steps in the process are also shown. It looks complex, but represents a logical and ordered approach to the strategic marketing planning process.

The key steps shown in this framework are universal inasmuch as they remain essentially the same, irrespective of the nature of a company, e.g. its size, nature of product markets, geographical dispersion etc, and may be followed by the marketing manager preparing a strategic marketing plan for an individual Strategic Business Unit. Although strategic planning frameworks tend to differ, the essentials, together with the sequencing of these, are now generally agreed. However, where marketing extends beyond domestic boundaries to include international markets a number of additional complexities, considerations and steps that international marketing gives rise to, are the subject of Chapter 16. As we shall see, markets and marketing are dynamic.

Marketing and marketers operate in a dynamic environment. As a result, marketing concepts and applications are constantly evolving and changing, so the strategic marketing planner must consider these when formulating plans. Because of this, although the basic elements shown in the framework for strategic planning remain essentially the same, it is useful to conclude this chapter by briefly outlining some of the more recent developments and trends in marketing thinking and application, together with some of the more important potential implications of these for marketing management.

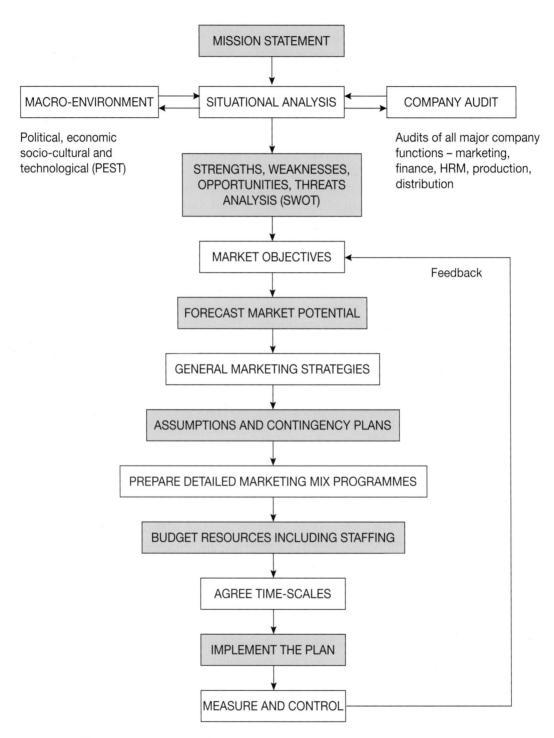

FIGURE 1.4 The strategic marketing planning process

TRENDS AND DEVELOPMENTS IN MARKETING CONCEPTS AND APPLICATIONS

Marketing and marketers operate in a dynamic environment. As a result, marketing concepts and applications are constantly evolving and changing, so the strategic marketing planner must consider these when formulating plans. We have selected the most important trends and developments for consideration.

An evolving marketing concept: relationship marketing

This concerns the evolving nature of the concept of marketing itself, and in particular the trend towards a concept of marketing based upon developing and maintaining long-term relationships with customers, referred to as **relationship marketing (RM)**. This represents a paradigm shift in the nature of marketing itself that gathered pace in the 1980s and still continues. Anthanasopoulou[19] argues that our understanding of relationship marketing concepts and techniques is still at a comparatively early and underdeveloped stage. However, the underpinning notion of RM is essentially simple in as much as it is based on the idea that an organization's marketing effort should be designed around a series of contacts with customers over time, rather than being based on single transactions (i.e. **transactional marketing**).

The conventional marketing concept centres on the notion of understanding customer needs so marketers can develop strategies that better meet these needs. As a consequence, the organization achieves its aims. The process of dealing with customers has traditionally been viewed as a one-off transaction where the customer receives satisfaction and the company achieves its objectives, whether these are for profit, or some other organizational objective. This transaction view is concerned with what marketing can do to buyers rather than do for buyers. In contrast, RM is built on creating and maintaining mutually satisfying commercial relationships which appears to be only a slightly different perspective from the traditional transactional view of marketing. In fact, it is a fundamentally different perspective on the marketing concept, and gives rise to potentially very different approaches to developing marketing strategies. Adopting a relationship marketing approach has implications for how we promote products and services, how we deal with customers and customer service functions and how we develop and use information about customers for targeting and other purposes. The growth of relationship marketing is so important that we consider its nature and implications in more detail in Chapter 9.

One of the reasons for the growth of relationship marketing is the recognition of the importance and value of customer loyalty and retention. Put simply, keeping an existing customer is more cost effective and profitable than creating new ones. In the same vein, loyal customers can become advocates for a company or brand, thereby helping to sell a product through word of mouth.

Many customer loyalty programmes that have been such a feature, particularly of retail marketing, and which commenced in the 1990s are in part based on the concepts and ideas of relationship marketing. Programmes such as Tesco Clubcard and Thomson Founders Club are based on the notion of developing relationships with customers to create customer loyalty. The essence of effective loyalty programmes is building communication and trust between the marketer and customers. Companies such as Waitrose, the grocery retailer, and B&Q in the home improvement market, place enormous importance on customer care tactics that embrace high levels of customer service.

Many of these loyalty schemes involve rewarding customers in some way for loyalty. This might involve the award of points as in for example the Tesco scheme or reduced prices/special terms as in the case of The Thompson founders club. Although loyalty schemes are now widespread in marketing, the marketer has to be careful not to assume that they actually generate genuinely loyal customers. Often customers passively claim 'loyalty points' simply because they are being given out. In this way loyalty schemes can become just another form of sales promotion with the customer being offered in essence a sort of financial or other inducement to purchase.

True loyalty schemes encourage customers to decide to remain loyal to a supplier or brand because they perceive this supplier or brand to best meet their needs. In other words true customer loyalty stems from a supplier or brand being viewed as the best solution for that customer. This applies in any type of product market, developed as well as developing ones. Customers want to feel special and valued and they need to feel they can trust the marketer. Ndubisi [20] found that customer loyalty was affected by four major factors namely: 'trust', 'commitment', 'communication' and 'conflict handling'.

Widespread though relationship marketing has become, we have to be careful if we assume that all marketing exchanges should be relationship marketing based. Ward and Dagger[21] have suggested that marketers should not always adopt a relationship marketing approach. For some customers and in some situations a transaction marketing approach is most appropriate; some customers do not want or seek a relationship with a supplier or brand. Sometimes, even if customers might welcome it, building relationships and loyalty may simply be too expensive compared to the potential benefits. The relationship marketing concept is 'complex' and as yet there is no set of 'rules' that tell us when a relationship marketing approach is needed.

Services marketing

A major development has been the growth of services marketing. Service industries have been the major growth area in most developed economies. Banking and finance, insurance, healthcare, tourism and leisure are all major service industries that need and use the tools of marketing. However there are differences in the application of marketing principles for the services marketer. A major difference is the need to consider the elements of the marketing mix from a slightly different perspective. The characteristics of service products have led to the notion of an extended marketing mix for service marketers. In addition to the conventional 'four Ps' of product, price, place, and promotion it is suggested that a fifth 'P' at least should be added to this mix, namely the '**people**' element. 'People' means anyone who directly interfaces with customers including: sales representatives, commission agents, distributors, franchise holders, service engineers, etc. In addition, two further 'Ps', namely '**process**' and '**physical evidence**' may be added (referred to as the '**3Ps' of service marketing**). Undoubtedly, the people element is crucial in the marketing of services, and must be considered and planned for by service marketers. We know that a key determinant affecting customer satisfaction and hence once again loyalty in services marketing is the customer's perception of the service providers personnel. For example, a recent study by Paul et al.[22] supports the view that the people element is a crucial factor affecting customer retention. The issues that services marketing gives rise to, along with extended marketing mix elements, are detailed in Chapter 17.

New technology: e-commerce and the Internet

This development has affected every facet of business over the past 20 years, but the marketing function in particular has been influenced by the impact and importance of new technology. There are so many ways in which this has affected marketing, ranging from developments in communications to technologies of transportation and distribution, and underpinning product technologies such as genetic engineering. Perhaps the most significant development for marketers has been the growth of e-commerce and the Internet. Originally confined to being another promotional technique and a channel of distribution, the Internet is now proving an invaluable tool in marketing applications ranging from market research (Schibrowsky et al.[23]), through to speeding the acceptance of new product innovations (Davidson and Copulsky[24]) or even scanning the marketing environment for marketing planning (Decker et al.[25]). In addition of course the Internet is now a major element in the continued growth of **direct marketing** which is the subject of Chapter 10.

Virtually every aspect of marketing management and planning, is affected by these developments, so marketing personnel need to be conversant with such developments. Because the impact of e-commerce and the Internet is so ubiquitous in marketing, we discuss the impact and implications of these facets throughout the text, but in particular in Chapters 9, 10, 11 and 17.

International/global marketing

Another major development in marketing has been an increasingly **international** and **global** approach to marketing. Marketers have extended their activities, and international marketing has been one of the fastest growing areas of trade and commerce. Factors like the continued liberalization of international trade, more cosmopolitan customers and potential for profit opportunities have led to the growth of global companies increasingly marketing global brands. Paliwoda and Marinova[26] have suggested that the enlarged single European market represents one of the most significant future marketing challenges and will require distinct changes in the marketing strategies and tactics of companies operating in this market. Again, the basic concepts and techniques of strategic marketing apply irrespective of whether we are marketing in domestic markets or across international frontiers. However, as with services marketing, the extra considerations caused by the complexity of marketing on an international or global scale mean there are a number of special issues for marketing that do not arise when marketing on a purely domestic basis. International and global aspects are considered in more detail in Chapter 16.

Internal marketing

It was earlier suggested that in the marketing oriented company it is essential for everyone in an organization to become customer oriented. This, in turn, has led to the growth of the notion of internal marketing. This idea of internal marketing centres on the notion of 'marketing' the importance of customers and of customer orientation to everyone in the organization. The idea suggests that employees of the organization can usefully be looked at and dealt with in the same way as external customers. For example, production staff are urged to consider, say, the sales force who have to sell the products as internal customers. At the same time the sales force should look at the production staff as one of their internal customers. There are several reasons and advantages for looking at other parts of the organization as customers in this way. Among the most important of these is the fact that it encourages functions that do not have a direct contact with external customers to appreciate the ideas of marketing and customers, and to understand how their activities can affect external customers with regard to customer satisfaction and service. Some even suggest that internal marketing has important implications for and is related to the happiness of employees at work Vasconcelos[27]). Internal marketing has important implications for the implementation of strategic marketing and in particular the development of marketing orientation. Detailed discussion of this issue is contained in Chapters 9 and 17.

Ethical and social aspects of marketing

Over the years, marketing and marketers have, sometimes with justification, sometimes without, generated antagonism and criticism regarding ethical and social implications associated with marketing activities. Occasionally this antagonism and criticism has been general in nature, for example, attacking notions such as the 'consumer society' or the 'waste of money' on advertising and packaging. At other times, antagonism and criticism has been focused on a particular company and/or incident such as the controversy when Greenpeace criticized Shell for plans to sink the Brent Spar oil platform in the North Sea. Overall, consumers are now much more aware of their rights and the responsibilities of marketers. Similarly, more and more consumers are concerned about protecting the environment and their health from the worst excesses of the marketer. The '**green consumer**' is now a permanent feature and not simply a fad of the 1990s. As Grant[28] shows, soon many marketers will have to plan around low carbon economies where sustainability is the order of the day. Related to this, increasingly marketers must plan within a complex and tough regulatory environment. We now have regulations related to every area of marketing ranging from aspects as diverse as direct marketing (Brubaker)[29] through to relationship marketing techniques (Murphy *et al.*[30]). Even where there are few regulations at the moment, marketers are learning the value of imposing self regulation on some of their activities. Because of these developments, modern-day marketing managers need to be aware of, take account of, and plan for, the social and ethical implications of their marketing strategies.

A controversial ethical area of marketing in recent years has concerned marketing to children. An example of one issue that has been the subject of considerable criticism has been the marketing of what some have suggested are unhealthy children's food products. Some marketers have responded positively to these criticisms. The Co-op, for example, undertakes to use its advertising to promote healthy diets to children; it has also banned the use of characters and cartoons on products which are judged to be high in fat, sugar or salt.

Extended applications for marketing

For many years, marketing concepts and techniques were associated with, and applied to, the marketing of consumer products in the **business-to-consumer (B2C)** sense. These applications spread into **business-to-business marketing (B2B)** such as component suppliers and industrial equipment suppliers. Increasingly, marketing concepts and techniques are being utilized by any organization that has exchange relationships with its public. This includes charities; public sector organizations like libraries, public amenities and the police service; political parties and candidates; causes and ideas; schools and universities; hospitals and other health services. It is now generally accepted that marketing concepts and techniques are not only useful and relevant to any organization where an exchange takes place between one party and another, but also that their application is, in principle, no different from the original applications for marketing in profit-seeking consumer goods organizations.

Cutting Back on Expenses

In 2009 *The Daily Telegraph*, a British national newspaper group, was offered details of expenses and allowances claimed by UK members of parliament. Although essentially confidential, the newspaper decided that releasing this information was in the public interest and began to publish details. The result was a bombshell. The details revealed dozens of MPs claiming as much as they could get away with and more besides.

For example, there were claims against second homes that had never been lived in by the MP. There were claims for duck ponds, garden mowers, expensive televisions and chandeliers. Understandably there was a public outcry. As a result several MPs resigned, there were questions in Parliament, apologies from party leaders and new legislation pertaining to claiming expenses and allowances was rushed through. But what has this to do with marketing? The answer is a lot.

In the first instance much of the problem was caused by a complete lack of understanding, even disdain by MPs of their 'customers' and markets. Many MPs were generally surprised by the furore caused. They apparently simply did not understand why the public was upset which suggests they were not in touch with the needs and views of their voting public. Voters expect lots of things from the politicians they elect, but above all they trust MPs to represent their interests in an honest way. The expenses scandal goes back to marketing basics in terms of understanding what your customers (voters) are buying. Having got into this position, MPs and Parliament itself need to use the tools of marketing to begin to remedy the situation. MPs need first to talk to their constituents and find out their real feelings. MPs need to come up with credible solutions to persuade their constituents and voters that this will never happen again. MPs need to communicate their proposals effectively to voters through announcements from Parliament and personal PR in their own constituencies. Only by marketing themselves effectively, beginning with understanding voters' needs, will MPs and Parliament begin the long and painful process of rehabilitation in the eyes of the British voting public.

SUMMARY

In this chapter we have traced the background to the development of marketing as a philosophy and a function in contemporary organizations. In particular, we have emphasized the importance of being marketing oriented, what this means, and how a company can improve in this respect.

We have also seen that at the same time as some companies struggle to come to terms with the meaning and application of basic marketing principles, marketing itself is changing.

A fundamental characteristic of this chapter has been to demonstrate that marketing is becoming more strategic in nature. The reasons for this are many, but include the pace of environmental and technological change, more aware consumers, increased competition, and increased organizational size and complexity.

A key point has been the discussion of the meaning of strategy and strategic planning together with the key elements of strategic marketing planning. These elements have been set against the framework of analysis and cross-checks necessary to develop a logical and effective planning process.

Applications of marketing have been extended far beyond organizations primarily producing consumer products and marketing itself is changing with developments such as increased use of Information Technology and its requirement for more effective relationship marketing, continued emphasis on the wider ethical and social aspects of marketing, growth in internal marketing and the expansion of global marketing.

KEY TERMS

Beckett Organics

John Beckett enjoys vegetables, so much so that he has given up his full-time job as a lawyer to concentrate on growing and marketing organic vegetables. He started growing vegetables 20 years ago in his back garden and eventually became fully self-sufficient in supplying vegetables for the family. Partly bored with his legal job and tempted by an attractive severance package, John decided he would try to establish his own vegetable supply business. Eighteen months ago he looked around for two fields to lease in which he could grow organic vegetables.

Organic products, including vegetables, are a growth market in the UK. Growers must adhere to strict guidelines in order to gain organic certification. Increasing awareness of the problems associated with many pesticides and fertilizers, coupled with an increased interest in healthy eating habits and 'wholesome' food, has meant that many consumers are now either purchasing or interested in purchasing organic vegetables. This is true not only of household customers, but in addition, many restaurants are using the lure of organic produce to give them a distinctive edge in the marketplace. All this has meant that many of the larger supermarkets in the UK have begun to stock more and more organic produce; from what was a relatively specialized market in the 1990s, the market has grown to where overall organic produce accounts for some 12 per cent of the total UK grocery market and in worldwide terms as of January 2010 it accounts for approximately 3 per cent of all food sales. The market for organic vegetables has grown more rapidly than other organic products and it is estimated that by 2014 some 25 per cent of all vegetables marketed in the UK will be organic. This growth has been sustained at a rate of around 20 per cent per year in developed countries. However, organic yields are between 10 and 20 per cent lower than conventional agriculture, with crops like potatoes some 40 per cent lower. Unsurprisingly, this makes organic produce on average around 40 per cent more expensive than non-organic produce.

A.C. Nielsen Co. cite the case of the United States where organic sales eased in the second half of 2009 as middle- and upper-income families have felt the strain of layoffs and declining investment portfolios. Sales in December 2009 were up 5.6 per cent, year on year, compared with a 25.6 per cent rise a year earlier.

Organic vegetables offer several advantages over their non-organic counterparts:

- They are generally tastier, and because they are not treated in the same way, are usually fresher than non-organic products.
- They are good for a healthy lifestyle as they contain no pesticides or chemicals.
- The fact that no pesticides or herbicides are used in their production means that they are much 'greener'. For example, they help to reduce the problems associated with nitrates in the soil and water supplies.
- On the downside, organic vegetables are generally less uniform, and as far as

. . . continued

some consumers are concerned, are less attractive in appearance. This lack of uniformity has also been a problem in the past with supermarket buyers who have traditionally looked for uniformity in fresh products to aid merchandising and marketing in retail outlets.

■ Generally, organic vegetables are more expensive than their non-organic counterparts. Currently, on average they are somewhere in the region of 40 per cent more expensive.

In the UK, anyone wishing to claim that their produce is organic, and market it in this way, needs to obtain the approval of the Soil Association, which checks the organic credentials of a supplier. For example in this case, they check the conditions under which the produce is grown and how the seeds used.

Two interesting developments are taking place in the organic produce market. One is the growth of home supplies. This is where the producer supplies direct to the householder. There are a variety of ways of doing this. Some smaller growers use mail-shots and leafleting to build up a client base. They then deliver locally to customers who order from a list. Very often the supplier will simply make up a box of a predetermined value or weight containing a selection of vegetables which are in season and ready for picking. Other suppliers are using a similar system, but take their orders via the Internet. This is particularly suitable for this type of product as customers can check on a regular basis what is available and order from home. The produce is then delivered at a pre-arranged time.

The second development in the organic produce market is the growth of farmers' markets. These markets are usually run by local authorities, often on Saturdays or Sundays. Local and other producers attend these markets, paying a small fee for a stall and then selling their produce direct to the consumer. These farmers' markets came about partly as a result of the frustration felt by many farmers and growers at the way they were being treated by retailers and at the margins they were receiving. In addition, such markets have been successful because consumers feel they are getting fresh produce at lower prices than they might be able to obtain through supermarkets.

Despite the growth in the market for organic vegetables, after 18 months in his business, John is worried. Quite simply, his business has not been as successful as he envisaged it would be, and as a result he is not earning enough to make a living. The real worry is that he is not sure why this is the case. His produce, he believes, is as good as anything in the business. He is a very good grower and the land he has leased is perfect for the range of produce he wishes to grow. Starting with organic potatoes he now produces a range of organic vegetables including beans, sprouts, carrots, lettuce and his latest venture: organic tomatoes and corn grown in polytunnels. Although customers he currently supplies are very loyal to John, indeed many are friends and acquaintances he has known over the years when he grew vegetables in his

... continued

back garden, there are simply not enough of them. As a result, his turnover, which increased rapidly over the first year of the business, has for the last six months has stagnated. He mainly supplies locally and has tried to increase his customer base by taking leaflets out and posting them through letterboxes in the area. He has done this by dividing up the housing areas in a 10-mile radius around his growing area and dropping leaflets throughout the area to as many houses as he can cover on a systematic basis. Only some 2 per cent of customers have responded with an order, usually contacting by telephone. These customers seem to come from the middle-class areas. He has considered taking a stall at one of the farmers' markets, the nearest of which is some 40 miles away and operates one day per month, but he realizes this would not be enough to reach the turnover levels he requires. He has in the past supplied one or two local restaurants and hotels, but usually only when they have contacted him because they have had a problem with their existing supplier. He has never followed these up. His growing area is currently too small to supply a major retailer, although he has been approached on an informal basis by the buyer of a voluntary chain of local grocers representing some 40 retail outlets in the county.

John is wondering where he goes from here. He cannot understand why his superior products are not selling well. A friend has suggested that John needs a more strategic approach to marketing. John is not convinced. He feels his business is too small to warrant any kind of marketing, never mind strategic marketing, and he has always felt that a good product should sell itself. He is, however, anxious to grow the business and become a leading organic vegetable supplier.

CASE STUDY QUESTION

What advice would you give to John about developing his business through more effective strategic marketing?

Suggestions as to how to approach and answer this question are contained on the accompanying website. In addition a number of longer strategic case studies, along with suggested solutions, are also contained on the website.

REFERENCES

1 Lamb, J. (ed.) with Marketing Staff at Ohio State University (1965), 'A statement of marketing philosophy', *Journal of Marketing,* January 1965: 43.
2 Cherington, P.T. (1920), *The Elements of Marketing,* New York: Black and East.
3 Mazur, P. (1947), 'Does distribution cost enough?' *Fortune,* November: 1,38.

4 Baker, M.J. (1998), *Dictionary of Marketing and Advertising*, 3rd edn, London and Basingstoke: Macmillan.

5 Smith, A. (1976 [1776]), *Inquiry into the Nature and Causes of the Wealth of Nations*, in W. Campbell, P. Skinner and S. Todd (eds), London: Oxford University Press.

6 Torrens, R. (1971), *The Economist Refuted* [Oddy 1805], p. 13, quoted by L.N. Rodger in *Marketing in a Competitive Economy*, 3rd edn, London: Associated Business Programmes, p. 24.

7 McCullough, J.R. (1833), *A Treatise on the Principles, Practice and History of Commerce,* Society for the Diffusion of Useful Knowledge; London: Baldwin and Cradock, p. 2.

8 Stanton, W.J. (1998), *Fundamentals of Marketing*, 8th edn, London: McGraw-Hill, p. 8.

9 Executive Office of the President (1963), 'Consumer Advisory Council, First Report', Washington, DC: US Government Printing Office, October, pp. 5–8.

10 Lancaster, G. and Massingham, L.C. (2002), *Essentials of Marketing*, 4th edn, Maidenhead: McGraw-Hill, p. 14.

11 Jobber, D. and Lancaster, G. (2009), *Selling and Sales Management*, 8th edn, Harlow: Prentice Hall, p. 17.

12 Levitt, T. (1960), 'Market myopia', *Harvard Business Review*, July–August: 45–6.

13 Kotler, P. and Keller, K.L. (2009), *Marketing Management*, 13th edn, New Jersey: Prentice-Hall, p. 90.

14 Lynch, R. (2006), *Corporate Strategy*, 4th edn, Harlow: Prentice-Hall, pp. 713–14.

15 Baker, M. (2007), *Marketing Strategy and Management*, 4th edn, Basingstoke: Macmillan, p. 54.

16 Kotler, P. and Keller, K. L., op. cit., p.103.

17 Cravens, D.W. (1999), *Strategic Marketing*, 5th edn, Homewood, IL: Richard D. Irwin, p. 20.

18 Weihrich, H. (1982), 'The TOWS matrix – a tool for situational analysis', *Long Range Planning*, 15(2): 54–66.

19 Athanasopoulou, P. (2009), 'Relationship quality: a critical literature review and research agenda', *European Journal of Marketing*, 43(5/6): 583–610.

20 Ndubisi, N. (2007), 'Relationship marketing and customer loyalty', *Marketing Intelligence and Planning*, 25(1): 98–106.

21 Ward, T. and Dagger, T.S. (2007), 'The complexity of relationship marketing for service customers', *Journal of Services Marketing*, 21(4): 281–90.

22 Paul, M., Hennig-Thurau, T., Gremier, D.D., Gwinner, K.P. and Wiertz, C. (2009), 'Towards a theory of repeat purchase drivers for consumer services', *Journal of the Academy of Marketing Science*, 37(2): 215–37.

23 Schibrowsky, J.A., Peltier, J.W. and Nill, A. (2007), 'The state of internet market research: a review of the literature and future research directions', *European Journal of Marketing*, 41(7/8): 722–33.

24 Davidson, A. and Copulsky, J. (2006), 'Managing webmavens: relationships with sophisticated customers via the internet can transform marketing and speed innovation', *Strategy and Leadership*, 34(3): 14–22.

25 Decker, R., Wagner, R. and Schol, S.W. (2005), 'An internet-based approach to environmental scanning', *Marketing Intelligence & Planning*, 23(2): 189–99.

26 Paliwoda, S. and Marinova, S. (2007), 'The marketing challenges within the enlarged Single European Market', *European Journal of Marketing*, 41(3/4): 233–44.

27 Vasconcelos, A.F. (2008), 'Broadening even more the internal marketing concept', *European Journal of Marketing*, 42(11/12): 1246–64.

28 Grant, G. (2008), 'Green marketing', *Strategic Direction*, 24(6): 25–7.

29 Brubaker, S. (2007), 'Ethics and regulation in direct marketing', *Journal of Direct Marketing*, 1(1): 55–8.

30 Murphy, P.E., Laczniak, G.R. and Wood, G. (2007), 'An ethical basis for relationship marketing: a virtue ethics perspective', *European Journal of Marketing*, 44(1/2): 37–57.

Chapter 2

Markets and customers

Consumer and organizational buyer behaviour and marketing strategy

LEARNING OBJECTIVES

After reading this chapter you will:

- appreciate the importance of understanding the behaviour of customers, both household and organizational
- grasp some of the key questions the marketer needs to address in developing this understanding
- be familiar with a framework for analysing consumer and organizational buyers, encompassing the steps and stages involved in the buying process, and factors affecting buyers at each stage
- appreciate some of the recent developments in thinking and research in this area
- understand the key strategic implications of buyer behaviour

INTRODUCTION

Environmental factors, company resources and competitive forces are key inputs into strategic marketing decision making. A key element in strategic marketing planning is an understanding of the buyer behaviour of individuals or organizations in the market.

In this, and the following chapter, we consider markets and customers and how they behave with regard to purchase decisions. The focus of this chapter is upon both **consumer** and **organizational decision making**. Marketers are concerned with how groups of customers behave and which groups they can best serve. In addition to understanding individual purchasing behaviour, the marketer must also understand the seemingly simple, but quite complex, concept of how individual needs combine to form markets and market segments. These concepts and the related issues of market targeting and positioning are the subject of Chapter 3. Here, we investigate buyer behaviour, and develop its strategic implications throughout the text. We also consider how to research buyer behaviour, and examine buyer behaviour in the strategic marketing process. First, it is important to look at the scope of buyer behaviour and to understand the complex nature of the subject area.

THE SCOPE AND COMPLEXITY OF BUYER BEHAVIOUR

Before we proceed, first consider the following seemingly simple questions:

- 'What was the last product or service you purchased?'
- 'Why did you purchase the product or service?'
- 'How did you decide between competing brands and/or suppliers?'
- 'Who, if anybody, other than yourself, was involved in the purchasing decision?'

You will have little difficulty answering these questions. You, the consumer, know the answers. Now think of these questions from the point of view of the supplier of the product or service in question. These apparently simple questions about your purchasing behaviour then become much more complex. Without answers to these questions, it is difficult to make effective strategic marketing decisions.

Most companies are able to resolve these questions with straightforward 'factual' answers, but unless they have some knowledge of buyer behaviour, they are unaware of, and unfamiliar with, the complex range of behavioural factors that impinge upon purchasing behaviour. The truth is that like much of human behaviour, purchase behaviour is complex and multifaceted. Many years ago some of the earliest marketing thinkers recognized the potential contribution of the behavioural sciences such as sociology, psychology and anthropology to understanding buyer behaviour. In doing so Tamilia[1] suggests academics such as Wroe Alderson 'revolutionised the way we now teach and do research in this area of marketing.' We now know that even the simplest purchasing decision is an amalgam of behavioural forces and factors of which even the purchaser might not be aware. For instance, the purpose of a lipstick is not simply to colour the lips. The purchaser may feel more attractive wearing lipstick, the colour may be purchased to match certain clothing or it may contain sunscreen or moisturizers that protect the lips. Partly arising from this complexity, researching and understanding consumer behaviour is a specialist area within marketing. In the context of this chapter, we cannot fully discuss all behavioural concepts and techniques relevant to understanding buyer behaviour. For a more detailed treatment of this area the reader is advised to consult one of the seminal texts, such as Blackwell, Engel and Miniard;[2] East, Vanhuele and Wright[3] or Schiffman, Kanuk and Hansen.[4] Even though consumer behaviour is complex, marketing planners should at least have an understanding of their customers' behaviour. For our purposes we are seeking to develop an appreciation of buyer behaviour in both consumer and organizational markets. Marketers are specifically interested in the behaviour associated with groups, or segments, of consumers as it would be impractical to serve the exact needs and wants of every individual in a market and remain profitable.

What does the area of buyer behaviour cover? Kotler[5] categorizes buyer behaviour into the '**seven "Os"** of the market place', namely:

Occupants	Who constitutes the market?
Objects	What does the market buy?
Occasions	When does the market buy?
Organization	Who participates in the buying?
Objectives	Why does the market buy?
Operations	How does the market buy?
Outlets	Where does the market buy?

Answers to these questions give a company an added advantage over less aware competitors and enable the company to fit their product offerings to customers more closely and satisfy customer needs better than competitors. Marketers need to know whether their controllable variables, e.g. marketing mix variables, will affect buying behaviour. There are many definitions of what constitutes **consumer behaviour**. One of the most popular is provided by Blackwell, Engel and Miniard:[6] 'Those acts of individuals directly involved in obtaining, using and disposing of economic goods, and services, including the decision processes that precede and determine these acts.' This not only encompasses observable buying decisions, but also the underlying, less measurable reasons for purchase decisions. The definition can also be applied to **organizational buyer behaviour** (or buyer behaviour in commercial settings) although many decisions in this area are made by groups. The concepts and implications associated with buyer behaviour can be applied to not-for-profit organizations e.g. charities suffering from 'donor fatigue' need to look at the motivation people feel to donate time and money, and respond to this. As discussed in Chapter 1, in connection with the expenses scandal

Keeping a Cutting Edge

Most men who shave use either an electric razor or a bladed safety razor. In the case of the safety razor, one might be tempted to think that choice and purchase processes might be relatively straight-forward. After all, for most men these are items that are used every day, are relatively inexpensive, and are purchased frequently, usually as part of a regular grocery shop at the supermarket. Unlike clothing or a car, the brand of razor and blades we buy does not say much about us to the outside world. Buyer behaviour in this case can hardly be complex! The American Gillette Company believe it is.

In marketing razors and razor blades the Gillette Company invest considerable time and effort in researching consumers' needs and wants and how these are changing. They know from this research that the behavioural forces and factors that underpin purchase and brand choice of these seemingly mundane items can be complex.

For example, there is a considerable amount of reference group influence when it comes to how men shave and what products they choose. Many men are heavily influenced by what products and brands their fathers used to shave with and are often very brand loyal. Razors are a good example of where the user is different to the purchaser in that it is often women who purchase these products during the weekly shop. Fashions change in shaving inasmuch as it affects appearance. Fifteen years ago, 'clean shaven' was the fashionable look, but this changed and 'designer stubble' became the look; then fashion changed again back towards a clean shaven look, including the shaving of heads. Price is an important factor in brand choice, but not an overriding one for many customers. Sporting celebrities are used heavily in this market. Gillette knows that buyer behaviour is complex and spend large sums understanding these complexities in developing new cutting-edge products for this market.

in UK politics, political parties and government organizations need to understand people who consume their services; location of parks and public transport services need to be researched for consumer wants, needs and usage rates.

The study of buyer behaviour has broad application and the term 'buyer' can be applied to numerous publics that organizations serve. Irrespective of the type of purchase or customer group, it is important to emphasize the potential complexity of buyer behaviour even for seemingly mundane items.

Before examining consumer and organizational buyer behaviour in more detail, it is worth reflecting on models of buyer behaviour.

BUYER BEHAVIOUR MODELS

The aim of buyer behaviour models is to take complex interrelated variables involved in purchase decisions, and simplify them to be of use to the marketer. **Buyer behaviour models** describe the characteristics affecting purchases of goods and services as well as giving insights into potential outcomes of marketing strategies. Many buyer behaviour models have been developed from a

FIGURE 2.1 A 'black box' model

'black box' model. The information that is processed by the buyer is not explained by the model. Figure 2.1 shows a **black box model** where the black box refers to the buyer.

This basic model has been developed into more complex models. In this model, the process and influences on the buyer's decision are not explained. **Multivariate models** try to explain in more detail what is going on in the buying decision. Most of these models view the buyer as a 'problem solver' and concentrate on the influences upon behaviour and the processes involved in purchase. Awareness of a problem arises from some stimuli (e.g. recognizing the need for a new item of clothing), information is processed, environmental and individual influences are evaluated and there is an output of purchase or non-purchase. Models have been developed for consumer, family and organizational buying. Discussions of the most popular models can be found in Schiffman and Kanuk.[7]

Criticisms have been made regarding the practicality of these models because of the difficulty in testing them empirically. Tuck[8] criticized multivariate models as they were not operational. He suggested that the approach took the basic 'black box' and merely broke it into many black boxes so the prediction criterion for a good model was not fulfilled. However, although this criticism is legitimate, most agree that multivariate models give valuable insights on the influences and processes involved in buying decisions and it is our view that these are fundamental to an understanding of customers. They provide a framework that marketers can use to evaluate important marketing opportunities in the buying process. Despite the contributions of multivariate models, in recent years the trend has been towards modelling specific aspects of buyer behaviour using partial models such as for example Damparat and Jolibert's model of buyer–seller relationships[9] or Talluri et al. and their model of 'buyer/supplier negotiations'.[10]

RESEARCHING BUYER BEHAVIOUR

The basis for research can start with the 'seven Os' of the marketplace outlined earlier. There is also the **introspective method** where marketers think about their own probable behaviour. Customers can be interviewed after purchasing their goods and questioned, which is termed the **retrospective method**. Prospective customers can be asked about how they will purchase the product i.e. the **prospective method**. These methods give insights into how consumers go through the process of buying. More difficult from a research point of view is information on the influences of buying behaviour. These are often not product related and involve less measurable aspects of human behaviour, such as perception and attitudes.

Of particular use in understanding some of the more complex underpinning factors affecting behaviour are the techniques of qualitative research. Much qualitative research has as its objective the exploration of matters like attitudes, perceptions and motives; to this end, during the 1960s marketers began to use techniques of 'motivational research'. These were derived from the tools and techniques of clinical psychology and were rooted in concepts and ideas of Freudian psychologists. More recently, concentration has been on qualitative marketing research into consumer behaviour using **focus group** discussions and **depth interviews**.

Focus groups

Focus groups involve a trained moderator guiding a group of selected customers or potential customers through a semi-structured interview. The moderator may have a psychology background, but should be a skilled marketing researcher and interviewer. Normally a focus group consists of between six and ten individuals. The idea is to encourage respondents to discuss factors which will reveal some of their innermost thoughts and feelings regarding a product or service in question. For example, if we were conducting research into consumer attitudes towards, say, the purchase and wearing of ties, the moderator might encourage the group to talk informally about their purchasing in general and then gradually, as the group began to open up and discuss between themselves, focus the discussion towards the product market in question: in this case, ties.

Skill and expertise are required to elicit useful information about the product market in question, without leading the group towards responses that are more in line with the ideas of the moderator than individuals in the group. In other words, care must be taken not to bias answers. A focus group

---

Kettling

'Kettling' is a tactic of crowd control increasingly being used by the British police force to ensure that example public demonstrations do not get out of control. Essentially, the technique entails the police corralling people by a perimeter of police officers usually to a pre-designated spot where the location makes it difficult or impossible to escape, for example into a cul-de-sac. The tactic was extensively used in crowd control at the G20 meeting demonstrations in London in April 2009. Some demonstrators were kettled for up to eight hours until the police determined the demonstration was over and they could be released.

Before these demonstrations and efforts to police them, not many of the public had heard of kettling. However, the demonstration and the policing of it received extensive television coverage not least because one unfortunate demonstrator who was being moved on by the police subsequently died, an event which was captured on television. As a result, the tactic of kettling, already controversial in some circles, became a national controversy. Many people think kettling is unacceptable, over-aggressive, undermines civil liberties, is dangerous and often self-defeating. Others, including senior police officers think it represents a safe and effective means of crowd control and particularly for defusing potentially violent situations.

Is kettling effective and should it be used to control public demonstrations or is it essentially undemocratic and potentially dangerous? Should it be outlawed or should more police be trained to use this tactic? If it is going to be used what should be the situations where it is deployed and should there be constraints on its use? The kettling controversy and questions raised about it are typical of issues for which the focus group technique is ideally suited. In fact, shortly after the G20 disturbances, Metropolitan Commissioner, Sir Paul Stephenson announced a review into the police tactic of kettling. No doubt this review process will include the use of focus group discussions.

interview will take anything between one to two-and-a-half hours and it will usually be recorded for later analysis. It would be common practice if, say, we were using focus groups in the development and launch of a new product in the UK market to conduct anything up to ten focus groups interviews which would be designed to provide a representative sample. At a current average UK cost per focus group of between £2,000 and £4,000, this type of interviewing is relatively costly. Respondents have to be paid as well as the facility that is being used (normally somebody's home) and of course the focus group moderator. It does, however, provide potentially rich information on which to base marketing decisions. Initially used for exploratory research prior to conducting quantitative research, focus groups are increasingly being used to explore further issues highlighted from initial quantitative research based on more traditional questionnaire research and analysis. Focus group interviewing is so useful that it is used by companies ranging from banks through to detergent manufacturers and political parties.

Although widely used in the USA, the use of focus groups to research consumer attitudes, potential voting patterns, and key issues amongst voters in the UK really came into its own in the run-up to the 1997 General Election. The Labour Party, in particular, made use of this type of research. Partly as a result of their success in the 1997 election, and the role focus groups were felt to have played in this, all the main political parties in the UK now use focus groups extensively on a regular basis to gauge voter opinions on various matters. Although there is some concern about the extensive use of these groups – some argue that it tends to detract from developing and implementing policies – there is no doubt that in the political arena, as in most other areas of marketing, focus groups are here to stay.

Depth interviews

Depth interviews are used less frequently than focus groups to research buyer behaviour, but can be useful when researching areas which are of a sensitive nature and where a group discussion situation would not be appropriate. The key difference between depth interviews and focus groups is that the respondent communicates on a one-to-one basis, and not in a group, with the researcher. The interview may be semi-structured or unstructured depending on the purpose and nature of the research. In other respects, with regard to skills required of the interviewer, the depth interview is similar to the focus group. As with a focus group, depth interviews can be used to explore what are more 'hidden' aspects of buyer behaviour and choice. Broad trends in society can be monitored constantly. In the UK there is an ageing population, most with occupational pensions, which means there are more opportunities for products aimed at older consumers. Changing cultural perspectives, such as attitudes to women becoming the main wage earners, and men assuming roles traditionally deemed to belong to women, can be monitored, using depth interviews, to enable marketers to use this attitudinal information in a strategic manner. As already mentioned, focus groups are widely used for researching buyer behaviour, but they are not without its limitations and its critics. In particular, some researchers have begun to question their usefulness, particularly for **futures research** on needs and wants or in assessing attitudes to revolutionary and novel ideas for new products and services.

Criticisms

Critics of focus groups argue that too often participants will knowingly, or subconsciously, tell the focus group leader what they feel he or she wants to hear. Similarly, some argue that there is a danger that group members simply say what they think the rest of the group want to hear. With regard to focus groups being weak at uncovering future trends and needs, the argument is that focus group members find it difficult to imagine or conjecture that product and brand usage will be any different in the future. In other words, there is a tendency for focus group to think along conventional lines.

As a result of these criticisms, some researchers have turned to alternative methods to gain insights into customer needs and wants, especially when trying to detect ideas and responses to new products and services for the future. These methods, now being used in marketing research are collectively referred to as 'futures research'.

Futures research

This is not solely about forecasting the future. Rather it is the application of innovative research techniques to gain insights into possible future needs and wants of consumers and the implications of these for the marketer with regard to possible new products. As this is a comparatively new approach to research in consumer behaviour, there are no definitive rules about how to conduct it. However, it has already generated several innovative and research techniques that are different from those conventionally used.

One of the leading companies in the UK using futures research at the moment, Brand Futures, uses several innovative approaches to its group consumer behaviour research, often coupled with traditional focus groups. Below are outlined some of the differences in this company's futures approach compared to traditional focus group methods.

- Instead of using 'representative' consumers, often the company will conduct interviews using panels of individuals who have previously been judged to be 'thinking ahead' in their particular field.
- Often the groups will deliberately include individuals with alternative views to the rest of the group. For example, a group assembled to investigate possible future meat-based food products might include a vegan.
- New techniques for uncovering attitudes and factors underpinning behaviour are used. One example is a technique known as 'deprivation'. With this, panel members are asked to go without a particular good or service for a period of time and are then interviewed to see what effect this has had on their behaviour. At the other extreme, another technique is 'inflation', where group members are asked to consume a product in much greater quantities than normal, again, with a view to gaining new insights into possible future consumer behaviour.

Using techniques such as these enables the marketer to gain more insights into possible future needs, areas for new product development, brand extension strategies and innovative and creative approaches to marketing existing products.

CONSUMER BUYER BEHAVIOUR

The distinguishing feature of consumer as opposed to organizational buyer behaviour is the fact that consumer buying behaviour consists of activities involved in buying and using products or services for personal and household use. To investigate this, it is advantageous to break down the purchase process into a model to simplify the process and factors influencing purchasing behaviour. Figure 2.2 shows a simplified model.

As can be seen, environmental influences that are external to the consumer affect purchase behaviour. The consumer also has influences that are individually determined. Both these types of influence are carried, consciously or subconsciously, within the consumer's memory. The third box in the diagram shows the decision-making process an individual goes through when purchasing a product. The feedback lines show that at any stage, information can be fed back and the purchase process can be stopped and resumed at an earlier stage. The model is now discussed in greater detail.

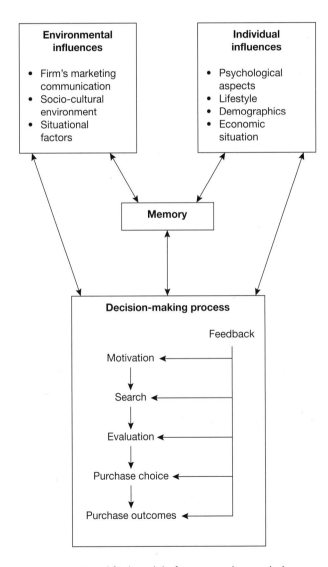

FIGURE 2.2 Simplified model of consumer buying behaviour

Environmental influences

Marketing communications are all around us. Some of these are retained in our memory, and we have an image of companies and the goods and services they provide. This may lead to an immediate motivation to purchase the product, or to be aware of the product, which might lead to purchase at a later stage.

Culture

As behaviour is learned, culture determines the broad values and attitudes an individual holds. Culture can be investigated by using an inventory of values. A child growing up in a certain culture learns its cultural values from socializing with other people, so the family, school and friends have a large impact on the cultural values with which the child grows up. Other aspects of culture are more dynamic. For example, the role of women in some societies has changed dramatically over the years. Even though culture is a basic foundation of society, in the strategic management process it has to be monitored for changes. In addition, culture is often assumed, and this has led to many mistakes when companies have tried to market their products abroad where there are often substantial cultural differences. Yapprak *et al.*[11] suggest there is a need for improved concepts and techniques of culture study in marketing and that an understanding of culture is essential for a whole range of marketing decisions from product development, advertising and communication to segmentation targeting and positioning. We explore these important international cross-cultural factors in Chapter 16, 'Global marketing'. Within a national culture, other aspects of the socio-cultural environment include subculture, social class, group and family influences.

Subculture refers to groups in society that have distinct cultural differences. This includes nationality groups such as Indian, Ghanaian, Italian or Japanese, who have their own individual lifestyles and values. Religious groups, such as Muslims, Jews, Christians and Hindus are a subculture within the larger cultural group. Blacks, whites and Asians are examples of broad racial groupings and geographical groups can include Northern Europeans, Southern Europeans or people living in Belgium or Spain as distinct groups. Subculture groups can vary in the products they buy, the outlets they buy from, prices paid and the media they read. Subcultures take on an array of influences; youth subculture takes on influences from fashion, music, sports personalities and family, for example.

By definition subcultures are different, but some are more different from others, sometimes bizarrely so. Below are eight of the world's most bizarre subcultures. Ever heard of them? If not, you are not part of one of them. Check them out and see what makes them bizarre!

1   Otherkin
2   Norwegian Black Metal
3   Bosozoku
4   Sukeban
5   Goths
6   Argentinean Floggers
7   Lolitas
8   Hardline

Social class

This is the grouping together of individuals or families who have certain common social or economic characteristics. Members of the same social class often exhibit similar patterns of behaviour and similar views and interests. As we shall see in Chapter 3, social class is often used to segment markets and determine targeting strategies. Criteria used for this type of grouping can be occupation, education or income. People from the same social class are more alike than people from differing classes. Social class is seen in terms of higher or lower classes (although individuals can move from one class to another) but this depends on the rigidity of the social system in a particular society. It is a major influence on buyer behaviour because it shows different product purchase behaviour in certain product categories. Examples are cars and holidays, where social class is a determining factor of the types of product purchased. The 'best' measures of social class include a number of factors rather than just one, such as occupation. Social class may determine not only the products people choose to purchase, but also the type of store chosen. For example, a department store, market stall, mail order, the Internet or independent retailer may be favoured by certain social classes.

Groups and family

Group influences affect purchase decisions. **Reference groups** are groups an individual is exposed to that have a direct or an indirect influence on behaviour and attitudes. **Primary groups** are ones with which contact is continuous and include family, neighbours, friends and colleagues. **Secondary groups** have less contact with individual members; e.g. members of a football team. People also have aspirations and may be affected by group pressure from an **aspirational group**; this is often used for example when marketing cosmetics with advertisements showing women from the aspirational group of beauty, wealth and desirability using the product. Reference groups affect people in three ways:

1   they influence self image and attitudes;
2   they expose individuals to new behaviour;
3   they create pressure to conform.

Reference group importance will depend on the product in question. If group influences are strong the marketer will seek to identify **opinion leaders** in the group. Opinion leaders have influence over members of their reference group. For instance, if you are about to purchase a computer and a friend you know is interested in them, then you may ask this friend for advice; then the friend is an opinion leader. The **family group** also has an influence on purchase behaviour and many purchases are made as a family group, e.g. the purchase of a house, a holiday, a car and furniture. In family decision making, individual members may assume different roles. Depending on the purchase and individuals involved they may perform one or many roles outlined below:

1   information gatherer;
2   influencer;
3   decision maker;

4   purchaser;
5   consumer.

For example, for the purchase of a holiday, a mother and daughter may go into a travel agent and pick up brochures; all the family will influence the decision, and the final decision might be made by the father, but the mother books the holiday and is then the purchaser. All the family are consumers. Some products within family decision making are dominated by the husband or wife; others are made jointly.

Marketers of many brands recognize that consumption habits, including brand choice and patterns of product usage, are often established early on in the consumer's life and once established can last a lifetime.

■   Procter & Gamble's 'Sunny Delight' was one of the most successful new brands to be launched in the UK. Introduced to the UK market in 1998, in just two years it had reached sales of £160 million, rivalling Coke and Pepsi. Kids loved it. But then it all went wrong. A stream of bad publicity hit the brand, centred round the fact that the product was not as healthy as it claimed. In addition one child turned orange through consuming too much of it. By 2003 Procter and Gamble sold the brand and it disappeared from the UK market. It's now back. Marketed once more as a healthy drink and called Sunny D. Guess what! The kids who loved it in the late 1990s still love it, even though many are young adults with children of their own. They now buy Sunny D for their children and a new Sunny D generation has been born.
■   One of the biggest user groups on the Internet is children. Unsurprisingly, brands like 'Slush Puppy' have been amongst the first to create websites on the Net that engage children. See: http://www.slushpuppie.co.uk/english/index.html.
■   Tesco launched its 'Computers for Schools' campaign which is sponsored by Pepsi, Tango and 7-Up brands. This is campaign is actually aimed at the parents of children, but uses the power of children to persuade their parent to buy.

Situational factors

Situational factors determine a purchase or consumption situation and can be a major aspect in purchase behaviour. If you were asked about your favourite food it would be acceptable to state that it depends upon the situation. At times you may prefer a snack, at others a meal with the family and at other times a meal in a restaurant. The consumption situation directly influences consumer brand perceptions and purchase behaviour, i.e. the place and situation in which the product is going to be consumed. Product availability, special offers and changes in price may also affect purchase behaviour.

In addition to environmental factors that influence a consumer's purchase decisions, there are individual differences that are personal or individual to the consumer. Psychological factors (see Figure 2.2) include perceptions, motivations, attitudes and personality. Perception is the way in which people select, organize and interpret stimuli. This includes how a person sees and interprets a company and its products. When a message is perceived it is modified by the individual's interpretation. An individual selects (subconsciously) exposure to, attention towards, comprehension and retention of stimuli. This information is organized so that it can be easily understood. This is done largely subconsciously by placing information in categories or combining these into brand images. It is, therefore, important that marketers build up brand awareness so a personality for the brand is developed in the minds of prospective buyers.

Attitudes are specific: an attitude is held about a certain product or supplier in the context of consumer behaviour. Attitudes are difficult to change, so companies finding that certain products are associated with a poor attitude might be better advised to change the product than try to change consumer attitudes.

Demographic variables describe individuals according to age, sex, income, education and occupation. Demographic factors have a bearing on the types of product individuals want, where they shop and how they evaluate possible purchases. For instance, a teenage girl might generally want different clothing products than those purchased by her mother. A concept similar to age is life cycle stage. Throughout life, people go through stages: single, married, married with children, children left home and retired. At each of these stages their product needs will be changing. Some never marry, but their needs change at different periods of life.

Lifestyle variables encompass an individual's *activities, interests and opinions* (called **AIO research**). A person's lifestyle is how they interact with their environment, which has implications for purchase behaviour. **Lifestyle concepts** and research are useful to the contemporary marketer, especially with regard to market segmentation and targeting and these are elaborated in Chapter 3.

The *economic situation* an individual faces affects purchase decisions. This not only encompasses how much income individuals have, but whether they have borrowing power and their attitude toward spending. Individual and environmental influences may then be stored in an individual's memory, which will be used during the decision-making process.

The decision-making process

In Figure 2.2 the **decision-making process** is shown in the lower box and encompasses five stages. The first stage is when an individual feels a need that a product will satisfy and is motivated to evaluate the goods on offer. People have many varying needs. If a need is intense they become motivated to purchase the product that will satisfy it. Abraham Maslow[12] described different needs of humans as being hierarchical as shown in Figure 2.3. This shows, at the bottom of the pyramid, physiological needs which are the most basic of human needs. When needs are met lower in the pyramid, individuals move up the hierarchy to fulfil 'higher' needs. Purchasing motivation can be stimulated by marketing. For instance, when people see an advertisement for a burger they may feel hunger and purchase one or they may seek alternatives like going to a restaurant to fulfil this need. This search for alternatives may be *external* i.e. physically looking for alternatives or *internal* i.e. searching through memory. Marketers need to research how they can stimulate need for their products and the types of information consumers require.

An example of how **Maslow's hierarchy** of needs can be useful to the development of strategic marketing plans is contained in research by Swoboda *et al.*[13] In a study which looked at the relevance of service in the retail environment they found that many customers had moved on from looking to simply meet their basic needs when purchasing. Instead they had moved up the hierarchy of needs and were looking for much more personal service from the retailers they shopped at. Personal

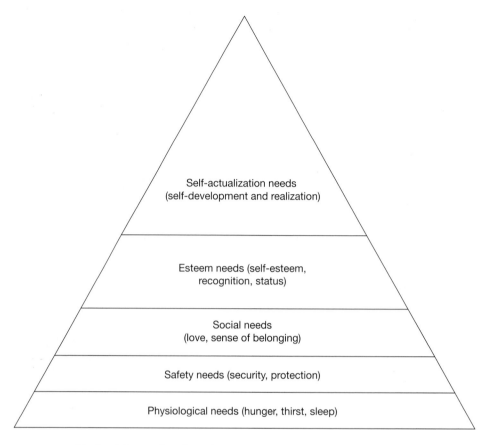

FIGURE 2.3 Maslow's hierarchy of needs

service quality appealing to what Maslow might have identified as social and achievement needs was extremely important in building an effective retailer brand image.

Ozuem, Howell and Lancaster[14] conducted research that suggested that the advent of the Internet and its widespread deployment as a means of communication was changing the information environment where once fragmentation was the ruling condition. Technology, they argued, is creating a 'defragmented' society. By providing a new common interface for shopping at 'lightning' pace in a competitive environment, the traditional idea that a valuable shopping experience depends on a human marketplace is now giving way to virtual computer-mediated marketing environments, and they concluded that the web-enabled marketing environment is best suited for information gathering.

There are numerous sources of information including that from friends or **word-of-mouth**, from advertisements and media sources such as press articles about a particular product or service. Another source of information is the handling of the products. When information has been assimilated by the individual, he or she can make judgements about alternative brands that are available. Marketers, as well as building awareness, need to ensure their products have **unique selling propositions (USPs)** so they stand out amongst competing brands.

When consumers have enough information they will evaluate alternatives. Criteria on which products are evaluated vary depending on the products and how many brands are available. The evaluative criteria used depend on what need is being fulfilled by the product. Most often highlighted is the role of price and the brand image. It is imperative that marketers know on what basis their products are being judged. If there are common themes from consumers for the evaluation of alternative products and the ideal product offering, this has implications for marketing management. It means that products can be tailored to suit consumer needs and marketing communications can respond to the evaluation criteria they use. Evaluating products often coincides with actually searching for the products.

When a product or brand has been evaluated, one product is selected for purchase. However, purchase intention can be affected by unforeseen factors e.g. a price rise or other people's opinions can have an effect on purchase choice even at this late stage. There may, therefore, be no purchase at all.

Purchase outcomes or *post-purchase behaviour* will be either satisfaction or dissatisfaction with the purchase choice. Again, the product will be judged against the needs that were to be fulfilled by it and by the criteria on which alternative brands were judged. Satisfaction occurs when expectations of the product are either met or exceeded. This is remembered next time it is purchased. The consumer may then tell friends about being satisfied with the product. If expectations have not been met, the consumer experiences some **post-purchase dissonance**. There are many ways in which consumers try to reduce post-purchase dissonance. They can find information to support their product choice, or avoid information that will not confirm their purchase. If dissonance is strong, the consumer may take action either against the company directly, perhaps asking for a refund, or indirectly by telling friends about problems with the product.

Marketers should be conscious of the importance of post-purchase feelings, and in particular the need to ensure that customers are satisfied with their purchase decisions. Effective marketers contact customers after purchase to enquire whether they are happy with their purchase and the way they have been dealt with. This cannot always be done on an individual personal basis, but it is possible to communicate with customers in writing to demonstrate that the company values their custom and are willing to respond to any dissatisfaction they may be experiencing as a result of having purchased the products or services. Similarly, companies can use **tracking studies** to assess levels of customer satisfaction or dissatisfaction over time. Research findings show that dissatisfied customers will on average express this dissatisfaction to nine other actual or potential customers. As we have seen in the context of reference groups, word-of-mouth is extremely important in influencing customer choice. In addition, marketers appreciate that it is more cost effective to retain existing customers than to attract new ones. Research has shown that attracting a new customer costs approximately five times the cost of retaining an existing one. The importance of this initial cost difference is further underpinned by the lifetime value of loyal customers, which can mean substantial amounts of revenue and profit to a company. It is vital to assess levels of customer retention and causes of customer attrition, and take steps to increase the former while reducing the latter. There is strong evidence that the customer's experience of relationship quality has a major impact on reducing post-purchase perceived value. Moliner *et al.*[15] contend that the higher the quality of the relationship, the greater will be the perceived value of the purchase and the greater will be customers' likelihood of purchasing again. Recognition of the importance of keeping customers and building loyalty is a major reason for the growth of relationship marketing as discussed in Chapter 1. This development in marketing is so far-reaching and important that we return to it in Chapter 9.

Whether or not all these behavioural stages are experienced, as well as the time spent at each stage, depends on the individual and the product purchased. Some products require extensive problem solving where a great deal of information is required to make a decision. This type of product is usually expensive, complex to understand, and/or has not been bought previously e.g. a house, a personal computer or a car. Limited search and evaluation will be used when there is some knowledge of the products on offer e.g. a small item of furniture or bed linen for the house. When customers know a great deal about the product, there is little search and evaluation. The purchase may be habitual e.g. repeat buying of the same brand of toothpaste or washing powder. This '**low involvement**' decision making causes some problems for marketers. Should they try to make such decisions ones of '**high involvement**'? Are consumers being brand loyal to products in an active way or are they displaying inertia? What is the best way of promoting the product in a low involvement market? Ways in which marketers try to increase involvement of consumers include:

1 Link the product with an issue, e.g. the marketing of relatively mundane products being described as being environmentally friendly or 'green'.
2 Use advertising that involves consumers, e.g. 'try the Pepsi challenge'.
3 Change product benefits, e.g. The washing detergent 'Radion' advertisements emphasize the benefit of effectively cleansing work-stained clothes and making them clean smelling.

Using a model such as Figure 2.2 shows the marketer how to break down consumer behaviour into aspects that can be analysed for effective strategic marketing planning. Many aspects of consumer behaviour can also be used to evaluate organizational buying behaviour and we now turn our attention to this.

A Shocking Example

A more extreme example of trying to increase levels of consumer involvement is the controversial approach to advertising used by the Benetton Company. Luciano Benetton's belief is that 'communication should not be commissioned from outside the company, but conceived from within its heart.' Their campaigns for clothing products have included pictures of dying Aids patients and kissing nuns. Although the advertising campaigns are complex and multifaceted they have nothing to do with Benetton clothing: as much as anything, they are designed to increase customer involvement with the product and brand by linking these products with issues.

These campaigns have gathered international awards, but at the same time have provoked fervent reactions, confirming that they are a focal point of discussion of confrontational ideas. When photographs of Death Row inmates were included in their advertising the backlash from families of murder victims was so severe that they convinced the Sears chain not to stock Benetton products, which was an enormous setback. This led to the end of the tenure at Benetton of Toscani, their photographer and creative marketing director, who specialized in confronting the public with challenging issues.

ORGANIZATIONAL BUYING BEHAVIOUR

There are three categories of organizational purchasers:

1   **institutional buyers** (e.g. buyers in the police service, fire service and public authority);
2   **retail buyers**;
3   **industrial buyers**.

These differences give rise to major differences between the three types of buying.

Organizations buy to enable them to provide goods and services that eventually reach final consumers. As has been explained, consumer buying behaviour relates to individuals (or families) buying goods and services for their own use. Both organizational and consumer buying behaviour involves people, individually and in groups, who are affected by environmental and individual factors. Organizational buying usually involves group decision making, which is known as the '**decision-making unit**' (DMU) or what Webster and Wind[16] referred to as the **buying centre**. In such a group, individuals have different roles in the purchasing process, categorized as:

1   *Initiators* – these people requisition or suggest purchasing a product or service;
2   *Users* – these are people in the organization who use the product. Sometimes they will also be involved in devising product specifications;
3   *Influencers* – influencers affect the buying decision in different ways e.g. they may be technical personnel who have developed product specifications;
4   *Deciders* – deciders make the buying decision (in most cases this is the buyer);
5   *Buyers* – buyers have formal authority to purchase the product;
6   *Approvers* – these people authorize actions of deciders or buyers;
7   *Gatekeepers* – gatekeepers control the flow of information to and from DMU or buying centre members e.g. a buyer's assistant or a telephonist.

One person might play all these roles, or each may be performed by different persons or groups of people.

Another difference in organizational buying is that many products are complex and require specialist knowledge to purchase. Where products have complicated specifications, there is more communication and negotiation between buyers and sellers. After-sales service is important and suppliers are evaluated after purchase. Organizational markets have fewer, larger buyers who tend to be geographically concentrated. Another aspect is the nature of **derived demand**, where demand for organizational (especially industrial) goods is derived from consumer markets. If demand for end product consumer goods falls this affects the entire **supply chain**.

Organizational buying decisions can be categorized into **buy classes** as to how complex they are, similar to low/high involvement decision making in consumer markets. A **straight re-buy** occurs often, is relatively cheap and usually a matter of routine. If the supplier is an '**in**' **supplier** they are on the company's approved list of suppliers; they have to perform well so they do not get taken off the list. If they are '**out**' **suppliers** they must try to get onto the approved list. A **modified re-buy** is a situation that requires some additional information or evaluation of suppliers. It is usually the case that specifications have been modified since the last purchase. A **new task** or **new buy** is the most complex purchase decision, when the company has not bought the product before. Search and evaluation procedures are extensive.

The process of organizational buying

The process involved in organizational buying has many similarities to consumer buying. Both go through a form of need recognition, search, evaluation, choice and post-purchase evaluation. Figure 2.4 shows the specific **buy phases** organizations go through when buying.

Need recognition occurs when the company has a need that can be fulfilled by the purchase of a product. Need can be stimulated internally from within the organization or through external means (e.g. if a salesperson visits with a new product). The company will then draw up general specifications. This can be done in consultation with the prospective seller, so more detailed specifications can be assimilated. **Value Analysis (VA)** (sometimes called Value Management) is a technique that evolved from Value Engineering that was first used in General Electric, USA during the Second World War. It can be used to reduce the costs of components in the production process by a team approach that critically examines the function and specification of each part in every component and sub-component. The team typically consists of people from design, manufacturing, marketing and purchasing, so different views can be incorporated e.g. if the manufacture of a particular product has tight specifications, this can be costly in terms of precision engineering components that must be produced; however, if marketing states that customers do not need such precisely engineered component parts, then the specification can be lowered with potential cost savings.

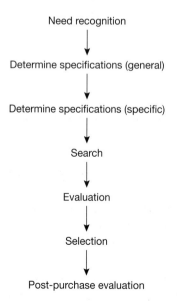

FIGURE 2.4 Organizational buying process

In the search stage of the organizational buying process, buyers use many information sources. They may advertise for tenders, investigate trade journals or directories, speak to salespeople, look at their own records or visit trade shows.

Marketing implications for suppliers include achieving a good reputation in the marketplace, attending trade shows, advertising and trying to identify prospective customers. By so doing the company can be considered early in the decision process and may even be involved in the formulation of specifications.

Evaluation may be systematic, involving some form of supplier evaluation technique. These can be detailed, covering quality, price, delivery and after-sales service. The buying centre will evaluate proposals and alternative product offerings and decide on the most suitable purchase choice. At this stage there may be further negotiations to alter the price on certain product specifications. The buying centre may choose to have a number of suppliers to protect it from being too dependent on one supplier. The selection stage may also incorporate some form of reordering system and the evaluation of the product after purchase, and such a procedure is often formalized.

Time spent, resources committed and whether all stages are passed through depends on the type of product bought. A 'new task' product means that all stages will probably be passed through. A straight re-buy will be a relatively quick process, missing a number of stages, and this type of purchasing is now often accessed by routine computerized buying. The people involved in the decision-making process can change over time, and it is important for the marketer to be aware of how marketing tactics can be modified because of this.

Members of the buying centre or DMU are influenced by both rational and emotional factors in their decision making. Marketers should be aware of different influences on the buying centre, although emotional factors are much more difficult to predict and interpret. Rational motives include price, service, quality and reliable delivery, whereas emotional motives include personal friendships between sellers and buyers and perceived risks of purchasing. Other influences on organizational buyers are now examined.

Influences on organizational buying

In consumer buying behaviour we discussed environmental and individual factors that influence purchasing behaviour. In organizational buying there is a more complex environment as illustrated in Figure 2.5 adapted from Hutt and Speh's model.[17]

Environmental forces on buyer behaviour include economic, legal, political, cultural, physical and technological factors, so general economic trends in the commercial arena in which the buying organization is located are important, as are specific economic trends in areas in which it trades (due to derived demand). When evaluating economic trends, the marketer should take a global perspective as world trade expands. The political and legal environment includes government spending, taxation and import and export controls, which should be evaluated for their influence on buying decisions. As global markets develop it is easy to disregard cultural differences, yet there are many different cultural climates and they should be addressed individually. Physical influences involve the geographical location of the organization and a changing technological environment also influences buying decisions. Marketers must also take account of group force purchasing influences:

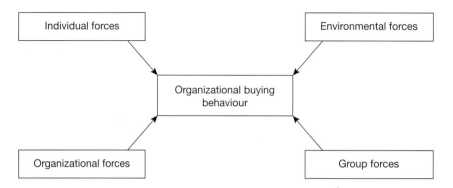

FIGURE 2.5 Influences on organizational buying

Source: Adapted from M.D. Hutt and Speh, T.W. (1999), *Business Marketing Management*, London: Dryden Press.

1   Who is involved in the buying decision?
2   What influence does each member have?
3   How does each member of the buying centre evaluate alternative products?

The type of information that is needed on *group forces* only becomes available when close contact is maintained with the buyer. This reinforces the role of the salesperson in the buying decision process. Members of the DMU are distinguished by the roles that each member carries out.

    Organizational forces, such as the organizational culture of the business, also have an effect on the buying decision. For instance, when marketing to an organization that has a highly centralized structure, including the buying function, this needs a different marketing approach to companies that have a decentralized structure.

    It might be assumed that organizational buying has little to do with *individual forces*. In any buying centre, individuals make buying decisions, not the organization. Different members of the buying centre may evaluate products using different criteria, which complicates the issue for the organizational marketer. Individuals try to reduce the level of risk they are exposed to in the purchase decision by using multiple sources or using an extensive information search. These factors have been developed into a comprehensive model of organizational buying behaviour by Webster and Wind.[18]

    There have been a number of trends over recent years within organizational purchasing that have implications for marketing management:

1   Purchasing is now more specialized and professional.
2   There is more centralized purchasing.
3   Computerized purchasing has increased.
4   There are new philosophies of purchasing, e.g. 'just-in-time', zero defects and materials management.
5   Supplier capability and performance analysis have improved.
6   Use of e-commerce purchasing and supply has increased.

TRENDS IN ORGANIZATIONAL PURCHASING

These trends are important in the sense that they have potentially significant implications for the development of marketing strategies and plans. However, three of these trends in organizational purchasing are felt to have been particularly important in this respect, and are now considered in more detail.

Just in Time purchasing

Originally devised in America, but first applied in the Toyota Company in Japan, many manufacturing companies have moved towards a system of manufacturing based on having parts and components for production in stock and available when, and only when, they are required by the production line or unit. For obvious reasons this system of manufacturing and inventory control has come to be termed **Just in Time (JIT)** although a more formal term is '**lean manufacturing**'. Used extensively in Japan for many years, it has now made major inroads into manufacturing companies in Western economies. A definition of JIT by Dion *et al.*[19] explains the meaning of JIT and captures its essential features:

> an inventory control system which delivers input to its production or distribution site only at the rate and time it is needed. Thus it reduces inventories whether it is used within the firm or as a mechanism regulating the flow of products between adjacent firms in the distribution system channel. It is a 'pull' system which replaces buffer inventories with channel member co-operation.

Companies realize that holding stock, including stock for production or sale, is costly. Not only is capital tied up, but there are potential costs in stockholding: for example, extra staff needed as stores personnel, pilferage, damage, changes in customer demand or product specification which renders stock obsolete. A JIT system aims to minimize stockholding and associated costs by supplying raw materials and component parts for production just at the time they are needed. The consequence of such a system for suppliers is that they must be able to provide parts and components on a continuous basis, typically within a four-hour time window, to consignees. In turn, this means there must be a close working relationship and exchange of information between customers and suppliers and to this end, as Lancaster[20] points out, close associations must be developed between marketer and customers.

JIT purchasing is the main factor underpinning the growth of 'relationship marketing' which we consider in more detail in Chapter 9. In addition to the need for close working relationships between suppliers and customers, supplying on a JIT basis increases the importance of effective distribution and logistical systems on the part of marketers. We consider some of the impacts of JIT on this element of marketing in Chapter 6 on logistics. The introduction of JIT purchasing by a customer means a reduction in supplier numbers, normally one for each item being supplied, and often with increasing numbers of parts being purchased from outside rather than being manufactured internally. In a properly synchronized JIT system customer demands can be met and profits maintained or increased through a reduction in stockpiles and inventory levels. An accounting rule of thumb says: 'on average the cost of holding stock can add 25 per cent to the costs of materials and component parts'.

There are however some drawbacks to JIT, principally through the need for synchronization. Suppliers might have commitments to other customers, so causing delays. A company's industrial relations must be excellent, which is why the first Japanese car manufacturer to set up in the UK (Nissan at Sunderland) insisted on single trade union representation with a 'no strike' clause written into workers' agreements, because to operate a successful JIT system means no downtime on the production line and the acceptance of flexible work routines.

Zero defects

Zero defects is closely related to JIT purchasing. The need for zero defects and reliable quality on the part of the supplier is critical as components are incorporated into the manufacturing process almost immediately following delivery. There is no time to test components or inspect for defective supplies. End customers demand totally consistent quality and this has pushed the need for quality back down the chain of manufacture and supply to involve all the different companies in the production and supply chain. For example, the Jaguar Motor Company in the 1970s, when experiencing substantial loss of market share and falling profits (particularly in export markets) due to the supply of poor quality components, turned the situation round by insisting on improved quality from their suppliers. Early recognition of the importance of quality, however, has now moved on with many companies now implementing and operating **total quality management (TQM)** systems. Lancaster[21] has shown that companies must focus on the total product quality of their goods to differentiate themselves from the opposition. JIT purchasing means that components and supplies must be 'right first time'. In the 1960s and 1970s it was typically sufficient to ensure that defects were within controllable and acceptable levels when supplying customers. Customers now insist that there must be no defects in supply. This has revolutionized manufacturing, quality control, design, marketing and logistics systems.

B2B markets

In business to business (B2B) markets, customer satisfaction is an evaluation by purchasers of suppliers, based on supply and consumption experience. The customer is the ultimate judge of supplier performance. Therefore, the organizational marketer has to ascertain how customers evaluate and hence choose between suppliers and in particular what, from the perspective of the customer, constitutes good and bad supplier performance. Business customers are becoming much more sophisticated in their supplier evaluation and selection systems. A study by Marzouk[22] illustrates just how sophisticated these systems can be. He proposes a model which allows a supplier-ranking process using a range of preference structures which can be used to rank potential suppliers with regard to the extent to which they have the required skills, resources and abilities.

As our earlier discussion of the decision-making unit shows, different functional areas have different criteria that determine their evaluation and selection of different suppliers. Engineers, for example, use different criteria with suppliers than purchasing or manufacturing personnel. In assessing the industrial buyers' perceptions of quality and satisfaction one must look at the buying group and not just the purchasing function. Despite these differences in perceptions of what constitutes supplier performance, there is no doubt that most organizations understand the importance of effective supplier evaluation and performance. A study by Cormican and Cunningham[23] shows how careful supplier selection can result in increased quality, reduced lead times and a reduction in the number of defects.

E-commerce and organizational buying

A major development affecting marketers in recent years has been the development of electronic commerce. **E-commerce** has major implications for marketing practice and it embraces a range of techniques and procedures for conducting business electronically. It is the use of electronic technologies and systems to facilitate and enhance transactions between different parts of the **value chain**. The value chain stretches from primary production of raw materials to the end customer, as opposed to the **supply chain** which stretches from the end product manufacturer to the primary source of supply. Just to complete this explanation the **demand chain** stretches from the end product manufacturer to the end customer, so the value chain is represented by the demand chain plus the supply chain.

One of the first applications of e-commerce was in the area of B2B marketing. In the 1980s companies began to use computers as a matter of course in purchasing and supply. Eventually, this developed into systems whereby suppliers and buyers could readily exchange information through linked computer systems. This developed into full **electronic-data-interchange (EDI)** systems which offer advantages to both parties in the transaction. For example, in the customer's company, when stocks reach a pre-ordained minimum level an automatic order is sent via the computer to the supplier's company whose computerized systems will in turn set in train the complete sequence of actions required to fulfil the customer's order. EDI systems are now so widely used in B2B markets that often suppliers are selected by a computer. All major motor companies in the world insist that their suppliers supply on an EDI basis with Japanese companies being at the forefront of this development.

Continuing the trend towards more and more electronically based systems, companies now have **extranet** systems that go further than linking just suppliers and buyers, as they seek to link together all members of the value chain including suppliers' suppliers and distributors and intermediaries. The extranet allows closer and more sophisticated relationships to be developed between the members of the value chain as it requires access to, and use of information between, members of the chain. This requires trust and commitment between all members.

We have discussed the main influences and processes of buyer behaviour in consumer and organizational markets, and examined some of the key trends and developments particularly regarding JIT purchasing, zero defects and the growth of e-commerce in B2B markets. This text is based upon a strategic as well as a tactical marketing outlook, so it is worth re-examining the application of strategic marketing concepts and assessing the insights that understanding buyer behaviour can offer.

STRATEGIC IMPLICATIONS OF BUYER BEHAVIOUR

Whatever definition of marketing is selected, consumer orientation is central. Implicit in a marketing-oriented company is the assumption that the wish is to satisfy customers. We now look at aspects of the strategic marketing process and discuss applications of buyer behaviour at each stage, starting with the **business mission**.

Business mission

Production and sales-oriented companies usually have 'company' based missions rather than 'customer'-based missions. A customer-based mission necessarily aligns the company with the marketing concept and affirms the importance of consumer behaviour to the firm.

SWOT analysis

Strengths and weaknesses that are internal to the organization are assessed to ascertain its capability and resources. Opportunities and threats are external to the organization and are evaluated to determine the broad environmental and competitive trends that have an impact on it. Companies that can diagnose threats and turn them into opportunities have an added advantage in the marketplace. This includes trends in consumer behaviour e.g. a change in lifestyle may have implications for the company; over recent years more people have been concerned with healthy eating, so food producers who monitored this trend and anticipated such changes were in a better position than competitors. Such companies changed their product offerings, e.g. Walkers put less salt into their potato crisps, or communicated existing healthy attributes about their products to consumers. Consumer behaviour can also be used in the strengths and weaknesses analysis to discover attitudes and awareness about their brands as well as those of competitors.

Market opportunity analysis

From an analysis of consumer behaviour it can be seen how existing products are perceived in comparison to those of competitors. **Market opportunity analysis** also shows whether or not there are any gaps in the market that your company can meet profitably with new products e.g. the shampoo brand 'Empathy' was launched to cater for the specific needs of older female consumers, a segment that was previously ignored. The theme of segmentation targeting and positioning is dealt with in detail in Chapter 3 as it has a strong link with the study of buyer behaviour. Suffice to say here that markets can be segmented into homogeneous groupings of consumers in a number of ways. Some of these ways are included in Figure 2.2, for example: demographics, lifestyle and social class. Therefore, consumer behaviour itself is used as a segmentation variable. When groupings of consumers are identified, companies decide which ones to target. Positioning strategies then aim to take the product offering and 'position' it in the mind of consumers to reflect consumer behaviour of targeted customers.

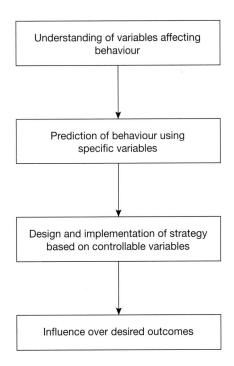

FIGURE 2.6 Knowledge of consumer behaviour facilitates development of successful marketing strategies
Source: Schiffman and Kanuk.[24]

Design of marketing strategies

Marketing strategies that companies decide to implement should be consistent with the consumer behaviour associated with the product or service. In Figure 2.6 Schiffman and Kanuk show how knowledge of consumer behaviour can aid the development of successful marketing strategies. First, the variables affecting purchase behaviour must be analysed and understood. This allows for the prediction of behaviour using the most important variables. Strategies based on controllable variables i.e. marketing mix variables of product, price, place and promotion, are designed and implemented which should influence the desired outcome of making a purchase.

Product

The study of consumer behaviour should indicate the types of product or service that will be successful. This can be extended into detailed product attributes and packaging decisions, including after-sales service. For example, a car manufacturer, to be successful, should look at consumer behaviour to see:

1   the preferred types of cars for certain groups of customers;
2   what product attribute/features are required, e.g. large boot, four doors, speed or fuel consumption;
3   warranties required after the sale.

In organizational markets we have already seen that with regard to the product, what is particularly crucial is control of the quality of the product or service being supplied, and the need to look at quality and its attributes from the perspective of the decision-making unit.

Price

Research into the relationship between price and consumer behaviour is important to the marketer. Consumers may not be aware of the prices of certain goods they purchase. This is especially true in **fast-moving consumer goods (FMCG)** markets. Consumers may be sensitive to price differentials between competing brands; in this case the marketer will have to monitor competitors' pricing strategies and either compete on price or try to add value to the product in another way. For many products, there is a relationship between price and perceived quality. An appropriate marketing strategy should therefore take into account consumer attitudes toward price for the product category in question.

In marketing to organizational buyers it is important not to make the mistake of believing and acting on the notion that organizational buyers buy only on price and will always select the lowest priced supplier. In both consumer and organizational markets it is overall value that is most important. Organizational buyers recognize that the lowest priced supplier does not necessarily equate with the lowest cost solution, particularly where this means lower quality.

Place

These decisions concern channels of distribution from the producer to the consumer. Different consumer groups have preferences for different retail outlets for certain products e.g. in ladies fashion some customers prefer to shop in department stores or in independent retail outlets, market stalls, mail order or chain stores. Consumer behaviour research can indicate how many outlets there should be, and where they should be located. A study of consumer behaviour can indicate to a company whether to provide out-of-town shopping facilities or to locate in a city centre. Where and how products are sold is also linked to store design. The layout of the shop is important as are 'atmospherics' within the store. Research has shown that consumers like the convenience of supermarket shopping but also want good quality fresh food. Fresh fruit and vegetables are usually displayed as a consumer enters a supermarket to indicate freshness and quality. In-store bakers are not simply there to provide fresh bread, but also to provide the smell of baking bread, and consumer behaviour research allows marketers to make decisions about enhancing 'atmospherics' in retail outlets.

The widespread adoption of JIT purchasing has meant that in organizational markets, reliable delivery and the design of distribution and logistics systems are crucial.

Promotion

Different consumer groups respond positively or negatively to marketing communications. Research into consumer behaviour will indicate to which promotional tools the target market will respond favourably. This can be used for general media planning e.g. when marketing a skin cream to teenage girls, research may help in deciding to conduct press advertising; further research may then indicate more specific media e.g. a monthly teenage magazine with further research indicating how often the advertisement should be inserted and the type of advertising copy and images to use.

Promotion can also be used to try to change a poor consumer image. In the UK, many companies have attempted to change their images by positive promotional campaigns.

As with price, there are some misconceptions about the role and value of promotion when marketing to organizational buyers. Many companies have a belief that the 'rationality' and 'hard-headedness' of organizational buyers has meant that the promotional element of the mix is less effective and important in forming attitudes of buyers. However, organizational buyers are individuals and in this context might be swayed by effective advertising and imagery provided as part of the marketing mix. Evidence suggests that advertising in organizational markets can help to substantially reduce costs of selling.

Control of marketing effort

By observing and analysing consumer behaviour we can evaluate the success of marketing programmes. Marketing strategies can then be refined to fit customer needs more closely.

SUMMARY

The concept of fulfilling consumer needs is central to successful marketing strategy. The study of buyer behaviour has become a specialist area of marketing owing to its complexity and it covers questions concerning who is in the market, what they buy, when they buy, how they buy and where. Marketing mix variables – price, product, place and promotion and the extra 3Ps of the mix for services – affect buyer behaviour, so the strategic marketer should be aware of the impact of these controllable variables.

Buyer behaviour does not simply encompass the straightforward decision process, but covers the underlying influences and motives to purchase. These are difficult to measure, but are nonetheless very important in gaining a thorough understanding of purchase behaviour. The principles of buyer behaviour theory can be applied to both consumer and organizational sectors, to non-profit-making institutions and service providers. A simple model has been used in this chapter to describe the factors that might influence purchase behaviour. Models range in complexity from simple 'black box' models to comprehensive multivariate models. They are useful in providing a framework for study. In the consumer model that was outlined, individual and environmental influences have an effect on the decision-making process of motivation, search, evaluation, choice and outcomes.

In organizational decision making, two additional influences are included. These are group influences and organizational factors. The decision-making process will depend on whether the purchase is a new task, a modified re-buy or a straight re-buy. The process involved is similar to the consumer decision-making process. Within organizational buying, motivation is not purely rational as emotional purchase motives can also play a part in decision making. Recent trends in organizational purchasing have implications for marketing management e.g. computerized purchasing and centralized purchasing have meant salespersons' roles and responsibilities have changed. In particular the growth of JIT purchasing and requirements for zero defects, together with developments in e-commerce have had an important impact on marketing in organizational markets.

The implications of researching buyer behaviour can apply throughout the strategic marketing process. The next chapter takes the concept of consumer behaviour further into the logical next step of market segmentation, targeting and positioning.

KEY TERMS

CASE STUDY

Six to Seven

Six to Seven is a telecommunications company marketing state of the art telecommunications equipment. The company is currently in the process of developing a new generation of mobile phones. When developed, this phone will not only enable users to make standard telephone calls and connect to the Web, but will have a small screen on which users can view the person at the other end of the line in high definition, unlike competitors' models whose definition characteristics leave a lot to be desired. Needless to say, investment to develop the technology and market the product is substantial.

As part of the development process, the company is eager to find out more about potential customers for this product. In particular, they are interested in finding out whether there is a market for the product, how big this market might be, and how customers will respond to this concept. They propose hiring a specialist market research agency with skills in the area of researching buyer behaviour, particularly for new product concepts.

CASE STUDY QUESTIONS

1 What areas of buyer behaviour should this proposed research encompass, and why?
2 What types of research techniques might be useful in researching these areas?

Suggestions as to how to approach and answer this question are contained on the accompanying website. In addition a number of longer strategic case studies, along with suggested solutions, are also contained on the website.

REFERENCES

1 Tamilia, D.R. (2007), 'Placing Wroe Alderson's contributions to buyer behaviour in historical perspective', *European Business Review*, 19(6): 468–94.

2 Blackwell, F.D., Engel, J.F. and Miniard, P.W. (2005), *Consumer Behaviour*, 10th edn, Hinsdale, IL: Dryden Press.

3 East, R., Vanhuele, M. and Wright, M. (2008), *Consumer Behaviour: Applications in Marketing*, London: Sage Publications.

4 Schiffman, L.G., Kanuk, L.L., and Hansen, H. (2008), *Consumer Behaviour: A European Outlook*, Harlow, UK: FT Prentice-Hall.

5 Kotler, P. (2006), *Marketing Management: Analysis, Planning, Implementation and Control*, 12th edn, Upper Saddle River, NJ: Prentice-Hall.

6 Op. cit. (2).

7 Schiffman, L.G. and Kanuk, L.L. (2007), *Consumer Behaviour*, 10th edn, Upper Saddle River, NJ: Prentice-Hall.

8 Tuck, M. (1976), *How Do We Choose?*, London: Methuen.

9 Damparat, M. and Jolibert, A. (2009), 'A dialectical model of buyer–seller relationships', *Journal of Business and Industrial Marketing*, 24(3/4): 207–17.

10 Talluri, S., Vickery, S.K. and Narayanan, S. (2008), 'Optimization models for buyer–seller negotiations', *International Journal of Physical Distribution and Logistics Management*, 38(7): 551–61.

11 Yaprak, A. (2008), 'Culture study in international marketing: a critical review and suggestions for future research', *International Marketing Review*, 25(2): 215–29.

12 Maslow, D. (1954), *Motivation and Personality*, New York: Harper & Row.

13 Swoboda, B., Haelsig, F., Morschett, D. and Schramm-Klein, H. (2007), 'An intersector analysis of the relevance of service in building a strong retail brand', *Managing Service Quality*, 17(4): 428–48.

14 Ozuem, W., Howell, K.E. and Lancaster, G. (2008), 'Communicating in the new interactive marketspace', *European Journal of Marketing*, 42(9–10): 1059–83.

15 Moliner, M.A., Sanchez, J., Rodriguez, R.M. and Calarisa, L. (2007), 'Perceived relationship quality and post purchase perceived value: An integrative framework', *European Journal of Marketing*, 41(11/12): 1392–422.

16 Webster, F.E. (Jr.) and Wind, Y. (1972), *Organizational Buying Behavior*, Upper Saddle River, NJ: Prentice-Hall, pp. 78–80.

17 Hutt, M.D. and Speh, T.W. (1999), *Business Marketing Management*, 6th edn, London: Dryden Press.

18 Webster, F.E. and Wind, Y. (1972), 'A general model for understanding buyer behaviour', *Journal of Marketing*, 36, April.

19 Dion, P.A., Banting, P.M. and Halsey, L.M. (1990), 'The impact of JIT on industrial marketers', *Industrial Marketing Management*, 19: 42.

20 Lancaster, G. (1993), 'Marketing and engineering: can there ever be synergy?', *Journal of Marketing Management*, 9: 141–53.

21 Lancaster, G. (1995), 'Marketing and engineering revisited', *Journal of Business and Industrial Marketing*, 10(1): 6–15.

22 Marzouk, M. (2008), 'A superiority and inferiority ranking model for contractor selection', *Construction Innovation: Information Process Mangagement*, 8(4): 250–68.

23 Cormicam, K. and Cunningham, M. (2007), 'Supplier performance evaluation: lessons from a multinational organisation', *Journal of Manufacturing Technology Management*, 1(4): 352–66.

24 Shiffman, L.G. and Kanuk, L.L., op.cit. (7).

Chapter 3

Markets and customers

Market boundaries; target marketing

LEARNING OBJECTIVES

After reading this chapter you will:

- appreciate the meaning and importance of the concept of market boundaries
- realize the relationship of market boundaries to the key process of target marketing
- be familiar with the steps in target marketing
- understand the different bases which may be used to segment consumer and organizational markets, including some of the more recent developments in this area
- be aware of the main considerations in evaluating markets for targeting strategies
- be familiar with the concepts and techniques relating to product positioning

INTRODUCTION

In Chapter 2 we explored key questions pertaining to analysing and understanding buyer behaviour in consumer and industrial markets. Although these questions were examined against a general framework for improving our understanding of how and why customers purchase, together with the broad range of behavioural forces and factors which impinge upon these decisions, the emphasis was on the behaviour of individuals, whether final consumers, or organizations. We now examine how individual customers aggregate to form **market segments**, and how these form part of a larger market, the boundaries, or limits, of which need to be clearly defined. The notion of boundaries in markets leads us to a key strategic process in contemporary marketing referred to as **target marketing**. We start by examining the concept of a 'market' and the important issue of defining **market boundaries**.

THE CONCEPT OF A MARKET: DEFINING MARKET BOUNDARIES

Until the strategic marketing planner has defined the market(s) the organization currently and potentially may operate in, few effective strategic decisions can be taken. Defining the market affects virtually every element of strategic marketing planning. Consider a question that practically every strategic marketing planner will need to ask and answer, namely: 'What is our market share?' The answer to this, and many other questions of importance to strategic marketing, depends on how we 'define' the market. A market definition is not always easy. Take, for example, the 'holiday market'; a company thinking about potential in this market, with a view to possible entry, could consider the 'holiday market' as comprising the total number and value of all holidays taken in any one year. However, within this total market there are many different types of holidays and ways of classifying them. For example, we can distinguish between winter and summer holidays, package holidays and self-catering holidays, domestic and overseas holidays, and so on. Although they are all 'holidays', they differ significantly. If the company was to assess, for example, market size, requirements for competitive success, market growth or market profitability it would probably find that each of these holiday markets would differ substantially. An example of the strategic importance of an organization identifying which market(s) it is in is given by Hooley *et al.*[1] when they describe a senior management meeting some years ago at the Parker Pens company. A new managing director challenged experienced senior managers to identify Parker's main competitors. Most suggested other marketers of writing implements; some suggested the telephone and other non-written forms of communication.

However, they were taken aback when the new MD identified the main competitor as being Ronson cigarette lighters. The reason was that at that time, many Parker pens were purchased as gifts. A leading alternative for a quality pen at that time was a quality cigarette lighter.

This example shows the importance not only of identifying the market you are in, but, as emphasized by Brassington and Pettit,[2] of looking at this from the perspective of the customer. The marketing planner must be careful to define market(s) and in so doing be aware of the different dimensions available. We now consider some of these dimensions, where appropriate, commenting upon their uses and limitations.

Product/industry-based definitions

Conventionally, many markets are defined, or at least thought of by those working in them, on the basis of products and/or industries, e.g. the computer software market or the industrial adhesives market. This definition centres on the nature of the product(s) or service(s) produced and marketed. As we can also see, even a product-based definition can lead to either very broad, generic product class definitions, which are akin to defining the market on an industry basis (e.g. the computer software market) or at the other extreme, a narrow product item-based definition, e.g. the writing instruments market.

Initially, this might seem a logical and simplistic way to define a market even if we still have the problem of how broad or narrow to pitch our product-based definitions. The problem with product based definitions is that although they accord with how many companies are in their existing and potential markets, they can be, and often are, misleading for marketing planning purposes. In particular, product-based definitions neglect the fact that customers purchase benefits, not products, and even where generic product class or industry-based definitions are used, as opposed to product item definitions, there is a danger of defining the market too narrowly.

This danger of product-based market definitions was recognized and highlighted in Levitt's[3] classic article on 'Marketing myopia' as long ago as 1960. He suggested that many companies were defining their businesses in product terms and hence too narrowly. This in turn, he suggested, was leading at best to missed opportunities and, at worst, business failure. Levitt cites the case of the American railroad companies who appeared to define and operate their businesses on the assumption that they were in the 'railway market'. Arising from this, he claimed that many of these companies had subsequently either gone out of business or were struggling to survive. The reason was that they had failed to define their market accurately. In short, according to Levitt, product-based market definitions are indicative of a lack of customer orientation in a business and result in a narrow and shortsighted view of marketing opportunities and threats. In order to avoid these problems, he suggests defining markets in terms of 'generic need'.

Generic need-based definitions

In suggesting a **generic** need-based **definition** of markets, Levitt argues that the market is better seen from the point of view of 'that which the customer buys' rather than 'what the organization or industry makes'. Accordingly, the railroad business would have been better to define their market as 'transportation' rather than 'railway market'. Similarly, a cosmetics company might define its market (generic need) as the 'beauty' market; an insurance company the 'peace of mind' market; and a camera company the 'memories' market. Using our previous Parker Pens example, their market was the 'gifts' market. This is a more customer and marketing-oriented method of defining markets. The advantages of a generic need-based definition include:

- It forces an organization to look at its markets from a customer perspective.
- It widens the perspective on what currently and potentially constitutes competition, i.e. it helps define competition.
- It helps in identifying future opportunities and threats.
- It helps identify key factors in competitive marketing success.

Taking the Mickey

Mickey Mouse, probably the most famous American Disney cartoon character and certainly the longest serving, is the official mascot of the Walt Disney Company. The survival of this character and its still central role in the company's public persona illustrates the debt Disney owes to its cartoon business. Walt Disney built his business on wonderfully produced cartoons using innovative animation skills. However, there is a limit to the market for cartoon characters. Furthermore, although there is an enduring quality to the cartoon genre, children today have been brought up on a diet of video and arcade-type games which means that the former novelty of going to the cinema and seeing adventures and characters on screen has over the years lost some of its appeal. However the Disney brand name and image was and still is very powerful. Most adults remember going to see Disney films such as *Snow White* or *Pinocchio* with great affection and nostalgia. Faced with a flattening demand, increased competition and changing customer needs and wants, Disney's dilemma in the 1970s became how to lever its powerful brand assets and company image into developing new markets. Wisely, Disney decided to build on its core brand and image strengths while looking for new growth markets. By identifying its markets as being broadly entertainment, Disney was able to diversify its portfolio without losing sight of what it was good at doing. One of Disney's earliest and most successful ventures outside of animated cartoons was theme parks. Initially developed in America, Disney theme parks and resorts have spread to other parts of the world such as Paris and Hong Kong. There is now a Disney cruise line.

Another venture has been into the non-animation film world. Included under the Studio Entertainment division is: Touchstone pictures, Dimension films, Miramax and Hollywood pictures as well as the original Walt Disney animation studios. The Disney television group includes ABC, ABC news, Disney Channel, Disney Family Movies, Radio Disney and more besides. Disney has also entered the interactive world with its Interactive Media group including: Disney.com, ABC.com, clubpenguin.com and espn.com. Under Disney Consumer Products there is: World of Disney Stores, Muppets Holding Company, Disney Store, Baby Einstein and Disney Publishing Worldwide. In 2008 total revenue was US$ 37.8 billion. Not bad . . . for a mouse!!

Source: Adapted from http://corporate.disney.go.com.

Given the Boot

The UK health and beauty group, Boots, began trading in 1849 selling herbal remedies from a small shop in Nottingham. It is now the UK's leading supplier and retailer of health and beauty products. However, recent years have not been easy for the group. Boots has faced intense and growing competition from some of its rivals particularly discount health and beauty retailers and supermarkets, many whom have opened their own pharmacies. There has been intense competition from manufacturers and marketers of many of the products that Boots themselves produce and market under their own brand names, such as toiletries, cosmetics and pain relief products.

A few years ago Boots management decided that the way forward was to expand their core health and beauty business by adding new products and services. The company introduced more health and beauty services in-store, such as manicure, pedicure and skin care clinics, 'minor' beauty surgery such as breast augmentation and 'Botox' treatment as well as introducing gym and fitness centres.

At face value, this seemed to make sense as these products and services were congruent with Boots' core business and positioning. After several experimental ventures in selected stores with some of these proposed ideas, Boots realized that even with their long experience in the health and beauty business this was a step too far and the idea was quietly dropped.

Drawing on Levitt's article to illustrate these advantages, consider the case of the film industry in the 1960s. Levitt suggested planners in this industry had defined their market and hence structure their marketing plans as being in the movies market. The generic need they were supplying however was in fact 'entertainment'. Therefore, they failed to anticipate the threat to their markets from the new 'competitor' television. Consequently, they lost out to this newer form of entertainment and could only watch with concern as their customer base dwindled, attracted to a cheaper, more innovative and more convenient way of fulfilling entertainment needs.

Most companies recognize the dangers of defining their markets and businesses too narrowly and have moved more towards these generic need-based definitions. Disney was once known as, and thought of themselves as, an animated film company. Their portfolio of businesses suggests they now think of themselves as being in the entertainment business.

Although the concept of generic needs for defining market boundaries is helpful in avoiding a myopic view of markets, in strategic marketing planning terms it also has drawbacks including the problem of precisely what is meant by 'generic needs' and how broadly we define these. We have seen that with this approach to defining markets, the intention is deliberately to push back the narrower market boundaries to which product/industry-based definitions give rise. However, the danger with using generic needs to define markets is that we can end up with definitions that are so broad as to be meaningless and are possibly misleading for marketing planning purposes.

Consider the example of cosmetic product manufacturers being in the generic needs market of 'beauty'. Clearly, there are many ways in which this need can be filled by customers. For example, the customer can meet this need by visiting a health farm or a plastic surgeon. Similarly, the customer could join a gymnasium, go on a diet, or purchase a new outfit; indeed, many other permutations are possible in terms of making an individual more attractive. From the point of view of the cosmetics company we ask: Is it helpful and realistic to define a market in such wide generic terms as beauty? For example, is a cosmetics company really in competition with a manufacturer of clothing or a plastic surgeon? The answer, of course, is 'no'. This is useful in reminding us that we must think of competition from outside the industry and helps prevent a myopic view of markets, customers and competition, but it is too broad to be of operational use in defining market boundaries and helping to develop marketing plans.

What is needed is an approach to defining markets that is neither too narrow nor too broad and is classified in terms of customer function or group and technology.

CUSTOMER FUNCTIONS, TECHNOLOGY AND CUSTOMER GROUP-BASED DEFINITIONS

Customer functions

We have seen that customers purchase benefits when they buy. For example, when we purchase a car it fulfils the functions of transport, prestige, convenience, etc. When we purchase a watch we purchase time measurement, status, etc. But similar products often serve different use functions (benefits) and hence different markets. Products and services with similar use functions are in similar markets, and hence they are in competition. In this context, let us consider computer software. Instead of defining the market in terms of generic needs, which might be 'rapid and accurate information processing', we might identify and define different markets according to the function(s) computer software serves or the ways in which it is used. For example, Function A might be 'games and entertainment' while Function B could be 'business problem analysis'. Clearly, each of these functions represents a very different market. We can see that the concept of functions served is very close to our previous generic needs basis of market definition. Identifying different functions, however, provides different customer benefits and represents more meaningful ways to define markets. We still have to decide how narrowly or widely to define functions (and hence markets); e.g. the 'business problem analysis' function could be broken down further into sub-functions as shown in Figure 3.1.

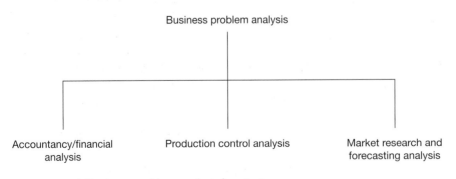

FIGURE 3.1 A 'business problem analysis function'

The question of how broadly or narrowly to define functions can only be resolved by reference to the strategic purpose of our definition. For example, if we are concerned to consider potential competition from outside conventional industry boundaries, we need to think at a higher level of abstraction than if we were evaluating direct competitor threats. The more broadly we define use-functions, the more expansive the market becomes. There is a stage where the definition of a use-function is so wide as to lose all value. Different use-functions attract different competitors and products and services that serve different use-functions serve different markets.

Technology

The second key dimension for market definition is the type of technology used to fulfil a function e.g. the function of 'convenience meals' can be met by technologies of canned foods, boil-in-the-bag or microwave. Similarly, the function of 'packaging' can be fulfilled by the alternative technologies of plastic, metal or glass. In defining the market, the strategic marketing planner must determine the technological bases to be used.

Customer groups

Most markets comprise sub-markets or segments, which comprise smaller groups of customers. Each of these sub-groups is homogeneous with regard to an important attribute, e.g. benefits sought, but heterogeneous when compared to other sub-groups with respect to these dimensions. The market for clothing, for example, can broadly be broken down into male and female subgroups. In turn, each of these broad sub-groups can be further divided into, for example, different age groups and/or income groups or 'fashion conscious' vs. 'traditional' groups. The definition of 'market' should specify which of these customer groups is to be served.

Combining factors to define market boundaries

Combining these three factors, we are in a position to illustrate how they may be used to define existing and potential market boundaries. An illustration of how these three elements might be combined is contained in Figure 3.2 for a supplier of drugs for medical use. Market boundaries in Figure 3.2 are defined by any combination of the three axes. There are different cells in the matrix of options each representing what are essentially individual building blocks for market definition. Each cell in the matrix may be defined in terms of customer function, customer group and technology. From the point of view of the drugs supplier, the current market boundary may be redefined using any one or combination of the basic dimensions e.g. new customer groups can be added, new functions served or alternative technologies used. The market cell shown in Figure 3.3 might represent the current 'served' market for the company. The remaining cells represent potential markets.

Practical illustrations of the different market boundaries, using the medical analogy, are:

Homeopathic drugs (technology) supplied to *chemists* (customer group) for the *prevention* (customer function) of disease (see Figure 3.3).

Synthetic drugs (technology) supplied to *private hospitals* (customer) for the *treatment* (customer function) of disease.

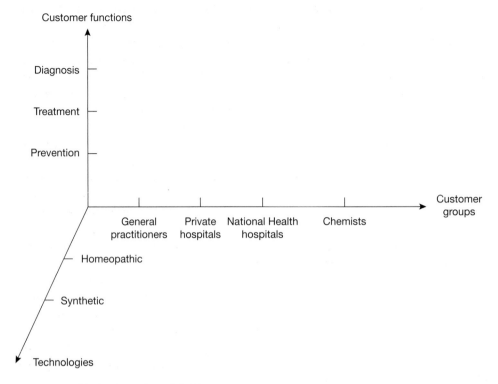

FIGURE 3.2 Market boundary definition

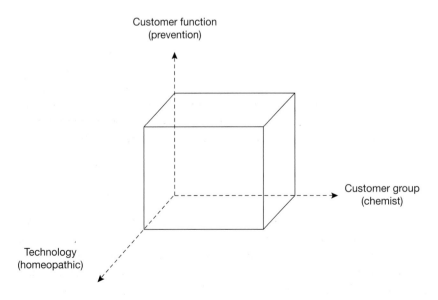

FIGURE 3.3 An illustrative market cell

In practice, the process of identifying and grouping market cells is complex. In particular, it requires detailed and objective market analysis combined with substantial managerial experience and insight.

Ultimately market boundaries are determined by customers and their perceptions, needs and choice behaviour rather than by the marketer. For example, we can establish how a market is divided into sub-markets by asking customers, or potential customers, how they choose between different product offerings. An interesting insight into the way customers, through their choice decisions, ultimately determine the limits of a market, and hence factors such as who or what constitutes competition, can be obtained by asking consumers to identify a list of products they feel could be used in a particular context or application. This approach is sometimes referred to as '**item by use analysis**'. For example, within the total market for chocolate, some customers may see a particular chocolate product as being most appropriate for snack occasions e.g. Mars Snickers which uses this theme in its advertising. So far as the customer is concerned, a key sub-division of this chocolate snack market is based on the primary need a particular product fulfils, in this case the 'snacks' market. However, Mars makes ice cream bars and here the product could be viewed as the 'dessert' market.

Despite the added complexities of this more sophisticated approach to defining market boundaries, it offers significant advantages over both product/industry-based definitions, and definitions based on generic needs. In order to use this three-dimensional approach, we need to understand how and why markets divide into different customer groups and also the range of customer functions which may be represented in the market. Identifying alternative technologies is less problematic. Advanced research techniques are enabling marketers to identify market boundaries more easily.

Understanding different customer groups and functions leads to what, for strategic market planning purposes, is a most important area of marketing, namely **market segmentation,** together with the related decision areas of **targeting** and **positioning**.

MARKET SEGMENTATION, TARGETING AND POSITIONING

In the example of the hypothetical supplier of medical drugs, the market served consisted of just one cell or segment. The total market, however, comprises several market segments. In other words, the market is not homogeneous, but rather is made up of separate cells of demand preferences. As Proctor[4] points out, the marketer's approach must be based on the acceptance that 'there are different demands in the market place'. It is this heterogeneity of markets that gives rise to the need for effective segmentation, targeting and positioning; three distinct steps in the process of what is known collectively as target marketing.

The meaning and importance of target marketing

The concept of target marketing is a logical interpretation of the basic philosophy of marketing. Essentially, it comprises the identification of different needs for specific groups or segments of customers, deciding which of these groups the organization should target or serve (and on what basis) and then designing marketing mix programmes so the needs of these targeted groups are then more closely met.

As explained above target marketing derives from the fact that demand within markets is heterogeneous. In the 'total' market for a product or service, different groups of customers will be looking for different clusters of benefits. In order to understand this better, you should reflect on the products and services you purchase. Do you purchase exactly the same kind of products as your friends and neighbours? Are your specific requirements with respect to purchasing certain products and brands different? Perhaps your friends and neighbours have different tastes in clothes or in the type of holidays they take. Perhaps they purchase and drive different cars or use different brands of toothpaste or breakfast cereals. Market segmentation, targeting and positioning starts by recognizing that within the total demand and market for a product, specific tastes and requirements often differ. We refer to a market that is characterized by differing specific preferences as being heterogeneous. Market segmentation therefore breaks down the total market for a product or service into distinct patterns or segments of customers who share similar demand preferences within each segment. This is illustrated in Figure 3.4(a) and (b).

In Figure 3.4(a) there is no market segmentation. Each and every customer in the total market is assumed to have similar demand preferences and wants, i.e. demand is homogeneous. In fact demand in most markets is heterogeneous as we have already explained. Hence, the total market can be broken down into segments of customers, as shown in Figure 3.4(b).

Effective segmentation is achieved when we group together customers who share similar patterns of demand and where we can differentiate each segment in the pattern of demand from other segments in the market. In other words, effective segmentation is achieved when the clustering gives rise to **homogeneous demand** within, and **heterogeneous demand** between, each segment. Most markets are capable of being segmented.

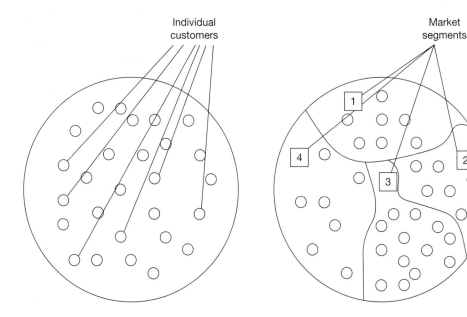

(a) Total market i.e. no segmentation

(b) Total market segmented into sub-groups/
     segments

FIGURE 3.4 The meaning of market segments

Salt of the Earth

Do all markets segment? Are there any markets where every customer wants the same thing i.e. demand is homogeneous?

When posed this question, people invariably suggest the market for salt is one where there are no different segments. After all, one salt is much the same as another. We put it in our food and apart from health issues think no more about it.

The mention of health gives us a clue as to the existence of a distinct market segment within the overall market for salt. We are now aware that too much salt is bad for our health, but many people do not like the idea of cooking and eating without salt. As a result there are now healthier versions of salt available with different constituents targeted specifically at this segment.

Once we recognize that there are different salt products aimed at different segments we find there is a whole range of different types of salt targeting the needs of different segments of the market e.g. 'up-market' sea salt, 'hand dried' crystals, basic salt products for price-conscious consumers, extra large packets for the catering trade and even rock salt for those who simply want to clear their paths of snow and ice. A bewildering range of salt products can by found by keying 'salt' into your search engine.

The fact that most markets are made up of heterogeneous demand clusters means companies have to decide which of these clusters to serve. Most companies recognize that they cannot effectively serve all the segments in a market. They must instead target their marketing efforts. Imagine you are a part of the project team developing a new car. Should the proposed new model be a two, four or five-seater model? Should it have a 1000, 2000 or 3000cc engine? Should it have leather or fabric seats? In deciding these issues, the overriding factor is customer demand, i.e. what are the customers' needs? Some customers (segments) may want a five-seater, 2000cc model with leather upholstery, while others may prefer a four-seater with a 1000cc engine and fabric seats. One solution is to compromise and produce a four-seater 1500cc model with leather seats and fabric trim. Clearly, such a model would go some way to meeting the requirements of both groups of buyers, but because the needs of neither market segment are precisely met and catered for, customers might prefer and purchase from suppliers who meet their requirements exactly.

ADVANTAGES OF TARGET MARKETING: CRITERIA FOR EFFECTIVE SEGMENTATION

Engaging in target marketing:

1   provides an understanding of competition;
2   gives insights into competitive advantage, and how this can be best applied;
3   allows the company to better appreciate of what customers need;
4   enables the company to produce more effective marketing plans;
5   uses company resources more effectively.

Stuck for Choice

Major car producers such as Ford, Chrysler and Fiat produce a model and variations on that model for virtually every segment of the market. The following is a list of the model range of passenger cars available from Ford in September 2009:

Ka
Fiesta
Focus
C-Max
S-Max
Kuga
Galaxy

Most of these main model variants are available with several engine options, several trim variants, a myriad of colours, and a huge range of accessories. Provided the customer wants a Ford they would be hard put not to find something that suited them. In short, the patterns of demand we referred to earlier require that marketers develop specific marketing mixes (i.e. products, prices, promotional appeals and distribution channels that are aimed or targeted at specific market segments). This 'targeting' vs. 'mass marketing' approach is referred to as using a '**rifle approach**' as opposed to using a '**shotgun approach**' to achieve market impact.

In order to secure these advantages, the base(s) used for segmentation should fulfil the following criteria:

1   *Measurability/identifiability*: The base(s) used to segment a market should lead to ease of identification (who is in each segment) and measurability (how large is each segment).
2   *Accessibility*: The base(s) used should ideally lead to marketers being able to reach selected market targets with their marketing efforts.
3   *Substantiality*: The base(s) used should ideally lead to segments that are sufficiently large to be worthwhile serving as distinct market targets.
4   *Meaningfulness*: The base(s) used should lead to segments that have different preferences/needs and show clear variations in market behaviour and response to marketing efforts.

Of all requirements for effective segmentation, this last one is the most important. It is an essential prerequisite in identifying and selecting market targets. These criteria are examined later in this chapter when we discuss the variety of bases for segmenting markets. Of course target marketing is not without its disadvantages which are:

1   It increases both production and marketing costs, i.e. economies of scale and the advantages of mass production are reduced and individual marketing campaigns need to be implemented for each market segment.

2   It requires more marketing research and information than if we do not segment and target.
3   There is a danger of brand proliferation and different company products competing against each other.
4   Critics argue that some approaches to segmentation and targeting help reinforce prejudices and stereotypes and are a form of 'customer abuse' by the marketer (see Rotfeld).[5]

We now examine steps in target marketing and how these steps work in practice.

STEPS IN TARGET MARKETING

Most marketers conceive of target marketing as comprising a series of steps or stages (see Solomon *et al.*).[6] The following is a sequence of steps to be taken when conducting a segmentation, targeting and product positioning exercise:

1   Divide the market into segments, selecting bases for segmentation.
2   Evaluate and appraise the market segments resulting from the above.
3   Select an overall targeting strategy.
4   Select specific targets in line with the previous step.
5   Develop product positioning strategies for each target segment.
6   Develop an appropriate marketing mix for each target segment to support the positioning strategy.

We now examine each of these steps to appreciate further what target marketing means.

Dividing a market into segments

In segmentation, targeting and positioning, we are seeking to identify distinct sub-sets of customers in the total market for a product. Any sub-set might eventually be selected as a market target, and on that basis a distinctive marketing mix can be developed. For example, we might find that in the market for hi-fi equipment we can identify a number of distinct sub-sets (segments) of customers based upon income levels. This is shown in Figures 3.5(a) and (b). Continuing the example, we may find that income segments can be broken down further into a combination of income and age segments as illustrated in Figures 3.6(a) and (b).

We need to recognize that in the example [Figure 3.6(b)] we assume that both income and age are associated with differences in buyers' behaviour towards the product, i.e. different age/income groups will have different needs/preferences with respect to hi-fi products (e.g. under 35s might prefer the same audio in an aluminium case and over 35s might prefer the same audio, but with a wooden case) and each might to respond to a different marketing approach. If we are correct in our assumption, this means that the bases selected for segmentation (age/income) are meaningful ones on which to segment the market. This is the most important criterion for effective segmentation. In addition, both these segmentation bases pose relatively few problems for the marketer in terms of identifying/measuring and reaching the segments to which they give rise; in the UK we know what proportion of the total population falls into discrete age groups (i.e. identifying/measuring). Furthermore, media habits of different age groups, e.g. television viewing and readership of

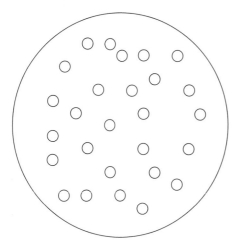
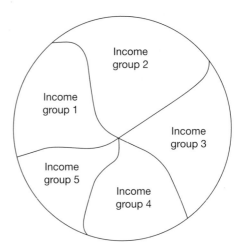

○ = Individual customers in a
non-segmented market

Income groups consist of groups of similar
income customers

(a)   Total market prior to segmentation

(b)   Market segmented on basis of income groups

FIGURE 3.5 Segmenting the market for hi-fi by income

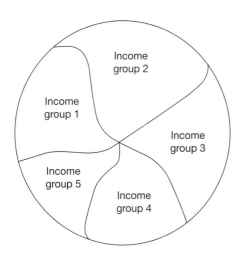
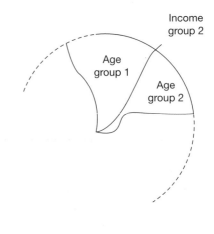

(a)   Market segmentation on basis
of income

(b)   Market segmentation on basis
of income/age

FIGURE 3.6 Further segmentation of each income group based on age

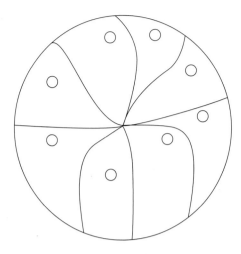

○ = A single customer who forms a single
    segment

FIGURE 3.7 Complete market segmentation

magazines/newspapers, enables marketers to use direct marketing for selected target age groups (known as **reachability**). These are 'ideal' criteria for effective segmentation and count for little if they are not associated with meaningfulness. With regard to the criterion of 'substantiality', the hi-fi example shows that a market may be segmented using a succession of different bases. This leads to the breaking down of the market into an increasing number of smaller and smaller segments. The ultimate point to which this process can be taken is illustrated in Figure 3.7 where the market has been completely segmented into individual buyers, i.e. a fully customized market.

The extent to which it makes business sense to continue to subdivide markets in this way depends on how worthwhile the resulting segments are in serving as distinct market targets with a separate marketing mix. In some product markets, complete segmentation (i.e. tailoring the marketing mix to individual customers) is not simply desirable, but essential; in shipbuilding or the supply of aircraft, each customer may be treated as a separate market. For many consumer product markets, such 'customizing' of the marketing effort would be unnecessary and prohibitively expensive.

In the hi-fi example we used the bases of income and age in segmenting the market. However, here is no 'right' way to segment a market, and different bases/combinations of bases, particularly motivational ones, should be sought by the marketer. A number of relatively common bases, which we now examine, are frequently used by marketers, starting with bases that are typically used in consumer product markets, followed by those used in organizational product markets.

Bases for segmenting consumer markets

Segmentation must fulfil various criteria for being effective. We now discuss some of these, starting with geographic and demographic bases and moving on to some of the more recent developments, in particular the use of geodemographic, lifestyle and combination bases and those that use the behaviour of consumers themselves as the basis for identifying market segments.

We begin with two conventional and widely used bases for segmenting consumer markets: geographic and demographic segmentation.

Geographic segmentation

This consists of dividing a market on the basis of different geographical units. In international marketing, different countries may be deemed to constitute different market segments. Similarly, within a country a market may be segmented regionally into, for example, north versus south segments. **Geographic segmentation** is still widely used, at least as one element in a combination of segmentation bases. Clearly, geographic segmentation is potentially at its most powerful and useful when considering international markets, and this is looked into in more detail in Chapter 16.

Demographic segmentation

This approach comprises a variety of bases and the more common ones include:

> social class/occupation;
> age;
> sex;
> income;
> education;
> family size;
> nationality;
> family life cycle.

Demographic bases were for many years the most popular for **segmentation** in consumer product markets, first because they were felt to be most strongly associated with differences in consumer demand (i.e. they are meaningful) and second because demographic information is relatively easy to obtain. With the exception of family life cycle and social class/occupation, their meaning and potential application is self-evident. Brief explanations of these two exceptions are now provided:

Family life cycle

This basis for **life cycle segmentation** centres on the idea that consumers pass through a series of distinct phases in their lives. Each phase is associated with different purchasing patterns and needs.

The unmarried person living at home may have very different purchasing patterns from a chronological counterpart who has left home and recently married. It is also recognized that purchasing patterns of adults often change as they move towards retirement.

The Newspaper Society together with the British Market Research Bureau (BMRB) have developed a 'life stage' classification system. Based on detailed market research and analysis, this life stage classification identifies the following life stage segments for classifying consumer groups:

live with parents;

left parents' home and live alone or in shared accommodation;

live with partner only;

no children;

children in household, majority pre-school age;

children in household, majority beyond school age;

children have all left home;

live with partner or alone.

These life stages can be grouped into three major categories, namely:

pre-family stages;

people with children at home;

people with children who have left home.

The developers of this system claim that it works well in distinguishing between different customer groups with regard to their lifestyles, media habits, and most importantly, their purchasing patterns.

Occupation/social class

These are linked together because official socio-economic group categorizations are based upon occupation. In the UK, this occupation is that of the 'chief income earner', because this is what is regarded as being the criterion that determines the social class of the household. It is a family classification unlike gender, which is an individual classification. Of all the demographic bases for segmenting consumer product markets, **occupational social class segmentation** is the most widely used as it so universally known and is simple to apply.

Social class scores highly against the segmentation criteria of 'identifiability' and to a lesser extent 'accessibility'. It is a simple task to classify individuals on the basis of occupation and then to reach the different social classes so categorized, according to their different patterns of media usage and shopping habits. Table 3.1 shows the system of social class gradings used in the UK together with an indication of the types of occupations associated with each.

TABLE 3.1 Occupation and social class

Social class grading	Occupation
A	Higher managerial
B	Intermediate management
C1	Supervisory/lower management
C2	Skilled manual
D	Semi-skilled/unskilled
E	Lowest levels of subsistence, e.g. state pensioners with no supplementary income

As occupation is the only factor in this system used to ascribe social class, it is important that the codex used to classify occupations into the six different social categories is valid, because the different occupations used to designate social class discriminate and distinguish between different customer groups who might have different purchasing patterns, to meet the 'meaningful' criterion identified earlier. Although this long established system of assigning social class is widely used in marketing, there is increasing doubt as to the extent to which social class is nowadays a 'meaningful' basis for segmenting some markets. This arises from the fact that they are no longer so strongly related to income groups. For example, it is often the case that the skilled manual group (C2) earn higher incomes than supervisory or intermediate management counterparts (C1 or B). Such groups are often in a position to purchase products and services that were traditionally the prerogative of higher social grades.

Many of the more traditional demographic bases including social class have become less meaningful to marketers as bases for segmenting consumer markets. Indeed, in the case of social class, there is evidence to suggest that this basis for segmentation may be a poor predictor of customer needs and behaviour, and might even be misleading. Because of this, the UK Office of National Statistics has developed an updated social class system which more nearly reflects the social groupings of today. This system, though still based on occupation, has eight new categories of socio-economic groups as opposed to the existing six, and these are illustrated in Table 3.2.

Although this system of classification is new, it is interesting in the way in which some of the occupations of the former system of social grading have been reassigned. The traditional system as shown in Table 3.1 is still the most popular for market researchers, but our notion of social class and its use in marketing is changing. For example, as we move towards new, more complex measures of social class this basis of segmentation is perhaps becoming more of a pschycographic/lifestyle basis of segmentation described below rather than a true demographic basis. Certainly, ideas about the nature, meaning and uses of social class in market segmentation are changing.

Concern regarding the predictive power of these more conventional demographic bases for segmenting consumer markets, coupled with improvements in data collection and analysis methods,

TABLE 3.2 Occupation and social class new classification

1	Higher managerial and professional
2	Lower managerial and professional
3	Intermediate occupations
4	Small employers and own account workers
5	Lower supervisory and technical occupations
6	Semi-routine occupations
7	Routine occupations
8	Long term unemployed

has led to the development of new bases in consumer markets. We group these newer segmentation bases into three types: 'geodemographic' bases; 'lifestyle/psychographic' bases and 'combination' bases.

Geodemographic bases

As the term implies, **geodemographic segmentation** of consumer markets is based on a combination of demographic and geographic factors. It is easier to understand the ideas behind geodemographic segmentation if we look at one of the first systems of geodemographic segmentation used in the UK, namely, the **ACORN system** (short for 'A Classification of Residential Neighbourhoods'). The ACORN system is produced by CACI, and like many of the geodemographic systems of segmentation, it is based on census of population data. In the UK this census data is collected on a decennial cycle during each year that ends with 1 and on a 10 per cent sample basis on every year that ends with 6, and consists of the collection and analysis of detailed information on every household concerning factors such as, for example, household size, incomes, occupations, car ownership etc. ACORN categorizes all 1.9 million UK postcodes, using over 125 demographic statistics in England, Scotland, Wales and Northern Ireland, and 287 lifestyle variables, giving a good understanding of clients and prospects. These districts can be described on the basis of the type of property and householder predominantly prevalent in each census enumeration district. Research has established that the different types of property and the neighbourhoods in which they are located, are strongly related to purchasing behaviour and patterns, so much so that in some cases it is possible from the type of neighbourhood and property to predict details such as average wine consumption by households in the area, holiday preferences and incidence of frozen food purchase.

The six major categories, together with the different 17 groups related to them, are shown in Table 3.3. The ACORN system is a good indicator of some patterns of purchasing such as brand choice and average spend, and goes some way towards fulfilling the 'meaningfulness' criterion mentioned earlier.

Among some of the marketing applications where ACORN is useful are:

- compilation of direct mailing lists;
- site location of new stores and distribution outlets;
- management of advertising campaigns, particularly in the local press;
- quantifying sales potential in any given area.

Another geodemographic system of segmentation is the **MOSAIC system**. This system classifies groups of homes on the full postcode. On average, 15 houses share a single postcode and each group shares a MOSAIC classification. According to the MOSAIC system (developed by CCN Marketing) there are 58 types of residential area in the UK (an example being M12: 'lower income enclaves in high income suburbs'). The system is used largely for targeting direct mailshots according to MOSAIC category. It allows users to 'cherry pick' and send personal communications to categories of household in specific locations that they wish to target.

Geodemographic segmentation systems are now widely available and are important to marketers. As with any segmentation base, these are not perfect. We know, for example, that in some census enumeration districts the types of neighbourhood and property can differ considerably even though

TABLE 3.3 ACORN groups in the United Kingdom

Gallery	Group	Type	
Wealthy Achievers	Wealthy Executives	01	Affluent mature professionals, large houses
		02	Affluent working families with mortgages
		03	Villages with wealthy commuters
		04	Well-off managers, larger houses
	Affluent Greys	05	Older affluent professionals
		06	Farming communities
		07	Old people, detached houses
		08	Mature couples, smaller detached houses
	Flourishing Families	09	Larger families, prosperous suburbs
		10	Well-off working families with mortgages
		11	Well-off managers, detached houses
		12	Large families & houses in rural areas
Urban Prosperity	Prosperous Professionals	13	Well-off professionals, larger houses and converted flats
		14	Older Professionals in detached houses and apartments
	Educated Urbanites	15	Affluent urban professionals, flats
		16	Prosperous young professionals, flats
		17	Young educated workers, flats
		18	Multi-ethnic young, converted flats
		19	Suburban privately renting professionals
	Aspiring Singles	20	Student flats and cosmopolitan sharers
		21	Singles & sharers, multi-ethnic areas
		22	Low income singles, small rented flats
		23	Student Terraces
Comfortably Off	Starting Out	24	Young couples, flats and terraces
		25	White collar singles/sharers, terraces
	Secure Families	26	Younger white-collar couples with mortgages
		27	Middle income, home owning areas
		28	Working families with mortgages
		29	Mature families in suburban semis
		30	Established home owning workers
		31	Home owning Asian family areas
	Settled Suburbia	32	Retired home owners
		33	Middle income, older couples
		34	Lower income people, semis
	Prudent Pensioners	35	Elderly singles, purpose built flats
		36	Older people, flats
Moderate Means	Asian Communities	37	Crowded Asian terraces
		38	Low income Asian families

. . . continued

TABLE 3.3 ACORN groups in the United Kingdom . . . *continued*

	Post Industrial Families	39	Skilled older family terraces
		40	Young family workers
	Blue Collar Roots	41	Skilled workers, semis and terraces
		42	Home owning, terraces
		43	Older rented terraces
Hard Pressed	Struggling Families	44	Low income larger families, semis
		45	Older people, low income, small semis
		46	Low income, routine jobs, unemployment
		47	Low rise terraced estates of poorly-off workers
		48	Low incomes, high unemployment, single parents
		49	Large families, many children, poorly educated
	Burdened Singles	50	Council flats, single elderly people
		51	Council terraces, unemployment, many singles
		52	Council flats, single parents, unemployment
	High Rise Hardship	53	Old people in high rise flats
		54	Singles & single parents, high rise estates
	Inner City Adversity	55	Multi-ethnic purpose built estates
		56	Multi-ethnic, crowded flats

Source: CACI LIMITED (2009) 'ACORN' is a registered trademark of CACI Limited.

they are grouped into, for example, one ACORN category. We must be careful to establish that the geodemographic system being used is appropriate to particular markets and products. Systems like ACORN are usually linked with market research survey systems such as the Target Group index survey conducted in the UK by the British Market Research Bureau. This is be used to assess the potential effectiveness of any proposed geographic segmentation basis for a particular market.

Lifestyle segmentation

A more contemporary basis for segmenting consumer markets is **lifestyle segmentation**, referred to as '**psychographics**'. It is based on the fact that individuals have characteristic modes and patterns of living that may influence their motivation to purchase selected products and brands, e.g. some individuals may prefer a 'homely' lifestyle, whereas others may see themselves as living a 'sophisticated' lifestyle.

Two examples of lifestyle/psychographic segmentation techniques serve to illustrate this approach to segmenting consumer markets.

Young and Rubicam's '4 Cs'

The advertising agency Young and Rubicam developed a lifestyle segmentation system that analysed how consumers perceive themselves and how these perceptions are reflected in their interests, values and activities, giving rise to different purchasing preferences and brand choices. Using marketing research involving in-depth interviews, focus groups and questionnaires, they identified three main lifestyle groups based on a Cross Cultural Consumer Characterization (**the 4 Cs**). Each of these three main lifestyle groups contains a number of sub-groups as follows:

Lifestyle Group	Sub-groups
The Constrained	Resigned poor
	Struggling poor
The Middle Majority	Traditionalists
	Mainstreamers
	Aspirers
	Succeeders
The Innovators	Transitionals
	Reformers

This classification was based on the notion that each group and sub-group, in this case because of their lifestyle/personalities, had differing needs and would exhibit different purchasing patterns and brand choices. For example, in the '4 Cs' system, in the Middle Majority group, mainstreamers were found to be consumers who were conventional in their lifestyle patterns and values. They found that mainstreamers prefer and purchase well-known brands. They tend not to purchase supermarket 'own label' brands. Similarly, mainstreamers tended to buy from domestic rather than overseas producers wherever possible. In contrast, aspirers, who were motivated to improve themselves, tended to purchase the latest products and brands which in their view would bestow higher status on them. They tend to indulge in the latest activities and pastimes and purchase conspicuously. Young and Rubicam therefore suggested that knowing the lifestyle group to which an individual belongs can be used in market segmentation and targeting, and in particular development of promotional campaigns to appeal to various target groups.

The VALS system

Developed by the Stanford Research Institute, this approach to lifestyle/psychographic segmentation is based on information collected from self-administered questionnaires embracing respondents' Activities, Interests, and Opinions (**AIO measures**) together with motives, attitudes, and aspects such as values. The updated system of **VALS** (and **VALS 2**) (which stands for Values and Life Styles) uses two key dimensions to classify customers into eight lifestyle types. These two dimensions are 'Self Orientation', and 'Resources Available to Sustain the Self Orientation'. These are used to classify a customer into one of the following lifestyle categories:

- 'fulfilled'
- 'believer'
- 'achiever'
- 'striver'
- 'struggler'

- ◼ 'experiencer'
- ◼ 'maker'

For example, 'experiencers' are action-oriented with regard to the self-orientation dimension and have a lifestyle characterized by a high degree of physical and social activity coupled with variety-seeking and risk-taking behaviour. With regard to the 'resources available' dimension, they have the most resources of any of the eight lifestyle groups to sustain their self-orientation. This lifestyle group seeks wealth, power and fame, and are substantial consumers of exercise and sports products, tending not to be conformist in their purchasing. The VALS2 system is now regarded as the major lifestyle/psychographic system in the USA. Like the '4 Cs' system, VALS 2 is used predominantly to develop promotional appeals.

These are two of a number of lifestyle systems for classifying consumers. In recent years, marketers have become increasingly interested in the potential of lifestyle segmentation for developing more effective marketing strategies. Not without problems with regard to underpinning concepts and problems of data collection and analysis associated with many lifestyle segmentation techniques, lifestyle segmentation has proved powerful for developing marketing and particularly promotional strategies.

These approaches to consumer market segmentation are examples of **associative segmentation**. That is, they are used where we feel that differences in purchasing behaviour/customer needs may be associated with them. If we use social class or lifestyle to segment a market, we assume that purchasing behaviour is a function of social class or lifestyle. Most problems with using such associative bases tend to be related to the issue of the extent to which they are truly associated with, or are a reflection of, actual purchasing behaviour. Because of this, many marketers believe it is more sensible to use **direct** bases for segmenting markets. Such bases take consumer behaviour as the starting point for identifying different segments, and they are referred to as **behavioural segmentation** bases.

Behavioural bases for segmentation

Examples of the more frequently used behavioural bases in consumer markets include:

- ◼ **Occasions for purchase**
  Here, segments are identified on the basis of differences in the occasions for purchasing the product e.g. in the market for perfume, occasions for purchase might include a Christmas gift, a birthday gift or a wedding anniversary present or simply an opportunity to try out the perfume brand.
- ◼ **User/usage status**
  The distinction here may be made between 'heavy', 'light' and 'non-user' segments.
- ◼ **Benefits sought**
  The total market for a product or service is broken down into segments distinguished by the principal benefits sought by each segment e.g. the shampoo market includes these benefit segments that can be observed from manufacturers' advertisements:

  - – cleanliness;
  - – protection from dandruff, greasiness and dryness;

– provides scalp medication;
– imparts feelings of 'well being'.

A 'benefits sought' basis for segmentation can provide useful insights into the nature and extent of competition and the possible existence of gaps in the market. Benefits sought bases of segmentation have been shown to be useful in markets ranging from student clothing[7] through to the market for beef in Brazil.[8]

■ **Loyalty status**

This direct approach is based on the extent to which different customers are loyal to certain brands (**brand loyalty**) or retail outlets (**store loyalty**). Identifying segments with different degrees of loyalty enables a company to determine which of its customers or prospective customers may be brand or store-loyal prone. Once they are convinced of the relative merits of a brand or supplier, such customers are unlikely to transfer their allegiances.

Where existing brand loyalty is already strong in a market, the would-be new entrant is faced with a difficult marketing problem. In such a situation, it may be necessary to identify and target the non brand loyal segment.

Combination segmentation bases

Often individual segmentation bases are used in combination to segment markets and delineate target customers e.g. the marketer may determine that targets are best identified in a particular market by using a combination of gender, income, social class etc. Some approaches to segmentation have been specifically developed to combine certain selected variables as the overall basis for segmenting a market. An example of this approach is **SAGACITY** developed by Research Services Ltd in the UK. This segmentation technique is based on a combination of family life cycle, occupation and income. These combinations are used to identify and describe some 12 consumer segments which the company suggests have differing purchasing needs and purchasing behaviour. Such a combination of individual segmentation bases in ways which are meaningful for a product market application represents a flexible way to delineate market segments.

DEVELOPMENTS IN CONSUMER SEGMENTATION TECHNIQUES: DATABASES, ONE-TO-ONE MARKETING AND THE INTERNET

Given its central importance to the development of marketing plans, segmentation is one of the most widely researched concepts in marketing. Marketers, academics and practitioners are constantly looking for new and more effective ways to segment and target markets. There is no totally right way to segment a market. Over time markets and customers change. We must, therefore, be constantly looking for new and more meaningful ways to segment markets. We now find many creative and thought-provoking segmentation bases that reflect the contemporary environment and market factors ranging through, for example, 'Green' segmentation (Paco and Raposo)[9] 'familiarity expertise and involvement' (Taloe-West *et al.*)[10] and even 'odd or even' price endings (Harris and Bray).[11] As we might expect, some of the most significant developments in market segmentation and targeting stem from developments in information technology and the Internet.

Effective segmentation and targeting, like many areas of marketing, requires information and analysis of consumer data. The development of inexpensive and readily available software programs puts this information increasingly at the disposal of the marketer. Modern data collection, storage and analysis techniques enable marketers to understand customer buying preferences and habits much better. It is now economically viable to profile buying patterns of individual customers and access this information through a database. Interrogation of company databases to search for information on customers, called **data mining**, is now extensively used by marketers with segmentation and targeting being one of the most fruitful of these uses (Liu and Chen).[12] This development is moving to a situation where instead of thinking of marketing to groups or segments of customers, the marketer is able to consider one-to-one marketing. The Internet plays a significant role here as the marketer can build an effective and detailed database on individual customers. Through this mechanism, the marketer can reach individual customers with tailored marketing programmes. Similarly, research has shown that the Internet and databases can be combined with effective segmentation and targeting to provide significant **cross-selling** opportunities (Ansell *et al.*).[13]

Perhaps one of the most significant developments in recent years, affecting potentially every facet of marketing has been the growth of '**mobile marketing**'. As the term implies, mobile marketing uses the technology of the mobile phone to target customers. Many think of mobile marketing as simply using their mobile phones to vote out a contestant on 'Big Brother' but in fact mobile marketing encompasses mobile advertising, mobile sales promotions, 'click and buy' technology, mobile CRM to allow customers to track their orders, and of course mobile applications which allow customers to access entertainment content such as games, ringtones and mobile videos, all using the ubiquitous five number short-code systems.

A recent report by the Internet Advertising Bureau (IAB) and PricewaterhouseCoopers[14] reported that the UK mobile advertising market was worth £28.6 million in 2008, a 99.2 per cent increase on the previous year. Mobile marketing in particular allows marketers to target individual customers and will continue to grow in importance.

BASES FOR SEGMENTING ORGANIZATIONAL/ INDUSTRIAL MARKETS

The basic approach to segmentation, targeting and positioning does not differ greatly between consumer and organizational markets. Segmenting industrial product markets introduces additional bases, whilst precluding others.

The most commonly encountered bases for segmenting organizational markets include:

- type of application/end use: e.g. fabric for curtains and fabric for fashion wear;
- geographical: e.g. north and south; the European Union; the USA;
- customer type: e.g. heavy engineering and light engineering;
- product technology: e.g. glass tubing, metal tubing and plastic tubing;

- purchaser loyalty status;
- customer size and usage rates;
- buying procedures: e.g. tender or non-tender; centralized and non-centralized buying;
- benefits sought.

Similar to consumer markets, organizational market segmentation may be on an indirect (associative) base or a direct (behavioural) base, and can use a variety of combined bases to obtain more precise segmentation.

A more neglected area of industrial segmentation has seen the emergence of powerful industrial segmentation frameworks, based on a step-by-step, hierarchical approach. A classic example is that developed by Wind and Cardozo[15] and illustrated in Figure 3.8. The approach is that customers in organizational markets be segmented in two stages. The first stage involves the formation of macro-segments, based on characteristics of the organization. The second stage involves dividing those macro-segments into micro-segments, based on characteristics of the DMU.

This hierarchical approach enables an initial screening of organizations and selection of macro-segments which, on the basis of organizational characteristics, provide potentially attractive market opportunities. Organizations that may have no use for the given product or service can be eliminated. Starting with the grouping of organizations into homogeneous macro-segments provides a reduction in total research effort and cost. Instead of examining detailed buying patterns and attempting to identify the characteristics of the DMU in each organization individually, such analysis is limited only to macro-segments that pass the initial screening.

Once a set of acceptable macro-segments has been formed, the marketer may divide each of them into micro-segments, or small groups of firms, on the basis of similarities and differences among DMUs within each macro-segment. Information for this second stage comes primarily from the sales force, based on salespeople's analysis of situations in particular firms or from specially designed market segmentation studies.

It is argued that the outcome from this segmentation model should include an important variable on which firms can be assigned to segments, i.e. the bases for segmentation, and a set of independent variables that allow marketers to predict where along the key dependent variable a particular group of customers may lie, as well as providing an insight into the key characteristics of the segment.

This concept of successively combining industrial market segmentation bases giving more and more precise and meaningful segments is taken further in another classic model developed by Shapiro and Bonoma.[16] Their **'nested' approach** is shown in Figure 3.9. This approach identifies five general segmentation bases that are arranged in the nested hierarchy shown. Moving from the outer towards the inner, we now examine each.

Demographics

This outermost nest contains general segmentation criteria that give a broad description of the segments in the market and relate to general customer needs and usage patterns. They can be determined without visiting the customer and include industry and company size and customer location. A good example of how demographics can be used in industrial market segmentation is provided by Powers and Sterling.[17]

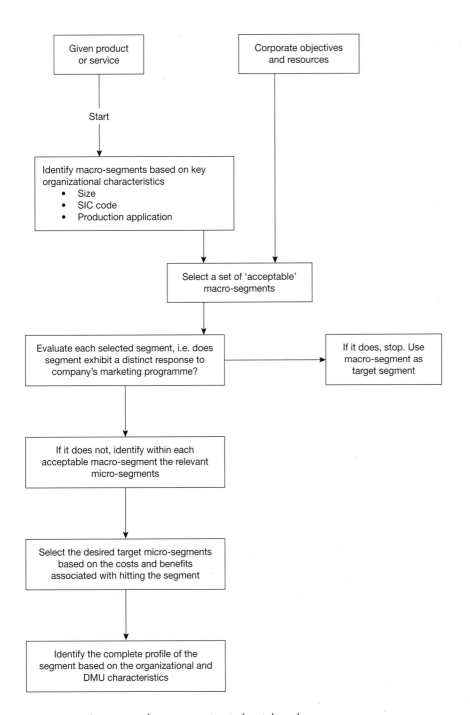

FIGURE 3.8 An approach to segmenting industrial markets

Source: Adapted from Wind, Y. and Cardozo, R. (1974), 'Industrial market segmentation', *Industrial Marketing Management*, 3(March): 156.

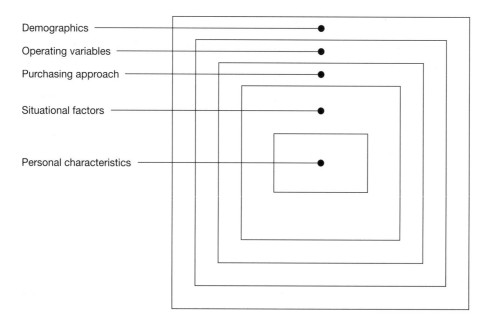

Demographics
Operating variables
Purchasing approach
Situational factors
Personal characteristics

FIGURE 3.9 A 'nested' appraoch to industrial market segmentation

Source: Adapted from Shapiro, B.P. and Bonoma, T.V. (1984), 'How to segment industrial markets', *Harvard Business Review*, May–June: 104–10.

Operating variables

The second nest contains a variety of segmentation criteria called 'operating variables'. These enable more precise identification of existing and potential customers within demographic categories. Operating variables are generally stable and include technology, user/non-user status (by product and brand) and customer capabilities (operating, technical and financial).

Purchasing approaches

A neglected, but valuable, method of segmenting industrial markets involves customer purchasing approaches and company philosophy. Factors here include formal organization of the purchasing function, its power structure, the nature of the buyer/seller relationship, purchasing policies and purchasing criteria.

Situational factors

The model has so far focused on grouping customer firms. It now moves to consider the tactical role of the purchasing situation. Situational factors resemble operating variables, but are temporary and require a more detailed knowledge of the customer. These include the urgency of order fulfilment, product application and the size of order.

Buyers' personal characteristics

People, not companies, make purchase decisions, although the organizational framework in which they work and company policies and needs constrain their choices. Marketers for industrial goods, like those for consumer products, can segment markets according to the individuals involved in a purchase in terms of buyer/seller similarity, buyer motivation, individual perceptions and risk-management strategies.

Having identified market segments, the next step in target marketing is to evaluate the attractiveness of these segments as a prelude to selecting target markets.

SEGMENT EVALUATION: CHOICE OF TARGETING STRATEGIES AND MARKET TARGETS

Determining whether, and on what basis, a market segments is the first step in the process of target marketing. Once market segments have been identified we must select a targeting strategy and if appropriate, select specific market segments to target. During this process we must evaluate the relative attractiveness of different segments.

Evaluating market segments

Whenever a market segments (and most markets do), as part of overall marketing strategy a company must decide on targeting which segments it wishes to serve and on what basis. To do this, the strategic marketer must first evaluate existing market segments. This evaluation process broadly involves assessing the attractiveness of the various segments in the market to determine which are worth serving. We must, therefore, consider the overall attractiveness of the segment, e.g. size and growth, as well as company objectives and resources.

Segment structural attractiveness

A number of factors influence the relative attractiveness of a particular segment. Each should be assessed before making targeting decisions:

1   *Segment size and growth*: Although larger segments are not always the most attractive (especially to the smaller company) an evaluation of market segments should include an assessment of current size, together with existing and potential future growth rates. As with market size, the most attractive segments are not always those that have the highest existing or potential future growth rates. Indeed, even a segment in decline may, because of lower levels of competition, offer attractive sales potential to the company able to supply e.g. spare parts for old model automobiles. After a period of time, the original equipment manufacturers may feel that declining demand for such spares no longer justifies supplying the market, and subject to meeting any statutory or contractual requirements with regard to supply, then withdraw. This leaves

the market open to smaller specialist suppliers who, for a time at least, can make sufficient profits to justify the investment.

This extends beyond the idea of evaluating the attractiveness of a segment from a purely volume perspective, to that of long-term profitable attractiveness. We can use Porter's model of industry/competitive advantage as discussed in Chapter 15, to indicate key areas for assessing segment attractiveness.

2   *Extent of segment competitive rivalry*: Some segments are characterized by intense and frequent rivalry, perhaps because they are high growth, high profit, but often because they are in decline with overcapacity. A more competitive segment will tend to be less attractive, particularly to the new entrant, unless it has some distinct and sustainable advantage it can use to compete.

3   *Barriers to entry or exit*: The most competitive segments, and the ones with the lowest profit margins, are those with low barriers to entry and high barriers to exit. What initially appears to be an attractive new segment can, if entry barriers are low, quickly become over-competitive and ultimately unprofitable.

4   *Threat of substitutes*: Existence of many substitutes reduces the attractiveness of a segment. An appraisal of substitutes should take in not only existing substitutes, but also likely future ones. Predicting these is difficult, although techniques of technological forecasting (TF) discussed in Chapter 11, can be useful.

5   *Bargaining power of buyers*: Some otherwise attractive segments are made less attractive by the bargaining power of buyers. In many retailing segments, the bargaining power of large multiple chain stores like Tesco is such that profit margins for suppliers can be slender. As with substitutes, not only should the current bargaining power of buyers be assessed, but also likely future developments should be anticipated.

6   *Bargaining power of suppliers*: This is the reverse argument of the previous factor. Assessing segment attractiveness should also take into account the extent to which present suppliers of materials, plant, finance, labour, etc. exercise strong bargaining power. Again, an assessment should be made of likely future trends and changes.

7   *Company objectives and resources*: This key area of segment evaluation concerns the extent to which the segment equates with a company's long-term objectives and strategic plans, skills and resources.

TARGETING STRATEGIES

Having evaluated the relative attractiveness of different market segments we can position to select a targeting strategy. A company can select from three broad strategies: **undifferentiated, differentiated** and **concentrated target marketing**.

Undifferentiated marketing

This is based on ignoring any segmentation in the market. Instead, a 'blanket' approach is used with a strategy aimed at the entire market rather than any single segment, or combination of segments.

A company will usually produce one undifferentiated product, relying on mass advertising and distribution to reach as many customers as possible. Undifferentiated marketing is most suitable where demand for a product is relatively homogeneous. It should also have the potential to yield significant economies of scale in both marketing and production. The existence of disaggregated/ heterogeneous demand renders this global approach to market segmentation and targeting unsuitable.

Differentiated marketing

This is based not only on the recognition that different segments exist in a market, but upon a decision to target several or all of these. The company designs a separate marketing programme for each market segment it decides to serve. Because each segment is specifically targeted, the company expects to increase overall company sales and market share. Any increase must be compared with the greater costs of having many individual marketing programmes.

Concentrated marketing

This strategy recognizes the existence of different market segments, but instead of serving several of these, a concentrated or **niche marketing** strategy focuses marketing effort on a single market segment. In this way, economies of scale in both production and marketing can be achieved, while at the same time more nearly meeting the needs of target group customers. The disadvantage of this strategy is that it renders a company vulnerable should anything threaten sales in the selected segment.

Many factors affect the choice of an appropriate targeting strategy. Smaller companies with fewer resources often have to compete by specializing in certain market segments and pursue a concentrated marketing strategy. Competition will also affect choice of strategy. Where competitors do not segment and target respective customer groups, a strategy of concentrated or differentiated marketing can produce a significant competitive advantage. The choice of marketing strategy is ultimately a question of comparing costs and benefits of each approach.

The selection of specific target markets only concerns companies that decide to pursue a concentrated or differentiated targeting strategy. With those two strategies, a company must decide which of the segments in the market it is best able and willing to serve. This decision must of course be based on the outcome of an evaluation process.

PRODUCT POSITIONING AND MARKET DEVELOPMENT

The final stages of target marketing involve the development of **positioning strategies** together with a supporting marketing mix.

Effective product positioning takes place in the mind of the customer and relates to psychology and understanding how people perceive products and brands. The concept is relatively simple and applicable in both industrial and consumer markets. The key aspects of this approach are based upon:

1 Products and brands have both objective and subjective attributes. Examples of objective attributes include those in Figure 3.10, and examples of subjective attributes are shown in Figure 3.11.
2 Purchasers use such attributes when choosing between products and brands in a particular segment.
3 The customer has individual ideas about how competitive products or brands rate on each attribute, i.e. 'positioning' takes place in the mind of the customer.

Using these precepts, it is possible to establish:

1 the important attributes in choosing between competing alternatives
2 how the customer perceives the position of competitive products in relation to these attributes, and how to ascertain the most advantageous position for the company within the segment of the market.

Let us assume a company seeks to enter the market for 'instant coffee' in which there are already competitors producing brands A, B, C, D, E, F and G. The company must establish what customers believe to be the appropriate attributes when choosing between brands and the perceived position of existing competitors with respect to these attributes. If we imagine that important attributes have been found to be 'price' and 'flavour', a **positioning map** (called a brand map) might be drawn as shown in Figure 3.12. With this information, the company must decide where to position its product

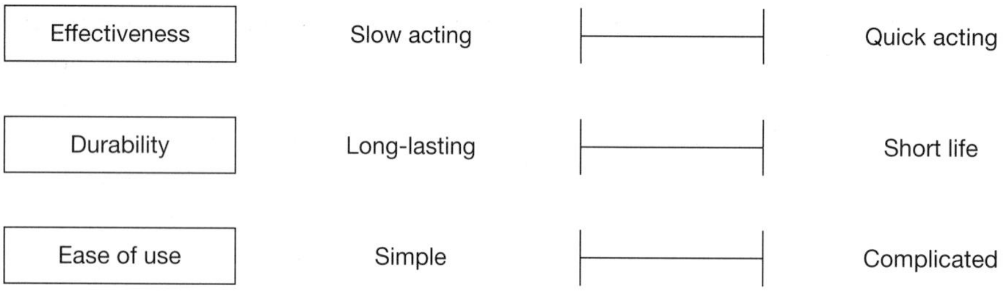

Effectiveness	Slow acting	⊢———⊣	Quick acting
Durability	Long-lasting	⊢———⊣	Short life
Ease of use	Simple	⊢———⊣	Complicated

FIGURE 3.10 Examples of objective attributes

Quality	High	⊢———⊣	Low
Style	Modern	⊢———⊣	Old-fashioned
Appearance	Attractive	⊢———⊣	Unattractive

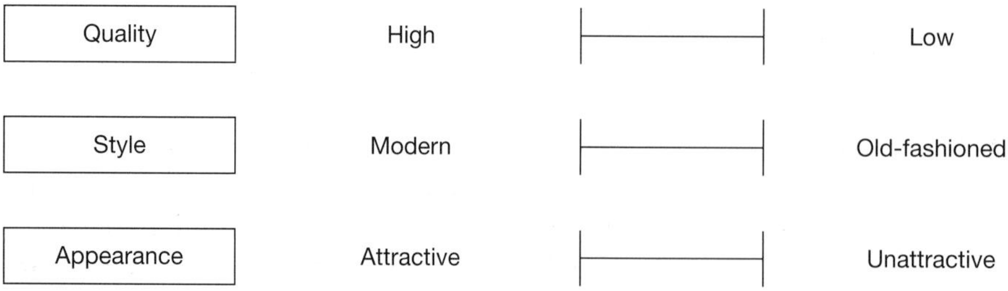

FIGURE 3.11 Examples of subjective attributes

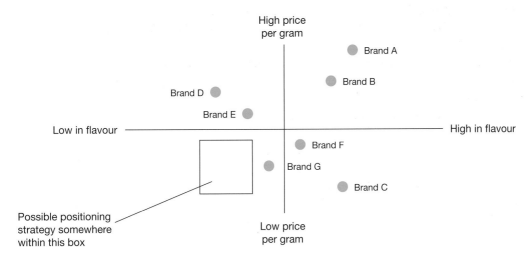

within this market segment. Possibilities are contained within the box, the parameters of which are low to medium price per gram and low to medium in flavour. Perhaps a 'caffeine free' product could also be considered? Such a product would give the new brand some distinctiveness, as opposed to positioning the brand next to another and competing 'head on' for market share.

What is the most appropriate position for the new coffee brand depends on its relative attractiveness. Similarly, we must assess the relative strengths of existing brands in the market and whether or not we want to tackle this competition head on. We must then consider our objectives for the new product are with regard to brand image. Once we have assessed brand positioning, the final step involves the design of marketing programmes that will support the positional strategy. In the instant coffee example, the company must determine what price, flavour, distribution and promotional strategy will be necessary to achieve the selected position in the market.

In the instant coffee market, 'Carte Noir' is positioned as a distinctly up-market and sophisticated product compared to its competition. All of the elements of the marketing mix for this brand serve to support this positioning strategy. The packaging is designed to convey an image of quality. The brand name itself suggests an air of sophistication. Although not necessarily the most expensive brand in the market, neither is it the cheapest. The promotion of the brand exemplifies the unique selling proposition extolled by the brand's marketers.

The example in Figure 3.12 illustrates positioning a new product based on attributes. There are, however, several alternative ways to position new products and brands. A product may be positioned on the basis of uses/applications e.g. car engine oil might be positioned as primarily for use in winter or a new brand can be positioned by associating it with particular groups of users e.g. being predominantly for 'executives'. Positioning can be achieved deliberately with respect to a competitor. This can be done by positioning with respect to the leading brand/competitor in the market using the attributes (good or bad) of the brand leader to make direct comparisons with the new brand, and so develop pre-determined perceptions with regard to the new product.

Although positioning is crucial when developing and launching a new product, it is also relevant to the management of existing products and brands. Because markets evolve and change over time, including changes in customer tastes, competition etc., the marketer must continuously assess the effectiveness of existing positioning strategies for products and brands. Often existing brands will need to be repositioned to reflect changing market dynamics. Some of the most common repositioning strategies are described below.

REPOSITIONING WITHIN EXISTING SEGMENTS

This approach to **repositioning** is often done to revitalize a brand which is losing sales/market share and/or has approached the end of its product life. This type of repositioning does not target new customers, but seeks rather to update the image and/or features of a brand. A good example of a brand which has been updated consistently over its life is 'OXO' which has changed its image, particularly through advertising, to reflect changing social and family attitudes.

Repositioning to attract new customers

Sometimes a company may deliberately reposition a brand to attract new customers. This may often involve significant changes to one or more of the marketing mix elements. This might be to take account of market dynamics or revitalize flagging sales. An example of repositioning is 'Lucozade' which over time has been repositioned from being for ill people to a brand that is for the fit and healthy, particularly where they participate in physical activities. An important consideration in such repositioning is the effect it has on existing customers and sales.

Innovative repositioning

Sometimes a marketer can create a new position in a market by introducing new criteria for brand choice based on attributes in which the marketer is strong e.g. Volvo has kept ahead of competition by deliberately positioning their products on the basis of the 'safety' attribute. Sometimes **innovative repositioning** can come up with entirely new attributes, e.g. Daewoo successfully introduced the notion of 'no hassle' showroom staff who sell cars.

Competitor depositioning

Here strategy is essentially based on repositioning competitor brands rather than changing the position of one's own brand. This means altering the perceived position of competitive brands from the perspective of customers. **Competitor depositioning** means repositioning competitor brands in a less favourable light, but it should be approached with caution because of legal implications where a competitive brand is denigrated through advertising, so facts must be checked to ensure accuracy. Sometimes it is safer to deposition competitors by more subtle veiled comparisons involving competitor brands.

SUMMARY

The delineation of market boundaries is seen as a prerequisite to strategic market planning and in particular the implementation of target marketing. Some companies still define their markets on the basis of product or industry classifications. Simple though this is, it can lead to a myopic view of markets. At the other extreme we have generic need-based definitions of market boundaries which, although offering advantages over product/industry-based definitions, are usually too broad to be used for strategic planning purposes. Between these relatively narrow and broad-based definitions of market boundaries is the delineation of markets based on a combination of customer functions, technology and customer groups. This approach affords a more useful perspective on market boundaries to planners, enabling the basic building blocks of a market to be assembled and analysed.

Recognizing that markets comprise individual blocks leads to consideration of segmentation, targeting and positioning. The importance of 'target marketing' stems from the fact that demand in most markets is heterogeneous. There are a number of advantages associated with the effective use of target marketing, but in particular a company is able to recognize marketing opportunities and avoid excessive competition. A market may be segmented using any one or a combination of bases, both associative and direct in nature. However, the base(s) used should lead to distinguishable market segments which may be selected as market targets to be reached with a distinct marketing mix. Used effectively, target marketing can lead to improved profitability. This is done by tailoring marketing efforts more specifically to customer needs, while at the same time selecting market segments that can be best defended against competition.

KEY TERMS

KEY TERMS . . . *continued*

CASE STUDY

Bon Voyage

The holiday market represents a highly segmented and targeted market. For example we have Saga type holidays aimed at the over 50s and designed to fill this group's needs. On the other hand we have had Club Med and Club 18–30, the latter in particular suggesting the age group these two operators were targeting.

You have been appointed as the new marketing manager for a large travel group, Bon Voyage, offering a range of holiday packages aimed at several parts of the market. The group includes package tour operations, a nationwide chain of travel shops and a fleet of aircraft.

One of the fastest growing parts of the travel market in recent years has been the cruise market. Once the domain of the privil-eged few, cruises are now available to a much wider target market as costs have come down and incomes have risen.

Until now, the company that has just appointed you has not been part of the cruise market. It now realizes it may have made a mistake in this respect and wishes to enter the market as soon as possible. The company has negotiated the provision of two cruise ships for the next season, which will sail round the Mediterranean and the Caribbean respectively. The ships have just been refurbished and offer the most up-to-date facilities. Other companies in this market have been predominantly targeting the middle-income groups. However, there remains a part of the market which is aimed only at the luxury end, with high prices and prestigious ships.

. . . continued

CASE STUDY ... *continued*

The company has asked you to give them some preliminary advice about how to segment this market and which target segments might be most appropriate and why. It also wants to know how its product offerings in this area might be positioned so as to differentiate it from existing competitors.

CASE STUDY QUESTION

Prepare a report on advice and information your company is seeking.

Suggestions as to how to approach and answer this question are contained on the accompanying website. In addition a number of longer strategic case studies, along with suggested solutions, are also contained on the website.

REFERENCES

1 Hooley, G., Piercy, N.F. and Nicolaud, B. (2008), *Marketing Strategy and Competitive Advantage*, 4th edn, Harlow, Essex: Pearson Education.

2 Brassington, F. and Pettit, S. (2006), *Principles of Marketing*, 4th edn, Harlow, Essex: Pearson Education.

3 Levitt, T. (1960), 'Marketing myopia', *Harvard Business Review*, 38, July–August: 45–56.

4 Proctor, T. (2008), *Strategic Marketing*, 2nd edn, London: Routledge.

5 Rotfeld, H.J. (2007), 'Mistaking demographic segments for people: another source of customer abuse', *Journal of Consumer Marketing*, 24(6): 332–3.

6 Solomon, M.R., Marshall, G.W., Stuart, E.W., Barnes, B. and Mitchell, V.W. (2009), *Marketing: Real People Real Decisions*, Harlow: Pearson Education.

7 Hyun-Hee, P. and Sullivan, P. (2009), 'Market segmentation with respect to university student's clothing benefits sought: Shopping orientation, clothing attribute evaluation and brand repatronage', *International Journal of Retail & Distribution Management*, 37(2): 182–201.

8 Canever, M., van Trijp, H. and van der Lans, I. (2007), 'Benefit-feature segmentation: a tool for the design of supply chain strategy', *Marketing Intelligence & Planning*, 25(5): 511–33.

9 Paco, A. and Raposo, M. (2009), '"Green" segmentation: an application to the Portuguese consumer market', *Marketing Intelligence and Planning*, 27(3): 364–79.

10 Tayloe-West, P., Fulford. H., Reed, G., Story, V. and Saker, J. (2008), 'Familiarity expertise and involvement: key consumer segmentation factors', *Journal of Consumer Marketing*, 25(6): 361–8.

11 Harris, C. and Bray, J. (2007), 'Price endings and consumer segmentation', *Journal of Product and Brand Management*, 16(3): 200–5.

12 Liu, S.S. and Chen, J. (2009), 'Using data mining to segment healthcare markets from patients' preference perspectives', *International Journal of Health Care Quality Assurance*, 22(2): 117–34.

13 Ansell, J., Harrison, T. and Archibald, T. (2007), 'Identifying cross-selling opportunities, using lifestyle segmentation and survival analysis', *Marketing Intelligence & Planning*, 25(4): 394–410.

14 IAB (2009), *Internet Advertising Revenue Report*, PricewaterhouseCoopers, March.

15 Wind, Y. and Cardozo, R. (1974), 'Industrial market segmentation', *Industrial Marketing Management*, 3(March): 142–64.

16 Shapiro, B.P. and Bonoma, T.V. (1984), 'How to segment industrial markets', *Harvard Business Review*, May–June: 104–10.

17 Powers, T.L. and Sterling, J.U. (2008), 'Segmenting business-to-business markets: a micro-macro linking methodology', *Journal of Business and Industrial Marketing*, 23(3): 170–7.

Chapter 4

Product and innovation strategies

LEARNING OBJECTIVES

After reading this chapter you will:

- appreciate the strategic significance of product and innovation decisions
- comprehend the notion of the 'product life cycle'
- understand the nature and scope of product and innovation strategies
- be familiar with the critical factors in the management of innovation
- understand the key steps in the development and launch of new products
- be familiar with recent developments in the strategic management of products and innovation

INTRODUCTION

We have discussed the analysis that precedes and is essential to the development of marketing programmes designed to meet corporate and strategic marketing objectives. In this, and subsequent chapters, we consider strategic decisions concerned with planning and implementing elements of the marketing mix; namely product, price, place and promotion (the four Ps).

This chapter examines the wide ranging nature and scope of product and service strategies (the term product covers services like banking and insurance so when we refer to products, this includes services). Products convey to customers more about a company than any other marketing activity. Not only are they the source of revenue and profit, but new products are the most important element in the marketing mix that establishes success in the future. A product can be a piece of machinery with physical characteristics or a service with intrinsic characteristics like hairdressing. The common denominator between products and services, whether physical or intangible, is that they need to meet the needs and requirements of customers and provide satisfaction. Product decisions determine the upper limit to a company's profit potential; the rest of the marketing mix determines the extent to which this potential is achieved. It is essential to manage a company's product mix effectively in a competitive marketplace. Companies are under increasing pressure to continuously develop new products which are timely and respond to customer needs. Successful businesses are able to develop new products to meet changing needs in a dynamic marketplace and it is this aspect of product management that is particularly emphasized in this chapter.

ELEMENTS OF PRODUCT STRATEGY

To illustrate the range of decisions which this key area encompasses, we consider product strategy as a hierarchy of related decisions ranging from product item to product mix elements. The nature and importance of service products are considered in a more detailed discussion of service product characteristics in Chapter 17.

Product item decisions

The first level of product decisions concern individual products/services that a company manufactures and markets. Some companies produce only one product, but most are multi-product. A **product item** is, by definition, any item that can be considered as a separate product entity and that may be distinguished from other products the company produces irrespective of its relationship to those other products. Provided that any product differs in some way from another, either through modification or market application, it is regarded as a product item. At the product item level, product decisions include: design, quality, features, packaging and branding.

Product line decisions

Individual product items that are closely related are classed as **product lines.** The relationship could be different variations of the same basic product, e.g. the range of different fillings as product items in a range of Sainsbury's sandwiches – the product line, or a range of industrial and domestic air conditioning filters as two product lines containing product items for different end use applications.

Product line decisions involve the marketing planner in considering the number of product items in a selected product line e.g. Ford Motor Company must determine how many models in the 'Ford Focus' line they should offer, and what the nature of these variations should be (engine, trim and accessory variations).

Product line decisions are not easy. A careful, detailed evaluation of demand and cost interrelationships between individual products in the line is vital. A sense of balance is needed; if too many variations in a line are offered, costs increase, but if a product line contains too few variations customer satisfaction may be unfulfilled through lack of variety. In competitive multi-product markets, it is essential to maintain balance within each product line to achieve and maintain market share. Product lines should focus on target markets to achieve market concentration and maintain competitive advantage.

Management of the product line means frequent appraisal of the range of product items in each product line, determining whether they are too extensive or too constrained. Policy must be set to add and delete items from product lines to meet financial targets while maintaining customer service levels. This can be a difficult dilemma as frequently opportunities arise to extend the product line either by moving up-market by adding higher quality products to the line or meeting 'budget market' requirements by adding economy lines. A clear rationale is needed for such decisions. Over time there is a tendency for product lines to extend in size as new products are added, while older outmoded ones, for many reasons, are not deleted. This calls for clear policy guidelines on the addition or deletion of product items from established product lines.

Over 30 years ago one of the UK Polytechnic institutions introduced the first undergraduate marketing degree in the United Kingdom. This was a straightforward marketing degree with no specialist options aimed at producing graduates who wanted to work in some area of marketing activity. During the first few years after the programme was launched there was little or no competition. Demand for the course built slowly but steadily, and there were good employment prospects with graduates proceeding to work in brand management, advertising, marketing research, retail marketing, and so on.

Over the years success of the product encouraged more competitors to enter the market, and potential students began to pick and choose. Some competitors, encouraged by increasing specialization in the marketing jobs market itself, began to introduce more specialized marketing undergraduate courses. Slowly at first, but then with increasing urgency, in response to increasing competition and changing demand, the original Polytechnic (now a University) provider began introducing new marketing degree course products to its range. Examples included: 'Marketing with a Foreign Language', 'Global Marketing', 'Sports Marketing' and Retail Marketing'. This University has over 20 different marketing degree specialisms in its product range, including the original programme introduced over 30 years ago. Only a small number of students apply for the original marketing degree. Most choose one of the more specialized degrees. Despite this, there is some residual nostalgia for the original course, coupled with a degree of inertia. This has meant that the original has never been dropped despite its now poor sales.

This situation can be found in many companies. Old, established products, which in the past were often the basis of the organization's initial success, are kept in the product range which simply continues to expand until it becomes unmanageable.

PRODUCT MIX DECISIONS

The **product mix** constitutes all individual product items and product lines the company markets. The product mix is described in terms or 'width' and 'depth'. This enables an analysis of the 'constituency' of the product mix to be made. Figure 4.1 illustrates a company that manufactures and markets three separate product lines: fountain pens, cigarette lighters and wrist-watches. Within each product line the company offers a number of separate product items. This is typical of diversified companies with multiple product lines. Here, the product mix represents the sum of the firm's products – in this case, 30. The number of product lines is three. **Line depth** refers to the number of products in each line – 9, 13 and 8 respectively – with the average depth being 10. **Line width** refers to the number of product lines offered.

By using the product mix concept a strategic assessment of the company's product offerings can be made e.g. product line three could be extended (and hence the product mix) by adding digital watches. The company can also assess the extent to which products in the same line are complementary to, or compete with, each other and hence which might be deleted.

Decisions about new products should reflect consistency with existing product lines. Conversely, is any one product so valued in terms of image and reputation that its deletion will damage the product mix? As Lancaster and Massingham[1] point out, ultimately the addition to the width of the mix and the depth within each product line should be compatible with long-term marketing strategy. Short-term opportunist decisions may be damaging the company's market position in the longer term.

Product mix analysis is a vital part of strategy review. In the case of Personal Products Ltd in Figure 4.1, the following are possible strategic options:

1   Augment the product line by adding rollerball pens. This would remove some measure of exclusivity and represent a strategy of being 'all things to people' in a bid to serve the whole market for ink-based writing implements.
2   Delete all but the most expensive men's lighters from line two. This would have the effect of making the company a market specialist in men's lighters, aiming at an exclusive market segment.
3   Delete lines one and two and become a specialist in a single product line i.e. wrist-watches, and options one and two would still be available to the company.
4   Delete all but one product and become expert in its marketing and production.

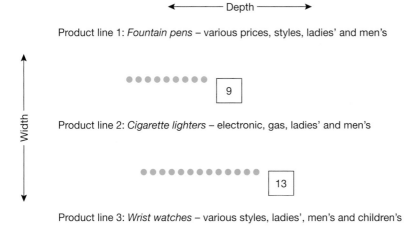

FIGURE 4.1 A hypothetical product mix for Personal Products Ltd

5   Add another product line. In the case of Personal Products Ltd, it could be a new line of pens aimed at the graphics market.

Given the existing product mix and the options available, the company must begin to take product decisions that are in line with long-term strategy and are consistent with that mix. The introduction of ball-point pens could influence the perception the consumer has of the company as a whole. Low-cost disposable pens might not be consistent with the firm's reputation for high quality lighters. Similarly, the firm may be technically capable of producing an industrial line, but lacks marketing expertise required to serve this new market effectively.

Analysis of the product mix examines every aspect of the company. Each decision has financial, technical, marketing and market implications. The critical nature of product strategy becomes more apparent when one considers the consequences of failure and the need for success. Strategic choice options that relate to product mix decisions should be carefully considered through a set of evaluation criteria, so decisions taken are rational and not emotional or opportunistic.

PRODUCT LIFE CYCLE

The **product life cycle** is a ubiquitous in marketing terms, but before we examine its uses and limitations in strategic market planning, we explain the concept.

The product life cycle proposes that like all life forms, products have finite lives. Hence, once a product is introduced to the market it enters a 'life cycle' and will eventually fade from the market.

In addition, the concept proposes that during its life cycle a product will pass through a number of different stages, where each stage has characteristic phenomena that suggest specific and different marketing strategies. This notion, together with the suggested shape and stages of the 'typical' product life cycle, are shown in Figure 4.2.

The characteristics of each stage are:

1   *Introduction*: At this stage the product or service is new to the market. The risk of failure is high and any initial sales are likely to be slow. Purchasers at this stage are likely to be innovators who are willing and able to take risks. Profit margins are likely to be small or non-existent due to the low volume of sales and high initial launch and marketing costs. Money spent during this phase should be regarded as an investment in the future.

2   *Growth*: Provided the product or service meets customer needs and there is a favourable market reaction, sales begin to accelerate as news of the product permeates the market. Customers take fewer risks than initial innovator purchasers, but they welcome novelty, and begin to purchase the product. Attracted by sales growth and potential profit, new competitors enter the market, often offering variations on the original product to encourage brand loyalty or to avoid patent infringement.

3   *Maturity*: Eventually the rate of sales growth will begin to slow down and then cease. A number of factors contribute to this process:

   ■   *Approaching market saturation:* Quite simply, there remain fewer and fewer potential customers left still to purchase the product as it is diffused through the market. Eventually, only replacement sales are made with comparatively few new customers left to purchase for the first time.

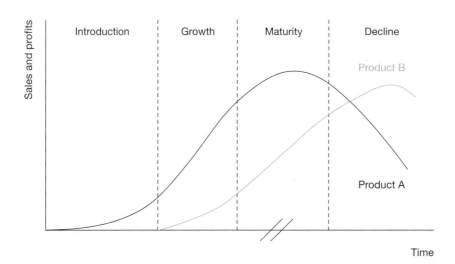

FIGURE 4.2 The product life cycle concept (PLC)

■ *Customer boredom/desire for novelty:* Customers are fickle when it comes to their appetite for new products. Customers who initially purchased the new product may become bored and switch to other products or brands.

■ *New products/technological change:* Successful new products carry within them the seeds of their own destruction. As sales and profits grow, competition is attracted to the market. Often they can only gain entry and market share by developing new or improved versions of the original product. If successful, new products and changes in technology begin to supersede the original product and sales begin to slow.

4   *Decline*: Eventually, forces and factors which contribute to the onset of maturity will erode the market to an extent that sales begin to diminish. The rate at which this will occur, and hence length of time the old product will remain viable, varies. Sometimes decline is rapid, as in fashion markets, or when a major technological breakthrough occurs. In contrast, the rate of decline may take many years e.g. when a hard core of loyal customers refuse to switch product category or brand.

The product life cycle concept has attracted much attention and criticism as a tool of strategic market planning. As a result, the basic concept described here has been developed and refined to include, for example, the notion of different levels of life cycle, i.e. life cycle analysis for brands, product forms and product classes and the notion of variations on the classic S-shaped curve. We examine some of these refinements and their relevance to the use of the concept in strategic market planning shortly, but first we look at some of the suggested uses of the basic concept in strategic decision making.

USING THE LIFE CYCLE CONCEPT

The basic product life cycle concept brings with it a number of suggested implications for strategic market planning.

Different objectives and strategies for each stage

The major use of the product life cycle concept in strategic market planning is based on the notion that characteristics of each stage of the life cycle lend themselves to particular objectives and strategies. We examine this by tracing through each of the stages.

1   **Introductory stage** At this stage, awareness of the new product is low, and competitors are few or non-existent. Considerable effort may have to be made to bring the product to the attention of distributors and consumers. Marketing efforts are likely to be focused on informing customers and promotional and distribution elements of the marketing mix will be targeted at innovator categories. Pricing strategies can be aimed either at 'skimming' the market through high initial prices that gradually reduce, or at 'market penetration', aiming to achieve high levels of market share quickly through low prices. Distribution will tend to be exclusive or selective, and advertising aimed at building awareness.

2   **Growth stage** If the new product is successful, we can expect a rapid growth in sales. During this stage new competitors can be expected to enter the market and marketing strategies will need to be focused on combating these new entrants. Although price wars are unlikely to develop at this early stage, considerable effort may be required to establish the intensive distribution required for ultimate mass market demand. Communications will be aimed at creating brand image.

3   **Maturity stage** Competition is at its peak. Market share needs defending, while at the same time preserving profit levels. Brand preferences and loyalties are likely to be already established by this stage, but there is likely to be considerable emphasis on trying to encourage brand switching through sales promotion. Price reductions feature here and distribution efforts are aimed at maintaining dealer relationships.

4   **Decline stage** Sales promotion may be reduced to a minimum as the market shrinks. Price competition and price cutting are likely to be intense. Emphasis is likely to switch either to looking for ways to extend the product life cycle or to new products, with the old product being 'milked' for profits.

As we can see from this outline of strategies, within broad limits the suggestion is that by identifying the life cycle stage of a product we can develop appropriate marketing mix strategies for each stage. These suggested emphases are not definitive, but they can serve as guidelines.

Criticisms and refinements of the basic product life cycle concept

Amongst the most cogent of these critics have been Dhalla and Yuspeh[2] who have challenged the whole concept of the product life cycle. Indeed, in their influential article we are counselled to forget the concept. They argue that there is a danger of allowing the life cycle concept to dull the planner's management judgement by over-relying on 'recipe marketing'. They suggest that its use can lead to costly and potentially irrevocable mistakes in strategy. There may be a danger of selecting entirely inappropriate strategies for a particular stage of the life cycle of a product because of the unique circumstances pertaining to that particular product.

Some critics have gone further in their assessment of the limitations of the conventional life cycle in strategic market planning. Essentially, such criticisms are based on the extent to which the concept is irrelevant or even misleading. The most fundamental criticism is that there is little or no consistent empirical evidence to support the notion of products following a natural and preordained life cycle with the distinct stages; in short, the product life cycle simply does not exist.

Doubt about the existence or otherwise of both the S-shaped life cycle and the distinct stages which it is supposed to comprise, can only be resolved by an appeal to the facts. With such a long-standing marketing theory, numerous empirical studies have been undertaken over the years designed to confirm or refute the PLC concept. Very early studies include those of Cox,[3] Polli and Cook,[4] and Day.[5] More recently, Baker and Hart[6] have provided further thoughts regarding the validity, or otherwise, of the PLC concept. In general, evidence from these and other studies suggests that the classic S-shaped life cycle does exist, but not for all products or for similar products on all occasions; in other words, we should not consider the traditional PLC concept as a universal law. If this is the

Keep Taking the Tablets

Developed in 1897, 'aspirin' is one of the world's longest established pharmaceutical products. Originally launched by the German company Bayer, aspirin was hailed as a wonder drug and was one of the most effective over-the-counter pain killers ever launched. By the late 1960s, however, it looked as if aspirin was approaching the end of its life cycle. New modern products were being developed to compete in the painkiller market: products which were heralded as being much more effective and with fewer side effects. As a result, many of the large pharmaceutical companies with aspirin-based products began to look to develop their own new painkiller products. Some withdrew their aspirin-based products completely.

In the late 1980s and the early 1990s research began to emerge that aspirin might have the effect of reducing the incidence of heart attacks if taken regularly in small and managed doses. The research appears now to be conclusive and aspirin can be effective in preventing heart attacks. As a result, it has enjoyed a resurgence of sales, seeming to defy the product life cycle and the decline stage it had appeared to have reached. Bayer now enjoy higher sales from aspirin than they ever have. Furthermore, ongoing research into aspirin is revealing that it may have other important uses in fighting a whole range of diseases from prostate to bowel cancer. Companies who withdrew their support for aspirin-based products are still feeling the pain.

Source: http://almaz.com: http://www.aspirin-foundation.com.

case, then where does this leave the strategic marketing planner with respect to the use of the concept with regard to suggested applications outlined earlier? We have counselled the use of judgement and experience in interpreting the concept for marketing strategy. The view is taken that critics and researchers of the concept, particularly those who have not supported the classic S-shaped PLC, have added to the debate concerning the usefulness of the concept to strategic marketing planning.

We can see that use of the product life cycle concept is one that raises uncertainty and debate as to its usefulness or otherwise in strategic market planning. The position taken here with respect to this debate, and hence with regard to this use of the life cycle concept, is well summarized by Brassington and Pettit,[7] with whose view we are in accord: 'Despite its weaknesses, the PLC is a well used concept. Product marketing strategies should, however, take into account other considerations as well as the PLC.'

Different PLC patterns

In addition to the S-shaped life cycle, other variations on this pattern have been observed. Some of these are shown in Figure 4.3. We see that the product life cycle can exhibit different patterns from that epitomized by the traditional notion of an S-shaped curve. Moreover, there is evidence to suggest that the 'typical' shape of the pattern may be associated with the type of product/market under construction.

Life cycle (a) is suggested as being frequently found in the market for many small household appliances. Initial sales growth after a new product launch is rapid, followed by a quite severe drop

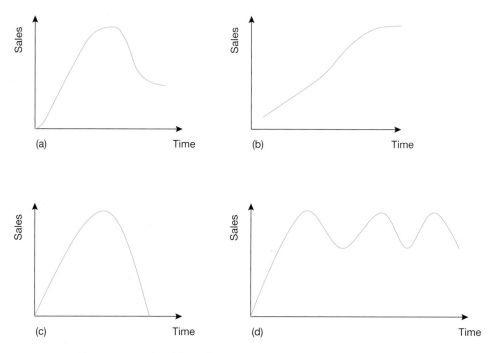

FIGURE 4.3 Alternative product life cycle patterns

in sales as the novelty wears off. Eventually sales decline will stop and the product enters a relatively long period of stability in sales as late adopters purchase the product and early buyers purchase again to become replacement purchasers.

The pattern shown in (b) represents a 'truncated' pattern. Its shape illustrates that there is no introductory period. Sales grow rapidly from product launch. This type of curve may be associated with new products, like petrol-driven motor cars where there is substantial market appeal and little learning is required or risk perceived.

Pattern (c) illustrates a rapid growth in sales, with no introductory stage, followed by an equally rapid decline with no maturity stage. Products that exhibit this shape of life cycle are typical novelty products or fads, such as many children's toys.

Pattern (d) illustrates a cycle/recycle pattern of a succession of product life cycle curves with a relatively short introductory period, rapid sales growth, a short maturity, followed by rapid decline. After this, the process is repeated when a new model is introduced. This pattern is frequently associated with fashion products like clothing or viewing a popular film a number of times.

Different categories (levels) of life cycle

Related to different life cycle patterns we note that there are different categories or levels of life cycle. The same 'product' market may be examined at a number of different levels, giving rise to different categories of life cycle:

1 *Product category life cycles*: Examples include the life cycle for washing powders, cars and cigarettes; i.e. the generic product. Product category life cycles may extend over considerable periods of time and may not even exhibit any sign of decline e.g. shoes.

2 *Product form life cycles*: Examples are laundry liquid or powder detergents, un-tipped cigarettes or leather shoes. Product form life cycles exhibit shorter cycles than those at the product category level. The S-shaped curve is most prevalent here.

3 *Brand life cycles*: Examples are Procter & Gamble's Ariel 'Ultra' washing powder, Ford 'Ka' cars, Gallagher's 'Park Drive' un-tipped cigarettes and Clark's 'big gripper' shoes.

In using the product life cycle for marketing decision making, we must be careful to distinguish between these different levels. Partly owing to criticisms of the product life cycle concept, and based on empirical research, our knowledge about the concept and how to use and interpret it in strategic market planning has improved. There is still controversy surrounding the utility of product life cycles, but like Brassington and Pettit cited earlier, most marketers agree that used with care, tempered by managerial judgement, the concept is of value as a tool of strategic marketing planning.

The product life cycle concept underpins many of the more recently developed tools of strategic market analysis, including some of the 'portfolio' planning tools which we examine in Chapter 14.

IMPLEMENTING PRODUCT STRATEGIES

It is necessary to consider ways in which the decision to choose any of the above options is taken while recognizing the absolute need for new products. If the rate of new product development and launch is not equal to, or better than, the rate of product deletion or obsolescence, the company will become unprofitable and unable to survive. A long-term view of product strategy must be taken. Product strategy is central to all company decisions and should emanate from and support the overall objectives of the company. Because organizations have different, and often multiple, objectives there exists a wide variety of possible product strategies that might be selected to support them. This notion, together with the range of possible product strategies which O'Shaughnessy[8] suggests, is shown in Figure 4.4.

Summarizing the discussion of product item, product line and product mix decisions, together with the range of possible product strategies as shown in Figure 4.4, it can be seen that product decisions are complex and multifaceted. Product strategies need to be evaluated in relation to both the strengths and weaknesses of the company itself, and to the opportunities and threats that are prevalent and likely in the future. Product strategy involves the management of existing successful products, the elimination of obsolete or non-profit-making ones and the development and introduction of new products. Each of these elements of product strategy is important in achieving company objectives. The pace of change, fierce competition and the product life cycle all heighten the significance of the new product development and innovation process, and it is to this particular aspect of product strategy and management that we now turn.

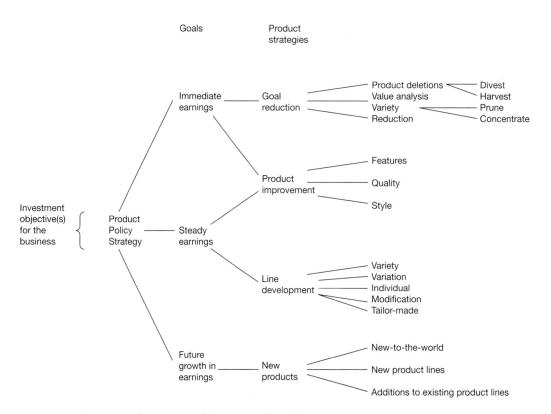

FIGURE 4.4 Company objectives and the range of product strategies

Source: Adapted from O'Shaughnessy, I. (1995), *Competitive Marketing: A Strategic Approach*, 3rd edn, Boston: Unwin Hyman, p. 334.

MANAGING THE PRODUCT LINE: NEW PRODUCT DEVELOPMENT; PRODUCT LIFE CYCLE EXTENSION STRATEGIES

A major use of the product life cycle concept in strategic marketing is in managing the product line and identifying the need for, nature of and timing of product development plans. The premise of this use of the concept is underpinned by the term 'life cycle'. In the absence of suitable strategies, especially if a company does not take steps to prevent it, the dynamics of the life cycle are such that over time, sales and profits will be eroded and eventually disappear. What is required is a constant programme of carefully planned strategies to ensure that long-run profit and sales objectives are met. In particular, the planner must consciously seek to develop a 'portfolio' of products to maintain long-run success. Using the concept in this way means the planner must undertake four steps:

1 Identification of current positions of different company products in their life cycles
The first task of the marketing planner is to locate the respective life cycles positions of the various products the organization markets. Obviously information is vital here. Unless the marketer has accurate and up-to-date information on where products are in their life cycles it is impossible to implement effective product life cycle management. Yang *et al.*[9] have proposed a life cycle information acquisition and management system. Jain[10] suggests that the following should be analysed for each product:

- sales growth pattern since introduction;
- any design and technical problems that need to be resolved;
- sales and profit history of allied products;
- number of years the product has been on the market;
- casualty history of similar products in the past;
- extent to which customers are becoming more demanding *vis-à-vis* price, service etc.;
- extent to which additional sales efforts are necessary;
- ease or difficulty of acquiring dealers and distributors.

Based on this analysis it is possible to relate the information to known characteristics of each stage of the cycle and pinpoint the position of each product in its life cycle curve, which is difficult as a dip in company sales and profits may be simply a result of poor marketing effort rather than a sign that the life cycle curve has peaked. The next step in the process is more difficult still.

2 Analysis of future sales and profit positions of products in their life cycles
The planner must now attempt to forecast the future shape of the life cycle curve. We examine forecasting techniques in Chapter 12, but critics have suggested that forecasting the life cycle curve is dangerous as the stages can vary enormously in their duration and there are several possible shapes for the life cycle curve itself. The view taken here is to concur with suggestions that forecasting life cycle curves is difficult, but that this should not deter the planner from making some attempt to forecast. After all, planning decisions reflect some view of the future so it is better to make some systematic attempt to predict what this future might be.

   Not only must the planner attempt to forecast future sales curves of products, but it is important to forecast the associated profit curves. The relationship generated between product life cycle sales curves and product life cycle profit curves is shown in Figure 4.5.

   The profit life cycle lags the sales life cycle for reasons discussed earlier. For example, in the introductory stage of the life cycle, losses and not profits are likely to occur, due to research and design, initial launch costs, etc. In addition, profits are likely to peak in the growth phase, as competition becomes fiercer and prices are cut to remain competitive.

3 Implications of current and future forecast sales and profits curves: 'gap analysis'
Once present and forecast future sales and profits curves have been established, results of this analysis can be compared with future corporate objectives for sales and profits. In particular, we should identify discrepancies between forecast and required sales or profit levels. This **'gap analysis'** is illustrated in Figure 4.6.

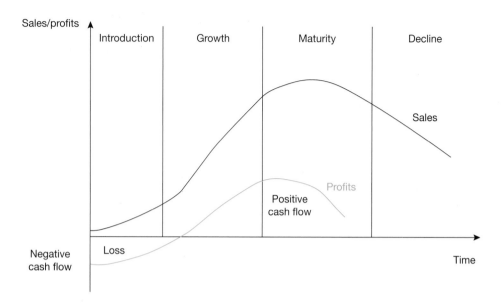

FIGURE 4.5 Sales/profit cycles

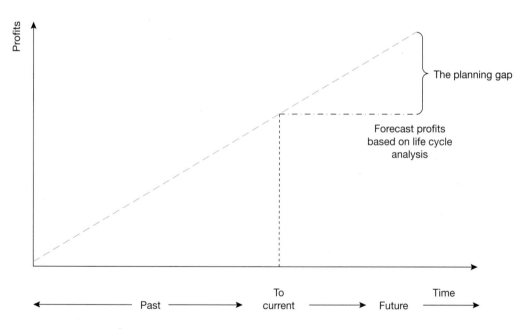

FIGURE 4.6 Gap analysis

Based on current and forecast profit life cycles compared to objectives for future profits, there exists a gap between what is required and what is forecast to be achieved. In the absence of any action to prevent it, projections of future sales and profit life cycles suggest that this gap will grow. Many other factors give rise to such 'planning gaps' such as adverse economic and other environmental trends and increased costs. However, product life cycle analysis will at least enable the planner to assess how much of this gap is attributable to life cycle forces and hence the 'balance' within the product range.

4 Developing innovation and extension strategies
The final step is the delineation and assessment of possible strategies to counter the underlying life cycle dynamics for the product range. In other words, we must determine how any gaps, if forecasted, are to be filled. Forecasted sales and profit gaps can be filled in many ways, e.g. we might determine that part of a profit gap can best be filled by reducing manufacturing costs or by diversification or exporting.

Which of the many strategies likely to be available when we eventually choose is dependent on a set of complex factors, including:

- competitive strengths and weaknesses;
- the nature of the environment;
- managerial attitudes towards risk.

Specifically, we need to consider ways of extending the life cycle of products that are beginning to mature or decline or the need to innovate and introduce new products, which we discuss shortly. As Hines *et al.*[11] show, product life cycle analysis provides a useful way of focusing new product development. We conclude our discussion of this use of the PLC concept by considering product life cycle extension strategies. The concept, and anticipated results of product life extension strategies, are shown in Figure 4.7.

Product life cycle extension strategies aim not simply to delay the seemingly inevitable onset of terminal decline, but to initiate a period of further sales growth. As can be seen, this process can be repeated, giving a series of enveloping curves, each one extending sales further. A number of strategies can be used to extend the product life cycle. Kotler and Keller[12] suggest some possible ways of extending the life cycle as illustrated in Table 4.1.

A popular electronic consumer product to hit the market in recent years has been the iPod. This is an example of how the product life cycle for a product/technology can be extended; in this case, from traditional means of recording music. An earlier example was video recording machines that were first launched in the 1970s. Over a period of 20-plus years they penetrated most households. Eventually then, other than replacement sales, the market was virtually saturated by the mid-1990s with comparatively few late product adopters still remaining to come on board. In an effort to revitalize sales, many manufacturers including companies like Sony, Panasonic and Philips looked to new technology to extend the life of their products. The DVD became the replacement technology for the VHS video. Launched in the late 1990s, DVD recorders quickly moved to the maturity stage of the life cycle and the majority of sales are now replacement sales. This technology was superior and offered several consumer benefits over its predecessor technology. Perhaps most

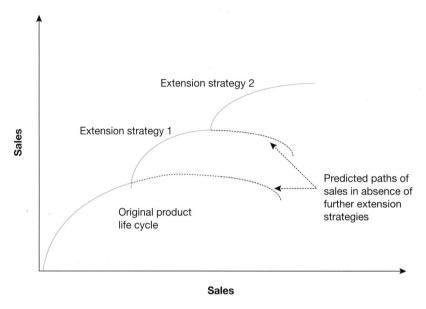

Sales

Extension strategy 2

Extension strategy 1

Original product
life cycle

Predicted paths of
sales in absence of
further extension
strategies

Sales

FIGURE 4.7 Extending product life cycles

TABLE 4.1 Life cycle extension

Broad thrust of strategy	Examples of means of achieving it
Expand number of brand users	Convert non-users; Enter new market segments; Win competitors' customers.
Increase usage of the brand by current brand users	More frequent use; More usage per occasion; New and more varied usage.
Product modification to attract new users/more frequent usage	Quality improvement; Style improvement; Feature improvement.
Marketing mix modification	Reduced prices/special offers; Improved penetration of distribution channels; Improved/more intensive advertising and personal selling; Better/improved service.

important of all in the growth of this new technology, was the desire of many customers to appear to be up to date and fashionable by having the latest electronic technology in their home. Not surprisingly, as the DVD recorder reached maturity, a successor technology was developed in the form of digital TV (e.g. the Sky plus product) which is simpler and more convenient for recording programmes. The Sky plus product is not a direct replacement for the DVD recorder as it will not play DVD discs. However, it is likely that it will be increasingly adopted as a convenient alternative for those who simply want to record programmes to watch them later.

SERVICE PRODUCTS

In some economies the service sector is now the largest sector. As we explained, there is no difference between more tangible physical products and their service counterparts with respect to their importance in overall marketing strategy, or in the importance of physical and service products meeting customer requirements. However, service products have characteristics that set them aside from their physical product counterparts and in turn give rise to additional considerations in their marketing.

The term 'service product' encompasses a myriad of different types of products and markets in which they are sold, but essentially a service is intangible involving some deed, performance or effort that cannot be physically possessed by the customer. The most important distinguishing characteristics of services is that they are essentially intangible, are often consumed at the same time and place as they are supplied, and customer and supplier often directly interact during the sale and consumption process. Because of these characteristics we find additional important elements in their marketing that are referred to as the 'extended marketing mix'. In addition to the conventional 4Ps for the marketing of physical products, when marketing service products, an additional 3Ps (making 7Ps in all) are added to the marketing mix. These three additional Ps are:

'**People**': because of direct contact with customers when marketing services, the service provider's staff, i.e. people, are an important element of the marketing mix.

'**Process**': in services marketing, how the service is provided is important, e.g. systems for serving customers and dealing with orders take on an important significance.

'**Physical evidence**': the intangible nature of service products means that customers often use other evidence such as the physical facilities of the service provider, their promotional and other literature as evidence of the potential quality of the service.

We consider special characteristics of service products and additional marketing mix elements in more detail in Chapter 17. Most products have a mixture of both tangible and intangible components. In some cases, the service element of a manufactured product is the most important factor in competitive success as it is the main means of differentiation. In reality, most products have a personal dimension.

NEW PRODUCT DEVELOPMENT AND INNOVATION

We have raised the importance of new product development and innovation, but now reiterate some of the arguments that serve to illustrate the importance of innovation in corporate and marketing strategy.

The pace of technological, market, social and economic change is accelerating. One of the most important implications of this accelerating change for marketing management is the shortening of product life cycles. Successful products stay successful for shorter periods of time. The pace of change is quickening as epitomized by aggressive competitive behaviour. Successful new products are often quickly copied or improved upon by competitors.

In many markets there is competition to speed innovation and new product development. Motor industry sources report that Honda is confronting its competitors by increasing the speed at which it can bring a new product to market. This not only allows Honda to respond to changes in market demand more rapidly, but it enables it to undermine both cash resources and confidence of its competitors by product proliferation. Amongst the best in the car industry, product development times needed to design and launch a new Honda model have reduced from an average of five to six years in the early 1990s to just over 30 months.

Life After Death

Many tend to think of innovation and new product development solely in the context of tangible, manufactured products. These days there is probably more innovation and new product development in service products. A good example is in the area of services available to the bereaved and their relatives.

Let's face it, death is inevitable. One would have thought that every possible service that could possibly be offered to the bereaved and their loved ones would have been thought of years ago. Not a bit of it! New products for the bereaved and their loved ones are constantly being developed. Here are a few:

- You can now be deep frozen at death with a view to possibly returning to life at some point in the future when medical science is more developed.
- If you want to light up people's lives after death, your ashes can now be launched into space.
- Alternatively, if you want to light up a loved one's life here on earth, for a fee your ashes can now be converted into a diamond.
- So your loved ones don't forget you, 'Eternal Space' lets loved ones create a customized online grave website which the bereaved can visit when they like.
- 'Legacy Locker' is a service which enables the pre-deceased to arrange to send messages and important information such as internet passwords and online account information to predetermined beneficiaries in the event of sudden death.

Innovation and new product development are essential to long-term competitive success. There is risk associated with new product development, and a high proportion of new products fail in the marketplace. With so many interpretations as to what constitutes a 'new' product and also what constitutes 'failure', estimates of new product failure rates vary. Taking estimates of new product failure rates we can say they are at least 20 per cent for industrial product companies and 40 per cent for consumer products. Often these estimates are far exceeded. When combined with the high costs and investments of developing and launching new products, this makes this area of marketing risky. Thus it is important that the process is managed effectively. Before we examine the steps in developing and launching new products we need to set the planning framework for innovation and establish the range of innovation activities in which a company can participate. Finally, we need to assess and draw upon a considerable body of research and evidence as to critical factors in managing innovation, which have largely been derived from studies into successful and unsuccessful innovation.

THE MEANING AND SCOPE OF INNOVATION

A way of distinguishing between different types of innovation and innovative activities is in terms of the degree of 'newness' of the product. Seven types of innovation can be classified in this way:

1 Entirely new products
Referred to as '**new-to-world products'**, such innovations perform an entirely new function and create new markets. Examples include the microwave oven, the mobile telephone, and Viagra. Such innovations are comparatively rare and pose the highest risks and often incur the highest costs.

2 Improved performance products
These are innovations that improve the performance of an existing function. This type of innovation is more common than the 'new-to-the-world' type, and is often the prime objective of innovation research and development activity. An example is the development of digital photography. 'Improved performance' encompasses a range of different types of innovation. At one extreme, it may involve the development and use of a brand new technology (e.g. digital watches); at the other, it may mean an extension or improvement of the technology currently used by improved design or better materials. An example in this category is the development of the Dyson vacuum cleaner.

3 New application products
A considerable amount of innovative activity involves developing new applications for existing products. The amount of development activity required can vary enormously. In some cases, the technology and product can be applied in a new context with little or no further development, e.g. in the case of the hovercraft, whereas for other products or technologies, widening the scope of application requires substantial research and development work, e.g. in finding new applications for laser technology.

4 Additional functions products
This type of innovation may be used to improve performance or extend functions of existing products. Typical was the addition of Internet capabilities on mobile phones and the ability to access Facebook from one's own mobile phone.

5 Lower cost products

This can be seen as a variation on the 'improved performance' product; a new product which performs the same functions as a previous product, but at a lower cost. A lower cost product may enable the marketer to extend applications of the product by reaching more buyers for whom the product was previously too expensive or not cost effective. Innovative activity aimed at reducing product cost is common for many products including computers, pharmaceutical and fashion clothing products.

6 Restyled products

Often, 'new products' are no more than an update or change in styling to old ones. This type of innovative activity is prevalent in the car and clothing markets. It is a progressive innovation that generally involves lower costs and risks than 'new-to-the-world' types of innovation. However, such low cost, low risk modifications sometimes turn into major investments carrying high risk which may not have been the original intention.

7 Repackaged or renamed products

At the opposite extreme to the entirely new product is the 'new' product which might simply be a result of repackaging, renaming or re-branding. Although requiring careful planning and management, this type of innovation involves fewer management issues than those raised by the development of products which are entirely new. One could argue that such products are not new at all, and should not be treated as innovations. The test of what constitutes a 'new product', and the degree of 'newness' is the extent to which the market (i.e. customers) perceive the product to be new. A repackaged or re-branded product, if perceived as new by the market, is in a sense an innovation and should be marketed as such. Repackaging, renaming and re-branding are tactical aspects of product innovation. They are really part of a 'product regeneration' strategy. Examples in recent years include the re-branding of Mars' 'Snickers' snack product (previously 'Marathon') and the 'repackaging' of British Airways.

We have seen that 'innovation' encompasses a broad spectrum of different types of activity, ranging from development of entirely new products and technologies to repackaging existing ones. It is entirely new products that pose greatest problems in terms of effective management and attendant risk, as shown in Figure 4.8. It is with managing this high risk type of innovation activity that much of what follows in this chapter is concerned.

Having established the variety of innovation activities we now examine some of the issues in the management of innovation, in particular the 'ingredients' in the successful management of innovation, and some of the current issues influencing the future environment for innovation and new product development.

Managing innovations: critical factors

Innovation is crucial to long-term success in an organization, yet the risks are high with significant rates of new product failure. The managerial issues and problems to which this dilemma gives rise are considerable. A combination of the recognized importance of innovation and the high risk of failure has meant that his area of company activity has attracted substantial attention and research in recent years. Much of this has focused on attempts to look for empirical evidence that can establish

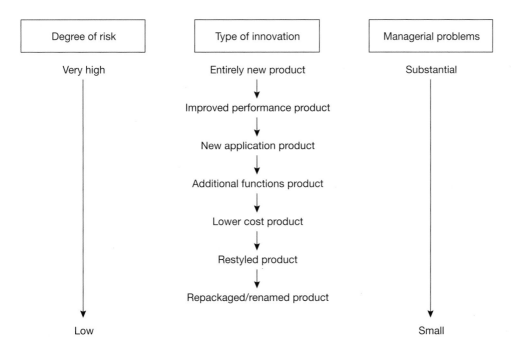

FIGURE 4.8 The continuum of product innovation

the key ingredients in the successful management of innovation. There are no 'recipes' for certain success, but research has been instrumental in establishing some of the critical factors in the process. By way of example, we have outlined a selection of research programmes in this area, together with a brief summary of their findings.

Successful product launches

Morley's[13] study of over 2,000 new product launches was very comprehensive. It found that only one in seven of the new product launches researched could be considered successful when considering sales and market share. Those that were successful exhibited the following characteristics compared to their less successful counterparts:

- sustained heavy promotion during the first three months of launch;
- more extensive and rigorous market research;
- less reliance on exaggerated claims for the new product to consumers;
- more awareness and receptiveness to distributors' needs and wants;
- use of a well-known company and/or brand name.

Conclusions drawn about successful new products were very much along the lines of what one would expect. For example, it is understandable that new products with a well-known company or

Project SAPPHO

One of the earliest systematic studies of success and failure in new product development was Project SAPPHO. Under the direction of Cyril Freeman[14] at the University of Sussex, an extensive and detailed research programme was designed to investigate the key factors for success in innovation. Twenty-nine pairs of similar innovation project were examined; in each pair, one project was successful and the other a comparative failure. Using a carefully designed statistical analysis, Freeman and his team were able to establish a pattern of factors which appeared to distinguish between success and failure in the various pairings. Project SAPPHO found that the successful innovator tended to be distinguished by the following five elements:

1 Successful innovators had a much clearer idea of user needs.
2 Successful innovators put much more effort into marketing their innovations – not just at the original idea stage by looking for gaps in the market, but throughout the process of development and launch.
3 Successful innovators paid much more attention to the development stage of their innovations than those innovators who failed. This often meant that the development work proceeded more slowly, but it was more effective.
4 Successful innovators were much more willing, and indeed able, to use outside help and advice in developing their products. However, most tended to perform more of the practical development work in-house.
5 Successful innovators were distinguished by a high degree of commitment to their innovations. Usually a senior manager with substantial activity in the organization was in charge of the successful innovation in each pair.

brand name that are heavily promoted stand more chance of success than their lesser-known weakly promoted counterparts. However, a finding from his study regarding successful new products is perhaps more surprising, namely that prices for successful new products tended to be above average for the sector.

Amongst the most difficult markets in which to succeed with new products is the grocery, particularly the luxury foods, market. Despite this, Ben and Jerry's brand of ice creams, which is not the cheapest of product ranges in this product category on the market, continue to be extremely successful. The brand's marketers have refused to be drawn into a price war against competitors and continue to support the brand's positioning at the top end of the marketplace to good effect.

Service products like HeartSWell Lodge, in Plymouth, are models of social and financial success. It opened in August 2001, having been funded by charitable donations. It provides support to families of complex high risk patients, yet it is run on business lines. Many units in the main hospital use the facility for carers of their patients in paediatrics, trauma, neurosciences and the hyperbaric oxygen centre.

The McKinsey Report

A slightly different approach to investigating innovative success of new products is exemplified by a report from McKinsey & Co.[15] which sought primarily to establish the essentials of a well managed company. They found certain factors associated with the success of a number of firms acknowledged as being leaders, especially in product innovation. The ten companies selected in the study were International Business Machines, Emerson Electric, Texas Instruments, McDonald's, Hewlett-Packard, Johnson & Johnson, ZM, Digital Equipment, Procter & Gamble and Dana.

The eight key factors for success McKinsey found were:

1   a bias towards action;
2   simple line and team staff organization;
3   continued contact with customers;
4   productivity improvement via people;
5   operational autonomy and the encouragement of entrepreneurship;
6   simultaneous loose and tight controls;
7   stress on one key business value;
8   an emphasis on sticking to what it knows best.

A summary of critical factors in successful innovation

These studies are a sample of empirical research done in this area. What emerges from these and other studies is that there are a set of critical factors in successful innovation which point the way to key areas for managing this activity. A summary of these ingredients is that offered by Twiss,[16] who lists seven critical factors:

1   a market orientation;
2   relevance to the organization's corporate objectives;
3   a source of creative ideas;
4   an effective project selection and evaluation system;
5   effective project management and control;
6   an organization receptive to innovation;
7   commitment by one individual or a few individuals.

He points out that there will be cases where innovations succeed in spite of poor management, but absence of one or more of the above factors is more likely to lead to innovative failure. Evidence suggests that companies seem to be learning to manage the process of new product development, especially the idea generation and screening stages, more effectively than in the past.

The future environment for new product development

In a résumé of the future for new product development, Crawford[17] isolated four sets of factors or trends that will influence the future for new product development:

1   reduced reward factors;
2   increased cost factors;
3   increased difficulty factors;
4   positive market factors.

Reduced reward factors: Crawford argues that a number of trends will tend to reduce the rewards (and the incentive) for product innovation in the future:

■   the increased use of segmentation, and therefore smaller markets;
■   the increased speed of competitive response, and therefore reduced period of price advantage;
■   shorter product life cycles.

All these factors serve to make innovation less rewarding (financially) for the innovator.

Increased cost factors: The increased pace of technological progress has increased costs of pioneering new technologies and products. Some of the more advanced technologies are beyond the resources of many individual companies. We are thus likely to see a much greater use of collaborative developments between companies or companies and government in the future.

An example of company collaboration on new product development was the development of the Advanced Photo system (APS) technology. The costs and risks of developing this technology were considered so great that collaboration between otherwise competitor companies comprising Kodak, Nikon, Canon, Minolta and Fujifilm took place.

An example of competitor and government collaboration for new product development is the development of the European Airbus which involved companies and governments in four European countries (Spain, Germany, France and the United Kingdom) forming a consortium to develop this product.

Increased difficulty factors: These are tending to increase the uncertainty and level of difficulty associated with innovation:

■   There are more government regulations pertaining to new technology.
■   The patent process is slow and not very reliable. For example, the average length of time to process a patent in the UK is three years. Moreover, it is notoriously difficult to establish patentability for a new invention. James Dyson was beset with problems of this kind when he invented and tried to patent the technology of his Dyson vacuum cleaner. Even if a patent is granted the responsibility for pursuing patent infringements lies with the patent holder and not the Patent Office. Pursuing alleged patent infringements is costly and time consuming.

■ Society has become more critical of constant innovation with its emphasis on 'newness', often at the expense of tradition, examples being consumer-oriented initiatives to bring back 'real ale' and 'real cheese'.

■ Managers are increasingly being urged to produce short-term results rather than the long-term commitment which much innovative activity requires.

Positive forces: A number of factors will tend to promote the progress of new product development in the future:

■ Despite the reaction towards new products and technologies, markets, customers are still responsive to them.

■ Linked to this, profit opportunities from successful new product development are still large.

■ In general, managers are now better trained to cope with uncertainties associated with innovation.

Strategies for innovation

Later we shall look at the stages in new product development, from idea generation to commercialization and launch. The first prerequisite for developing and launching new products is to determine the overall strategic approach to innovation and its use within corporate strategy. Twiss[18] distinguishes the following possible strategies for innovation:

1   offensive strategy;
2   defensive strategy;
3   licensing strategy;
4   **interstitial strategy**;
5   market creation strategy;
6   **maverick strategy**;
7   acquisition of personnel;
8   acquisition of companies.

We now examine these to see what is involved in the variety of corporate approaches to innovation strategies:

1 Offensive strategy
This strategy can be high risk, but with high potential pay-off. It requires an effective research and development department, also a positive marketing element that recognizes new market opportunities that can rapidly change new product ideas into commercial products. This type of strategy is usually undertaken by larger players and often occurs in an industry dominated by a small number of major companies. An example of an organization which practises this approach to innovation is Apple who are often at the forefront of new technologies.

2 Defensive strategy
This is the opposite of an offensive strategy: it is a low risk, low pay-off strategy. The company offering it needs an established market share, and has to be able to maintain profit levels through

low manufacturing costs even when price competition is intense. At the same time, the company must possess appropriate technological ability to react swiftly to technological advances by competitors. This approach is best suited to companies whose strengths are in marketing rather than research and development. An example is IBM, which uses its well established corporate credentials and service and quality levels rather than competing at the edge of technological development.

3 Licensing strategy

A licensing strategy is also known as 'absorbtive strategy'. This allows the company to make profits by buying technological innovations of another company, so reducing the need for an effective in-house research and development department. There is little to gain from discovering what can be obtained from another source more cheaply. Licensing out your own technology to competing companies also has its advantages. It may reduce the company's market share in the long run, but licensing fees can be obtained from the sale of an innovation which competition would eventually develop and match itself. Pilkington's have used licensing strategies very effectively and profitably with their 'float glass' production technology. The Dutch company, Philips have also pursued a strategy of licensing to good effect. Philips has a strong technology and innovation base and the company has been responsible for many of the most successful 'new-to-world' products. Examples of Philips' inventions range from the cassette tape through to the laser disc. Leading consumer goods companies throughout the world, including Sony and others, have licensed Philips' technologies, and as is the intention with licensing, to the benefit of both parties.

4 Interstitial strategy

This strategy aims to avoid direct competitive confrontations. Instead, the company analyses existing market leaders to discover their strengths and weaknesses and related gaps in the market. This technological strategy fits in with a more general 'niche marketing' corporate strategy, and it is applied usually by smaller companies in a large and expanding market. The Wharfedale speaker company, famous for producing very high quality speakers, have always sought to avoid challenging their often much larger competitors, instead concentrating their new products on those segments who seek professional quality sound reproduction.

5 Market creation strategy

The company may be in the position to create a completely new market because of technological advances facilitating the development of entirely new products. This strategy has the advantage of there being little initial competition and it can be very profitable. Sony established a whole new market when they developed their then revolutionary 'Walkman' product.

6 Maverick strategy

This strategy is one that is applied to a product, which owing to technological advances, reduces the total market size for the old product. It allows a company to apply new technology to someone else's market, so benefiting their own company, but harming others in the market with a subsequent reduction in total market size. This type of strategy will succeed in the long run only if the company follows its maverick strategy with an offensive strategy to retain its technological lead over the competition. An example of a company pursuing a maverick strategy for a product range is

Procter & Gamble's range of 'Fairy' brand products. Most of the products in the 'Fairy' cleaning product range are claimed to be much more effective in their cleaning properties than those of competitors. This means much less of the product is needed for each cleaning operation, and although initially more expensive, is claimed to be much better value.

7 Acquisition of personnel

Rather than licensing to gain a competitor's innovations, a company could try to 'poach' the opposition's personnel. This strategy is not wholly ethical, although it is a low cost method of acquiring technology and can prove to be fruitful. A further problem is the fact that such personnel will tend to rate low on loyalty and will probably be equally likely to leave your company if they are given a better offer elsewhere.

8 Acquisition of companies

An alternative to acquiring personnel is to acquire a whole company through takeover or a merger. Some small companies are highly creative, entrepreneurial and strategically offensive. They do, however, have limitations regarding research and development funds, and may not be effective in production and marketing. This makes them attractive and easy targets for large companies who are less likely to create such innovation and adopt such offensive strategies themselves. The takeover of an already established small company can be much less of a risk to a large company than trying to develop the technology itself.

As we can see from this typology of innovation strategies, there are a number of alternatives for achieving innovation objectives. In fact we can now add another strategy which has emerged in recent years, namely, a **guerrilla marketing strategy**. This is a strategy that relies on imagination rather than a large marketing budget. Guerrilla marketing tactics target customers in unexpected places which makes the idea of what is being marketed memorable. Such tactics involve public relations stunts, giving the product away in public places and using mobile digital technologies to engage customers and create a memorable event.

Clearly, innovation strategies have a major bearing on the focus of new product development and the means of achieving product innovation. The selection of appropriate innovation and new product development strategies will depend on many factors, including company, competitor and customer considerations. However, a key input to innovation strategies and decisions is technology itself, and in particular the way that technology is developing and likely to change in the future. No discussion of innovation, particularly the formation of innovation strategies, would be complete, therefore, without some consideration of technological forecasting.

TECHNOLOGICAL FORECASTING

The allocation of corporate funding to innovation is an investment decision that commits resources now with a view to a return in the future; yet that future is likely to be different from the circumstances that pertain today, particularly with respect to the nature of future technologies. The pace of technological change and the high risk and costs of developing new products mean that technological forecasting is essential.

What to forecast?

The first issue is the question of what we need to forecast. As with any forecast – the weather, the economy or sales forecasts – the purpose is to improve decision making. A technological forecast might be used to make better decisions in the following areas:

- levels of research and development spending;
- overall innovation strategy – offensive vs. defensive;
- allocation of resources to specify innovation programmes for technological investment.

To help in such innovation-related decisions, the decision maker ideally needs to know the answers to the following:

1 'What will be the nature of future technology as it relates to my business?' A *qualitative* aspect.
2 'What will be the performance level of future technology?' A *quantitative* aspect.
3 'What time-scale are we talking about; when will it happen?' A *temporal* aspect.
4 'What is the assessment of the likelihood of events described in the above questions?' A *probability* aspect.

The information that answers these questions provides means the decision maker is in a stronger position to make informed decisions about innovation.

Techniques of technological forecasting

The techniques of technological forecasting are numerous and what follows is a brief description of the more frequently used categories, together with an indication of their merits and drawbacks, as a more detailed overview of forecasting and its implications for marketing planning is provided in Chapter 12.

Trend extrapolation is one of the simpler techniques that consists of using past technological trends to predict future levels of performance in a technology. Imagine that we are concerned to predict likely levels of future performance in computing technology, where 'performance' is measured in terms of 'speed of calculation'. The first step is to ascertain what the past trend in this performance parameter has been, plotting past trends in this performance over time. As with the time series analysis method of sales forecasting, the performance figures over a time period will fluctuate, but beneath this is a trend which the forecaster wishes to know in order to apply the forecast. If improvements in technological performance do not follow a trend then it is not possible to forecast the future using past performance, but there is considerable evidence to show that technological progress does tend to follow a regular pattern when performance is plotted over time. The essence of the extrapolation technique is illustrated hypothetically in Figure 4.9.

In using trend extrapolation for technological forecasting, careful consideration should be given to:

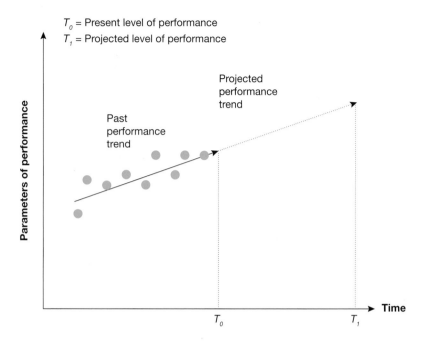

T_0 = Present level of performance
T_1 = Projected level of performance

FIGURE 4.9 Trend extrapolation forecasting

1   *Selection of the parameter of performance*
     Care should be taken to ensure that the performance characteristic selected is one which truly does represent the 'correct' measure of 'functional' performance, i.e. one that is not technology specific and is related to the needs of the marketplace.
2   *Sufficient and accurate historical data*
     As with any forecasting technique that relies on past data to predict the future, forecasting accuracy relies on both the quantity and quality of this past data.
3   *Factors which may cause discontinuities in the shorter-term trend*
     While there may be substantial continuity in the long-term progress of technological performance, in the shorter term there can be substantial discontinuity. The race to put a man on the moon by the end of the 1960s hastened the development of many technologies, as increased resources were devoted to this single aim.

Overall, the merit of technological forecasting is that it is relatively straightforward to understand and apply. The major disadvantage is that it provides only the quantitative and temporal aspects of information on new technology that the decision maker requires.

   Delphi forecasting: here the forecaster recruits experts in the technology, and using a questionnaire, solicits their opinions as to likely future technological developments. The questions may relate to matters of a technological breakthrough (such as new developments in pollution-free engines or the treatment of cancer). Respondents may also be asked to predict likely time-scales, levels of performance, and estimates of probability.

A Delphi forecast is normally 'played' in a number of rounds. Once the original (first round) questionnaires have been circulated and completed, the results are summarized and then re-circulated to respondents who are then asked to reconsider their forecasts in the light of summarized results. The questions themselves may become more pointed as a result of feedback. The rounds of questioning continue until a consensus emerges or sufficient useful information is available to make effective innovation decisions. Respondents do not meet face to face (as in a committee). Therefore, any 'bandwagon' effect of majority opinion is eliminated.

The advantages of Delphi relate to the fact that it can provide information about all areas in which the decision maker is interested. The major disadvantages are associated with difficulties in designing an unambiguous set of questions, and the selection of the panel of experts.

Scenario writing first became known through the work of 'think tanks' such as the Hudson Institute in the United States. Now many companies have such 'think tanks' where a team of experts is responsible for forecasting possible future technological developments based on a wide-ranging technological and environmental analysis. A number of potential scenarios are generated, each one being considered further with respect to probabilities and implications. Scenarios considered highly probable, and with a significant projected impact on the organization (e.g. a future technological or market threat) may form the basis of a research and development programme.

Relevance trees are used systematically to explore all possible routes to achieving given stated technological objectives. The process starts by defining the desired objectives and then tracing backwards to determine possible viable routes for achieving the objective, and the implications for research and development. A simple example is shown in Figure 4.10 where the stated objective is

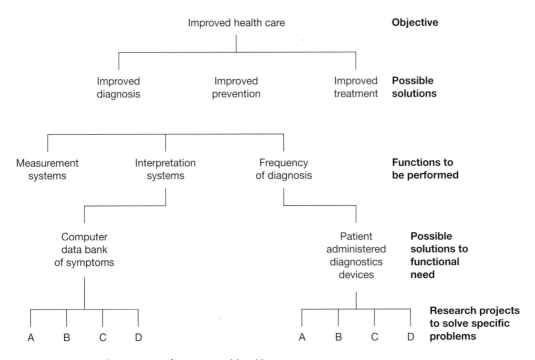

FIGURE 4.10 A relevance tree for improved health care

'improved health care' by a computer company that is involved in this market. A complete relevance tree will be much more complex than this simplified version.

The relevance tree approach can be used:

- to explore the feasibility of various technological decisions;
- to establish the optimum research and development programme according to feasibility, cost and timing considerations;
- to determine and select between detailed research projects.

These are a few of the techniques of technological forecasting. Our discussion has been brief in what is a specialist area in terms of strategies for innovation. Technological forecasting remains somewhat under-utilized in innovation planning, especially in Europe. The techniques have their limitations, but in the future more and more companies are likely to have to use them if they are to cope with an uncertain technological future.

DEVELOPING AND LAUNCHING NEW PRODUCTS

So far we have set the background to new product development decisions. Not all innovation strategies involve in-house development of new products, but where this route is selected evidence on successful new product development suggests that a systematic approach is essential. The following sequence of steps in new product development was originally suggested by the American consultants, Booz, Allen & Hamilton following research they conducted initially in 1968 and followed up in 1981. It is still in widespread use in marketing textbooks today. This enables us to outline some of the key marketing issues involved at each stage of developing a new product:

- idea generation
- idea screening
- concept development and testing
- strategy development
- business analysis
- product development
- market testing
- commercialization
- launch

Idea generation

Good ideas are the life blood of new product development. This raises the question: 'What constitutes a "good idea"?' Evidence on the mortality rates involved in developing new products means that we need a lot of ideas before we are likely to find one that constitutes a winner. Two key aspects are involved in increasing the number of ideas for new products, namely:

1   an effective scanning process for new ideas which systematically collects ideas for possible new products from the widest range of sources possible;

2   the use of the techniques of 'creativity' to encourage idea generation.

Product screening for new ideas

Screening should encompass both internal company sources and external sources. The most obvious sources are those departments charged with this responsibility that include:

■   technical departments i.e. mainly research and development and design departments;

■   the marketing department;

■   in some organizations, the new product development department.

In some ways it is sources of ideas outside of the above departments that represent some of the richest and frequently untapped sources of new product ideas such as:

■   **Employees** There are usually many with substantial potential for being helpful as sources of new product concepts. Sales personnel are an obvious group, but so are manufacturing, customer service, packaging and persons who use the products. They need to be told that their ideas are wanted, and mechanisms must be constructed to gather these ideas. Employee suggestion systems turn up ideas, but the most useful suggestions come from employees whose work brings them in contact with the customers and their problems. Salespeople know when a large order is lost because a company's product is not quite what the customer wanted. Complaint-handling departments become familiar with consumers' use of products.

■   **Customers** are a productive source of new product concepts and improvements as these are users of the firm's products or services. Many approaches are used to gather consumer ideas, but the most popular are street and mail surveys, continuing panels and special focus groups.

■   **Resellers** Depending on the industry, brokers, manufacturers' representatives, industrial distributors, large jobbers and large retail firms may be worthwhile information sources. Many manufacturers' agents are so skilled that they serve as industrial advisers to their clients.

■   **Suppliers/vendors** Large suppliers near the beginning of the production chain often provide advice to their customers, e.g. many manufacturers of plastic housewares are small and look to the large plastic firms for advice. Virtually all producers of steel, aluminium, chemicals, metals, paper and glass have technical customer service departments who give advice to their customers.

■   **Competitors** Competitors' activities are of interest, and their products may be an indirect source of a leap-frog or add-on new product. Leaf[19] suggested a five-step approach to studying competitors' products:

1   Purchase the competitive product.

2   Tear down the product, literally: i.e. remove every nut, bolt and weld, and get back to the basic pieces.

3   Reverse engineer the product: while tearing down the product, figure out drawings, parts lists and manufacturing methodology.

4   Build up the costs: using available labour, material and overhead costs, estimate exactly what it cost the competitor to make.

5   Establish economies of scale: given known and estimated production runs combined with selling prices, estimate the competitor's profits.

■ **Miscellaneous** Among the other sources of new ideas are:

- consultants
- advertising agencies
- market research companies
- universities/colleges
- research laboratories
- governments
- printed sources.

Appropriate records for all ideas put forward, but not used, should be kept for future reference. Although we have been concerned to discuss ways of generating more ideas for new products, it is important to note that quality as well as the quantity of ideas matters. The ideas need to be relevant to overall corporate objectives and strategies.

Product innovation charter

Crawford[20] has suggested the notion of a 'product innovation charter' to ensure that idea generation is conducted within this framework. The charter specifies, as a prelude to idea generation, the goals of new product development, the product/market areas to which new product development should be aimed, and the corporate objectives towards which the new product development programme should contribute.

Risks in new product development

Product screening is a preliminary assessment of ideas with a view to determining which should be dropped and which retained for potential development. Screening is a means of increasing the quality of managerial decisions, since selection based on judgement is more likely to result in two sorts of error:

1   A *drop-error* is failing to develop an idea with potential. Losses due to such errors are difficult to quantify.

2   A *go-error* occurs when the company lets a poor idea proceed to further development and commercialization.

New product screening methods are used to reduce the risk, but are nevertheless imperfect since there is always an element of judgement. The use of pre-specified screening criteria and product idea rating systems, i.e. a formal screening approach, can help. We now discuss the most frequently used screening techniques.

The simplest form of screening technique is the use of a checklist of all criteria to be taken into account in evaluating the product, i.e.:

- corporate objectives, strategies and values;
- marketing criteria;
- financial criteria;
- production criteria.

Each of these broad areas is broken down into a number of marketing sub-criteria for evaluation:

- extent of clearly defined market need;
- estimated size of market;
- estimated product life;
- competitive position;
- estimated launch costs.

A development of the checklist approach is the use of either **profiling**, or **merit number systems**. Here the criteria to be used for assessment are given a numerical weighting according to their judged relative importance. Each new product idea is then scored against each of the pre-established criteria, say on a 1 to 10 basis, with 1 being a poor score and 10 the highest (i.e. a strong product idea). Scores and weightings are then multiplied to give an overall score for the product idea. A profiling system uses exactly the same approach but the weighted total scores against each criterion are presented in the form of a visual profile for each new product idea.

High Profile

Screening new product ideas is inevitably subjective. Consider the breakfast cereals company which has come up with five different ideas for a new breakfast cereal, but can only afford to develop one. At a senior management meeting called to discuss the relative merits of each product the following managers are asked to select their favourite product from the five proposed and give their reasons.

1   The marketing manager chooses product **one** because he feels it would generate most sales.
2   The accountant chooses product **two** because it has the highest forecast profit margin.
3   The production manager chooses product **three** because it is easiest to produce using existing machinery.
4   The human resource manager chooses product **four** because in his view it is 'greener' than the rest in terms of the ingredients it contains.
5   The managing director liked product **five** best because it tasted nicest.

With so many different views and reasons, how would one decide which product to choose? By listing each criterion used by each manager (sales potential, profit margin, ease of production, greenness and taste), we can then ask each manager to score each new product, against each criterion. The score for each can then be represented in a simple bar chart for each product. The product with the highest visual profile wins the day.

The benefit of such formal systems is that they force assumptions (and prejudices and vested interests) about new products into the open. They also induce systematic and sometimes more objective, appraisals of new product ideas, where over-enthusiasm and excitement can blind management to potential dangers.

Although we have discussed screening as the second stage in new product development, screening effectively takes place throughout the development of a new product, right up to (and after) launch. The idea of preliminary screening is to spot 'no win' products early, before development resources are wasted. Effective screening requires the consideration of a wide number of criteria. It is important to have a wide range of viewpoints and skills from different functions in the organization. Analysis of past failures points to over-enthusiasm of either research and development or marketing as a prime cause of 'go-errors'.

Concept testing

Crawford suggests a number of functions of **concept testing**. It tries to identify sure losers that can be eliminated from further consideration. Presuming the concept is acceptable, the company must then obtain an estimate of the sales that the product would enjoy. This has brought some contention amongst researchers to the subject.

He states that the most common format for gathering respondents' reactions on their likelihood of purchase form is a five-point scale:

1   definitely would buy;
2   probably would buy;
3   may or may not buy;
4   probably would not buy;
5   definitely would not buy.

It is customary to combine the number of people who answered that they probably or definitely would buy and to use that number as an indication of group reaction. This is called the 'top-two-boxes' figure.

It is not particularly important whether precisely that many people would or would not buy the product. In the first place, the product that will eventually be offered will almost certainly be different from the description offered in the interview, as much development and further testing needs to be done. However, if the company doing the research has an inventory of percentages from past studies, the figure from the current study may provide a good indicator.

Research methods in concept testing

However the specific data is presented, methods used for analysis are conventional:

Personal interviewing can be done by a one-to-one interview survey or by focus group where a creative researcher approaches a group of people in a controlled situation with a concept statement that is discussed or refined. The focus group technique is a powerful tool in the new product development process and in the hands of a skilled researcher can be used to achieve in-depth understanding of consumer behaviour, attitudes, perceptions and reactions to new product concepts

Arising from the importance of concept testing, many researchers use a sequenced system of interviewing. Here they start with several focus groups, themselves in a sequence from exploratory to confirmatory. Then for consumer products the testing is carried over into individual interviews in shopping arcades or homes; for industrial interviewing, people involved in the buying decision are interviewed on site. This research method is constructed differently to fit each situation.

Telephone interviews Using modern computer-based interviewing technology, this method is quicker and cheaper and is tending to replace traditional in-home personal interviews. It is also useful for obtaining more superficial background information. However, telephone focus groups are not very effective.

Mail Portfolios of concepts can be mailed to potential users, although sample selection and response can pose a problem because of its low response rate. This is more successful when a mail test of a new product concept is combined with a telephone follow-up.

The Internet is being increasingly used in researching new product concepts. The obvious advantage here is speed of response, but in addition its interactive nature allows new product concepts to be explored with a wider range of potential customers (Schribowsky et al.[21]).

Information gathered concept testing

Exactly what information should be gathered in a concept development study is a function of the situation, but several general issues are suggested by researchers:

- current practice in the category – for a new concept in an established product field, one would want to know how customers responded to the old product;
- attitudes towards current options – one would want to know not only what respondents like about what they are getting now, but also their opinions on the options they reject;
- any specific experience prior to this time that seems relevant to the concept about to be discussed;
- do respondents understand the concept?
- reactions to the concept – such information can run deep, including product positioning, hidden thoughts, probable uses visualized, reactions of others to the idea, further information wanted about it and possibilities of breakdown when using the product;
- changes the respondent would make in the concept, even if only in vague verbal form;
- comparative data to be used relating this idea to others previously studied. Purchase intentions come in here, but so do other scorings like how the concept compares with those currently on the market.

Advantages and limitations of concept testing

The advantages of concept testing are:

1 It can be undertaken quickly and easily, well before prototypes are available.
2 It provides invaluable information for later decisions about the product, e.g. applications, user types and preferred attributes.

3   Proven market research technology exists.
4   It is confidential since small samples are taken and most concept particulars can be restricted.
5   Bad ideas can be easily detached particularly if there is one clear reason for this being so.
6   Such research permits gaining an understanding of buyer thinking, misunderstanding and prejudices.
7   Segments and positioning can be developed in tandem with the concept.

Weaknesses are:

1   There are many opportunities for misunderstanding new items – newness, vague concepts and multiple attributes. Ziegler[22] suggests that one of the problems might be that traditional concept-testing techniques may not be effective for researching many of the new technology-based products now coming onto the market.
2   People find it difficult to react to entirely new concepts without a learning period.
3   Testing occurs long before marketing, so many variables in the situation may change by the time the product is marketed. People are asked to be judges and endorsers which is hypothetical.
4   Considerable interview skill is required, especially in focus groups, although it looks deceptively simple. Thus there can be a degree of misinterpretation.
5   Certain attributes cannot be measured in a concept test, e.g. rug texture or softness produced by using a fabric conditioner.
6   It is difficult to establish the validity or reliability of a concept test.

Concept testing for new products can be particularly difficult when the new product is unlike anything else on the market. In this situation it is difficult for consumers to have any frame of reference against which to judge the concept. The Red Bull drink product was completely different to any of its predecessors on the market. Products like this require careful attention to the context and application of concept testing techniques.

Marketing strategy development

If the results of the concept testing stage are encouraging, the next step in the new product development process is the formulation of preliminary marketing strategy plans for the product launch which include:

- preliminary marketing objectives;
- delineation of possible market targets;
- product positioning strategies;
- preliminary marketing mix decisions;
- preliminary budget estimates.

By now, the new product will have progressed to the stage where it is possible to more precisely assess its likely sales and profit potential. At this stage, few resources may have been committed to the project. However, the stage is rapidly being approached where further progress may involve substantial investment – including, for example, investment in pilot plant and the development of prototypes.

Before a decision can be made about the product development stage, a detailed analysis of the business potential of the new product is required. If these results are satisfactory, the stages of product development and market testing, preceding market launch, can take place.

Business analysis

As far as possible, a company must be sure that the launch of a new product will contribute to the profitability of the firm. For this reason the company should conduct an analysis of the likely financial outcome as a central issue in the 'go'/'no go' decision.

The approach to business analysis is to compare alternative new projects, with each other or some in-company standard, using criteria that give indications of future profitability. Like screening, business analysis is a process and not an event. Business analysis involves estimation of likely sales and profit levels. This stage precedes development of the product itself, so in later stages, particularly in test marketing, initial estimates of the business potential of the new product are likely to become firmer as information on which to base the estimates becomes clearer. Product development will also enable more accurate cost estimates to be made, including direct and investment costs. Business analysis and test marketing can thus be thought of as a continuation of the screening process carried out earlier in the development of the product.

Business analysis requires that estimates be made for the product in three areas:

1 **Sales estimates** should include, in volume and value terms, estimates of likely total market potential, estimates of company demand and time-scales, i.e. the pattern of sales which will vary according to whether the product is a singular long-term purchase, bought infrequently, or frequently purchased like food. Forecasting sales for new products is notoriously difficult. For example, sales of the first Sony 'Play station' were said to be nearly four times those forecast by the company.

2 **Cost estimates** are easier to make than sales estimates. However, such estimates can sometimes be highly inaccurate. The Concorde aircraft was estimated at £250 million and eventually cost £2,000 million. All costs need to be estimated, including direct costs, total investment costs and overhead costs. It is important to estimate the timing of costs to plan cash flow. It is wise to build a substantial contingency element into the estimation of both fixed and variable costs to reduce the impact of under-costing a new product development.

3 **Margins, profits, return on investment and cash flow** Once sales and cost estimates have been made we can estimate the financial aspects of performance. Not only should absolute profits be estimated, but so should the return on investment. Conventional investment analysis techniques such as discounted cash flow and calculation of payback periods are appropriate here. Companies like IBM require their new products to earn a minimum return on investment. Using return on investment measures not only enables different new product proposals to be evaluated, but also allows comparison of investment in new products with other alternative uses of company funds.

Payback period is defined as the time required to repay the initial investment, which is calculated by summing predicted successive yearly net profits until the original outlay is exceeded. Provided accurate information is used, this technique is quick and simple. However, it does not take into account the likely life of the product and cannot be an adequate measure of profitability.

Return on capital is defined as the percentage annual net profit to the net assets employed in the product. The analysis is applied to each year of the forecasted life cycle and provides a means of direct comparison with alternative investment options. Account is then taken of the changing value of money over time.

Discounted cash flow is a technique that takes into account the time value of money by effectively weighting the value of cash flows by an amount that depends on when they occur in relation to the initial investment, i.e. money received during the early part of the life cycle is considered more valuable than that received years later. This technique has gained universal acceptance as a means of investment appraisal as conventional capital investment appraisal techniques give insufficient evidence to allow the decision maker to take the development decision to the next logical stage.

There is significant difference between venture capital required to set up the development and working capital requirement needed to maintain necessary levels of marketing activity after the launch stage, so projections for working capital needs are vital. It is also essential to consider financial pressure that new product introductions can have upon the liquidity position of the company. There is a lagged effect during market development that can place a company in severe liquidity crisis, attributable to the rate of growth.

Survival through innovation, growth and competitive advantage is an interactive triangle, bounded by time. Financial implications of innovation and new product development necessitate an understanding of start-up capital and working capital needed to stay in business. It is vital that a cash budget is developed to forecast incomes and expenditures pertaining to the new project that impact on the company's entire product portfolio.

Pre-tax profits, i.e. the bottom line, and return on capital invested are goals for achievement. The means of their attainment is through an effective budgetary control system with concurrent variance analysis based on the forecasted cash needs of the project to survive and achieve growth. Cash flow forecasting is therefore essential.

Margins can be eroded through an inability accurately to determine costs and cost behaviour in relation to output. A comprehensive understanding of fixed and variable costs in relation to projected levels of performance is vital to establish a financial control climate within which the new product development process can be nurtured. Absolute profits can be disappointing in the short term. Therefore, objectives have to be set clearly in relation to the time horizons of the development plan to monitor progress towards targeted profits. Attention to these aspects of financial control is advised to provide a balance between marketing enthusiasm and the requirements to achieve and maintain a stable financial position for the new enterprise.

Product development

If business analysis points to a favourable decision, the next major step is product development which is where costs tend to rise substantially. Once a physical product e.g. a prototype, has been developed, further testing, both technical and consumer, should be carried out. Even at this stage an objective and critical view needs to be taken about further investment in the product.

Test marketing

This is the penultimate stage before full scale commercialization and launch. Here, the new product is tested in a way that involves consumers purchasing in a normal shopping situation, or in the case of a more durable product, being tested in an environment in which it is finally used (usually in the home). This process is conducted towards the end of the development process when the concept, product and marketing strategy are at a refined stage. The objective of the test marketing exercise is reduction of risk in any subsequent decisions that are made. The need for this research is to reduce the risk of a costly mistake in a national launch.

In an unusual context for new products, an embarrassing launch in recent years was that of British Airways' new tail fin designs. British Airways felt it was time to move away from the traditional red, white and blue British flag logotype design on their aeroplane tail fins, replacing them with a series of ethnic and abstract designs designed to appeal to a more cosmopolitan and global flying public. The result was subsequently felt to be a public relations disaster and it was universally disliked, especially by the then Prime Minister, Margaret Thatcher, who very publicly placed her handkerchief over the new tailfin design while being videoed for a news programme with a model of a British Airways plane carrying the new logo. The concept had been researched, although it would have been difficult to conduct true test marketing in this situation, but a small-scale roll-out of the new designs would probably have quickly established that consumer reaction to them was unfavourable.

The argument in favour of test marketing is that it measures consumer behaviour in a real situation. The results give an indication of overall consumer response to the marketing mix, whereas product testing measures only individual aspects. Test marketing also removes a major problem in product research, which is that the consumers know that they are being studied, and this alters responses accordingly.

By definition, the exercise takes place in an area substantially smaller than that covered by the entire market. Choice of area is dependent on the nature of the product. Since the objective is to create a scaled-down version of the national launch, test markets for products developed by major companies in the consumer field generally take place in areas defined by the target market coverage. Test marketing is a theme to which we return in Chapter 12.

Increasingly, companies are looking to cut costs and time-scales of market testing by using laboratory test or simulated market tests. In industrial product markets, product user tests and dealer tests are commonplace.

Commercialization

The final stage of new product development is 'commercialization', or bringing the product to the market. If the company goes ahead with commercialization, it is likely to begin to incur its highest costs, involving as it does investment in plant and production and marketing costs. As a consequence care and planning is required if the product is to succeed: many otherwise excellent products have failed because of an inadequately managed launch phase.

Amongst key questions to be addressed at the launch stage are:

- *When to launch?*
  Timing of new product launches is critical: too early and the market or product may not be ready; too late and the opportunity may have passed or a competitor has arrived in the market.
- *Where to launch?* (coverage)
  A major decision at the launch stage is the geographical coverage of the launch e.g. should it be on a local/regional basis first or national or even international? This decision involves selection and timing of areas for the launch. In some cases it pays to go first for the more profitable segments of the market only. In others, circumstances will dictate an all-over launch attack to cover the whole market simultaneously. Critical to this decision are company resources and the existence or absence of competitors i.e. how quickly might they move in?
- *How to launch?* (launch plans)
  By this stage a detailed plan of attack for the launch should be drawn up, including sales forecasts, budgets, allocation of resources and detailed timings. Most important at this stage is an understanding of target markets and the processes of **diffusion** and **adoption**.

These key issues must be resolved at the launch stage right as they provide the platform on which the product's future performance will be built. As Green *et al.*[23] have shown, changes to the product's competitive position after entry may be very difficult and expensive to achieve. Because of this, they have developed an 'Entry Strategy Performance Model' as shown in Figure 4.11 which attempts to capture what they feel are some of the key determinants of performance for a new product and which must be considered at the entry and commercialization stage.

Diffusion and adoption of innovations

The adoption process relates to the stages that every prospect for a new product has to pass through in terms of their buying perceptions i.e.:

- awareness;
- interest;
- evaluation;
- trial;
- purchase.

These are important processes, particularly in marketing communications. If a prospect has already passed through the awareness stage of adoption, then advertising copy must seek to encourage interest in the product or brand.

Individuals differ in their attitudes towards new product acceptance. Of particular relevance to the new product market are the '**innovator**' and '**early adopter**' categories that are shown in Figure 4.12. By definition these are the first to adopt new products and services and so represent prime market targets (Munnukka[24]). Little evidence has emerged to support the notion of a generalized attitude to innovativeness as it tends to be product specific, although if a company can identify likely innovators within a product market, initial marketing programmes should be targeted at this group.

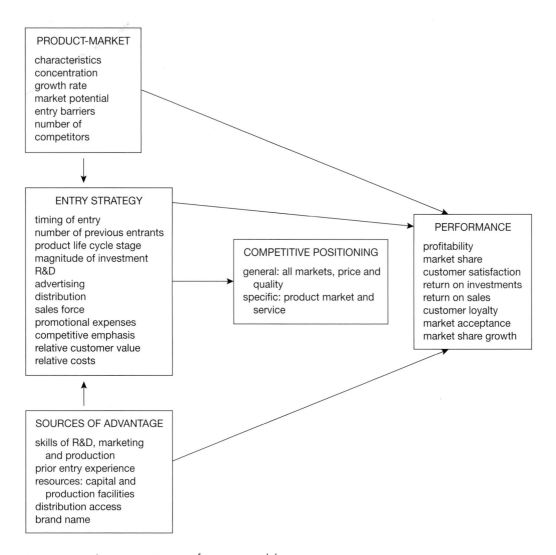

FIGURE 4.11 An entry strategy performance model

Source: Green, D., Barclay, D.W. and Ryans, B. (1995), 'Entry strategy and long-term performance conceptualization and empirical examination', *Journal of Marketing*, October, 59(4): 6.

Consumers can be grouped into five 'adopter categories', each of which has distinct characteristics, so specific strategies need to be formulated that suit individual needs of each group at a given time. The marketing of a product should be seen in as many dimensions as possible e.g. the 'early majority' will require a specific approach to advertising, pricing and distribution. Competitors will be employing the marketing mix in a similar way and will, in turn, create market conditions that require decisions and action of a strategic nature, which in this case should be relevant to the 'growth' stage of the product life cycle (see also Figure 4.2).

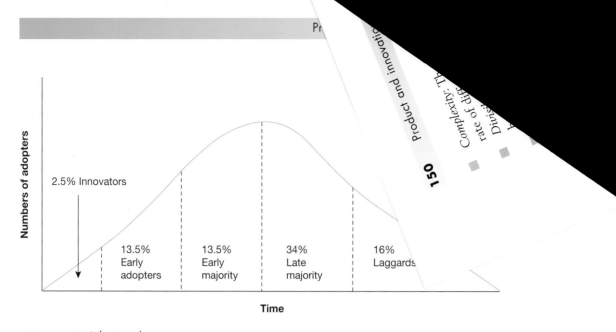

FIGURE 4.12 Adoption theory

Source: Rogers, E.M. (1962), *Diffusion of Innovations*, New York: Free Press, p. 162.

The following typifies customer characteristics in each group:

- Innovators are more adventurous risk takers and purchase early because it is exciting.
- Early adopters are the opinion leaders who purchase after careful analysis, but are willing to take a reasonable risk. Later adopters tend to look to them for a lead.
- Early majority are more averse to risk and represent those who deliberate more and try it after others have tried it. They tend to be better educated and better off than later categories.
- Late majority consumers need contagion and reassurance about the benefits of the product, and will not try it until it is well established and respected customers have adopted it. At this stage the product will have reached the maturity stage of the product life cycle.
- Laggards are traditional and do not see any urgent reason to change. They tend to be older and of lower socio-economic status and not so well off as earlier categories.

Diffusion processes relate to the speed and extent of take-up of a new product. In most circumstances the new product marketer is interested in securing the widest adoption at the highest rate. Clearly, diffusion is related to the adoption process of individual customers, but five particular product characteristics tend to favour a more rapid and extensive adoption and diffusion process:

- *Relative advantage*: The greater the perceived advantage of the new product to customers, the faster it will diffuse.
- *Compatibility*: The greater the extent to which the new product is compatible with existing customer lifestyles, values and uses, the faster it will diffuse.

       e more complex the new product is to understand or use, the slower will be its
       usion.

       ability: The better the ability of the new product to be tried or used on a limited scale
       before full commitment, the faster it will tend to diffuse.

- *Communicability*: The easier it is for the advantages or features of the new product to be demonstrated or communicated by early purchasers to other potential purchasers, the faster will be the rate of diffusion.

New product development and innovation

In an area of marketing that is characterized by change, in recent years a number of key developments have taken place regarding the management of new product development and innovation. In part, these developments reflect improvements in our knowledge regarding key factors in managing this process more successfully. In part, they reflect changes in the competitive and market environment. Some of the more important of these developments are now discussed.

Design and new product development

Design of a product is a major source of product differentiation in a competitive marketplace. The importance of design in new product success has long been recognized by some, but not since the 1930s has design been so strategically used to gain advantage in the marketplace. Block[25] suggests that distinctive design can render older competitors obsolete. He suggests that more durable product designs can have an impact on both users and non-users for many years. To be durable, a product design does not have to be complicated; a good product design is one that satisfies the needs of the customer and makes a product eye-catching in the marketplace. A company recognized for its design skills, which are a major facet of its marketing success, is the Apple Corporation.

As well as helping to differentiate a company's products from those of competitors, the design process determines product attributes such as functional capabilities and product lifespan. Price[26] shows how the life cycle cost of a product is significantly influenced by how it is designed and this affects ease of manufacture and serviceability. Simplifying design results in benefits like reduced costs and marketing benefits of improved quality and potentially shorter product development lead times. Lee and Sasser[27] have suggested that the total cost of producing and delivering a product is determined by the design. At the time of design completion only 5 per cent of the budget for new product development may have been spent, but 80 per cent of the remaining budget has been committed.

How products are designed has changed significantly in recent years. Customer-focused designs have replaced the expensive, slow, product-oriented, engineer-dominated design processes of the past. Neff[28] proposed that **quality function deployment** (QFD) be introduced to ensure customers' ideas are incorporated into the product design process from the outset. Marketing has the responsibility of relating customer requirements to technical departments including design, so in a well run organization marketing research should be used to evaluate the marketability of new designs at an early stage. Customer requirements should be translated into technical requirements at each stage of product development, but it is at the early design stages that they are most important.

Competitive benchmarking is also an approach that can be used to ensure that proposed new product designs improve on those of competitors in aspects which have greatest importance and value to customers. The effect of QFD requires far-reaching changes in how a company operates with respect to design and new product development. In essence it requires different functional groups to interact simultaneously, to identify and solve problems through greater teamwork and communication, particularly between marketing and design functions. An example of how QFD can be used in new product design and development is outlined by Lockomy and Khurana.[29] In particular, they stress the significance of the role of QFD in integrating functions horizontally through the process of design and new product development as illustrated in Figure 4.13.

In the diagram we can see that quality function deployment starts at the beginning of the process of new product development, and as explained, centres on identifying customer needs. QFD then helps translate these needs through each stage of the design and development process including manufacturing and production. The idea is to ensure that customer needs and wants remain paramount in each and every successive stage of the process right up to and including production. It is suggested that one of the key advantages of implementing a system of QFD is that 'a pioneer'

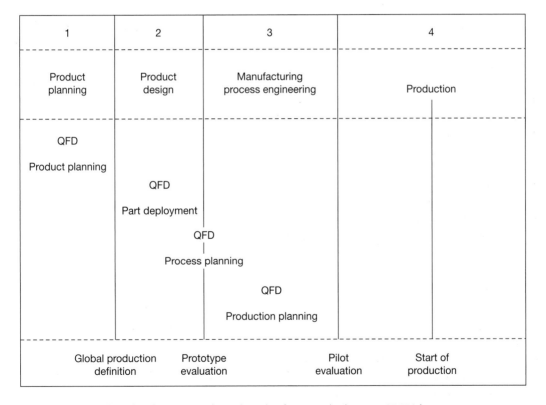

FIGURE 4.13 Product development cycle and quality function deployment (QFD) key events

Source: Lockomy, A. and Khurana, A. (1995), 'Quality function deployment in new product design', *International Journal of Quality and Reliability Management*, 12(6): 75.

in a market can charge premium prices in the early years of a product's life cycle, and then use process improvement initiatives to generate savings in later years.

Overall, effective management of the design process is essential if products are to compete successfully in the marketplace. Most companies realize this and have elevated their design function to a more important role in the process of innovation than was afforded in previous years.

Speed and flexibility in the new product development process

With competitive environments changing rapidly to meet changes in markets, technologies, and user needs, product life cycles have become shorter. There is an increased premium on speed and flexibility in managing new product development. Because of this, companies have sought to find ways of improving their performance with respect to these attributes and the most important development in this respect has been to move from the traditional sequential approach to product design and development to one which is characterized by shorter, overlapping phases between the different stages of new product development and with interaction and feedback from cross-functional and multi-functional areas. Takeuchi and Noanaka[30] suggested a holistic approach to new product development where several phases of development overlap as shown in Figure 4.14.

The process in Figure 4.14 (a) represents the traditional sequential process of new product development with each functional area completing its part in the process independently before passing the project on to the next department in the sequence. For example, the first department might be R&D with ideas for a new product. These ideas are then passed onto, say, the design

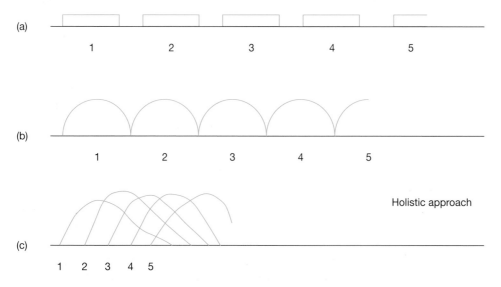

FIGURE 4.14 Sequential (A) versus overlapping (B and C) phases of new product development

Source: Adapted from Takeuchi, H. and Nonaka, I. (1986), 'The New Product Development Game,' *Harvard Business Review*, 64(1): 139.

department who translate them into a preliminary design. The design is then passed to production to manufacture and finally the marketing department comes up with plans for marketing the new product. This is a slow process as work on one stage cannot take place until the previous stage has been completed and 'signed off'. In the process shown in (b) we are beginning to see some overlap between the stages. Each stage is still managed independently and in sequence, but there is beginning to be communication between one department and the next in the process. In (c) the stages overlap. There is teamwork and communication. Responsibilities for each stage are still divided, but work on production and marketing plans might begin earlier; indeed, while R&D and design work is still ongoing. Clearly, this reduces the amount of time needed for developing new products.

With the sequential approach to product development, the new product goes through each phase in a step-by-step manner, moving from phase to phase only after all requirements of each phase have been completed. The 'Type B approach' shown in Figure 4.14 has moved from the traditional sequential approach to a process where development overlaps at the borders of each phase. The final truly holistic approach shown in Type C is where the different phases of product development run together. This inevitably means an end to functions being specialized, where marketing examines customer needs, engineers produce designs and production builds the product. This Type C process is akin to running a relay race with each function passing the baton from one to another, rather the new product development process being organized around multi-functional teams who take charge of the product development process, developing products, manufacturing processes and marketing plans simultaneously to collapse time. The increased speed of product development to which this gives rise can represent a major source of competitive advantage. For example, Ray[31] cites the case of Canon. In the early 1980s Canon's top management set an objective of reducing product development cost and time by 50 per cent. Ultimately, Canon reduced its development costs by 30 per cent and achieved its objective of reducing time to market by 50 per cent. This enabled Canon to increase its market share by 10 per cent over a ten-year period. Similarly, when Yamaha threatened Honda's leadership in the motor cycle market, Honda unleashed 30 new motor cycle models within a six-month period, effectively thwarting the Yamaha threat.

Similarly, Brassington and Pettit[32] cite the example of Renault. By bringing all new product development activities for a new model into a 'technocentre', Renault reduced the time and the costs of new product development. They suggest that costs for Renault have been cut by up to 25 per cent and development times for new products reduced from nearly eight years to just three.

Inter-company collaboration in new product development

As products become more complex, design and manufacturing requires more resources, so some companies are turning towards collaboration when developing new products. Each collaborating company concentrates on activities that reflect their competencies so the product development process is shared between the different members of the supply chain. Collaboration is increasingly being promoted as an effective strategy in dealing with some of the more complex aspects of product development. Littler and Leverick[33] suggest that collaboration offers a means to secure access to technologies, skills and information, to share costs and risks of product development and again reduce the time taken to develop products. Styles[34] contends that pooling resources and capabilities can generate synergistic growth between organizations in terms of developing a current product or service, or through the creation of an entirely new venture. Collaboration between different companies for new product development has been increasing in recent years in addition to licensing, joint ventures and strategic alliances. This is particularly the case for new technology and high cost/high risk products.

A successful example of a strategic alliance between companies to develop new technology and products was that described earlier in this chapter, where co-operation between Kodak, Fujifilm, Minolta, Nikon and Canon led to the development of the Advanced Photographic System (APS). This was a new type of film that was easier to use, load and change than conventional 35mm and other format films. These companies combined to share development costs up to the point where the technology was proven. They then went their separate ways in developing specific products and features on cameras incorporating the new technology. The technology would probably never have been developed unilaterally by individual companies in the industry.

THE INTERNET AND NEW PRODUCT DEVELOPMENT

Internet technology allows a more flexible approach to the process of innovation as the marketer can involve customers in the process. This means that the Internet provides a basis for the introduction of the quality function deployment process referred to earlier. The interactive nature of the Internet enables the marketer to solicit customer participation in the product development process and at the same time reduce development times.

New IT systems have enabled Toyota to make constant and rapid improvements to its design processes, meeting the racing team's requirements to redesign up to 15 per cent of the car in only two weeks between Grand Prix races to continually improve speeds and road-holding abilities. Intel-based servers have enabled faster, more accurate simulations and design calculations to optimize racing car aerodynamics, processing virtual tests significantly faster than on the old legacy RISC-based platform, and have delivered a marked reduction in car development time.

The following represent some of the ways in which increased flexibility and customer involvement are achieved in new product development using the Internet:

- A database can be used to identify key innovators in the market. The company can then communicate with the selected customers to gain information about their particular needs and the implications of these for the concept of the product.
- Product concepts and customer response to these can then be fed into the design process and outcomes in the form of design options can be evaluated directly and immediately with customers.
- Ultimately, as product development progresses, customer needs can be integrated with technical solutions using both the Intranet and the Extranet to integrate the process and to encapsulate customer response as the project evolves.

Implications for marketing in relation to the Internet and developments in IT are important and discussion here is introductory. We consider this development more fully throughout the rest of the text and more specifically in Chapters 9, 10 and 17.

SUMMARY

Product decisions lie at the core of marketing strategy development. Product management starts with the management of existing products and includes decisions about product items, product lines and the overall product mix.

In relation to innovation and new product development, the logic of the product life cycle provides the imperative for a constant search for new products. In short, companies must innovate or face decline. However, new product development is inherently risky. We need to be aware of the critical factors in successful innovation and follow systematic steps in the new product development process.

The importance of new product development in today's competitive environment has caused companies to look at ways in which product development and innovation process can be improved. Because of this, in recent years we have seen several significant developments in this area of strategic marketing. In particular, companies have recognized the importance of the design function in new product development and in particular the importance of relating design to all the elements of new product development from manufacturing through to final marketing of the product. Similarly, there has been considerable focus on how to reduce product development times, in particular through more effective teamwork and better sequencing through the new product development process. The increased cost and problems of new product development have led many companies to enter into collaborative ventures with other members of the supply chain to develop new and improved products. The Internet is important in new product development as it helps speed up and qualitatively improve the process by facilitating consumer interaction and responses throughout the new product development process.

KEY TERMS

Novelty Creations

Howard Boothroyd is disappointed. His company, Novelty Creations, has just withdrawn from its latest venture after three unsuccessful months of trying to market a new product.

The company markets a range of novelty 'lifestyle' products using a direct mail brochure and the Internet. Products marketed include a rainwear range for dogs and cats, an automatic odour protection device for bathrooms and 'make-your-own' birthday card kits. In its outdoor collection it markets a range of garden lights in the shape of garden gnomes and self-erecting clothes dryers. It has over one hundred individual personal items including nose-hair clippers, blood pressure monitors and earwax removal systems.

The company is always looking for new product ideas as the essence of keeping sales moving is novelty and interest. The product just withdrawn after three months in the brochure, and slightly longer on the website, was an extended toenail clipper whereby a person could clip their toenails without having to bend down. Not all new products succeed, but Boothroyd's problem is that this is the tenth recent new product failure and he is worried that the company is losing direction.

New product ideas come from an in-house team consisting of Boothroyd and two other directors. All are from technical backgrounds. Customers are not consulted at the stage of idea generation as it is felt that they would be unable to grasp many early stage concepts. Idea generation sessions take place on the last Friday of every month and usually result in about ten new ideas being put forward and discussed. As the major shareholder of the company, Boothroyd takes it upon himself to select which, if any, of these ideas should be taken further with a view to including them in the product portfolio. He uses his own judgement in this screening process as he feels that the growth of the company is down to his 'feel' for the market.

Once a product idea is selected, Boothroyd and his team find someone who can make the product and it is then incorporated in the brochure and on the website. He believes that the best test of a product is whether it sells or not and for this reason no marketing research is conducted before its inclusion in the product portfolio. Once the product is launched, a small sample of customers are contacted randomly and asked to complete a questionnaire regarding their views on this product and other company products.

Boothroyd is seriously concerned about recent product failures and is wondering if a different and perhaps more systematic approach to developing new products might be appropriate. He is looking for advice about what the company might be doing wrong and how it might improve its new product development procedures.

CASE STUDY QUESTION

Evaluate the company's approach to new product development and suggest how the company might improve its success rate for future new products.

REFERENCES

1 Lancaster, G. and Massingham, L.C. (2002), *Essentials of Marketing*, 4th edn, Maidenhead: McGraw-Hill, p. 186.

2 Dhalla, N.K. and Yuspeh, S. (1976), 'Forget the product life cycle concept', *Harvard Business Review*, Jan./Feb.: 102–12.

3 Cox, W.E. (1967), 'Product life cycles as marketing models', *Journal of Business*, October, 40(4): 375–84.

4 Polli, R. and Cook, V. (1969), 'Validity of the product life cycle', *Journal of Business*, October, 42: 385–400.

5 Day, G.S. (1981), 'The product life cycle: analysis and application issues', *Journal of Marketing*, Fall: 60–7.

6 Baker, M.J. and Hart, S. (2007), *Product Strategy and Management*, 2nd edn, Harlow: Prentice-Hall.

7 Brassington, F. and Pettit, S. (2007), *Principles of Marketing*, 4th edn, Harlow: Prentice-Hall, p. 200.

8 O'Shaughnessy, I. (1995), *Competitive Marketing: A Strategic Approach*, 3rd edn, Boston: Unwin Hyman, p. 334.

9 Yang, X., Moore, P.R., Wong, C. and Pu, J. (2007), 'Product lifecycle information acquisition and management for consumer products', *Industrial Management and Data Systems*, 107(7): 936–53.

10 Jain, S.C. (1985), *Marketing Planning and Strategy*, 2nd edn, Cincinnati: South Western Publishing, p. 473.

11 Hines, P., Francis, M. and Found, P. (2006), 'Towards lean product lifecycle management: a framework for new product development', *Journal of Manufacturing Technology Management*, 17(7): 866–87.

12 Kotler, P. and Keller, K. (2009), *Marketing Management*, 13th edn, Upper Saddle River, NJ: Prentice-Hall, p. 325.

13 Morley, C. (1999), 'Set for a splash', *The Grocer*, 3 April: 28–9.

14 Freeman, C., Rothwell, R., Horsley, A., Jervis, V.T.P., Robertson, A.B. and Townsend, J. (1972), *Success and Failure in Industrial Innovation*, Brighton: Centre for the Study of Industrial Innovation, University of Sussex.

15 McKinsey & Co. (1980), 'Putting excellence into practice', *Business Week*, July: 20–32.

16 Twiss, B. (1996), *Managing Technological Innovation*, 4th edn, London: Pitman.

17 Crawford, C.M. (1997), *New Products Management*, 5th edn, New York: Irwin, pp. 22–5.

18 Twiss, B., op. cit.

19 Leaf, R. (1978), 'How to pick up tips from your competitors', *Director*, February.

20 Crawford, C.M., op. cit., pp. 64–85.

21 Schribowsky, J.A., Peltier, J.W. and Nill, A. (2007), 'The state of internet market research: a review of the literature and future research', *European Journal of Marketing*, 41(7/8): 722–33.

22 Ziegler, B. (1999), 'Old market research tricks no match for new technology', *The Wall Street Journal*, November: 131.

23 Green, D., Barclay, D.W. and Ryans, A.B. (1995), 'Entry strategy and long term performance, conceptualisation and empirical examination', *Journal of Marketing*, October, 59(4): 1–16.

24 Munnukka, J. (2007), 'Characteristics of early adopters in mobile communications markets', *Marketing Intelligence and Planning*, 25(7): 719–31.

25 Block, P.H. (1995), 'Seeking the ideal form: product design and consumer response', *Journal of Marketing*, July, 59(3): 16–29.

26 Price, H.L. (2003), 'Delivering cost effective innovations: new methods to link innovation with detailed design', *Strategic Direction*, 19(3): 29–32.

27 Lee, H.L. and Sasser, M.M. (1995), 'Product universality and design for supply chain management', *Production Planning and Control*, May/June, 6(3): 270–7.

28 Neff, R. (1992), 'Number one and trying harder', *International Business Week*, 2 December: 26–9.

29 Lockomy, A. and Khurana, A. (1995), 'Quality function deployment in new product design', *International Journal of Quality and Reliability*, 12(6): 73–84.

30 Takeuchi, H. and Nonaka, I. (1986), 'The new product development game', *Harvard Business Review*, January, 64(1): 137–46.

31 Ray, M.B. (1995), 'Cost management for product development', *Journal of Cost Management*, Spring, 9(1): 52–9.

32 Brassington, F. and Pettit, S., op. cit. (7) pp. 411–12.

33 Littler, D. and Leverick, F. (1995), 'Joint ventures for product development: learning from experience', *International Journal of Strategic Management and Long Term Planning*, 23(2): 58–68.

34 Styles, J. (1995), 'Collaboration for competitive advantage: the changing world of alliances and partnerships', *International Journal of Strategic Management and Long Term Planning*, 28(5): 109–12.

Chapter 5

Pricing strategies

After reading this chapter you will:

- appreciate the strategic significance of pricing decisions in marketing strategy
- understand the approaches to pricing of the economist and accountant, together with their contributions and limitations in the context of the price setting process
- apply a framework to pricing decisions based around the key inputs to these decisions
- understand the main pricing methods and their relative advantages and disadvantages

INTRODUCTION

The price of a company's products and services represents the vehicle for that company to achieve its financial objectives. It is through price and volume that revenue is generated. Price equates to the financial sacrifice that the customer is willing to make to purchase the product or service desired.

The important criterion of pricing is problematical to marketers. This is attributed to the uncertainty associated with pricing decisions as it is a complicated area of decision making. It is with a view to examining this problem and the ways in which it can be resolved that his chapter is framed. The pressures of today's market environment place increasing burdens on management. It is important, therefore, that the decision maker has a framework for making pricing decisions. We start by examining the traditional economist's view of price to illustrate both the shortcomings and potential contributions of this approach as a prelude to discussing more strategic pricing approaches for the decision maker.

THE ECONOMIST'S VIEW OF PRICING

Traditionally the economist has looked at price and pricing decisions from the perspective of price being determined by the interplay of demand and supply. At a broader level, the economist views pricing decisions as an 'allocatory' mechanism, with prices being used as the signal to solve the basic problems of an economic society; namely, the allocation of scarce resources between competing users and individuals in that society so that resources are used in the most effective way. From the perspective of the price setter, traditional economic theory suggests that the 'optimum' price is one that equates marginal costs to marginal revenue so as to 'maximize' profits.

This summary of the economist's view of price and pricing decisions is most striking by its lack relevance to the practising marketing manager. In short, although the economist has some useful concepts to offer the marketing manager when it comes to setting prices (for example the relationship between demand and price) much of what traditional economics has to offer in this area of decision making is not helpful.

The main problems associated with bringing together the theoretical and practical side of pricing can be explained by the apparent reluctance of the economist to take full cognizance of the implications associated with the setting of either a particular price, or an overall pricing strategy, when considered in the context of an organization and its overall corporate and marketing objectives. Essentially, the economist's viewpoint is based on a set of assumptions which, in many cases, are unrealistic and hence would be difficult to apply in the business environment.

An example of such an assumption is when the individual customer is considering the price of a given product. Economic theory suggests that the customer will act in a totally rational economic manner, such that his or her total utility (or satisfaction) is maximized. In deciding whether or not to 'try' the product our 'totally rational' consumer will carefully equate whether or not buying the product at the asking price set will maximize his or her utility. In making this judgement, the economist 'assumes' that the consumer has 'perfect information' about both the prices and utility of all other competitive products in the market, and that price is the only consideration in choice. Clearly these are unrealistic assumptions.

Another example of unrealistic, and unhelpful, assumptions is that which we mentioned earlier in our introductory summary of the economist's concepts of pricing; namely the assumption of 'profit maximization'. Although profits are an essential element of long-run survival in many organizations, and as such are likely to be enshrined in overall corporate and marketing objectives, these are much more likely to be couched in terms of a required level of profits rather than 'profit maximization'. Most importantly, it is well known that there are many other objectives a company might pursue through its pricing strategies. For example, if a company wanted to maximize market share or simply survive, a different set of prices would be delivered than if the objectives were to maximize profits. Again, we can see that the assumptions of the traditional economist, as to the objectives of the price setting exercise, are somewhat restrictive and unhelpful to the practical price setter.

Set against this seemingly dismissive view of the economist's approach to pricing decisions is the fact that in some areas the economist has provided a number of useful concepts and tools for the marketing practitioner when it comes to making pricing decisions. In particular, the economist has made an important, if only partial, contribution to price setting in the area of the relationship between price and demand. Notwithstanding this, it is unsurprising that a gulf has opened between the theoretical/economist viewpoint and the practical/marketing side of pricing. It is important that we develop a structure for strategic pricing decisions that is helpful to marketing and which can be implemented in the 'real world' of business and it is to this that we now turn our attention.

A FRAMEWORK FOR PRICING DECISIONS: KEY INPUTS

The starting point for developing a pricing structure is the delineation of a framework for pricing decisions. Specifically, we need to establish key inputs to pricing decisions. Although there are a myriad of considerations for arriving at a price for a product or service, the following are considered to be key inputs for the pricing decision maker that are now discussed:

- company and marketing objectives;
- demand considerations;
- cost considerations;
- competitor considerations.

Company and marketing objectives

Pricing decisions are salient to the achievement of corporate and marketing objectives, so it is essential that pricing objectives and strategies are consistent with and supportive of these objectives. Oxenfeld,[1] in Table 5.1, illustrates both the potential range of pricing objectives and their clear relationship to overall corporate and marketing objectives.

This selection from an even wider range of possible pricing objectives which Oxenfeldt[1] delineates, illustrates the fact that the pricing decision maker must establish what objectives the pricing strategy is to achieve. The continued link between corporate objectives and pricing strategies is confirmed in a more recent studies by Kehagias *et al.*[2] and Indounas and Avlonitis.[3] We can also see that according to the precise objectives, we might arrive at very different prices for our product and services. Where a company has multiple objectives, pricing strategies may need to consider trade-offs between different possible price levels, such that these different objectives are met.

In addition to these broader corporate objectives, pricing decisions must also reflect and support specific marketing strategies. In particular, pricing strategies need to be in line with market targeting and positioning strategies, which were outlined in Chapter 3. Clearly, if a company produces a high quality product or service aimed at the prestige end of the market, it would not be sensible to set a low price even if cost efficiency allowed this. Pricing, therefore, must be consistent with the other elements of the marketing mix and the selected positioning strategy. Effectively, the selection of company and market objectives, market targets and the formulation of a positioning strategy constrains or delineate the range of pricing strategies and specific price levels.

An example of how price must reflect and support the overall positioning strategy of the company is the price set for the Aston Martin DBS. The car is positioned at the top end of the market and with just 500 made in the UK for sales worldwide the emphasis is on exclusivity. Many people still associate Aston Martin with the James Bond character, 007, again emphasizing the racy and prestigious image intended. Prices start at £160,000.

TABLE 5.1 Pricing and corporate/marketing objectives

Pricing to maximize long-run profits;

Pricing to maximize short-run profits;

Pricing to expand market share;

Pricing to maintain a price leadership position;

Pricing to discourage potential new entrants;

Pricing to avoid the attention of government and legislators;

Pricing to establish and maintain dealer loyalty;

Pricing to improve corporate image;

Pricing to improve the sales of weaker products.

Demand considerations

A key parameter affecting pricing decisions is customer based. The upper limit to the price to be charged is set by the market, unless the customer must purchase the product and we are the sole supplier. In competitive markets, demand, i.e. the price customers are willing and able to pay, is a major consideration in the selection of pricing strategies and levels. It is in analysis and interpretation of demand and demand schedules that the economist has much to offer the marketer in terms of concepts and techniques.

Ideally, the marketing manager needs to know the **demand schedule** for products and services to be priced. The demand schedule relates prices to quantities demanded and can be illustrated by the use of a diagram shown in Figure 5.1.

The demand curves in Figure 5.1 indicate the number of units that can be sold at any given price. In addition, the slope of the demand curve is directly related to the price sensitivity of demand. Demand curve D_1 slopes less steeply than D_2 where demand is more price-sensitive. Even simple demand curves represent powerful tools for pricing decision makers, showing, as they do, both the number of units that can be sold at any given price and the effect on this quantity of any changes in price. However, price is only one of the determinants of the demand for a product or service. In addition to price the following represent some additional factors which combine to determine demand:

- income/budget of the purchaser;
- attributes of the product;
- tastes of the purchaser;
- price of other products;
- the time it takes to deliver.

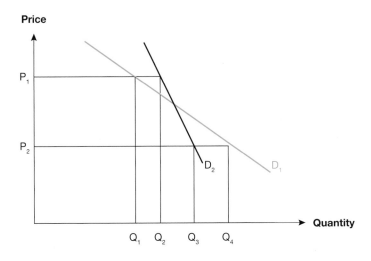

FIGURE 5.1 Examples of simple demand curves

Price per unit

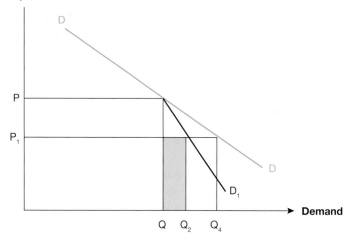

FIGURE 5.2 Oligopoly

Although the views put forward by economists are sometimes difficult to envisage in reality, they are useful in terms of being able to relate to in marketing terms because these theoretical positions tend to relate to certain kinds of marketing behaviour. With this background in mind, an industry or service provision that more or less equates to perfect competition, oligopoly (as explained in Figure 5.2) and monopoly is:

- perfect competition – the restaurant trade;
- oligopoly – motor cars; petrol
- monopoly – the electricity generating industry.

Figure 5.2 explains the theory of oligopoly:

At price P the law of demand states that quantity Q will be demanded. If the price is then reduced to P1, then Q1 will be demanded, so Q–Q1 will be the additional amount demanded. However, in a situation of oligopoly where price as an instrument of competition is less effective, then the demand curve will kink to D1 and the dark area covered by Q–Q2 will be the additional amount demanded. A price reduction in these circumstances is less effective as customers will have been 'pre-sold' their existing products through non-price factors like advertising and branding; this is termed 'non-price competition'.

Income/budget of the purchaser

The ability of the purchaser to buy products and services according to individual income level and purchasing power converts the purchaser's needs and wants into actual purchasing. The economist refers to this willingness to purchase as 'effective demand'. For an organizational buyer, the ability to purchase is directly related to budget requirements and constraints set on the purchaser.

Attributes of the product

Demand for a product or service and the price the customer is willing to pay, is related to the attributes of competitive products being offered. Demand for a product is closely related to how the customer perceives the various attributes of competitive products. These attributes include physical/tangible attributes e.g. quality features and packaging, and 'non-tangible' attributes, such as brand/corporate image and status.

Tastes of the buyer

Related to attributes, another factor affecting demand is the tastes of the buyer. Although a somewhat nebulous concept, 'tastes' are a powerful influence on demand. Changes in taste can give rise to the growth of entirely new markets and the demise of mature ones.

The growth in popularity of hybrid powered cars over recent years is an illustration of changes in taste. However, their demise might be just as rapid as a result of negative publicity surrounding their use e.g. the relatively short range and difficulties of recharging vehicles.

'Tastes' can be of an industrial nature such as being associated with variables like emphasis on productivity improvements, quality management and employee care and protection.

All's Fair

One of the fastest growing areas in retailing in recent years has been the growth of 'fair trade' products. The Fairtrade Foundation was established in 1992 with the aim of providing a better deal for the poor and disadvantaged in their trading with large multinationals. In particular, the foundation exists to help farmers, growers and producers in the developing parts of the world. For example, it is a fact that in the past coffee growers have received a poor deal from their large and powerful customers. Small farmers, with few resources, were required to sell their crops for extremely low prices and often at a loss. The foundation wanted to remedy this by helping negotiate better terms and conditions for their members.

A key part of this initiative was the establishment of a 'Fairtrade' label. Under this label, brands could demonstrate to customers that the suppliers of the product had received a fair deal, usually meaning a fair price. Strict conditions were imposed for a brand to qualify for the Fairtrade label. The real issue was whether customers would be prepared to pay the inevitably higher prices which fair trade brands required. The answer has been a resounding yes. Many people apparently are prepared to pay a price premium to protect developing world suppliers.

As a result the market for fair trade products in the UK has boomed and includes such well known brands as Clippper Teas, Green & Black's chocolate, Starbucks coffee and the Body Shop. UK supermarkets now have their own brand range of Fairtrade products, underlining that it is here to stay. In July 2009, Cadbury re-launched its Dairy Milk bar as a certified Fairtrade product.

Price of other products

The price of competitive products is a key area affecting demand. Inevitably buyers tend to consider prices of substitute products when evaluating the effect of prices on demand. However, if the consumer has to spend more disposable income on essential items due to increases in the prices of these items, e.g. food and mortgage repayments, then the consumer's disposable income demand for other apparently unrelated products can be affected. Clearly, in the case of substitute products, how the price of one item compares to the price of another is central to the selection process of the buyer. In the current recessionary climate this is of heightened relevance as witnessed by increased numbers of price comparison websites.

The time factor

When discussing demand for a product or service, we must consider the time factor, i.e. demand must be specified for a given time period. For example, it is conventional to distinguish between 'short', 'medium' and 'long run' time horizons when discussing demand. Demand can vary over these different time periods. The time period must be explicit when evaluating demand concepts in the context of marketing.

From the perspective of the pricing decision maker, it is essential to assess sensitivity of demand. From discussion of the slopes of the demand curves shown in Figure 5.1, the slope of the demand curve indicates what the effect on quantity demanded will be for any given change in price. This effect is referred to as the **price elasticity of demand**.

Elasticity of demand

Price elasticity of demand means demand for a product is **inelastic** if consumers will pay almost any price for the product and very **elastic** if consumers will only pay within a narrow band of prices. Inelastic demand means a producer can raise prices without affecting demand too much, and elastic demand means consumers are price sensitive and will not buy if prices rise too much.

A medical cure that will save a person's life has inelastic characteristics in that the person whose life is at risk will pay anything for the cure, so price is inelastic. However, demand for cars is elastic because if prices rise too much consumers will switch to alternatives like shared lifts or public transport or car hire.

Elasticity can be expressed by:

$$E = \frac{\% \text{ change in quantity demanded}}{\% \text{ change in any demand determinant}}$$

The demand for a product to be responsive, or not, to changes in price can be summarized as a function of:

- the number and closeness of substitutes;
- the necessity of the purchase to the buyer;

- the importance of product performance to the buyer;
- the cost of switching suppliers.

The number and closeness of substitutes

Of all determinants of price elasticity of demand, this is probably the most important. If the product is in competition with a number of others that are similar in quality, perform similar functions and are being offered at a lower price, then it follows that demand for the lower priced product will be greater.

The marketer can modify price-sensitivity of demand for the company's products and services by differentiating them from those of competitors. For example, the market can be 'desensitized' to differences in price by, say, better quality or improved packaging. Unless a company is in a position to compete and win purely on price, every effort should be made to gain a competitive edge by differentiating products from close substitutes.

The market for detergents and cleaning products such as washing powders, washing up liquids and bleaches is extremely competitive. To avoid competing purely on price, companies have made substantial efforts to differentiate their brands from those of competitors. An example of a brand successfully differentiated from its competitors is Fairy Liquid. For many years Fairy Liquid successfully based its differentiation on its 'kindness' to the hands of the user. When other brands began to blur this differentiation through their marketing efforts, introducing their own claims for gentleness in use, Fairy Liquid switched the differentiation to one of the brand being both long established and more effective and, by implication, better value for money compared to its competitors.

The necessity of the purchase

Some product categories are essential purchases for the consumer, whereas others can be classified as luxuries. For example, food, water and electricity are 'essentials'. Total market demand for products and services in this category tends to be less sensitive to changes in price than products and services we count as luxuries. We should note though that individual products and brands, even within the 'necessities' category, can be extremely price-sensitive where there are available substitutes. In addition we should note that what is a 'luxury' for one consumer may be a 'necessity' (or utility good) for another, depending on disposable income, attitudes and lifestyles.

For example, many of us only buy flowers for special occasions and even then might balk at paying more than say £40. In 2009, French President, Nicolas Sarkozy and his wife Carla Bruni were reported as spending over £660 per day on flowers.

The importance of product performance

In certain industrial markets, where the buyer is primarily concerned with performance specifications, demand will tend to be inelastic with regard to price. If a situation arises where the product fails and the buyer would suffer severe penalties in the form of cost, production time or convenience, then demand would be inelastic to price.

Cost of switching suppliers

Hutt and Speh[4] have pointed to the importance of '**switching costs**' in industrial markets. For example, in some situations an industrial user of a component part may align certain part specifications of its products to that of the supplier. The firm may have also made a heavy investment in tooling charges or in installing a supplier's equipment, e.g. a dedicated computer system. The cost here of turning to another supplier would probably be prohibitive and not in the best interests of the purchasing organization.

Cross elasticity of demand

As far as demand is concerned, products can be related in any one of a number of ways. First, they may be competing products or substitutes, in which case, an increase in the purchase of one product may result in a decrease in the demand of another. Next, when products are of a complementary nature, an increase in demand for one product may result in an increase in demand for another. Finally, when two products are of an independent nature then a purchase of one product will have no effect on the demand of another. **Cross elasticity of demand** is a measure for interpreting the relationship between products. It measures the percentage change in the quantity demanded of a product to a percentage change in the price of another product, shown by:

$$Sxy = \frac{\% \text{ change in quantity of } y}{\% \text{ change in price of } x}$$

Possible shapes of demand curves

Marketers need to be aware of the way customers react to a given price level, which in turn is related to the shape of the demand curve, In fact there are a number of possible shapes for demand curves. Each curve illustrates sets of customers reacting to a change in price by plotting the price of the product against the level of sales. In plotting these curves, all other factors are kept constant in line with the assumptions of the microeconomic theory of pricing. A variety of possible shapes for demand curves are shown in Figure 5.3 (a)–(d).

Figure 5.3(a) is a traditional economic demand curve. Assuming 'rationality' on the part of consumers, the lower the price, the higher the quantity demanded. The majority of markets are characterized by this shape of demand curve.

Figure 5.3(b) also shows a frequently encountered demand curve, though one that is often not appreciated by pricing decision makers who use traditional economic principles. Here, lowering the price of a product increases demand up to a point, but below this threshold, the desirability of the product, and hence demand, decreases due to suspicion of 'poor quality' signalled by the lower prices. Such suspicions may or may not be justified, but it is customer perceptions that count.

Figure 5.3(c) shows a market where regardless of price charged, demand remains unchanged. This seemingly 'unrealistic' market situation is a characteristic of markets where the customer must purchase the product and where there is only one supplier of that product i.e. a monopolistic situation.

Figure 5.3(d) illustrates a market where increased prices result in increases in demand. Markets where this might occur are those where the consumer is eager to signal that the product is affordable

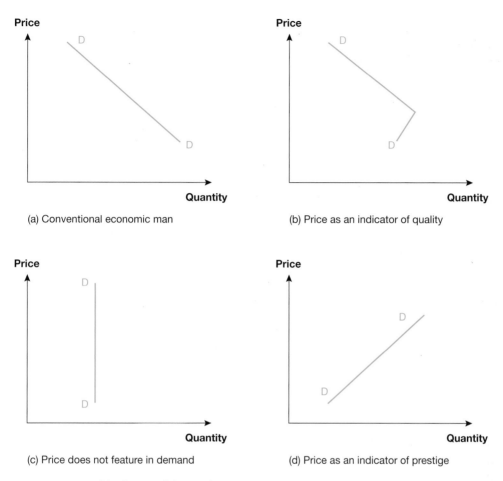

(a) Conventional economic man

(b) Price as an indicator of quality

(c) Price does not feature in demand

(d) Price as an indicator of prestige

FIGURE 5.3 Possible shapes of demand curves

with the higher price being an indicator of the prestige and status of the buyer. An example here is well known brands of perfume.

An understanding of price/volume relationships is crucial to pricing decision making. In practice, particularly for new products, estimating these relationships can be difficult. It is essential in analysing demand to examine the buyer's 'perception of value' as the key to demand and pricing decisions; a factor we return to later.

COST CONSIDERATIONS

If demand considerations effectively set the upper limits to price, then cost considerations determine the lower limits. Relevant up-to-date cost information is essential to formalize pricing strategy. Accurate information allows the pricing decision maker to identify costs on a specific basis directly related to each product, activity or customer. In this way, management is able to make informed decisions about pricing to target market segments.

Relevant cost information is information which is presented and analysed in such a way as to be pertinent and helpful to marketing decision making. In particular, the cost analysis should enable the marketer to distinguish between fixed and variable costs and the relationship between these and volume. The importance and use of the distinction between fixed and variable costs is illustrated by a breakeven chart shown in Figure 5.4.

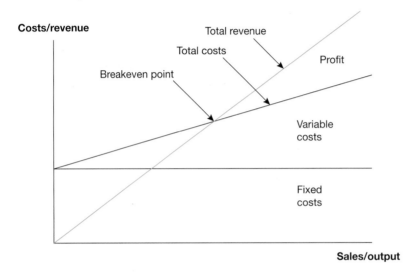

FIGURE 5.4 Simple breakeven chart

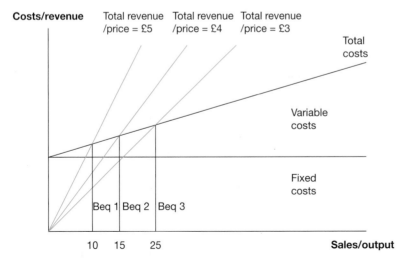

FIGURE 5.5 Breakeven versus different prices

Fixed costs are those that do not vary with levels of output, examples being rates, heating, lighting and security of premises and are represented by the horizontal fixed cost curve in Figure 5.4. **Variable costs** directly relate to production and sales and include labour and direct materials. Increases in output or sales lead to a proportional increase in these costs. Taken together, fixed and variable costs combine to give total costs. The remaining information contained in a breakeven chart is the revenue curve. This shows the total revenue that will accrue to the company at a given price-quantity combination.

The **breakeven point** is the point at which total revenue exactly matches the total costs, i.e. there is neither profit nor loss. This information on cost/revenue relationships is useful to the pricing decision maker e.g. when comparing breakeven points associated with different possible prices for a product. This idea is shown in Figure 5.5. The effect of charging a higher price is to steepen the total revenue curve and as a consequence lower the breakeven quantity. The decision maker can then evaluate the effect of charging different prices in terms of what these different prices and breakeven points mean to the company. Specifically, the information in a breakeven chart includes:

- profit (or losses) at varying levels of output;
- breakeven point at varying prices;
- effect on breakeven points and profits (or losses) if costs change.

Breakeven points can also be calculated using the following information:

Selling price per unit − variable cost per unit = contribution per unit

$$\text{Breakeven quantity} = \frac{\text{Total fixed costs}}{\text{Unit contribution}}$$

e.g. Selling price = £20
Variable costs = £10
Fixed costs = £50,000
Contribution = 20 − £10 = £10.

$$\therefore \text{Breakeven quantity} = \frac{50,000}{10} = 5000 \text{ units.}$$

The notion of **contribution** is a valuable addition to the pricing decision. It illustrates that in the short run at least, it may be advantageous to sell a product at a price that is less than the full cost of producing it. The distinction between fixed costs and variable costs is particularly useful where a company is attempting to penetrate a market with a new product. It is also useful in times of recession where prices have to be cut to maintain demand. The essential issue is to cover variable costs as a minimum and have a clear understanding of the contribution to fixed costs and profits.

Although fixed, variable and total costs are of major importance to pricing decisions it is also useful to consider how these costs change with different volumes of output, i.e. economies of scale and experience curve effects that we considered earlier.

If a company has a downward sloping experience curve, i.e. costs fall as a function of production experience, then the company might then adopt an aggressive pricing strategy based on increasing volume through low prices. There are risks such as aggressive competitor reaction and the creation of a down-market image.

Although costs are just one of the inputs to pricing decisions, in many organizations they are given more emphasis than any other factors in setting prices. Cost-based pricing is criticized, but it is still a widely used approach. Before looking at cost-based and other approaches to pricing along with their respective merits, we need to look at the final key input to pricing decisions: competitors.

COMPETITOR CONSIDERATIONS

It is increasingly recognized that in today's competitive environment, effective strategic marketing plans are as much about being competitor-oriented as customer-oriented, as evidenced in the following quote from Porter:[5]

> Competition is at the core of the success or failure of firms. Competition determines the appropriateness of a firm's activities that can contribute to its performance, such as innovations, a cohesive culture, or good implementation. Competitive advantage is the benefit derived through competitive strategy aimed at establishing a profitable and sustainable position against the forces that determine industry competition.

Business can be compared to running a competitive race, with all the awards going to the winner. It behoves the marketing manager to make a careful analysis of the company's competitors before devoting resources to marketing strategies. This involves examination of competitors so the planner can develop and sustain superior competitive performance. This deceptively simple statement belies the fact that to do this we must establish where competition stems from now and in the future. We also have to consider and appraise competitors' present and likely future objectives and strategies as well as their likely reactions to the competitive moves we might make.

The marketing strategist must also widen the focus to include in the analysis not only 'competition' in the more traditional sense, but also the competitive structure of the industry. This includes the assessment of factors such as barriers to entry and exit and hence, for example, the threat of new entrants; the assessment of potential substitute products or services; the bargaining power of suppliers and the bargaining power of buyers. In short, competitor analysis is complex and multifaceted. Consider how we might seek to conceptualize the competitive structure of an industry, starting with the more traditional approach based on the number of sellers (competitors) and degree of product differentiation in a market.

No pricing decision can be taken in isolation from the nature and extent of prevailing or latent competition in any industry. The most important considerations with regard to competitor pricing include:

- competitors' prices, including discounts, credit terms and terms of trade;
- competitors' resources, especially financial;

- competitors' costs and profit margins;
- likely competitor responses to our pricing strategies and decisions;
- likely potential competitors and barriers to market industry entry;
- substitutes from other industries;
- competitor marketing strategies, especially targeting, positioning and product differentiation.

Three of the most important competitor considerations which directly affect the extent to which an industry will be price competitive are:

- the number of competitors;
- the degree of product differentiation between competitors;
- freedom of entry.

For example, where there is only one supplier, i.e. a monopoly, then the pricing decision maker has substantial discretion over price. On the other hand, where products are undifferentiated, price competition is likely to be fierce. Finally, where competitors can enter an industry with relative ease, then the price setter will have less discretion over price and may be forced to set lower prices than might otherwise be the case in order to deter new entrants.

We have outlined four key inputs to pricing decisions: company, cost, customers and competitor factors. There are many other considerations, ranging from those involving distributor and channel arrangements to possible legal considerations in price setting. We now consider how prices might be set, i.e. pricing methods.

PRICING METHODS

There are several methods through which a company can set prices. We can distinguish between three broad categories according to the emphasis that predominates as the basis for price setting:

- internal cost-based methods;
- competitor-based methods;
- customer value-based methods.

Internal cost-based methods of pricing

The most widely used method for determining prices involves setting prices predominantly on the basis of the company's costs. This method is referred to as **'cost-plus' pricing**. In its simplest form it involves a company calculating average costs of production and then allocating a specified mark-up, which may be related to rate of return required by the company, to arrive at the selling price.

The major advantage of this method is its simplicity. However, despite its widespread use, it has been criticized. Before we examine the basis of these criticisms we need to examine further the mechanics of cost-plus pricing, as well as some of the reasons why this apparently 'simple' approach to pricing may be more complex than it seems at first glance.

As we have seen, the mechanics of cost-plus pricing involve calculating variable costs per unit and adding to this an allocation of the total fixed costs. The first problem with cost-plus pricing is in both the calculation and allocation of these fixed costs. Lancaster and Massingham[6] highlight these problems as follows:

> Both the calculation of total fixed costs and the methods of allocating this total between products give rise to serious problems when using this method of pricing. For example, the amount of fixed costs which will be added to each product, and consequently the price clearly depends on the number of products produced. In turn, the number of products that a firm will produce will, ignoring stockholding, be a function of how many it can sell. How many will be sold, in turn, depends upon the price charged. Pricing in this way then is nonsensical; it means that for a given production capacity, if a company finds that it is selling less and cuts its production its market prices will need to increase. This, in turn, will probably lead to fewer sales, a further cut-back in production and even higher prices. To say the least this is an unsatisfactory state of affairs.

In many multi-product companies the allocation of fixed and semi-variable costs to individual products is often arbitrary. In practice, total fixed costs are allocated on the basis of either a standard volume or a forecast level of output.

A second problem with cost-plus pricing is in determining mark-up. Often the percentage mark-up is derived from a pre-determined target rate of profit or return. The problem with such pre-determined mark-up rates is that they take no account of demand conditions. Where rigid percentage mark-ups are applied, particularly where these are based on internally determined requirements for profit, cost-plus has major disadvantages:

- it ignores demand and market conditions;
- it ignores competitors and competitive considerations;
- it ignores factors such as target marketing and positioning;
- it ignores potential substitutes.

With these disadvantages there must be good reason why cost-plus remains widely used by companies and the advantages are as follows:

- The pricing decision maker does not have to consider the difficult (if essential) area of demand and price sensitivity.
- Where other companies are using cost-plus pricing, and provided they have similar costs and mark-ups, it can lead to price stability.
- It is claimed that because prices are directly related to costs it is 'fair' to both competitors and customers.

None of these potential advantages can compensate for the fact that cost-plus pricing, in its most rigid form, is not market oriented, and can lead to significant strategic disadvantages in the market.

Variations on cost-plus pricing

It would be strange if companies had not realized the problems of cost-plus pricing. Thus a number of variants on this approach, although still based on costs, may be needed.

Marginal or direct cost pricing is where prices are based not on full costs that include fixed costs, but direct or marginal costs. Fixed costs are not charged to production as they are treated as a period charge and written off to the profit and loss account. In this way, the problems associated with having to cover costs, and the methods of having to allocate fixed costs, are avoided. This makes use of the notion of 'contribution' discussed earlier. Needless to say, in the long run all costs, including fixed costs, must be covered, but marginal cost pricing does at least allow a company to take advantage of market opportunities and to use price as a more strategic tool of marketing. This approach is particularly useful for services marketing where the service cannot be stored, i.e. is highly perishable, such as cinema seats or hotel bedrooms. Prices can then be based on making a contribution to fixed costs by charging prices which cover variable, but not total costs.

EasyJet and Ryanair make good use of marginal-cost pricing in their marketing strategies. These operators cover their variable costs when selling an airline seat rather than let the plane fly with empty seats. Provided of course that there are enough 'full price' paying passengers, this is an effective way of not only making a contribution to profits, but at the same time making life difficult for cost-plus competitors.

Another example of marginal cost pricing can be found in the hotel industry. Hoteliers know that if a hotel room is not sold on a particular evening then the revenue that letting the room would generate for that evening is lost for ever. This is due to the service product characteristic of 'perishability', i.e. a service cannot be stored and sold again on another occasion. This makes it imperative that demand and supply of services be balanced and matched. Price is the primary mechanism for achieving this match. In the case of the hotel reducing the price of unsold rooms, this allows the marketer to generate some contribution and the room should be let at a discount if the full price cannot be achieved. Marginal pricing, especially for services, makes sense and is popular. However, it necessarily leads to price variations which as Palmer and McMahon-Beattie[7] show can lead to customer dissatisfaction and mistrust.

Variable mark-up pricing is an alternative to the fixed mark-up system of traditional cost plus pricing, and here the percentage added to costs can be varied. This approach has advantages over the fixed mark-up approach:

- mark-up, and hence prices, can be varied to take account of demand, competition and market conditions;
- mark-up can take account of marketing objectives and strategies;
- overall it represents a much more flexible approach.

Despite these variations on rigid cost-plus pricing, it is a fact that cost-based pricing is an indication of a company that has failed to appreciate the significance of the marketing concept. This is not to deny the importance of costs, and cost information in pricing decisions, but costs are perhaps better used in an evaluative, rather that a decision-making role when it comes to setting prices.

Competition-based pricing as a method of determining a price uses the price set by competitors to orient the pricing decision. This method is based on assumptions, including that of product image and the position of the company, as being the same or similar to those of the competition. This can be improved upon with a more sophisticated method, involving setting a differential between the company operating it and the competition. The marketer may, for example, set a price 5 per cent below that of the market leader to allow for the market leader's stronger reputation within the industry. This approach to pricing has the disadvantage of being somewhat passive in nature, which tends to restrict the management of the company in terms of individualistic flair and style. Another drawback of this method, known as **going rate** pricing, is that it tends to ignore the company's own cost and demand situation. Going rate pricing is popular in markets where costs are difficult to measure or the response of competitors is uncertain.

Going rate pricing is used extensively in the university sector to price undergraduate degree programmes. For government-funded universities, easily the largest sector, upper limits to fees are set by the government. However, there is no lower limit to these fees. Universities can charge what they want below the upper limit. Notwithstanding difference in costs, objectives, competitive structures and so on, virtually every University charge exactly the same price for their products.

Although it is vital to consider competitors' prices and costs, this information should be used to influence decisions on price rather than as a 'formula' for setting it.

Customer value-based pricing is a market-oriented method. Although complex in nature and application, this method moves away from a focus on costs or competition and concentrates on customers. With this approach, prices are determined on the basis of the perceived value of the product to the customer. The basic idea is that when customers purchase a product they go through a complex process of balancing benefits against costs.

In consumer product markets, the 'benefits' the customer derives correspond to the economist's notion of 'utility' or satisfaction and may include both functional and psychological elements. For example, the customer may derive satisfaction, and hence value, from the quality of a product, or a particular product feature such as a satellite navigation system built into a new car. An example of a psychological element of value might be the benefit which the customer derives from the status of a prestigious brand name. Clearly, the more benefits the customer perceives a product as offering, the more value that customer will place on this product and the more the customer will be prepared to pay. Again, we should note that it is the customer's perception of value that matters and not that of the supplier.

Needless to say, a customer will not purchase a product where costs are seen as being greater than benefits. It is important to stress that costs may include more than just the purchase price, and it is the customer's perception of these costs that is used in the evaluation process. For example, in assessing the cost of, say, a new car it is not just the initial purchase cost, but also maintenance, insurance, fuel and depreciation costs that the purchaser may consider. In addition, just as there are psychological benefits, so too are there psychological costs. For example, a new car purchaser may well consider the costs of 'loss of status' if an otherwise 'good value for money' purchase might be ridiculed by peer groups. Certain Eastern European car manufacturers faced this problem in trying to market their models in parts of Western Europe.

The Czech company, Skoda, in their advertising, actually acknowledged this problem as initially, the brand was regarded as a joke, but this is no longer the case. Effective marketing has now made the Skoda car a success story of recent years. Product improvements, the backing of German group, Volkswagen and a repositioning of the brand have served to make Skoda one of the best value cars in the market. Although the car is still low priced compared to some of its competitors, this low price base has been turned to advantage by the company by building the value for money aspect. Customers who were attracted to this car become brand loyal and saw themselves as being astute in their choice. After all, they argued, they were securing the advantages of a Volkswagen product at a Skoda price.

Basically, the marketer must determine what the market will bear i.e. the highest price the customer will pay which is:

Benefits – Costs other than price = Highest price the customer will pay

For the pricing decision maker the difficulty in this method is in measuring how the customer perceives the product the company is offering against the competition.

One method that can be used is to weigh product attributes against those of the competition. First, the customer is asked questions concerning different attributes of a product, e.g. quality and delivery. The customer is then asked how important each criterion is, e.g. the customer might think that after-sales service is more important than delivery and would then give this criterion a higher rating than delivery. The customer is next asked how the organization fares in comparison to other companies in the market place on these criteria. The customer's perceived value of different competitive offerings can then be calculated.

Let us assume that competitor C has the highest overall value rating over competitors A and B. On this basis that company should be able to charge higher prices than competitors A and B for the product. If, say, the average price for this particular product in the industry is £10.00 and the average value rating is 36.5 then company C should be able to charge £10 x 36.5 ÷ 33.3 = £11.00 approximately, and still be competitive. If all three companies set their prices proportional to their value rating, then they would all be offering the same value to price. However, if company C sets a price of less than £11.00 it should begin to steal market share from its competitors because it will be perceived to be offering better value for money. This illustrates just one method of analysing how the customer perceives the relative benefits of the products on offer.

Taking this approach a stage further, it is useful to establish the Economic Value of a product to a Customer (EVC). **Economic value pricing,** sometimes also referred to as performance pricing, is a powerful pricing tool that is used principally in pricing industrial products. It requires extensive market research to allow the pricing decision maker to analyse:

- how the customer uses the product;
- the financial benefits the product offers to the customer in each usage situation;
- costs involved over the lifetime of usage of the product;
- the cost/benefit trade-off.

How the customer uses the product – Different customers may use the 'same' product in different ways and make different cost/benefit evaluations e.g. one contractor may run earth-moving machinery 24 hours a day and place a premium on a machine which offers greater reliability and parts back-up to minimize 'down time'. Another, perhaps smaller, contractor in the same business might only operate its machines 12 hours a day, but may not be able to afford a permanent team of mechanics. This contractor is likely to place more emphasis (i.e. value) on supplier/dealer servicing facilities. In short, the marketer must study and understand how the product fits into the operation of the customer.

Benefits – When we understand how the customer will use the product we can proceed to evaluate the 'cost out' of financial benefits of the product to the customer. Focusing on benefits helps develop a more detailed picture of the overall desirability of the product. When analysing benefits the product gives, it is useful to break them into core product benefits and augmented product benefits. Core attributes could be quality, reliability or other functional aspects. The augmented attributes could be delivery, service, guarantees and maintenance offered by the supplier. Focusing solely on physical and core attributes can lead marketers into the trap of marketing features of the product as opposed to benefits the product has to offer.

Costs – Just as benefits can be a group of core and augmented attributes, perceived in differing ways by different customers, so the same can be said for costs, in that costs are not just the price the customer forgoes. One aspect of this is when a buyer decides to change from an existing supplier to a cheaper source. The buyer may be thinking of lowering cost, but in fact the opposite may be the case as the alternative products may not be of as good quality as the previous products, or the new supplier may not be able to deliver the goods on time. The lost time from reject products and subsequent breakdown in the production runs can make savings achieved on price irrelevant. Total lifetime operating costs, including residual value of the product, should be calculated for each customer.

Trade-off between benefits and costs – If the customer makes a trade-off between costs and benefits it would seem sensible for the selling company to do the same. The simplest method is by analysing only the core attributes and price. Once again, it is important therefore that the selling company looks at the use of the product and evaluates this in conjunction with costs and benefits offered.

As the customer looks at price as part of the overall product package, so too must the marketer. If the firm wishes to adopt a value-based approach to pricing it must follow certain guidelines:

- a commitment to the philosophy that the customer chooses products by measuring product benefits against product costs;
- an understanding that benefits involve more than the core attributes, and in many choice situations it is augmented product benefits that differentiate products;
- a realization that costs involve more than just the purchase price alone;
- an awareness that different customers view costs and benefits differently.

Despite the inherent wisdom of value-based pricing evidence shows it is still resisted by many companies (Hinterhuber[8]). Certainly customer/value-based pricing involves more analysis, time and effort than cost-based or competitor-based pricing, but it is essentially marketing oriented. Because of this, value-based pricing is useful in guiding other elements of marketing strategy. For example:

1 Value-based pricing can help in market segmentation and targeting, with marketing efforts being focused on those parts of the market (customer groups) where the perceived value of a company's offering is highest.

2   Value-based pricing can point the way to developing effective promotional and selling strategies. The customer must be made aware of, and convinced about, any extra value that your products or services can potentially offer.

3   Value-based pricing can be used in the early stages of designing and developing new products and services with a conscious effort being made to 'build in' value to the product or service for the envisaged target market.

4   Many agree that value based pricing represents the truly marketing-oriented approach to pricing, but as Ingenbleek[9] shows it is still poorly researched and understood.

Other considerations in setting prices

We have discussed inputs to pricing decisions and merits of different pricing methods. In arriving at a final price, other considerations may influence the decision, such as:

Price/quality relationships

In the absence of other information, price is often used as a singular indicator of quality. The pricing decision maker must be careful to ensure, particularly for a new product, that a low initial price does not put off customers because they suspect the quality.

'Psychological pricing'

It is now recognized that pricing sends many complex signals to customers. Moreover these price signals don't always mean the same thing to each customer. As a result, they are often interpreted and acted upon in different ways. There are behavioural forces at work with respect to price involving psychological factors such as perception, learning and personality. These behavioural forces have led to the notion of considering the psychology of pricing processes. Examples include:

Odd pricing: Often prices are set to end in an odd number (e.g. £4.99 instead of £5.00). There is some evidence that customers then see the product as falling into the lower priced category (i.e. £4.00) rather than the higher one to which it is actually much nearer.

Price and perceptions of quality: Price is often used by potential customers as an indication of quality, particularly where they are unfamiliar with a brand or supplier. This means that a low price may be taken as a sign of low quality and vice versa for a high price meaning it is possible to price a product too low.

Price and social status: Related to price as an indicator of quality, the marketer needs to be aware that some customers will connect the prices they and other people pay as being an indicator of status. Again, some customers may be deterred by low prices even if they know it represents the best possible value, because they feel it detracts from their social status.

Other products in the line/mix

In a multi-product company many products have interrelated costs and/or demand. When setting a price on an individual product in the line, consideration should be given to the overall profitability of the product mix, e.g. we might decide to set a lower price on an individual product than we might otherwise do because it helps to sell other, perhaps more profitable, items in the line.

Other elements of the marketing mix

As with all marketing mix elements, it is important that pricing reflects, and is consistent with, other elements of the mix. A high quality, expensively packaged product may be looked at with some 'suspicion' by potential buyers if it carries a 'bargain' price tag.

Product life cycle

The competitive situation for a product changes throughout the life cycle of a product. Each different phase in the cycle may require a different strategy. Pricing plays a particularly important role in this respect. Care should be used in interpreting the possible strategic implications of each of the life cycle stages.

Pricing in the introductory stage of the life cycle – With an innovatory product, developers can expect to have a competitive edge for a period of time. With innovatory new products, a company can elect to choose between two pricing strategies:

- price skimming: the setting of a high initial price, that is lowered in successive stages;
- price penetration: the setting of a low initial price.

Price skimming is where the setting of a high initial price can be interpreted as an assumption by management that eventually competition will enter the market and erode profit margins. The company sets a high price so as to 'milk' the market and achieve maximum profits available in the shortest period of time. This 'market skimming' strategy involves the company estimating the highest price the customer is willing or able to pay, which will involve assessing the benefits of the product to the potential customer. This strategy has been successfully carried out by firms marketing innovative products that have substantial consumer benefits. An example of price skimming was Apple's iPod. Launched in 2005, the initial price was set at £450. It now is possible to purchase variants of the iPod for less than £100.

After the initial introduction stage of the product the company will lower the price of the product in successive stage so as to draw in the more price-conscious customers. When a company adopts this strategy the following variables are usually present:

- demand for the product is high;
- the high price will not attract early competition;
- hHigh price gives the impression to the buyer of purchasing a high quality product from a superior firm.

Price penetration is where setting a low price or a 'market penetration strategy' is carried out by companies whose prime objective is to capture a large market share in the quickest time period possible. Conditions which prevail in such circumstances include:

- demand for the product is price sensitive;
- a low price will discourage competitors from entering the market;
- there are potential economies of scale and/or significant experience curve effects and manufacture has to be large scale from the outset;
- a manufacturer will be prepared to wait longer to recoup capital investment costs.

Pricing in the growth stage For a period of time after introduction, the market will continue to grow. The fact that new companies are entering the market means the market will be divided between competing companies, but as the market is still growing, new companies may not take any sales away from the innovator for some time. When new companies come in to the market they tend to emphasize non-product attributes of their product, as opposed to the innovator. If this occurs, the innovating company will usually lower the price of its own product so as to discourage competition.

Pricing at the maturity stage As the market for the product continues to expand and develop, the use of the product becomes more widespread, and with the entrance of new competitors, the price of the product will become increasingly important in competitive strategy. A new supplier entering the market or an existing company can only increase market share by taking share away from other companies. The means for achieving this is often on the basis of price competition, since by the time the market reaches maturity stage, product differentiation and other forms of differentiation may have been eroded.

Pricing in the decline stage During this stage, price-cutting initiated in the maturity stage will tend to continue. At this stage, a careful appraisal of profit margins will need to be made. Prices may be eroded to the point where either total or even only marginal costs are no longer being covered. As we considered in Chapter 4, at this stage in the product life cycle, decisions as to whether to harvest or divest the product need to be made. These decisions will need to take account of possible ways of reducing costs to try and maintain profit margins.

Other interested parties

Pricing decisions will need to take account of various other parties that might be interested in, or be affected by, the pricing decision. For example, there may be legal aspects to pricing decisions, with possibly government departments and/or 'watchdog' bodies playing a key role in pricing decisions. For example, some privatized companies in the UK, such as gas, electricity and water companies, have to meet stringent regulatory requirements with respect to their pricing. A further 'interested party' to take account of in pricing decisions is the distributor. Where products and services are marketed using intermediaries we need to remember that in many markets the final selling price may not be determined by the producer, but by intermediaries. There is now no longer resale price maintenance which means that a supplier to a retailer can only recommend (not stipulate) a retail price. The final price is set by the retailer who adds a mark-up, so to this extent the supplier can try to influence the final market price. The extent that intermediaries are free to set prices effectively means that the marketer has little control over final price.

In addition, we must also determine factors like credit terms and discounts as part of pricing strategy. Many branded product marketers have sometimes been incensed by their inability to force distributors to sell their brands at the prices they would like. Tesco supermarket chain sold Levi jeans at a lot less than the manufacturer's 'recommended' prices. Challenged by Levis, Tesco won the right to sell the brand at these reduced prices in their stores subject to certain conditions being met. Perfume houses, haute couture clothing brands, books and over-the-counter pharmaceuticals are examples where the branded marketer has effectively lost control over prices charged.

This does not mean that unless you own or control the channel of distribution that planning and managing pricing and much of what we have discussed in this chapter are unimportant. In fact, just the opposite is the case. The increasing power of intermediaries to control price in many markets means that the brand marketer must increasingly search for ways to counteract this power. One of the most powerful tools is to use dominant brands. Even the most influential retailers would not like to lose some of the best known and best selling brands from their shelves. They know that such brands command price premiums and serve to attract customers to shop at their stores. Brand marketers must also work closely with distributors to mutually agree price and promotional campaigns. Another way to gain control over price is to market direct to customers. Needless to say, with the popularity of the Web, this is the route that many marketers are choosing to go.

PRICING/MARKETING STRATEGIES FOR DIFFERENT COMPETITIVE POSITIONS

It is suggested that a company's competitive position in an industry is one of the most important determinants of marketing strategies. A significant contribution to thinking in this area has stemmed from the work of the Arthur D. Little Consultancy Company. They suggest the following alternative categories of competitive position for a company in an industry. Associated with each category of alternative competitive position we have given a brief indication of some of possible implications for strategic marketing:

Dominant: As the term suggests, the dominant competitor in an industry is the company which overtly or tacitly controls all competitors. Dominance may stem from a number of factors such as size/resources, control of raw materials, control of distribution channels and control of technologies. Needless to say, the dominant company is in a strong position as it can exercise considerable choice over pricing strategies.

Strong: These companies do not dominate the market, but their size and strength enables them to exercise considerable discretion over their marketing strategies. Although other competitors cannot be ignored, strong competitors are understandably treated with caution by other companies.

Favourable: These competitors in a market have particular strengths which enable them to compete effectively even though they may not be amongst the largest and strongest companies. Often their favourable position derives from a particular aspect of their marketing such as a strong brand name or a reputation for technological innovation. Often such strengths may be used to lever a stronger position within a market. Companies in this position can in the long run, become strong or even dominant in a market.

Tenable: Although these competitors can make profits and survive, they are often at the mercy of dominant, strong and favourable competitors. Companies in this position have no particular significant differential advantages over their competitors and must follow the market leaders in much of their elements of marketing strategy including pricing.

Weak: These competitors are at a considerable disadvantage in the market. Their weakness may stem from factors such as small size, weak brands or poor quality. Weak competitors must improve in those areas where their weaknesses are significant or they will be driven out of the market.

Non-viable: As the term implies these competitors should not be in the market as they are in no position to compete, nor do they have any avenues left that will enable them to improve their position, so they should leave the industry before they are forced out.

An alternative perspective on competitor position and marketing strategies is proposed by Kotler and Keller[10] who distinguish between the strategies available to the following types of competitor in an industry:

- **Market leader** or a company with the largest market share. This competitive market position can give a company significant cost and power advantages. There is strong evidence that market leaders invariably have the highest rates of return on capital employed. Market leaders may shape prices, industry standards and methods of competing in a market and are often a competitive target for other companies, so they should make every effort to maintain market leadership by, for example, expanding the total market through new uses or more frequent usage. Market leaders tend to benefit disproportionately from increases in overall market size, which strengthens their market share position. The market leader must do everything in its power to defend its market share against market challenges and constantly seek to innovate.
- **Market challengers** are companies that market leaders need to defend their position against. They might be second in market share terms or lower, but they are distinguished by their desire to become market leaders. Market challengers often take advantage of the potential for complacency by market leaders. Many companies have risen from relatively low market shares to become dominant market leaders. This is particularly pronounced in the case of many Japanese companies. They must seek to outperform the market leader in some way which may involve finding new ways to attract customers in a market and attacking the weaknesses of the market leader.
- **Market followers** are companies that do not want to challenge for market leadership, but prefer instead to follow the strategies of the market leader. This does not necessarily mean that they will do exactly the same as the market leader with respect to price, but it means that their strategies are primarily shaped by the market leader. There are disadvantages to being a market follower although many companies have found that this is a viable and profitable strategy.
- **Market nichers** concentrate on specialist parts of the market that larger companies have either consciously or unconsciously ignored. This strategy is useful for the smaller company and is called 'concentrated marketing' as discussed in Chapter 3.

An interesting development in the formulation of marketing and pricing strategies has taken these notions of competitive market positions, and the importance of building strategies around these and relative competitor strengths, and linked them to some of the concepts and techniques developed by military strategists when considering techniques of warfare. In part, this in itself is recognition of extreme competition in many markets, and the notion that companies must either 'kill' or 'be killed' by competitors. This notion of marketing as 'war' involves using the concepts of military strategists and thinkers such as Carl von Clausewitz[11] and Basil Liddell-Hart[12] and applying these to marketing plans and strategies As Kolar and Toporisic[13] show, the concept of marketing as warfare and the application of principles of battlefield command have now become popular amongst marketing academics and practitioners.

PRICING OF SERVICES

Lancaster and Withey[14] suggest that the basic methods of price determination and alternative pricing strategies, such as market skimming versus market penetration, apply equally to services. You will recall that the perishability of services means that the careful matching of demand and supply is crucial. Because of this, we should expect to find that a much more flexible approach to pricing and margins is appropriate for services. Differential pricing with different prices for different market segments is widely used in the pricing of services to try to ensure a matching of demand and supply.

We should also note that the intangible nature of service products also tends to heighten the use by customers of price as an indicator of quality.

CLUES TO EFFECTIVE PRICING STRATEGIES

It is interesting to observe that many companies fail to price effectively, even when they employ effective marketing strategies. A reason is that they do not apply to their pricing decisions the same fundamental principles of marketing that they apply to other marketing decisions. Success in marketing comes from understanding how customers evaluate marketing decisions, since the customer's response to those decisions will ultimately determine their success or failure.

Shrewd managers reason that by creating exceptional value through careful attention to customers, they can reduce the importance of price in the buying decision. They also acknowledge that price is of primary importance to their companies and conclude that it is appropriate to evaluate product, promotion and distribution strategies from a customer perspective while evaluating pricing from the company's perspective. However, there is a tendency to forget about the customer when pricing, focusing instead on the company's need to cover costs, to maintain cash flow, or to achieve a target rate of return. Clearly, this is a strategic mistake and goes a long way towards explaining why many pricing decisions are ineffective from a strategic marketing point of view.

The customer's goal is to obtain the most value for their money. For commodities, that often means buying the cheapest offering. For differentiated products, that often means paying a little more for the perceived superiority of a particular brand. Whether the product is common or unique, customers will base their decisions on the value of the transaction to themselves rather than to the selling firm. A few pence difference in price may be of great importance to a firm selling millions of units, while being of little consequence to a customer who buys just one, yet that will not stop potential customers from rejecting any price that is a few pence more than they are willing to pay. Customers are not concerned with the seller's need to cover production costs, to improve cash flow or to meet a target rate of return. Their concern is to get value for money.

An effective pricing strategy cannot be achieved unless it is co-ordinated with other elements of marketing strategy. The crucial relationship between pricing and other aspects of marketing is particularly important with new products.

Pricing depends as much on good judgement as on precise calculation, but since it relies on reasoning, there is no justification for pricing decisions based on intuition. Good judgement requires understanding. One must comprehend the factors that make some pricing strategies succeed and others fail. The manager must understand how costs, price sensitivity and competition determine a product's pricing environment. In some companies when the time arrives to make a pricing decision, managers simply meet at specified times and make a decision. They do not study the firm's costs to find out how they will change with changes in sales. They do not talk first to potential buyers to learn what role price will play in their purchase decisions, and they do not analyse past behaviour and likely actions of competitors. Consequently, the pricing process becomes internally oriented and ignores key information necessary to setting effective prices. All too often price is considered and implemented as an essentially tactical decision. There are times when price can, and indeed has to be, used tactically, particularly when reacting to competitors' price changes. Even then, the marketer must know when to follow competitor price changes and when to ignore them, so tactical pricing decisions need careful consideration before they are implemented.

DEVELOPMENTS AND FURTHER ISSUES IN PRICING CONCEPTS AND PRACTICE

It is tempting to think that pricing is one of the less dynamic areas of the marketing mix. One might think, pricing is either cost-based, demand-based or competitor-based and considerations in pricing decisions are in many ways just the same as they were decades ago. In fact pricing is just as dynamic as any of the other elements of the marketing mix.

Below is a brief summary of some the more important developments affecting pricing:

The Internet and pricing

As with all areas of the marketing mix the Internet is affecting how marketers approach pricing. One facet of this is the increased ability of customers to compare and contrast prices. The Internet moves us close to the notion of 'perfect information' on prices central to the economist's notion of perfect competition. Markets may still not be perfectly competitive with respect to price, but it is much more difficult now for the marketer to avoid extensive price comparisons. As we saw earlier in the chapter, the Internet through direct distribution allows the brand marketer to potentially regain some control over pricing decisions. Yan[15] shows that for the marketer who sells through a mixture of online and traditional retail channels there can be real issues of integration and control in price setting.

Increased legislation and regulation

In many countries marketing's power to set and control prices to consumers has been substantially reduced. We have already discussed this in the context of the growing power of the retailer to set prices. In addition, in many markets there is substantial legislation and regulations relating to price setting. For example, in many countries the price of pharmaceutical products is regulated and controlled. Similarly, through 'quangos' and consumer protection bodies, prices of many essential products and services such as gas, electricity, water and public transport are controlled. Finally, and overarching all this, is increased regulation pertaining to pricing in and between trading blocks such as the EC. For example, changes in legislation and the atmosphere concerning competition have meant that European car distributors and franchisees now have almost limitless freedom over the prices charged for cars they sell on behalf of the major car companies.

The Single European Currency

Staying with developments in the EU, one of the most significant developments affecting marketing pricing strategies in Europe is the single Euro currency. At the moment only Denmark and the UK have opted out, and some newer European Union countries will join when they fulfil the right conditions to join the single currency. There are arguments both for and against joining, but undoubtedly the single currency is a major factor in setting prices.

Price comparisons and negotiating

Modern consumers are more motivated and sophisticated in their desire to compare and contrast prices to obtain best value for money and shop around to get the best deal. Bargaining and negotiation is now commonplace in the UK even at the retail level. Moreover, as we have noted, developments in communication and IT are facilitating the ease with which customers can compare and contrast prices all made possible through the Internet.

Methods of payment

Finally in our brief overview of developments in pricing, marketers have increased their efforts looking for new ways to make it easier for customers to buy and make payment. Recent years have witnessed a plethora of financing and payment schemes for purchasing expensive consumer durables. Cars, jewellery, holidays and homes can be purchased using a myriad of payment methods like leasing, leasing and buyback schemes, tracker mortgages and timeshare all of which all examples of strategies designed to make it less 'painful' for customers when it comes to paying. These help to justify the contention that pricing is perhaps one of the most dynamic elements of the marketing mix.

SUMMARY

Pricing decisions are more than just a 'mechanical' exercise of adding margins for profit to costs. Price setting must become an integral part of the marketing strategy of the company and must be consistent with corporate and marketing objectives and other elements of the mix. In addition to these inputs to pricing decisions, the marketer must also consider demand, cost and competitors.

Although cost-based and competitor-based pricing methods can be used, they suffer from major weaknesses. The most useful approach is a marketing-oriented one that does not neglect costs and competitors, but is one that is essentially based on customers and their perceptions of value.

A whole set of complex factors affect pricing decisions, making this in fact one of the most complex and difficult areas of strategic market planning. If anything, this complexity is compounded by the dynamic nature of pricing with so many developments affecting the pricing process.

KEY TERMS

CASE STUDY

ACME Engineering

Pamela Spencelayh has been the accountant at ACME Engineering for over 20 years. During that time one of her responsibilities has been to help set prices for new products launched by the company. In her view this has never posed problems.

As an experienced cost and management accountant, Spencelayh has taken the approach of estimating the average cost of producing any new product and then simply adding on a pre-determined mark-up for profit set by the managing director in line with required rates of return. In her and the company's view, this pricing method has worked well and has a number of advantages. She feels it is the simplest method and it 'ensures' that costs are covered and a profit is made. Finally, she sees it as a 'fair' method of pricing which can be justified both to customers and the outside world.

Over this 20-year period not all new products launched by the company have been successful. Of the unsuccessful ones, no one has ever blamed price as being a reason for failure. The view has been taken that price could not be wrong if it was based on a factual assessment of average cost with a fair margin for profit added.

. . . continued

CASE STUDY ... *continued*

Spencelayh has never had to think or consider the effect of price on product success and failure, and has left these considerations to the design team and the marketers who are, after all, collectively responsible for new products.

Things have now changed. As a result of appointing a new marketing manager who has had a new innovative product developed quickly, Spencelayh found her position as regards pricing decisions challenged. The new marketing manager has simply asked Spencelayh for some cost estimates. When she asked how these were going to be used and proposed a price for the new product based on these estimates, she was told that the new product would be priced using a customer-value based method. Spencelayh had never heard of this.

It was explained that for the new product it was necessary to establish the economic value of the product to the customer (EVC) and that Spencelayh was expected to help in the costing side of this exercise. She was now extremely worried. Not only did she wonder why it was not sufficient to use cost-plus, but she had no idea what establishing the economic value of the product to a customer meant and what information and analysis would be required to establish the EVC.

CASE STUDY QUESTIONS

1   What arguments can be used in this context to justify a customer-value based pricing method as opposed to the simpler cost-plus method?
2   What information and analyses will be required by Spencelayh to assess the EVC of the new product, and what problems might there be in using this approach to pricing?

REFERENCES

1 Oxenfeldt, A.R. (1973), 'A decision making structure for price decisions', *Journal of Marketing*, 37, January: 50.

2 Kehagias, J., Skourtis, E. and Vassilikopoulou, A. (2009), 'Plaiting pricing into product categories and corporate objectives', *Journal of Product & Brand Management*, 18(1): 67–76.

3 Indounas, K. and Avlonitis, G.J. (2009), 'Pricing objectives and their antecedents in the services sector', *Journal of Service Management*, 20(3): 342–74.

4 Hutt, M.D. and Speh, T.W. (2009), *Business Marketing Management: B2B*, 10th edn, Cincinnati, OH: South Western Educational Publishing.

5 Porter, M.E. (1985), *Competitive Advantage: Creating and Sustaining Superior Performance*, New York: Free Press, p. 32.

6 Lancaster, G. and Massingham, L.C. (2002), *Essentials of Marketing*, 4th edn, Maidenhead: McGraw-Hill, p. 230.

7 Palmer, A. and McMahon-Beattie, U. (2008), 'Variable pricing through revenue management: critical evaluation of affective outcomes', *Management Research News*, 31(3): 189–99.

8 Hinterhuber, A. (2009), 'Customer value-based pricing strategies: why companies resist', *Journal of Business Strategy*, 29(4): 41–50.

9 Ingenbleek, P. (2009), 'Value-informed pricing in its organizational context', *Journal of Revenue and Pricing Management*, 8: 396–8.

10 Kotler, P. and Keller, K.L. (2009), *Marketing Management*, 13th edn, London: Pearson Education, pp. 341–53.

11 von Clausewitz, C. (1997), *On War*, London: Wordsworth Editions Ltd.

12 Liddell-Hart, B.H. (1991), *Strategy*, New York: Praeger.

13 Kolar, T. and Toporisic, A. (2007), 'Marketing as warfare, revisited', *Marketing Intelligence and Planning*, 25(3): 203–16.

14 Lancaster, G. and Withey, F. (2007), *Marketing Fundamentals*, Oxford: Elsevier Butterworth-Heinemann.

15 Yan, R. (2008), 'Pricing strategy for companies with mixed online and traditional retailing distribution markets', *Journal of Product and Brand Management*, 17(1): 48–56.

Chapter 6

Channels of distribution and logistics

LEARNING OBJECTIVES

By the end of this chapter you will:

- comprehend key elements and decisions in distribution channel design
- be able to evaluate different configurations of channel structure
- be familiar with recent trends and developments in channels of distribution
- appreciate the importance of managing the physical flows of products, services and information into, through, and out of the organization to its customers
- grasp the meaning and scope of physical distribution and logistics management
- be aware of developments and trends in production and manufacturing, particularly the growth of 'lean manufacturing' and implications for logistics
- recognize the role of Information Technology and marketing in logistics

INTRODUCTION

This chapter deals with the 'place' element of marketing strategy (i.e. 'placement' of goods and services from their respective providers into the hands of customers). Before we discuss the structure of marketing channels, followed by logistics, it is useful that we look at their emergence and the functions that channels perform.

THE CONSUMER WANTS CYCLE

The word 'channel' has its origins in the word for canal, which for marketing can be interpreted as a route taken by products as they flow from production to points of intermediate and final use. Marketing is a key factor in a continuous cycle that begins and ends with consumer wants. It is the role of the marketer to interpret consumer wants and combine them with empirical market data such as location of consumers, their numbers and preferences, to establish the starting point for manufacture. On completion of manufacture, the finished product is moved to the consumer and the cycle is complete when he or she obtains satisfaction resulting from product ownership.

THE PRODUCER–USER GAP

Despite the growth of direct marketing (to be discussed in Chapter 10) in today's complex economy, most producers still do not sell directly to final users. Between them and consumers lie marketing intermediaries. A distribution channel bridges the gap between user and producer, and so plays an integral role in the operation of the marketing concept.

Relationships among channel members are influenced by the structure of the channel. Marketing channels can be described as sets of interdependent organizations involved in the process of making a product or service available for use or consumption.

DEMAND STIMULUS

In addition to marketing channels satisfying demand by supplying goods and services in the right location, at the correct quantity and price, they should stimulate demand through promotional activities of retailers, manufacturers and wholesalers. In this way, a marketing channel should be viewed not just as a demand satisfier, but as an orchestrated network that creates value for consumers through the generation of form, possession, time and place utilities.

We start by examining ways in which distribution systems are designed and how channel policy is determined, depending on the degree of market exposure sought by a company.

DISTRIBUTION SYSTEM DESIGN

The starting point for marketing channel design is the end consumer. Although an understanding of consumer purchasing patterns is essential, there are other factors that influence channel organization:

■ There may be a restriction in choice of outlets available to suppliers, e.g. retail outlets may already have been secured by established manufacturers.

■ Channel design will be influenced by the number, size and geographic concentration of consumers. If customers are few in number, but large and geographically concentrated, it may be that direct channels will be suitable. If customers are dispersed, the mechanics of direct channels become increasingly difficult and there will be a need for a large number of intermediaries.

■ Product characteristics affect channel design. Industrial goods manufacturers tend to use direct channels, but there are other factors that influence the decision. Perishable goods, for example, need to be turned over quickly so direct methods are often applied. Non-perishable, non-bulky goods can be handled via indirect channels.

■ Some products are more suited to indirect channels because of environmental characteristics. For example, in some countries shopping is seen very much as being a leisure activity especially for items like clothing and furniture, so much so that companies such as the Swedish company IKEA have made this a central part of their business model.

■ Some organizations have limited discretion over marketing channel choice owing to economic conditions and legal restrictions. In certain of the Eastern European and Baltic countries such as Estonia, Latvia and Uzbekistan there is still restricted choice in terms of the range and scope of retail outlets for marketers.

Any channel decision will have long-term implications for the company, e.g. price will be affected depending on the number of levels between the manufacturer and the end user. A decision to change channels is likely be long term so it is important that existing channel structures are constantly reviewed to exploit opportunities.

STRATEGIC CHANNEL CHOICES

An important consideration when formulating channel policy is the degree of market exposure sought by the company. Choices available include:

- **Intensive distribution** where products are placed in as many outlets as possible. This is most common when customers purchase goods frequently, e.g. household goods such as detergents or toothpaste. Wide exposure gives customers many opportunities to buy and the image of the outlet is not important. The aim is to achieve maximum coverage.
- **Selective distribution** where products are placed in a more limited number of outlets in defined geographic areas. Instead of widespread exposure, selective distribution seeks to show products in the most promising or profitable outlets, e.g. high-end 'designer' clothes.
- **Exclusive distribution** where products are placed in one outlet in a specific area. This brings about a stronger partnership between seller and re-seller and results in strong bonds of loyalty. Part of the agreement usually requires the dealer not to carry competing lines, and the result is a more aggressive selling effort by the distributor of the company's products, e.g. an exclusive franchise to sell a vehicle brand in a specific geographical area, in return for which the franchisee agrees to supply an appropriate after sales service back-up.

We can see that there are several key decisions to make when determining the company's distribution system. Its importance is underlined by the fact that the choice of distribution channel has an effect on all elements of the marketing mix and these are long term.

TYPES AND CLASSIFICATION OF CHANNELS

Marketing channels can be characterized according to the number of channel levels. Each institution that works to bring the product to the point of consumption is included. The number of intermediaries involved in channel operation determines on how many levels it operates. There are four main types of channel level in consumer markets as shown in Figure 6.1. The first three levels (zero, one and two) are self explanatory. The three level channel includes a 'jobber', or merchant

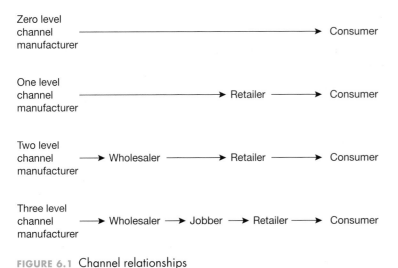

FIGURE 6.1 Channel relationships

wholesaler who intervenes between the wholesaler and retailer. It is the jobber's role to buy from wholesalers and sell to smaller retailers, who are not usually serviced by larger wholesalers.

Within each channel, intermediaries are connected by three types of flow:

1   **Physical flow** describes movement of goods from raw material that is processed in various stages of manufacture until it reaches the final consumer. In the case of a towel manufacturer raw material is cotton yarn which flows from the grower via transporters to the manufacturer's warehouses and plants.

2   **Title flow** is the passage of ownership from one channel institution to another; when manufacturing towels, title to raw materials passes from the supplier to the manufacturer. Ownership of finished towels passes from manufacturer to the wholesaler or retailer and then to the final consumer.

3   **Information flow** involves the directed flow of influence from activities such as advertising, personal selling, sales promotion and publicity from one member to other members in the system. Manufacturers of towels direct promotion, and information flows to retailers or wholesalers, known as trade promotion. This type of activity may also be directed to end consumers, i.e. 'end user' promotion.

Conventional marketing channels comprise autonomous business units, each performing a defined set of marketing functions. Co-ordination among channel members is through the bargaining process. Membership of the channel is relatively easy, loyalty is low and this type of network tends to be unstable. Members rarely co-operate with each member working independently of others. Decision makers are more concerned with cost and investment relationships at a single stage of the marketing process and tend to be committed to established working practices. Most food grocery products in the European Union are marketed through conventional marketing channels; independent food and grocery producers are responsible for growing, rearing and manufacturing products and brands. These are sold through a series of wholesalers and retailers such as Sainsbury's, Aldi, Lidl, Tesco or Carrefour each operating as independent businesses in the chain and selling to their own customers.

Vertical marketing systems are in contrast to conventional channels where members co-ordinate activities between different levels of the channel to reach a desired target market. The essential feature is that participants acknowledge and desire interdependence, and view it as being in their best long-term interests. For the channel to function as a vertical marketing system, one of the member firms must be acknowledged as the leader; typically the dominant firm, which can be expected to take a significant risk position and usually has the greatest relative power within the channel. An example of a vertical marketing system is that of franchising. The franchiser, usually on the basis of having a powerful brand or perhaps a patent/copyright, for a fee, allows franchisees to produce or distribute the product or service. The franchiser effectively controls the channel, including aspects such as product ingredients, advertising and marketing, pricing, etc. through formal and legally enforceable agreements. Franchising is an example of what are termed contractual vertical marketing systems which we consider again shortly.

Corporate vertical marketing is when a company owns two or more traditional levels of the channel. In many economies corporate vertical channels have arisen as a result of a desire for growth on the part of companies through vertical integration. Two types of vertical integration are possible with respect to the direction within which the vertical integration moves a company in the supply chain: when a manufacturer buys, say, a retail chain, this is referred to as forward integration with respect to the chain. Backward integration is moving upstream in the supply chain, e.g. when a retailer invests in manufacturing or a manufacturer invests in a raw material source. Although the end result of such movements is a corporate vertical marketing channel, often the stimulus to such movement is less to do with channel economies and efficiencies, and more with control over access to supply or demand, entry into a profitable business or overall scale and operating economies. Much vertical integration activity which took place during the 1990s in many economies resulted in lower overall profitability levels, and in some cases, the demise of companies involved, as companies overextended themselves and/or moved into areas where they had little expertise. Because of this, many companies have now turned their attention towards contractual systems for achieving growth and more control through the vertical marketing system. Many of the large oil companies are examples of corporate vertical marketing. They prospect for oil, extract it, process it, distribute and retail it through their petrol stations. Other companies operate partial corporate vertical marketing systems in that they integrate only one way. Zara (the clothing retailer) is integrated vertically backward with manufacturing facilities. Firestone (the tyre manufacturer) on the other hand, is vertically integrated forward owning its own tyre retailers.

Many companies formalize their obligations within channel networks by employing legitimate power as a means of control achieved by using contractual agreements. Nearly all transactions between businesses are covered by some form of contract, and as such the contractual agreement determines the marketing roles of each party within the contract. Indeed, the locus of authority usually lies with individual members. The most common form of contractual agreement are *franchises* and *voluntary* and *co-operative groups*.

Franchises are where the parent company grants an individual person or relatively small company the right or privilege to do business in a prescribed manner over a certain time period in a specified place. The parent company is referred to as the franchiser (or franchisor) and may occupy any position in the channel network. The franchise retailer is termed the franchisee. There are four basic types of franchise system:

- Manufacturer/retailer franchise, e.g. service stations where most of the garage petrol stations such as Shell and Esso are franchisees of the large oil exploration and refining companies.
- Manufacturer/wholesaler franchise: e.g. Coca-Cola sell drinks they manufacture to franchised wholesalers, who in turn bottle and distribute soft drinks to retailers. This type of arrangement is common in the food and drinks markets with many of the large companies franchising part of their manufacturing and or wholesaling activities to others.
- The wholesaler/retailer franchise. Many retail chains are franchisees of large wholesalers. These wholesalers saw the value of securing a measure of control, and of course a share of the retail profits, from marketing their products and brands. The most notable example is 'Spar' which advertises itself as 'Spar, your 8.00 till late shop', and of course all retail members must abide by this promise.
- The service/sponsor retailer franchise e.g. McDonald's, Kentucky Fried Chicken, Subway, Car Rental companies like Avis and Hertz and services like DynoRod and Prontaprint. This is the best known and certainly most ubiquitous of franchising arrangements and it has enabled many organizations to rapidly expand their global operations.

There are different types of franchise arrangement, e.g. McDonald's insists that franchisees purchase from official suppliers; they provide building and design specifications, help locate finance for franchisees and impose quality standards to which each unit must adhere in order to hold its franchise. Rigorous inspection through 'secret shoppers' (explained in Chapter 12) ensures franchise 'rules' are being obeyed.

Franchises share a set of common features and operating procedures:

1   A franchise essentially sells a nationally, or internationally, recognized trade name, process, or business format to the franchisee.
2   The franchiser normally offers expert advice e.g. location selection, capitalization, operation and marketing.
3   Most franchises operate a central purchasing system at national or international level to enable cost savings to be made at the individual franchise level.
4   The franchise is subject to a contract binding both parties that normally requires the franchisee to pay a franchise fee and royalty fees to the franchiser, but the franchisee owns the business as opposed to being employed.
5   The franchiser often provides initial and continuous training to the franchisee.

Contractual vertical marketing systems like franchising have been one of the fastest growing areas of marketing and distribution. Substantial advantages derive from the franchising system. From a system that essentially involves two independent parties voluntarily agreeing to contract with each other, advantages accrue to both the franchisee and franchiser. Advantages to the franchisee are:

- The franchisee gains the benefit of being able to sell a well-known product or service which has been market tested and known to work.
- The franchisee enjoys access to the knowledge, experience, reputation and image of the franchiser. Because of this the franchisee is able to enter a business much more easily than setting up from scratch. The learning curve is shortened, expensive mistakes can be avoided, and there is less chance of business failure.
- Although the franchisee has the backing of what is often the large organization of the franchiser, the franchisee is still essentially an independent business with all that this implies for motivation to succeed.
- The franchisee is often helped by national or international advertising and promotion by the franchiser which would be beyond the means of a small independent business.
- The franchisee enjoys the use of the franchiser's trademark, continuous research and development and market information.
- The franchiser will normally provide a system of management controls such as accountancy, sales and stock control procedures.

Advantages to the franchiser are:

- Finding and recruiting a network of franchisees enables rapid growth as wider distribution can be achieved with less capital.

- The individual franchisee is more motivated than a hired manager might be.
- The franchiser secures captive outlets for products or services, especially in the case of trade name franchising and private labels.
- Franchise and royalty fees provide a regular stream of income for the franchiser.
- The terms of the franchise contract normally give the franchiser substantial control over how the franchise is operated and normally the franchiser can terminate a contract should the relationship turn out to be unsatisfactory. The costs of such terminations are likely to be less than if the franchiser was operating a corporate owned facility with staff on the payroll. Normally, terms and restrictions on location and sale of the business by the franchisee ensure that the franchiser is able to maintain territorial exclusivity for its franchisees.

There are disadvantages, but the franchise relationship combines the strengths of both small and large scale businesses. The franchisee is the small business person who is able to respond to local market conditions and offer personal services to customers. The franchiser passes on economies of scale in national advertising and bulk purchasing. For a franchise to be successful both parties need to work towards a common goal and avoid conflicts which requires frequent and open communication between partners if the system is to meet changing market conditions while maintaining its integrity.

What constitutes the main disadvantages of franchising depends from whose perspective we are looking; the franchisee or the franchiser. The main disadvantages of franchising from each perspective are:

Disadvantages to franchiser:
- The franchiser loses some control over the provision and marketing of the brand. Poor service on the part of the franchisee can result in problems for brand image.
- Ideas and techniques can be copied even if seemingly well protected by patents and copyright arrangements.
- Some proportion of profit has to be foregone.
- There may be less commitment and enthusiasm from the franchisee.
- Often franchisees lack business skills or experience.

Disadvantages to the franchisee:
- lack of support from franchiser;
- franchiser may go out of business;
- lack of flexibility/scope to use initiative;
- close control from franchiser.

Franchising is not solely confined to consumer products like fast food. It is used for a wide range of products and services in both consumer and industrial markets.

Voluntary and **co-operative groups** emerged in the 1930s as a response to competition from chain stores. The scope of co-operative effort has expanded from concentrated buying power to the development of programmes involving centralized consumer advertising and promotion, store location and layout, financing, accounting and a package of support services.

Generally, wholesale sponsored voluntary groups have been more effective competitors than retail sponsored co-operative groups. Primarily this is because of the difference in channel organization between the two. In the former, a wholesaler can provide strong leadership, because it represents the locus of power within the voluntary system and this is normally supported by a brand name like 'Spar'. In the latter, power is diffused throughout the retail membership and role specification and allocation of resources are more difficult to accomplish. The principal purpose here is in bulk purchasing. In voluntary groups, retail members have relinquished some of their autonomy by making themselves highly dependent on specific wholesalers for expertise. In retail co-operative chains, individuals retain more autonomy and this tends to depend much less strongly on the supply unit for assistance and direction.

This type of organization is not to be confused with the Co-operative movement that was founded in 1844 by the Rochdale, Lancashire, Society of Equitable Pioneers who were a group of 28 weavers and other workers. As mechanization of the Industrial Revolution pushed more and more skilled workers into poverty, tradesmen banded together to open their own store selling items they could not otherwise afford. Over four months they pooled together £28 of capital. They opened their store with a basic selection of dry goods and foodstuffs and quickly moved into higher quality unadulterated produce. They devised the internationally famous *Rochdale Principles*:

1   open membership;
2   democratic control (one person, one vote);
3   distribution of *surplus* in proportion to *trade*;
4   payment of limited interest on *capital*;
5   political and religious neutrality;
6   cash trading (no credit);
7   promotion of education.

Administered vertical marketing systems (VMS) do not have the formal arrangements of a contractual system or the clarity of power dependence of a corporate system. It is a co-ordinated system of distribution channel organization in which the flow of products from the producer to the end user is controlled by the power and size of one member of the channel system rather than by common ownership or contractual ties. Member organizations acknowledge the existence of dependence and adhere to the leadership of the dominant firm, which may operate at any level in the channel. Large retail organizations like Marks & Spencer typify this system.

In administered systems like Marks & Spencer, units can exist with disparate goals, but there is informal collaboration on inclusive goals. Decision making occurs by virtue of interaction between channel members in the absence of a formal inclusive structure. However, the locus of authority still remains with individual channel members. As in conventional channels commitment is self-oriented and there is a minimum amount of system-wide orientation among the members. As McCammon[1] observes:

> Manufacturing organizations ... have historically relied on administrative expertise to coordinate reseller marketing efforts. Suppliers with dominant brands have predictably experienced the least difficulty in securing strong trade support, but many manufacturers with

'fringe' items have been able to elicit reseller co-operation through the use of liberal distribution policies that take the form of attractive discounts, financial assistance, and various types of concessions that protect resellers from one or more of the risks of doing business.

An example of a successful administered VMS in is that of the furniture/lifestyle retailer, IKEA who has developed close working relationships with its suppliers. Acting as the channel co-ordinator, IKEA is committed to cost-effective supply and their suppliers benefit from the channel leadership of an effective and marketing-oriented retailer.

Administered VMS are one step removed from conventional marketing channels. In an administered system, co-ordination of marketing activities is achieved by the use of programmes developed by one or a limited number of firms. Successful administered systems are conventional channels in which the principles of effective inter-organizational management have been correctly applied. Before we discuss how such marketing channels are co-ordinated, it is important that we discuss their structure.

STRUCTURE OF MARKETING CHANNELS

The marketing channel has two basic aspects:

1   the placement of intermediary types of channel in relation to each other i.e. the order in which they occur;
2   the number of different intermediary levels or stages in the channel i.e. how many different separate types of intermediary are involved, so types of intermediary and number of levels determine the structure of a marketing channel.

There are several types of channel structure, dependent on the type of goods. An example of a structure for consumer goods such as food and clothing is shown in Figure 6.2. This figure is based on three assumptions:

1   The channel consists of complete organizations.
2   Manufacturers' agents and selling agents are included with the merchants even though they do not take title to the goods.
3   Physical movement follows exactly the movement of ownership.

We must understand the underlying reasons for the emergence of channel structures. Four logical steps can be identified:

1   The efficiency of the process can be increased via an intermediary.
2   Channel intermediaries arise to adjust the discrepancy of assortments through the performance of the sorting processes.
3   Marketing agencies remain together in channel arrangements to provide the routine of transactions.
4   Channels exist to facilitate deliveries and to avoid inventory stock-outs.

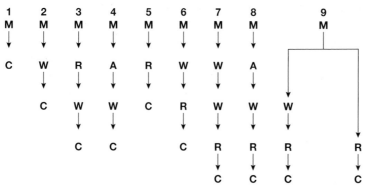

M = Manufacturer
W = Wholesaler
A = Agent (sells for manufacturers)
R = Retailer
C = Consumer

FIGURE 6.2 A typical example of structure for consumer goods

Rationale for intermediaries

As numbers of transactions increase, the need for intermediaries becomes greater. The marketing channel is a 'canal' which contains the physical flow of products. Because of the complex array of intermediaries operating within a channel, which may be involved in one or all aspects of channel function, the channel may also be visualized as a chain-link arrangement where each intermediary unit is effectively a link. Manufacturers are dependent on the effectiveness of their intermediaries if their channels of distribution are to meet their marketing goals.

Intermediaries of a channel specialize in more than one function. Their inclusion primarily depends on their superior efficiency in the performance of basic marketing tasks. Such intermediaries, through their experience, specialization, contacts and scale of operation, offer other channel members more than they can achieve on their own. However, this type of specialization leads to some important behavioural concepts.

Position and role

Each channel member chooses a position or location in the channel. 'Role' refers to the functions and degree of performance expected of the firm filling a position. Channel intermediaries perform the distribution function at a lower unit cost than the manufacturer who is the intermediary most distanced from the consumer, and they balance the production efficiencies of the supplier to the purchasing needs of the customer.

Another reason is to break down large volumes into smaller quantities, termed 'breaking bulk', e.g. a furniture retailer places an order for 100 tables, but the individual buys only one. When we consider the selling process, the number of intermediaries can reduce the number of transactions contained within the selling process. See Figure 6.3. Figure 6.3 shows that there are four manufacturers and ten retailers who buy goods from each manufacturer. Here the number of contact lines amounts to 40 (i.e. 4 × 10). If all four manufacturers sell to 10 retailers through one intermediary, the number of contacts is reduced to 14 (i.e. 4 + 10). The number of contacts increases as the number of intermediaries increases, e.g. when the number of wholesalers is increased to 2, contacts will increase from 14 to 28 (i.e. [4 × 2] + [10 × 2]). Thus, greater numbers of intermediaries result in diminishing returns per contact.

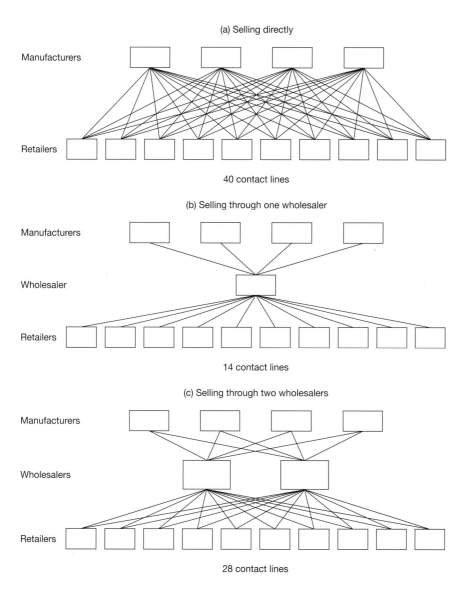

FIGURE 6.3 The economics of intermediary systems

Assortment and sorting

In addition to increasing the efficiency of transactions, intermediaries smooth the flow of goods and services by creating what economists refer to as 'possession', 'place' and 'time' utilities. This smoothing requires that intermediaries perform a sorting function to overcome the discrepancy that arises between goods produced by manufacturers and goods demanded by the consumer.

In addition, intermediaries bring together a range of similar or related items into a large stock, thus facilitating the buying process. A supermarket will buy in thousands of lines to provide shoppers with choice, and a builders' merchant will provide everything from sand and gravel to light fittings that the builder can use. In this way, intermediaries play an important role in facilitating the flow of products from the manufacturer to the consumer.

Routine transactions

The cost of distribution can be minimized if transactions are routinized. In effect, through routinization, a sequence of marketing agencies is able to hang together in a channel arrangement or structure. A good example is automatic ordering, whereby the cost of placing orders is reduced when retail inventory levels reach the necessary re-order point.

Searching

Buyers and sellers are often engaged in similar activities within the marketplace. There is a degree of uncertainty if manufacturers are unsure of customer wants and needs, and consumers are not always sure what they will find. In this respect, marketing channels facilitate the searching process in two ways:

1 Wholesale and retail institutions are organized by different product groups; for example, fashion, hardware, grocery.
2 Many products are widely available from wide ranging locations.

FLOWS IN MARKETING CHANNELS

When we discuss marketing flows, there will be times when the word 'function' could be used, but here we refer to marketing 'flows' in channels as a better method of describing movement. In this way, we can show that various intermediaries that make up a marketing channel are connected by several distinguishable types of flow, summarized in Figure 6.4, which depicts eight universal flows. The figure shows that physical possession, ownership and promotion are typically forward flows from producer to consumer. Each of these moves is 'down' the channel; a manufacturer promotes the product to a wholesaler, who in turn promotes it to a retailer, and so on. Negotiation, financing and risking flows move in both directions, whereas ordering and payment are backward flows. Financing is the most important of these flows; at any one time, when stocks are being held by one member of the channel, financing is in operation. When a wholesaler takes ownership and physical

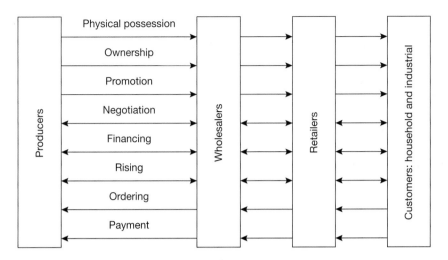

FIGURE 6.4 Marketing flows in channels

Woolly Thinking

Under the auspices of the Confederation of British Wool Textiles (CBWT), groups of British wool textile manufacturers exchange information and ideas. The Confederation is organized into distinct groups in the industry with each group representing a particular stage in the manufacturing and processing of wool. For example, there is a group representing 'Raw Fibre Producers', another representing 'Spinners', another representing 'Fabric Manufacturers' and one representing the interests of 'Dyers and Finishers'.

possession of a portion of the output of a manufacturer, the wholesaler is essentially financing the manufacturer.

This notion is apparent if the costs of stock are considered. Stock held in stores as dormant stock is 'dead money', but if this is freed via a wholesaler, this 'dead money' is available for reinvestment. The furniture industry exemplifies the flow. Traditional furniture retailers operating on a sold-order basis do not participate in the backward financing flow. However, 'warehouse type' furniture retailers participate in this flow directly, and receive benefits from manufacturers in the form of lower prices and preferential treatment. This backward flow of financing is not solely associated with stockholding, another example being prepayment for merchandise.

The problem is that in the event of any downturn in sales the warehouse type retailer with large sums of money tied up in stock is very vulnerable to cash flow and liquidity problems. To underline this, blaming the downturn in the UK housing market in July 2009, the UK's second largest carpet retailer, Allied Carpets, called in the receiver.

Forward flow of financing is more common. All terms of sale, with the exception of cash on delivery and prepayment, may be viewed as elements of the forward flow of financing. In addition to these flows there is information flow. Typically, information regarding product attributes is passed 'down' the channel, often with the dominant channel member having greater influence on this function. Marketing information is passed 'back' up the channels. In addition, information flows horizontally, i.e. with intermediaries operating at the same level, such as fibre manufacturers, communicating for mutual benefit.

CHANNEL CO-ORDINATION

However well designed a marketing channel may be it is important that it is organized and co-ordinated, otherwise activities and flows will not operate effectively, and the full potential of the system will not be realized. Emphasis should be placed on understanding behavioural dimensions of inter-organizational relationships, because through such understanding, the manager can organize, manipulate and exploit available resources.

The long-term objective of channel management is to achieve, at a reasonable cost, the greatest possible impact at the end user level, so that individual members of the channel can obtain satisfactory returns (e.g. profits, market share) as compensation for their specific contributions. The behaviour of intermediaries within any given structural arrangement should thus be directed towards achieving high yield performance.

Once the marketing management of an organization isolates the market targets to attack, and the products and services which it must supply in order to satisfy needs and wants in those various segments, the question of how best to make products and services available for consumption arises.

Figure 6.5 identifies four major steps that represent the co-ordination process. The first step is to determine the level of service outputs demanded by end users of the commercial channel system. Service outputs that are among the most significant in distribution are, for example, lot size. Some companies insist on a minimum order level. Under this limit they will not accept the order. In contrast, often smaller companies are unable or unwilling to supply orders over a certain size.

A second type of service output is delivery or waiting time, or how long it takes from order to delivery.

A third service output relates to market decentralization or spatial convenience, namely, to where the provider will deliver. For example, some suppliers will only deliver locally whereas at the other extreme some will undertake to deliver anywhere in the world.

Finally, there is breadth and depth of product or service assortment. This refers to whether or not the provider is able to supply a full range of products and services or only a selected range, i.e. a 'one -stop shopping' facility.

The second step involves identifying the marketing tasks that need to be carried out in order to achieve the service outputs, and which channel members have the capability to perform the tasks. Management must then determine whether, through the use of channel control strategies, they will be able to control the behaviour of existing channel members or be compelled to integrate channel flow vertically so the required service outputs are provided to end users.

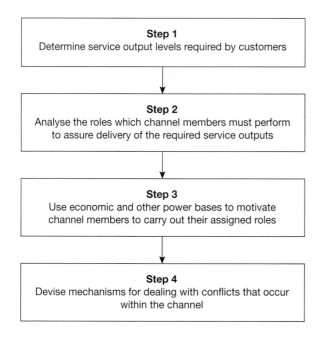

FIGURE 6.5 Stages in the channel co-ordination process

For example, if a desired level of service output is that orders must be fulfilled within five working days then the channel and logistics system must be designed to reach this service level. If intermediaries in the channel are unwilling or unable to meet this service output then alternative channel arrangements must be found. Without effective channel management and control there is no guarantee that the desired service outcomes will be achieved, so a major issue in channel management relates to where, and to what extent, marketing flow participation should be assumed to generate the desired service outputs; e.g. if a car buyer needs finance, the manufacturer, the retailer or an outside intermediary should provide it, but lending services must be readily available if the consumer is going to feel comfortable in considering a specific purchase that requires finance. In a situation where no channel intermediary is willing to accept the risk of financing, the initial supplier may have to assume this, i.e. it would prefer to specialize in those flows that it can perform at a comparative advantage.

The third step in the co-ordinative process is to determine which strategies should be used to achieve the desired results, irrespective of whether management decides to invest in integrating functions or whether it deals with independent companies. Essentially this is an issue of where and how 'power' is applied in the channel. Power is the ability to get somebody to do a task. In the context of a marketing channel it can be defined in terms of how one channel member can exert influence on another channel member. For example, due to their size and purchasing power, many retail multiples in the UK like Marks & Spencer are able to exercise substantial power over their suppliers. Power is the mechanism by which congruent and effective roles become specified, roles become realigned when necessary, and appropriate role performance is enforced. There are several bases of power, which include reward, coercion and expertise.

The fourth step involves setting up mechanisms to deal with conflict issues that may arise so that the channel will continue to provide the desired service outputs even if channel members disagree. Very often channel members perform unique roles. Thus, manufacturers specialize in production and national promotions, while retailers specialize in merchandising, distribution and promotion at a local level. This specialization means that channel members become reliant on each other to achieve objectives. There has to be co-operation between channel members, as without it, the task will not be completed. Such co-operation does not always come easy and needs to be cultivated.

CHANNEL CONFLICT

There is a danger that there will be conflicts of interest and distribution channels will exhibit levels of conflict. For example, suppliers may want to deliver weekly to a retailer, but the retailer wants to hold less stock, so may want daily deliveries. Ideally, channel members should attempt to co-ordinate their objectives, plans and activities with other intermediaries such that performance of the total distribution system to which they belong is enhanced. Evidence supports the view that such integrated activity throughout the length of the marketing channel is rare and channel participants are not too concerned with transactions that occur between each of the various channel links. Channel intermediaries are more concerned about dealings between channel members immediately adjacent to themselves, from whom they buy, and to whom they sell. Channel intermediaries do not function as component members of a distribution system, but operate independently, making decisions concerning their own methods of operation, functions performed and clients served as well as deciding their own objectives, policies and programmes. Therefore, a marketing channel should be a set of interlocking and mutually dependent elements and it is in the interests of all channel members for there to be a substantial degree of co-operation, but an almost inevitable feature is potential conflict between members which should be taken into account when making channel arrangements. It is possible that healthy competition can lead to conflict and management should seek ways to reduce this conflict. Conflict in distribution channels can occur in different forms as follows:

1   **Horizontal conflict** – is related to competition among similar types of intermediaries at the same level in the channel – e.g. two household textile stores in competition with each another.
2   **Intertype conflict** – refers to competition among different types of intermediaries at the same level in the channel. This kind of competition has intensified since the advent of 'scrambled merchandising' by retailers (where retailers add new product lines that are unrelated to their normal lines of business) e.g. supermarkets have added homewares and clothing to their product lines, offering consumers a wider product range and attaining higher margins. Intertype conflict is significant as it reflects a way in which industries remain efficient and respond to changing market conditions.
3   **Vertical conflict** – refers to competition among different levels in a channel. Such problems can be damaging to existing co-operative relationships e.g. in recent years some of the major car producers have been in conflict with their distributors over matters like pricing and discount policies, stockholding levels and exclusivity agreements.

Stress and conflict can be in a dormant state; times of change cause existing stress to peak, leading to hostility among channel members. Some conflict is inevitable in channels and may even be positive in that it can prompt needed changes. The earlier example regarding retailers selling manufacturers' brands at lower prices than manufacturers wish is an example of vertical conflict. Selling of brands like Levis and Calvin Klein at prices lower than those recommended by manufacturers has given rise to vertical conflict in the channel. Other examples of this type of conflict in the UK recently have been the selling of discounted books and discounted pharmaceutical products by the large retail supermarket groups.

Goal incompatibility

Channel members appear to share a common goal – maximizing the efficiency and effectiveness of the total system. However, each firm exists as a separate legal entity, each with its own employees, owners and other interested parties who help shape its goals and strategies. Some firms' goals may be incompatible with the aims and objectives of other channel members. This incompatibility can be a primary cause of stress which will ultimately result in conflict. The distribution of channel profits is a typical example. Each institution will desire the highest possible profit for the whole channel and the natural tendency will be towards co-operation to achieve maximum profit levels. However, each individual firm can be expected to desire the largest obtainable share of total channel profits. The predictable result is conflict over the allocation process.

Even if goals are compatible, there may be disagreements about methods employed: all channel members may agree that increases in volume of a product are desirable, but may disagree on the means employed to accomplish it. Wholesalers may desire more shelf space for better positioning of products in retail stores; retailers may feel that more advertising and promotional effort by the manufacturer would accomplish the objective of an increase in sales. The result is conflict over which method to use.

Position, role and domain incongruence

In a channel consisting of a manufacturer using only wholesalers who sell to retailers, there will be a realignment of the roles and domains of each party. By serving large retailers direct, positions will be re-specified. Changes in position specification, or poorly defined positions, can precipitate conflict among channel members, so the manufacturer must anticipate and understand the expected behaviour of such members. In situations where consensus does not exist, conflict can be expected.

Because each role represents a code of conduct defining the channel member's expected contribution, adequate performance is critical to maintaining harmony within the channel system. Inadequate performance, or failure to behave in the prescribed manner, frustrates attempts by one firm to predict what the other will do and such frustration is a major cause of channel conflict.

Conflict may also arise when there is lack of agreement concerning who is the channel leader (termed the '**channel captain**'). If channel members disagree on the domain of firms in the system, there will be conflict and an inability to achieve goals. If domains overlap, and two or more firms lay claim to the same functions, products or customers, disagreement might lead to hostility. The conflict between car producers and their distributors just described, in part stems from the issue of who controls the channel. In the past it has been the car companies who have been channel captains but market and legislative changes have shifted the balance more towards distributors, giving rise to conflict.

Communication breakdown

Communication breakdowns may cause conflict in two ways:

1   The failure of one firm to pass on vital information to other channel members. A manufacturer wishing to maintain a competitive advantage may decide not to announce a new product until a national distribution programme has been developed. Retailers, on the other hand, need information about new products as soon as possible to prepare their own strategy for the introductory period.
2   Distortion within the message process is called '**noise**' that often arises from confused language nuances. When channel members attach different meanings to language and terminology (e.g. if their roles are unclear and confused) stress results and there is potential for conflict. Speculation surrounding the health of Apple boss Steve Jobs caused problems for the company and its distributors. In January 2009 the annual MacWorld conference normally used to announce new products and developments was cancelled. This caused speculation in the trade about whether or not Jobs would continue. The problem was not so much Jobs' illness bur rather the rumours about it. In July 2009 it was announced that Jobs was making a good recovery from a liver transplant.

Communication breakdowns are common in specialist business areas. Noise arises when functional specialists develop terminology that means little to those outside that business environment. Unclear communication with non-specialists can play a part in developing conflict so the specialist should ensure that communications have been understood.

Differing perceptions of reality

Different solutions to mutual problems can lead to confliction behaviour. Even when channel members have a strong desire to co-operate and goal agreement exists, conflict can occur when perceptions of the real facts differ.

Bare Bellies Update

Dear all, further to my e-mail yesterday, I've had clarification that a new system for producing bare belly information will be in place. Please note there will no longer be blank bare belly sheets available in departments. Confused? So was this organization's staff who received this e-mail.

   The e-mail was from the organization's publicity department and was sent to all staff. 'Bare bellies' is a term used by printers to denote blank sheets to be printed on. The e-mail related to the production of company promotional material.

Each channel member brings to the relationship different backgrounds and prejudices; facts are likely to be interpreted according to prior experience. All members may agree that the channel is not functioning as effectively as desired; each channel member may perceive a different reason for this lack of effectiveness. Manufacturers may feel that a retailer's lack of stock is due to failure to maintain adequate safety stock levels and realistic reorder points. The retailer may feel that inventory policies are realistic and that the problem is caused by the manufacturer's inability to meet scheduled delivery times. Each party is interpreting the situation based upon experience and natural prejudices associated with its own position and role.

Ideological differences

Sometimes there may be a fundamental ideological conflict in channels which stems from big business and small business perceptions of management, particularly concerning the appropriate level of sales effort. For example, a manufacturer may be so satisfied with the performance of a wholesaler in a given territory that pressure is exerted on the wholesaler to expand the line of products on offer, whereas the wholesaler may be satisfied with allowing the business to continue to run in its present form.

In this way, pressures exerted by the manufacturer will lead to stress and conflict in the relationship. If this is an established channel, it is in the interests of everybody to settle the dispute or misunderstanding quickly.

There are several methods of resolving conflict, and it is a task of management to seek ways in which to manage it to avoid it becoming dysfunctional and to harness the energies in conflict situations to produce solutions. Depending on which underlying cause is identified, different strategies can be employed in isolation. Another important factor in the resolution of the conflict will be the weight of power of the channel member seeking to resolve the conflict.

Problem solving

Adopting **superordinate goals** is a method that refers to goals that are desired by all members caught up in the conflict. Often such goals cannot be achieved by individual channel members, as concerted efforts of all parties are required. Such disputes become more pronounced when the channel is confronted by an external threat, and conflict only dissipates when alternative channel systems emerge.

The threat to existing channel members of new channel arrangements for car retailing in the UK has brought about a reduction in conflict between traditional channel members. Car manufacturers and dealers were challenged by the fact that consumers were increasingly purchasing new cars through a variety of new channels including sourcing them from countries where prices might be lower, the growth of 'car hypermarkets' where cars are sourced on the 'grey market' and through the Internet. The result has been for existing traditional channel members to adopt superordinate goals and this has resulted in a reduction of conflict between them in an effort to survive.

Permanent conflict resolution requires an integration of the needs of both sides to the dispute so they find a common goal without sacrificing their basic economic and ethical principles. The problem is developing a common goal on which all parties agree.

A solution exists to alleviate **communications noise** in distribution channels. A more efficient flow of information and communications in channels permits members to find solutions to their conflict based on common objectives. Channel communication efforts should be designed to decrease or avoid conflict, e.g. using sales representatives to convey information from wholesalers or retailers implies that the manufacturer is trying to encourage the attainment of both individual and common goals; the function of the sales representative in such cases is that of 'problem solver'.

Persuasion

This implies that institutions involved draw on their leadership potential. If effective channel management is to be achieved, it is often the case that there will be a need to locate an institution or an agency within the system that is willing to assume this role. Channel leadership is the intentional use of power to affect the behaviour of other channel members and cause them to act in a manner that contributes to the maintenance or achievement of a desired level of performance. Often channel control results from channel leadership and like channel power, the level of control achieved by one firm over others in a channel may be issue specific, e.g. while the manufacturer may have control over pricing, retailers may have control over stock levels. Whether or not control can be exerted depends on the power base of each channel member.

By its nature, persuasion involves communication between conflicting parties. Emphasis is on influencing behaviour to resolve conflict; the primary intention is to avoid or reduce conflict concerned with domain or sphere of influence. Persuasion allows members to reach a consensus resulting in agreement without formal bargaining.

Some years ago a well-known company launched its own brand of cola. The new brand was eagerly stocked by many leading grocery supermarkets who were persuaded to make space for the new brand on their shelves. Inevitably this meant less shelf space for existing brands including some of the best known cola brands in the world. As if this loss of shelf space was not bad enough, the world's leading cola brand claimed bitterly that at first glace the new Virgin cola looked remarkably like their own cola brand. They subsequently asked Virgin to withdraw the new brand in its present form and at the same time asked their supermarket customers not to stock it. Needless to say, there were protracted discussions, but after a little time all parties were persuaded to come to a compromise which avoided costly litigation and loss of face. The new cola was altered slightly in appearance, some of the lost shelf space was restored and the new brand gradually made inroads into the market.

Bargaining/negotiations

The difference between bargaining and persuasion is that in the bargaining process stress continues to exist in the system long after agreement is reached. In negotiation, no attempt is made to fully satisfy a channel member. Instead, the objective is to reach an 'accommodation' to stop conflict among members. Such a compromise may resolve the episode, but not necessarily the fundamental stress over which the conflict erupted. If stress continues, it is likely that some issue will cause conflict again at some later date.

Compromise is a means by which bargains can be reached in the channel. Each party gives up something it desires to prevent or end conflict. Often compromise is necessary to reach domain consensus where persuasion and negotiation draw on abilities of parties involved to communicate.

Politics

Politics refers to resolution of conflict involving new organizations in the agreement-reaching process. Mediation involves a third party, usually to secure settlement of a dispute by persuading the parties to continue negotiation or consider recommendations made by the mediator. Mediation involves understanding the conflicting views of parties in such a way that opportunities are perceived that otherwise may have been missed. The fact that solutions are being offered by a mediator, i.e. somebody external to the dispute, can often lead to a settlement if both parties deem the solutions acceptable. Effective mediation keeps the parties together and clarifies facts so the communication process does not break down. While mediation offers solutions to disputes, channel members are not obliged to accept the solutions.

In arbitration, however, the solution suggested by the third party is binding upon the conflicting parties. Arbitration can be compulsory or voluntary, and when it is the former, parties are required by law to submit their dispute to the third party and be bound by the decision. Voluntary arbitration is a similar process whereby parties are bound by the decision, but the dispute is settled voluntarily.

The question of relying on law enforcement to settle disputes in distribution is imprecise as it is doubtful whether solutions enforced by law can be applicable to future channel disputes in different circumstances. In purely domestic channel management, these mechanisms are not greatly used because of the inability to find a neutral third party whose decision will be accepted by everybody involved in the dispute. However, arbitration is a normal and accepted part of international channel management and is part of the contractual agreement between the parties in channel activities. For example, if an exporter feels that an overseas agent has not fulfilled the terms of an agreement between him or herself and the principal, but the two parties cannot agree as to the remedies for this, then normally the terms and conditions for instituting an arbitration process are written into the original contract and will be instituted to resolve the problem.

Diplomacy

Channel diplomacy is the normal method by which inter-organizational relations are conducted, adjusted and managed by 'ambassadors', envoys or other persons operating at the boundaries of member organizations. Normally channel members rely on diplomatic procedures, especially in non-integrated systems. Channel diplomats should be the 'eyes and ears' of the firms they work for, and should report anything that may be of interest. Such 'diplomats' are commonplace in distribution channels at executive level. In this way, the diplomat's power base is such that it is obvious to the parties with whom the diplomat will interact. Effective channel management strategies provide for more rational decision making within the channel.

THE DYNAMIC NATURE OF CHANNELS

Marketing is characterized by constant change, and there is a need for the marketer to adapt to these changes, making marketing channels subject to change and innovation. Channels represent a dynamic area of marketing as they are constantly evolving to meet changing customer and market needs which reflect underpinning wider changes and trends in demography and lifestyles. Marketers must be aware of the changing nature of channels and respond to them. An example of recent developments that are indicative of the innovation and changing nature of this area is the growth of **multi-channel systems** of direct marketing and Internet marketing which are dealt with in Chapter 10.

The growth of multi-channels

Companies now use a variety of channel arrangements to reach their target customers. Once, companies tended to use only one type of channel configuration in their marketing; now they use several. The use of multi-channel systems can be for a number of reasons:

- to increase market coverage by reaching new customers;
- to reduce costs of selling to certain customers where for example such customers require less service than that provided through the company's normal channels;
- to achieve a more customized service to particular customers than would be available through the company's normal channels.

In multi-channel marketing, a company might sell to one group of customers using telephone selling and no intermediaries, while another target group may be marketed to through a network of dealers, since these customers require after-sales service and technical advice.

Although there are advantages to be gained through using several different channel configurations to different target customers, multi-channels can give rise to increased costs if not controlled. They can also give rise to problems of conflict between different channel members where several channels are used, particularly where one type of channel member feels that their contractual rights are being infringed. An example is where the marketer uses a system of 'appointed' distributors for the company's products. In return for being granted 'exclusive' distribution rights in a particular geographical area a retailer may enter into a formal agreement with a supplier. In exchange for these 'exclusive' rights, the dealer may agree not to stock and supply other competitive brands.

Unsurprisingly, 'exclusive' dealers feel aggrieved if they find that the brand they have been appointed to sell in a given are can be purchased direct over the Internet often at a price the dealer cannot hope to match.

Growth of direct channels

As Chapter 10 discusses the growth of direct marketing, suffice to say here that besides being an element of the promotional mix, direct forms of marketing can be considered as sales channels. Clearly, the growth of direct marketing methods such as catalogue selling and direct mail are examples of developments in channels as well as promotion. In addition to direct marketing channels, another key area of growth in direct distribution is the development of home shopping mainly through the Internet.

Internet channels

The Internet has brought about significant changes to existing channels e.g. traditional booksellers, travel agents and record stores have had to cope with major changes in how customers purchase.

Jeff Bezos founded Amazon in Seattle in 1994. It started as an Internet bookseller and shocked traditional retailers. From virtually nothing, Amazon built substantial sales in a very short space of time. Without having to support expensive retail outlets, Amazon was able to undercut the prices of conventional book retailers. The company added the facility for buyers to write their own book reviews. People began to look at Amazon as more of an on-line community and not just a place to make purchases. Amazon diversified into DVDs, video games, toys, clothing, beauty products, household goods and other items.

Mail order shopping at home has been around for a long time. In 1744 Benjamin Franklin formulated the basic mail-order concept in the USA when he produced a catalogue selling scientific and academic books. New forms of home shopping take this concept of selecting goods at home and ordering further. Access to cheap computing power at home has enabled marketers to develop systems of real time shopping where customers call up descriptions and pictures of products on their computer screen, search through computer-based catalogues, and order and pay over the Internet through charge cards. Virtual reality shopping is now commonplace where the home shopper calls up the shopping mall onto their screen and moves to different selected outlets, taking trips down different aisles in the retail outlet, and even selecting products from the 'shelves' for closer inspection. The customer places an order through the Internet and has it delivered. Large supermarket groups offer such facilities.

A fast growing area of home shopping has been shopping channels on the television. Cable television in particular has fostered this growth; in the United Kingdom many television companies have a shopping channel where customers view products and services and buy direct using only the television, a credit card and the telephone. Home shopping is advantageous for the elderly and infirm and it is likely that this type of retailing will continue to grow. As Ozuem, Howell and Lancaster[2] conjecture:

> Marketing communication is in need of reinvention in respect of its key concepts, methodologies and prevailing procedures to ensure their appropriateness for the evolving global interactive market-space. This is a challenge for both theoreticians and communications specialists.

PHYSICAL DISTRIBUTION AND LOGISTICS

We switch our emphasis away from the more abstract concept of channels, towards more practical issues that were, until recently, undeveloped aspects of marketing and corporate strategy; namely, the physical flows of products, services and information into, through and out of the organization to its customers. Physical distribution and logistics are part of the 'place' element of the marketing mix and these have had a major impact on channel strategy and design. Effective management of physical distribution and logistics has a substantial impact on a company and its customers' costs, efficiency and effectiveness. If these are well planned and implemented, they are competitive tools that can build sustainable competitive advantage. A total **systems approach** to physical distribution i.e. the science of moving items from production to consumption in a timely, economical manner, is referred to as logistics.

Reasons for increased attention to this function are the result of a continued search for cost savings in distribution and stockholding. Much research for cost savings has centred on the production area. Labour-saving technology, replacement raw materials and effective production planning have accounted for considerable effort being made to reduce costs and improve output. This has meant that increasingly the potential for further cost savings in these areas has become limited. If management is going to continue to look for cost savings it has to look elsewhere.

Lancaster[3] suggests that distribution and stockholding costs can add 25 per cent to direct materials costs. Unsurprisingly, in the search for further cost efficiencies in companies, physical distribution and logistics have figured highly. It has become increasingly clear that not only is there substantial potential for improving efficiency and reaping cost savings, but more importantly for the marketer, this area offers substantial potential for developing sustainable competitive advantage.

Part of the explanation for neglecting research in this area lies in the fact that conventionally individual elements of physical distribution and logistics have been dealt with in a fragmented manner, with separate parts of the business incurring what appeared to be relatively small costs of distribution. As a consequence, information on total costs has not been available or has 'disappeared' in the accounting system. Some of the major costs of physical distribution have accelerated. A major element of cost is transport, which is increasingly expensive as road, sea and air networks have become increasingly congested. Similarly, increases in fuel prices have contributed to increased transportation costs.

The emergence of a total systems (logistics) view of distribution is based on analogies and ideas drawn from the military. It became recognized that effective distribution depended on **logistics**, or an integrated approach to elements which help move products and services to the right place, in the right quantity and at the right time. It was recognized that 'optimizing' one part of the system, e.g. inventories of stocks and work-in-progress, might have a detrimental knock-on effect on other parts of the distribution system, thereby reducing the effectiveness of the system as a whole. Such systems thinking is an essential component of modern logistical management. Systems thinking applied to distribution has proved a powerful impetus to the importance of this area.

Alongside the development of the total systems approach to distribution has gone the development of more sophisticated and powerful tools of analysis. The notion of interrelationships in the total system of distribution makes the problems of managing it difficult and complex. Developments in modelling, allied to more powerful computer power, have enabled this complexity to be managed. We now have the tools to handle logistics through IT.

The main reason for the growth in importance and interest in physical distribution and logistics is the fact that the logistics system offers substantial potential for achieving a competitive edge and winning and keeping customers. Particularly in industrial markets, where products may be relatively undifferentiated and margins are slender, companies find they can gain a competitive edge by using their logistical system to improve customer service levels and this might be critical in terms of customer choice. This may allow a company to increase volumes of sales and/or increase prices. Because of this, identifying appropriate levels and types of customer service to be achieved by the logistics management system is a key aspect of planning in this area.

Developments and trends in manufacturing and purchasing have heightened the importance attached to the service elements of the logistics systems of suppliers. This was discussed in Chapter 2 when we considered organizational buyer behaviour. With modern continuous flow and large batch manufacturing systems a stock-out situation of a minor and inexpensive component may incur substantial costs in down time. This problem is heightened where a firm's customers have moved towards the implementation of 'lean manufacturing' purchasing and production. These developments in manufacturing and purchasing are so important that they need to be considered in more detail.

Perspectives on what constitutes an effective production process in a company have undergone considerable changes, which have been as a result of increased competition and more demanding customers. One of the major implications of these factors has been the recognition that production needs to be built around flexibility, while at the same time achieving cost efficiencies and consistent quality of output. Lancaster[4] suggests this flexibility of the production process is essential because:

> It transforms production operations enabling one machine to produce a wide variety of models and products – it provides the corporate capability to produce more varieties and choices even down to offering each individual customer the chance to design and implement the 'programme' that will yield the precise produce, service or variety that is right.

Amongst others Womack[5] termed these new production processes **'lean production'** – fundamentally different from traditional mass production processes developed by Ford in 1913. Bolwijn and Kumpe[6] suggested that this new production was part of an overall change in world manufacturing during the 1990s. They describe a number of manufacturing developments over the past 40 years. The first stage of development was based on the notion of the *efficient firm* where cost and price was all important. The emphasis was on producing competitively priced products on a mass-production scale. As a result of increasing competition, the end of the 1960s saw the need for the *quality firm* which was the next development in the evolution of production and where quality specifications were strictly applied in the manufacturing process. The third development was the transition to the *flexible firm*. This phase involved a distinct change in the production process with flow production and small batch runs of a wide assortment of products operated by teams of multi-skilled employees. Increasingly, companies have turned to this new form of flexible lean production based on flexible cells and working arrangements Accompanying this growth of lean manufacturing has been the introduction of **'Just in Time'** (JIT) systems of manufacturing and purchasing. First used extensively in Japan, JIT took time to make inroads into the West. As the term implies, in the context of manufacturing and purchasing, JIT is based on a company securing supplies of raw materials and components needed for the manufacturing process at the precise point in time when they are required to enter this process. Dion *et al.*[7] defined JIT as:

> An inventory control system which delivers input to its production or distribution site only at the rate and time it is needed. Thus it reduces inventories whether it is used within the firm or as a mechanism regulating the flow of products between adjacent firms in the distribution system channel.

The JIT approach contrasts with the more conventional approach to stockholding delivery and manufacturing which was based essentially on the *just in case* principle. Oliver[8] provides a comparison between Just in Case and Just in Time approaches in Table 6.1. Implications of the introduction of JIT/lean manufacturing systems for the marketer have been wide reaching. In the context of logistics, successful servicing of customers using a JIT system fundamentally alters the design and operation of the logistical process. For example, to be successful needs precise synchronization from supplier right through to production units to retailers to consumers. In turn, this synchronization requires a complete exchange of information, so the supplier is fully aware of raw material deliveries and the need for component deliveries to manufacturers. Manufacturers need to know that they will receive deliveries at the right time. Lynch,[9] using the Dell case analogy, has shown how JIT systems require close contact between suppliers and customers. Increasingly, this contact and the exchanges of information involved utilize computer linkages.

Womack *et al.*[10] have shown that at a consumer level this system can work through retailers who provide information to manufacturers in two forms: firm orders and tentative orders. Working

TABLE 6.1 Just in Case versus Just in Time

Issue	Just in Case	Just in Time
Official goal	Maximum efficiency	Maximum efficiency
Stocks	Integral part of the system	Wasteful: to be eliminated
Lead times	Taken as given and built into production planning routines	Reduced to render small batches economical
Batch sizes	Taken as given and economic order quantity is calculated	Lot size of one is the target because of flexible system
Production	Various means – MRP (Manufacturing Resources Planning) models	Centralized forecasts
Planning and control	Existing system and optimizes within it. Information 'pull' for hot orders	In conjunction with local pull control
Trigger to production	Algorithmically derived schedules. Hot lists. Maintenance of sub-unit efficiencies	Imminent needs of down-stream unit via Kanban cards
Quality	Acceptable quality levels. Emphasis on error detection	Zero defects. Error prevention
Performance focus	Sub-unit efficiency	System/organization efficiency
Organizational design	Input-based; functional	Output-based; strategic
Suppliers	Multiple, distant, independent	Single or dual sourcing. Supplier is extension of production

through retailers in this way and ascribing more importance to firm orders, means the company can respond closely to customer needs and changes in the market. Thus, in the volume car market in Japan, nearly all cars are made to orders taken in the distributor's showroom and lead times are as low as ten days. A study by Frazier et al.[11] suggests that in fact some distributors have realized that sharing strategic information with suppliers can be a powerful competitive weapon helping to reduce supply uncertainties and reduce risks

These trends towards lean manufacturing are indicative of the recognition of cost savings associated with elements of logistical processes including stocks of raw materials, work-in-progress, stock-outs and problems of defective components. The result of these factors is that effective supply and the logistical systems on which this is based – logistics – are now key factors in supplier choice in industrial markets. Table 6.2 is taken from a study by Perreault and Russ[12] and discussed in Hutt and Speh.[13] They found that when a stock-out notice for a product was received, purchasing managers switched to another supplier 32 per cent of the time. Over a 2-year period, 50 per cent of purchasing managers stopped using a supplier because of slow or inconsistent service. They investigated what happens if a rush order is not acted upon by the supplier and found that after one such inaction 42 per cent of purchasing managers would change suppliers. If this problem persisted, 54 per cent would change suppliers.

This study indicated that logistics was big on the list of supplier evaluation criteria, ranking second only to quality. Another implication is the need for closer working partnerships between suppliers and customer (Manna[14]). In a study based on the automotive supply industry, Jayaram et al.[15] suggest that building close relationships with key supply chain partners is essential in order to be competitive. This underpins the importance of Relationship Marketing to which we return to in Chapter 9.

A company at the forefront of developing Just-in-Time techniques in its relationship with suppliers is the Toyota Motor Company. Toyota has over the years built up close relationships with its component suppliers, many of whom are, as a result of these close relationships, actually sited

TABLE 6.2 Importance of logistics in how purchasing managers evaluate suppliers

Supplier characteristics	Importance ranking
Product quality	1
Distribution service	2
Price	3
Supply managerment	4
Distance to supplier	5
Required order size	6
Minor/small business	7
Reciprocity	8

next to the Toyota production units that they supply. Toyota was one of the first companies to recognize that effective supply chain management could be a key factor underpinning competitive success.

The nature of physical distribution and logistics

At its simplest, the subject of **physical distribution** and logistics can be defined as having the right quantity of an item, in the right place, at the right time. In marketing terms we could add: at the right price, as discussed in Chapter 5.

This description of physical distribution and logistics belies the complexity of decisions and planning in achieving these objectives. Defining this business activity in this way does not provide guidance as to how to manage it. As we have seen from the importance attached to logistics, physical distribution and logistics are not passive tools. They can be important demand creators (as well as customer losers). Product availability, prompt delivery and efficient and accurate order processing

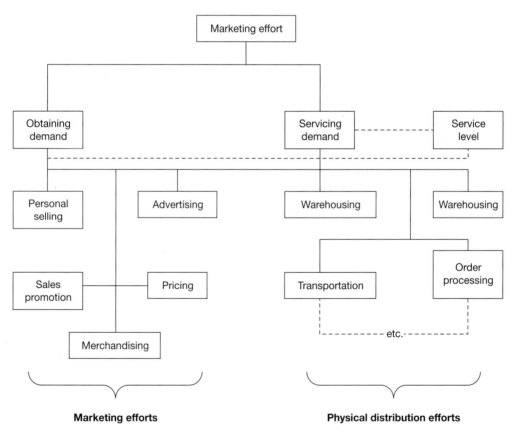

FIGURE 6.6 The demand-creating role of physical distribution efforts

Source: Adapted from Ballou, E.H. (1987), *Basic Business Logistics*, 2nd edn, Upper Saddle River, NJ: Prentice-Hall.

help to capture and keep customers. Determination of the nature and level of physical distribution service elements is crucial to effective planning of this area if it is to be used as a demand-generating tool. According to Ballou[16] physical distribution and logistics can be considered in the same way as product, price and promotional elements of the mix as shown in Figure 6.6.

Some of the elements that comprise physical distribution can be used through service levels to influence demand as shown. There are others. Before examining these elements that contribute to customer service, we need to clarify the distinction and relationships between the terms we have used interchangeably; namely physical distribution and logistics. To explain the business meaning of the latter term, we need to introduce the concept of materials management.

'Physical distribution', 'logistics' and 'materials management' are often used as alternative terms when discussing flows of materials into, through and out of an organization. Although they are interrelated, the scope of each of these terms together with their interrelationships is shown in Figure 6.7.[17] Physical distribution relates primarily to those elements that facilitate the flow of materials from the company to its distributors, retailers, final customers or all three. **Materials management** is primarily concerned with elements that facilitate the flow of goods and raw materials into and through the organization. Business logistics encompasses all of these in a total systems view of the 'place' element of marketing.

The term 'system' is used to denote the fact that all elements need to be integrated and planned as a whole to achieve specified objectives. We return to the implications shortly, but we see that the most comprehensive and useful term for planning and co-ordinating the place elements of marketing is business logistics, and we use this term throughout the rest of our discussion. It is

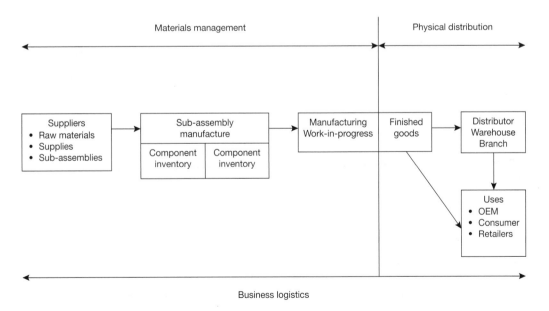

FIGURE 6.7 The relationship between materials management, physical distribution and logistics

Source: Firth, D. (1988), *Profitable Logistics Management*, Ryerson, Canada: McGraw-Hill.

important to stress that in addition to the physical flows of materials into, through and out of the organization as shown in Figure 6.7, a business logistics system includes flows of information and planning and decision-making systems; e.g. sales forecasting is an important information and planning input to the logistics system as are order processing procedures, production scheduling and planning and quality control. We can now define business logistics as follows:

> A total systems approach to the management of all those activities required to acquire, move and store raw materials in process inventory and manufacturing inventory from the point of origin to the point of the end user or consumer.

Implications of the total systems approach

Before considering the design and planning of the business logistics system and its relationship to marketing strategy, we need to consider some of the major implications of the total systems approach to business logistics.

Complexity

The first and most obvious implication is that the web of interrelationships it introduces poses considerable problems in its planning and management, particularly when trying to optimize the performance of the system. This is a reason why the growth of business logistics has been dependent on the development of appropriate IT tactical planning tools.

Trade-offs between elements

A second implication is that in trying to optimize the performance of the total system we are confronted with trade-offs between the different elements; attempts to optimize performance of one part of the system without regard to the other elements tends to result in lower performance for the system as a whole. We might have to trade off optimum performance in one element of the business logistics system to optimize overall performance, e.g. where we try to minimize the costs of holding raw materials inventory by cutting down the stocks, if we cut these too far, we might find that the effect is to increase costs elsewhere in the system such as losing production through stock-outs and being unable to fulfil customer orders. As shown in a study by Shang et al.,[18] if designed effectively, the system should be able to both reduce operating costs and at the same time increase customer service, clearly a very powerful competitive combination.

Effective co-ordination and organization

Related to complexity and trade-offs is the need in a systems approach for individual elements to be effectively coordinated and planned. Rarely are organizations structured in a way to achieve this. The far-reaching nature of the elements of the business logistics system invariably means it cuts across functional boundaries such as marketing, production, purchasing and finance. Some companies have distribution managers whose responsibilities are limited to duties like route scheduling, fleet

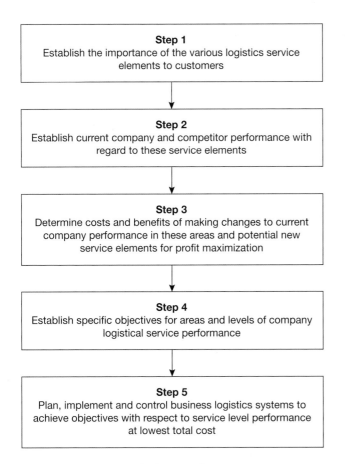

Step 1
Establish the importance of the various logistics service elements to customers

Step 2
Establish current company and competitor performance with regard to these service elements

Step 3
Determine costs and benefits of making changes to current company performance in these areas and potential new service elements for profit maximization

Step 4
Establish specific objectives for areas and levels of company logistical service performance

Step 5
Plan, implement and control business logistics systems to achieve objectives with respect to service level performance at lowest total cost

FIGURE 6.8 Designing the business logistics system

Step 2 Establishing current company and competitor performance with regard to service elements
The next step is to establish how well the company and its competitors are performing in areas of logistics services seen as important by customers. Underperformance will result in lost sales. There are significant marketing opportunities available to a company that is able to improve service performance. In assessing competitor performance we also need to look at areas where we are significantly outperforming our competitors to assess whether or not our extra performance justifies the additional cost of providing it.

Step 3 Determining costs and benefits of making changes to current company performance in levels of logistical service: profit maximization
Before we make decisions about specific objectives for service elements and design of the logistical system to achieve them, we need to assess likely costs and benefits and profit potential associated with different service levels. This brings us to an important point about the overall design of the

logistics system. Improvements in these services are likely to be costly. In determining the appropriateness, or otherwise, of current logistical services and any proposed changes, we need to assess the impact on company profits. The optimal logistics system is not likely to be one that operates at lowest cost, as we may lose too many sales, nor is the optimal system likely to be one that generates greatest demand, as these sales will probably be generated at too great a cost. The best system generates maximum profit where the logistics contribution is maximized. The notion of optimizing profit contribution is shown in Figure 6.9. We see that maximum contribution is obtained neither at the lowest nor the highest service levels. Too low a level of service and we lose revenue; too high and we incur too high costs for extra revenue generated. In theory, maximum contribution is obtained where the marginal cost of additional service levels is equal to the marginal revenue generated by these additional service levels. In reality, deriving the revenue curve with respect to different levels of service can be difficult. Nonetheless, steps of identifying customer service requirements and current company/competitor performance in this area should give some indication of likely responses to increases/decreases in service levels.

In practice the system should be designed from a demand perspective. Following earlier analysis of customer needs, we should define service level objectives based on the role we have determined for logistical services in overall competitive strategy. The design of the total logistics systems should be aimed at delivering this pre-determined level of logistical services at minimum cost.

Step 4 Establishing specific objectives for areas and levels of logistical services

Overall objectives for logistical service levels need to be translated into specific objectives for the various areas of logistical service. Possible customer service elements have been outlined in Tables

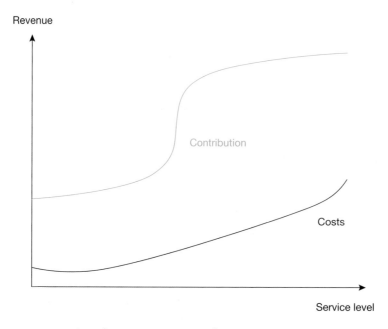

FIGURE 6.9 Contribution vs. revenue and costs

6.2 and 6.3, but we need to set quantified objectives for order cycle times, response to emergencies and order cycle time consistency.

Step 5 Planning, implementing and controlling the logistics systems
From a marketer's perspective, planning, implementation and control of logistics is paramount in providing the level of service support needed for customers. This involves purchasing, inbound transport, production, planning, inventory control, warehousing, order processing and outbound transport. Even though customer and market needs must be paramount when designing a logistics system, this can only be achieved through expertise in functions like materials management and production planning and control. In addition, we need to consult channel members and suppliers. We should note that continued operation of an effective logistics system requires ongoing information from sales and marketing including sales forecasting, customer feedback and competitor information. Of all the elements of the marketing mix, perhaps the 'place' element requires more inter- and intra-firm communication and co-ordination than any other.

Having established what types and levels of customer service the logistics system is to provide to support a competitive market strategy, the task of the logistics manager is to provide this at minimum cost. Here it is important for the marketer to understand and recognize the existence of 'trade-offs' between the elements of the logistics system. We have already come across the notion of a trade-off, but in this case it is for the system as a whole where the costs of the total system are traded off against revenue. In planning and operating the system the logistics manager must make trade-offs between individual elements of the system to achieve the desired levels of customer service at minimum cost. This requires what logistics planners refer to as a '**total cost approach**' that recognizes interdependence between the demands of logistics activities, e.g. minimizing costs in one area like inventory may lead to more than proportional increases in another, say transport.

Effective planning, implementation and control of the business logistics system is greatly enhanced by the introduction of a service policy and quantified service standards. Again, these need to be determined on the basis of customer and market needs. Service policy should include written statements concerning levels of customer service in the form of promises to customers which the company will fulfil. These can represent both a powerful promotional tool in helping to secure and keep customers, and a way of informing staff about the role and value of a logistics service in overall company and marketing strategy. Policy statements may be relatively simple, such as 'all orders received by noon will be shipped the same day' or more elaborate, covering in detail factors such as time, condition of goods, order communication and service contingencies. The policy statement may then be translated into detailed operating standards for the logistics system. In turn, these standards form the basis of the logistics control system, against which logistics inefficiencies and service problems can be quickly addressed.

DEVELOPMENTS AND TRENDS IN LOGISTICS

A number of developments and trends in the area of logistics have implications for the marketer with regard to the design and operation of their marketing logistics systems. Some of the more important of these developments and trends are now outlined.

Information Technology and logistics

As we have seen, the impact of developments in IT on marketing management has been profound. This impact is particularly pronounced in the area of logistics with IT acting as an enabling factor in more effective logistics management. There are a number of major trends that are having an impact on the use of IT in logistics. Integration and flexibility are important. Advance transaction processing systems which enable management to monitor inventory at all locations throughout the organization are commonplace. The level of flexibility and sophistication in software is continually being enhanced, enabling organizations to manage the whole supply chain system to give them competitive advantage. We have seen developments such as **Electronic Data Interchange (EDI)** where customers and suppliers interact through an on-line system to conduct transactions. EDI is not a new concept, but increasingly the emphasis on the way it is being used is moving from one-off tactical benefits to strategic benefits i.e. its use for developing closer supply chain relationships. Suppliers and customers are now able to work more closely for mutual benefit by co-ordinating integration. A series of developments in IT has enabled a totally paperless supply chain.

Much IT hardware is small, fast and cheap enabling it to be implemented in parts of the logistics process that were previously never considered because of space and cost considerations, e.g. the use of hand-held bar code scanners. Various developments such as point of sale terminals, satellite tracking, electronic funds transfer and EDI systems have resulted in substantial gains in logistical efficiency.

Another area of IT development that has affected logistics is developments in mobile communications. The growth of cellular technology-based mobile voice communications and developments in digital service provision offer the possibility of voice and data services, and more one-to-one contact has led to better client–supplier relationships. Developments in computing power and software systems have enabled marketers to cope with the complexities of managing interactions and trade-offs.

Channel partnerships/supply chain management

The earlier example of Toyota illustrates that the notion of developing channel partnerships with a view to managing the overall supply chain is not new. However, companies like Marks & Spencer have developed effective channel partnerships and supply chain management; Toyota is different, in that they work to 4-hour tactical time windows for delivery of critical supplies whereas Marks & Spencer's time windows are longer and less critical from an operations point of view. In part, this is linked to the application of IT inasmuch as this technology facilitates the complex management and exchanges of information required for effective channel partnerships and supply chain management. Channel partnerships take many forms, ranging from simple information sharing and joint facilities like warehousing through to joint management of the whole supply chain by its members. **Supply chain management** includes every facet of the supply chain from the manufacturer through to raw material suppliers. The **demand chain** refers to the chain from end customers to the manufacturer. The supply chain plus the demand chain is known as the **value chain**.

As one would expect, much greater trust between different members of the supply chain is required together with exchanges of information. This is one reason for the growth of the relationship marketing approach that is explored in more detail in Chapter 9. As a result of supply chain management, companies use a smaller number of suppliers so these must be 100 per cent reliable.

The output of the logistics system is the level of service received by the customer, so effective supply chain management must reflect this. An interesting further development that reflects this output-based view is the growth of the concept of **enhanced consumer response (ECR)**. Initially developed in the USA for manufacturing industry, ECR represents the application of total supply chain management to the retailing sector with Asda supermarket group being one of the first companies in the United Kingdom to adopt this. By working in close partnerships with other members of the supply chain, not only as regards logistics, but also in areas like promotion, product development and packaging, they have found that non-essential costs can be cut out of the system.

THE INTERNET

The trend in logistics planning has been to minimize levels of stock held. One of the problems for Internet marketers is that although it is easy to place an order, many sometimes fail to deliver. In the run-up to Christmas 2009, some disgruntled customers who ordered Christmas presents via the Internet found they were not going to be delivered until the middle of January. Internet supply requires holding larger stocks than would be considered 'normal' in conventional channel systems. However, it has beneficial effects on managing logistics. Effective supply chain management requires good communication between channel members and from the extent to which the Internet facilitates this we see advantages that accrue through the application of Internet technology to logistics.

International/global sourcing

Global aspects of marketing are covered in detail in Chapter 16. A trend with regard to logistics and supply chain management has been the growth of a more international and global outlook with regard to sourcing. In part this is a reflection of a more global outlook in company operations, but it has also been facilitated by developments in communication, transport and infrastructure which make it easier for the marketer to consider sourcing components and supplies from any part of the world according to which offers the best competitive advantage.

SUMMARY

The need for effective distribution channel management is exacerbated when economic conditions turn down. Distribution arrangements are relatively long term in nature so channel decisions tend to be strategic rather than tactical or operational. As a result, manufacturers need continually to monitor the distributive environment and reassess their existing channel structure with a view to exploiting and capitalizing on any changes.

Channel strategy must be derived from channel objectives. Commonly, such objectives are derived from profit growth, return on investment and sales growth. Because of the strategic nature of channel decisions, a decision to change them is infrequent as such a move would be high risk, often requiring the approval of senior executives within the company. We need to consider the way a company is perceived in the marketplace so any change in channel selection can radically affect perceptions of the company.

Three major strategies are: *intensive* (every available outlet), *exclusive* (a single outlet) and *selective* (a few outlets). Each has merits depending on the type of product made by the company. Despite relative advantages and disadvantages of each strategy, there is often a trade-off in selecting the right one e.g. if a company decides on a strategy of intensive distribution, it might lose some control over the marketing of its products. To maintain control of its own destiny, the company needs to assume greater participation in each of the marketing flows. Differences between *conventional marketing systems* (based on isolated and autonomous units) and *vertical marketing systems* (where participants desire interdependence) are important.

The role of intermediaries in the management of channels is critical in that that each channel member has a *position* and a *role*. In this context, 'position' is defined as where each channel member chooses to locate in the overall scheme of things, and 'role' refers to the functions and degree of performance expected of the firm filling the position.

As in all forms of organization, the interaction of people, companies and organizations will inevitably lead to some form of conflict. If handled properly, good management will result in more rational and functional collective decision making within the channel. We need to understand that there will always be some element of conflict when organizations interact.

Distribution can present opportunities for gaining distinctive competencies relative to competitors. While an enterprise can offer good products at competitive prices, when communicated effectively to the right people, this can be let down if products are not available in the right place and at the right time.

Physical distribution represents a substantial cost element in business, but managed as a total logistical system it can be a powerful competitive tool which is a major issue in supplier choice. Effective management of logistics requires a total systems approach. This makes management of this area complex, requiring effective co-ordination and organization of a large range of elements, cutting across different functional areas of the company. Levels and elements of customer service need to be based on an appraisal of customer requirements and in particular levels of service they value and will pay for and what competitors are offering in this respect. This can be translated into likely costs (to the marketer) and benefits (to the customer). Service levels should be designed to maximize the logistics contribution.

Developments in IT and the Internet have produced sophisticated systems of logistics management. We have witnessed the growth of total supply chain management and increases in numbers of channel partnerships.

KEY TERMS

Intensive distribution	193	Title flow	194
Selective distribution	193	Information flow	194
Exclusive distribution	193	Conventional marketing channels	194
Physical flow	194	Vertical marketing systems	194

CASE STUDY

Starfish (channels of distribution)

The founder of Starfish Products is Pandora Truelove who started by making jewellery as a hobby at home. Eventually Pandora began to sell some of her jewellery at small craft fairs in the district where she lives. Her jewellery proved to be very popular, especially amongst the age group 14–18. It was low priced, but well made and very fashionable. Quite simply, Pandora discovered that not only was she good at making jewellery, but she had a feel for the market and jewellery fashions that would sell to younger customers.

From this humble beginning, in just three years Pandora has expanded her business and sales to the point where she now works full-time and employs three people helping her make the jewellery in a small workshop. At the moment she is selling mainly through craft fairs, but now at much larger national events.

Pandora wants to expand the business; demand is still strong and she has retained her flair for judging the market. She has the option to move to larger premises where she could take on more production staff. She has a small budget for promoting her products. Her main problem in relation to expanding the business she feels is distribution. To expand quickly she must secure retail outlets on a national basis through which she can market. Alternatively, she has considered whether franchising might be an answer, with sales direct to customers in their own homes rather like Tupperware or Ann Summers parties.

CASE STUDY QUESTION

What distribution alternatives might be available to Pandora to expand her business, and what are their relative advantages and disadvantages?

CASE STUDY

Radiance Products (logistics)

David Cundy is feeling the pinch. He is marketing manager of Radiance Products, a company supplying lighting components to companies that in turn supply some of the major car manufacturing plants in the UK. His customers' customers include companies such as Honda, Ford and Toyota. He has had several complaints recently from his customers concerning the level of service his company is providing with regard to some key areas. These key areas include the following:

■ *The order cycle time*: this is felt to be too long compared to what the industry requires. Companies like Honda are constantly looking for reductions in this time.

■ *Order status information*: customers complain that it is difficult to obtain information regarding the status of particular orders when they enquire. Currently a customer can only enquire about order status through writing or the telephone.

■ *Responding to emergencies*: Cundy's company is not felt to be flexible enough when it comes to dealing with unplanned events, such as emergency orders.

■ *Damaged goods*: Cundy's customers are beginning to insist on a zero defects policy. Currently, the defect rate is approximately 0.25 per cent of products delivered.

CASE STUDY QUESTION

What steps can David Cundy take to improve the design and operation of the business logistics system in Radiance Products?

REFERENCES

1 McCammon, B.C., Jr. (2008), 'Perspective for distribution programming', in A. Coughlan, E. Anderson, L.W. Stern, and A.I. El-Ansary (2008), *Marketing Channels*, London: Pearson International Edition.

2 Ozuem, W., Howell, K.E. and Lancaster, G. (2008), 'Communicating in the new interactive marketspace', *European Journal of Marketing*, 42(9–10): 1079.

3 Lancaster, G. (1993), 'Marketing and engineering: can there ever be synergy?', *Journal of Marketing Management*, 9: 141–53.

4 Ibid.: 143–4.

5 Womack, D. (1992), 'Developments in production', *Business Quarterly*: 19–22.

6 Bolwijn, P.T. and Kumpe, T. (1990), 'Manufacturing in the 1990s – productivity, flexibility and innovation', *Long Range Planning*, 23: 44–57.

7 Dion, P.A., Banting, P. and Halsey, L.M. (1990), 'The impact of JIT on industrial marketers', *Industrial Marketing Management*, 19: 42.

8 Oliver, N. (1991), 'JIT: issues and items for the research agenda', *International Journal of Physical Distribution and Materials Management*, 13: 3–11.

9 Lynch, R. (2006), *Corporate Strategy*, 4th edn, Harlow, Essex: Prentice-Hall, pp. 308–10.

10 Womack, D., op. cit., p. 25.

11 Frazier, G.L., Maltz, E., Antia, K., and Rindfleisch, A. (2009), 'Distributor sharing of strategic information with suppliers', *Journal of Marketing*, 73(4): 31–43.

12 Perreault, W.D. and Russ, F.A. (1976), '"Physical distribution" in industrial purchase decisions', *Journal of Marketing*, 40: April.

13 Hutt, M.D. and Speh, T.W. (2009), *Business Marketing Management: B2B*, 10th edn, Cincinnati: South Western Educational Publishing.

14 Manna, D.R. (2008), 'Just-in-time: case studies of supplier relationships across industries', *Journal of Applied Business Research*, 24(1): 75–83.

15 Jayaram, J., Vickery, S. and Droge, C. (2008), 'Relationship building, lean strategy and firm performance: an exploratory study in the automotive supply industry', *International Journal of Production Research*, 46(20): 5633–49.

16 Ballou, E.H. (1987), *Basic Business Logistics*, 2nd edn, Englewood Cliffs, NJ: Prentice-Hall.

17 Firth, D. (1988), *Profitable Logistics Management*, Ryerson, Canada: McGraw-Hill.

18 Shang, J., Yidrim, T.P., Tadikamalla, P., Vikas, M. and Brown, L. (2009), 'Distribution redesign for marketing competitiveness', *Journal of marketing*, 73(2): 146–63.

19 Firth, D. op. cit.

20 Ballou, E.H., op. cit.

Chapter 7

Communications strategy

LEARNING OBJECTIVES

By the end of this chapter you will:

- appreciate the role and scope of communication decisions in marketing strategy
- understand how the communication process works
- be familiar with issues in planning and managing individual elements of the communications mix
- be aware of developments and trends in promotional strategy

INTRODUCTION

The promotional element of marketing strategy is one of the most potent elements of marketing. **Promotion** is of course one of the four Ps, but in a broader context the correct term is communications. This involves communicating with a pre-determined audience to elicit a desired response. Understanding the nature and meaning of this process and its relevance to marketing objectives and strategy is a prerequisite to communications planning. Promotional expenditure is one of the more difficult areas of marketing to manage well. Considerable money is wasted; causes of this waste, and how it can be reduced, are the concern of much of this chapter.

UNDERSTANDING MARKETING COMMUNICATIONS

Effective planning of promotional elements of the marketing mix requires an appreciation of how communication works which can be summarized by answering these questions: 'Who says what?' 'In what channel?' 'To whom?' 'And with what effect?' These questions encapsulate the elements and process of communication as shown in Figure 7.1.

IMPLICATIONS OF THE COMMUNICATIONS PROCESS

Figure 7.1 illustrates that communication starts with the sender having a message or meaning to send or share with an intended audience and to do this the communicator requires **encoding** of these into signs and symbols that incorporate the message or meaning. These can be visual (words and pictures) or oral (speech and other sounds). There are many ways in which the message or meaning can be encoded, but to be effective, the encoding process needs to be done such that the target audience can readily interpret (decode) the intended meaning. In other words, the encoding process must take into account, and be consistent with, the target audience. An example of its importance is where a company is communicating through advertising across international and cultural boundaries. What may be readily understood in one culture may be interpreted in different ways in another. This is discussed more fully in Chapter 16 when we consider global marketing. Suffice to say that international marketers have encountered problems because they have not encoded meanings in a way that allows for accurate understanding of the target audience e.g. the brand name 'Nova', a Vauxhall car that was marketed in the UK, would not have been appropriate in the Spanish market, where the name translates as 'no go'. Even in domestic markets, communication is most

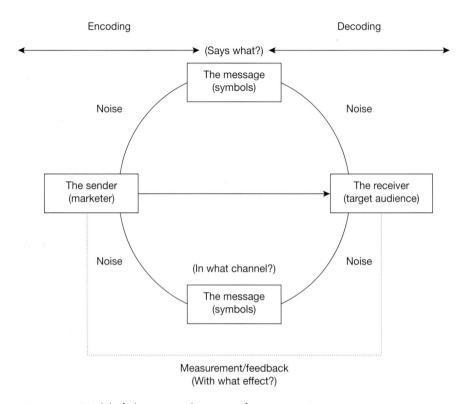

Encoding   Decoding

(Says what?)

FIGURE 7.1 Model of elements and process of communication

Source: Adapted from Lancaster, G. and Massingham, L.C. (2002), *Essentials of Marketing*, 4th edn, Maidenhead: McGraw-Hill, p. 283.

effective where symbols used are consistent with the target audience, e.g. advertisements aimed at the 'Yuppie' market segments so prevalent in the 1980s and early 1990s would now be perceived as being brash and inappropriate to the softer, less up-front current lifestyles. Symbols of financially successful young city traders in costly designer wear and driving expensive sports cars are less appropriate now, so encoded messages are being delivered through a variety of media channels to appeal to these segments.

Conventionally, we think of media channels as including television, the Internet, commercial radio, newspapers, magazines and posters. In addition, messages are delivered via a company's sales force. A key planning area in marketing communication is **media planning**. Not only are media one of the major costs in promotional budgets, but a plethora of choice of media, their scheduling and their coverage makes the choice of channels for communicating messages a key one.

The receiver is the intended target audience at whom communication is aimed. This audience may be actual or potential customers. However, organizations may wish to communicate with publics like financial institutions, shareholders, the local community or government. Irrespective of the target audience, communication requires that the encoded message be decoded by the intended recipient and this **decoding** process needs to result in the target audience accurately receiving and interpreting the message that the sender intended. A number of factors serve to detract from the accuracy of the decoding process. Receivers often have pre-determined attitudes that influence how they perceive messages e.g. a confirmed left-wing voter will, because of strong attitudes, tend to have expectations about what they will receive in a party political broadcast on behalf of a right-wing party. Because of this, the left-wing receiver will tend only to hear what they 'expect' to hear, and will subconsciously add to or remove important meanings when decoding the message. In communication terms, this process is referred to as **selective perception** and **distortion**. Only by understanding the decoding process, and factors that affect it, can the sender ensure that messages are received and interpreted as intended.

To ascertain that messages have been received and interpreted accurately and have had the intended effect, another important element is feedback that may occur in a conversation between two individuals. The sender might receive feedback through verbal or non-verbal affirmation. In much marketing communication there is no direct personal contact between sender and receiver, so it is more difficult to gauge the effect of how the communication has been received. In managing the process, accurate feedback is important in ascertaining its effectiveness. By measuring this we can determine whether promotional budgets are well spent and if the communication needs to be improved.

Noise is anything that serves to reduce the quality of communication that occurs in any part of the system as described in Figure 7.1. Selective perception and distortion in the decoding process is an example of noise. A major source of noise in marketing communications is that introduced by other senders of messages. We are constantly bombarded with messages from marketers vying for our attention and spending power. As well as noise, there are other factors that serve to distract, e.g. television advertisers are concerned about viewers 'zapping' to another channel with their remote control when advertisements appear during the commercial break. Noise may also appear in the feedback process when, for example, interviewer bias creeps into a market research exercise designed to evaluate the effectiveness of communications.

For successful marketing communications, the marketer needs to understand the process of communication. Figure 7.1 is a simplification and is not a communications planning tool. However, it illustrates that for effective communication the sender needs to know the target audience and the purpose of the communication. Messages need to be sent in a way the target audience can interpret as intended. The communicator must send these messages through appropriate media to reach the intended audience with the use of feedback to monitor audience response and so reduce or counteract noise in the system.

MARKETING COMMUNICATIONS

Having outlined the process of communication, we turn our attention to the elements of planning marketing communication strategies. Promotional elements of the marketing mix must be planned and managed in a systematic and strategic manner to be effective. For marketing communication to become strategic it needs to be planned and implemented so that it is consistent with, and supportive of, overall corporate and marketing strategies. Other elements of the marketing mix often have a strong communications element and these are now considered.

Product communication: For many consumers, products represent symbols denoting characteristics of lifestyles and personality. Packaging, in particular, communicates certain things like status, quality, atmosphere and image. A product's physical properties or brand name can communicate an image.

Place communication: Distribution channels can communicate messages to the market e.g. certain distribution channels such as up-market stores, may communicate quality and status, whereas others may communicate a particular lifestyle. A retail outlet may communicate messages to the market, e.g. untidy shops may create a bad image, whereas well-stocked and well-managed shops may build confidence. Conversely, an untidy shop might communicate that its prices are more economical.

Physical distribution can convey messages. The state of a company's delivery vehicles may convey a careless message and companies now pay considerable attention to the livery of their vehicles as this becomes part of the corporate image.

Prices and communication: As we saw in Chapter 5, particularly for new products, or for brands with which a customer has no previous experience, pricing conveys powerful signals to the market. The price of a product may signal the perceived quality of a product or service. Similarly, regular discounting of brands can lead to consumers forming an image that the brand is inferior.

The communication emphasis of these marketing mix elements illustrate an important point about planning marketing communications, namely, that virtually everything a company does or says can communicate something to the market. Because of this, an effective marketing communications strategy requires more than just management of the promotional elements of the mix. Marketing communications must be part of an integrated communications strategy with promotional tools being integrated within overall marketing strategies.

PLANNING MARKETING COMMUNICATIONS STRATEGIES

Strategic management of marketing communications requires a systematic and ordered approach. A number of approaches that fit these criteria have been developed. Although these approaches vary in their precise detail, there is sufficient commonality between them to propose a generalized framework that is integrated with other elements of marketing strategy. This framework is shown in Figure 7.2. Each of the above stages is now discussed:

1 Target audience, marketing strategies and mix elements

Unsurprisingly, effective marketing communications starts with selection of the target audience and delineation of broad strategies and marketing mix elements designed to achieve objectives in these target markets. We are primarily concerned with communication aimed at customers, but as we have seen, communications may be aimed at any one or a combination of several target audiences. We have also seen that the specific promotional elements of the marketing mix need to be part of,

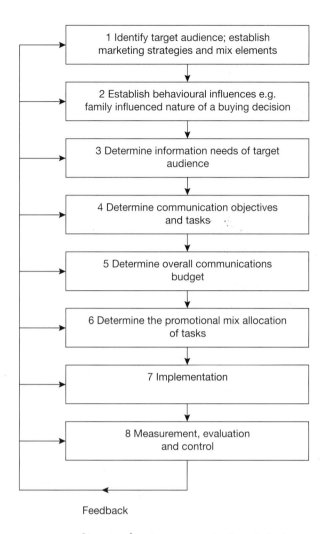

FIGURE 7.2 Steps in planning communication strategies

and consistent with, the communication elements of remaining marketing mix elements. Until the target audience is delineated, it is impossible to proceed in an effective way with remaining elements of the marketing communications planning process.

An example of identifying the target audience for marketing communications is the fact that a considerable amount of women's lingerie is purchased by men. These purchases are bought as gifts usually by men for women. Because of this, if you look at the marketing communications efforts of some of the lingerie marketers a lot of it is slanted at this important male target audience. This is reflected in the fact that the media selected for advertising is male magazines, and advertising copy and visual content is geared very much to the male psyche.

2 Behavioural characteristics of target audience

It is not sufficient to simply delineate target audiences: the marketing communicator must also understand the target audience as well as the buying decision process. The importance of understanding this process was discussed in Chapter 2. In the context of communication decisions, the stage at which the target audience is in the buying decision process provides important information for planning communication.

In the case of the purchase of a new car, communication will stimulate the start of the buying process by encouraging problem or need recognition. In addition, the marketer must understand where the customer will search for information about the new car and what information they are looking for, and also who is involved in the purchase process and what the key behavioural and other influences on this decision process might be. If the customer does purchase the marketer will need to know how the customer feels about the purchase and take steps to reassure them that they have made the right decision so that they can reduce post-purchase anxiety.

Major car manufacturers take active steps to reduce post-purchase anxiety on the part of customers. For most of us, purchasing a new car is one of the most substantial financial outlays we make. Because of cost and the wide range of alternatives we have to choose from, it is understandable that having taken delivery of our new vehicle we begin to wonder if we made the right choice. Did we get the best possible deal? Is the colour right? Should I have bought a different make or model? To allay these anxieties car marketers use a number of communication tools. A simple but effective one is a follow-up phone call from the dealer two or three days after delivery of a new vehicle to check if the customer is happy and that there are no problems. Another is to send out details of the owners' club perhaps with an edition of an owners' magazine containing stories about satisfied buyers of a similar vehicle.

As mentioned, in addition to understanding how the target market buys and the stage of the buying process they have reached, it is important to understand who is involved in the purchase process. In Chapter 2 we saw that we can usefully distinguish between different roles in the buying process e.g. if we are launching a new brand of breakfast cereal, it is important to distinguish between 'influencers', 'deciders', 'purchasers' and 'users'. All these roles might be embodied in the one target group, but as we have seen, both in consumer and organizational markets, these roles may be filled by a range of individuals.

Sometimes it is important to establish existing preferences and attitudes of the target audience as we are concerned with image, so it might be important to establish the target audience's current image of the company and its products.

3 Establishment of information needs

Analysis of the target audience helps the marketing communicator to assess information needs of customers, e.g. analysis of search and alternative stages of the buying process should help establish where the target market looks for information, the degree of reliance on word-of-mouth versus marketer-dominated sources of information and the type of information sought.

4 Determining communication objectives and tasks

Each step in planning a communications strategy helps contribute to the establishment of quantified communication objectives. In the communication process the marketer must determine what effect the communication is intended to achieve, but the problem is that the list of possible communications objectives is endless. Marketing communication objectives are best thought of in the context of what are termed '**audience response repertoires**'. These are similar to the stage or step models of buyer behaviour, in that they posit that the buyer passes through a series of stages or steps en route to making purchase decisions. A variety of such audience response repertoires have been developed. Two of the earliest and best known are Strong's **AIDA** model,[1] Lavidge and Steiner's **Hierarchy of effects model**[2] and Colley's **DAGMAR** model.[3] Later, Jones[4] suggested that marketing communications in general, but advertising in particular, has a much weaker effect on consumer behaviour that earlier models such as AIDA suggested. One model that reflects his view of a weaker effect for advertising is the **ATR model,** which stands for the steps of Awareness, Trial and Reinforcement. This model suggests that advertising works by first creating awareness, which may lead to tentative trial of the advertised product by the customer. Having trialled the product, the customer can then be reinforced or reassured about the purchase through further advertising. These four influential models of how advertising might work are shown in Figure 7.3.

These sequential models of the step-by-step process can be used to help determine appropriate communication objectives, although they need to be interpreted and applied with care; customers need not necessarily always pass through all stages of the various models in the manner prescribed. Factors such as nature of purchase, previous experience and time pressure affect the nature and speed of a consumer's progress through the various stages. By using audience response models, the marketing communicator is able to set communication objectives in terms of what is required to move the target audience through the various steps in the process e.g. in the AIDA model, if the target audience is at the early stage of the buying process the primary objective of communication will be to bring the company and its products to the attention of customers. At later stages the objective of marketing communications may be to produce action. We examine these stages of hierarchy models of audience response later when we discuss advertising.

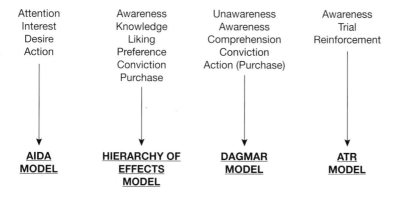

FIGURE 7.3 Examples of audience response repertoires

As with all objectives, it is important to couch these in quantitative terms whenever possible. This makes the final stage of measurement and control easier. It also allows preliminary cost estimates to be made regarding research required to meet the objectives, thereby facilitating budget decisions for communication. In setting objectives for marketing communication, it is important to remember that a consumer can rarely be moved through all response stages by a single promotional campaign. Because of this, like corporate objectives, communication objectives may need to be both long term and short term.

For many years the British public have been exposed to government-sponsored campaigns aimed at persuading drivers not to take alcoholic drinks and drive, aimed of course at safety. More recent campaigns have highlighted the effects of taking drugs and driving. In recent years, most of the money spent on these campaigns has gone on television advertising around the Christmas period for drink driving and throughout the year for taking drugs and driving. Increasingly, the campaigns have been designed to shock viewers by using graphic images of the possible results of drinking and driving, including death and injury, social approbation or imprisonment. Unfortunately, many people are still not deterred and continue to drink and drive and take drugs and drive. Does this mean that the advertising is not working and that the government would be better spending this money in other ways? You will no doubt have your own views on this, but the advertiser, in this case a government department, has to appreciate that often advertising works slowly.

5 Determining the communications budget

Having decided communication objectives we are in a position to determine the budget required to meet those objectives. A budgeting method that is often used is to take a percentage of sales, either current or projected. This represents a simple way of setting budgets for communication. However, the problem is that communication budgets will be high when sales are high and low when sales are low, which is not logical.

Another approach is to set the budget at the same level as that of the competition, or at least on a pro rata basis using market share. The problem here is that this assumes that competitors have similar objectives and strategies, and they are budgeting effectively in the first place. Neither of course might be the case.

Setting clear and quantified objectives for communication allows us to determine what tasks need to be done to achieve these objectives and allows these to be costed. This method is referred to as the 'objective and task' approach.

6 Determining the promotional mix: allocation of tasks

This stage of communications planning requires decisions to be made on allocation of communication tasks, and relates the budget to the variety of promotional tools available to a company. Communication tools are embodied in all elements of the marketing mix. However, in the promotional area of the mix, marketers distinguish between a number of promotional tools (termed **promo-tools**) and collectively these elements are referred to as the **communications mix** that encompasses the following:

1 Advertising: paid for non-personal promotion of ideas, goods or services through media of print, broadcasting, TV, outer packaging and inserts, cinema, posters and leaflets, billboards, display signs, point-of-sale (POS) displays, the Internet, logos and symbols.

2 Sales promotion: incentives that stimulate purchase of products and services by consumers or the trade e.g. coupons, samples, demonstrations, contests, trade allowances, premium offers, low-interest finance, entertainment, trade fairs and exhibitions and competitions.

3 Public relations and publicity: promotion and protection of company image and products through press releases, 'in-house' company magazine, company reports and lobbying persons like Members of Parliament who might influence events.

4 Sponsorship: where the company's name is displayed in support of a particular event or cause.

5 Personal selling: verbal sales presentations aimed at prospective purchasers to make sales, but also including sales meetings, incentive programmes and provision of samples.

6 Direct marketing: post, telephone, e-mail, Internet and fax to communicate directly with potential customers, e.g. mail shots, fax, voice mail and telemarketing.

7 Events marketing: sponsored activities intended to create brand interactions e.g. sports events, entertainment, cultural activities and festivals.

8 Interactive marketing: On-line activities that connect with customers or prospects to improve image, raise awareness or generate sales e.g. e-mail, TV shopping, intranet and Internet websites.

9 Word-of-mouth communications: Oral, written or electronic communications relating to experiences of purchasing and using particular products or services, an example being recommendations from friends to dine at a particular restaurant.

Each of the communications tools has advantages and disadvantages which, together with the precise nature of the communication tasks, means the marketing decision maker should be able broadly to determine the most appropriate mix, e.g. advertising, sales promotion and publicity are usually the most cost-effective tools at the buyer awareness stage, more so than 'cold calls' from sales representatives. Advertising produces comprehension. Buyer conviction is influenced by personal selling and supplemented by advertising. Placing an order is usually, but not always, a function of the sales call with assistance from sales promotion. Additional factors influencing this decision include:

■ company objectives and resources;
■ the stage in the product life cycle;
■ competitor considerations;
■ type or product market.

At the extremes of fast-moving consumer goods versus capital and industrial goods, the promotional mix differs with emphasis switching from a non-personal, advertising-dominated promotional mix for fast-moving consumer goods to one dominated by personal selling in capital and industrial goods. This is unsurprising as organizational buying involves purchasing large volumes and technical products. Organizations are less susceptible to 'glitzy' advertising and want to negotiate on a personal face-to-face basis, but this does not mean that advertising should be discounted. We know, for instance, that in industrial markets, advertising helps substantially to augment the effectiveness of personal selling by increasing awareness of a company and its products, thereby reducing the difficulty and costs of selling 'cold' to customers. It is not simply a choice between advertising and personal selling or a combination of these. There is a wide range of effective promotional tools to choose from, and more proactive marketers are constantly searching for improved ways to promote products and services.

In this constant search for new and effective promotional tools we have seen the development of more direct ways of marketers communicating with their target audience. So rapid and far reaching have been these forms of promotion that the direct marketing element of the promotional mix is as important as the tradition elements of advertising, sales promotion, PR and personal selling. Direct marketing includes a number of dynamic and innovative tools of marketing communication and is set to continue to grow in importance as an element of the promotional mix. We shall, therefore, be considering this relative newcomer to the communications mix tools in more detail in Chapter 10. In common with the other broad categories of promotion, direct marketing includes the promotional tools of direct mail, telemarketing and Internet or e-marketing.

7 Implementing the promotional mix

Having determined how communication tasks are to be allocated between different elements of the promotional mix, the next step is to develop detailed action programmes for each promotional tool being used. This entails the development of advertising, sales promotion, personal selling, direct marketing and publicity programmes. These need to be co-ordinated one with another and with other elements of the marketing mix. Often, advertising, sales promotion, direct marketing and publicity programmes will be developed and implemented with an outside agency, so careful selection and briefing of an agency are essential.

Planning and implementing each area of the promotional mix requires a detailed understanding of issues and steps involved and we investigate these later. Management of personal selling and direct marketing are discussed in Chapters 8 and 10 respectively.

8 Measurement, control and feedback

The last stage of effective communication management is concerned with the measurement of how effective the communication has been against pre-determined objectives and standards. Evaluating effectiveness is difficult, but with such substantial expenditure close control is important. According to how effective the communication programme has been, some readjustment may be necessary. Measurement and control should not simply assess the extent to which communication objectives have been met, but should also provide reasons for variances like advertising expenditure not producing sales that had been forecasted. This information can then be used to adjust the communications programme.

In the remainder of this chapter and in Chapters 8, 9 and 10 we examine in more detail the strategic management of each of the five major promotional tools – advertising, sales promotion, publicity and PR, personal selling and direct marketing.

ADVERTISING

Perhaps one of the most visible promotional tools we think of is that of advertising. Partly because of this high visibility, advertising is also one of the most controversial elements of the promotional mix. Some believe that much advertising is a waste of money or even immoral. We start by examining what advertising is (and is not) before looking at how it works. Our main concern is how advertising can be managed so it is cost-effective and helps support both overall and marketing communication strategies.

What is advertising?

A number of elements distinguish advertising from other tools of promotion and at the same time indicate its key characteristics. These key elements are:

- **Non-personal** Unlike personal selling, advertising affords no direct personal contact with the customer. Although this is a limitation, especially in industrial markets, it means that the advertiser has less control over what is said and to whom.
- **Paid for by an identified sponsor** Advertising is directly sponsored and paid for by the advertiser. It is intended to create a favourable response on the part of the consumer and is identified as being for commercial or organizational gain on the part of the sponsor.
- **Promotion of ideas, goods or services** The word 'promotion' rather than 'selling' is used; although some advertising is intended to create a sale in its own right, such as in classified advertising or some forms of direct marketing, most advertising is only part of the process of moving consumers nearer to making a purchase. A distinguishing characteristic of advertising compared to personal selling and to some extent direct marketing is that it is normally aimed at a mass audience through mass communication.

In the case of commercial advertisers, the objective of spending on advertising is to increase sales and profit. However, we must be careful not to exaggerate the power of advertising in this respect, as advertising is but a part of the communications mix; and the communications mix, in turn, is a component of overall marketing strategy. This point is best evidenced, albeit negatively, by illustrating what advertising cannot do:

- Advertising cannot secure repeat business for a product or service that is not value for money.
- Advertising cannot remove problems of insufficiently trained or motivated sales staff.
- Advertising cannot work if the brand is not in stores when the consumer wants it.

Advertising is only powerful when it, and the rest of communication and marketing strategy, is well planned, implemented and integrated through **Integrated Marketing Communications (IMC)** – communications and messages are carefully linked so they work in consistent harmony rather than in isolation as their sum is greater than their individual parts. This means that communications tools like direct marketing, media advertising, interactive/Internet marketing, sales promotion, publicity/public relations and as Mulhern[5] illustrates, increasingly these days digital communication, are planned as an integrated whole to provide maximum communications impact by being clear and consistent. There are other levels of integration, namely:

- horizontal (across the marketing mix and also business functions like finance, production and distribution);
- vertical (so communications objectives support higher level corporate objectives);
- internal (keeping company staff informed about new developments like new corporate identity, better service standards and new strategic partners);
- external (ensuring that external partners like PR and advertising agencies work together to deliver a cohesive message, integrated message);
- data integration (where sales, direct mail and advertising help each other; this requires a marketing information system that collects and shares relevant data across different departments.

IMC means that the whole organization works together and everyone is conscious that their decisions and actions send messages to customers. Furthermore, viewing sales as the objective for advertising is narrow and limiting from a planning perspective. Smith[6] et al. suggest that it is particularly important to integrate communications at the marketing–sales interface In discussing what advertising is (and is not) it is important to recognize that the term 'advertising' covers many different types of activity; we can distinguish between retail advertising, trade advertising and consumer advertising. Similarly, we can categorize different types of advertising according to objectives.

The objectives of consumer advertising might be to create preference for a specific brand; that of retail advertising to create traffic through a store; manufacturers' trade advertising might be to encourage dealers to stock a product, announce important forthcoming price deals or new product launches, or simply to increase trade confidence and loyalty. With government advertising, objectives can vary from presenting public information, to exhortations to behave or vote in a certain way. Newspapers provide classified advertising, from announcements like births, deaths and marriages to the sale of products and services.

One of the most useful ways of distinguishing between broad categories of advertising is on the basis of the intended communication effect. In this way we can distinguish between three main categories:

1 **Informative advertising** is particularly relevant when a company wants to tell the market about a new product, suggest new ways of using an existing product or inform the market of changes to the product, e.g. price changes.
2 **Persuasive advertising** is used to build up a brand following or encourage customers to switch brands, or when potential customers have unfavourable attitudes towards a product or company in an attempt to change these attitudes.
3 **Reminder advertising** is aimed at maintaining brand loyalty. It can also be used to encourage former customers who have ceased to buy to return.

An example of the widening scope and application of advertising is the continuous advertising campaign to attract new recruits to the police force in the UK. The Home Office use nationwide television advertising to attract new recruits. National campaigns are backed up with newspaper advertisements and promotional techniques such as open days. An example from the USA was when California State Highway Patrol ran a 'click-it or ticket' campaign explaining the risks involved in not using a seat belt.

How advertising works: behavioural models of advertising

Given the plethora of types of advertising and the underlying complexity of behavioural issues involved, it is not surprising that there exist many conflicting views as to how advertising works. From our perspective, the reason for attempting to understand how it works is to improve our planning, implementation and control of this element of promotion. In this respect, audience response repertoire models have proved to be the most fruitful.

The four examples of possible audience response repertoire shown in Figure 7.3, i.e. AIDA, Hierarchy of Effects, DAGMAR and the ATR models, are designed to explain how advertising, or more generally communication, works. We can see from these that the precise nature and number of steps vary, but their essence is essentially the same. Specifically, they share common characteristics of suggesting that advertising, as an element of marketing communications, works by nudging the audience through a series of steps or stages in the buying process en route to making a purchase decision. The AIDA and Hierarchy of Effects models suggest that good advertising can potentially exert a powerful effect on customers creating, in the case of the AIDA model, 'desire' and 'action', and in the Hierarchy of Effects and DAGMAR models, 'conviction/desire' and 'purchase/action'. The ATR model, although based on a step-by-step process, suggests that even where advertising is effective, it is much weaker, serving only to encourage 'trial' and/or create 'reinforcement'. Rodgers'[7] **'Product adoption model'** adds to these when he cites the stages as:

- awareness;
- interest;
- evaluation;
- trial;
- adoption.

By understanding these steps, and knowing where our target audience currently is in the sequence, we can better plan, implement and control advertising decisions. Adoption models have proved to be particularly robust and useful to marketers and are still widely used. They have been used in product markets as diverse as the adoption of mobile shopping in Korea (Ko *et al.*[8]) and the adoption of Internet banking in Estonia (Eriksson *et al.*[9]).

These models suffer from the fact that they are not based on empirical evidence. In other words, they represent hypothetical constructs which may or may not reflect reality. It is true that many lack any empirical support, although others have been extensively tested, and on the basis of this, subsequently developed and refined. Evidence, however, is mixed. Certainly some consumers pass through the stages shown in the models, but not always. Palda[10] has criticized the hierarchy model, suggesting that consumers may first purchase a product and then become convinced about its value.

These models are also difficult to translate into practice because although they may point to a level in the hierarchy at which advertising should be aimed, it is still necessary to develop a specific campaign. Many of the models lack detail as to how best to achieve an objective. Refinements to some, such as the DAGMAR model, are attempts to operationalize hierarchy models further. However, there remain difficulties associated with measurement, as conceptual problems are still associated with constructs such as awareness, conviction and preference. In addition, some believe that these models focus on the wrong dimensions. Specifically, it is argued, sales and not communication effects are the underlying objective of advertising; in the absence of a direct and measurable relationship between awareness, or attitudes and sales, the models tend to focus attention on objectives which may not be related to sales. Smith *et al.*[11] review the various hierarchy models with particular relevance to creativity in advertising.

An interesting criticism is that these models tend to restrict creativity in advertising by over-specifying what has to be achieved. Certainly, many practitioners and writers on advertising subscribe to the view that the creative element, which effectively establishes and sells the brand image and appeals to the emotions, is the most important element of successful advertising.

It is safest to say that the arguments remain unresolved. Certainly we have gone some way to understanding the complex process of how advertising works and how to manage it more effectively. The stance taken here is that the models are useful provided they are applied and interpreted with care.

Managing advertising: campaign planning

The following represent the six basic elements of managing advertising effort:

- identification of the target audience;
- determination of clear, realistic and measurable objectives for advertising;
- determination of the advertising budget;
- message selection and creative platform;
- media selection and scheduling;
- control and evaluation of advertising effectiveness.

External factors also need to be taken into account, including social and legal constraints, attitudes and ideas of the advertising agency, competitors and customers (particularly their needs and motives). This wider framework for advertising decisions is shown in Figure 7.4.

Identification of target audience is the first step in planning advertising campaigns. Much of what follows in campaign planning stems from this essential step. Together with overall marketing and promotional objectives, the target audience determines creative context, media planning and scheduling.

Frequently used methods of defining target markets include demographic factors of age, sex, income and social class. However, particularly useful for advertising decisions are the more behavioural/psychological bases e.g. the ACORN system, discussed in Chapter 3, and newer 'lifestyle' approaches to classifying target markets. This is because these bases give us a fuller, richer description of target markets, encompassing not just consumer characteristics such as age and sex, but also their

FIGURE 7.4 Managing advertising: a systematic approach

Source: Adapted from Aaker, D.A. and Myers, J.G. (1982), *Advertising Management*, 2nd edn, Upper Saddle River, NJ: Prentice-Hall, p. 30.

personalities, spending habits, attitudes, interests and opinions. Where information on these aspects is not available, market research will be required to establish a full profile of target customers.

Setting advertising objectives: Once we have determined the target audience for advertising, we need to determine what advertising is intended to achieve with that audience. In broad terms, using the earlier classification of types of advertising, it might be intended to inform, persuade or remind. While this might be useful in beginning to delineate the reasons and role of advertising in the overall marketing and communications mix, these broad classifications are not a sufficient guide to the next steps in the advertising management and campaign planning process. Ideally, we need to specify precise communication goals for advertising. This is where models of the sequences in buyer behaviour related to communication are useful. For example, Colley's DAGMAR model translates into some 52 possible communication goals for advertising. Notwithstanding the controversy over these models, they are helpful in setting specific objectives for advertising, couched in terms of objectives for communication designed to move customers through the buying stages. These objectives should, whenever possible, be defined in quantitative terms and specify a time-scale.

Determining advertising budgets: Earlier we discussed some of the approaches to setting the overall budget for marketing communications, together with factors that would determine the allocation of this overall budget to the individual elements of the promotional mix. Having gone through the process of broadly determining the thrust or emphasis of promotional strategy between the different promotional tools, we should have at least a preliminary idea as to how much of the total budget will be allocated to advertising. However, at this stage we need to refine this process to arrive at a precise budget for advertising. In fact, the advertising budget can be arrived at on the same variety of bases as the overall budget for communications, i.e. based on percentages of sales and/or profits, based on competitiors' spend or based on the objective and task method. Once again, the only justifiable method is the objective and task approach, as this is distinctly advantageous when setting clear and quantified communication objectives for advertising in the preceding stage.

With a thorough understanding of what the advertising objectives are, these can be translated into specific tasks for advertising, and in turn those tasks can be costed in conjunction with the advertising agency.

Deciding on the message/creative platform is an area which potentially has the greatest impact on the success or failure of an advertising campaign. Unfortunately, it is an area that generates controversy as to what makes a successful creative advertisement. The basic direction for the creative programme is provided by product strategy that defines the market position towards which (for consistency) the product is to be directed. Advertising objectives are the second vital input to the creative programme. They influence both what the advertising says and the manner in which it is presented. The third input to the creative programme is information developed in the consumer, product and market analysis. In particular, the creative programme should be based on a clear description of the characteristics of the target consumer and the problem that the consumer is trying to solve. It also depends on information about the product to be advertised and detailed information about competitive products.

It is here that the manufacturer and the advertising agency have to decide what the advantages of the product are when compared with those of its competitors. Is it less expensive? Is it of improved quality? Is it smaller or larger? Does it have new features? Does it offer a new experience? Does the product have several outstanding advantages to offer the consumer? If it has one truly outstanding feature that can be exploited in the advertising, this is the **unique selling point** or **proposition** (USP).

In developing a creative programme the advertiser must determine the content of the message. Advertising content serves the advertiser by carrying out the strategy and objectives set for the product. The content serves the consumer by providing information about solving problems. In addition to deciding what is to be said, the programmes must also consider how it is to be said. The creative programme must determine how the advertising will be produced.

The advertiser faces difficult choices in weighing up the promise or appeal. It has been suggested that the advertiser should use rational appeals when their prospects face utilitarian problems. Emotional appeals on the other hand work best when problems are social or psychological.

Controversial, but widely used types of emotional appeal are those based on creating fear or shock in target audience. These have been used in campaigns as diverse as trying to reduce the spread of AIDS, protecting children from cruelty/abuse, anti-smoking campaigns and even in the marketing of Benetton's fashion clothing. Some believe that with the advent of reality TV type programmes, advertising has lost its power to shock. Williams[12] suggests that used with care, shock advertising still works today.

Think about the promotion of household cleaning products such as polishes and detergents. Often the advertising approach is to extol the cleaning or ease of application properties of the brand. Increasingly, advertising agencies are using less of an intuitive subjective approach to developing the creative content of advertisements. Instead, they are turning to a range of market research tools designed to improve the design of creative content based on careful and systematic research. It is over 40 years since one of the most successful advertisers, Leo Burnett,[13] advocated using in-depth interviewing techniques to provide information on a suitable **copy platform**. This is a written statement of creative strategy that specifies work to be done before writing the advertisement. Similarly, in the 1960s Maloney[14] developed a framework for designing advertising copy content based on encouraging representative target customers to associate with the type of reward or benefit they expected or hoped to get from either having used or consumed the product or service in question, or from an aspect of the product or brand in question which was 'incidental' to the usage experience. For example, we can appreciate that a major benefit from using real ground coffee instead of instant for dinner guests is the feeling that we are making a special effort for them. Put another way, making real coffee makes us feel better about ourselves. Many leading brands of non-instant coffee use ideas like this in their creative content.

Determining media selection and scheduling This element of advertising management should be prepared concurrently with the budget decision. A wide variety of media vehicles are available to the advertiser. Media planning is made easier by adherence to the preceding steps in the advertising management programme. Overall marketing strategy, advertising objectives, budgets and creative strategy serve to delineate and point to the required media strategy which is determined by the target audience.

A four step media planning approach proposes:

1   definition of media requirements, specifying the target audience, required exposure, creative requirements of the media and budget available;
2   selection of media to be used against media requirements;
3   selection of specific media vehicles utilizing media requirements to gauge their potential effectiveness;
4   specifying time length of advertisements and scheduling their appearance.

With such a variety it is difficult for a non-specialist to decide which media are best suited to a particular campaign. There is considerable competition between media to provide a service to advertisers. Most media owners publish information about their media and its coverage/audience. We examine sources of such information shortly, but generally, media selection requires asking and answering a number of questions:

■ To whom is the appeal to be directed and what kind of appeal should be made? On the basis of decisions made, the media department (usually in the advertising agency) will begin to examine characteristics of available media.

■ To what extent are various media categories and vehicles appropriate for reaching the target audience and the particular appeal selected?

■ What is the credibility of the various media vehicles?

Having decided a shortlist of various media which appear to be suitable for a campaign, the media buyer must consider which one is the 'best buy'. It is rare for only one medium to be selected and usually the best results are obtained by using a combination. When the media buyer prepares the shortlist, he or she will prepare a cost comparison. This will be based on rates issued by media owners. A summary showing the cost per thousand readers or viewers in the 'target' market for each of the media, will be submitted to the advertiser with the agency's advice. At this stage, a decision will be taken.

There has been a trend towards 'media shops' or media agencies. Essentially different names for the same thing, before the arrival of these independents, agencies had to run their own media departments. These media independents book space or time and specialize in this kind of work. An agency has to consider whether using a media shop gives a better service or whether to integrate the function in-house.

Advertising agencies are paid by the media on the basis of a percentage (between 10 per cent and 25 per cent and an average of 15 per cent) of advertising expenditure that the advertising agency places with the media. The agency's client agrees the advertising budget, advertising copy and message with the agency, and the agency receives commission from the media based on the advertising spend (often more than £10 million for a major campaign). Advertising is sometimes referred to as 'above-the-line promotion', and the 'line' refers to the line above which the agency receives commission for placing their client's advertising. 'Recognition' of the agency is needed in the UK from the Institute of Practitioners in Advertising (IPA) before commission can be paid, so non-recognized advertising agencies cannot draw commission. In other countries, similar organizations to the IPA exist with similar 'recognition' rules.

A number of research sources and tools are available to help in the task of media planning and buying. Some of these are provided by the media owners and the more important of these UK and European based sources are now outlined.

British Rate and Data (BRAD) This gives information on issue date and price, copy date, circulation, mechanical data and the advertising rates of:

1 national daily newspapers;
2 national Sunday newspapers;
3 provincial daily newspapers;
4 London and provincial newspaper groups;
5 weekly newspapers;
6 consumer publications;
7 trade, technical and professional publications.

Advertising rates and other relevant information are included on:

1 television;
2 radio;
3 posters;
4 transportation;
5 cinema;
6 telephone directory advertising;
7 local free distribution papers;
8 house-to-house distribution.

Media Expenditure Analysis Limited (MEAL) produces a monthly report covering product groups within product categories; analysis of advertising expenditure by category, product group and brand, product description and expenditure via press and television.

British Audience Research Bureau (BARB) measures TV audiences in the UK by monitoring a sample of 4,500 homes using a special meter installed in each household. The meter records which stations are turned on and, using a remote control unit, a record is made of who is watching the programmes at any point in time. This data is then downloaded from monitors direct to BARB for analysis. BARB provides a monthly chart involving the top programmes as well as publishing a weekly top ten of the most popular programmes. In addition, it publishes weekly regional lists of the top programmes and the monthly ratings share of each channel.

Radio Joint Audience Research (RAJAR) Established in 1992, RAJAR measures and analyses radio audiences in the UK.

Cinema and Video Industry Research (CAVIAR) produces statistics on cinema and video audiences.

National Business Readership Survey This is commissioned by the *Financial Times* and the results are published at six-monthly intervals. Its purpose is to help in the planning of advertising aimed at business people in the UK.

Audit Bureau of Circulation (ABC) Most large publishers belong to the ABC, to which their auditors return sales figures. The Bureau has the right to investigate these figures, and random checks are made. The Bureau issues an ABC Certificate at the end of each half year. This gives the ABC figures for publication by ABC in the *Circulation Review* issued as a supplement to British Rate and Data (BRAD). ABC also measures and verifies website traffic.

The Commission Luxembourgoise pour l'Ethique en Publicité (CLEP) was officially re-launched on 20 May 2009 as the Luxembourgish self-regulatory advertising organization, which had been restructured according to the Best Practice Recommendations of the European Advertising Standards Alliance (EASA). As the CLEP had been inactive for several years, a project was initiated in 2008 to restructure and re-launch the advertising watchdog. This was done with the support of EASA and the Belgian self-regulatory advertising organization, Jury voor Ethische Praktijken inzake Reclame/Jury d'Ethique Publicitaire (JEP).

Once these planning stages have been completed, advertising is produced and media booked. Normally, both planning and production of advertising will be done in conjunction with an advertising agency.

Evaluating and controlling advertising Given the importance and expense of advertising, it is vital to assess its effectiveness. This is where the importance of the stage of setting clear and quantified objectives comes in. When we discussed objectives for advertising, it was suggested that although sales and profits may be the ultimate reason for advertising in profit-making organizations, there are difficulties in relating these to advertising. Because of this, it was suggested that advertising objectives be set in communication terms, e.g. increasing recognition and brand awareness. Advertising and creative/copy content must be evaluated prior to implementing the campaign as well as post-campaign. An overview of research techniques for pre-testing and post-testing advertisements is now set out.

An evaluation programme begins by defining elements from the advertising budget, the media programme and the creative programme. An 'effectiveness evaluation procedure' is designed for each element. This includes specification of a standard as a base for comparison; when actual performance is measured it is compared to the standard, to determine whether or not performance is satisfactory. Budget evaluation methods involve the sort of standards and control applied to any financial budget, namely, measuring and evaluating any differences between planned and actual advertising spend. Perhaps, as with most budgets, the tendency is to overspend. Reasons for this in the context of advertising can include: overruns on production costs, delays in casting or filming, and unforeseen competitor actions. With regard to the media programme element, we might establish standards with regard to required media reach and frequency i.e. the number of target customers who have an opportunity to see the campaign and on how many occasions it has been seen. With regard to the creative programme, this can be evaluated against more qualitative measures such as: ability to recall or changes in attitude.

For each programme element to be evaluated, the evaluation programme should specify the measurement technique to be used, e.g. *media audience measurement* evaluates the effectiveness of media programmes, *recognition and recall tests* measure the effectiveness of individual advertisements, and techniques such as *consumer and retail audits* measure the effectiveness of overall campaigns.

Media audience measures were mentioned earlier. As we saw, many of the audience measurement systems are run by independent bodies, and for obvious reasons, not by the advertising industry itself. Measures of audience figures essentially assess how many might potentially be exposed to an advertisement, how many actually did see it and on how many occasions. Media is priced and purchased on the basis of figures such as these so they are important. Increasingly the various audience measurement bodies are adding qualitative assessments of their target audiences to the more qualitative ones. Recognition and recall tests have long been used to measure and evaluate advertising effectiveness. Recognition tests are based on simply asking respondents if they can recognize a brand and/or its advertising. For example, a photograph of a brand or advertisement may be shown to a respondent without the brand name being visible. The respondent is asked to identify the brand in question. If this is done with respondents pre- and post-advertising we obtain a measure of the effectiveness of advertising in aiding brand recognition.

Recall tests are more involved than recognition tests and ask respondents exposed to the advertising being evaluated what they can 'recall' about the advertising. Clearly, this is a much sterner test of the effectiveness of a campaign than simply measuring recognition. Recall tests may be aided, where the respondent is given some kind of prompt; or unaided, where the respondent must rely totally on their memory. Both recall and recognition tests are used widely by advertisers and can be used to assess a wide range of factors. Recall tests in particular are usefully when assessing the effectiveness of the creative content of promotion (Baack *et al.*[15]).

As regards the use of consumer and retail audits, these are aimed at measuring the sales effect of advertising. In the case of retail audits the measure is of the effect of advertising on moving products into and out of retailers. Consumer audits measure the pattern of purchases by the customer, often using participants who agree to record and report the products and brands they have purchased during the week.

Techniques of measuring and evaluating advertising are quite sophisticated. We now know much more about what to measure and how to do this through increased use of electronic systems for collecting and analysing information.

Developments in advertising research and practice

Advertising concepts and methods represent one of the most dynamic areas of marketing. The importance of advertising, coupled with the amounts of budgets and resources devoted to this area, have meant that it is an aspect of marketing that attracts considerable research attention to extend our knowledge and management expertise. We are constantly increasing our knowledge about how advertising works (and does not work) to manage advertising more effectively. In addition to developing this knowledge, advertising is affected by trends and changes in macro-environmental factors; particularly technological trends and changes. Some of these more important developments and trends are now discussed.

The notion of brand equity

Kotler and Keller[16] define **brand equity** as the added value endowed to products and services through individual elements of the communications mix especially advertising. This is explained graphically in Figure 7.5. The arrows from each element that forms the marketing communications programme and brand equity respectively, illustrate that each of these is an integral part of the box they are joined to.

The marketing communications programme delivers communications tactics in relation to the brand shown on the left hand side. This imparts more abstract impressions about the brand to consumers such as feelings about the brand, loyalty towards the brand, brand image, brand relationships and awareness of the brand. The most powerful brands, therefore, have a strong brand equity comprising elements on the right-hand side of Figure 7.5. The diagram also helps reinforce the notion of integrated marketing communications discussed earlier. Each of the different communication tools potentially conveys something, positive or negative, about a brand to a customer, thereby adding (if positive) or detracting (if negative) the standing of the brand (its equity) in the eyes of the customer. For example, the customer may be exposed to an advertising campaign for a brand which he or she finds interesting and amusing. As a result, brand awareness is increased together with a favourable brand image. These add to the equity of the brand by increasing the opportunity of making a sale or increasing brand loyalty. However, if, persuaded by the amusing advertising, a customer visits the company website intending to find out more about the brand, but in so doing, finds the website unattractive and difficult to negotiate, then the value of the brand in

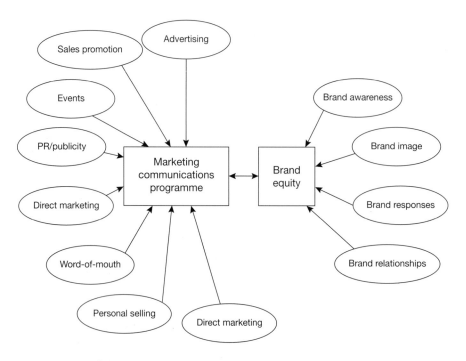

FIGURE 7.5 Marketing communications and brand equity

the eyes of the customer is diminished. Therefore, each and every element of the promotional mix affects the standing of the brand in the eyes of the customer.

The proliferation of advertising and advertising clutter

Increases in availability and types of media, more advertisers and greater advertising spends have contributed to a proliferation of advertising activity and messages. Consumers are inundated with advertising and the result is that it is difficult to gain the attention or interest of consumers, so often the message intended by the advertiser is lost. This phenomenon is known as '**clutter**' or more technically '**information overload**' which occurs when the number of advertisements to which an audience is exposed reduces interest in, and the capability to receive, any specific message. Kent[17] investigated clutter with respect to television advertising on UK network channels. His results showed that television is cluttered with advertisements for directly competing brands and this damaged the ability of target audiences to recall particular advertisements. The suggestion is that advertisers attempting to seek target audiences may be inadvertently compromising the effectiveness of their advertising. The conclusions of this and similar experiments are that highly cluttered times should be avoided and advertisers should negotiate for greater protection against clutter. More contemporary research by Rotfeld[18] has taken this research further in terms of providing a partial solution to declining audience attention to advertising. In another study Chen *et al.*[19] researched the effects of information overload on consumers' subjective state towards buying decision in the internet shopping environment.

Direct response television/interactive digital television

Direct response television (DRTV) includes television advertising that asks consumers to respond directly by calling an 0800 number, visiting a website, calling for more information, or visiting a retailer There are two types of DRTV, short form and long form. Short form is a DRTV commercial that is two minutes or less in length. Long form is longer than two minutes and is known as an **informercial**. Long form is used for products that need to educate and create awareness. Research indicates how such advertising works best and how to manage it more effectively. In an early study, Carter[20] found that longer DRTV advertisements were more effective than shorter ones. She also found that advertisements which displayed a telephone number for more than ten seconds were six times as efficient as those that displayed a telephone number for less than ten seconds. A voice-over of the telephone number gave a much better response. Most DRTV experts now agree that adverts must be at least 60 seconds long, but surprisingly compared to conventional TV ads, generally the longer the better

DRTV advertising has become popular for fast moving consumer goods (FMCGs) and some more durable products. Developments in IT have facilitated the growth of two-way communication of television advertising with target audiences. This is relatively new, but is destined to grow with advances in digital technology and opportunities for application on the Internet.

Zipping, zapping and muting

Television sets have remote control and programme recording facilities. This has led to phenomena known as '**zipping, zapping and muting**'. Zipping is the term given to the fast-forwarding of advertisements on pre-recorded TV programmes. Zapping is the term used for channel-hopping, and muting is turning down the sound on the set when advertisements are on. Advertisers are worried

Rubbermaid

Rubbermaid is a company that supplies a large range of household and industrial products. These include cleaning and storage products, office products, promotional gifts and much more. This company has run a series of DRTV advertisements for some of their products. One, which runs for just over two minutes, features a storage system for garages called 'fast track'. Because the advertisement runs for over two minutes there is plenty of time to explain the product and how it works. Running for two minutes would be too expensive to buy on a main television channel, and the properties of the product take time to explain unlike a detergent, so the company uses a specialized digital channel.

about these phenomena as they reduce the effectiveness of advertising spend. However, the effects on advertising are complex. Early research by Gilmore and Secunda[21] found that as a repetition of a zipped advertisement increased, so did its recall. However, product recognition and product recall depended on having seen the product advertisement before seeing the zipped advertisement. They concluded that a zipped television advertisement can lead to product retrieval and reinforcement of previously learned information. This recognition and retrieval can have a positive effect on attitudes towards a product. Such findings suggest that extensive research is needed with regard to implications for the marketer.

Fragmentation of media

Technology has led to an explosion in the range and types of media available to the advertiser. This is particularly true in television advertising. The growth of satellite and cable television means that audience figures for many programmes are much smaller and often more specialized than they have been previously. While this means that the advertiser can reach fewer potential customers through television advertising, they are able to target selected audiences more accurately. There are many implications of this fragmentation of target audiences e.g. many marketers are moving away from large-scale 'blockbuster' promotions on national TV networks towards more selective promotional campaigns involving more of an emphasis on 'push' rather than 'pull' promotion. **Push promotion** is the use of sales promotional incentives by manufacturers to distributive intermediaries with the objective of persuading retailers and distributive intermediaries to stock (e.g. by offering additional discounts). **Pull promotion** is the use of advertising and branding and customer-oriented sales promotions by manufacturers aimed at 'pulling' customers into stores to search for specific brands like Kelloggs. Manufacturers using pull techniques can exercise greater control over wholesalers and retailers.

Advertisers increasingly use global websites through the Internet to promote products, and this is explained more fully in Chapter 10.

We have seen how advertising strategy fits into overall marketing and promotional strategy, together with the steps in its effective planning and management. In the remainder of this chapter we consider sales promotion and PR/publicity. Other elements of the communications mix, namely selling and direct marketing, are considered separately. Much of the framework for planning sales promotion, direct marketing and publicity i.e. the need to relate these to an overall promotional and marketing strategy considering target customers, competitors and social/legal factors applies in the same way as advertising. Similarly, these elements of promotion must be planned systematically, with clear measurable objectives and effective control and evaluation.

SALES PROMOTION

In consumer markets, typically spend on **sales promotion** outstrips that of media advertising. It offers buyers a supplementary attraction as an incentive to engender an instant sale. As such it is regarded as a short-term promotional tool. The category of sales promotional tools includes some of the best known communications used in marketing such as coupons, self-liquidating offers, sample, bargain packages and giveaways which are explained later.

Scope and objectives of sales promotion

As consumers have developed a resistance to advertising, the use of sales promotion has increased. There is scope for a variety of activities with sales promotion and companies seek to create a promotion that singles it out from competitors. Advertising is partly restricted by the media that can be used.

The role of sales promotion is to encourage purchase by temporarily improving the value of a brand. However, it is part of the overall marketing mix and should tie in with advertising, product performance and pricing. The purpose of advertising is to improve dispositions towards a brand, while the objective of sales promotion is to translate favourable attitudes into actual purchase. Advertising cannot normally close a sale because its impact is too far from the point of purchase, but sales promotion can.

Sales promotion is often managed in isolation from other elements of marketing, because there is the need to gain shelf space through retailer support and in this context it is referred to as 'the silent salesman'.

Collectively, these tools of sales promotion are often referred to as '**below-the-line promotion**' which contrasts to advertising which, as discussed earlier, is termed 'above-the-line' expenditure. We now describe and discuss some of the more frequently used tools of sales promotion. With such variety of techniques, we need to be sure that the planning of sales promotion is systematic, so the key steps in planning sales promotion, along with appropriate techniques, are now discussed.

Planning sales promotion

The starting point is the identification of the target audience and the specific objectives that the sales promotion intends to achieve. Sales promotion can be aimed at one or more of the following:

- consumers;
- the 'trade' (retailers, wholesalers, distributors etc.);
- the sales force.

In consumer sales promotion, typical objectives include encouraging customers to switch brands, to try a new product or encourage heavier purchase/consumption. Much of the literature on sales promotion relates to the use of this tool in markets for fast moving consumer goods. It is also prevalent and effective in industrial product markets, through the use of, for example, trade fairs, executive gifts and sponsorship. Sales promotion can play an important part in a market where competition is fierce and where relatively minor 'incentives' to purchase might swing the balance in favour of a particular supplier.

In trade sales promotion, objectives might include encouraging the trade to stock a new line or exhorting them to put more effort into selling a company's brands to the final customer. Naturally, the trade will only be interested in doing any of these if it is profitable. Because of this, effective trade sales promotion needs to be supported by imaginative marketing, including sales promotion efforts to the trade's customer. More importantly, the trade will need to be convinced that there is a market for the product.

Promotion aimed at motivating the company's own sales force might include these objectives: stimulating greater effort to support a new product launch, encouraging the opening of new accounts and encouraging more visits per day.

We see that achieving a given objective may require targeting sales promotion at various parties. Where this is the case, it needs to be effectively co-ordinated and controlled along with other elements of the marketing and promotional mix. The next step is to select the most appropriate and cost-effective sales promotional tools. There is little empirical evidence to suggest which tools work best in which situation and why. As an indication of the types of sales promotion tools available for each target audience, we outline the major ones used for consumers, trade and the field sales force.

Consumer sales promotion

Coupons The consumer must be in possession of a coupon or voucher of a particular value which can then be 'redeemed' at a local store to obtain the product or products named on the voucher at the usual price, less the value of the voucher. There is usually a deadline, and the offer often applies to a particular size in the range of products, which usually means that the consumer, in order to take advantage of the offer, must purchase the product within a shorter space of time than normal. The effect of this is to increase the rate of stock-turn for both the retailer and the manufacturer.

A problem is that most redemptions are made by people who would normally have bought the product, so the true value of the scheme is difficult to ascertain, although in oligopolistic situations (explained in Chapter 5) some might switch brands as a result of the offer. However, where the voucher constitutes an introductory offer on a relatively new product, the 'bargain' element sometimes persuades consumers to switch brands.

Self-liquidating offer An example here is where a manufacturer of a brand of canned food purchases a quantity of kitchen knives from a supplier at a price of £1 per knife. The food manufacturer then 'offers' to sell the knives to the consuming public at the cost price of £1 or thereabouts, plus proof of purchase (e.g. the till receipt) from a particular size of the manufacturer's brand of canned food. The advantage to the retailer and the manufacturer is that stock-turn rate is increased. The consumer benefits by being able to purchase the knives at trade price. This type of operation is termed 'self-liquidating' because capital used by the manufacturer in purchasing the knives is returned by the consumer.

Until relatively recently, manufacturers making such offers used to ask for proofs of purchase in the form of the actual label or a token from the can's label. Legislation has now made this illegal, as the view was taken by the UK and other countries that the public should not be coerced into making purchases that they may not want, particularly in relation to those purchasing simply to take advantage of the offer. This, incidentally, is the main reason why there are now fewer consumer competitions on offer, as the rule now is that no purchase should be necessary to enter a contest, so manufacturers are naturally reluctant to offer expensive contests when they cannot directly see the benefits of such promotions.

Sampling Many manufacturers, particularly in the areas of fast moving consumer goods (FMCGs), give away free samples of their products. The sample is often of a smaller size than the normal pack size and it is hoped that customers will try the product, like it, and purchase it in future. Again, this is usually reserved for new entrants to a market and its advantage is that if consumers are given a sample of shampoo for example, they are unlikely to buy their usual brand until they have used the free sample, by which time they might decide to switch from their usual brand next time they purchase.

Bargain packages There are two main forms of this promotional technique. One is where the product is advertised at a particular price, but the pack is marked '50p off' (known as a flash pack) which means that the purchase price will be reduced by that amount, but only on products so marked, which is another way of saying 'while stocks last'. Many people take advantage of this type of offer, but they include regular purchasers, many of whom stock up with the product at the bargain price and do not purchase again until their stocks have run down. Legislation was enacted in the UK that makes it difficult for manufacturers to use this tactic as the problem is '50 pence off what?' The fixing of retail prices by manufacturers is not legal as a result of the Resale Prices Act (1964 and 1976) and retailers can sell at whatever price they feel is appropriate. In 2001 Levi's jeans were being imported by Tesco from South America from what is called the 'grey market' and sold in its stores at a discount. Levi's insisted that its retailers sell at stipulated prices and stopped Tesco selling its goods without permission through the European Court of Justice, who ruled that Levi's had the right to stipulate who sold its products. In this way Levi's was able to exercise control over distribution of its products and at what price. Manufacturers now find it easier to use tactics like '10 per cent extra free'.

The second form of this technique is where the offer is advertised as 'buy one, get one free' (BOGOF) which is two for the price of one. Sometimes, attached to the large size pack (of toothpaste, for example) is a smaller sized pack (termed a 'limpet pack'). This method does not help the retailer so much as the manufacturer, who is able to increase turnover of large packs, sales of which may have been sluggish, and at the same time maintain the turnover of the smaller pack. Competitive brands of toothpaste are unlikely to be purchased by the customer until their stocks have run down.

Give–aways This is often aimed at the younger end of various market segments, and has been used extensively by breakfast cereal companies. Into every packet of cereal is put a small toy or gift in an attempt to use the influencing power of children.

Many FMCG marketers 'bundle' their promotional offers using a combination of promotional tools in a campaign, e.g. a two-for-one offer on a brand may be combined with a promotional offer of a free product with the purchase, such as free Bolognese sauce with a pasta purchase. Bundled promotional campaigns are successful in persuading customers to purchase or switch brands, as they offer good value for money, although the can be expensive for the marketer.

Trade promotions

Frequently used trade promotions include:

- *Discounts/cash allowances*: a percentage discount or cash allowance given for each bulk case purchased;
- *Additional products with order*: extra products given with each unit ordered e.g. if a case of 12 is purchased, one extra case is given free (colloquially called a 'baker's dozen');

- *Merchandising allowances*: financial allowances to a retailer for featuring and selling the manufacturer's products;
- *Advertising allowances/co-operative advertising*: compensates retailers for featuring a manufacturer's products in a newspaper advertisement featuring the retailer; alternatively, the supplier may organize collaborative advertising with the trade.
- *Exhibitions*: in some trades are almost obligatory. A well known example in the UK is the Ideal Home Exhibition, which is held annually. It features all possible goods which can be used in a home, and exhibits 'model homes' which are fully furnished and can be visited and inspected. Another international example is the annual Frankfurt motor show.

Many exhibitions are on an industrial scale, including examples like the Motor Show, the Office Equipment Exhibition and the Hardware Trades Fair. Many of these exhibitions are mounted solely for the trade and the public are not allowed admittance.

Sales force promotions

This is a popular area for the application of sales promotional techniques like sales contests, bonus prizes and sales incentives and gifts.

Appropriateness of sales promotions

The most appropriate tools in this context vary according to type of product market, sales promotion objectives, target audience and the emphasis of marketing strategy, e.g. a 'push' versus 'pull' strategy. Often consumers, trade and the sales force will be targeted, so it is important that multifaceted campaigns are well co-ordinated.

Before a full-scale sales promotion is launched, as with advertising, it is advisable to pre-test the promotional vehicles selected. This can be done by using focus groups, selected in-store tests or full-scale test marketing. If testing is successful, indicating that the sales promotion will achieve its required objectives, a full-scale campaign can be implemented.

An important factor in assessing the success of a sales promotion campaign is the effect on sales which should be compared with the costs of the campaign and alternative ways of spending this budget. In measuring the sales effectiveness of such a promotion, it is important to monitor sales over a longer period than the duration of the campaign. This is because there can be a 'lagged' effect. If the promotional campaign has been aimed at generating a short-term increase in sales and market share, any such increases will often be followed by a downturn in sales and market share compared to immediately before the campaign. This drop is due to customers having stocked up as a result of an effective sales promotion campaign. After a time, sales will return to normal, albeit at a new and hopefully higher level than before the campaign. A complicating factor concerns what is known as a 'lead' effect which is where, in anticipation of the sales promotion, customers delay purchases they would otherwise have made. Similarly, salespersons may hold back on selling effort if they expect a sales contest with prizes to be introduced in the future. Such factors add to the need to evaluate and control sales promotion.

Developments in sales promotion research and practice

Sales promotion is constantly being researched and techniques are being developed and used alongside traditional methods. Some interesting developments are:

In-store sales promotion: promotional kiosks: In-store sales promotions have traditionally used techniques like leaflets, demonstrations and merchandising. Allied to developments in IT, promotional kiosks have been developed. These are in-store kiosks where potential customers are presented with visual and verbal information regarding products in the store, their features, uses, unique selling points and stock availability. Interactive video is used in these kiosks. Advantages for in-store kiosk systems include:

- They provide a means of showing an extended range of products.
- Customers can consider alternatives if desired items are not in stock.
- The customer can browse through a range of products and pay for specific products in stock.
- They can be used to offer a 24-hour 'through-the-wall' shopping service like automatic teller machines that are used for banking services.

A variation is touch screens used in large grocery supermarkets. Touch screens are located in the entrance foyer of the stores and are activated by customers swiping their loyalty cards through the sensor. Having done this, the customer is able to trace through promotional offers in the store on that day. The use of customer loyalty cards, backed up through the database system, enables the promotional offers displayed to be to a degree tailored to the personal shopping profile in terms of product and brand choice of the individual customer. If the customer is interested in any of the promotional offers on the screen then he/she presses the screen, and the appropriate promotional coupons are issued.

Packaging design: This is powerful area of promotion. Innovative packaging design is able to demonstrate market share and profitability improvements for the marketer. Companies are turning their attention to the potential for this below-the-line promotion element of marketing. Blair and Rosenburg[22] have shown the potential impact of effective packaging design. They cite the effect of a redesigned package for McVities Jaffa Cakes. When this long established product was languishing in the market, the company rejuvenated the product packaging and market share increased rapidly. In the UK a reform to the Trademarks Act has allowed shapes, sounds and smells to be registered as trademarks. The large number of applications is testament to brand owners' perception of the need to redesign packaging and to protect this as quickly as possible.

Point of sale material and in-store merchandising: Trends in the use of sales promotions in the communications mix is recognition of the importance of **point-of-sale promotion (POS)** and in-store merchandising activities. Increasing power of retailers and the ensuing fight by manufacturers for limited shelf space has made this activity more popular. Research has shown that up to 70 per cent of customers make their brand choices in store, so there is increased need to reinforce brand differentiation at the point of sale. As a result, in-store merchandising and POS are sophisticated and fully integrated into the promotional mix as a key part of a brand's long-term positioning.

Have One On Me

An example of how point-of-sale can be used as part of a planned promotional campaign is that developed by the design and promotional agency, The House, for J. D. Wetherspoon Company. The promotion was based on a 19-day beer festival which centred on introducing Wetherspoons' customers to a range of beers they had not heard of, let alone tried, and hence to widen their tastes. A central facet of the campaign was the use of point-of-sale material designed by The House. This included a range of special ⅓ pint glasses so it was possible to try three different ales and still only drink one pint. In addition to these special glasses, staff wore special 'taste three ales' T-shirts. Special beer mats were produced for the bar areas and there were tasting notes on the beers on offer for customers to pick up and read. The result was success in which point-of-sale promotion was crucial.

Source: http://www.thehouse.co.uk.

Increased use of information technology is having a major effect on the marketer e.g. more sophisticated and powerful databases enable better targeting of sales promotional campaigns. As mentioned earlier, Sainsbury's stores use touch screens, enabling promotional offers to be linked to individual customer purchasing patterns. Many retailer loyalty schemes and the ensuing databases which stem from them, enable the marketer to identify targets for promotional campaigns. The effects of a promotional campaign can be rapidly and accurately measured and evaluated using developments in IT. This enables the marketer to evaluate a campaign while it is on-going and make any modifications to increase its effectiveness.

Emphasis on building loyalty: What has traditionally been seen as a promotional tool used to encourage short-term brand switching on the part of customers is increasingly being used to encourage and develop company, brand or store loyalty. The use of loyalty cards in retailing is one approach to using promotional techniques to engender customer loyalty. The growth in the recognition of the importance of customer loyalty is linked to the growth of relationship marketing which is discussed in Chapter 9. At this stage, it is sufficient to note that marketers are increasingly aware of the value of customer loyalty as a marketing asset and have put more effort into building and maintaining this loyalty. Sales promotion campaigns which lock in customers have increased in recent years. There is a danger, however, that customers become loyal to the loyalty scheme rather than to the marketer or the brand.

The introduction of a loyalty card scheme was a factor in Tesco becoming the largest grocery supermarket retailer in the UK. The loyalty card was introduced to enhance customer loyalty directly by offering rewards as an incentive to shop there regularly. Launched in February 1995 Tesco's loyalty card was the first such successful scheme in the UK. Many competitors felt the scheme would be a short-term gimmick and customers would tire of it. Not long after, these competitors realized that the scheme was very successful and quickly moved to introduce their own schemes. Sainsbury's said when it introduced its scheme in June 1996 that it was motivated by the perception of being at a competitive disadvantage without one. Asda introduced a scheme in 1994 which was not successful and discontinued it in mid-1999, to focus on its price rollback campaign to enhance customer loyalty.

Morrisons have not participated in loyalty cards as they believe that competitive pricing is more effective at retaining customers than a loyalty card.

Controversially, a considerable amount of sales promotion directed at building customer loyalty is aimed at children. Research in the UK reported in *Marketing Week*[23] showed that children are susceptible to some sales promotional campaigns, especially for example the use of free gifts, T-shirts, models etc. This susceptibility is heightened where the campaign can be linked to a film character or theme. For example, some of the most successful sales promotion campaigns of the late 1990s made use of the interest in dinosaurs due to the popularity of the *Jurassic Park* series of films, the first of which was introduced in June 1993.

Direct marketing: This major element of the promotional mix is a relative newcomer. In some ways, direct marketing is not new: direct mail catalogue as a basis for marketing products has been around for many years. However, the use of these techniques has grown considerably in recent years. As with other categories of the promotional mix, direct marketing encompasses a plethora of different tools and techniques. As a promotional tool direct marketing can also be considered under the 'place' element of the marketing mix as a channel of distribution in its own right. Within the context of direct marketing we include telemarketing and electronic marketing (e-marketing) whose application is normally direct from **Business-to-customer (B2C)** or **Business-to-business (B2B)**. Techniques of direct marketing have become increasingly important, and Chapter 10 considers these techniques and their application in a promotional context.

PUBLIC RELATIONS AND SPONSORSHIP

Recent years have witnessed an increasingly professional approach to managing this area of marketing communications. **Public relations (PR)** has replaced the term 'publicity' for this type of promotion. Publicity, somewhat confusingly, is often used to denote these activities. PR is a broader concept than publicity as it relates to more strategic issues.

Sponsorship can be included as a promotional category in its own right or sometimes as a sales promotion technique. We feel that because sponsorship is normally associated with promoting the company's image and name amongst its publics, it is most appropriately considered alongside other PR activities. We now outline the main issues in managing these elements of the promotional mix.

Public relations (PR)

PR's concern is to promote the image of a company, its products and services. Unlike other promotional activities, PR does not necessarily involve the company in direct costs e.g. the company may issue a press release with a view to having its contents published free if the publisher feels it is sufficiently newsworthy or interesting to their readers. News items that are generated through this means tend to be more 'believable' than 'paid for' advertising, so from the company's point of view it can be very effective. The fact that it is sometimes not paid for does not mean it is unimportant, not to be integrated with other elements of a company's promotional mix. The old adage that there is 'no such thing as bad publicity' is simply not true. Bad publicity can seriously affect a company's image and sales.

The launch of the now highly successful Mercedes 'A' Class model was marred by bad publicity. The so-called 'moose test' conducted in Sweden in 1997 by the journalist Robert Collin from the motor magazine *Teknikens Värld* was designed to test the ease with which a new model could be steered around an object such as a moose appearing on the highway. The test showed that in its original design form the 'A' Class was susceptible to rolling over. The tests and the failure of the 'A' Class to pass them made worldwide news as the test was done independently. To make the situation worse, a much older widely mocked design of Trabant car, from the former German Democratic Republic, managed the test perfectly. In short, publicity for the safety-conscious and highly respected engineering image of Mercedes was a disaster. The product had to be recalled and redesigned.

Public relations tools include:

- *Press release*, which is basically news that a company issues in objective, journalistic form in the hope that it will be printed in the form in which it is received by the editor.
- *Press conference*, a meeting where a major announcement is made and at which guests are invited to ask questions. A press conference may be given in preference to a press release if the matter under review merits some explanation which may not be covered adequately in the press release itself.
- *Press receptions* (not a substitute for a press release). It is at press receptions, which are major events in themselves, that important announcements are made e.g. a new model of car. Such receptions need to be well planned and guests receive 'programme invitations'. A press reception is not as formal as a press conference as it is normally done in a more relaxed and sociable manner usually accompanied by some kind of hospitality.
- *Facility visits*, where representatives, often including the media, are given the opportunity to inspect some special aspects of a firm's operations. A visit may involve a tour around a new factory.

Effective PR management requires building up good and trusting relationships with opinion leaders, especially in the press and magazines. **Publicity** is a tactical tool within the broader framework of PR. PR is a deliberate, planned and sustained effort to establish and maintain mutual understanding between an organization and its publics. In this context PR has a wider role to play than simply publicity as illustrated below when we examine what is termed 'the publics of PR':

- *Community activities* are where the organization acts in support of local and national activities and partakes in the development of a community relations programme.
- *Employee relations* is an important internal aspect of PR as there are benefits involving the workforce in terms of establishing and maintaining a mutual understanding.
- *Government relations*: both local and national politicians are important sources of information for an organization e.g. legislative changes that might affect the business; lobbying politicians is not without criticism, but it is a perfectly acceptable procedure in industry and government relationships.
- *The financial community* involves commercial and merchant banks, investors and share analysts as well as city journalists who are all 'publics' with whom an organization needs to communicate in the context of financial matters.

■ *Distributors* are intermediaries in the distribution channel and these include wholesalers, retailers, agents, brokers, dealers, etc. They all need information about products and services to have the knowledge and confidence necessary to become effective resellers.

■ *Consumers* are often though of as the only 'public' and they need to be co-ordinated with other areas of marketing communications like advertising and sales promotion. Educating consumers and creating and maintaining interest among target audiences can lead to favourable attitudes being generated towards a company's products and services.

■ *Opinion leaders* include trade associations and pressure groups. PR must attempt to understand the position of all important external groups, even if the group is opposed to them. If effective communication through PR takes place, it is better for factual information to be the basis of debate rather than hearsay or exaggeration.

■ *Media* Here PR has a role to play in the development of relationships with the broadcasting media. As mentioned already, the aim is to achieve appropriate broadcasting of information a company may create as part of a well organized PR campaign.

Recognition of the communications role of PR is – it means that it is seen as a sub-set of marketing communications planning with clear marketing communication objectives for PR, well managed campaigns and effective evaluation and control.

Sponsorship

Sponsorship is sometimes viewed as being a sales promotional activity, but it should be considered as a component of PR. It involves a company supporting in some way something or someone it feels will help in the overall marketing and sales of its products or services, albeit indirectly. The 'something' or 'someone' being sponsored can be a sportsperson, or an event like the Olympics, or a cause such as Aids prevention.

Commercial sponsorship has been a rapidly growing area of promotion. There are many reasons for this. The sponsoring of a particular event or person enables the sponsor to achieve more cost-effective awareness with the target audience generated by the event, or by the publicity associated with the individual, than might otherwise be possible through conventional promotional tools like advertising. Millions watched the March 2009 Oxford–Cambridge University boat race on Independent Television, which is a large audience for any sponsor whose name might be attached to one of the boats for a relatively modest outlay. Who cares about it? ITV's 7.6 million peak viewers, plus more than 100 media people and 250,000 spectators lining the towpath in one of London's largest annual public events. In a wider context, 112 countries requested film of the race to screen live or as highlights for an estimated 200 million people around the world.

Large investments are made by marketers on event and celebrity endorsement contracts. Tripp and Jensen[24] have suggested that the use of such promotion is based on the premise that source effects (i.e. the celebrity her- or himself) play an important role in persuasive communication. They give examples of the impact of such endorsement on sales. Michael Jordan, the US basketball star, signed a multi-million pound sponsorship contract with Nike and the company's market share increased by 20 per cent over the previous quarter. However, their research points to the possible detrimental effects of celebrities becoming involved in promotion, especially when the celebrity is involved in multiple product advertising. It is suggested that too many endorsements might damage credibility which may have a negative impact on sales. Sponsorship based on celebrity endorsement in particular is not a panacea for marketers. Another risk associated with using celebrities is that if, for some reason, the reputation or image of the celebrity becomes 'tarnished', this may have a detrimental effect on the sponsor's image.

SUMMARY

To understand and plan the promotional element of the marketing mix, it is important to appreciate how communications works. Marketing effectiveness is highly correlated with the effectiveness with which the marketer communicates to the target audience, and this requires coordinating the variety of ways in which this communication is achieved. All the elements of the marketing mix, and not just communications, potentially contribute to this process. In particular, advertising, sales promotion, direct marketing, public relations, sponsorship and personal selling must be seen as a total marketing communications package and managed from this perspective.

When it comes to managing individual elements of the promotional mix, there are differences in application, purpose and implementation; the overall process is the same. Clear objectives must be set, couched in communication terms, and wherever possible quantified. On this basis, budgets can be set and promotional campaigns developed. Each of the promotional tools and the overall marketing communications strategy must be carefully evaluated and controlled. Only by following a systematic, planned and co-ordinated approach to marketing communications can expenditures on this area of strategic marketing be justified.

KEY TERMS

Promotion	235	Promo-tools	242
Encoding	235	Communications mix	242
Media planning	236	Integrated marketing	
Decoding	236	communications (IMC)	245
Selective perception	237	Informative advertising	246
Selective distortion	237	Persuasive advertising	246
Noise	237	Reminder advertising	246
Audience response repertoire	241	Product adoption model	247
AIDA model	241	Unique selling point (USP)	250
Hierarchy of effects model	241	Copy platform	251
DAGMAR model	241	Above-the-line promotion	252
ATR model	241	Recognition	252

CASE STUDY

Global International plc

Toby Kelly is the recently appointed Marketing Director of Global International plc. The company is multinational marketer of sports equipment, selling a range of well-known brands in virtually every part of the world.

As a company, and somewhat unusually compared to competitors, it has never considered commercial sponsorship for the company or any of its brands. In fact, several of its branded products are used by leading sportspersons in a number of sports. For example, Mia Rees (currently the world's number 1 female tennis player) uses the company's 'Spinner' brand of tennis racket. Similarly, most of the Australian cricket team use the company's 'Century' brand of bat. Their basketball brand 'Bouncy' is the official ball of the American Basketball Association. None of these brands or usages are connected in any way with any form of sponsorship.

The company has considered sponsorship on several occasions, particularly as it has seen its major competitors use this form of promotion to good effect. The main reason why the company has not considered sponsorship before is that the chairperson, the original co-founder of the company, feels that any form of sponsorship is demeaning to the company and its products. The view held by the chairperson is that a good product will sell itself, a viewpoint in some ways substantiated by the selection of many of the company's brands by leading sportspersons and sports organizations without any sponsorship. In addition, there was a feeling in some parts of the company that sponsorship through product endorsement by a leading sportsperson was not particularly effective inasmuch as everyone knew that this person would receive large sums of money for endorsing the product. In other words, there was a source credibility problem. Finally, there was always a concern

. . . continued

CASE STUDY ... *continued*

about what would happen to the company's brand image if there was some sort of scandal with the sponsored party.

Toby Kelly is a firm believer in sponsorship. His previous company used it to good effect. Global spends large amounts of money on advertising and sales promotion. He has decided to make his case to the rest of the Board for introducing sponsorship as a major part of the promotional mix. He needs to prepare his case for the next Board Meeting.

CASE STUDY QUESTION

Prepare Toby's case for the company investing in sponsorship.

REFERENCES

1 Strong, E.K. (1925), *The Psychology of Selling*, New York: McGraw-Hill.

2 Lavidge, R.J. and Steiner, G.A. (1961), 'A model for predictive measurements of advertising effectiveness', *Journal of Marketing*, October.

3 Colley, R.H. (1983 [1961]), *Defining Advertising Goals for Measured Advertising Results*, New York: Association of National Advertisers.

4 Jones, J.P. (1991), 'Over-promise and under-delivery', *Marketing and Research Today*, November: 195–203.

5 Mulhern, F. (2009), 'Integrated marketing communications: from media channels to digital connectivity', *Journal of Marketing Communications*, 15(2/3): 85–101.

6 Smith, T.M., Gopalkrishna, S. and Chatterjee, R. (2006), 'A three stage model of integrated marketing communications at the marketing-sales interface', *Journal of Marketing Research*, 43(4): 564–79.

7 Rodgers, E.M. (1962), *Diffusion of Innovations*, New York: Free Press.

8 Ko, E., Kim, E.U. and Lee, E.K. (2009), 'Modelling consumer adoption of mobile shopping for fashion products in Korea', *Psychology and Marketing*, 26(7): 669–87.

9 Eriksson, K., Kerem, K. and Nilsson, D. (2008), 'The adoption of commercial innovations in the former Central and Eastern European markets: the case of internet banking in Estonia', *International Journal of Bank Marketing*, 26(3): 154–69.

10 Palda, K.S. (1966), 'The hypothesis of a hierarchy of effects – a partial evaluation', *Journal of Marketing Research*, 3(1): February.

11 Smith, R., Chen, J. and Yang, X. (2008), 'The impact of advertising creativity on the hierarchy of effects', *Journal of Advertising*, 37(4): 47–61.

12 Williams, M. (2009), 'Does shock advertising still work?', *Campaign*, 16: 11.

13 Burnett, L. (1961), *Confessions of an Advertising Man*, Chicago: Leo Burnett Co., p. 61.

14 Maloney, J.C. (1966), 'Attitude measurement and formation'. Paper presented at the Test Market Design and Measurement Workshop, American Marketing Association, Chicago, Illinois, 21 April.

15 Baack, D., Wilson, R. and Till, B.D. (2008), 'Creativity and memory effects', *Journal of Advertising*, 37(4): 85–94.

16 Kotler, P. and Keller, K.L. (2009), *Marketing Management*, 13th edn, New Jersey: Prentice-Hall, p. 513.

17 Kent, R.J. (1993), 'Competitive versus non-competitive clutter in Television Advertising', *Journal of Advertising Research*, March/April: 40–6.

18 Rotfeld, H.J. (2006), 'Understanding advertising clutter and the real solution to declining audience attention to mass media commercial messages', *Journal of Consumer Marketing*, (4): 180–1.

19 Chen, Y., Shang, R. and Kao, C. (2009), 'The effects of information overload on consumers subjective state towards buying decision in the internet shopping environment', *Electronic Commerce Research & Applications*, 8(1): 48–58.

20 Carter, M. (1994), 'Direct response ads gain respect', *Marketing Week*, 1 July: 24–5.

21 Gilmore, R.F. and Secunda, E. (1993), 'Zipped TV commercials boost prior learning', *Journal of Advertising Research*, Nov./Dec.: 29–38.

22 Blair, M.H. and Rosenburg, K.E. (1994), 'Convergent findings increase our understanding of how advertising works', *Journal of Advertising Research*, 34(May/June): 35.

23 'Power Points', *Marketing Week*, 3 February 2000: 43–7.

24 Tripp, C. and Jensen, T.D. (1993), 'Effects of multiple product endorsement', *Journal of Consumer Research*, 20(4), March: 548.

Chapter 8

Sales management

LEARNING OBJECTIVES

By the end of this chapter you will:

- understand the role and importance of selling in the marketing programme and how it should be managed
- be familiar with the different steps in selection, training, and organization of the sales force
- appreciate the considerations in planning sales force structure and territory and journey planning
- be aware of the elements of the personal selling process
- recognize different ways of controlling and evaluating the sales force including remuneration systems
- understand the changing nature of personal selling and the developments taking place in this area of marketing

INTRODUCTION

Selling is a universal activity; everybody sells something. In a modern market economy, selling is an important and sophisticated activity. In less advanced societies, selling is low level, often amounting to simple barter. In this chapter we examine the important role of the sales force in overall marketing activities, and the relationship between marketing and sales functions.

Selling is a process to make a sale, but personal selling is more than this. Selling can be done remotely through mail-shots or advertisements; personal selling is done face-to-face which demands interpersonal skills and training and it is a highly professional activity. We examine the key steps in managing the sales force from recruitment and training to territory design, sales call planning, and control and remuneration as well as the steps in personal selling and considerations in managing these effectively as well as examining emerging trends in selling and sales management.

ROLE OF THE SALES FORCE

Depending on the type of organization, a sales force may consist of a few salespeople with infrequent contact with customers, or many salespeople operating in a highly organized system with regular and frequent contact. The latter would apply to companies selling consumer goods like confectionery where it is necessary to have a regular, day-to-day contact. A company that constructs bridges needs fewer salespeople as there are fewer customers and it is more appropriate to have technical sales-persons to negotiate contracts and resolve problems that customers may face during the construction process.

The sales force provides a flow of information to the company which needs to know what is happening 'in the field' to keep up with changes in demand or fashion.

Personal selling is an integral part of the firm's communication mix which is made up of non-personal communication tools. Generally, personal selling is more important in organizational settings. As much as 80 per cent of the total marketing budget is spent on selling because of the necessity of a one-to-one relationship. This is because of:

- the technical complexity of products;
- the commercial complexity of sales negotiations;
- the degree of commercial interdependence and interaction between the buying and selling organizations.

These factors are not present in many consumer marketing situations. Personal selling is less critical and more of the budget is spent on non-personal communications like advertising which features strongly for products such as lager, coffee and detergents. Consumer advertising attempts to 'pull' these goods through the distribution channel. Personal, face-to-face selling, attempts to 'push' goods through the channel.

Selling is the main task of the sales force, although are other tasks include:

- obtaining information;
- maintaining and creating goodwill;
- building business for the future.

TYPES OF SALES FORCE

A variety of different types of sales force take account of different sales situations:

Selling consumer goods to members of the channel where regular contact must be maintained. Personal relationships are important; typically used for FMCGs and consumer durables. Salespersons must be well organized to provide regular coverage. Selling to retailers requires a large sales force to call on customers at pre-determined intervals (termed the **sales journey cycle**). Large sales forces can be split into regions with regional sales managers, and regions are split into areas with an area manager in charge of individual representatives. Channel members (retailers and wholesalers) are business customers, so processes and considerations pertaining to organizational buyers apply as they are professional purchasers using systematic buying processes and purchase in large lots.

Industrial goods selling where products are often made to individual specification, so customer needs have to be satisfied on an individual basis. Products range from machinery to component parts to raw materials and services such as the provision of IT products and systems on behalf of clients. Much time is spent finding prospective customers. Often, products are sold at such infrequent intervals that when the customer is ready to re-order, specifications have been modified substantially. Salespeople tend to be well qualified and can discuss customer technical problems and offer solutions so cementing relationships with industrial buyers.

Retail selling: Despite the ubiquitous nature of self-service, considerable selling activity takes place in this setting. These activities are not confined to durable products or services like cars, televisions or holidays, but also relate to lower value items like shoes and clothing, and even non-durables like foodstuffs and meals. Think back to the last time you purchased shoes in a retail outlet. How helpful was the person who served you? Did they have any influence over whether you bought or not? Did they suggest a particular pair of shoes? Did they get you to spend more than you intended? Did they get you to purchase another item like shoe polish with the shoes? Will you ever return and buy again from the same retailer? Shoe retailers are aware of the importance of sales activities to customers. Staff training involves how to sell to customers including encouraging them to trade up and extend their purchasing.

TYPES OF SELLING JOB

A classic description of different types of salesperson was devised by McMurry:[1]

1   The salesperson's job is mainly concerned with delivery e.g. milk, beer, bread and lemonade. They possess little in the way of selling responsibilities. Increases in sales are more likely to stem from a good service and a pleasant manner.
2   The salesperson is predominantly an inside order taker, e.g. a sales assistant in a retail outlet. Opportunities to sell are limited as customers have often already made up their minds.
3   The salesperson is predominantly an order taker, but works in the field, e.g. the wholesale or retail grocery salesperson. Selling to an account like a large retail chain is usually done by senior executives at head office. The field salesperson simply records and processes customer orders and makes sure the customer is carrying sufficient stock. Good service and a pleasant personality may lead to more orders, but the salesperson has little opportunity for creative selling.
4   In 'missionary selling' the salesperson does not actually take orders, but builds up goodwill, educates the actual or potential user and undertakes various promotional activities, e.g. salesperson for a pharmaceutical company.
5   In technical selling, companies tend to use technically qualified salespeople where product and application knowledge is a central part of the sales function.
6   Creative selling involves both tangible and intangible products and services, e.g. vacuum cleaners, washing machines, encyclopaedias, insurance, banking and investment advice. The last three are more difficult because the product cannot easily be demonstrated.

Classification of the nature and range of selling positions is useful in that it provides clues to effective management of sales and selling activities, e.g. they help recruitment and selection procedures; different selling positions may require different training and remuneration schemes. Since McMurry's early classification scheme other schemes have been developed. Donaldson[2] has developed a classification of types of selling job encompassing 12 categories of selling, ranging from 'industrial direct' through to 'franchise selling'. Anderson[3] identifies three categories of selling encompassing 'order taking', 'order supporting' and 'order getting' categories.

A useful view of different selling jobs is proposed by Pickton and Broderick[4] as shown in Figure 8.1 together with examples of selling categories. Their classification system is based on two key dimensions, the degree of communication and relationship building skills required and the degree of complexity and value of the sales involved. One type of selling job in this system is '**key account management' (KAM)** where high levels of communication and relationship building skills are required and where transactions are relatively complex, involving high values. At the other extreme is the example of retail shop sales involving simple low-value sales where levels of communication and relationship-building skills are low. Relationship-building skills are cited as a key dimension and this notion is expanded in Chapter 9.

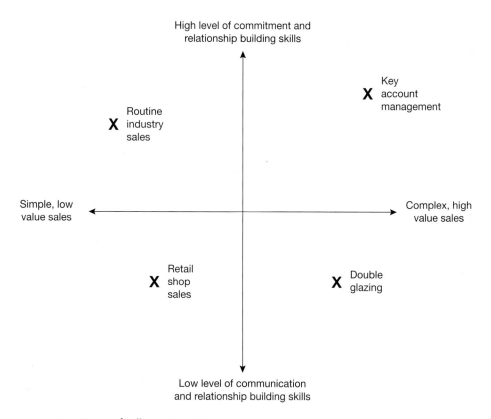

FIGURE 8.1 Types of selling categories

Source: Adapted from Picton, D. and Broderick, A. (2004), *Integrated Marketing Communications*, Harlow, Essex: Pearson Education.

ROLE OF SELLING WITHIN MARKETING

Selling is one of a number of tactical activities within marketing such as pricing and advertising. Co-ordinating these is essential for effective marketing. Differences in importance depend on the companies and industries involved. A successful sale depends on whether or not the product concerned fulfils the customer requirements and results in satisfied customers.

Relationship with marketing research

Marketing research finds out what people want and why they want it. Information might result in changes in the product. Such information is fed to the sales department and can be used by them to counter competition. Cowan[5] argues that in the past market research has often failed to identify significant changes in markets or new innovatory products. Because of close contact with customers and markets however, the sales force in particular can be used to provide market intelligence information that feeds into the Marketing Information System (MkIS) and helps shape marketing strategy.

Relationship with other elements of the promotional programme

The relationship of the sales force to the other aspects of promotion should be one of mutual co-operation, e.g. the sales force can obtain agreement from customers for the company to use a retail customer's window for displaying promotional materials. The Integrated Marketing Communications (IMC), introduced in Chapter 7, suggests that all elements in an organization's communications mix have a specific part to play. Malcolm *et al.*[6] explain why integrated marketing communications is so important but essentially each component of the communications mix has a key role to play. Non-personal communication, in the form of advertising, public relations and sales promotions, aims to push customers who were previously unaware of the firm's products into buying them. It is the role of personal selling to capitalize on preceding communications and close the sale. Personal selling and other communications tools should contribute to an overall communications strategy. To achieve this requires sales to be managed effectively in terms of recruitment, selection, training and planning and control. This is critical and it is to this area and the elements within it that we now turn our attention.

RECRUITMENT AND SELECTION OF SALESPEOPLE

Salespersons vary in accordance with the product/service to be sold and the nature of the selling situation. We set out four key elements in a typical sales job description:

1 *Responsibility* The representative is responsible directly to the sales manager.
2 *Objective* To achieve the annual sales target across the product range in the area for which the salesperson is responsible as economically as possible and within the limits of company policy.
3 *Planning* To be familiar with company policy plus the ability to plan and achieve defined objectives within the limits of that policy. To submit a periodic plan for a specific territory to higher management.
4 *Implementation* To act as a link between customer and head office; organize travel itinerary effectively; develop skill in selling; maintain and submit accurate records; gather market intelligence and report this to head office; assess potential of sales territory in terms of time available for visits, outlets for company products and activity of the opposition; protect and promote the company image; protect the company's business by avoiding unnecessary expense; be a good team member, and set a good example by maintaining loyalty towards superiors.

Many customers do not see representatives of companies with whom they deal other than the salesperson who calls on them, so frequent changes of representative can have an unsettling effect on customers and their ordering habits. In a sense, the salesperson is the company ambassador. It is reassuring for the customer if the same salesperson calls regularly to build up a good working relationship, for the salesperson's role is important in upholding the company's image and for building trust. The salesperson is relied on to provide goods that are suitable and to supply them when required at a fair price.

Because of the differential performance between 'good' and 'average' sales staff, which Jobber and Lancaster[7] contend may be as high as 30 per cent, it is important that the right type of person is selected for the job. Their research finds that nearly 50 per cent of sales managers find recruiting good sales staff difficult. For this reason, what might normally be regarded as a human resource issue is highlighted here, because salespersons are the conduit through which revenue is generated for the company. Recruiting and selecting sales staff sales (staff recruitment) requires a systematic and ordered approach for reasons of:

- checking that all duties are covered;
- enabling selection decisions to be made;
- providing criteria against which to appraise performance and identify training needs;
- giving motivation as the salesperson knows the job's limits and opportunities;
- providing basis for the advertisement.

The job description should include information like: job title; job location; job objectives; person to whom the successful applicant will be responsible; subordinates (if any); duties of the position; evaluation of performance and remuneration. The job description needs to be drawn up on the basis of a job analysis which includes the personnel profile of the type of person required to fulfil the job

---

McDonald's

As a service marketer, companies like McDonald's recognize that sales and service staff perform an 'ambassadorial' role for the company in their direct contact with customers. This role is acknowledged and reflected in the company's selection, training and motivation systems. McDonald's was one of the UK's first large employers to receive 'Investors in People' status and in 2007 they were declared 'winner of winners' in the 'Best Places to Work in Hospitality' awards. McDonald's recognize the importance of the 'people' element of their marketing mix by paying careful attention to staff selection, training and motivation. They select new staff on attitude and not just qualifications or experience. They have introduced several innovative schemes and initiatives to make staff feel more valued and enhance their qualifications whilst working with the company, For example, McDonald's have a staff website which members of staff can access for training and development advice. It even includes on-line tutors and lifestyle advice. They have experimented in allowing two family members working in the same restaurant to exchange rotas without consulting management. In an industry where staff turnover can be high, that of McDonald's is low. The company takes pride in how many of their most senior staff started by working in their restaurants.

Source: http://www.catersearch.com/Articles.

description, setting out qualities, skills and experience that an ideal salesperson should possess. Quantitative factors such as age, experience, qualifications, intelligence and health are easy to identify, but character traits such as willingness to work hard to achieve results; perseverance; interpersonal relationships; loyalty; self-reliance; empathy; persuasiveness; flexibility and resilience are difficult to assess on an application form, so these are best assessed in an interview setting.

Some salespeople expect to be rewarded directly by results and this type of person is best suited to a position paid on a commission basis, or part salary, part commission. Straight salary jobs suit people who feel security is more important than risk taking.

During the 1990s many financial product salespersons were remunerated on a commission-only basis. In selling products such as pensions and life insurance schemes, the inducement to sell in return for high commissions resulted in many inappropriate schemes being sold to unsuspecting customers. This is termed the 'pensions misselling era', the effects of which still impact on the financial services industry. As a result of this, new legislation was introduced and some financial services companies were removed, while others now have substantially modified remuneration schemes to replace those that were based on commission only.

Selling jobs vary in the degree of social status they confer. Door-to-door selling is perceived as ranking low, and generally selling positions do not offer much scope for the exercise of power. Jobs involving detailed specifications, like selling drugs to doctors or dealing with architects, are more suited to specific personalities. The importance of competitiveness depends on how the company views the selling task and some introduce a spirit of competitiveness by running sales contests. Desire to serve is a trait that salespeople should possess.

A personnel specification for a sales job may include factors that are difficult to appraise and assess in a candidate. Lancaster and Simintiras[8] conducted research from the point of view of salespeople. This indicated that the best efforts by salespeople do not always lead to performance maximization and factors like role clarity and social interaction with management can lead to greater job satisfaction, rather than simply financial reward.

As the nature of the selling job itself changes so too must our ideas about the qualities and skills we are looking for in the salesperson. In particular we must be careful to dispense with what many feel are outdated preconceptions of the effective salesperson such as for example that they should always be extroverts or have 'the gift of the gab'. Piercy and Lane[9] have suggested that the role of selling has changed from being based on 'conventional transactional sales activities' to one of strategic customer management.

In turn this requires new types of sales skills and activities and hence different attributes in the salespeople we are seeking to employ.

Elements of sound sales recruitment are to provide continuity of representation in individual territories and economy in generating sufficient applicants for appraisal. A source of recruitment is the company's marketing department as such people have a thorough grounding in the company's methods, products and policies, so if they have the right temperament they are likely to be successful. Another is through recommendation from friends, customers, employees or educational establishments. The obvious source is through the press and through the company's website.

'Short-listing' is an important stage of selection when potential candidates are called for interview. The interview should be structured using an interview record form. It consists of questions that explore work history and personal details. The interview should begin by informing the candidate

---

Selling to the Sellers

Hewlett Packard (HP) have introduced an extensive sales training programme for their value added reseller (VAR) network. HP want to extend their sales to small businesses and realize that their VAR network is crucial to this, but many of their distributors need better training in HP products and marketing methods. They have introduced free on site training for all their small business VARs. This training includes training in how to generate and follow up sales leads, training in how to close sales and training in how to trade up customers across the HP product portfolio. Initial results from this training look promising. Many of HP's smaller distributors have moved into HP's 'elite' designation which entitles them to extra product discounts and greater levels of sales training and support.

Source: http://www.channelinsider.com.

---

of the purpose of the interview and the time it should take. A detailed explanation of the job should be given and the candidate should be allowed the opportunity to ask questions. Next, questions should be asked about the candidate's present or last job, widening out into a detailed questioning of the candidate's work history and ability to perform the job that is vacant.

Some companies favour group interviews where short-listed candidates are requested to attend at the same time. They might be asked to discuss a specific subject or topic that is sometimes controversial. Human resource and sales staff might be brought in to listen. Each senior staff member is usually assigned a particular candidate and the staff member assesses the candidate by means of a rating chart. The group interview is usually followed by a conventional interview.

TRAINING

The saying: 'salespeople are born and not made' can lead to a neglect of training. New recruits need to undergo training as learning by observing the skilled performance of an experienced salesperson is not enough. A training programme should be devised that sets out to achieve the objectives of giving knowledge and developing selling skills. Training should not be restricted to a company's own sales force, but where appropriate should be extended to an organization's intermediaries.

Training curricula

Knowledge goals should relate to matters like learning company history and background. At the end of training, the salesperson should have achieved defined knowledge goals such as being able to name six major benefits of a particular product and explain how these benefits are derived from relevant product features. Goals should reflect a statement in the job description like: 'The salespeople must be knowledgeable about company products and their applications' or 'The salesperson must ensure that the company's products are well displayed' where the knowledge goal would be in terms of learning merchandising techniques and in-store promotion schemes.

Skills goals spell out what the salesperson needs to do. In the first example under knowledge goals above, skill goals would be an ability to relate product features to consumer needs and find and interest new customers. In the second, the skill goals would be concerned with display building and selling merchandising ideas. The salesperson needs knowledge of the company relating to its structure, product mix and customer policy and needs to understand how the remuneration system can affect earnings. Product knowledge is important in understanding applications and related consumer benefits. Market knowledge involves continuous updating in relation to competitors' products so that the salesperson can converse with conviction to buyers. Sales interview training should be broadened beyond sales procedures, to include the salesperson's role, pre-sales preparation and after-sales service.

Good work organization usually results in more business. The salesperson should be trained in time management procedures so more time is spent with customers and less on travelling or waiting.

Reporting from the field is an essential aspect of selling and sales reports help a company to take appropriate action in areas like customer relations, competitive activity and market changes which are pertinent to the 'market intelligence' input into the marketing information system, covered in Chapter 12.

Methods of training

Lectures, demonstrations, case studies, videos and seminars help, but the salesperson will derive greater benefit from participation in sales situations or simulations. This is more effective if feedback is provided quickly. Ideally, this should be by video where scenarios are acted out and replayed by the trainer to trainees in a constructive manner. The **SPIN model** of selling developed by the Huthwaite Research Group and described by Rackham[10] emphasizes the importance of questioning skills in identifying customer requirements in the selling process, and hence the overall need for strong communication skills on the part of the salesperson and indeed this company specializes in sales training.

Field performance assessment

There should be a set of standards against which a salesperson's performance in the field can be evaluated. The job description plus related knowledge and skill requirements should provide the necessary criteria. The sales manager should sometimes accompany the salesperson on a normal day's work and should observe, but not interfere. After the period of observation, the manager and salesperson should meet to discuss the latter's performance. Evaluation can be formalized through use of an appraisal form that will include product knowledge, selling methods, work habits and organization, mental attitude, development needs and general commitments. Figure 8.2 shows a typical appraisal form. The salesperson, when being appraised, is given marks or a letter rating. There is a section for the last grade awarded to see if there has been an improvement, no change, or a decline since the last appraisal. The salesperson should be allowed to see comments and together with the manager, should sign the form. An advantage of the appraisal form is that it acts as a record of abilities. It can also be compared with the previous year's results to see whether progress has been made and act as a basis for quantifying qualitative attributes.

APPRAISAL FORM

Grade

	A	B	C	D	E	Last grade
Product knowledge						
Selling method						
Work habits						
Organization						
Mental attitudes						

A = Excellent   D = Below average
B = Very good   E = Poor
C = Average

Date: ....

Signature of manager: ....

Signature of salesperson: ....

Department: ....

FIGURE 8.2 Salesperson appraisal form

The sales manual

The sales manual, issued to salespeople for reference, is a useful source for initial training and for established salespersons to improve performance. It contains information on methods of operation and guides salespeople in their duties covering such matters as:

- a statement on company sales policy and methods;
- background information about products;
- prices, terms and conditions of sale;
- distribution methods;
- publicity and display policies;
- regulations regarding use of company vehicles;
- rules governing expenses;
- sickness and accident rules;
- **journey planning** procedures;
- rules for granting credit and obtaining trade references;
- account collection procedures;
- order procedures;

- rules governing the issue of samples;
- methods of requisitioning stationery and supplies;
- reporting and correspondence procedures.

Personal development and training

Continuous development through updating courses, seminars and conferences ensures that the salesperson is equipped to deal with changing marketing conditions and competitive activities. Company policies and specific sales objectives can be imparted to salespeople at these regular sessions with a specific agenda or theme.

Sales force structure

Territory design and journey planning can be organized for the sales force in a the following ways:

- *Geographically-based sales force* where each salesperson has a specific area in which the company's products are sold. The main advantage is that as the salesperson's responsibility is clearly defined, the territory is intimately known, and in co-operation with management, its sales potential can be fully developed. The salesperson can develop business and personal ties with the locality, and if the territory is of a manageable size, expenses can be lessened.
- *Product-based sales force* is suitable if a company has large, complex and diverse product lines. The sales force is more effective because of product specialization e.g. a computer producer selling hardware and software applications to banks, education establishments, retail outlets and manufacturing companies.
- *Customer-based sales force* Customers vary according to type of industry, size and distribution channels so a sales force may be organized according to different categories of customer. A thorough understanding of customers is necessary. This approach is popular in 'key account' structured selling efforts which are discussed in Chapter 9.

Territory management

Because of the complexity of representational arrangements, some companies employ executives whose main task is to 'build' territories, and readjust them as situations demand. These are known as **sales engineers**, even though they are not engineers in the accepted sense. The 'building' analogy is taken further by the development of territories by using '**sales bricks**' which relate to geographical area in which all known buyers are listed. The bricks are about equal in sales potential e.g. one brick may contain 10 buyers of furniture and another brick may have 15. In such an example, the brick would have been calculated on the basis that the 10 buyers are, on average, likely to make slightly larger purchases than the 15, but total purchasing capacities are about the same. As the bricks are built up, they can be transferred in units from one territory to another. Once this is done, schedules listing all customers can be prepared and linked to their buying potential.

Many pragmatic or personal factors contribute to the final design, so decisions are not necessarily clear cut; if a customer has a distinct preference for a particular salesperson then it would make sense for this person to make visits. Other practical considerations are:

- potential business;
- number of active customers;
- number of potential customers;
- location of customers;
- methods of physical distribution and storage facilities;
- the existing sales situation in terms of individual workloads;
- frequency of sales calls;
- mixture of trades which representative call on;
- salesperson boundaries and limitations.

A long-term view should be taken in relation to territory design taking into consideration prospects for future growth. A loss may even be tolerated at the beginning in the interests of higher potential later. Some companies, particularly in the food trade, use 'brokers' to sell for them because of the high total costs of employing sales representatives.

Factors that may point to the necessity of revising an existing territory include:

- change in consumer preference;
- intrusion of competition;
- diminution in the usefulness of chosen distribution channels;
- the closure of an outlet or group of stores;
- increases in cost of covering territories.

Once design of the territory i.e. size and number of customers is agreed, salespersons can play an important role in helping sales management to be more effective. This will depend on self management by the salesperson and important criteria are:

- *Know the decision maker* i.e. not to waste time contacting the 'wrong' person in a company. The 'right' people to see are key members of the decision-making unit as discussed in Chapter 2. It is not always clear who these people are, so it is advisable to find out from the company itself through people like a receptionist or a junior buyer who may be able to suggest the most suitable contact.
- *Carry out research* by investigating buyers and their companies. This creates a good impression and can done from market intelligence sources.
- *Make appointments* as they save time are part of an organized travel plan. Ideally, a future appointment should be arranged while the salesperson is with the prospect.
- *Make manual and electronic record cards and diaries work* These are invaluable sources of information, especially if somebody else has to take over an area at short notice. Data to be recorded includes name, address and telephone number of the company; name of contacts and

position in the company; type and size of business; number of employees; best days and time to call; a record of what discussions have taken place; invoices raised and date for next call.

- *Organize the territory* which can be divided into sectors, with salespersons making regular calls in one sector at a time, thus cutting down on travelling. This is referred to as the 'sales journey cycle'.
- *Plan each interview* Once an appointment has been made the interview needs to be planned. A decision should be made beforehand as to its aim. The salesperson should have realistic expectations of how to close a sale within the allotted time. Documents and samples should be included for presentation and careful planning enables the salesperson to know what will be needed according to the aims, including:

  - to get a final decision;
  - to arrange for a demonstration to take place;
  - to obtain consent to carry out a survey;
  - to provide sales benefits;
  - to find out about competition;
  - to find the decision maker.

Journey planning

Planning, activity controls, and better organization of sales routines help the sales force become more productive. Systematic journey planning is important and it involves:

- *Developing a call frequency* Each salesperson will have a mixture of accounts. Most buyers allocate a certain amount of time to seeing salespeople. The more time a salesperson spends with a customer, the less time will that customer be able to see a competitor. A **call frequency** is needed where some customers receive a visit as frequently as once a week, and others say once every three months, according to the sales journey cycle.
- *Establishing priorities* Customers should be given priority according to the value of business done with them. Accounts that order in small quantities might not justify a call and it might even be worthwhile either abandoning them or linking them with a wholesaler, as the cost of invoicing and administration may exceed any profits.
- *Minimizing travelling time* is a responsibility of sales management who should ensure that the salesperson is not sent out for unduly long periods dealing with matters other than selling, and territories are not too large in the geographical sense.
- *Evolving a call pattern* Having graded customers according to their value or potential, the salesperson should develop a call pattern or a sales journey cycle.
- *Assessing the workload* ensures a salesperson's effort is not wasted by too many calls of a short a duration. A decision should be made as to the optimum number of visits to be made each day, allowing for achievement of quotas that sales management anticipates.
- *Combining a programme with flexibility* Occasional changes of activity may take the form of test marketing or task force selling, where a number of salespeople descend upon one territory with the aim of '**saturation selling**' so building up sales quickly. Other activities might include:

- developing a certain market segment;
- forestalling a competitive activity in a given area;
- forestalling competitive promotional activities;
- introducing a new product;
- training a new recruit;
- balancing the product mix;
- moving obsolete products from stock;
- announcing a revised price structure;
- entering a new market;
- opening new accounts.

THE SALES SEQUENCE: THE SEVEN STEPS MODEL

Planning is essential for personal selling time to be maximized, so one must adopt a general sales sequence and a specific plan for each individual interview. The sales process or sequence is a basic framework that must be flexible and adaptable, as each individual sales situation is different and presents its own problems. The one that follows is widely used to distinguish the key steps in the sales sequence and for obvious reason is often referred to as the 'seven steps' model.

1   *Preparation* – where the salesperson should have a good general knowledge of:

   - *the company* – its systems, procedures, prices and terms;
   - *the product* – especially new products and/or uses for existing products;
   - *market knowledge;*
   - *customer knowledge* – and maintenance of a good customer records;
   - *equipment, samples and sales aids* – ensuring that the right equipment, including order books and trade directories is carried;
   - *journey planning* – an organized journey plan giving details of appointments covering existing customers and time for generating new business or prospecting;
   - *personal preparation* – i.e. personal grooming and dress.

2   *First impressions* – A sales meeting should start in a pleasant yet businesslike way. Time is important, but so is being polite. Likewise, good personal selling involves listening as well as asking questions. It is also about being accommodating. If a buyer sets a time limit, this should be respected, although an offer to stay longer is often necessary and can be useful. Mention should also be made at this early stage of other business to be dealt with, such as expediting invoices due for payment. Such matters should be discussed and settled at the beginning of the meeting in the knowledge that it will then be simpler to discuss the real business on hand.

3   *Preparation and demonstration* – Salespersons should a list major selling points relating to the products or services they are selling. The most important of these will be points that give some advantage over competitors' products. In the presentation and demonstration the salesperson should concentrate on the **unique sales propositions (USPs)** that are appropriate to that particular customer's needs and interests. In a sales situation involving the need for a sales

presentation or a demonstration, the salesperson should be prepared for this and secure the potential customer's active involvement. What should be avoided is running both the demonstration and presentation together, as this can be confusing. The salesperson should use terms at a degree of technical detail that the customer can understand. During the presentation the salesperson should ask questions and listen to the answers to probe the customer's interests further. Some products are impossible to demonstrate and here the salesperson should use models or audiovisual aids. A salesperson should avoid being too 'long-winded' or sales might be lost. Selling signals as simple as the buyer looking at his or her watch should be sought and attempts then made to close the sale as over-presentation often loses a sale.

4   *Negotiation* – The principal role for the salesperson is to know the limits of acceptance and non-acceptance. The salesperson may negotiate with the customer aspects like price, discounts, credit and selling rights. Often the final margin of **negotiation** is retained by the sales manager. The salesperson should obtain as much information as possible about the buyer's needs and level of potential business and assess its potential worth. Concessions should be held back as long as possible. If not, they cease to be concessions. Negotiation is a key element of major sales activities.

5   *Overcoming objections* – These might be commercial **objections** that relate to matters like price, credit or delivery. These are common and salespersons should be trained in techniques for handling them. An objection on commercial grounds could be a disguise for a real objection or even simply be a buying ploy e.g. a buyer might argue that a competitive product has a better finish, but not fully explain how the quality of finish is better. When it is a disguise, or excuse, it is up to the salesperson to discover, by shrewd questioning, the real objection. A skilled salesperson can use customer objections to close a sale by suggesting that if the objection is answered, will this result in a sale. However organizational buyers are experienced enough to recognize when salespeople are using objections as a closing technique, and will be skilled enough to be able to pose an apt reply.

6   *Closing the sale* – The objective of most sales interviews is to obtain a sale, although others might be to discuss matters like service provision. There are a variety of **closing techniques**, which the salesperson can use:

   - basic close: when the salesperson thinks there is a sale and starts filling in the order form;
   - alternative choice: offer a choice as a trial close, e.g. 'Do you want grey or black?'
   - summary questions: from a prepared list, ask the buyer questions like: 'Is this a problem?' Here an answer of 'no' might represent a step towards closing a sale;
   - closing on a final objection: if a final objection still exists, identify it and then offer to do something about it. The customer cannot then object any more.

7   *Follow-up* – is needed to avoid loss of contact or to bring about repeat business. After closing a sale it is important that the salesperson 'ties up' loose ends such as delivery times. To this end a follow-up call should be made, and if unforeseen problems occur, the salesperson can rectify them and not lose the sale or future business.

The seven steps model is probably one of the oldest paradigms in the sales discipline and it is still used widely in sales training, in sales textbooks and in selling itself. However, some have questioned its relevance in an increasingly relationship selling era (Moncrief and Marshall[11]).

EFFECTIVE COMMUNICATION

Good communications require listening as well as speaking skills. Charts, models and brochures may also help in the sales process. Sales personnel can be trained to be good speakers, knowing what to say, and how and when to say it. Listening and speaking are dual parts of effective communication.

As well as developing selling skills, salespeople should develop technical expertise that can be applied during the presentation process. There are occasions when a customer might ask questions that appear simplistic. Salespeople represent a limited number of products to a variety of customers, so what is an unusual problem to one customer may seem routine to the salesperson. Each sales situation is different, so patience is required in explaining to the buyer what might seem to be a simple matter.

Showing customers you are listening is important. This can be done by non-verbal communication like eye contact, facial expressions or other forms of 'body language'. Using non-verbal cues, the salesperson is able to signal understanding of what the customer is saying without speaking and so regulate the speed of the conversation as well as the depth and detail of the customer's discussion. What we do not want are people who talk while we are speaking or show other signs of lack of interest. This is emphasized, because salespeople, by their nature, tend to be talkers rather than listeners.

When talking there is often a feeling of control where one is asserting one's beliefs, and with this there is a feeling that by so doing, one will succeed. The problem is that this ignores the needs of others. Salespeople should aim to satisfy others by offering goods and services that fit precise requirements. Such requirements can be practical or can relate to less tangible buyer behavioural needs.

MANAGING AND CONTROLLING THE SALES FORCE

We have thus far examined elements of sales management that encompass recruitment, selection and training of sales personnel. Additionally, we have looked at the important area of organizing and structuring the sales force, specifically looking at such factors as territory design, journey planning and bases for structuring a sales force. Finally we have examined the sales sequence. We now examine the remaining elements of sales management, including setting sales quotas, evaluating and controlling sales effort and design of remuneration systems.

Setting sales quotas

'Sales targets' and 'sales quotas' are terms that are often interchanged. The *target* which is given to a salesperson is, strictly speaking, something that should be aimed for. A *sales quota* is something that should be achieved, but the difference is semantic. Whatever term is used, the salesperson should be given a clear indication of the level of performance that is expected to be achieved.

If a salesperson's quota is fixed on a co-operative basis rather than being imposed, there is more likelihood of it being acceptable. It also raises the salesperson's level of confidence in management.

An imposed quota may result in resentment and unwillingness to co-operate with management that fails to consult its salespeople on such important matters. Salespeople, after all, are the ones expected to meet quotas that are set so there is a need for joint consultation. The individual salesperson is best placed to help in setting realistic estimates of what can be achieved. It is helpful for both parties if the area, branch or regional manager consults with the salesperson, and by the process of consulting customers more realistic estimates of sales can be ascertained for each customer. There are other means of forecasting sales that are dealt with in Chapter 11. This not only applies to fixing new quotas, but also to changes in quotas. The salesperson needs to appreciate why changes are necessary; the arbitrary raising of quotas might be seen as being unjustified to the salesperson and can lead to mistrust of sales management, and a cut in earnings resulting from arbitrary alterations is not appreciated.

Sales volume achieved in the previous period is a good starting point when setting quotas. However, other factors may influence future sales such as changes in demand, business conditions, marketing and sales policies, territory potential and competitive actions. The sales quota should be an accurate measure of market potential, tempered by workload and experience factors. Territories are differentiated by the density of the market. A rural area will involve salespersons in more travelling between calls than an urban area. The amount of physical effort and time involved, or the **workload factor**, should be considered when setting quotas.

The experience of individual salespersons and that of the company makes up what is termed the **experience factor**. Higher sales targets will be expected from experienced salespersons, and inexperienced salespersons will find sales easier if the company is well established in the market area. Sales quotas stem from the sales forecast and are used to:

- set targets of performance;
- monitor this performance;
- serve as incentives;
- serve as a basis for payment to the sales force.

SALES PERFORMANCE

Unlike performance measurement in production, which deals with material that can be seen and easily measured, a salesperson's routine activities cannot be directly seen, so measurement is difficult, especially when sales are of a long-term nature e.g. a construction company that is seeking a contract to build a hospital. Some sales operations are simple; when selling to retailers the number of calls made, number of orders obtained and their value can be calculated reasonably accurately. Sometimes effective sales performance will require the salesperson to carry out activities that are not easily measured such as giving advice to customers about how best to display their stock in the retail outlet. In effect, this is **merchandising** where sales representatives visit retailers to take orders, and organize displays to stimulate consumer purchases. Merchandising is recognized as an essential skill in retailing and often it is the sales force who provide merchandising advice to their retail customers.

Numark markets to pharmacists who are by necessity of course experts in dispensing but often do not necessarily know the best way to lay out their merchandise. A common mistake is to pack too much stock into one area which can lead to products slipping behind other products or facing the customer side-on, making it hard for customers to find what they are looking for. Numark maintain that gondola ends, or end of aisles, are '**hotspots**' that are not used to their full potential as they are often full of inappropriate products, so pharmacists lose out on impulse purchases. Numark offers retail pharmacists data on top selling lines, collected from the individual store's **electronic point of sale (EPoS)** system. Better performing products in each category of merchandise are identified, and information is provided about which ones are moving up or down the best-sellers' list. Numark maintains that in the late 1990s hair care and baby care products were big sellers in pharmacists. Now these sectors have been lost to supermarkets, but many pharmacists still over-allocate space for their display instead of concentrating on more appropriate merchandise. They suggest that pharmacists could learn a lot from a trip to their local supermarket to see how gondola ends are designated to promotions.

Although performance standards are necessary to ensure that the sales force is operating efficiently, they need to be applied with forethought and in consultation with the salesperson from the outset. They should also be relevant to the kind of operation being conducted and these are now discussed.

Sales analysis and performance analysis

Sales analysis begins with a detailed breakdown of the company's sales records, while performance analysis seeks exceptions or variations from planned performance. Sales analysis is the listing of facts and figures, but performance analysis is comparing pre-determined standards with results that are useful in pinpointing operating problems as well as identifying areas in which the company may be performing well or not so well.

Continuous use of sales and performance analysis enables operating problems to be detected before they become serious; they cannot uncover the cause of the problem, nor can they provide the solution.

We now define what is meant by a '**sales performance index**' which is computed by dividing actual sales for an area (or salesperson or product) by the sales quota and then multiplying this figure by 100 as follows:

$$\frac{\text{Sales (for area and the salesperson)}}{\text{Sales quota}} \times 100$$

Performance indices enable sales management to compare what ought to have happened to what did happen. Analysis of sales for evaluation purposes is usually based on a geographical breakdown; other ways include analysis by product line or by customer category, e.g. industrial customers or key customers.

Analysis of sales may not be enough. Such analysis may present a favourable picture as far as sales volume versus quota is concerned. Actual sales can be equal to, or over the quota and yet the company might be losing its market position because the area that the firm is operating is expanding at a greater rate than the firm's expansion of sales, as illustrated Figure 8.3.

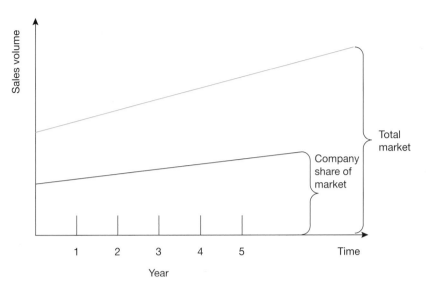

FIGURE 8.3 Market share analysis

The Devil's in the Detail

Harold Bird, sales manager of Trust Care Products, a marketer of financial advice services, was pleased with himself. He had just received the sales figures from the six territories that his sales force cover. Every one of his sales force team has exceeded their sales targets. These targets were set at the start of what everyone agreed was one of the worst economic downturns since the 1930s and most of his team felt at the time that targets were too high. Even Harold was unsure about the targets at the time, but he was under pressure from senior management to improve results. Harold wondered if he should try to negotiate better bonuses. He was still pondering this when the phone rang. It was his manager. He informed Harold that he had just received the market share figures from the company's market research team and it appeared that sales in the sector had not just held up in the recession, but had soared as more and more people turned for expert advice about how to protect their financial portfolios from the worst ravages of the global recession. As a result, Harold was congratulating himself on sales of Trust Care Products that had increased by some 10 per cent. Unfortunately, total market sales, Harold boss informed him, had grown by over 20 per cent. As a result, Trust Care's share of the market was substantially down from the last period.

Evaluating performance – quantitive criteria

The effectiveness of the salesperson is evaluated against pre-determined performance standards. To help the sales manager determine whether or not corrective action is required the control technique deals with three elements:

1 information on performance;
2 standards;
3 evaluation of performance (against standards).

While types of standard used in a company vary; most are linked to the following:

- sales volume;
- profit contribution on sales/product mix;
- number of service calls made;
- number of calls for an order;
- percentage of quota achieved;
- amount of market intelligence gathered.

All these performance standards (targets against which results are measured) are quantitative measures. Such standards, when communicated to the sales force, become a basis for sales planning. Where, then, does sales management obtain information about the salesperson/s performance?

Reports that include the following:

- call reports, showing which customers were visited, competitive brands used, best time for calling, degree and type of sales resistance, results achieved and future account promise;
- expense reports, showing a breakdown of expenses incurred;
- new business reports, showing new accounts opened and potential new business which evaluates the extent and effectiveness of the salesperson's prospecting work;
- lost business reports, showing what business was lost and why;
- work plan reports, showing what calls the salesperson will make and the routine he or she will use for a future specified period (providing a basis for comparing plans with achievements);
- Reports on a local market condition and competitive activity. Care must be taken when interpreting and evaluating this report as the salesperson might distort the local picture if it is to be linked to sales targets.

Observation is where the district sales manager goes out with the salesperson and observes him or her in the real situation. This can be a meaningful input to the evaluation-control system.

Checklist of quantitative standards for performance evaluation

1 *Sales*

- sales volume in money terms;
- sales volume in previous year's sales;
- sales volume in units;
- sales volume in quota;

- sales volume in relation to market potential;
- sales volume by customers;
- sales by outlet type;
- sales by product or product line;
- sales volume per order;
- average sales volume per call;
- amount of new account sales;
- amount of repeat sales.

2   *Accounts*

- percentage sold to existing accounts;
- number of new accounts;
- number of accounts lost.

3   *Profit*

- net profit by salesperson.

4   *Orders*

- number of orders delivered;
- number of orders booked;
- number of cancelled orders.

5   *Selling expense*

- compensation in relation to sales volume;
- salesperson's expenses in relation to sales volume or quota;
- total direct selling expenses per sales value.

Evaluating performance – qualitative measures

A salesperson can be assessed qualitatively through a number of measures:

- How does the salesperson demonstrate knowledge of markets, competition, the company's lines and each customer's business and how is it applied?
- How does the salesperson break down the quota given into separate goals, customer by customer?
- How does the salesperson create effective plans of action?
- How capable is the salesperson in preparing and making sales presentations?
- How well does the salesperson deal with awkward customers?
- How well does the salesperson evaluate results and take corrective action?

These questions are at the base of qualitative evaluation, and other qualitative measures of performance are in the areas of:

- motivation;
- personality characteristics e.g. general manner, speech, appearance, tenacity, patience, temperament;
- contribution to the flow of market intelligence;
- managerial ability;
- personal development;
- self-organization (time management).

REMUNERATION

Since profitability is important, management needs to seek ways to stimulate salespersons to sell more profitably using equitable **remuneration methods**. Thinking in terms of profitability moves away from traditional remuneration schemes geared to turnover. The three main methods are commission, salary plus commission, and salary only, although there are variations.

Commission is a simple method. If the salesperson works, and achieves results, he or she gets paid. The advantage of a commission-only scheme is that the employer knows exactly how much cost of sales will be, and the salesperson knows that he or she will only be paid if they work to achieve sales. This is simple, but there is a strong element of insecurity in a commission-only system. It is not wholly satisfactory in that sometimes the salesperson may not wish to work so the employer is left without any sales coverage. Much depends on the nature of the product and the way it is sold. A major disadvantage of commission-only remuneration is the potential for misselling as mentioned earlier and the reputation of the company might suffer as a result of negative publicity.

Sales and commission is the most common method of remuneration. Commission includes bonuses and profit sharing. It offers more security to the salesperson. The proportion of salary to commission varies depending upon the company and its products.

Salary Although it may appear to be lacking as a means of creating incentive, it is popular with salespeople who prefer a more straightforward arrangement. It must be considered that some situations are more suited to this type of payment. Sometimes it is not possible to establish what has been sold by individual salespeople, or total sales effort might due to background technical personnel e.g. the attainment of an IT consultancy contract. In addition, in lean manufacturing situations, the task of the sales representative concerns non-selling duties as the company they represent might be the only source of supply; a topic that is considered more in Chapter 9. In addition, in the case of capital goods like the construction of an oil refinery, the time delay between enquiry and receipt of order can be too long for a commission payment system to be an incentive.

Variations to the methods cited include:

1   A basic salary plus commission above a certain figure. Here the salesperson, once the target has been reached, starts to earn commission on amounts above this sum.
2   A basic salary plus an escalating scale commission. Here the salesperson receives a salary plus a commission e.g. ½ per cent on the first £5,000 sales, 1 per cent on the next £5,000 and 1½ per cent on amounts over this. This figure can be related to monthly sales targets.

3   A basic salary plus commission on the type of outlet to which the goods are sold. Here, the salesperson might receive a salary plus commission as follows:

- ½ per cent on wholesale orders;
- 1 per cent on multiple chain orders;
- 1 per cent on co-operative store orders;
- 1½ per cent on independent orders;
- 1¼ per cent on department store orders.

Incentives include group incentives, where a team of salespeople form a group, and if the group fulfils its performance, all members benefit. Some companies use incentives that benefit the salesperson's family, perhaps in the form of holidays or gifts like domestic appliances or children's presents.

It is important to ensure that the pay and benefits structure corresponds with:

- the company's market segments;
- the company's stage of development;
- the company's goals and objectives for the future.

A company can implement a marketing strategy via remunerating differently for diverse kinds of work. It can be weighted towards **missionary selling** (i.e. seeking out new customers) as this will involve more time and effort than servicing existing clients. If a company's marketing objective is not specifically that of growth, expanding the customer base through missionary selling is less important. The company may wish, for instance, to put maximum effort into account servicing to consolidate existing customers. Remuneration policy should reflect this objective although it might need to be adapted for companies selling multiple products. Salespeople working on a commission plan understandably tend to concentrate on products that offer most commission. Setting sales targets by volume is only a partial answer since salespeople will tend to concentrate on higher value items. A solution is to offer higher commission on sales of particular products or extra commissions or bonuses for sales of excess or obsolescent stocks.

Creatively designed incentive plans are useful for achieving corporate and marketing objectives other than sales volume. Straight salary may be a poor motivator for increased sales, but it may be instrumental in helping to achieve other company objectives, since the salesperson, being free of the pressure to sell, can concentrate on these other objectives such as providing exemplary service.

By using financial incentives imaginatively, the sales manager can motivate the sales force to ensure the company's objectives are carried out. A clearly defined remuneration policy helps to achieve the following objectives:

- attracts sales personnel of the right calibre;
- encourages sales personnel to achieve their job objectives;
- rewards sales personnel in accordance with the value of their contribution;
- prevents losses made through dissatisfaction with levels of pay;
- encourages good sales personnel to stay with the company;
- enables sales personnel to move up or across departmental, divisional or company boundaries.

Salespeople tend to work alone, unsupervised for long periods and visits by supervisors tend to be brief and infrequent. It is important to provide clear objectives and standards. **Management by objectives (MBO)** enables managers to lay down a clear and precisely defined sales job. Setting realistic sales targets in co-operation with the salesperson makes their achievement more likely, and the salesperson has a clearer idea of what is expected to achieve results.

SALES FORCE SIZE

Calculating optimum sales force size is a sales management task. Account must be taken of:

1   the firm's financial resources;
2   the number of customers to be reached;
3   the average number of calls required per customer, per week, per month;
4   the average number of calls that can be made by a salesperson in a given period;
5   distribution policy of the firm i.e. whether the company operates a policy of exclusive, selective or mass (intensive) distribution.

SALES OFFICE ADMINISTRATION

Its main function is sales force support which is done by a regular supply of information, following up queries and attention to matters arising from sales representatives' reports.

Responsibilities vary according to the nature of the company and its products, but most sales offices have the same basic managerial responsibilities and the sales office should fit the needs of the organization. The office is normally under the control of a sales office manager and responsibilities include:

- general correspondence dealing with matters like quotations, complaints, requests for information and queries about individual orders;
- maintaining records of customer accounts and correspondence;
- preparation of activity budgets in financial terms for the forthcoming period;
- sales statistics;
- planning administration of the sales office and the sales force;
- organizing day-to-day work – handling orders, correspondence, complaints, administering to needs of the sales force, control and administration of the sales force in matters such as examination of expenses and reports;
- in some companies, an estimating department to which purchase enquiries are submitted (this is sometimes the responsibility of the sales office);
- distribution arrangements and arranging for the handling and storage of goods;
- keeping records of progress and sometimes the ledger accounts of customers;
- planning, co-ordinating and communicating the sales plan.

DEVELOPMENTS IN SELLING AND SALES MANAGEMENT

Growth of key account management

Recent years have witnessed a growth in the use of key account management (KAM) approaches to organizing the selling process. An important factor that has led to this is the trend towards more centralized buying. Here, a shift in the balance of power, particularly in retail markets, towards the buyer has meant that such accounts must be handled carefully in terms of retaining goodwill. It makes marketing sense to identify and manage key accounts professionally.

Millman and Wilson[12] suggest that a key account is a customer of strategic importance to the supplier. This definition does not necessarily mean large customers or important ones in terms of share of sales, but rather customers who can affect the future of the company in some important way. All customers are important, but it is useful to assess the differences and the bases regarding the variation of this importance between them.

Key account selling requires the development of different selling and sales management skills (Ivens and Pardo[13]). For example, key account selling heightens the consultative and ambassadorial roles of the salesperson. In addition, the salesperson must have regular meetings and communication with key account customers, and normally the task is assigned to a senior salesperson, as key account customers require much more support than their non-key counterparts. Brehmer and Rehme[14] suggest that key account management is a very effective way to develop existing relationships, thereby increasing sales, but it needs a proactive approach on the part of the supplier

Telesales

This form of direct marketing has increased dramatically in terms of usage in recent years. Starkey[15] states that one facet of the overall process of telemarketing is a key part of this process; that of **telesales.** This can involve dealing with calls into the company and calls out to customers. Increased use of telesales is because of potentially lower costs. However, lower costs can only be justified to the extent that teleselling actually creates sales. Like key account management, teleselling requires

Looking up to 'Big Blue'

Some companies are looked up to and respected in an industry. Such companies are often market leaders or have a reputation for innovation and forward thinking. Some are respected because of their 'green' credentials or because they are leading business thinkers. Suppliers to companies like this can benefit from the reputation of the company being supplied. For example, being a supplier to 'Big Blue', or IBM, to give the company name, confers a degree of business legitimacy to suppliers. IBM is known as being a very stringent and demanding customer. To supply IBM, you have to be an effective supplier with excellent products and service. Used as a form of marketing testimonial in securing other business, being an 'approved IBM supplier' carries some weight.

special skills and training. In addition there is a danger of alienating some customers when using telesales staff to contact customers at home. In this respect there are ethical and legal issues involved with this type of selling. A broader discussion on telesales is contained in Chapter 10.

The Internet

Virtually every company uses the Internet as an aid, or sometimes exclusively, to sell products and services. B2B marketers, where, as we have noted, personal selling predominates in the communications mix were some of the first to recognize the potential for computer-based interchanges between themselves and customers through Electronic Data Exchange (EDI) systems. The often close relationships required between buyers and suppliers in B2B markets encouraged supply chain members to 'link up' electronically to exchange information. As a result, EDI systems were developed. These have now developed further into B2Be networks. In a sense, the Internet reduces the need for personal selling. The major impact of the growth in Internet marketing has meant a reduction in the size of many companies' sales forces, and can be seen by some sales persons as 'cannibalizing' their customers (Sharma and Gassenheimer[16]). However, these days sales personnel recognize the potential of the Internet combined with selling skills to help generate sales and customer loyalty. For example, the Internet is a powerful aid to generating sales leads. In addition, it is a powerful communication tool, especially when managing key accounts. Day and Bens[17] show that the Internet can be used to reduce customer service costs and build sales. Research by Samaniego et al.[18] suggests that the Internet is particularly useful in the early stage of the buying process and/or for new adopters where perceived risk is high and information low. The Internet and its uses in marketing are so important to the contemporary marketer that discussion on this topic is expanded in Chapter 10.

RELATIONSHIP MARKETING

Several times we have mentioned the importance and the growth of relationship marketing. A detailed analysis of the reasons for this development as well as the implications for the marketer are the subject of Chapter 9. In the context of this chapter it is important to point out that one of the most important areas of marketing that relationship concepts have affected is that of personal selling and sales management.

We have highlighted the changing nature of markets and marketing and in particular increased competition and have pointed to the emergence of more co-operation and interdependence between suppliers and their customers, evidenced by the growth of strategic alliances. Discussion on this, together with developments in lean manufacturing is the subject of Chapter 9.

With greater consumer choice it is realized that customer loyalty can no longer be relied upon unless positive steps are taken by the marketer to develop and maintain such loyalty. Most marketers feel that marketing must now seek to develop customer loyalty by integrating customers into the company and trying to develop a new relationship between the company and its customers. Some believe that relationship marketing is not new and that effective marketers have always practised a relationship marketing approach (Zineldin and Phillipson[19]) however most are agreed that with relationship marketing there has been a fundamental shift in the role and purpose of marketing from manipulation of the customer to genuine customer orientation Lancaster[20] argues that there has been a shift from a perspective that is concerned primarily with generating sales on a one-off basis to one which looks for longer-term and interactive exchanges between the company and its customers based on true partnership and sharing.

As a result of these changes there has been a realization that we must develop new approaches to customers. Today's marketing environment requires that the marketer develop a new more co-operative approach to dealing with customers and in particular close, long-term relationships. The wider consequences of relationship marketing are discussed in detail in Chapter 9, but at this stage we should note the key implications of relationship marketing with regard to the process of selling.

Relationship marketing requires a fundamentally different approach to selling than that found in transaction marketing. The following represents shifts in perspectives and emphasis in the sales process when a company moves towards relationship marketing:

- The salesperson must take a longer-term perspective than that of simply making a one-off sale when dealing with customers.
- Effective relationship selling requires more of a team effort, not only between individual members of the sales force but between the salesperson and other functions in the supplying company.
- Salespersons must be proactive with customers e.g. calling or visiting customers at times other than when they think the customer is ready to place an order.
- Salespersons must act as problem solvers rather than order takers or order winners.
- Salespersons must act as an exchanger of information between their own company and the customer, and between the customer and their own company.
- The emphasis must be more on levels of customer service than simply on low prices when attempting to generate sales.

All of this means that skills, attitudes and ideas of what constitutes an effective salesperson have changed. The relationship salesperson must be skilled at listening to customers and interpreting their problems. Job satisfaction and remuneration for the salesperson must be geared towards developing customer loyalty and trust rather than immediate sales. Relationship marketing is evolving and changing the nature of selling.

SUMMARY

Although selling is part of the communications mix, its importance is paramount, not only within the communications mix, but within the wider context of the marketing mix. This is relevant to salespeople, as it is largely they who apply sales tactics especially in relationship marketing settings in terms of customer care. In most companies, particularly in intermediate product and service B2B providers, selling is the singular most important element of the marketing mix; indeed, in many situations it is sales management that is senior to marketing management where marketing's role is simply one of managing marketing services.

In this chapter we have discussed strategic and tactical sales management issues including sales force size and management and control of the sales force including recruitment, selection, evaluation, motivation, training and remuneration. Sales office support issues have also been considered.

Face-to-face communication will always be important in commercial transactions. Such contact directly involves human beings, with their idiosyncratic ways, and this makes the subject of selling complicated, dynamic and interesting.

Some of the more significant developments in recent years that have impacted directly on the sales function have been the growth of key account management, relationship marketing, direct marketing and more recently, the Internet. So important are these that the next two chapters are devoted to their development and implementation.

KEY TERMS

CASE STUDY

Shakesheff Web Design

Malcolm Shakesheff is at a crossroads in the development of his business. Three years ago, he left his job as a successful sales representative to develop his own company, Shakesheff Web Design, which has grown beyond his wildest expectations. The company was an extension of what was initially Malcolm's hobby in terms of a practical skill he possessed in designing simple Internet websites for friends and family. The company's success is

. . . continued

principally down to Malcolm who has single-handedly performed the sales function. However, his wife, Penny, has been the bedrock behind the scenes as she has managed the everyday running of the business. Malcolm has received backing from the bank that means doubling the size of his business. In particular, Malcolm now needs to employ three new salespeople who will be based in London, Birmingham and Edinburgh respectively to provide countrywide coverage.

Although he has always been successful in selling and indeed his new company's growth is down to his personal selling skills coupled with his knowledge of IT and web design, he has never before had to manage a sales force, and certainly not for his own company. Within the next three months, however, Malcolm has to decide what sort of people he needs and then recruit and select them. He must then train and manage them.

Quite simply, despite his extensive experience as a salesperson, he is concerned about where to start. He recognizes the importance of getting this right, as the whole future of his company will depend on the qualities and management of his own sales force.

CASE STUDY QUESTION

Advise Malcolm regarding what you feel should be the key elements in recruiting, training and managing his new sales force.

REFERENCES

1 McMurry, R.N. (1961), 'The mystique of super-salesmanship', *Harvard Business Review*, 26(March–April): 114–32.

2 Donaldson, B. (2007), *Sales Management: Theory and Practice*, 3rd edn, London: Macmillan.

3 Anderson, R. (1995), *Essentials of Personal Selling*, London: Prentice-Hall.

4 Picton, D. and Broderick, A. (2004), *Integrated Marketing Communications*, 2nd edn, Harlow: Pearson Education.

5 Cowan, D. (2008), 'Creating customer insight', *International Journal of Market Research*, 50(6): 719–29.

6 Malcolm, S., McDaniel, H.C. and Langett, J. (2008), 'Philosophical bridges for IMC: grounding the practice', *International Journal of Strategic Communication*, 2(1): 19–30.

7 Jobber, D. and Lancaster, G. (2009), *Selling and Sales Management*, 8th edn, London: Prentice-Hall.

8 Lancaster, G. and Simintiras, A. (1991), 'Job related expectations of sales people: a review of behavioural determinants', *Management Decision*, 29(2): 32–48.

9 Piercy, N. and Lane, N. (2005), 'Strategic imperatives for transformation in the conventional sales organisation', *Journal of Change Management*, 5(3): 249–66.

10 Rackham, N. (1995), *SPIN Selling*, Farnham, Surrey: Gower.

11 Moncrief, W.C. and Marshall, G.W. (2005), 'The evolution of the seven stages of selling', *Industrial Marketing Management*, 34(1): 13–22.

12 Millman, T. and Wilson, K.J. (1995), 'From key account selling to key account management', *Journal of Marketing Practice, Applied Marketing Science*, 1: 9–21.

13 Ivens, B.S. and Pardo, C. (2008), 'Key account management in business markets: an empirical test of common assumptions', *Journal of Business and Industrial Marketing*, 23(5): 300–10.

14 Brehmer, P. and Rehme, J. (2009), 'Proactive and reactive: drivers for key account management programmes', *European Journal of Marketing*, 43(7/8): 961–84.

15 Starkey, M.W. (1997), 'Telemarketing', in D. Jobber (ed.), *CIM Handbook of Selling and Sales Strategy*, Oxford: Butterworth-Heinemann.

16 Sharma, D. and Gassenheimer, J.B. (2009), 'Internet channel and perceived cannibalisation: scale development and validation in a personal selling context', *European Journal of Marketing*, 43(7/8): 1076–91.

17 Day, G.S. and Bens, K.J. (2005), 'Capitalizing on the internet opportunity', *Journal of Business and Industrial Marketing*, 20(4/5): 160–8.

18 Samaniego, J.G., Gutierrez Arranz, A.M. and Cabazudo, R. (2006) 'Determinants of internet use in the purchasing process', *Journal of Business and Industrial Marketing*, 21(3): 164–74.

19 Zineldin, M. and Phillipson, S. (2007), 'Kotler and Borden are not dead: myth of relationship marketing and the truth of the 4Ps', *Journal of Consumer Marketing*, 24(4): 229–41.

20 Lancaster, G. (1993), 'Marketing and engineering: can there ever be synergy?', *Journal of Marketing Management*, 9: 141–53.

Chapter 9

Customer care and relationship marketing

By the end of this chapter you will:

- understand the importance, scope and meaning of customer care and relationship marketing and the links between these two areas of marketing
- appreciate why customer care and relationship marketing have become important in contemporary marketing
- know how to develop policies and programmes to improve standards of customer care in an organization
- understand how and when to develop policies and programmes of relationship marketing
- be aware of recent developments in customer care and relationship marketing, and in particular the role of new technology and its impact on these areas

INTRODUCTION

Marketing is an evolving body of thought and practice. We have seen that marketing is a concept and a management function that has developed over the years. We have seen how use of the marketing concept and tools has widened from its original primary application in marketing consumer goods in profit-seeking organizations to spread to industrial markets, service markets and not-for-profit organizations. Similarly, we have seen how new technology and technological developments are changing the practice of marketing. So much is happening with regard to developments in contemporary marketing thinking and practice that it is difficult to select what are the most important and far-reaching of these for the modern marketer. However, among the most significant changes in recent years have been the interlinked developments of an increased emphasis on **customer care** activities, coupled with the growth of **relationship marketing (RM)**. Developments in these areas represent what constitutes an almost seismic shift in marketing thinking and practice. Why this is so we shall see shortly, together with the implications of this shift. We start with customer care. It is important to stress that these two areas of contemporary marketing are interrelated. The term **customer relationship management (CRM)** is also used to link relationship marketing to customer care.

CUSTOMER CARE

We have seen that the marketing concept centres on the importance of customers and the absolute necessity of identifying and satisfying their needs and wants. The marketer puts the customer at the centre of the business and the development of organizational strategies. This idea is fundamental to marketers and even non-marketers in that other business functions would not disagree with the notion of the importance and centrality of customers. If this is the case, why has there been an upsurge in the importance of customer care in marketing programmes in recent years, and how does the notion and scope of customer care differ from the traditional marketing concept? How can a company plan and implement effective customer care programmes?

Meaning and scope of customer care

Amongst the many views of the meaning and scope of customer care, the view taken here is that it involves planning all the activities involved in the customer–supplier relationship including pre-, during- and post-transaction stages to ensure that customer expectations are met or exceeded.

This view emphasizes the fact that customer care is all-embracing covering every aspect of customer–supplier relationships. It also illustrates that customer care involves planning in both the strategic and tactical sense.

Customer care entails much more than the notion of customer service, as this focuses more on 'order-cycle' related activities. Customer service is an important facet of overall customer care, but centres more on those activities that involve direct contact with the customer. Customer care is a much more holistic way of looking at customer satisfaction. It necessitates the involvement of every facet of the company's marketing and customer-related programmes and should affect every stage of the marketing planning and implementation process. Why then do we need customer care, and why has it grown in importance in recent years? These are questions that we now examine.

Cost of poor customer care

It is increasingly recognized that should customer expectation at any point in the supplier/customer relationship not be met, this will result in customer dissatisfaction. The extent to which the customer feels dissatisfied depends upon the circumstances. For example, the customer may be simply mildly dissatisfied or at the other extreme might be 'hopping mad'. Particularly where the latter is the case, we know that every displeased customer is likely to talk about this dissatisfaction to other customers or potential customers. Young[1] suggests that customers with bad experiences are twice as likely to tell others about it as those with good experiences. Quite simply, poor customer care loses not only the customer involved, but many more as well.

Benefits of good customer care

We know that satisfied customers are more likely to return to buy again, and over time, become loyal. This illustrates just one of the links between customer care and RM. This is particularly important when we look at the costs of acquiring customers compared to keeping them. Kotler and Keller[2] have suggested that in organizational purchasing settings it can cost as much as ten times more to acquire a new customer than it does to keep an existing one. Certainly, the marketing costs required to persuade a new organizational customer to purchase are much greater than those required to persuade a satisfied customer to purchase again. In this respect, the notion of a 'ladder of loyalty' has been developed. Peck et al.[3] show this as involving the steps or rungs shown in Figure 9.1.

The first rung on the ladder, 'Prospect', represents an individual or an organization which the marketer could possibly persuade to do business. Once the prospect has been persuaded in this way they become a 'Purchaser', having done business at least once with the organization. The 'Client' is someone who has done business with the marketer's organization on a repeat basis, but is still at best neutral towards the supplier. A 'Supporter', however, is someone who has done business with the marketer on a regular basis, but now begins to like the supplier's organization and gives support if only passively. The penultimate stage, the 'Advocate', is a customer who recommends the marketer's organization to others, i.e. effectively someone who helps to do your marketing. The highest rung of the ladder is represented by a 'Partner' who is a customer who effectively has the relationship of a strategic partner with the supplying organization.

FIGURE 9.1 The relationship marketing ladder of loyalty

Source: Peck, H. *et al.* (1999), *Relationship Marketing*, Oxford: Butterworth-Heinemann, p. 45.

As we shall see, RM is aimed at moving customers up the ladder of loyalty until they ultimately become partners. The lifetime value of loyal customers can be huge as measured in sales and profit terms. Given that customer care is a major facet in moving customers up the ladder of loyalty, we can see why marketers have become increasingly interested in the customer care aspects of marketing yet this does not explain in itself the growth in importance of customer care.

Customer expectations

Perhaps the major reason for the growth in importance of customer care is the fact that customer expectations have changed over the years both in organizational and consumer contexts. Quite simply, customers expect higher levels of customer care and satisfaction from the marketer. In part, this is as a result of changes in education on the part of many customers. Customers are now more ready to challenge poor levels of customer care and are much better informed as regards their rights in this respect. Another factor is that customers have much better access to information about failings and shortcomings in customer care through more media exposure in this area and information that is posted on the Internet. Customers are also better protected through legislation regarding their rights as customers and what they can realistically expect with respect to customer care.

Spread the Word – But Be Careful!

Word-of-mouth implies personal one-to-one communication. One person telling another person in a face-to-face conversation or telephone call about a bad experience with a brand is a common occurrence. Imagine the problems when a dissatisfied customer can tell millions, and all virtually at the same time! Not possible, unless that person owns say a television channel or newspaper or presents a popular programme or writes a well read column. Well, it was not possible for the disgruntled customer to tell this many people, but now it is. How? Through the growth in use of social networks on the Internet such as YouTube or through the myriad of blogging sites, many of which are global and able to reach millions. In January 2009 there were estimated to be over 120 million blogging sites. If you upset customers it can be very costly. We should remember, of course, that upset customers have to be careful about what they say about companies and brands. By 2009 defamation litigation related to blogging sites in the US reached over $17 million.

Today's customers are more willing to complain if they feel their expectations have not been met. Moreover, they are increasingly likely to follow up these complaints through some form of formal procedure and even litigation if necessary. It is important to stress, however, that the average customer, even in the USA, where perhaps the highest levels of customer expectation with regard to customer care in the world exist, is still reluctant to complain. For example, a report by The US Office of Consumer Affairs[4] suggested that the average business does not hear from 96 per cent of its unhappy customers, and that for every complaint received there were as many as 30 customers with problems or serious problems. In countries like Germany, Ireland and the UK where customers are more reluctant to complain, these figures are likely to be even higher. One might be tempted to believe that most customers are simply not that concerned about customer care, to the extent that they perhaps do not think it is worth complaining. Certainly, many customers do not feel it is worthwhile, but this is more a reflection of the fact that they feel that their complaints will go unheeded. Other customers simply may not know how to start to complain in a formal way. This does not mean that such customers are not concerned about customer care or that the marketer need not be too concerned. Just the opposite is the case; it is probably customers who do not complain that are most important with regard to focusing improved customer care efforts. Such customers represent a majority of customers who never purchase again, and who represent the main source of negative information about a company, and this is passed by word-of-mouth to other potential customers.

STEPS IN ESTABLISHING A CUSTOMER CARE PROGRAMME

There are clear benefits of having an effective customer care programme. Mere acceptance of this is not sufficient to ensure effective customer care. A series of practical steps must be implemented in establishing effective programmes. The main steps in this process are in:

Incorporating a customer care philosophy into company mission statements

The first and most important step in establishing a customer care programme is to ensure that a commitment to customer care is enshrined in the corporate mission statement. By so doing a company has taken the first step in a commitment to customer care. Moreover, being the mission statement, this commitment can be seen to come from the top. This should serve to form and guide a customer care culture and philosophy throughout the organization

Establishing a customer care culture and philosophy

Effective customer care is not something that can be left solely to marketing and sales departments. Customer care is everyone's business. In the same way as the adoption of the marketing concept necessitates a cultural change within many organizations, so too does the adoption of the customer care concept. However, instilling this philosophy is not easy. As with the marketing concept, customer care is often seen as being someone else's responsibility. Adopting a customer care philosophy starts at the top and must have the full support and commitment of senior management. The importance of customer care must be 'marketed' throughout the organization. This is part of the process of 'internal marketing' that we referred to in Chapter 1. Individuals and functions in the organization must be persuaded and shown how their activities relate to overall levels of customer care and the impact they can have on this area. Implementing this philosophy throughout an organization requires that people's tasks, activities, responsibilities and even promotion and remuneration are linked to customer care. Customer care responsibilities are part of everyone's job in the organization.

Needless to say, the marketing function has a primary role to play in this process; in particular the marketer or marketing function should be responsible for providing up-to-date and reliable information about what it is that customers want with regard to customer care, how various activities in the organization contribute or otherwise to the satisfaction of customer needs and any problems or shortcomings in this respect. The marketer must also ensure that track is kept of competitor levels of customer care and any trends in these levels.

Identifying customer needs and perceptions

As with all marketing programmes, the start point of effective customer care is the identification of customer needs. Customer care is about ensuring these needs are met and in particular that customer expectations are fulfilled or exceeded. Many companies still do not appreciate what their customers' needs and expectations are with regard to various facets of the transaction process. For example, most new car customers want a full tank of fuel when they collect their new cars. In spite of this, even some of the most expensive new cars have only enough fuel in them to reach the first filling station.

As mentioned already, customers are often reluctant to complain, and in any event if the customer does complain it is already too late. The marketer must therefore research customer needs to establish precisely what constitutes customer satisfaction and the customer expectations with regard to the various facets of the transaction process. The marketer must also at this stage consider perceptions that customers have with regard to the company and its standards of customer care.

Focus group interviews with both potential and existing customers can be useful. Customers are often more willing to reveal their true needs or, in the case of existing customers, feelings of satisfaction and dissatisfaction in a group setting. Many companies use follow up phone calls or mailed questionnaires to check on customer satisfaction. For example, 'Home Care', an insurance product for householders covering plumbing repairs, kitchen appliance breakdowns, etc., regularly contact a sample of customers who have had a call-out to check levels of service and customer satisfaction. As with all marketing the marketer must be careful not to assume he/she knows what the customers needs are.

Establishing customer care standards and specifications

This step in the process involves the company establishing specific levels for customer care and the key activities and processes to be included. These must relate to customers' expectations and needs established in the first step. For example, we need to establish delivery standards, standards for customer responsiveness, courtesy and credibility and product quality. Every facet of the company that may impinge on customer satisfaction needs to be incorporated here; not just marketing activities. Specific standards for customer care that can be measured and evaluated need to be established at this stage. Although customer care programmes should meet the highest level of standards in line with customer expectations, it is important to establish a basic minimum level below which levels of customer care should not drop under any circumstances.

Again, regular surveys and feedback from customers are essential. Consumer panels which allow for such regular feedback from customers are useful. In addition, the marketer should consult dealers and other intermediaries on a regular basis for their views.

Specifying jobs and activities

Related to required standards and specifications for customer care there needs to be detailed specifications of what this means for people's activities and jobs within the organization. It should include, for example, the designation of tasks and activities, allocation of responsibilities, motivation and monitoring and control systems necessary to successfully implement customer care and the information systems required to facilitate effective customer care programmes.

Ensuring adequate systems for monitoring and evaluating levels of customer care

It is important that effective systems are established for measuring and evaluating standards of customer care including tracking and monitoring systems, market research and customer evaluation procedures. Clear systems and procedures for ensuring effective responses to problems with customer care levels, including complaints are necessary. These are the practical steps in implementing customer care programmes, but effective customer care also requires an organization-wide commitment. In this respect it is important to stress that this is not just a marketing department responsibility and activity. The importance of customer care and an acceptance of this importance throughout every level and function of the organization is a critical issue. Customer care must be part of overall corporate culture. Moreover, it should impinge on every facet of the marketing programme. It is to these two aspects of implementing customer care programmes that we now turn our attention.

CUSTOMER CARE AND THE MARKETING PROCESS

Where commitment to customer care becomes part of a company's philosophy, we find that customer care impinges on the whole of the marketing process. This notion can most easily be seen by returning to the typical steps in the marketing planning process established in Chapter 1 and extended in later chapters. We can see from this how a company-wide philosophy and commitment to customer care affects the whole marketing process. Each of the steps in the marketing planning process, together with an outline of how customer care relates to each of these steps is now outlined.

Corporate objectives/business mission

Commitment to customer care should be reflected and enshrined in the overall corporate objectives and mission statements of the organization. At this stage, mission statements about overall customer care objectives feed into and shape the subsequent stages and strategies of the marketing plan.

The marketing audit/SWOT analysis

This encompasses an appraisal of the internal and external environments of the company. With regard to the external environment analysis, this should help shape required levels of customer care in, for example, changing cultural and social values. These, in turn, are reflected in customer requirements and expectations for customer care levels. Competitor customer care levels should also be appraised in the external audit. The internal part of the audit requires the organization to assess standards of performance regarding customer care and any shortcomings. As we have seen, the internal and external audit feed into the SWOT analysis. Part of the SWOT analysis should be an assessment of strengths, weaknesses, opportunities and threats with regard to customer care levels and programmes e.g. a company may establish through the audit that it has major weaknesses in certain elements of its customer care activities that need to be remedied. Alternatively, a company may identify possible future opportunities by building on strong levels of customer care compared to competitors.

Marketing objectives and strategies

Marketing objectives and strategies should include customer care elements. Overall, marketing objectives may relate to, for example, growth and market share, but should also include specific objectives with regard to levels of customer care. Again, tools such as **gap analysis** can be used. As the term implies, gap analysis looks at any difference between planned levels of customer care and service and achieved levels with a view to correcting these differences. For example, a company may specify a maximum number of rings before a call is answered by a customer service operative. Possible reason for gaps may include operative overload or inadequate call queuing systems.

As regards marketing strategies, different strategies for growth such as diversification will often have customer care implications. If the intention is to pursue new markets e.g. as a strategy for growth, the marketer will need to establish customer needs and expectations regarding customer care levels in these markets.

Marketing tactics/marketing mix decisions

Perhaps one of the most important facets regarding customer care and the marketing mix is to ensure that marketing mix decisions and in particular specific marketing tactics that can often be short term in nature, do not conflict with or detract from overall planned levels of customer care. For example, pricing strategies designed to attract new customers may result in lower levels of customer care than is necessary or required for existing customers. Many companies only make special offers available to new customers e.g. a new subscriber to a cable TV service may be offered an initial three months at a reduced price and free installation of the latest set top box. Existing subscribers, however, must pay the full rate for the service and pay an upgrade fee for the new box. In this way, existing customers who may have been with company for a long time are dealt with less favourably than new customers when it comes to offers and price deals. Needless to say, this can result in considerable dissatisfaction amongst previously loyal customers and is a major cause of high customer 'churn rates' in some markets.

Virtually every facet of the marketing mix has implications for customer care. Thus, delivery and after-sales service stem from distribution and logistics decisions; product and augmented product decisions (as discussed in Chapter 4) have a major effect on customer care; promotion should be aimed at building long-term customer relationships. Therefore, pricing should reflect overall customer care strategies.

Implementation

We have seen that overall objectives for customer care need to be translated into specific action programmes with the allocation of responsibilities, systems and procedures that should include training and motivation of staff. Suitable organizational structures need to be in place to implement effective customer care programmes.

Evaluation and control

It goes without saying that effective customer care, like other areas of marketing, needs to be evaluated and controlled. Systems for monitoring achieved levels of customer care, responses to customer complaints, etc. must be built into the company's overall evaluation and control systems.

Customer care affects, and is affected by, every single facet of the marketing planning process. Before we consider the development of relationship marketing, including how this relates to customer care, we need to consider the relationship between customer care and quality, and the distinction between customer care and customer service.

CUSTOMER CARE AND QUALITY

There is a close, but complex relationship between customer care and quality management in the organization. Quality has been a major issue in competitive strategy in recent years, and in particular the pursuit of improved and consistent quality has mainly been due to the fact that we know now that good quality is a major factor in competitive success.

Note that 'good quality' does not necessarily mean simply high quality. In consumer terms, good quality means 'fitness for purpose'. In other words, the marketer must ensure that the product or service is of a quality that meets customer needs and expectations. For example, if we purchase a shovel or spade then we must at the very least be able to dig with it. Used for the purpose intended, it should not bend or break and should last what can be considered a reasonable life-time. Over and above this, the customer might be looking and paying for higher quality levels like stainless steel construction.

The PIMS programme[5] developed by the Marketing Science Institute and the Harvard Business School in the early 1970s, has long established the link between management strategies and profitability. The **PIMS** project (Profit Impact of Management Strategies) looked at the return on investment (ROI) of a large sample of American and European businesses and compared this with information on the various strategies these businesses were using. The essence of PIMS is the use of empirical evidence to establish which strategies are associated with higher levels of profitability in an industry and thereby to steer managers in these industries towards better (more profitable) courses of action.

Some of the basic questions that PIMS seeks to answer include:

■ What is the typical profit rate for each type of business?
■ Given current strategies in a company, what are future operating results likely to be?
■ What strategies are likely to help improve future operating results?

To obtain this information for a particular company, the company must subscribe to the PIMS project and provide detailed information, including, for example:

■ competitors and market information;
■ balance sheet information;
■ assumptions about future sales, costs, strategies, etc.

This information is then compared with the PIMS database and a series of reports prepared for the subscribing company as follows:

1   A 'Par' report showing the ROI and cash flows that are 'normal' for this type of business given its market, competition, technology and cost structure. Also included is an analysis of strengths and weaknesses that are regarded as explaining high or low par figures compared with other businesses in the database.

2   A 'Strategy analysis' report which computes the predicted consequences of each of several alternative strategic actions, judged by information on similar businesses making similar moves, from a similar starting point and in a similar business environment.

3   A 'Report on look-alikes' (ROLA) that examines possible tactics for achieving strategic objectives such as an increase in market share, by analysing strategically similar businesses more closely.

4   An 'Optimus strategy' report aimed at predicting the best combination of strategies for that particular company, again based on the experiences of other businesses in 'similar' circumstances.

The advantages of PIMS to an individual business are that not only can management assess the likely outcome of its proposed strategies, but it can also identify those strategies that will yield the highest return on investment.

Why doesn't every company subscribe to PIMS for its strategic planning? First, there is the question of cost. The full range of PIMS services is expensive. Second, the amount of data required to be supplied by a company for a PIMS analysis is extensive. This can be costly and time consuming. Most important of all, there are limitations to PIMS:

■   PIMS data is historical and may be misleading in conditions of rapid change.
■   The underlying assumptions of the PIMS model are not clarified and must be taken on trust.
■   The statistical basis of PIMS can give rise to problems of interpretation and understanding.

PIMS is not a panacea for strategic decision making in individual companies. It is best used as an aid to managerial judgement. In general terms, analysis of the PIMS database has shown that some 37 variables together account for almost 80 per cent of the variations in return on investment. These, therefore, are the key factors that most strategic marketing planners will need to consider in their marketing plans. From the viewpoint of our discussion, good quality was found to be a major factor accounting for differences in success for the companies in the PIMS database as measured by return on investment. Put simply, quality pays! PIMS offers access to a comprehensive, empirically based strategic planning tool although the full advantages of PIMS are available only to a company that subscribes to the PIMS database. However, even for the non-subscribing company, the general published findings of PIMS regarding key determinants of return on investment consistently underpin the importance of good quality and company success.

Given our definition of customer care, effective standards of customer care are impossible where the quality that the customer experiences or perceives does not match their expectations. Customer care and quality are inextricably linked.

A major development in recent years has been the **total quality management (TQM)** approach to business that is applied when managing every aspect of the company's activities. Given that quality management revolves around meeting customer requirements and expectations, and what represents acceptable quality is essentially determined by customers and their requirements, then customer care and TQM are closely related. Quality programmes encompass many other areas than dealing with customers, while customer care programmes are specifically focused on customers and how to improve care. The major influence of TQM on customer care activities is the notion that with TQM processes, all activities, not only in-company activities, but also partners in both the **demand chain** and the **supply chain** (i.e. the entire **value chain**) can affect quality. Total Quality Management also gives central place to the customer in designing quality systems. Customer-driven quality is one of the key distinguishing features of TQM as a philosophy.

Companies can make two types of mistakes when it comes to quality and customer needs. The first of course is producing products and services which do not come up to the target customer's quality requirements and expectations. The quality is too low. In our previous example of the spade, obviously if on first use the spade bends or breaks then the customer to say the least is going to be disappointed. Less obvious, however is the mistake of supplying products and services which exceed the target customer's quality requirements and expectations. The quality is too high. This may result in a product which either has too high a price, lowers company profits or both. Many British engineering companies have in the past made this mistake, producing things that were of too high a quality or specification for market needs hence leaving the way open for other lower priced, 'lower quality' competitors.

In many ways, TQM and customer care go hand in hand in the contemporary organization, but what is the relationship between customer care and customer service?

CUSTOMER CARE AND CUSTOMER SERVICE

A degree of confusion exists regarding the relationship and distinction between customer care and customer service. In fact, although the two are closely related there are also some major differences. Some of the key differences are captured by Stone and Young[6] and shown in Table 9.1.

Taking each of these differences in turn, customer service emphasizes the tasks involved in servicing customers rather than customer needs. It is more a supplier's view of the elements of customer requirements as opposed to the customer's perspective. Customer service also focuses primarily on the costs associated with customer requirements, whereas customer care centres on long-term profit and revenue implications. With customer service, more attention is given to procedures, management processes and hierarchies and on technical and administrative requirements. Customer care, on the other hand, emphasizes the importance of procedures that encourage

TABLE 9.1 Differences between customer services and customer care

Customer service	Customer care
Emphasizes tasks	Emphasizes customers
Focuses on costs	Focuses on profit and revenue
Procedures restrict responsiveness	Procedures enable responsiveness
Hierarchical management	Supportive management
Technical/administrative environment	Commercial environment

Source: M. Stone and L. Young (1992), Competitive Customer Care: A Guide to Keeping Customers, Kingston-upon-Thames: Croner, p. 20.

responsiveness to customer needs and ways in which management systems and procedures can support this with a view to achieving commercial, as opposed to technical or engineering, aims and goals. Having said this, in many companies we still find customer service departments. There is nothing wrong with this so long as the elements of customer service and the activities of the customer service department are set and managed in the context of a wider overall company approach and perspective regarding customer care. Put another way, customer service is but a part of overall customer care activities.

RELATIONSHIP MARKETING

Another major development in marketing thinking and practice in recent years has been the growth of relationship marketing (RM). We emphasize that RM is very much linked with the notion and practice of customer care. We shall, therefore, highlight these links between the two areas where appropriate as we discuss relationship marketing. For many RM represents an even more significant shift in marketing thinking and practice than the growth of the philosophy of customer care, so much so that it is referred to as involving a paradigm shift in the marketing concept itself. Certainly there is no doubt that the development of RM has had, and will continue to have, major implications for the marketing manager. What follows is an overview of these aspects of relationship marketing.

Essentially RM is based on the notion that instead of the marketer looking at the exchange process as one where two protagonists, supplier and customer, each look to maximize the benefit they receive from each transaction or exchange. It is more effective to look at customer and marketer as partners in an exchange, whereby both parties benefit by working together on a basis of mutual trust and loyalty. This deceptively simple statement represents a new and revolutionary marketing paradigm though there are some who dispute this (Zineldin and Phillipson[7]).

There are different views as to the precise nature and definition of RM. For example, Gronroos[8] stresses the element of mutual exchange and trust in relationship marketing:

> Relationship marketing is a process including several parties or actors, the objectives of which have to be met. This is done by mutual exchange and fulfilment of promises, a fact that makes trust an important aspect of marketing.

Gamble *et al.*[9] put more emphasis on the traditional tools of sales, communications and customer care techniques and again we see the overlap between these areas:

> Relationship marketing involves the use of a wide range of marketing, sales, communications and customer care techniques and processes to: identify named individual customers, create a relationship between the company and these customers, and manage that relationship to the benefit of both customers and company.

Perhaps one of the most powerful summaries of what relationship marketing represents is that provided by Buttle:[10]

> At its best, RM (relationship management) is characterized by a genuine concern to meet or exceed the expectations of customers and to provide excellent service in an environment of trust and commitment to the relationship.

He goes on to indicate what is involved in successful relationship marketing and the commitment of the company, required to generate this success:

> To be successful relationship marketers, companies must develop a supportive organizational culture, market the RM idea internally, intimately understand customers' expectations, create and maintain a detailed customer database, and organize and reward employees in such a way that the objective of RM, customer retention, is achieved.

This illustrates that as suggested RM has major implications for how we think about marketing and our approach to the practice of marketing. It affects and includes the provision of marketing information, organizational systems and procedures and the elements of marketing strategy. We must then consider the characteristics of an RM approach, and in particular how it compares and contrasts with the more conventional transactional marketing approach. We must also consider why RM emerged as a suggested new paradigm for marketing and the implications of this for the practice of marketing management.

RELATIONSHIP AND TRANSACTIONAL MARKETING COMPARED AND CONTRASTED

RM first became evident in B2B marketing, but this approach is now evident in the services sector and in consumer marketing. Conventional **transactional marketing**, based on the notion of mutual exchange, is where the seller offers immediate and hopefully attractive combinations of product, price and technical support to generate a sale. The emphasis, albeit implicitly, is on completing this individual transaction. In turn, this completion of the transaction is the measure of success of the exchange. The marketer then moves to consider the next order the customer might place and attempts to generate another individual transaction. The buyer is interested in the best possible value, and the marketer with revenue from the exchange. There is little emphasis on customer service or long-term relationships by either party – typically found in a relationship where a buyer of a raw material such as steel plate purchases purely on price, specification and delivery.

With RM the emphasis switches to developing a longer-term and more interactive set of relationships between the marketer and customer based on partnership and sharing. In particular, the marketer's concern is to move the customer up the ladder of loyalty to the point where the customer becomes a partner with the supplier. Although transactions and immediate satisfaction are still important to both parties, in RM the success of the exchange is the extent to which both parties benefit thorough co-operation and agreement. In the most successful examples of RM, the two parties grow more trusting, more knowledgeable about each others' interests and needs, and more interested in helping each other. Transactions cease to be negotiated each time and become part of a longer-term routine. The outcome of successful relationship marketing is the development

TABLE 9.2 Transactional marketing vs. relationship marketing

Transaction marketing	Relationship marketing
Focus on single sale	Focus on customer retention
Orientation on product features	Orientation on product benefits
Short timescale	Long timescale
Little emphasis on customer service	High customer service emphasis
Limited commitment to customer	High commitment to customer
Moderate customer contact	Extensive customer contact
Quality is primarily concern of production	Quality concern of all functions

Source: Adapted from Kotler, P., Armstrong, G., Saunders, J. and Wong, V. (2001), *Principles of Marketing*, London: Prentice-Hall, p. 408.

of solid, dependable supplier–customer relationships which form the basis of a marketing network and represent a valuable marketing asset. By so doing, the bureaucratic process of sending out enquiries, receiving quotations, placing the order and following up the order can be short circuited.

RM, as opposed to traditional transactional marketing, can be seen as opposite ends of a continuum. The distinctions between transaction marketing and RM already highlighted, together with additional key areas of difference are summarized by Kotler *et al.*[11] and are shown in Table 9.2. We can see from this table that relationship and transactional marketing are different in several respects. But why has RM emerged and what has given rise to this paradigm shift in the concept of marketing?

Reasons for the growth of relationship marketing

The well established notions of 'exchange' and 'interaction' in marketing provide the theoretical antecedents for the emergence of RM. However, as Lancaster and Massingham[12] point out, the growth of RM has more pragmatic causes. Put simply, they assert, both marketer and customer have increasingly recognized that relationship marketing, and in particular the requirements needed to develop effective relationship marketing such as the building of strong trust and confidence between the two parties, the exchange of information and effective communication, and mutual support, simply makes good sense. In particular, this commonsense approach concerns the building of strong trust and confidence between the two parties, the exchange of information, effective communication and mutual support, and this can only be good for business relationships.

To these antecedents, Gummesson[13] adds the notion of 'networks'. By 'networks' he is referring to the fact that in many exchanges there are more than two parties involved, especially in B2B markets. For example there is a whole network of parties involved in the chain of supply, manufacture and marketing including raw material suppliers, suppliers of finance, distributors and intermediaries and a whole array of service agencies like advertising and market research agencies. The suggestion is that we plan marketing strategies around the whole network of supply and marketing.

Perhaps this explains why RM first began to emerge in B2B markets, where it was readily seen to make good commercial sense in terms of improving customer retention rates. Estimates vary, but on average it can be up to six to eight times more expensive to create a new customer than to keep an existing one. For the marketer, building long-term relationships with customers can lead to substantially lower marketing and other costs, e.g. lower costs are incurred in advertising and promotion to attract and keep customers. Selling costs can be lower, particularly in B2B markets where salespeople spend less time having to prospect for new customers. Both implicitly and explicitly, RM focuses on customer retention. As we have seen with customer service, companies have realized the financial value of keeping customers and the life-time value of loyal customers is huge. This recognition of the financial pay-off of building long-term, lasting relationships with customers is now increasingly recognized in consumer goods markets.

An RM approach is felt to bestow benefits on the customer in consumer goods markets, especially if customers feel they can purchase the same brand every time because they trust the brand or supplier. This can substantially help reduce the time, effort and risk in making a purchase. In addition, many RM campaigns used in consumer markets involve some sort of financial inducement for the customer to become involved in a long-term relationship with the marketer – loyalty cards, air miles and bonus points are examples of inducements designed to encourage the customer up the ladder of loyalty. RM would not have increased if there were no benefits for the customer. Again, in the case of B2B customers these benefits are readily identified and easier to communicate as they are principally financial in nature, e.g. for the manufacturing customer, developing effective relationships with suppliers enables more cost-effective systems of purchasing to be put in place if production operates a just-in-time (JIT) lean manufacturing system. Through RM, companies are able to develop collaborative ventures with customers or suppliers with regard to developing new products. Clearly, JIT and collaborative new product development require long-term relationships between customers and marketers.

Overall, as one would expect from any successful relationship, both parties need to feel they can benefit if RM is to be appropriate and successful. In this respect, Bund-Jackson[14] suggested that the development of a RM approach is not always appropriate for all customers. She suggests that some customers are better managed through the traditional transaction marketing approach. These customers she refers to as 'always-a-share' customers. Such customers include those who have low switching costs in terms of changing suppliers and brands and find making such change relatively easy. Because of this, they do not value long-term relationships with suppliers and for more expensive durable goods items prefer to negotiate individual transactions each time a purchase is made. Other types of customer in this category include customers who are make one-off purchases and are not interested in supplier relationships. Such customers are 'brand promiscuous' and want to try out as many different brands as possible in seeking variety. For this category of customers, any would-be supplier is always in a position to gain a share of this type of customer's business so RM is less appropriate. In contrast, she terms customers who are best suited to a RM approach as 'lost-for-good' customers. The characteristics of such customers are that they have high switching costs in terms of changing suppliers, tend to have longer time horizons, make a series of purchases over time and view commitments to particular suppliers or brands as important and preferably relatively permanent. Once a supplier has won this type of account, the customer is likely to remain loyal to the supplier for a long time. If lost, however, the customer often never returns, so is 'lost-for' good' to the supplier. If anything, the incidence of 'lost-for-good' customers, particularly in business-to-business markets, has grown in recent years, again related to developments such as JIT manufacturing and collaborative ventures between companies. Such collaboration requires close co-operation between supplying and purchasing companies that can only be achieved by supplier and buyer taking a long-term RM approach. One of the first steps in developing RM, and in determining whether a RM approach should be used, is to identify which customers merit a relationship approach.

There are those who feel that RM is more relevant in B2B marketing and is not suited to marketing consumer goods where it is suggested that customers do not seek relationships with marketers.

BRANDING AND RELATIONSHIP MARKETING

When it comes to consumer goods marketing, do customers want or need a relationship with suppliers other than ensuring smooth transactions? The emergence of powerful brands has changed this. Many customers now want to develop a relationship in their purchasing, and what they seek and value is a relationship with the brand rather than the marketer.

Brands are big business and are estimated to drive nearly two-thirds of purchases in consumer markets. Coca-Cola, Sony, McDonald's and Microsoft are global brands that transcend national boundaries. What is the link between brands and relationship marketing? The most successful brands over time develop a relationship with customers. Initially a customer may purchase a brand simply for novelty, perhaps to try something new or because of the recommendation of a friend. If the brand delivers, i.e. the customer is satisfied, then it increases the chance of the customer purchasing this brand again. Over time, provided the brand continues to deliver, the customer will become brand loyal. From a mere liking of, or satisfaction with, the brand, the customer becomes committed, seldom considering purchasing another brand and eventually possibly becoming an advocate for the brand.

Brands make the process of purchasing easier and less stressful. They reassure and build trust. Some confer status on purchasers and become 'badges' that send signals out about the customer and what they feel about themselves. Reast[15] suggests that the marketer can build on a customer's relationship with a brand to develop brand extensions. In the case of retail brands, Binniger[16] shows how strong retail brands are associated with store loyalty, providing a powerful basis for retailers to develop relationships with customers in consumer markets.

THE IMPLICATIONS OF RELATIONSHIP MARKETING

There are far-reaching implications for the marketer associated with the emergence and growth of relationship marketing. RM heightens the need for a more effective two-way communication between the marketer and customers. In B2B markets, electronic data interchange (EDI) systems have facilitated the growth of RM. In consumer markets, direct on-line communications help in developing effective customer relationships. Marketers and consumer can now communicate on a more personal basis through the Internet. We receive e-mails from organizations with whom we have had some contact and, annoyingly for many, sometimes from those with whom we have not. Most companies have extensive databases on their customers linked to, for example, loyalty card systems that they can 'mine' to reveal patterns and preferences in purchasing, giving a more detailed insight into the needs and wants of individual customers which can then be personalized for direct communications.

A second major implication is that everyone in the supplying company, not just marketing, needs to be concerned with generating customer satisfaction. This is an area where RM and customer service overlap and interact. Any failing in customer service inevitably leads to the loss of customers. Like customer service, RM needs an appropriate supportive organizational culture where everyone in the company is seeking to build relationships with customers. This heightens the importance of internal marketing in companies. The notion of **total relationship marketing (TRM)** is suggested by Zineldin[17] who asserts that the main philosophy behind the TRM approach is to facilitate, create, develop, enhance and continuously improve all internal and external relationships with customers, employees and collaborators.

RM means an organization's marketing effort should be designed around a series of contacts with customers over time, rather than focused on single transactions. This means that more non-marketing people are involved, and has led to the notion of what Gummesson[18] terms the 'part-time marketer'. Here, non-marketing people are increasingly brought into contact with customers at an operational level. This has always been the case in B2B marketing where, for example, engineers come into direct contact with customers, but with the growth of service industries and markets it is now true for many consumer products where the customer comes into contact with the service provider's personnel. Non-sales personnel need to be educated in marketing principles and this has led to the notion of **internal marketing** whereby all employees are encouraged to develop a customer-oriented perspective, whatever their function and role in the organization. Mele[19] suggests TQM is an integrator between production orientation and marketing orientation while Mehra and Ranganathan[20] suggest that TQM should focus on enhancing customer satisfaction. Combining customer satisfaction and TQM requires new attitudes and approaches by both marketing and non-marketing personnel. In some companies, customers are still seen as being the sole responsibility of marketing, and customer contact by staff from other functional departments is sometimes seen as being counter-productive. RM, however, demands a move away from such rigid demarcations of responsibilities for customers. Some companies have moved to cross-functional multi-disciplinary teams to build relationships with customers. In industries ranging from cars and computers to jet engines and industrial controls, this inter-functional team approach is useful and it uses RM in the process of developing new products, where close relationships with, and inputs from, customers are essential.

A further implication of RM is the way the customer often leads the whole of the marketing process. This notion is central to the original marketing concept, but with RM the marketer makes a conscious effort to encourage customers to explain what is required and the marketer develops an appropriate marketing programme to respond to this. This process is referred to as **reverse marketing**. This is prevalent amongst buyers in retail chains like Tesco and Sainsbury's; buyers source appropriate suppliers and enter into contracts with them; they initiate and often help fund long-term commercial manufacturing relationships such as helping to set up a farmers' co-operative in an overseas country to grow, process, pack and despatch agricultural products that cannot be grown in the UK.

RM puts greater emphasis on systems for enabling constant tracking and assessment of customer satisfaction and needs. Customer databases and other sources of information on customers are central to its successful implementation. Organizations can access extensive databases on customers. Such data can be analysed for patterns of behaviour and purchasing that help reveal insights into consumers and their needs. In addition, it is now possible to access external sources of information on customers ranging from their credit profile to their driving records and in some cases even their medical histories.

RM potentially affects every element of the marketing mix. As with customer care, the elements of the mix should be used carefully to encourage customers to become, and stay, loyal to the company. The use of short-term tactics such as special promotional deals, while possibly encouraging new customers, may attract the wrong sort of customer who is not interested in long-term relationships with a supplier or brand. Of all the areas of the marketing mix, it is in the area and process of personal selling that we see some of the most far-reaching implications of a relationship as opposed to a transaction approach to marketing. The following represents just some of the shifts in emphasis and perspectives in the selling process when a company moves towards a RM approach:

- The salesperson must take a longer-term perspective than that of simply making a one-off sale when dealing with customers.
- Effective relationship selling requires much more of a team effort not only between individual members of the sales force, but between the salesperson and other functions in the supplying company.
- The salesperson must be proactive with customers, calling or visiting customers at times other than when they think the customer is ready to place an order.
- The salesperson must act as an exchanger of information between his or her own company and the customer, and vice versa.
- The emphasis must be much more on levels of customer service rather than simply on special deals and attempting to generate sales.

This means that RM requires different skills and attitudes for successful selling. The relationship salesperson must be skilled at listening to customers and interpreting their problems. Moreover, systems for managing and motivating salespersons may need to change. For example, remuneration may need to be geared much more to developing customer loyalty and trust, rather than on immediate one-off sales.

The notion of customer retention is central to the practice of RM. Kotler and Keller[21] discuss three ways in which a company can attempt to build and maintain stronger relationship with existing customers thereby helping to retain them over time:

1 *Adding financial benefits*: Essentially this involves rewarding customers financially for being loyal. Loyalty schemes mentioned earlier, such as reward points or air miles, are examples of these types of benefits. There is some debate about the extent to which such schemes actually encourage truly loyal customers, or simply encourage customers who are looking for the best deal or value.
   The supermarket group Tesco was amongst one of the first retailers in the UK to introduce a loyalty card system. At first, competitors thought that this was a throwback to the 1960s when

consumers were offered trading stamps with their purchases which they could later trade in exchange for products from a catalogue. Many of these competitors felt that customers would not be bothered to collect their reward points let alone be induced to shop at Tesco because they were available. They very quickly changed their attitudes when they found they were losing market share to Tesco partly as a result of Tesco's loyalty scheme. Needless to say many of these competitors were quick to follow Tesco's example when they saw how successful the scheme had proved to be.

2 *Adding social benefits* This involves company personnel increasing their personal and social bonds with customers e.g. by learning about customers' individual and specific needs and requirements, and by giving more personal service, 'customers' are turned into 'clients', thereby strengthening the ties and the loyalty they have to the supplier. The salesperson can play a key role in this approach to building customer loyalty, but in addition, the use of more sophisticated databases to analyse individual customer needs and tailor specific marketing programmes to individual customers is growing in importance with developments in IT.

The banking industry has increasingly been using the notion of social bonds to improve customer retention rates. At one time, up to the 1970s and early 1980s, many banks had personal relationships with their customers, with customers often knowing and dealing with a bank manager on a close personal basis. During the late 1980s and early 1990s the banks moved away from this personal approach in an effort to reduce costs and become more like retailers than bankers. Recently, however some of the banks have been making determined efforts to rebuild bonds with individual customers by learning about their customers' individual and specific needs and by giving personal care. NatWest Bank introduced a product for its current account holders who may, for a fee, be given access to a range of banking services which are specifically designed to meet their individual banking needs, thus returning personal service to part of the UK banking system.

3 *Adding structural ties*: There are ways in which this approach to building customer loyalty and relationships can be implemented. Essentially, it involves providing customer support in the form of expertise or equipment. This provides helps to 'lock' the customer into the supplier. In other words, this approach increases switching costs for a customer. Examples include companies providing computer software to a customer which helps the customer run production schedules, but which is specific to the supplier. Another example would be the supply of electronic data interchange systems for purchasing.

Research by Dodourova[22] concludes that behavioural characteristics such as commitment, co-ordination and communication are found to play a more significant role in explaining overall partnership success compared with organizational characteristics like structure and control mechanisms. Hewlett Packard provide comprehensive technical and after-purchase support systems for their customers. This is so comprehensive that customers do not need to turn to other suppliers for this service.

The implications of relationship marketing

Systems must be in place with RM to enable constant tracking and assessment of customer satisfaction and needs. Customer databases and the introduction of total quality management are important in implementing an effective relationship marketing approach.

RM, as we have seen, is based on developing long-term relationships with customers and hence heightens the need for building and maintaining customer loyalty. Although there are many reasons for their introduction, customer loyalty schemes, as introduced by many retailers, are examples of how companies are concentrating on customer retention. Similar inducements through 'frequent flier clubs' in the airline industry also illustrate this approach. Such benefits tend for be largely, but not exclusively, financial in nature. Obviously, if a customer feels they can purchase the same brand every time this can substantially help reduce the time and effort required to purchase. Similarly, having a trusted brand reduces the risks to the customer of making wrong or ill-advised purchase decisions.

As we saw in Chapter 4, more and more companies are involved in collaborative ventures with regard to developing new products with their suppliers. Clearly this requires effective long-term relationships.

These are just some of the ways in which a company can build and maintain stronger relationships with their customers. In turn, the application of some marketing mix elements is affected by the adoption of a relationship marketing approach. As we saw in Chapter 8, personal selling in particular requires a fundamentally different approach under the relationship marketing concept compared to transaction marketing.

Overall, and together, customer care and relationship marketing are changing the way in which marketing is practised.

SUMMARY

The two interrelated areas of customer care and relationship marketing represent some of the most significant changes in marketing thinking and practice. Both, however, reflect the essential and core concept of marketing inasmuch as they stress the importance of identifying and satisfying customer needs, but with the emphasis on building long-term partnerships with customers. Both concepts effectively add further layers to the notion of consumer orientation. Marketers now recognize that building long-term customer loyalty, paying careful attention to retaining customers and developing effective systems of customer care can provide major long-term benefits to customer and marketer alike.

KEY TERMS

Customer care	304	Demand chain	313
Relationship marketing (RM)	304	Supply chain	313
Customer relationship		Value chain	313
marketing (CRM)	304	Transactional marketing	316
Gap analysis	310	Total relationship marketing	
PIMS	312	(TRM)	320
Total quality management		Internal marketing	320
(TQM)	313	Reverse marketing	320

CASE STUDY

Infotech

Infotech is a small engineering company producing quality engine components. The company's management team are keen for the company to grow and have been exploring the possibility of becoming a supplier to an international car manufacturer in the North East of England.

Preliminary discussions have proved promising and the manufacturer's engineering team seem pleased with Infotech's engineering skills and production systems. The issues of Infotech possibly becoming a supplier to this company lie not so much with the engineering and design skills of Infotech, but rather with its current systems of customer service and quality management. In particular, at the moment Precincts has no experience of EDI (Electronic Data Interchange) systems with its customers, nor does it currently operate a TQM system.

CASE STUDY QUESTIONS

Why would it be necessary to implement EDI and TQM in this company, and how might this help them get this business?

REFERENCES

1 Young, L. (2008), *From Products to Services: Insights and Experiences from Companies Which Have Embraced the Service Economy*, Chichester: John Wiley & Sons Ltd.

2 Kotler, P. and Keller, K. (2009), *Marketing Management*, 13th edn, Harlow, Essex: Pearson Education, pp. 238–42.

3 Peck, H., Payne, A., Christopher, M. and Clark, M. (1999), *Relationship Marketing: Strategy and Implementation*, Oxford: Butterworth-Heinemann, p. 45.

4 US Office of Consumer Affairs (1992), *Customer Complaints Incidence and Practice*, Washington, DC: The White House.

5 Buzzell, R.D. and Gale, B.T. (1984), *The PIMS Principles: Linking Strategy to Performance*, New York: Free Press.

6 Stone, M. and Young, L. (1992), *Competitive Customer Care: A Guide to Keeping Customers*, Kingston-upon-Thames: Croner, p. 20.

7 Zineldin, M. and Phillipson, S. (2007), 'Kotler and Borden are not dead: myth of relationship marketing and the truth of the 4Ps', *Journal of Consumer Marketing*, 24(4): 229–41.

8 Gronroos, C. (1994), 'From marketing mix to relationship marketing: towards a paradigm shift in marketing', *Management Decision*, 32(2): 4–20.

9 Gamble, P.R., Stone, M., Woodcock, N. and Foss, B. (2006), *Up Close and Personal?: Customer Relationship Marketing at Work*, London: Kogan-Page.

10 Buttle, F. (2008), *Customer Relationship Management*, 2nd edn, London: Paul Chapman.

11 Kotler, P., Armstrong, G., Saunders, J. and Wong, V. (2001), *Principles of Marketing*, London: Prentice-Hall.

12 Lancaster, G. and Massingham, L. (2002), *Essentials of Marketing*, 4th edn, Maidenhead, Berkshire: McGraw-Hill, p. 343.

13 Gummesson, E. (2008), *Total Relationship Marketing*, 3rd edn, Oxford: Butterworth-Heinemann.

14 Bund-Jackson, B. (1985), 'Build customer relationships that last', *Harvard Business Revenue*, 63(November–December): 120–8.

15 Reast, J.D. (2005), 'Brand trust and brand acceptance: the relationship', *Journal of Product and Brand Management*, 14(1): 4–13.

16 Binniger, A.S. (2008), 'Exploring the relationship between retail brands and consumer store loyalty', *International Journal of Retail and Distribution Management*, 36(2): 94–110.

17 Zineldin, M. (1999), 'Exploring the common ground of total relationship management (TRM) and total quality management (TQM)', *Management Decision*, 37(9): 709–18.

18 Gummesson, E. (1991), 'Marketing orientation revisited: the crucial role of the part-time marketer', *European Journal of Marketing*, 25: 60–75.

19 Mele, C. (2007), 'The synergistic relationship between TQM and marketing in creating customer value', *Managing Service Quality*, 17(3): 240–58.

20 Mehra, S., and Ranganathan, S. (2008), 'Implementing total quality management with a focus on enhancing customer satisfaction', *International Journal of Quality and Reliability Management*, 25(9): 913–17.

21 Kotler, P. and Keller, K.L. (2007), *Marketing Management*, 13th edn, Basingstoke: Macmillan.

22 Dodourova, M. (2009), 'Alliances as strategic tools: a cross-industry study of partnership planning, formation and success', *Management Decision*, 47(5): 831–44.

Chapter 10

Direct marketing

LEARNING OBJECTIVES

By the end of this chapter you will:

- appreciate why direct mail has become so popular during recent years
- understand the individual elements that form direct marketing
- be aware of the value to marketers of direct marketing tactics
- know how to mount a direct marketing campaign

INTRODUCTION

We discussed some of the changes taking place in channels of distribution in Chapter 6. It was suggested that one of the growth areas of channels has been direct marketing. The term 'direct marketing' was first coined by Leslie Wunderman in 1961 following work he had done with American Express and Columbia Records. However, the principles of mail order catalogue marketing, which was an early form of direct marketing, can be traced back to Europe in the fifteenth century following Gutenberg's invention of type and production of trade catalogues from printer publishers.

The principal feature of direct marketing is that it sends messages direct to consumers and not via intervening media. This involves the use of direct mail, e-mail and telemarketing through business to consumers (B2C) and business to business (B2B) communications that are normally unsolicited. It attempts to persuade customers to make purchases that emphasize explicitly a 'call-to-action' that involves a prominent message to gain a positive measurable and trackable response from potential customers.

Direct marketing is a pro-active approach to marketing that takes the product or service to potential customers rather than waiting for them to come to a store or other point of access. It is a form of **'non-shop' shopping** and is sometimes referred to as **'precision marketing'** or 'one-to-one' marketing.

Rather than the marketing firm sending out a general communication or sales message to a large group of potential customers, even if these constitute well-defined market segments, direct marketing tends to target specific individuals or households. In a B2B context this would be an individual or a specific organization. Direct marketing is not just concerned with marketing communications. It is also concerned with distribution. In using direct marketing, the firm is making a choice to cut out the use of marketing intermediaries and sell the product or service direct to customers. This has implications for both channels of distribution and logistical decisions.

Direct marketing comes in a variety of forms. It is one of the fastest growing areas of marketing and is being propelled by technical advances, particularly in the field of computer technology and the worldwide web (www). It has been taken up with enthusiasm in a wide variety of contexts. This medium of communication is not new, as many companies have sold products direct to the public for many years. For example, Kleeneze was established in 1923 by Harry Crook in Bristol. Another long established direct marketer is Avon Cosmetics, established over 120 years ago by David McConnell as the California Perfume company. Direct mail through the post and mail order catalogues has been utilized for a long time and all are forms of direct marketing.

Direct marketing originated in the early 1900s and the Direct Marketing Association (DMA) was established in the USA in 1917. It became an important force in the UK in the 1950s, but at this stage of its development it was generally concerned with direct mail, mail order and door-to-door personal selling. Today the scope of direct marketing has expanded dramatically largely due to the use of the telephone and in particular the use of the Internet. Its scope includes all marketing communications elements that allow an organization to communicate directly with prospective customers, or prospects. This includes direct mail, telephone marketing, direct response advertising, door-to-door personal selling and the Internet.

Another form of direct marketing, which many think of as new, but has been with us for many years is 'Party Plan' selling. As the name suggests, party plan selling is selling products direct to customers in their own homes by throwing a 'party' for friends and relatives to attend. During the party they are sold the products by an agent. Perhaps the most iconic name in party selling is 'Tupperware'. Earl Silas Tupper introduced his new plastic kitchen storage products in 1942 in the USA. By 1946, Brownie Wise, one of his employees, was marketing products by organizing parties.

The telephone has been used for B2B sales for many years, particularly for the regeneration of 'routine' orders and for making sales appointments. It is now being used increasingly in domestic direct marketing programmes often to 'follow up' a posted personalized mail shot. Motoring organizations, such as the RAC and AA in the UK, have used direct personal selling for many years to sell membership of their organizations and today use direct mail extensively to keep members informed about product and service benefits. However, direct marketing has evolved with advances in computer technology. The use of computers to store, retrieve and manipulate customer information has revolutionized the way direct marketing firms operate. Companies can make use of the Internet and computer databases which allows them to access data 'warehouses' and gives them the capability to sort and aggregate or use what is termed **data fusion** to increase its value as a marketing resource.

As a component of direct marketing, the Internet has the potential to be the most powerful direct marketing tool ever. Owning a computer workstation that is wired to the Internet is now becoming almost as common as owning a TV. Children being taught at schools using new technology today and playing computer games at home take the use of the Internet as a shopping medium for granted. The Internet will continually evolve. We are at the beginning of the next business revolution that will affect the way we live, work and play. Online marketing using a computer, a modem and the Internet has been the fastest growing form of direct marketing in recent years and is set to grow substantially over coming years. Virtually every product or service that one can think of can now be bought directly through the Internet. Products and services such as books, travel and entertainment, have proved particularly suitable for this type of marketing, but now one can purchase houses, cars education, and even cosmetic surgery over the Net.

The telephone derives its power as a direct marketing medium from its transactional nature (i.e. one human being in a controlled conversation with another). What originally began as 'ordering by telephone' evolved into **telemarketing** which creates and exploits a direct relationship between the supplier and the customer through interactive use of the telephone.

There are still opportunities for traditional methods of communication that are well proven. Some of the more long established forms of direct marketing methods, like door-to-door selling, are still effective and widely used, and direct mail and telephone marketing techniques are still widely used. Computer technology continues to develop and ideas are change constantly. It will be interesting to see what direct marketing will look like in 10 or 20 years' time. Figure 10.1 illustrates its development.

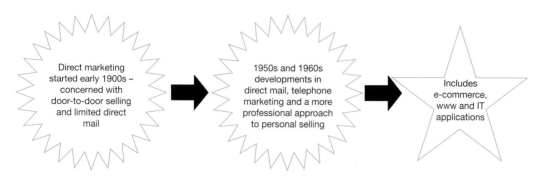

FIGURE 10.1 Direct marketing

OBJECTIVES OF DIRECT MARKETING

Much direct marketing activity is intended to result in a sale. However, in some situations a direct sale might be unlikely or inappropriate. In such cases some other form of measurable response might be used. For example, a direct mail campaign and a telephone-marketing programme may be used in the engineering industry to invite and encourage buyers to attend a machine tool exhibition. A leaflet drop for double-glazing might contain a free telephone number for the prospect to request a brochure or estimate. The result may not be a sale, but some specific, measurable action that will hopefully contribute to an ultimate sale. Although a sale may not be the immediate objective of a direct marketing campaign, some form of direct response on behalf of the recipient of the message will be. This, in turn, will contribute to the eventual sale. Hence, direct marketing is not necessarily the same as direct sales. It might be used to keep customers informed of new product developments or to send them specific discount offers.

Direct marketing should not only be used as a simple tactical marketing communications tool, but should be integrated with the rest of the communications mix. All marketing communications elements interact to some extent. Direct marketing is likely to form a major part of communications strategy of many companies and not simply be used as a tactical adjunct. Other forms of communication are likely to be used in conjunction with direct marketing programmes even if these are only general corporate advertising programmes. Many firms use direct marketing predominantly, but not to the exclusion of other communication methods. Direct marketing is often used as part of integrated CRM programmes, as discussed in Chapter 9, and such CRM programmes, by their very nature, are long term and strategic in nature.

The goal is to provide customers with information relative to their needs and interests. A profile on the direct and interactive marketing industry offers a useful way of looking at it as a cyclical process with six distinct phases:

1   the creative stage and design phase, where the marketing plan is constructed and appropriate media channels are selected;

2   data compilation where both internal data, such as customer lists and outside data from a
     database company or list broker is assembled in preparation for the next stage in the programme;
3   database management, where information is mined, fused, aggregated or disaggregated, enhanced
     and standardized for use in the programme;
4   database analysis, or fine tuning the database which further focuses on an optimal target
     market;
5   execution and fulfilment where customer inquiries and orders are acted upon and information
     on response rates is collected for final post programme analysis;
6   response analysis where the results of the campaign are examined for effectiveness before the
     cycle begins again.

SCOPE OF DIRECT MARKETING

Direct marketing is broadly defined as any direct communication to a consumer or business recipient
that is designed to generate a response in the form of a direct order, a request for further information
(lead generation) or a visit to a store or other place of business for the purchase of a specific product
or service (traffic generation). The emphasis is on direct marketing communication.

Dibb and Simkin[1] define direct marketing as:

> A decision by a company's marketers to select a marketing channel that avoids dependence
> on marketing channel intermediaries, and to focus marketing communications activity on
> promotional mix ingredients that contact directly targeted customers.

Pickton and Broderick[2] describe the essence of direct marketing with emphasis on its use of customer
information:

> Direct Marketing is a marketing system based on individual customer records held on a
> database. These records are the basis for marketing analysis, planning, implementation of
> programmes, and control of this activity.

Fill[3] defines direct marketing as a strategy:

> A strategy used to create a personal and intermediary free dialogue with customers. This
> should be a measurable activity and it is very often media based, with a view to creating
> and sustaining a mutually rewarding relationship.

Direct personal selling formed the bedrock of the direct marketing industry at the time of the
establishment of the Direct Marketing Association (DMA) in the USA in 1917. The World
Federation of Direct Selling Associations was founded in the USA in 1978 as a non-governmental,
voluntary organization representing the direct selling industry globally to support direct selling
associations in areas of governance, education, communications, consumer protection and ethics in
the marketplace.

We have examined the nature of direct marketing and its role in the communications mix. The discussion that follows is not exhaustive, but it covers the main direct marketing tools and examines their application in different marketing situations. We start with direct mail and e-mail and its use which has seen enormous growth as a direct marketing tool over the past 30 years. We then discuss the use of telephone or telemarketing, which has been used particularly in B2B marketing. Telemarketing and the use of direct mail were the two main pillars of the direct marketing industry when the DMA was established. Direct marketing tools include developments in applying Internet technologies including database marketing and techniques of data mining and data fusion that are central to the direct marketing revolution. We also examine direct response in television, newspaper and radio applications.

DIRECT MAIL

Direct mail is not a new promotional tool, but it has been a major growth area. Many factors have fuelled this growth, but of particular importance in this respect have been access to more accurate, detailed and up-to-date mailing lists allied to extensive consumer database systems. Most direct mail involves the marketer sending out promotional material through the mail direct to homes or offices of target customers.

Direct mail may involve sending out technical information, notice of special offers and general information about a company and its products, and it can include free samples, questionnaires, promotional gifts and order forms, to name but a few. It may be sent to householders or to organizational buyers and directed at existing or prospective customers (this is discussed in more detail later).

Greater accuracy in mailing lists and more sophisticated databases on customers have made such mailings more cost effective. A major issue when using direct mail marketing is response rates. Response rates can be very low. In direct marketing there are estimates that response rates vary from approximately two per cent for mail shots to existing customers down to one per cent when mailing new or lapsed customers, http://www.gaebler.com.

Direct mail campaign planners realize that one of the most critical factors in success is getting the addressee to open the envelope. Careful targeting and skill in the design of the direct mail package can significantly increase the percentage of consumers who will open the direct mail envelope and proceed to read the promotional material. Undoubtedly, direct mail remains one of the most unpopular techniques of promotion amongst many consumers. Improved techniques and increased social and customer conscience on the part of direct mail marketers, possibly backed up with an effective regulatory system, might be required if direct mail is to achieve its full potential as a constructive promotional tool. Unsolicited direct mail is disparagingly referred to as **junk mail**. This derogatory term has been reinforced by the fact that the sheer growth in direct mail in recent years has meant that consumers in many developed economies are inundated with direct mail on a daily basis. Post Office/Royal Mail statistics show a continuing rise in the annual volume of direct mail and in the number of organizations using it for business and consumer communication. A number of factors account for this increased use and acceptance of direct mail, the most significant of which is the increased fragmentation of media. There are three UK terrestrial commercial television channels as well as a wide choice of satellite and cable television available to subscribers. In the USA there are literally hundreds of commercial channels. In the print media, there has been the rapid growth of 'free-sheets' alongside traditional local press, coupled with proliferation of special interest magazines.

This fragmentation has meant that media buyers and advertisers either have to spend more money to ensure they reach as wide an audience as previously, or spread the same amount of money more thinly over a range of media. Developments within the direct mail industry have removed many difficulties that have previously deterred large advertisers, particularly in respect of the inferior quality of large mail shots that have led to the 'junk mail' terminology. IT advances have made it possible to 'personalize' good quality mail shots, targeted to individuals by name. There have been tremendous technical strides in all areas of direct mail, including computer aided design of direct mail material and use of mail merge software that produces results that look like letters. Direct mail uses mailing lists that have usually been purchased to target recipients considered most likely to respond positively, e.g. a person might be on a database for having an interest in rugby so will be a good target for rugby-related products. This is referred to as database marketing. Bulk mailings are popular for businesses operating in the financial services, home computer and travel industries and also charities. Bulk mailout rates enable marketers to send mail at ecomomical rates. To effectively segment and target markets and gain best value for money, organizations are increasingly opting for the benefits of direct mail i.e. flexibility, selectivity and personal contact.

A direct mail campaign may be aimed at eliciting an immediate response, or simply to increase awareness or interest. In other words, the purpose of direct mail is very wide ranging. In essence, it represents an impersonal promotional activity sent directly to prospective customers in their own homes or offices. A direct mail shot may consist of anything from a letter to weighty catalogues of product offerings. Regular users of direct mail techniques are the Readers Digest and the Automobile Association. It is a method of communicating a message directly to a particular person, household or firm. As such it falls under the more general heading of direct marketing, which includes many other forms of direct communication.

Direct mail and direct advertising are subsets of direct marketing. The latter consists of printed matter that is delivered by the advertiser direct to the prospect. This material is sent by mail and other means like house-to-house leaflet drops, handed out to passers-by, or put under the screen wipers of parked cars.

E-mail and viral marketing

One of the latest tools available to the direct marketer is **e-mail**. Most people regularly send and receive e-mails both in our homes our places of work. To a large extent e-mail has replaced the letter as a form of communication. Just like the letter an e-mail can be personalized to a particular individual and sent direct to a previously identified receiver. Compared to communicating by post, e-mails have the advantage of being much cheaper, easier to produce and customize and have an increasing global reach. Not surprisingly marketers and direct marketers in particular were quick to spot the potential for e-mails in marketing campaigns. As a result e-mails are now a major tool of the marketer. Brassington and Pettit[4] show that e-mailing is now widely used to generate awareness, attract customers to a website, extend the mailing list through third party referrals and in the context of direct marketing specifically, in some cases to generate a direct order.

Systems have been developed that can delineate and select target customers for unsolicited commercial e-mail (Moustakas *et al.*[5]). A major disadvantage of e-mail as a direct marketing tool is when e-mails arrive in e-mail boxes unsolicited. This type of e-mail from a company we have not contacted, or asked to send information, is known as **'spam'** and has become a major problem in the direct marketing industry. Quite simply, most customers object to receiving unsolicited e-mails especially when a lot of it is for products in which they have no interest. There is now a strict code of regulation and industry practice in many countries to protect customers from the worst excesses of spam marketers (Brubaker[6]). Many anti-virus systems now include programmes for blocking unsolicited commercial e-mails.

Related to e-mail marketing is the growth of **viral marketing.** As the term implies viral marketing is based on the idea that an e-mail sent to one person may, if planned effectively, be forwarded on by that person to their friends and acquaintances so 'spreading the message' about a product or brand. In this way, the marketer can overcome some of the problems with unsolicited commercial e-mails. After all, we are more likely to open an e-mail if it comes from someone we know personally. In this way, viral e-mails make use of the known effectiveness of 'word-of-mouth' communication. The real issue for the marketer in using viral e-mail based marketing is to ensure that the initial receiver passes the e-mail on. Marketers have used a number of devices for this, ranging from straightforward financial inducement, to the use of humour or simply inherent interest which persuades a recipient to pass the message on to others.

We are still in the early stages of using viral marketing and particularly, as shown by Cruz and Fill,[7] when it comes to evaluating viral marketing efforts, but as a means of communication, viral marketing is now firmly established in the armoury of the direct marketer.

DIRECT RESPONSE ADVERTISING

This is a strategy of using specially designed advertisements, usually in newspapers and magazines, to invoke a direct response rather than a delayed one. The most familiar type is the coupon-response press advertisement, in which a coupon is provided that the reader may use to order the product or service or request further information or a sales call. Other variants involve incentives to visit the retail outlet immediately, such as preview invitations and money-off coupons. Direct mail can also be used for **direct response advertising**.

Improvements in database software have revolutionized the direct marketing industry. Nothing has driven the direct marketing industry forward more than IT developments, especially in database software and applications. **Database marketing** is a system that continually gathers, refines and utilizes information and data that drives relevant marketing and sales communications programmes. It is used extensively, but not exclusively, in direct marketing. Examples are sales calls, direct mail and advertising to selected companies to acquire new customers, retain customers, generate more business from existing customers and create long-term loyalty. The Internet, e-commerce, rising costs of direct marketing and more emphasis on customer retention over customer acquisition are only a few salient factors affecting the way firms carry out business today. Firms have to move quickly and keep up with the latest developments and trends and invest in appropriate software and systems to stay ahead of the competition.

Database marketing describes a way of organizing a company's total marketing and sales processes. It is broad and can impact through market research and product development to customer service. Accurate information about customers that is readily available can transform marketing. It allows you to take information you have in your customer databases, analyse it to find patterns like purchasing associations and relationships, and use information that has been gained to produce and instigate better marketing and sales programmes. This means targeting specific groups with specific messages about products that are important to them. This means more resources can be spent on prospects that are most likely to buy, increasing the return on marketing and sales investment.

Proper use of databases gives marketing better tools through which to operate and improves the effectiveness of marketing campaigns, allowing for the more effective allocation and utilization of marketing resources. Database marketing is sometimes referred to as **precision marketing** and directing a marketing programme from a well constructed and managed database is analogous to shooting a rifle at a target using a precision telescopic sight rather than a conventional sight. Developments in database marketing have done more to drive the direct marketing industry forward than any other development.

PRACTICAL ASPECTS OF DATABASE MARKETING

Illustrations are provided below of basic principles and applications of database marketing. This is not an exhaustive or definitive list, but it serves to illustrate the main principles:

- Consider characteristics your best customers have in common so you can target your next programmes to prospects with similar characteristics. Evaluate which market segments buy from you. You might think you know this, but analysis could uncover market segments you have sold a significant amount to, but did not realize it. This process enables the firm to improve its segmentation by refocusing and redefining existing segments or it may highlight unexpected new segments.
- Ascertain whether different market segments buy different products. This allows you to spend marketing and sales resources more effectively by marketing each of your products to the best potential industries, firms or prospects. Study which market segments bring most revenue and which ones bring highest average revenue. This is the application of differentiated marketing, which divides the total market into segments, and then has a slightly different marketing strategy for each segment.
- Find out what types of industries, firms or individuals respond to which types of marketing communication, so you can decide where to spend advertising and marketing resources next time. Ascertain that they not only respond to your programmes, but also actually buy, and which customers buy from you repeatedly. These might have been different demographic profiles or different in some other way, which might be commercially exploitable, and you may then decide to modify your targeting tactics and only market to segments that buy more frequently.
- Calculate the average lifetime value of customers. This can be done using discounted cash flow (DCF) procedures which is a method of valuing a project, company, or an asset using the time value of money. Here, future cash flows are estimated and discounted to obtain their current

present values. This information can be used to find out which customers are not achieving their potential. Programmes can then be devised to encourage more purchases. Reward the most frequent buyers and buyers that bring the highest revenue. The concept of lifetime value is central to the idea of customer retention and long-term relationship marketing.

Database marketing has grown because more and more information about individuals and households can be collected, stored, retrieved and analysed. Moreover, developments in computing technology and systems mean that data storage and analysis is now more cost effective. Databases can be readily combined to provide detailed profiles of customers including for example data on purchasing patterns, life styles, credit ratings, incomes and even health and medical histories.

Database marketing has grown to the extent that data collection and analysis is an industry in its own right. The marketer can purchase any number of data types from companies that specialize in providing this type of information. Marketers, however, need to be careful about what to collect, handle, analyse and disseminate on consumers. Most countries have strict regulations about data protection and the penalties for contravening these can be severe.

CONSUMER DIRECT MAIL

The uses of consumer-targeted direct mail are only limited by the scope of imagination. Some of the more common uses are:

- *Selling direct* – Direct mail is a good medium for selling to customers without the need for middlemen. Product offerings can be described fully and orders can be sent straight back to the advertising company.
- *Sales lead generation* – If a product requires a meeting between the customer and a specialized salesperson (e.g. fitted kitchens, central heating and insurance) direct mail is a useful method of acquiring potentially useful, qualified leads for the company's salespeople. Sales calls are expensive, so anything that improves success rates is welcome. A well planned mail shot can act as a sieve, pinpointing the best prospects and ranking others in terms of sales potential. The 'warmer' the lead, the more effective will be the sales discussion with fewer wasted calls. Responses, indicating potential interest can be followed up by direct mail, a telephone call or a personal visit by a salesperson. Potential customers can be placed in a personal selling situation by issuing an invitation to view the product in a retail outlet, showroom or exhibition. This is useful for products that salespeople cannot take to prospects for demonstration because of their size or function. Direct mail creates a receptive atmosphere for the company's salespeople through 'cordial contact' mailings that build on the reputation of the company and through the impression created. Well executed mailing places the company in a favourable light to prospects, setting up goodwill or creating a latent desire that might be triggered into action by a later mailing.
- *Sales promotion* – Direct mail can send promotional messages e.g. money-off vouchers and special offers to selected targets. This is a useful way of encouraging people to visit a shop or exhibition.

Book a Place in History

Interested in the crusades, or perhaps Henry the VIII and his dissolution of monasteries? Whatever your specific interest happens to be, the History Guild Book Club probably has a book or more on it. This well established book club provides its members with a monthly magazine from which they can choose from a range of books on topics selected on the basis of information provided by the member.

In addition, members can interact with the company's website 24 hours a day 7 days a week to obtain information on new topics, new titles etc. The company claims to offer titles at up to 40 per cent off the published price and payment can be by credit card, direct billing on-line, phone or post. With all this there really is no excuse to be ignorant about the past.

Source: http://uk.book-club-offers.com/history-guild.

- *Clubs* – Book clubs are an example of the use of direct mail as a medium of communication and transaction between a club and its members. Other items can be marketed by the club system particularly 'collectibles' e.g. records, porcelain and miniatures.
- *Mail order* – Mail order companies use direct mail to recruit new customers and local agents as well as direct selling.
- *Fundraising* – An advantage of direct mail is its ability to communicate personally with an individual. This makes it a powerful method of raising money. It can carry the 'long copy' often needed to convince recipients of the worthiness of the charity, and make it more likely that the reader might respond with a donation.
- *Dealer mailings* – If a product is sold through dealers/agents, direct mail can be used to reach prospective customers in their area just as a producer might do.
- *Follow-up mailings* – The company's name can be promoted to customers by following any kind of sales activity with a mailing e.g. checking that the customer is satisfied with their purchase or informing them that perhaps a car they bought last year is coming up for its annual service. Most of the major car brands do this including, for example, Mercedes-Benz who contact every customer shortly after purchasing a new car, asking them to complete a customer satisfaction survey. Customers are kept informed of new developments, latest products and improved services. They regularly and systematically use their customer database to contact customers about new models and launch evenings. 'Exclusive offers' are made and invitations issued. Using direct mail in this way helps maintain contact quickly, personally and effectively and this can increase repeat sales.

BUSINESS DIRECT MAIL

Business markets are made up of closely defined, discrete groups of individuals. These groups cannot be best reached by mass advertising. Direct mail can be used to accurately identify different market sectors and provide messages appropriate to each sector. Some of the more common uses are:

- *Product launch* – Often the launch of a new industrial product or business service entails getting the message across to a small, but significant, number of people who will influence buying decisions e.g. catering managers and car fleet managers.
- *Sales lead generation* – As in consumer markets, direct mail can effectively reach qualified sales leads for a company's sales force.
- *Dealer support* – Direct mail can keep dealers, retail outlets, franchise holders, etc. more fully informed of tactical marketing promotions and plans.
- *Conferences and exhibitions* – These are means of communicating with potential customers and business colleagues. Direct mail can be used to invite delegates, who may be attracted if the event relates to a specific theme of direct interest to them.
- *Follow-up mailing using the customer base* – Much business takes the form of repeat sales to existing customers. Since these are existing clients it can be worthwhile mailing them regularly, as long as the content of the mail-out relates to something that is new or of specific interest rather than simply being 'junk mail'.
- *Marketing research/product testing* – This type of direct mail is suitable both in a consumer and business context. Marketing research can be conducted amongst existing and potential customers. Questionnaires can be used as part of a regular communication programme, with levels of response being increased by some kind of incentive. Small-scale test mailings can be made to sample a target market. The results can give a quick and accurate picture of market reaction, with minimum risk. An approach that is successful in a 'test mailing' can later be mailed to the full list.

MAIL ORDER

This form of direct marketing uses a catalogue or brochure from which the customer places orders. Often the catalogue is part of a mail shot, or it may have been provided in the company's retail outlet. Some catalogue marketers use agents who generate orders from friends and acquaintances. The first catalogue mail order company was reputedly established in the USA by Benjamin Franklin in 1744, selling scientific and academic books. Specialist mail order companies have seen a resurgence of its popularity. In part, this is due to increasingly busy lifestyles, making it difficult for many customers to visit retail outlets. Mail order marketers have also improved their marketing techniques. Catalogues now tend to be well produced and are used by up-market brands and retailers, whereas in the 1960s mail order had a down-market image. New and easier methods of payment via credit and debit cards have helped facilitate the popularity of this direct marketing method.

An effective catalogue marketer is the NEXT Company. Although essentially a retailer, NEXT appreciate that many of their customers are busy working women for whom shopping through a catalogue at home represents a significant advantage. NEXT was one of the first companies to move up-market with catalogue marketing. Their catalogues are expensively produced and designed to show their fashion products in the best possible light. Back-up systems for NEXT's catalogue marketing activities include easy delivery, payment and return systems. Unlike many of the established mail order companies NEXT charge potential customers for their catalogue, a practice which has become more and more widespread amongst top end mail order catalogue marketers.

Planning direct mail

The following represent the key steps in conducting a direct mail campaign:

1 *Identify target recipients/compiling the mailing list*

The greatest proportion of direct mail is thrown away unopened. Any that is opened is often only partly read, and even less is acted upon. The principal reason is that most direct mail is unsolicited by the recipient. One of the most important factors determining the effectiveness of direct mail is the identification on the part of the direct mail campaign planner of the target recipients of the mail campaign. It is vital to identify recipients who are most likely to be interested in the subject of the direct mail campaign and are most likely to respond positively. Identifying and understanding the target audience are essential in planning any marketing communications. In the case of direct mail, this identification is normally done using a mailing list. A mailing list obviously contains the names and postal and/or e-mail addresses of targets for the mail campaign, but, in turn, the mailing list itself must be based on customer details and information that allows only the most appropriate recipients for the mail shot to be identified. Because of this, in addition to straightforward names and addresses, a mailing list is built using information and data about potential recipients. This information and data may include details of, for example, lifestyles, incomes, qualifications, family details and past purchases.

A major reason for its growth is the increase in consumer information and databases. A mailing list, therefore, is the driving force of direct mail planning and any data and information on which the mailing list is based must be relevant and up to date. Increasingly, commercial market research companies, advertising agencies, and specialist direct mail and mailing list agencies supply appropriate mailing lists for a campaign. For example, CACI, the developer of the ACORN system also supply mailing lists, in this case linked to ACORN groups. Similarly, the Royal Mail is a major supplier of UK mailing lists.

2 *Setting objectives*

As with all marketing activities it is important to determine the objectives of a direct mail campaign. Specifically, the marketer needs to consider what response the direct mail campaign is designed to elicit from the target recipients. For example, we need to determine whether the mail shot is designed to elicit, say, a telephone enquiry from a customer, or whether it is designed to 'break the ice', the direct mail shot being followed up by a telephone call. At this stage it is important to determine what constitutes an appropriate target for the campaign so the marketer needs to determine what percentage rates of return are being sought.

3 *Producing the direct mail package*

This step in conducting a direct mail campaign includes decisions such as what to include in the direct mail shot e.g. samples, the covering letter, any free gifts, money-off or discount vouchers. In addition to what is inside the direct mail package, decisions must be made about the outside of the package i.e. the envelope or parcel the recipient will receive, and about what to say in the direct mail campaign. Designing effective direct mail packages is a specialized and skilled task, and the resultant end products must ensure that at the very least the customer is interested enough to open the package in the first place. This is a crucial step when determining the effectiveness of the campaign. To be effective, a mailing list should be built upon information about target customers.

4 *Evaluation, control and follow-up*

All spending on direct mail should be evaluated and controlled. The marketer must consider whether pre-determined objectives have been met, and if not, why not. Direct mail often requires a planned follow-up by contacting mailed customers by telephone. A campaign will only be as good as the quality of the follow-up.

USING THE INTERNET AS A DIRECT MARKETING TOOL

Customers now have more products and services to choose from and more information available to them to help them make purchasing decisions. Conventional communications, principally media advertising, is not as effective as it used to be. This is partly because there is more for consumers to digest, and partly because people have learned to ignore it. The rise of the Internet means that companies can go further than conventional communications would allow them to in the past.

There is a new group of products and services that relies on customers registering their interest in them with the company. Amazon.com for example, encourages customers to review books and publishes their comments on the website, so both the firm and other users can read and make use of them. A US airline invites customers to register their preferences for last-minute offers via its website, and then emails potential customers with details of weekend breaks at their preferred resorts. These are examples of the precision that can be achieved with direct marketing.

There have been some disasters as regards some of the newer Internet companies and there are still problems for the consumer in purchasing using this medium: security and non-delivery being examples. www.Boo.com in the UK and www.Webvan.com in America are just two high profile examples of spectacular Internet start-up failures. These two companies are amongst the most spectacular failures from the dotcom boom in the late 1990s. Both companies went from nothing to multi-million pound businesses in the space of a few months. www.Boo.com specialized in selling branded fashion apparel over the Internet, but despite spending an estimated $135 million of venture capital money within 18 months, it went into receivership. Similarly, www.Webvan.com started selling grocery products on its website and in eighteen months had spent over $1 billion on expansion. After 18 months the company was liquidated with the loss of over 4,000 jobs. In both cases these companies had tried to expand too quickly giving rise to problems like slow delivery, cash flow troubles and poor customer service.

The Internet has demonstrated that it is significantly changing the way people interact with each other, particularly in the sphere of direct marketing. The Internet crosses boundaries of geography, politics, religion, time zones and culture. Some areas of marketing are totally underpinned information technology. The Internet has reduced the planet to a global village, accelerated the pace of technology, opened up possibilities for direct marketers and altered the way they think about doing business. It has started the new revolution in direct marketing which is the most important since the development of commercial advertising. The e-commerce revolution is projected to rebuild the economy and change the way marketing and business is conducted.

TELEPHONE MARKETING

This is a long established direct marketing tool, mainly in B2B situations. Much routine reordering can be handled over the telephone without the need for an expensive personal visit. The telephone is used to keep in touch with customers between visits. It can be used to make 'cold call' appointments and re-appointments with established clients. In consumer markets it is now used extensively and has grown in importance as a marketing tool. Services like banking are offered over the telephone and customers can give instructions to pay bills and receive a balance on their account using special access codes.

Telephone marketing is divided into incoming and outgoing call telemarketing. With incoming call telemarketing the prospect makes the call to the marketing firm, usually in response to a direct mail advertisement or direct response television advertisement giving a free phone or toll free telephone number. Hence, telemarketing is often used with other direct marketing tools as a part of an integrated programme. The caller may wish to sign up to a service such as insurance, apply for a loan over the telephone, order a product seen on the television or in a direct response advertisement or ask for further details. The call is logged. The caller is followed up with an outgoing telephone call later, or sent information through the post. A personal visit might be arranged for example from a kitchen surveyor. Outgoing telephone marketing may simply be the return of an incoming call. Often existing customers are telephoned to ask if they want to take advantage of a special offer. For example, if a loan has been taken out with a finance company by a good customer, the firm may ring that customer to offer another loan at a special discount rate. A bank may telephone a customer to ask if they would like to make an appointment at the branch to have their house borrowing reviewed or discuss house insurance.

Often telemarketing involves making telphone calls to individuals in their own homes or businesses which are unsolicited. The marketer has not obtained or even sought the customer's permission to call and usually has had no previous contact with the customer. This is referred to as **cold calling** and is often outsourced to specialist call centres. This type of telephone selling can cause annoyance to some customers and many believe it is intrusive and should be outlawed. This has led some countries to introduce legislation including fines. In the USA, a national 'do-not-call' list came into effect in 2003 and it is now illegal for telemarketers, who are fined, if they call anyone who has registered themselves on the list. After one year over 62 million people in the USA had signed up. The telemarketing industry is opposed the creation of such lists as it restricts their commercial activities.

Jobber and Lancaster[8] cite a set of guidelines that have been suggested by Bell Telephone Systems of America in relation to best practice for this type of telemarketing, particularly in B2B situations, as follows:

1 identify yourself and your company;
2 establish rapport: this should come naturally since you have already researched your potential customers and their business;
3 make an interesting comment (e.g. to do with cost savings or a special offer);

4   deliver your sales message: emphasize benefits over features (e.g. your production people will like it because it helps to overcome down time through waiting for the material to set);
5   overcome objections: be skilled at objection handling techniques;
6   close the sale: when appropriate – do not be afraid to ask for the order (e.g. 'Would you like to place an order now?') or fulfil another objective (e.g. 'Can I send you a sample?')
7   action agreement: arrange for a sales call or the next telephone call;
8   express your thanks.

Like direct mail, telemarketing has developed something of a poor image. As already mentioned, many householders and businesses resent unsolicited telephone calls to sell something. As we have discussed, there are codes of practice in the industry regarding the use of this tool, but the more unscrupulous telemarketers can legitimately be accused of pestering customers in their own homes.

Despite these problems and criticisms, telemarketing's importance as a marketing tool is underlined by a growth rate, in the UK at least of approximately 20 per cent per year over the past ten years. The advantages of telemarketing include easy and widespread access to customers in their own homes or offices; low cost per contact compared to personal selling; and the ability to contact customers outside normal shopping hours.

When setting up a telemarketing system staff must be recruited and suitably trained. In addition, suitable equipment and software packages must be acquired, and in the first instance many newcomers to telemarketing use agencies at least as the first step.

Companies can exploit the telephone as a marketing tool in a number of ways:

■   *Cost savings* – Telephone selling provides customized communications. Greater sophistication in telemarketing equipment and services, new marketing approaches and developments in applications have turned the use of the telephone into 'telemarketing'. The telephone may not have the quality of a personal sales call, but it is significantly cheaper. Sometimes in the initial stages of a direct marketing programme a personal visit is not necessary or appropriate.

■   *Supplement to a personal visit* – Professional salespeople use a system of differential call frequency to plan their visits to customers. Salespeople may have to prioritize their calls on a key account basis. Although they may not be able to visit less important customers with the same frequency as more important customers, they can make a telephone call on a regular basis to keep customers informed and build and maintain relationships.

■   *Gaining marketing intelligence* – Marketing firms can speak to customers on a regular basis, not only to maintain relationships, but also to ask questions about their needs and wants and purchasing intentions. This information can be recorded and fed into the organization's marketing information system (MkIS) for future use. Buying intentions can be used to produce sales forecasts for future planning. On establishing customer needs, telephone marketers can introduce new products to clients and use the call to sell further products.

■   *Supplement to direct mail and other advertising* – Many direct mail and other forms of direct response advertising, on television, press or radio for example, will carry a free phone message. This enables the prospect to make telephone contact at no cost. Prospects can make an immediate commitment to purchase while the advertising message is still fresh in their minds.

If they do not ring to make a purchase, they may telephone for further information, which in turn produces a qualified lead for further marketing action.

The above list is not exhaustive, but it serves to demonstrate how versatile the telephone can be as a direct marketing tool. As we have seen, the use of the telephone is still growing as a marketing tool and advances in technology and the linking of the telephone to television and the Internet is bringing further developments, thus making it an even more important marketing medium.

OTHER DIRECT MARKETING APPLICATIONS

Broadcast faxing is less common than other forms of direct marketing. This is largely due to laws in the USA which make it illegal, and also because the fax has declined in popularity as a communications medium, coupled with the fact that other forms of direct marketing, especially through the Internet, are more advanced and more effective.

Another type of direct marketing in the context of telemarketing is **voicemail marketing**. Due to the omnipresence of e-mail marketing and the expense of direct mail, an economical means by which to reach people has been developed through the medium of the human voice. However, like telemarketing, applications of this technique have resulted in a profusion of 'voice-spam', and have quickly brought about legislation to curb its excesses. Some businesses use **guided voicemail** where pre-recorded voicemails are guided by live callers to achieve a more personal B2B aura that was previously the province of telemarketing.

Leaflet distribution services are used widely by fast food companies and other B2C businesses that have a local focus. Similar to direct mail, this method is targeted by area and is less expensive than mailshots due to not having postage charges or having to buy address lists.

Couponing is used in print media where a coupon which the reader cuts out is presented at the retail checkout which provides a discount.

Direct marketing on television (**DRTV**) can be in a long form (typically half-hour or more segments explaining a product in detail and termed **infomercials**) and in shorter forms of around 30 seconds that ask viewers for an immediate response, usually to call a phone number on screen or go to a website. DRTV advertisements that are intended to produce a direct sale through an order by the customer are part of direct marketing. Although it can be used to build brand awareness or develop a customer database, most frequently it is used to generate an immediate sale. For example, the viewer may be given a telephone number to ring to place a direct order. Direct response television marketing is growing. It is particularly suited to fundraising marketing for charities, causes, etc. It is widely used for products such as CDs, chat lines and novelty products.

Direct response advertising has witnessed an enormous growth over recent years. It is a major part of direct marketing. It uses carefully crafted marketing communications to generate a response directly from the advertisement itself. This could be a telephone call to you asking for an appointment to provide further information, or an order in the post, a request for a brochure or a coupon presented for a discount or free sample. Credit cards are convenient charging platforms when selling direct over the telephone, and these have helped to expand this type of business. Many products are advertised on television that cannot be purchased elsewhere, and the only way to obtain the product is to telephone a free phone or toll free number given in the advertisement. There is sometimes a related 'free gift' such as an extra product if you place the order within a short period of time.

Since the firm is generating and monitoring responses, management can measure the contacts and income produced by each individual advertisement or mailing. Conventional advertising is difficult to evaluate in terms of sales response, where it is more appropriate to evaluate the communications effect rather than the sales effects following advertising. Management can test different forms of advertising in consecutive issues of the same publication, or schedule the same advertisement in different publications, and learn which is most effective in producing the desired response. Direct response is a unique type of advertising, as it allows evaluation of the effectiveness of operations in relation to specific, measurable objectives.

It is sometimes difficult for a firm to evaluate specific sales responses from conventional advertising because of 'multiple causation'. An advertisement is only one of a number of communications being used by firms simultaneously. It is difficult to separate out the effects, particularly sales effects, in respect of each of these forms of promotion. As they do not have any response generator or tracking mechanism in place for quantifying sales results, it is difficult to ascertain which medium is working and which is not. Lord Lever of household detergent fame once said: 'I know that half my advertising is wasted, but I don't know which half'.

Direct Response Advertising relies on compelling and persuasive material whose objective is not merely to inform, but to bring about a desired specific response that can be objectively measured. With direct response advertising, creative writers use artwork copy, page layout, plus carefully crafted text, to explain salient reasons to purchase a product or service.

DIRECT PERSONAL SELLING

Marketing communications can be classified into personal and impersonal methods, and in the context of direct marketing, selling is now discussed. A detailed discussion of selling has, of course, already been provided in Chapter 8.

In the context of direct marketing, selling is personal and involves interaction with a prospect. This interaction can be at a distance e.g. over the telephone. However, most personal selling is carried out on a face-to-face basis and this dimension is a key strength of personal selling. Selling is more expensive on a cost-per-contact basis, but sometimes there is no substitute for a personal approach as building personal relationships is a key element in the context of customer care, which was the theme of Chapter 9. Consumers can benefit from direct selling because of the convenience and service it provides, as it includes personal communication, demonstration and explanation of products to a higher standard than in conventional retail outlets or through the printed media.

The task of direct selling differs according to products or services being marketed. In some situations it is more a matter of keeping customers satisfied and the task then calls more for skills of personality and caring. In other situations, contractual negotiations might be the main emphasis of selling where skills of prospecting, negotiating, demonstrating and closing a sale will be greater criteria for success. In organizational marketing, reliance is placed on personal communication, and in this context the proportion of selling within the total market budget can outweigh all other marketing expenditure. Owing to its personal nature, direct selling provides a channel of distribution for companies with innovative or distinctive products not readily available in traditional retail outlets. It may be that products on offer are produced by a relatively small firm that cannot afford to compete through advertising and promotion, because of the costs associated with gaining space on retail shelves of major outlets. Hence, customers gain by being able to purchase products that would have been unavailable had the marketing company to operate through conventional retail outlets. Direct selling enhances the retail distribution infrastructure and can serve customers with a convenient source of products that may not be available elsewhere.

Direct selling is described as marketing products and services directly to consumers face to face generally in their homes, at their workplace and other places away from permanent retail locations. It typically occurs through explanation or personal demonstration by a direct salesperson, or direct seller.

Products and services sold by direct sellers are varied as are people involved in the direct selling industry: insurance, financial services, cosmetics, skin care products, personal care items, home appliances, household cleaning products, nutritional products, toys, books, clothing, jewellery, fashion accessories, etc. Sometimes, such products are sold in the context of group presentations (party plan selling). We saw earlier how the Tupperware were one of the first companies to successfully use the idea of party plan selling with its range of kitchenware and food and drink storage boxes. The normal approach in party plan selling is for an appointed company demonstrator/salesperson to persuade individuals to invite friends and relatives to a 'party' in their home with perhaps food and drink being provided. Invited guests are informed that products will be on sale and that a demonstrator will be present. During the party, the direct salesperson demonstrates products to the group of guests and afterwards they are invited to place orders which are then delivered to their homes, often by the party organizer. The company sales agent receives commission on any orders and the party organizer usually receives a 'free' gift of some of the company's products. Tupperware has now departed from this type of selling, but many companies find that party selling works for them including companies such as Virgin Vie (cosmetics) and Anne Summers (adult products).

By contrast other types of direct home selling often explain and demonstrate the products being offered to customers in the comfort of their homes at a time that is convenient for them on a personal one-to-one basis rather than in a party group. Avon Cosmetics uses freelance agents to visit people in their own homes and demonstrate and explain the use of a range of beauty products.

Direct selling provides benefits to individuals who desire an opportunity to earn income and build their own business. It also offers an alternative to consumers who want something different from traditional shopping.

MULTI-LEVEL MARKETING (MLM)

Like many innovative marketing systems, MLM was developed in the USA and exported to other parts of the world. Some suspicion surrounds MLM as there is confusion with **pyramid selling**. This was an unethical business practice that is banned in the UK. It is also referred to as **network marketing**, **structured marketing** or **multi-level direct selling**, and has proved to be a successful and effective method of compensating direct sellers for marketing and distributing products and services direct to consumers. Unlike 'pyramid selling' MLM is an ethical business practice that uses the principle of '**team building**' in terms of stimulating salespeople to aspire to better levels of performance to sell products. Direct salespersons are usually self-employed people working on a freelance basis for commission on sales. However, as salespersons are self employed there is an obvious inducement on their part to sell, and enthusiastic salespeople will obviously tempted to use 'high pressure' sales techniques to obtain the sales upon which their commission and income depends.

Figure 10.2 shows how MLM is structured.

Salespersons normally start by selling goods and services to the public, often in the first instance, to people they know such as friends and work colleagues. They then move up the hierarchy to not only sell products themselves, but to recruit other direct sellers to sell as part of their own team. They not only receive commission on the goods they sell themselves, but also earn 'downstream' commission on products the people they have recruited have sold. Eventually they may move from selling direct themselves, and concentrate on managing others in their team. As the team grows so does the 'downstream' commission that accrues to the original team organizer. Eventually the team leader may have a network of many direct selling staff at different levels in the hierarchy. Some will be content to sell some products direct on a part-time basis. Some may want to recruit a small team. Some may want to be senior team leaders and put in effort to lead a whole networking team of direct personal selling staff and reap the rewards of commissions based on the selling effort of their team, combined with their own motivational, leadership and managerial skills.

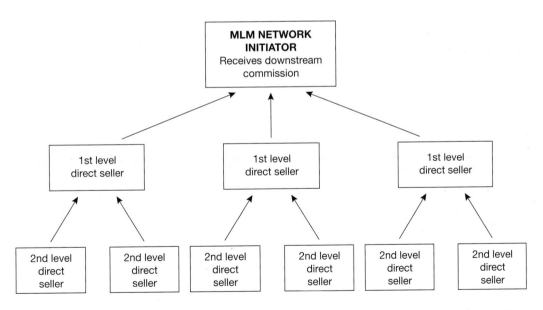

FIGURE 10.2 Principles of multi-level marketing (MLM) showing team originator receiving downstream commission from those lower in the network

SUMMARY

Direct marketing refers to a collection of methods that allows companies to communicate with, and obtain a direct response from, prospects. It allows firms to target customers more precisely than conventional non-direct marketing techniques and they are collectively referred to as precision marketing. It is a branch of marketing that has witnessed rapid growth and technological change over the past 30 years. It is an important marketing process and some organizations base their entire marketing strategy on direct marketing methods. Worldwide, the direct marketing industry is huge. As firms seek ways of obtaining more value from marketing budgets, direct marketing is likely to become even stronger in the future.

Direct marketing techniques are constantly being improved and developed, and new innovative media are likely to be developed in the future. At present, the main methods employed within the direct marketing industry are the use of the telephone, direct mail, the Internet, direct 'face-to-face' personal selling and direct response advertising using television, radio and newspapers, trade journals, magazines and the Internet. The industry is being driven by a desire for greater accuracy and economy in marketing operations and by developments in IT that can be applied to direct marketing. Database marketing in particular has revolutionized the way organizations use direct marketing and has increased efficiency in areas like direct mail and telephone marketing, yet direct marketing is not solely driven by IT. Some traditional methods that were used in 1917 when the Direct Marketing Association was founded are still being used successfully, particularly face-to-face direct personal selling. However, even these traditional techniques have benefited from the information revolution in terms of retrieval of customer information and improved targeting. Direct marketing is a major force within marketing and its influence is likely to increase in future.

Direct marketing has a number of strengths including for example: low cost, flexibility and of course direct contact with the customer. On the other hand its weaknesses include: low response rates for some direct marketing tools, the risk of customer annoyance, and in some countries, a stringent regulatory framework.

KEY TERMS

CASE STUDY

Woodvale Products Ltd

Karen Rees, director of marketing at Woodvale Products Limited, has called an urgent meeting with her fellow directors of the other functional areas of the business. The overriding reason for calling this meeting is that Rees feels her efforts to improve the marketing standing of the company through improved customer orientation are being thwarted by other functional managers. In addition, and as part of the overall problem, over the past twelve months since Rees was appointed there has been considerable conflict between members of her marketing team and other members of the company.

One of the first things that Rees organised when she was appointed marketing director was an update of the product range, including the introduction of several new products. In Rees's view, the product range was badly out of date and this was directly affecting sales and market share. However, the battle that Rees had to fight in order to get the design team and the engineering and production staff in the company to go along with her ideas had been very bruising indeed. In short, they had vehemently resisted these innovations. Rees felt vindicated now because the new product range had been welcomed by the existing customer base.

However, this was not the only battle that Rees had to fight. Over the past twelve months she has had battles with finance over pricing and costs of delivery and distribution, complaints about customer service, battles with personnel over proposed customer awareness training for all company employees (which had been turned down on the grounds that such training would be too expensive), and even battles with the sales department, which was independent from marketing, over suggestions for increasing call rates by sales representatives on key accounts. In short, Rees was not happy with the way things were in the company.

The company is currently organized on a functional basis, including her own marketing department. Most of the sales team come from engineering backgrounds and the company is strongly engineering and product oriented. At the moment, she feels that she does not even have the support of the senior management team regarding her views that the company needs to become more customer focused.

CASE STUDY QUESTION

What problems and issues might Rees highlight to her follow directors at the forthcoming meeting as regards the marketing organization and culture in the company? She is also thinking of a move towards direct marketing which would allow control over sales. What proposals might Rees make in order to try and resolve some of these problems and issues?

REFERENCES

1 Dibb, S. and Simpkin, L. (2004), *Marketing Briefs: A Revision and Study Guide*, Oxford: Butterworth-Heinemann.

2 Pickton, D. and Broderick, A. (2004), *Integrated Marketing Communications*, 2nd edn, London: Prentice-Hall.

3 Fill, C. (2007), *Marketing Communications: Engagement, Strategies and Tactics*, 4th edn, Chapter 21, On-line and Interactive Media, London: Prentice-Hall, pp. 580–606.

4 Brassington, F. and Pettit, S. (2006), *Principles of Marketing*, 4th edn, London: FT Prentice Hall.

5 Moustakas, E., Ranganathan, C. and Duquenoy, P. (2006), 'E-mail marketing at the crossroads: a stakeholder analysis of unsolicited commercial e-mail (spam)', *Internet Research*, 16(1): 38–52.

6 Brubaker, S. (2007), 'Ethics and regulation in direct marketing', *Direct Marketing: An International Journal*, 1(1): 55–8.

7 Cruz, D. and Fill, C. (2008), 'Evaluating viral marketing: isolating the key criteria', *Marketing Intelligence and Planning*, 26(7): 743–58.

8 Jobber, D. and Lancaster, G. (2009), *Selling and Sales Management*, 8th edn, London: Prentice-Hall, pp. 342–3.

Chapter 11

Sales forecasting

LEARNING OBJECTIVES

By the end of this chapter you will:

- understand the role of sales forecasting in the marketing planning process
- appreciate the distinction between short-, medium- and long-term forecasting
- be aware of the importance of accurate sales forecasts to different functional areas in the business
- know the relationship between sales forecasts and sales budgets
- be familiar with the major types forecasting techniques available to the marketer

INTRODUCTION

The task of business management would be simpler if industry was not in a continuous state of change. This change is precipitated to a large extent by the growth of global competition. The widespread adoption of IT-based commercial applications has speeded up the way that business transactions take place. IT-based innovations in manufacturing and service provision have meant that new ideas and procedures are more quickly adopted and implemented. This makes it increasingly important and necessary for organizations to predict future prospects in terms of sales, costs and profits, otherwise there is a danger that they will stagnate and be overtaken by competition.

AID TO MARKETING PLANNING

Forecasting can be described as the act of giving advance warning in time for beneficial action to be taken. The value and importance of advance information is a cornerstone of planning activity. Modern businesses are aware of sales forecasting and its overall purpose, but many managers do not pay due regard to its importance. Only in recent years has the value of forecasting become clear. This has resulted in the development of sophisticated forecasting techniques that can be applied directly to businesses.

To predict the future we must examine the past to observe trends over periods of time and establish the degree of probability with which these trends are likely to repeat themselves in the future. Forecasts cannot be totally exact; management must be aware of this, and decide on the degree of inexactitude that can be tolerated when planning the future.

Incorrect forecasting (or no forecasting) is at the base of many business failures. In a production-oriented environment goods might be sold on company reputation alone and forecasting is less important. In a more competitive environment sentiment does not apply, and firms that do not attempt to make an accurate forecast on which to base their future production and subsequent corporate planning find it difficult to survive.

When attempting to forecast we must ultimately forecast for a specific market segment at which the marketing effort is aimed. However, one can attempt a macro-forecast for, say, the world market for a particular commodity that the company produces, in the knowledge that the company's marketing effort will only include a portion of this. The skill lies in determining what percentage of that total potential market is likely to accrue to the company, given its anticipated marketing effort. It is here that management planning must determine the resources that must be apportioned to individual parts of the business to achieve the forecasted sales that the company anticipates.

Back to Your Roots

2008–9 was a difficult time for many marketers. Perhaps the most severe economic depression since the 1930s hit virtually every country in the world. As a result many companies' sales were severely depressed as customers cut back on their spending. Amongst some of the most severely hit markets were those for non-essential luxury products, hence in most countries sales of, for example, electrical products, cars, and holidays, were substantially down.

Another market badly hit was the personal care and beauty market. For example, many women cut back on their visits to the health centres and hairdressers. Surprisingly, marketers of some of the leading hair care brands forecast a large increase in sales for some of their products and expanded their marketing and production budgets accordingly. Were they crazy or just poor forecasters?

In June 2009 sales of Clairol's Root Touch-up home hair colouring products were 20 per cent up on the previous year as more and more women shifted from having their hair coloured by their hairdresser to doing it themselves at home.

Source: http://web.ecohost.com.

Forecasting occurs at different levels: internationally, nationally, by industry, etc., until we ultimately reach a specific product forecast. Normally a company does not have to produce general international or national forecasts on such matters as economic growth or inflation. These are provided by government and other agencies. Company forecasters take this information and adjust their individual forecasts in the light of these macro-level predictions. In some industries, forecasts for the industry are sometimes supplied in general terms by an agency such as a Manufacturers' Association. As Shahabuddin[1] shows, industries such as the automobile industry are particularly well supplied with this type of information for forecasting. Forecasts for the industry are termed market forecasts, as opposed to a sales forecast that pertains to an individual company. The method where company forecasts are derived from macro-data is termed **top-down forecasting**. Conversely, a company can forecast from its own data by extrapolating company sales. This is termed **bottom-up forecasting**.

Management planners are thus only interested in a forecast when it relates to the individual firm and specific products or services, because it is from there that they can prepare plans and budgets. It is this pragmatic level of forecasting in which we are interested; what makes the situation better is that management can now place more confidence in forecasts, because more sophisticated techniques are now available.

SHORT, MEDIUM AND LONG-TERM FORECASTING

Marketing and other managerial functions need these three types of forecasting horizon because each directly affects a different business function, and more importantly, medium and long-term forecasting are critical to the corporate planning process.

Short-term forecasts are usually made for tactical reasons that include production planning and control, short-term cash requirements and adjustments that need to be made for seasonal sales fluctuations. This latter factor can be very important for production, whereas the general trend may be of less consequence. Such forecasts are for periods of less than one year, with a normal range between one and three months.

Medium-term forecasts are made for minor strategic decisions in connection with the operation of the business. They are important in the area of business budgeting for the operating budget, and it is from this forecast that company budgets are built up. Incorrect forecasting can have serious implications for the rest of the organization, for if it turns out to be over-optimistic, the organization will be left with unsold stock and will have overspent on production. Money will be owed to the bank and other creditors, and stock may have to be sold at a loss to raise money to satisfy these creditors. Many bankruptcies among smaller firms can be ascribed to insufficient attention being paid to medium-term sales forecasting. This forecast is used for such matters as the staffing levels that are required to achieve expected sales, the amount of money to be spent on sales effort, and short-term capital requirements for such items as machines to be purchased to meet increased production. The time period for a medium-term forecast is normally one year.

Long-term forecasts are for major strategic decisions to be taken within an organization, and they very much relate to resource implications. They deal with general rather than specific items, and as shown by Raspin and Terjesen[2] rely more heavily in their computation upon such factors as government policy, social change and technological change. They are, therefore, concerned more with general trends, and in the light of these trends, attempt to predict sales over periods greater than two years. In some strategic, heavily capitalized industries, predictions might be needed for a decade or more. The problem is that for these lengths of time the forecast cannot be more than vague, and planners in retrospect blame the forecast when things go wrong (often for reasons completely outside the possible knowledge of the original forecaster) and forecasting thus receives criticism.

CORPORATE OBJECTIVES

A major reason for forecasting is to provide a basis for medium and long-range plans. Businesses must plan in order to achieve goals established on the basis of such forecasts, and these plans will affect various functional aspects of the business. At the base of such plans is long-term profitability, for without this the company may not be able to meet its future commitments in achieving the planned-for sales. Company planners will have to assess whether or not such potential sales can be achieved within the confines of the business as it stands and, if not, what resources will be needed in order to achieve these sales.

Medium-term forecasts are also used for business planning, but less so for strategic reasons. They are of particular importance for costing, and through the sales budget, for marketing management in controlling the marketing function while it goes about achieving the forecasted sales. With a reasonably accurate sales forecast such plans will be more realistic, and when they are put into action they have a better opportunity to work.

Management decisions within a manufacturing concern, together with such external changes as new technology, fashion and the cost of raw materials, affect the accurate prediction of future sales. It is the accuracy of this prediction that can single out the successful firm from the unsuccessful. In the current competitive climate there is little margin for error, and efficiency of operation is a major factor for success. Consequently, prediction of a change in demand is essential for continued prosperity. If a company is able to forecast a change in demand and the extent of that change, it can plan ahead to operate in the most efficient and profitable manner.

Managers are surrounded by a multitude of factors that can affect the future operation of the business. By using the best available forecasting method they can assess their present position and provide more accurate predictions for the future. Whatever circumstances surround the situation in which the manager makes a forecast there is one clearly defined objective, which is to profit eventually from this prediction in terms of revenue or knowledge.

Companies prepare for change by planning. This requires forecasts to be made, followed by an assessment of how these planning goals are to be reached. In practice, the sales forecast acts as the planning base upon which all internal forecasting and budgeting takes place. The effect of considering expected levels of sales in making such decisions is to reduce uncertainty and lower costs. Forecasting is thus central to the planning process and should not be used as a substitute for effective decision making, or management will simply tend to react to short-term fluctuations as they affect sales instead of developing long-term strategies. The company should first work out its selling plan, because this is really what is going to determine the level of sales. For example, a price reduction can be expected to influence a company's share of the total market, and such considerations should be noted by the sales forecaster. Consequently, the forecaster predicts what will happen for a set of decisions in a given set of circumstances, whereas planning states that by taking certain actions, the decision maker can alter subsequent events relating to a particular situation. Thus, if a forecast is made which predicts a fall in demand, management can prepare a plan to prevent sales from falling. The future is not immutable; if it was, there would be little strategic point in forecasting or planning.

The objective of the sales forecast is to predict a company's sales for some period in advance, and this can be done in one of two ways.

1   It can predict the company's sales directly from past sales data and from anticipated orders the company expects to receive (called a **sales forecast**).
2   It can forecast the total market and then determine the company's share of it (called a **market forecast**).

For many companies, the latter course is the most logical, because a company's future strategy will affect its market share and this strategy is directly linked to what is happening in the marketplace. Consideration must also be given to what competitors are doing, and in many cases sales action by one manufacturer will merely cancel out similar action by another.

It has been said that forecasting is often a fruitless adventure, but difficulties when forecasting should not be used as an excuse for inactivity. Forecasting is not a 'crystal ball' that enables the manager to foresee the future more clearly. It is an aid to more informed and better decision making.

FUNCTIONAL OBJECTIVES

Forecasts are needed for many different purposes, including production planning; ordering raw materials; ensuring a steady supply of trained personnel; controlling stocks or inventories; estimating short-term cash requirements, and a variety of other reasons. All these applications have different 'time horizons'. That is, the forecast is needed at different times before the event if it is to be of any practical value. The sales forecast is thus not merely used for planning marketing; it has company-wide applications.

It is marketing and sales personnel who should prepare the sales forecast. In fact according to Geiger and Guenzi,[3] the sales force itself has a key role to play in sales forecasting. This point is made because in many companies, sales forecasting is left to the finance department, as they have an immediate need for the forecast for business budgeting purposes. When forecasts are left to finance in this manner it is an abrogation by marketing of its responsibilities. The reason is that finance personnel are not expected to be forecasting experts and they will simply take sales from earlier periods and do extrapolations from past data. Marketing, above all other functions in business, should be in the best position to ascertain potential sales, including downturns and upturns, of which accountants will be less aware, since they are much further removed from customers than the marketing department. Forecasting is a risky business, which is all the more reason why marketing should not abrogate its responsibilities in this regard.

We now consider the business functions that are most directly concerned with sales forecasts.

Production needs forecasts for each product line in order that manufacturing can be planned and scheduled on an orderly basis. Thus machines and manpower can be more effectively utilized. When the transport element of logistics is organized by production, it is helpful to have advance warning of bulky or awkward items that have to be packed and moved, particularly when overseas considerations are involved. In the longer term, production needs to make decisions on levels of plant operation in order to be able to meet production levels to achieve the planned-for sales. Production's main need will thus be for accurate short-term forecasts for production planning and control.

Human resource management (HRM) needs forecasts in order to be able to ascertain staffing levels in the future. It will then be able to recruit personnel to achieve the forecasted sales. There will be training implications for employees taken on to achieve an increase in sales, so the concern of HRM will be mainly in respect of the medium-term forecast, but the long-term forecast will be needed for formulating management succession plans.

Purchasing needs accurate forecasting so that raw materials and component requirements can be met on a timely basis. As the forecast will give the purchasing officer more time in which to purchase, rather than having to wait until the requisition is received from production, he or she may be in a position to purchase on a more favourable basis because of the increased lead time. The purchasing department can also operate more effective stock control for raw materials and part manufactured goods and work out optimum stock levels. The danger of overstocking, with the risk of deterioration and obsolescence, will be less, and because less stock will need to be carried, this will result in a saving on working capital. Better forecasting will also avoid the possibility of stock-outs resulting in disruption to the production programme. In general, the purchasing function will be more interested in short-term forecasts, although the medium-term forecast will be of value. Clearly the techniques of JIT supply and lean manufacturing as discussed in Chapters 1 and 9 have altered the nature of the need for short-term forecasts in this regard.

Finance needs forecasts in the medium term to establish budgets based on the planned-for sales. Here, accuracy is important, because if the forecast is incorrect, then all the company budgets will be incorrect, with consequent overspending in the case of an optimistic forecast. Cash requirements to fund working capital need to be budgeted, and an incorrect forecast could mean that the company has to make a request to the bank for increased borrowing. Many bankruptcies are a result of a shortage of working capital, and better forecasting could, in many instances, have avoided such an event. Also, finance needs to engage in long-term profit planning and must predict income flow. It must make provision for long-term capital needs in terms of plant, machinery etc., and here the long-term forecast is of importance if the organization is to be ready to produce appropriate products in the correct quantities at the time these are needed.

Marketing should make the forecasts, and these are needed for the entire company as just illustrated. However, marketing also needs these forecasts in order to plan promotional campaigns and sales strategies to complement these campaigns. It needs the forecast in order that the correct types of sales and marketing personnel can be recruited and trained to achieve the planned-for sales. Remuneration plans will also need to be formulated, particularly when these are linked to sales targets or sales quotas, and these targets or quotas will be a reflection of the sales forecast broken down among individual sales personnel. When 'off-the-shelf' delivery is offered to customers, the sales forecast will help to determine maximum and minimum stock levels, and here an incorrect forecast will result in either stock-outs (and possible loss of custom) or overstocking (with a resultant drain on working capital). In the longer term, more precise goals can be set for members of the marketing channel, both in terms of the supply chain and the demand chain. Channel arrangements tend to be of a more stable, long-term nature, and if potential sales are predicted to be much higher in the long term, then new channel arrangements might be called for. Thus, marketing is in need of short, medium and long-term forecasts.

Research, Design and Development (R,D&D) requires technological forecasts. Marketing is the conduit through which changes in the marketplace can be relayed to the R,D&D department. Design features and new technology will affect company sales, and products need to be updated or changed at intervals. Marketing is in close touch with customers and should be aware of competitive offerings, so marketing is best placed to give advice in this respect. It might be that a particular product line is becoming obsolete, in which case R,D&D will need to plan and develop a new product or make modifications to an existing product in conjunction with marketing research. Only by doing this will an organization be able to keep ahead of, or apace with, its competitors and continue to produce products that are appropriate for the marketplace. Marketing, through the medium of marketing research, will liaise with R,D&D and from medium and long-term forecasts will co-ordinate new product developments and ultimately product launches.

With an accurate forecast, departments can plan more effectively with the reassurance that these action plans can be carried through and will not have to be modified, as they might be if the forecast was inaccurate. There is thus an interrelationship and interdependency between the plans and operations of each of the above functions, because they are all based on the sales forecast. If the original sales forecast proves to be incorrect, then it will affect each and every function within the business, because each department uses the sales forecast as its starting point. The importance of an accurate and timely sales forecast cannot be overemphasized. What we must do is reduce the extent of the wrongness of the forecast, or at least provide guidelines as to the extent to which it might be incorrect.

SALES BUDGETS AND THEIR USES

Budgets, which are also discussed in Chapter 14, stem from the sales forecast, and the sales budget is the vehicle through which sales are generated. Thus the **sales budget** comes after the sales forecast, and this is a representation of each salesperson's sales broken down by product type, by customer type and by individual territory. The sales department budget then follows, together with other departmental budgets. Although we use the term 'sales department budget', its true description reflects more than purely selling. It includes forthcoming investment in promotion, such as different forms of advertising, displays, exhibitions, consumer and trade promotions, etc. It also includes investment in distribution, which includes distributive intermediaries and facilities such as warehousing and physical distribution of finished goods to customers. Additionally, it includes marketing research expenditure, selling expenditure and all the various costs that go into winning orders. For definition purposes, cost accountants subdivide the sales department budget into the selling expense budget, the advertising budget and the sales department administrative budget. These terms of course reflect production orientation, and better descriptions might ultimately be found for each of the subdivisions which reflect a more modern marketing orientation. However, accountants use these terms that are now universally accepted, so for these reasons they are included here.

A budget differs from a forecast in that it is a representation of what is planned to happen, whereas a forecast is concerned with what is expected to happen. The forecast is far more uncertain, because it is affected by extraneous factors, whereas the budget is to do with internal matters, and these can be controlled directly by the organization. The relationship is explained diagrammatically in Figure 11.1.

It has been explained that the budget is derived from the sales forecast, and business budgeting cannot commence until the forecast has been agreed. Budgeting requires detailed planning of all duties to be undertaken during the budget period (normally one year ahead). The total sales budget is divided among the individual product lines to be sold in terms of apportionment of expenditure on advertising, packaging, personal selling etc. The way the total sales budget is apportioned is, of course, a decision for marketing management.

It is important to ensure that the sales budget co-ordinates with other budgets in the organization. For instance, the sales budget should not plan to achieve more sales than production is budgeted to manufacture. Budgets must also be flexible to allow for changing conditions or unforeseen circumstances, and in some companies it might be necessary to prepare more than one budget as a contingency measure. Thus flexibility is important, because if during the budget period it seems as though another set of circumstances is likely to prevail, then the budget might need to be altered to cover such a contingency.

When actual expenditure differs from the budgeted expenditure, the departmental manager should explain the deviation. Cost accountants refer to each item of cost as a budget or cost venture,

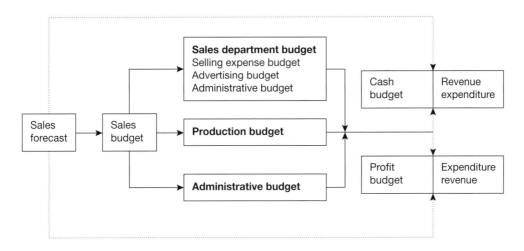

FIGURE 11.1 Sales budgetary procedure

and they describe these differences as 'variances'. The term used to describe this process of control is 'management by exception', and the philosophy implies that only when events do not go as planned does an investigation need to be made. Budgeting is not merely a matter of planning; it is also used as a method of control. Furthermore, realistic evaluation cannot take place unless detailed plans have been agreed before the budget period.

In short, budgets provide a financial statement of the company's plans and policies, and reflect the co-ordinated efforts of all departments (or cost centres) within the organization. The sales department budget is thus the marketing function's share of the company budget and this, in turn, is broken down into constituent parts covering promotion, selling, administration etc., and then allocated between each product within the range of products.

NEED FOR PROFIT PLANNING AND ITS DERIVATION

Profits need to be planned on the premise that in a well run organization, they should grow. Actions within the company that can bring about such profit growth include: better working practices, provision of incentive schemes to bring about increased productivity, better computerization with resultant efficiency in the performance of clerical tasks, automation in the workplace, better stock control of raw materials, components and finished goods with resultant savings in working capital, standardization and variety reduction exercises to bring about a reduction in inventories, less obsolescence and better quality control, and many other cost saving exercises.

Sales forecasting must precede **profit planning** exercises, and it is emphasized that such forecasts should be as accurate as possible, for such efforts as those just described are time-consuming and costly in their implementation. To be meaningful, they should take place in the light of anticipated production and resultant sales, which is based on the forecast.

Companies need to plan in order to make provision for fixed and working capital expenditure. Such fixed capital expenditure plans are necessary because old assets deteriorate, new additional plant and buildings may be needed to accommodate increased production, and new production methods may become available, rendering the old plant and machinery obsolete. Similarly, working capital needs to be planned, and this means forecasting stock investment because sales can fluctuate on a cyclical basis or for economic or other reasons. As a result, raw materials, components and finished stock levels will fluctuate in accordance with demand. Working capital in terms of liquid cash assets must be planned to accommodate the value of stocks to be held plus the costs of holding such stock.

The sales forecast precedes all planning, and the need for fixed and working capital expenditure forecasts has just been outlined. Once this has been done, it is necessary to translate all of these statements showing how they will affect the finances of the business. This is called the **cash forecast**, which encapsulates the sales forecast and resulting business plans in terms of money. Preparation of the cash forecast is a specialized cost accounting activity, but it starts with the basic premise that profits should increase the amount of cash in the business. Therefore, a net profit figure is forecast, and from this is taken away corporation tax, increases in stock and work in progress, loans and overdrafts repaid, dividends and interest, increases in debtors, decreases in creditors, and expenditure on capital equipment. To the end figure must be added sales of assets, receipts from share or loan issues, decreases in stock and work-in-progress, depreciation, increases in creditors and decreases in debtors. The amount left at the end is profit, and how it is distributed is a decision for the board of directors. The fact is that a plan is needed in order that business management can organize its activities in a responsible manner and such planning, of necessity, stems from the sales forecast.

TECHNIQUES OF FORECASTING

There are two basic techniques:

1 **Objective methods** that are of a mathematical or statistical nature;
2 **Subjective methods** based on experience, judgement and intuition rather than on quantitative analysis.

The wide acceptance of objective techniques in recent years is primarily because objective methods have developed a record for accuracy and thus have inspired confidence in managers who use them as an aid to decision making. As we shall discuss in Chapter 12 the development of better forecasting software has greatly improved its accuracy. Subjective methods still rely largely on intuition, but the practice of objective forecasting is more advanced. Marketers recognize that the pace of change in the marketing environment, and the increased uncertainty which this gives rise to, is making the use of such intuitive techniques more appropriate.

The discussion that follows relates to specific practical and managerial problems that can be encountered when using such techniques.

Objective methods

Moving averages This method of time series analysis involves compilation of the arithmetic average of a number of previous consecutive points in a time series. It is best employed in a situation where an extrapolation of a trend that is gradually increasing or decreasing is present. It has a low cost with ease of manual computation. Problems occur in the choice of the number of points to average, and the effects of a non-typical item in the time series. Seasonality and cyclical trends can be catered for by the application of relevant indices, provided they are known.

The major disadvantage of this technique is that it is purely quantitative in its approach and thus extremely introspective. It does not take into consideration any salient factors in the environment that may affect future sales.

Exponential smoothing Using a moving average has the problem that it gives equal weight, or significance, to all the items in a time series. More recent points in a time series will represent the present situation more accurately than older items, and it is therefore, only logical to attach more significance to more recent items by using a weighting method. The different weight attached to an item in a time series can be calculated either simply by using an arithmetic progression or, more sophisticatedly, by using a geometric progression. When a geometric progression is used and a graph is drawn, raw sales data are smoothed into an exponential curve; hence the name 'exponential smoothing'. In the case where an arithmetic progression is used, this is simply known as a weighted moving average.

Exponential smoothing provides a forecast which is equal to the old one, plus or minus some proportion of the past forecasting error(s). There are many variations of exponential smoothing, ranging from the very simplistic to the more complex methods involving a greater number of data points and proportions of forecast errors. These techniques, because of their statistical nature, lend themselves particularly to purely quantitative data, thus neglecting other important market factors. A more realistic prediction is gained through the use of this technique than moving averages because it allows for new factors and influences that have emerged in the most recent sales period.

Trend projections By fitting a trend line to a mathematical equation it is possible to make forecasts about future sales using the equation. Figure 11.2 shows four typical growth curves that a firm may experience. The danger of using the trend approach alone is that when the analyst extrapolates, the assumption is that what affected sales in the past will continue to affect sales in the same way over future periods. An adequate number of past measurements or observations are also required for adequate statistical significance, but care must be taken not to include too many past observations or history will be too heavily weighted. Trend projections, like moving averages and exponential smoothing, are not ideal for short or medium-term forecasts. They are more fitting for predicting a 'broad sweep' trend over the long term.

The Box-Jenkins forecasting method is a special case of exponential smoothing in which the time series is fitted with an optimizing mathematical model that attributes minimal error to historical data. Once the model has been identified and constructed, the parameters must then be estimated.

Of the available statistical routines, this is one of the most accurate and flexible in that it can cope with almost any type of data pattern. However, accuracy involves complexity, which, along with flexibility, results in a relatively high cost and the need for a skilful operator with plenty of time to reap the full benefit s of this technique. As this method's accuracy is limited to the short

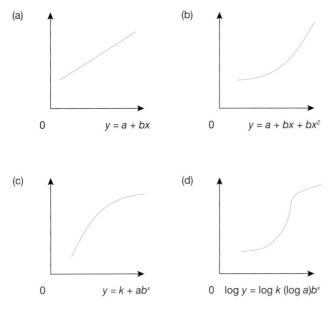

(a)

$y = a + bx$

(b)

$y = a + bx + bx^2$

(c)

$y = k + ab^x$

(d)

$\log y = \log k\, (\log a)b^x$

FIGURE 11.2 Company growth curves

term it is not very often used in practice, as there are many other cheaper and easier techniques that can be employed, and although they do not give as much accuracy, these are often adequate for short-term decisions.

Spectral analysis Incorporated in the classification of spectral analysis is the technique of Fourier analysis, where a time series is mathematically decomposed into its constituent sine wave forms. Thus, from one time series, a spectrum of time series are produced having the name 'power spectrum'. The mathematical complexities of this method put it beyond the use of all but the most competent analyst, whose skill and understanding of the technique are imperative for its successful implementation.

X-11 technique is similar to spectral analysis in that it decomposes the original time series into a spectrum of time series. However, it only separates out the seasonal and cyclical trends, and then fits a time series to the remainder. It takes the best of spectral analysis and Box-Jenkins and combines them in one technique. Used by a skilled analyst, it rates as one of the most effective short to medium-term forecasting methods, with its ability to identify turning points being a major asset.

Causal methods are still objective techniques, but they all involve some degree of subjectivity. One of the best known causal methods is that of **regression analysis**, which attempts to assess the relationship between at least two variables: one (or more) independent and one dependent, the purpose being to predict the value of the dependent variable from the specific value of the independent variable. The basis of this prediction generally is historical data. This method starts from the assumption that a basic relationship exists between two variables, and the least squares method of estimation is used to formulate the mathematical relationship which exists. Various forms of regression analysis exist, one being multiple regression analysis, where any number of variables can be considered at one time. Another form is stepwise regression analysis, where only one independent variable is considered at one time. The value of this technique is difficult to assess other than in individual cases, as the accuracy is dependent upon the degree to which the independent variables explain characteristics of the dependent variable. This relationship may vary considerably, but improved computing techniques have meant that the value of regression analysis is increased dramatically on a cost/benefit basis.

Through techniques such as regression analysis, the Newspaper Society has established clear links between their different life stage categories with levels of demand for a range of products. Unsurprisingly, Mothercare shoppers are almost four times more likely to have pre-school-aged children than the national average.

Econometric models are an extension of the regression technique whereby a system of independent regression equations is evolved. These equations describe a particular sector of economic activity whose parameters are usually estimated simultaneously. Generally, these models are relatively expensive to develop, the precise cost being dependent on the amount of detail incorporated in the model. However, the inherent systems of equations in such models express the causalities involved far better than an ordinary regression equation, and thus will predict turning points more accurately.

Input-output models are particularly applicable in the field of industrial marketing since they are concerned with inter-industry or interdepartmental flows of goods or services in a company and its markets. The technique is based on the theory that the output of one industry comprises the basic inputs of products and materials of another, thereby providing an inter-industry/interdepartmental flow of goods and services within the economy/industry. Major inputs required for this type of model are not in the operation of the model, but in the collection and presentation of data. This is because tables and government statistics showing the extent to which one industry obtains its basic inputs from another are very broadly defined in standard industrial classifications.

The cost of these models in producing a sales forecast, especially when they are combined with econometric models to produce economic input-output models, is often high but as Lackman[4] shows this should be offset against the relatively high accuracy produced by these more sophisticated models.

Diffusion indexes use the many economic indicators available that represent general economic activity, or the activity within a particular industry or product class. By formulating an index based on a certain combination of these indices, an indication of future trends can be compiled. The accuracy and applicability of the index can be tailored to fit specific requirements, such as predicting turning points in the short term by choosing appropriate economic indicators. A forecasting technique of this nature can be accurate and relatively economical to apply in certain industries and product classes.

Tied indicators are used where the sales of one product are closely related to sales of another product and the sales trend of one product precedes that of the other. The preceding product is the indicator, and in the case of leading indicator models, the sales of more than one product may be utilized along with indicators of general economic activity. The leading indicators generally increase or decrease prior to the pending increase or decrease in the dependent variable, and they usually take the form of a time series of economic activity. As a forecasting method the real value of this type of model is its ability to predict turning points rather than as a predictor of future trends in general.

Life cycle analysis is particularly applicable where there is no historical data. Sales of similar products are analysed over time and usually a particular 'S' curve (see Figure 11.2 (d)) is found to apply for a certain product class. The phases of product acceptance by various groups i.e. innovators, early adopters, early majority, late majority and laggards are essential to the analysis (see Chapter 4, Figure 4.12, Roger's 'Diffusion of innovations'). Consideration of the concepts of life cycle analysis by individuals is often more valuable than a thorough detailed expert analysis, as the database for this type of model is conceptually weak. A manager can readily appreciate that the product has to pass through the various stages in its life cycle and subjective opinion might even be as accurate as any expert analysis.

Subjective methods

Market research involves studying a representative sample of a market involving a systematic formal procedure for evolving and testing hypotheses about a market. For any valid information to be obtained, two reports should be made over a period of time so one can be compared with the other and conclusions drawn. This necessitates the collection of market data from questionnaires, surveys, published statistics, marketing intelligence reports and time series analyses of market variables. Due to the relatively high cost of this technique, it is only used in cases where there is a considerable financial risk, which generally means it is restricted to large companies. The major application of this technique for sales forecasting is in the area of predicting new product sales by investigating consumer reaction to a new product concept or prototype. A variety of market research techniques are available for this purpose, and these are discussed in Chapter 12.

The **Delphi method** is a technique that involves the marshalling of expert opinion to cope with the problems of eradicating the 'bandwagon effect' of majority opinion. Its workings and implications have already been discussed in Chapter 4.

Panel consensus is not unlike the Delphi method, except that the panel of experts are encouraged to communicate and discuss matters in relation to the future prospects of what is to be predicted. Developed primarily for long-term forecasting, this method is rarely used due to the problems of personal and social bias influencing the members of the panel. Methods of this nature often do not arrive at a true consensus of opinion because of the effects of such bias.

Experts are not infallible. Predictions regarding the growth in access to the Internet in the UK proved to be too conservative. Growth rates in the diffusion of this technology into UK households have been much higher than the experts predicted.

Visionary forecast is where 'visionary' forecasters or 'futurologists' attempt to prophesy through personal opinion and judgements. The method is characterized by subjective guesswork and imagination, and in the method is non-scientific. A set of possible scenarios about the future is prepared by a few experts in the light of past events. At one time, visionary forecasts were felt to be too subjective to be used in marketing decision making. However, as mentioned earlier, the pace of chance and dynamic nature of the marketing environment have begun to make companies appreciate some of the advantages of visionary forecasts even though they may sometimes be wrong.

Many believe that at least in part the success of Microsoft in being ahead of its competitors in many areas is down to visionary forecasts. The company has a system whereby senior managers are encouraged to think about the future in the widest possible sense, including, for example, social trends and developments, and how these developments, might potentially open up new opportunities for Microsoft for future product development.

Historical analogy is a comparative analysis of the introduction and growth of similar new products, and this bases the forecast on similarity patterns. By comparing a new product with a similar previous new product, forecasts of future sales performance can be made. This technique, however, is conceptually weak, as a true new product will not be similar to any previous product, and even a new version of a product will probably not be similar enough to make any comparison really valid.

Sales force opinion is where members of a sales force are in constant contact with customers, and are in a position to predict their buying plans, attitudes and needs. An obstacle to gaining true estimates is that salespeople often tend to be pessimistic, owing to their compensation system. It is common practice for salespeople to be remunerated according to the degree to which they attain sales quotas which, in turn, are based on sales forecasts. Thus it is in their own interest to underestimate future sales, resulting in low quotas and possibilities of high compensation. However, Jobber and Lancaster[5] provided evidence that being involved in the sales forecasting and hence quota setting process can actually increase salesforce motivation, therefore making the achievement of agreed sales quotas more likely. This method has the advantage of being relatively cheap and easy to introduce and administer through the existing sales organization.

APPROPRIATENESS OF TECHNIQUE CHOSEN

There can be no general conclusion drawn as to which is the best forecasting technique to employ, but it is certainly true that a forecast should consider both objective and subjective aspects. The analyst can only consider what is required, and with the resources that are available, try to match them against a method that will provide the best result.

The techniques considered cover a range of objective and subjective, quantitative and qualitative techniques that require various resources and data for their employment. It is the situation, within various constraints, that should determine the method to be used for forecasting, not external constraints of cost, simplicity and personal preferences.

MEASURES OF VALUE OR VOLUME?

In theory, a manager should use sales forecasting where the benefit is greater than the effort needed to generate the forecast. The problem of measuring the effectiveness of a forecast is a major obstacle. A manager can accurately cost the use of a forecasting technique in terms of current time and money, but not the benefits that could possibly be enjoyed in the future by having a more accurate forecast.

One of the problems the analyst has to face when preparing a sales forecast for a product or product group is what units should be the units of measurement for future sales? Even if a total market prediction is undertaken, the forecaster still has to determine what units to use for the forecast. In most commercial situations this results in a choice between value and volume, dependent upon whichever is the most consistent over time and likely to provide the most accurate measure of future sales, assuming data are available in both forms.

Volume measures are likely to be confusing where the product mix is not homogeneous, e.g. two products may have similar physical characteristics that classify each of them as one single unit, but they may have widely differing sales values. A volume measure may state a market of so many units, but the value of this market could vary to a large extent as the value of the constituent units is not precisely known. However, volume forecasts have the advantage of not being affected by inflation or deflation because once a physical unit is defined it is not affected by external factors.

On the other hand, value predictions can be adjusted for variations in the buying power of a currency, but the application of many of the available inflation/deflation indices is not representative of the same fluctuation experienced by the product. Indices are invariably computed on the basis of price changes and reflect only one aspect of inflation/deflation, neglecting to compare the product with other products. The consumer can be regarded as having a disposable income for which many companies compete by means of their products, and a consumer's choice of product is a function of that consumer's perception of the worth of that product in relation to other products. A price increase index does not reflect the inflation/deflation experienced by a product in relation to other products.

IMPORTANCE OF ACCURATE FORECASTS

Should actual sales fall short of, or exceed, forecasted sales, management must investigate the reasons for the difference, and from their inquiries determine whether or not it is necessary to adjust the sales forecasting technique. Thus sales forecasting is a continuous process. The changing nature of the economic and physical environment means that forecasts should be under continuous scrutiny and revision. Every projection can be improved, and in competitive situations even fractional increases in accuracy can be translated into higher profits.

It has already been said that all sales forecasts are wrong; they only differ in the extent of their wrongness. Perfection is unattainable, and the organization must decide what level of accuracy is required within pre-determined time and cost constraints. Management must fix the level of inaccuracy that can be tolerated, and this will allow it to compare cost with value when selecting the appropriate technique.

An illustration of how this notion of comparing the costs of different techniques of forecasting can be traded off against their degree of accuracy in order to arrive at the best-value techniques is illustrated in Figure 11.3.

THE SALES FORECASTING SYSTEM

Sales forecasting involves the determination of the expected levels of sales in the future, based on past and present sales data, the intentions of management and environmental influences upon the enterprise. The forecasting of sales can be regarded as a system having inputs, a process and an output. This may be a simplistic viewpoint, but it serves as a useful tool for the analysis of the true worth of sales forecasting as an aid to management, and is illustrated in Figure 11.4.

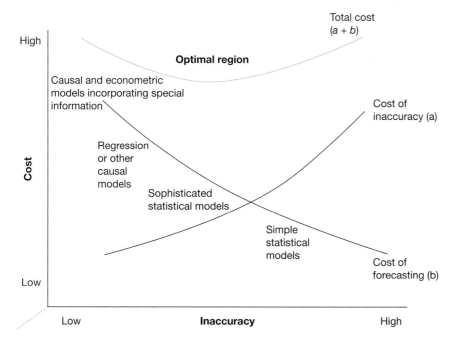

FIGURE 11.3 The cost/sophistication trade-off

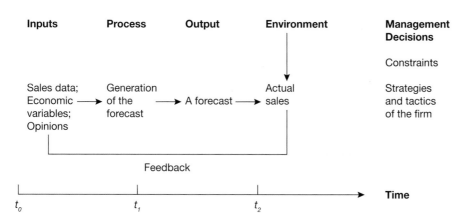

FIGURE 11.4 The sales forecasting system

THE TIME FACTOR

It could be said that the main concern of forecasting is the elimination of the phenomenon of time, in that it attempts to negate the effects of time by the logical and probabilistic determination of future events. To appreciate this, you only have to consider the effect time has on the validity of inputs to a forecasting technique. In Figure 11.4, at time t_0 all the inputs may be correct, but by time t_1, when they are collated, some may well have varied to reflect changing situations, yet this is not shown in the inputs to the forecasting process. Certainly by time t_2 (the lead time) the inputs could be totally inaccurate due to changes in the market and this is without considering the changes that may occur in the projection time of a forecast.

Although the analyst may strive to reduce the lead time for a forecast to a minimum in order to ensure that the output is based on the most recently available data, any forthcoming changes in the inputs will ultimately occur in the projection time. As forecasting should be a continuous process, analysts should constantly be updating the inputs to reflect any changes and produce revised forecasts. It is thus the job of the analyst to reduce lead time to an optimum point where a forecast is based on the latest data without sacrificing accuracy, or involving disproportionate costs for the value of the prediction obtained. On the whole, quantitative methods lend themselves to economical revision far more readily than qualitative techniques owing to the nature of the data involved and the cost of generating and processing them.

A common fallacy is that forecasting is an activity that takes place at periodic intervals, such as once a year, and ceases entirely between these intervals. In fact, in order to reflect changes in the environment and internal structure of the firm, forecasts should be continually evaluated and revised to maintain their credibility. Such factors as price alterations by competitors, government legislation, technological breakthroughs, changes in the organization's own advertising strategy and alterations of any one of the factors in the marketing mix which has not been previously foreseen can substantially alter sales.

Sometimes a forecast can be rendered totally wrong by completely unforeseen events which would have been impossible to forecast using any method. During the fuel crisis in the UK in the early weeks of September 2000, panic buying caused sales of some products to increase by up to 75 per cent over a three-day period. Few of the companies affected by this could have forecast such a dramatic increase in short-term sales.

The importance of the feedback loop cannot be overemphasized. For the ongoing forecasting process, the feedback loop constitutes a major input to the forecasting process, as can be seen by considering the value attached to error analysis in many quantitative methods. In the case of qualitative techniques, significant weight is attached to any variance between what was forecast and what actually occurred, and the related reasons. Future forecasts thus attach considerable significance to the reasons for past performance and try to incorporate these in any new forecast. The feedback loop is the control on the process.

SUMMARY

Forecasting is of utmost importance to business as it is the precursor to all planning activities and lies at the base of corporate strategic planning. The strategic plan determines how the company will go about achieving its share of the total forecasted sales. Thus sales forecasting and strategic planning are interlinked.

Sales forecasting does, however, have three principal dimensions, short-term (about three months), medium-term (normally one year) and long-term (usually two years minimum and a lot longer in some industries). Each of these dimensions is for specific tactical (normally short or medium-term) or strategic (normally medium or long-term) purposes.

Once the sales forecast and the strategic plan have been agreed, business budgeting can take place and the sales budget is the medium through which sales are generated.

Forecasting therefore lies at the base of all company planning. It is of paramount importance that this forecast is the best that can be produced within the resource constraints of the company, for if the sales forecast is incorrect in the first place, then the whole planning exercise for the organization will have been in vain.

KEY TERMS

CASE STUDY

Scalar Products

Sonia Miller cannot believe what she has just heard. Having joined Scalar Products as a Market Analyst and Planner she has just been informed that the company has no sales forecasting system and Finance simply examine previous sales when doing next year's estimated sales for budgeting purposes. She cannot understand how the company has managed to operate effectively without one.

Her marketing manager, however, a very competent technical engineer who has over the years moved through sales and into marketing in the company, believes that all forecasts are simply a waste of time. His view is that what is going to happen will happen and no amount of forecasting will affect this. Moreover, he has pointed out that in his experience forecasts are usually wrong and so it is better to do without them. Although Sonia has already pleaded her case regarding the need for and uses of sales forecasts, her manager is adamant that she should spend her time on other 'more useful activities'. Sonia, however, feels that she cannot effectively do her job with regard to helping prepare marketing plans without an effective system of sales forecasting.

CASE STUDY QUESTION

How can Sonia persuade her manager that sales forecasts are not only useful, but essential, in the marketing planning process? What should she advise her manager in relation to the types of forecasts and forecasting techniques might be useful in any newly established system of forecasting?

REFERENCES

1 Shahabuddin, S. (2009), 'Forecasting automobile sales', *Management Research News*, 32(7): 670–82.

2 Raspin, P. and Terjesen, S. (2007), 'Strategy making: what have we learned about forecasting the future?', *Business Strategy Series*, 8(2): 116–21.

3 Geiger, S. and Guenzi, P. (2009), 'The sales function in the twenty first century: where are we and where do we go from here?', *European Journal of Marketing*, 43(7/8): 873–89.

4 Lackman, C.L. (2007), 'Forecasting sales for a B2B product category: case of auto component product', *Journal of Business & Industrial Marketing*, 22(4): 228–35.

5 Jobber, D. and Lancaster, G. (2009), *Selling and Sales Management*, 8th edn, Harlow: Prentice Hall, p. 483.

Chapter 12

Marketing information systems and research

LEARNING OBJECTIVES

After reading this chapter you will:

- understand the importance of information in effective marketing planning
- appreciate the nature and meaning of the marketing information system and its role in providing information for decision making
- become acquainted with the principal problems in designing a marketing information system
- recognize the contribution of contemporary marketing information system technology to information provision and processing
- be aware of key sources of information and inputs to the marketing information system, including the marketing research process, and with contemporary developments in this area
- be familiar with marketing research techniques in terms of their application and importance in the marketing information system

INTRODUCTION

Marketing orientation places customers at the forefront of planning activities. It is a philosophy of total business thinking that is not merely confined to the realms of the marketing department. Organizations face changes and challenges from outside as well as inside their boundaries. The role of marketing is to anticipate and identify such changes and advise the organization on how to respond to challenges in the context of a competitive marketplace.

Marketing needs information to carry out this task. Marketing research collects information and a **marketing information system** (MkIS) analyses and acts on such information. According to Kotler and Keller[1] a marketing information system consists of: 'People, equipment, and procedures to gather, sort, analyze, evaluate and distribute needed, timely and accurate information to marketing decision makers.' This definition highlights that the marketing information system is more than just marketing research. Information provided by marketing research is one input to the marketing information system, albeit a crucial one. The whole purpose of the marketing information system is to enhance the marketing manager's decision-making capabilities.

In practice, an MkIS provides a store of historical customer data. This produces better efficiency internally due to better organized data, thus ultimately leading to more effective strategic improvements; better identification of opportunities that might lead to the development of new products and services, and the development of better long-term relationships with customers arising from increased customer loyalty. Chapter 11 was concerned with forecasting, and the forecast is the starting point when constructing a business plan. It is, therefore, critical that forecasting information is lodged on the MkIS. To achieve this requires a study of an organization's current information base and its ability to monitor existing marketing activities. It also needs the ability to use information to match the dynamics of a changing market and to report such changes to marketing management in order that appropriate planning action can be taken.

INFORMATION REQUIREMENTS

An organization's strategy, planning and operational control is dependent on information that is available to the decision maker. A **situation analysis** is a method of considering this information, and then relating it to the operations of the organization. Environmental scanning should then be undertaken, as well as studying the internal marketing system, and this should then be made available to key decision makers. This forms the basis for strategic marketing decisions which are monitored to ensure that objectives are achieved. The MkIS provides the medium through which information is collected, channelled, focused and communicated.

Information requirements depend on:

- the type of industry or environment;
- the size of the organization;
- the marketing decisions to be taken;
- the dynamics of the industry or environment.

It is difficult to generalize about the individual needs of an organization. However, information is collected from internal and external sources that include customer, market and competitor information. Quite often this information exists, but is not in a form suitable for use by marketing. Much is collected for invoicing purposes, where its strategic value is not recognized. Customer inquiries and customer complaints need to be channelled into the MkIS to ensure that they are valued and used for planning and controlling marketing operations.

Information on existing customers will form the core of the database, e.g. invoices record information that can be used by marketing as can be seen in Table 12.1.

As the volume and sophistication of the information collected increases, an organization will build up its database of existing and potential customers, which will allow the application of more sophisticated targeting and segmentation strategies through a more thorough understanding of buying behaviour in the marketplace. Gounaris et al.[2] show how far we have come with building and evaluating marketing information systems in today's organizations. They demonstrate that an effective marketing information system in modern organizations improves not only internal performance, including functional performance and organizational climate, but also external performance such as better adaptability to market conditions and customer responsiveness.

The nature of the marketing information function has changed over recent years, and so too has computing technology such as laser scanning of bar coded grocery products. This has resulted in revolutionary changes to business as information is more accurate and more quickly obtained. This is a key reason for the expansion of the large retail groups like Walmart, Lidl, Aldo, Tesco, Asda, Morrisons and Sainsbury's.

TABLE 12.1 MkIS utilization of accounting invoice information

Information	Marketing use
Customer name	Identification
Customer address	Geodemographic profiling and census data
Date of sale	Tracking of purchase rates; repurchase intervals
Items ordered	Benefit/need analysis; product clusters
Quantities ordered	Heavy/light user; crude segmentation
Price	Value calculation of profitability
Discount (if any)	Price sensitivity
Terms and conditions	Customer service needs; special requirements

Decisions support systems (DSS) were developed in the late 1970s and these are designed from the viewpoint of an individual decision maker. They are computer-based systems that are interactive and flexible, so results can be generated on the spot and then sorted and regrouped and manipulated as required. Managers can probe for trends and isolate problems.

The MkIS is an invaluable aid to decision making and is a specialized subset of the corporate **management information system (MIS)**. The term 'management information system', along with that of MkIS, is synonymous with data processing and forms a framework for managing information that is gathered from both outside and inside the organization. The MIS consists of five separate planning subsystems, namely: Production or Operations; Human Resource Development; Finance; Logistics and of course Marketing's MkIS that itself consists of four subsystems as shown in Figure 12.1.

1   The **internal accounting system** is a system that reports orders, sales, dispatches, inventory levels and cheques receivable and payable.
2   The **market intelligence system** is a set of procedures and sources used to obtain everyday information about pertinent developments in the marketing environment, largely built up from data like reports from sales representative.
3   The **marketing research system** is the systematic design, collection, analysis and reporting of data findings relevant to a specific marketing situation facing the company.
4   The **analytical marketing system** analyses marketing data using statistical procedures and models. This analysis feeds into strategic marketing plans.

Subsystems 1, 2 and 3 are data collection methods, whereas subsystem 4 is an analytical method. Together they provide a framework for marketing managers to marshal their thoughts into tactics, and to assist management in seeing the important elements of a particular situation and examining

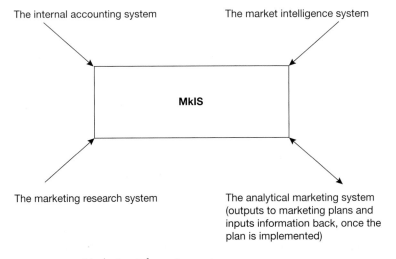

FIGURE 12.1 Marketing information system

the relationships between these elements. A successful MkIS provides a structure for analysis, planning and control of a given set of activities. Creating an MIS and MkIS for any business is a complex, individualized process.

Lancaster and Massingham[3] distinguish between an MkIS and marketing research. Marketing research is concerned with the task of generating information, whereas the MkIS is focused on managing the flow of information to marketing decision makers. This distinction is important because information is worthless unless it is relevant and effectively communicated.

INPUTS TO THE MKIS

The three inputs to the MkIS as shown in Figure 12.1 are now examined individually:

The internal accounting system

Internal company data can be a fruitful source of information, but it is often not fully utilized. Administrative and documentary procedures vary between companies, but most start with the customer's enquiry and end with the customer's invoice. In B2B environments it is possible to build a picture of the overall system from individual employees to the total departmental system and ultimately to the firm as a whole.

Data from marketing/sales departments

These are the main points of commercial interaction between an organization and its customers. Consequently, a great deal of information should be available, including:

- *Total sales*: every company keeps a record of its total sales over specific periods e.g. daily, weekly, monthly.
- *Sales by products*: few companies sell only one product; most sell a range and keep records of each kind of product or product group.
- *Territorial sales*: statistics are kept partly to measure the progress and competence of the salesperson (sometimes to influence earnings because commission may be paid on sales) and to measure the degree of market penetration.
- *Sales by trade classification* e.g. textiles, engineering or chemicals. This will give an indication of market penetration for each class when compared to the official census of distribution which analyses sales by trade classifications.
- *Sales volume by market segment* may be geographical or by type of industry. This gives an indication of segment trends in terms of whether they are static, declining or expanding.
- *Sales volume by type of channel of distribution*: where a company has a multi-channel distribution policy it is possible to calculate the effectiveness and profitability of each type of channel. This allows for trends to be identified in patterns of distribution that can then be taken into account in planning future channel requirements. Such information allows marketing to identify and develop promising channel opportunities resulting in more effective channel management.

- *Sales volume over time* covers actual sales and units sold. Such information enables seasonal variations to be identified, and inflation cost adjustments can be taken into consideration.
- *Pricing information*: historical information relating to price adjustments by product allows the organization to establish the effect on demand of price increases or decreases and to judge the likely effects of any future price changes.
- *Communication mix information* includes past data on the effects of advertising campaigns, sponsorship, direct mail programmes or exhibitions, levels of expenditure on marketing communications and the effect on sales of increases or decreases in such expenditure. Such information can act as a guide to the likely effectiveness of future communication expenditure plans.
- *Sales representatives' records and reports* A visit card or file on every 'live' customer should be maintained. Sales representatives frequently send reports to the sales office on such matters as orders lost to competitors and possible reasons why, as well as on firms that are holding future purchasing decisions in abeyance. Such information could help in determining future levels of demand or point to possible necessary improvements in marketing strategy.
- *Inquiries received and quotations sent*: buyers send inquiries to potential suppliers who then send quotations. Such information is useful in terms of establishing a pattern of inquiries that mature into purchase orders. Such a pattern will expose levels of economic activity in the marketplace.

Other records

As well as sales records other departments also have records that may be of direct value:

- *Material purchased* comprises raw material and components used in the manufacturing process. Profitability measures can be established from such analyses.
- *Wages records*: knowing the proportion of direct labour that goes into prime cost (prime cost being made up of direct labour, direct materials and direct expenses) can give a guide to manufacturing productivity.
- *Despatch records* are kept that include details of goods despatched and methods of transport which then allows the company to build up a picture of logistical effectiveness.
- *Accounts department* provides cost data, as well as documents like past management reports. In addition, past budgets, with variance analyses, show budgeted figures against actual figures.
- *Departmental plans*: not only should past and current internal information be available to marketing, but so should short, medium and long-term plans of individual departments. Future planned activity and changes in company policy or methods of operation can be evaluated and taken into account.

Sources of information available from the internal accounting system are multifarious and represent the most obvious data that can be of use within an MkIS. Other departments can input valuable data and such information can be collected from Research and Development, Human Resource and Production in particular where measures of output and productivity can be used. A fully co-ordinated corporate MIS, of which the MkIS is a component part, is an invaluable aid to strategic corporate planners and marketing planners.

THE MARKET INTELLIGENCE SYSTEM

The market intelligence system is concerned with collection and analysis of ongoing developments in the marketing environment. This is normally regarded as a sub-set under marketing research where it is referred to as 'desk research'. However, we are considering this as a component part of the MkIS, so it is logical that it is included here, and marketing research follows later. The main sources are **secondary data sources**, the principal ones of which are now summarized.

Government sources

In most developed countries of the world government-supplied information is probably the most valuable of external sources of secondary data. The more potentially useful types of government information include:

- *Census data*: most governments conduct a regular census of their citizens. Census data is necessary for government planning and policy making but it is also a valuable source of information for the marketer. Census information includes information on numbers in the population, household and individual data such as number in household, age, sex, marital status, socio-economic class, country of birth, education and economic activity.
- *Economic activity*: most governments collect and publish statistics about occupations and the employed population classified into branches of industry. In most developed countries key statistics, covering age, distribution, socio-economic status, housing conditions, housing tenure, car ownership and many others are available. These statistics are used by marketing organizations to evaluate potential markets and often form the basis of segmentation and targeting strategies as discussed in Chapter 3.
- *Income and expenditure statistics* contain information on national income and expenditure; population statistics; labour; social services; production; agriculture and food; energy; chemicals; textiles; construction; retailing and catering; transport; external trade; wages and prices; entertainment and overseas and home finance.
- *Social statistics* usually contain information on aspects of social conditions and services and education.
- *Distribution statistics*: governments also collect and publish information on distribution such as information on numbers, sizes, type and turnover of different types of retail outlets.
- *Production statistics* provide information on employment; wages and salaries; stocks; capital expenditure; purchases of materials and fuel; sales and work done.
- *Economic trends* usually contain information on aspects such as the value of imports and exports; volume of retail sales; index of production; retail prices; gross domestic product; personal disposal of income; saving and borrowing; consumer expenditure; investment; relationship of stocks and output and changes in stocks.
- *Household expenditure*: these types of government surveys collect information on household expenditure on about 100 grouped items and are analysed by factors such as household income, household composition, occupation and age of the head of the household.

- *Overseas trade statistics* involve a summary of imports and exports by commodities and countries.
- *Business monitors*: the object of individual business monitors is to bring together the most up-to-date official statistical information covering production, imports and exports relating to a particular industry. Most countries produce such information, and in the UK, such monitors cover:

  - *The Production Series* detailing such items as food, drink and tobacco; coal and petroleum products; chemicals and allied industries; metal manufacture; engineering; textiles; clothing and footwear; printing and publishing; timber; furniture; pottery; glass and cement.
  - *The Service and Distribution Series* covering food shops; clothing and footwear shops; durable goods shops; catering trades; and finance houses.
  - *The Miscellaneous Series* detaining motor vehicle registrations; cinema; insurance companies; overseas travel and tourism; acquisitions and mergers and company finance.

Government statistics are collected for the purposes of government, and not specifically for marketing firms. Consequently, such data may not always fit a particular marketing purpose and may have to be extensively modified or re-tabulated to be of use. A further point is that many of these statistics have been collected by government for general macro-economic policy making. For such decision making, broad aggregates of data are usually sufficient, and various government agencies will often use a number of assumptions and conventions when compiling statistics which can affect their validity, especially when they are used out of context in situations other than those for which they were originally compiled. Government statistics are generally free of charge and are a useful information source which must be used prudently when making marketing plans. Detail of the range and sources of government-published information in different countries is beyond the scope of this text but can be found in appropriate marketing research texts.

Trade associations and other bodies

There is a wide variety of statistics on particular trades or industries issued by trade associations, chambers of commerce and other bodies. Generally, these statistics are issued only to the members of such associations, depending on what they make or sell. Data available from such sources are more detailed than government statistics and relate to a narrower field, e.g. statistics issued by a trade association for tool manufacturers would include figures for volume and value of the production of various tools. They will also show the destination of manufactured tools exported from rival countries, and this gives valuable leads as to the areas where there is a market for such products.

Other published information

Statistics are only part of desk research. A great deal of information can be obtained from published reports, yearbooks and reference books on relevant subjects. This is a wide field, but researchers know where to look for such information and find the information services of technical and reference libraries and city business libraries useful sources. Such sources, however, are researched and authored by consultants and there are cost implications in using them.

Official handbooks

In most countries or regions, 'official' books give a mass of general background information on that country e.g. *Hong Kong – an Official Handbook*, issued by the Hong Kong government. Similar publications are available for most countries and are normally provided free of charge from information departments of embassies. If one is carrying out research relating to a particular country, such a handbook will supply general background data.

Directories

A wide range of trade and regional directories lists information on businesses in a particular trade or a particular town or area. Even a classified telephone directory can yield a wealth of information in terms of listing contact details of companies providing a variety of products and services under different alphabetical headings e.g. electric motors; electrical appliances – rental and hire; electrical appliances – repairs and parts; electrical components and wiring; electrical engineers; electrical inspecting and testing; electrical supplies, etc.

Economic surveys

As well as government, banks and Chambers of Commerce, stockbrokers often issue reports on a particular industry, mainly in relation to those firms whose shares are quoted. Sometimes findings of research sponsored by a firm or trade association are published and many such reports are provided by national or local newspapers.

International sources

- *The United Nations*: apart from its political role, the UN operates through many agencies. Those which concern the industrial and trade researcher are the United Nations Development Programme (UNDP) and the United Nations Industrial Development Organization (UNIDO) both of which are mainly concerned with helping the progress of developing countries. Each has an international staff and is engaged in a wide variety of international operations. To support these operations, regular research is undertaken and reports are published on industrial and commercial problems throughout the world.
- *International bodies*: apart from organizations sponsored by the UN there are some which are associated with the UN and others which are independent but co-operate. Such sources are generally very reliable and the main ones are:
  - *World Health Organization (WHO)* is mainly concerned with world health problems such as combating disease and giving guidance on hygiene. Its activities are of interest to marketing people who are engaged in the pharmaceutical trade.
  - *International labour Office (ILO)* is principally concerned with trying to find work and create employment in under-developed areas. To a certain extent, its activities run parallel with those of UNDP and UNIDO, but it concentrates mostly upon employment and training labour.

- *World Trade Organization (WTO)* is mainly concerned with international negotiations on trade and tariff reforms, but also issues publications on trade and industry.
- *European through Eurostat Union* is mainly concerned with the development of trade and industry in Europe. It has a range of publications on trade and industrial issues that are mainly concerned with Europe. Since non-European countries have ties with the European Union, some publications also have studies and reports on other countries' activities.
- *Food and Agricultural Organization (FAO)*: associated with food and agriculture is the use of fertilizers and insecticides.
- *Organization for Economic Co-operation and Development (OECD)*: this organization's objective is to achieve in Europe the highest sustainable growth, employment and standard of living, to contribute to economic development and to expand world trade on a multi-lateral and non-discriminatory basis. As a result, the OECD produces many publications like *Food Marketing and Economic Growth* and *Organizing and Operating a Voluntary Food Agency*.

Companies House

Information about all UK limited companies can be accessed at Companies House or in person or through agencies that conduct searches for a fee, or online. Most developed countries have their equivalent of Companies House whereby information can be found on registered companies in that country. There are many private suppliers of information on registered companies in different parts of the world.

Miscellaneous

Examples here include company annual reports, promotion and publicity literature and competitors' price lists. Visits to trade exhibitions are a useful way of gathering this material as well as giving the opportunity to study competitors' products and promotional material at first hand. A further source of information is published market research reports. These can be purchased when required, examples being Economic Intelligence Unit reports, Euromonitor (which produces reports on European markets), Henley Centre for Forecasting and MINTEL publications surveys whose reports cover a number of different markets, usually four or five in each publication, although periodically a whole issue is devoted to one market. They give many useful comments, statistics and predictions and the work of compilation is carried out by market researchers employed by MINTEL or commissioned from other professional market research firms.

'Off–the-peg' research data

In addition to the variety of published secondary research data, a company may decide to make use of syndicated research data usually purchased from a marketing research company which itself has carried out certain surveys. This type of data is a 'hybrid', falling somewhere between true secondary data and primary data. The difference between this type of data and **primary data** that is collected by the company itself through primary research, is that data are normally not collected for an individual client, but rather are sold to whoever will buy. For this reason, such data is often referred to as 'off-the-peg' research data. The following are examples of such data.

Consumer panels serve the purpose of providing marketers with a continuous check on the market and a record of the behaviour of consumers and their reactions to changes in household products, methods of marketing or advertising. They comprise a reasonably permanent set of consumers, consisting of a sample of consumers selected on a statistical basis to represent accurately a cross-section of the target market. In the UK, the Attwood Consumer Panel consists of 5,000 consumers in Great Britain and 500 women in Northern Ireland. Members of the panel are defined by age, ACORN group, social class and income group. Each member of the panel is given a diary in which he/she records information on all household product purchases such as products and brands bought, prices paid, from which retailer, day and time of purchase, promotional offers, etc. This information is then fed back to the market research company, usually via a computer link, for detailed analysis, thus providing manufacturers and advertisers with a continuous check on the market and a record of the behaviour of consumers and their reactions to changes in products, methods of marketing or advertising.

Panellists return the diary to the market research organization who then sells reports of this activity to individual manufacturers. Diaries are intended to reveal:

- the performance of brands;
- the total number of people buying specific products;
- sales volume by type of shop and geographical area;
- the effect of promotions, price changes or competition;
- consumer purchasing patterns concerning brand switching.

Brand barometers are a service offered by market research firms to subscribers on a quarterly basis. Each covers a particular market, e.g. the private motorist's market or the household products market. In each market barometer, a range of products is covered; in the household products market, areas such as pet foods, bread, cereals and cleaning materials are included. Respondents are questioned regarding purchases or otherwise of each product category. Where respondents indicate they have purchased within a commodity class they will be questioned as to when, what brand and from which retail outlet. Data in brand barometers is analysed by geographical area, age, social class and Acorn categories.

Retail audit research is a well tried method of research that was first started by A.C. Nielsen Company in the USA, but is now applied in most countries. The principle is that an inventory is made at regular intervals of the stock and purchases of certain products at selected retail outlets in such fields as food, confectionery and cigarettes. This detailed inventory is carried out by field researchers with the co-operation of retailers, who are remunerated for their help. The audits are accurate and provide a picture of what the trade buys and sells and the quantities it carries in stock. Once the manufacturer's products leave the company, there is a time lag before they are bought and consumed. The longer this gap becomes, the more difficult it is for the producer to exercise control over supply to meet changes in demand and modify production. By the process of adding purchase invoices to opening stocks and then deducting closing stocks, sales of each item can then be determined.

Reports issued to subscribers are along these lines:

- retail purchases by brand and by product;
- retail stocks by brand and by product;
- consumer sales by brand and by product;
- percentage of shops handling the product;
- percentage of shops out of stock of various brands;
- retail and wholesale prices of various products;
- average size of retail order from average retailers;
- proportion of retailers buying direct from manufacturers and from wholesalers;
- display material, promotion and advertising carried out for various brands.

Nielsen claim this gives a better understanding of consumer behaviour and preferences; increases **up-selling** (i.e. satisfying the customer with a better and more expensive product than had been initially envisaged) and **cross-selling** opportunities (i.e. selling other products in addition to the ones that have been purchased); gains a comprehensive analysis covering consumers, brands, retailers and promotion and pricing practices; integrates sales, consumer profiles and attitudinal data; compares online and off-line performance and gains visibility into distribution gaps, competitive strongholds and pricing disparities to uncover tactical opportunities.

This is now a competitive market and several companies as well as Nielsen provide retail audit type services and data, increasingly providing information online. Websites enable the marketer to access a wide range of information sources quickly.

THE MARKETING RESEARCH SYSTEM

This is the final input to the MkIS and the method used can be one, or a combination of observation, **experimentation** and **survey research**.

Observation

The generation of primary data is based on watching and sometimes recording market-related behaviour. Techniques using **observation** are more suited to investigating what people do rather than why they do it. An example might be the posting of a researcher in a retail outlet to observe patterns of shopping behaviour. Another is the use of meter-recording devices in television audience research. Observational research varies from simple non-recorded personal approaches to complex, non-personal, permanently recorded ones, including the use of eye cameras and video cameras. A major advantage of observational techniques is that they may be used without the observed respondent's knowledge. This is particularly useful when such knowledge would influence or bias the results, or where perhaps respondents would not be willing to participate at all. Understandably, use of observation without the knowledge of the respondents raises a number of ethical and legal issues.

Several commercial research companies have introduced an observational marketing research service whereby a researcher actually moves in and lives with a selected family for a few days. During this time, the observer will note details of product and brand usage by the family followed up by a detailed analysis and report for the client. This relatively new approach to marketing research is often referred to as 'sleeping with the customer' (not literally we would add); the researcher actually lives with the subject family for several days including overnight stays. The idea is that this provides very rich data on how customers actually use products and brands in their everyday lives. After a time it is argued that the family will begin to forget they are being observed and simply proceed as normal.

Observational research is now well established in marketing. Lee and Broderick[4] argue that the potential for this marketing research approach is heightened by developments in technology which for example enable much more effective recording and interpretation of the behaviour of customers.

Experimentation

This is a more formal approach to primary data collection. As in any experimental design, the essence of this approach is to determine causal relationships between factors and to support or refute hypotheses about these relationships. The most usual marketing research application is that of test marketing. This is a technique in which the product under study is placed on sale in one or more selected localities or areas and its reception by consumers and the trade is observed, recorded and analysed. Performance in test markets gives some indication of performance to be expected when the product goes into general distribution and it includes likely sales and profitability of the product when marketed on a national scale, and feasibility of the marketing operation, meaning the soundness and integration of all elements that enter into it.

It is often an economic necessity to reduce new product risk by using one or more small and relatively self-contained marketing areas, wherein the marketer can apply a full-plan marketing strategy in order to gain at least a reasonably reliable indication that the product can be sold profitably in the eventual total marketplace.

The problem with the experimental approach to marketing is the difficulty of designing and administering the experiment in a scientific way. It is difficult controlling extraneous factors that might affect test results. The marketer may want to use experimentation to assess the impact on sales of different prices. It would seem relatively simple to do this by running several test markets using different prices while holding the other elements of the marketing mix constant. In these circumstances, any differences in sales between the test markets would be purely down to differences in prices. However, extraneous factors may serve to interfere with results and hence confound the marketer's assessment of the effect of different prices. For example, a competitor may introduce a special promotional offer in the test market region, or perhaps a local major employer in the test market area may suddenly lay off many workers thereby depressing the local economy. Such uncontrollable factors can affect experimentation results in marketing.

Mystery/secret shopping

Marketing research companies contract with retailers, banks, restaurants, beauty salons, motor dealerships, hotels, etc. to provide mystery or secret shopping evaluations. A shopper poses as a 'real' customer and goes to a particular outlet and evaluates the service received according to some pre-determined criteria. The mystery shopper is normally an independent contractor from an agency. Discretion and a good eye for detail are requirements of a good mystery shopper.

Companies might want to monitor staff product knowledge, availability of goods and services, response to promotional campaigns, compliance to standards of service and procedures, cleanliness of the premises, attitudes of staff to customers or the time it takes to obtain service.

Many customers have their first dealings with business over the telephone. Telephone call surveys provide a report and digital recording of each call. Online mystery shopping evaluates matters like access response time and the quality of response to e-mails and the efficiency of the website. Similarly, postal mystery shopping can reveal the speed and quality of a request for information. Secret video surveyors can film staff in everyday situations and then report this back to the sponsoring company.

The results of a mystery shopping programme can give an opportunity to gauge employee effectiveness in terms of performance and indicate areas where training might benefit employees or where there might be a need for action on the part of management.

Neuromarketing

Recently, marketers, and in particular, market researchers, have begun to explore the potential for using technologies which get inside the mind of customers in order to understand their buying behaviour. Senior *et al.*[5] refer to this approach as *mapping the mind*. Many of these technologies are used by members of the medical profession and in particular neuroscience. Fugate[6] designed a system to explore how the brain works in relation to marketing. Other technologies include functional magnetic resonance imaging (fMRI) which measures activity in parts of the brain; electroencephalography (EEG), another technique for measuring brain activity; and techniques for measuring heart rate, respiratory rate and galvanic skin responses. According to Kenning *et al.*,[7] fMRI in particular looks promising for the market researcher. Using these techniques the neuromarketer is hoping to be able to assess the effects of aspects such as different colours or packaging, different advertising copy platforms, different tastes etc., on customers' most deep-seated physical and cognitive processes. In fact, the idea of **neuromarketing** research is not new. Marketers were using the psychogalvanometer (lie detector) in their research as long ago as the 1950s. Although in its early days, neuromarketing research techniques are appealing and innovative.

Survey research

Survey research, based on sampling and questioning respondents, represents, both in volume and value terms perhaps the most important method of collecting data and covers: customer attitudes, customer buying habits, market trends and potential market size. Unlike experimental research, survey research is aimed at generating descriptive rather than causal data; unlike observational research, survey research usually involves consumers actively engaging with the researcher. Because of the importance and diversity of survey research in marketing, it is on this particular aspect that we now concentrate.

Sampling: contact with consumers and users is fundamental to marketing research. It is impractical and expensive to interview more than a proportion of the total who might purchase. This total number is known statistically as the 'universe' or the 'population'. In marketing terms, it comprises the total number of actual and potential users of a particular product or service. The total number of consumers who could be interviewed is known as the 'sample frame', while the number of people who are actually interviewed is referred to as the 'sample'. Scientific sampling techniques aim to achieve samples that are reflections, in miniature, of the universe from which they are drawn i.e. a microcosm of the universe.

If we can define clearly the universe or population to which the study relates, we have then to see if there is a suitable frame. If random or systematic sampling is to be used in a market survey, the availability of a suitable sampling frame is of prime importance. National lists, such as the Register of Electors, fall out of date, while commercial directories and professional registers are only reflections of subscribers or members who may not represent the entire population.

For example sampling companies from a local business directory would only encompass those businesses that have felt it necessary or useful to be listed in the directory, thereby leaving out perhaps smaller businesses who cannot afford to subscribe, or better established businesses who feel they do not need to. In this way the sampling frame is not representative.

Five criteria are important when evaluating sampling frames:

1   Size: is it big enough?
2   Completeness: *all* units of a population under survey should be included.
3   Accuracy: totally up-to-date sampling frames are rarely available. The frame may contain units which no longer exist.
4   Duplication: bias will result where names of sampling units occur more than once, e.g. some firms may have multiple listings in telephone directories.
5   Convenience: sampling lists should be accessible and suitable for sampling purposes.

Basic statistics texts explain random sampling, systematic sampling, multi-stage sampling, cluster sampling, stratified sampling and quota sampling along with an understanding of how deviation or bias can enter into a sample and its potential effects upon the results of a survey.

Contact methods Contact methods are a balance between time, the degree of accuracy required and costs.

■   *Personal interviews* can be formal '**on-street**' or '**mall intercept**' surveys using structured questionnaires and a less structured 'depth' or 'focus' interview format that is done at the interviewee's home or in a group setting.
■   *Postal surveys* demand a straightforward formalized questionnaire as personal intervention is not possible to explain questioning areas which might be unclear.
■   *Telephone interviews* are popular owing to relatively low costs, especially for consumer research, but increasingly for B2B industrial research as respondents might be geographically spread, so travel costs are eliminated.

Contact medium: the questionnaire This cannot be designed until precise information requirements are known. It is the vehicle whereby research objectives are translated into specific questions.

The type of information sought and the type of respondents to be researched will have a bearing on the contact method to be used. This will influence whether the questionnaire is an unstructured schedule of discussion points for depth interviewing or a structured closed-ended type questionnaire for 'on-street' interviews.

Qualitative research

Data such as market size, numbers of competitors and average purchasing prices provide hard data on market facts. Marketers are also interested in **qualitative** data on markets and customers. This data encompasses areas like underpinning customer attitudes, customer perceptions and beliefs, psychological and sociological influences on consumer behaviour, and such techniques are aimed at providing this information.

Marketers have used several techniques for researching these more complex aspects. Many have been adapted from psychology and sociology. In the 1960s for example, marketers began to use what became collectively referred to as **motivation research**. Examples of specific techniques include thematic apperception, Rorschach ink-blot tests and word association tests. During the 1980s and 1990s many of these techniques fell into disrepute and motivation research in general was used less and less by marketers who felt it to be unscientific. Two techniques of qualitative research which remain viable and widely used are focus groups and depth interviews that were discussed in Chapter 7, Marketing Communications.

Marketers have again begun to look at innovative research techniques to gather and analyse qualitative data. Futures research, described earlier, is a good example. In the main, marketers are becoming more amenable to innovative techniques of qualitative market research if they afford insights into the underpinning behavioural processes and attitudes of customers.

Guinness is a good example of a company that has been willing to try out new techniques of qualitative research to try and find out customers' innermost thoughts. Guinness's research company have used techniques such as role playing, psychodramas and psycho-drawing in this process. Some of the findings from this research have found their way into multi-million pound advertising campaigns for the Guinness brand. Using this research, Guinness found that many of their customers drank Guinness because they felt it set them aside from the crowd. Many Guinness drinkers apparently see themselves as individuals. The famous Guinness 'It's not easy being a dolphin' advertisements starring Rutger Hauer were the result of this type of research.

INDUSTRIAL MARKETING RESEARCH (B2B)

Marketing research is traditionally associated with consumer goods. However, industrial goods marketers face similar problems – assessing market size and share; identifying customer needs; ascertaining the most appropriate price structure and determining levels of competitive activity. As we saw in Chapter 2 the principal differences between consumer and organizational buyer behaviour are motives for purchase and the context within which buying takes place. With this background in mind, it is useful to consider some differences in emphasis in relation to marketing problems:

- marketing mix emphasis, where purchasers of consumer products are more affected by appearance, packaging and advertising and often buy on impulse. Industrial goods purchasers are more concerned with quality, performance, specifications, price and delivery;
- different end uses of industrial products, which include finished articles like machine tools or fuel injection systems for cars, and components which need further work in order for them to fit into an end product (e.g. castings which will then require machining and polishing);
- customer requirements which can vary according to how closely they specify e.g. some specify dimensions, materials and tolerances, whereas others may simply purchase standard parts of materials.

It follows that industrial marketing research is more concerned with researching individual buyers and more use is made of depth interviews. These are costly, as more skilled interviewers must be used and respondents tend to be more widely scattered. Such disadvantages are offset against 'richer' data that can be generated.

In industrial marketing research it is less possible to generalize, as too much depends on such factors as numbers of potential customers. For example, a total market may contain six large buyers who make 70 per cent of all purchases, and 50 small buyers who make the other 30 per cent. In such a situation it would be sensible to census survey the six large buyers and sample the 50 smaller buyers.

INTERNATIONAL MARKETING RESEARCH

As we shall see in Chapter 16 there are added complexities when marketing across international frontiers. These include the process of marketing research. Differences in the availability and quality of secondary data are important considerations, so care should be taken to verify the accuracy of such data. Social and marketing practices differ widely between countries, as can political and commercial institutions and of course, language.

In researching export markets, it is important to note that conditions may vary from country to country so each has to be investigated individually. It is important not to assume that because a product or service is a commercial success in one country, it will automatically be so in another. This is true even of countries that share similar customs, lifestyles and languages. There are examples where, because some basic but small difference has been overlooked, a great deal of money and effort on the part of the exporter has been wasted. For example, German male customers usually want their trousers to be fully lined to the knee. In the UK this is unusual. In China the colour for mourning is white; in most other parts of the world it is black. Similarly, in certain parts of Africa the colour red is considered unlucky. Quite simply, it is easy for the marketer to miss subtle differences between cultures when marketing their products.

Even within a country, regional variations may be sufficient to require a different marketing strategy. These variations add to the complexity of research in international markets, and should be considered at a very early stage in research design. As a simple example we can define potential export markets:

- geographically;
- administratively (by divisions imposed by the company);
- by economic zones or trading blocs;
- politically.

These extra dimensions add complexity and more uncertainty to the international marketing research situation.

Before we complete our discussion of the MkIS, we are going to examine the stages in the conduct of a marketing research exercise.

THE RESEARCH BRIEF AND THE RESEARCH PROPOSAL

Before research is commissioned and undertaken it is important to ensure that the objectives, scope, time-scale and costs of the proposed research are fully understood and agreed. This is of particular importance when the marketing research is to be undertaken by an outside market research agency. The document which accompanies this stage of the research procedure is known as the **research brief**. The research brief should specify the nature of the problem to be investigated, the objectives of the research, research methods, analysing the results, time and budget. Most importantly, these aspects of the research must be understood and agreed between the party commissioning the research and those who will undertake it. A good brief must:

- clearly state the objectives of the research;
- mean the same to both the client and the researcher;
- not ask for irrelevant information;
- define the population to be sampled;
- state the accuracy required;
- state the variables to be measured and how these relate to the problem;
- specify analyses.

Once the research brief has been discussed and agreed, the marketing research team can then draft the *research proposal*. The main considerations here are to:

- restate the problem to confirm understanding;
- specify the research methods and reasons for choice;
- specify the sample method/size/construction/frame;
- specify the interviewing method/location/supervision;
- specify the data processing methods;
- specify the length of the survey and costs.

These responsibilities are important, because the conduct of marketing research and the decisions arising from it are the cornerstones upon which subsequent marketing policies are based. It is, therefore, important for an activity that can have an influence on the future prosperity of a company to be organized and controlled effectively.

NEED FOR AN MKIS

Marketers must increasingly consider building long-term relationships with their customers, especially those who operate in lean manufacturing environments as discussed in Chapter 9. Lead times are shorter and emphasis is now placed on quality and supplier reliability and less on price.

Lancaster[8] contends that these trends have affected all aspects of marketing. Normally dominated by the idea of the unique selling proposition, corporate marketing is now being forced to practise the small business philosophy of staying close to customers, understanding and meeting their needs and treating them well after the sale. Through having an MkIS it is possible to apply these principles in practice.

Tesco is a company that uses an effective marketing information system to get close to customers and their needs. Using their extensive database on customers, based primarily on their loyalty card scheme, Tesco are able to identify key customer groups to target special promotional offers, send direct mail shots and evaluate in-store campaigns. Often the integration of computer processes with decision making can be complex. Galliers and Sutherland[9] suggest possible reasons for this:

1   Much of the information that is gathered and communicated by individuals and organizations has little decision relevance.
2   Much of the information that is used to justify a decision is collected and interpreted after the decision has been made, or substantially made.
3   Much of the information gathered in response to requests for information is not considered in the making of decisions for which it was requested.
4   Regardless of the information available at the time a decision is first considered, more information is requested.
5   Complaints that an organization does not have enough information to make a decision occur while available information is ignored.
6   The relevance of the information provided in the decision-making process to the decision being made is less conspicuous than is the insistence on information.

In short, organizations and individuals collect more information than they can reasonably expect to use in the making of decisions. At the same time, they seem to be constantly needing or requesting more information, or complaining about inadequate information.

The authors conclude that organizations are systematically inept, or have severe limitations in understanding the nature of information and decision making. A situation exists where turbulent environments are increasing the need for information on the changes taking place. Yet, information technology does not always make the contribution it could to provide this information in a form suitable for decision makers. Technical problems of designing and implementing an MkIS are many, but it is problems faced by the user of the system that are of most importance to marketing management. These problems can be summarized under the headings of misinformation; lack of user orientation; the nature of management decision making; the user–system interface and organizational problems.

A final set of problems relates to difficulties of integrating the system into the organization. Often, systems are designed which fail in their implementation, not due to failures of the system, but because of the designer's ignorance of how it will be used. This can be a problem with systems where marketing decisions affect other parts of the organization. After all, marketing decisions relate to customers, and customers are the starting point of all business planning in a marketing orientated organization. This 'boundary spanning' role is an essential aspect of an integrated marketing approach, but is often resisted by departments who guard their own power in the form of information they control. Clearly, management support at board level is necessary to overcome such problems. Overcoming these problems, especially the problem of too much information from the system, needs careful system design.

A well designed information and decision support system should:

- Be based on a careful appraisal and analysis of the decision making requirements of marketing management. This involves establishing what types of marketing decisions are made, what sorts of information are required for these decisions and how this information is to be supplied. Clearly, this involves consulting end users of the system before it is designed and implemented.
- Be designed to be 'user-friendly'. Information is wasted if it cannot be used. A problem in the provision of information to marketing is that often the system is designed to suit the information specialist rather than the decision maker.
- Be designed to be 'interactive' and allow analysis rather than simply be a system for retrieval of information.
- Be cost effective. Information costs money, so an effective system of marketing information supply should be based on a careful evaluation of how the system will contribute to more cost-effective marketing decisions.

It is by paying attention to these key areas of the design of the marketing information system that potential problems of having information overload or the system being too costly can be minimized.

APPLICATION OF AN MKIS

Tactical applications are in areas like customer loyalty measures, generation of sales leads, testing price levels, promotional effectiveness and customer segmentation. When analysing the most profitable consumer profile for a product or service, the analyst can locate a list of actual and prospective customers with those characteristics. Promotional material can then be targeted to the specific needs of the identified market segments.

Sales force activities can be better co-ordinated by selecting the contact tactics most suitable for different groups of customers. Customer loyalty can be built up through logging all customer contacts which will provide an opportunity for repeat sales and maximizing sales of other company product lines. For example, through an effective marketing information system the marketer can build up a detailed profile of customers for the sales force. This can include details such as: the composition

TABLE 12.2 Strategic application of an MkIS

Competitive opportunity	Marketing strategy	Role of information
1 Changing the basis of competition	Market development or penetration, Increased margins, Alternative sales channels, Reducing cost structure	Prospect/customer information, Targeted marketing, Better control
2 Strengthen customer relationships	Tailored customer service, Providing value to customer, Product differentiation, Create switching costs	Know customer needs, 'Individual' promotions, Response handling, Identify potential needs, Customers as 'users' of your system
3 Strengthen buyer/supplier relationships	Superior market information, Decreased cost of sales, Providing value to supplier, Pass stockholding to supplier	Internal/external data, Optimization of sales channels, Measure supplier performance, Identify areas of inefficiency
4 Build barriers to new entrants	Unique distribution channels, Unique valued services, Create entry costs	Knowledge of market allows improved service and value, 'Lock in' customers, suppliers and intermediaries, Immediate response to threats
5 Create new or substitute products	Market led product development, Alliance opportunities, New products/services	Market gap analysis, Customer dialogue, User innovation, Information as a product

and operation of the decision-making unit (DMU), company-specific purchasing policies and procedures, average order size and effects of special promotions. Clearly, this type of information puts the salesperson in a much stronger position when approaching and selling to customers.

Strategic applications where information is used to develop strategic plans especially in areas of targeting, new product development and direct marketing. An effective MkIS generates huge amounts of customer and market data. It thus has the potential to input into marketing policy and can be seen to operate strategically when its information is used in the ways illustrated in Table 12.2.

DEVELOPMENTS IN MARKETING INFORMATION SYSTEMS TECHNOLOGY: DATABASES

Technological developments have had a major impact on marketing information systems. These developments are underpinned by relatively cheap yet sophisticated computing power which is facilitating improvements in data collection storage, manipulation and retrieval. A technology that speeds up results from a market research survey uses computer assisted telephone interviewing that provides instant data feedback to the control centre as interviews are conducted and questionnaires completed through a hand-held computer in a wireless Internet location.

Databases Developments in information collection, storage and analysis are making information an important competitive asset. The key to this information revolution is the use of **databases** in marketing. Essentially, a database represents a pool of information on markets and customers which can be interrogated and analysed to facilitate improved marketing decision making. Databases are not new, as even a system of manual sales records kept on customers in a filing cabinet is a database.

A database can be built from a variety of sources. Examples include customer orders, loyalty cards, customer enquiries, subscription lists and ad hoc market research studies. There is a wealth of information available to the point of it being overwhelming. Not only do modern database techniques and technologies help to overcome this problem, but we now know much more about the key factors in developing and using successful databases. In developing a database attention needs to be paid to:

- clear and specific objectives for the database, including types of information required and why;
- effective systems and strategies for data capture;
- effective systems for data storage, including database maintenance;
- effective systems of analysis and interpretation of data to provide information for decision making.

Data capture involves systems for providing and collecting data for the database and includes many of the sources mentioned above. Marketers use sophisticated IT-based data collection techniques. In some countries there is legislation relating to the collection and use of data on customers which is designed to cover customers' rights in several respects with regard to such data. Online sales enable the marketer to capture more information than shop-based transactions because the customer provides their address, email, telephone and mobile numbers, etc. as a matter of course, whereas many shops do not do this.

Data warehousing is a term used to describe collecting data on customers and markets from several possible sources in a company and storing it in one central database. This has developed because companies have different departments in the organization, each of which has a unique database that is not always made available to the rest of the organization.

Data mining enables the marketer to use database information in ways to improve the effectiveness of segmentation and targeting, promotion and direct marketing strategies as well as the development of relationship marketing strategies. Marketing managers can now use statistical analysis and modelling techniques to look for important patterns of cause and effect in the database through data mining.

Some companies, because of the nature of their business, have considerable information on their customers which can be used effectively through data mining. Banks and credit card companies are good examples. A company such as the logistics company, Federal Express, has a wealth of information encompassing not only their card holders' personal details, but also what purchases they are making at what price, how often and from where. Imagine how information like this can be used by the marketer: for example, to develop direct marketing programmes, design new products to meet specific customer needs, target specific customer groups and adjust the marketing mix.

It is important to ensure that databases are regularly maintained and updated. Customers and information on them change all the time and if the database contains inaccurate information we run the risk of making wrong or embarrassing decisions. One of the most embarrassing effects of obsolete database information is where direct mail is sent to a deceased person's address perhaps offering the chance of a 'holiday of a life-time'.

SUMMARY

It is becoming increasingly important for marketing management to have up-to-date information to carry out its tasks. Marketing is becoming increasingly proactive, and must seek to identify changes and trends in the macro-environment and then translate these into action plans. In order to carry out this task, the concept of the marketing information system (MkIS) has been developed and this forms an integral part of the corporate management information system (MIS).

Inputs to the MkIS are:

- the internal accounting system;
- the marketing intelligence system;
- the marketing research system;
- the analytical marketing system which is the output.

Internal accounting information is collected as is market intelligence, the latter particularly by the field sales force, and this inputs to the MkIS. Marketing research should be well planned from a good research brief to provide tactical and strategic information, also an input to the MkIS. Developments in marketing information systems technology and databases have helped to develop sophisticated marketing information systems which are useful for marketing planning purposes as will be demonstrated in Chapters 13, 14 and 15.

KEY TERMS

Marketing information system (MkIS)	370	Marketing research system	372
Situation analysis	370	Analytical marketing system	372
Decision support system (DSS)	372	Secondary data sources	375
Management information system (MIS)	372	Primary data	378
Internal accounting system	372	'Off-the-peg' research data	379
Marketing intelligence system	372	Consumer panel	379
		Brand barometer	379
		Retail audit research	379

. . . *continued*

CASE STUDY

Dashdish

John Oldfield is feeling under pressure. His desk is covered with market research reports, data from the accounts department regarding sales and profits figures, sales representatives' records and reports for the last three months, and any number of secondary reports, including government publications, Chamber of Commerce reports and bank reports pertaining to his company's product markets. His problem is that he simply cannot make sense of what it all means. His boss, the marketing director of Dashdish, has asked John to sort through all this information, which was previously on the marketing director's own desk, and to come up with a report that makes sense of it all. The marketing director's view is that there is plenty of information to go on, and that some of it must mean something for the company. John is not even sure what information his marketing director wants, and why, let alone what the format and precise content should be.

Having studied at the local university for a marketing qualification, which helped John secure his job as a marketing assistant, he is convinced that the company needs a properly designed marketing information system. He is aware that the marketing director feels it is simply a question of getting lots of information and then sifting through it. John feels his first priority will be to explain to his director the nature and purpose of a modern marketing information system in a company and the key facets in the design and operation of such a system. He has decided to write a brief report setting out his thoughts on these matters for his marketing director.

CASE STUDY QUESTION

Write the report.

REFERENCES

1 Kotler, P. and Keller, K. (2009), *Marketing Management*, 13th edn, London: Prentice-Hall, p. 107.

2 Gounaris, S.P., Panigayrakis, G.G. and Chatzipanagiotou. K.C. (2007), 'Measuring the effectiveness of marketing information systems: an empirically validated instrument', *Marketing Intelligence and Planning*, 25(6): 612–31.

3 Lancaster, G. and Massingham, L.C. (2002), *Essentials of Marketing*, 4th edn, Maidenhead: McGraw-Hill, pp. 175–6.

4 Lee, N. and Broderick, A.J. (2007), 'The past, present and future of observational research in marketing', *Qualitative Market Research*, 10(2): 121–9.

5 Senior, C., Smyth, H., Cooke, R., Shaw, R.L. and Peel, E. (2007), 'Mapping the mind for the modern market researcher', *Qualitative Market Research: An International Journal*, 10(2): 153–67.

6 Fugate, D.L. (2007), 'Neuromarketing; a layman's look at neuroscience and its potential application to marketing practice', *Journal of Consumer Marketing*, 24(7): 385–94.

7 Kenning, P., Plassman, H. and Ahlert, D. (2007), 'Applications of functional magnetic resonance imaging for marketing research', *Qualitative Market Research: An International Journal*, 10(2): 135–52.

8 Lancaster, G. (1993), 'Marketing and engineering: can there ever be synergy?', *Journal of Marketing Management*, 9: 141–53.

9 Galliers, R.D. and Sutherland, A.R. (2009), 'The evolving information systems strategy', in Galliers, R.D., Leidner, E.D. and Baker, B.S.H. (eds), *Strategic Information Management*, 2nd edn, pp. 31–60.

Chapter 13

Analysing the environment

(Opportunities and threats) and appraising resources
(strengths and weaknesses)

LEARNING OBJECTIVES

After reading this chapter you will:

■ appreciate the importance of analysing the environment in the development of strategic marketing plans

■ understand the range and types of key environmental factors

■ be familiar with a systematic approach to identifying forecasting and appraising environmental forces and factors

■ appreciate the key importance of assessing competitors and competitive industry structure in the development of strategic marketing plans

■ be aware of the importance of appraising the resources of a company

■ comprehend how this appraisal should be organized and conducted

■ recognize how Strengths and Weaknesses assessment feeds into and affects the process of strategic market planning

■ understand how to translate the internal appraisal into an assessment of the Opportunities and Threats elements of the SWOT analysis

INTRODUCTION

In Chapter 1 we outlined the nature and significance of strategic marketing together with an introduction to the essential components of analysis, planning, implementation and control required to develop a strategic approach to this function. We now return to this strategic theme by looking at the importance of analysing the environment for strategic marketing. Changes and trends in the environment are the primary source of major marketing opportunities and threats so it is essential that the strategic marketer monitors, interprets and responds to such changes and trends. However, the word 'environment' encompasses many factors, often complexly linked, which affect the survival of any enterprise. Specifically, this chapter examines the range of environmental factors, discusses how to assess the impact of these factors, and suggests a framework for environmental scanning.

The identification of opportunities and threats represents one half of SWOT analysis. The other half entails the appraisal of organizational resources in order to ascertain strengths and weaknesses. As shown in Chapter 1, assessment of possible opportunities and threats and the appraisal of strengths and weaknesses only make sense if we consider both internal and external factors together. It is difficult for the individual company to assess the strategic implications of environmental trends and changes and the extent to which they will pose opportunities or threats, without considering these trends and changes in the context of organizational resources. In addition, selection and implementation of strategies are dependent on organizational strengths and weaknesses. Resource analysis and assessment of organizational strengths and weakness that stem from this analysis are a key task of strategic marketing management. This important task poses a difficult and complex dilemma.

IMPORTANCE OF ANALYSING THE ENVIRONMENT

Consider the following:

- Problems with processing nuclear waste at the Sellafield plant in Cumbria in the UK has had a profound effect on attitudes towards the nuclear power industry.
- The future of the pound sterling remains uncertain whilst Britain decides whether or not it will ultimately recommend adoption of the Euro currency.
- The near collapse of the banking system in 2009 had worldwide repercussions.
- Global warming and the melting of the ice caps has had a profound effect on attitudes towards 'green issues'.

- In the UK more than half of homes have access to the Internet and the percentage is growing.
- Discussions about expanding the European Union to include more former Eastern European bloc countries and Turkey continues.
- Marketers have been faced with an expansion in the 'grey market' where their products and brands are bought and sold in international markets outside conventional channels and therefore their control.

These are a small selection of 'environmental' forces and factors that have had (or will have) an impact upon the marketing strategies of many companies. Not every company will be affected by these specific trends and changes, nor will all companies be affected equally. What is certain is that changes and trends in the environment of a company, such as those listed, give rise to some of the most significant opportunities and threats that an organization faces. Companies that have failed to recognize and take account of changes in their environment have failed to capitalize on opportunities or have realized that their markets have disappeared with the closure of factories and redundancies.

The importance of environmental analysis is self-evident, but if further confirmation of this importance is required this can be underlined by tracing through an example of failure to identify and respond to environmental change.

Marks & Spencer were, until the late 1990s, one of the most successful clothing and food retailers in the United Kingdom. Since then, the company has faced increasing problems with regard to sales and profits. Marks & Spencer are still faced with sluggish sales and reduced market share. There are several reasons for this, but it has been suggested that the company has not kept pace with changing market and customer needs. In particular, critics have argued that many of its product ranges are not fashionable enough. Certainly, over the past decade the company has faced increasing competition both from domestic and overseas retailers who have entered the UK with exciting merchandising and retail formats. In the food area, the competitive advantages which Marks & Spencer once had, such as being amongst the first to offer good quality ready-made/chilled foods, are being eroded. The company now recognizes that it is operating in a different trading environment and has embarked on a series of major changes in its approach to sourcing, merchandising and marketing. It is experimenting with new formats for its stores, new merchandising and ranges and major television advertising campaigns. In addition the company has made several major changes to its management structure from the chief executive down. It remains to be seen whether these changes will be sufficient to restore its former market position.

This example illustrates the negative effects or threats posed to companies by changes in their marketing environment, or rather their failure to respond to these changes. Equally, environmental trends and changes can give rise to major marketing opportunities, even to the extent of spawning whole new industries.

An example of major opportunities arising out of technological, economic and social changes has been the growth of the Internet. Technological developments linked to social and economic changes such as a desire to work more from home, have combined to facilitate the growth of new companies, using Internet technologies to market their products and services direct to customers. Companies like Amazon have shown exceptional growth.

This illustrates that environmental trends and changes are important in posing major opportunities or threats to organizations. Some of these environmental trends and changes are long term and take place gradually, but some take place extremely rapidly and are more difficult to predict. The environment comprises a wide range of factors, the relationships between which are complex. Our first step in analysing the environment, therefore, is to identify and classify environmental influences.

RANGE AND LEVEL OF ENVIRONMENTAL FACTORS

The term 'environment' in the context of strategic marketing planning can be used in a variety of ways. Environmental analysis involves analysing three key environments: the external environment (i.e. macro-environment); the customer environment (i.e. micro-environment); the organization's internal environment (i.e. intra-firm environment). Marketers distinguish between different categories of environmental factors in this way. This distinction is drawn by conceptualizing successive 'layers' of the environment, as shown in Figure 13.1. This illustrates examples of key environmental influences for each successive 'layer' of the marketing function's environment. Examples of environmental

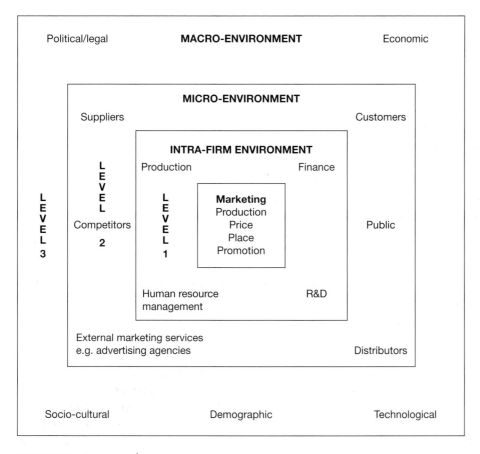

FIGURE 13.1 Layers in the environment

factors shown at each level are not the only factors, but they represent what are felt to be the key factors pertaining to each level of the environment in turn.

INTRA-FIRM ENVIRONMENT

Firms have finite resources. The marketing function has to compete with other management functions to obtain resources needed to complete its task. Similarly, the marketing function must co-operate with these other functions. This interaction and interdependency between the marketing function and other functional areas of management is the **intra-firm environment**. To understand the influence of factors in the other two layers of the environment, it is important that marketing has the ability to carry out its role of monitoring and adapting to these factors as influenced by its relationship with other functions within the company. Marketing managers make decisions that have a bearing on other functional areas of the firm. Similarly, decisions taken by other departments directly affect the ability of marketing to perform its role.

Chapter 14 examines organizational aspects of strategic marketing planning and considers how these intra-firm elements of the environment affect the marketing function.

MICRO-ENVIRONMENT

These middle-level environmental factors, which impinge on marketing management, comprise factors which unlike the lowest level intra-company components lie outside the normal boundaries of the organization. Unlike the top level, macro-environmental factors, which we shortly examine, the organization has some measure of control over its **micro-environment.** The more important elements of the micro- or task-environment include: competitors, distributors, suppliers, customers and external marketing services, e.g. market research companies and advertising agencies, and the organization's publics. Micro-environmental factors are self-explanatory, although their significance to strategy formulation is such that many of them, including competitor, customer and distributor analysis, are considered in more detail later. The micro-environmental factor 'publics' is any group that has an impact on a company's ability to achieve its objectives.

As would be expected from such a broad definition, a company's public(s) are diverse and include groups such as the local community, the general public, shareholders, the financial community in general and governments.

The key points for the marketing strategist are to acknowledge the importance of such publics to the process of planning and ensure that relationships with significant publics are effectively managed. Traditionally these relationships have been the concern and responsibility of the public relations function in companies, but many now think that this is too narrow a view and that everyone in a company can contribute to effective relationships with an organization's publics.

An example of the importance of a company's publics in developing strategic marketing plans is the increased influence and power that company shareholders now have. At one time the interest of shareholders was restricted mainly to the level of financial return and profits which they received from their investment. Increasingly, shareholders are taking a greater interest in how companies are managed, including their marketing strategies.

MACRO-ENVIRONMENT

We have considered those environmental forces and factors that are within the marketing function's organizational boundaries or in its immediate task environment. The top level of environmental factors comprises broader factors in the wider **macro-environment** of the organization over which the individual company has little or no control. It is from changes and trends in these macro-environmental factors that the most significant and far-reaching marketing opportunities and threats for the organization will stem. These are now discussed in more detail.

Socio-cultural environment

Changes and trends here present significant challenges to the strategic marketing planner. Basic beliefs, attitudes and values are shaped and conditioned by the society in which people grow up, and their general behaviour, including purchasing behaviour, is influenced by societal and cultural norms as discussed in Chapter 2.

Cultural and social values are firmly established within a society and are difficult to change. If and when they do change, they do so only slowly. In the short term they should be treated as parameters within which marketing strategies are formulated. Over longer periods we can expect some social and cultural values to have changed and these include changes in attitudes towards credit, an increasing awareness of and interest in healthy lifestyles and changes in attitudes towards women in society. Although core cultural and social values change relatively slowly some changes are more rapid e.g. attitudes towards work and leisure, the place of women in the home and at work, bringing up and disciplining children and sexual attitudes and behaviour. In some societies, political, religious and economic forces and factors still combine to limit the nature and speed at which social and cultural changes take place.

In the UK, Channel 4's *Big Brother* programme has been very successful. The programme centres on continuously observing a group of selected people living together in a house, with each week a member of the group being nominated for expulsion by the others. The programme attracts large viewing audiences, while at the same time making its participants overnight celebrities even when they are expelled. The format has been imitated by other channels including the popular *I'm a Celebrity: Get Me Out of Here*. The format of such programmes and their content would probably never have been envisaged, and certainly not have been as successful, even ten years ago. Essentially, the participants in the programme have no privacy whatsoever. The camera observes and records them 24 hours a day, seven days a week. This observation extends into the most private activities of the group, and is effectively an invasion of privacy.

The surprising success of the programme is in part due to the fact that it was a product of its time. There was a demand for this sort of voyeuristic entertainment. The somewhat ruthless nature of the expulsions satisfies some of the viewing public with regard to what is now a more aggressive and individualistic approach in society.

Political/legal environment

The outcome of political decisions can often be seen in the economic policies of governments. In the UK, major marketing opportunities and threats in recent years have stemmed from the policies and legislation of successive governments irrespective of their political hue. For example, Margaret Thatcher and then John Major's Conservative Government with its belief in the free market mechanism created significant marketing opportunities for many companies and threats for others through its policies of privatization. The Labour Government of Tony Blair and Gordon Brown which replaced it similarly created marketing opportunities through its policies regarding public–private co-operation and funding in many sectors of the economy. For the marketing strategist, what matters in a planning context is not whether these and other policies and the legislation which has accompanied them have been 'right', but more the implications for marketing strategy. Indeed, the 'melt down' of the world economy in 2009 caught all governments unawares. Not only must strategies be planned to take account of existing policies and legislation, but account must also be taken of likely future changes. It is important to realize that the political and associated legislative environment is of great significance to the marketer and is likely to have a direct bearing on the formulation of marketing strategy.

Economic environment

This is closely related to the political/legal environment and the marketing strategist must understand the variety of economic variables that can shape marketing plans.

Rates of inflation, interest rates, exchange rates, industrial output, levels of disposable income and the balance of payments are some of the factors of concern to marketing management because these influence costs, prices and demand. Not just domestic, but international economic developments and trends must be considered.

The Euro issue still dominates economic debate in the UK, and although the Conservative arm of the Conservative/Liberal Democrat coalition Government favours keeping the Pound Sterling, the Liberal Democrats favour entry to the Euro, so commitment to enter the single currency still remains. Therefore, this aspect of the economic environment continues to be a subject of debate and an area of uncertainty for companies with regard to their future planning.

Technological environment

This is a major environmental influence on marketing strategy and its influence is manifested in terms of developments and breakthroughs in technology that are the basis for new products and even new industries. Home computers, compact disc players, video recorders, i-pods and electronic cameras are just a few of the products which have emerged in recent years. Biotechnology, information technology and energy conservation are some of the new industries.

Equally important is the fact that technology also affects the way marketing is practised; e.g. in the marketing research area questionnaires can be designed and administered directly via computer terminals. Such IT developments have enabled the use of sophisticated forecasting techniques. In retailing, electronic point of sale (EPOS) data capture is now used by retailers through laser checkouts and direct transfer of funds.

Technological changes affect the way products are produced. Robotics, flexible manufacturing systems and fully automated factories are examples of the ways in which the basis for competitive advantage can be changed. So ubiquitous and far-reaching have been these technological developments that virtually every area and aspect of marketing is affected and the modern marketer must be aware of such trends and changes together with the implications for their businesses.

The physical environment

Sometimes referred to as the 'natural' or 'ecological' environment, this element of an organization's environment was, until the end of the last century, felt by many strategic planners to be of little direct relevance to the formulation of future strategies. This was primarily because it was assumed that it had little direct effect upon organizations. Recent trends and events have shown this assumption to be ill founded and myopic.

As long ago as 1962 Rachel Carson[1] warned of the dangers to the physical environment from industrial and commercial activities. Frequently such warnings were dismissed on the grounds that they represented the views of a small number of 'environmentalists' who were misguided or overly pessimistic. This 'small' number of critics proved to be in the vanguard of what has now become a popular, powerful and global movement concerned to protect the natural environment in which we live. We each have our views on issues such as the use of the world's natural resources of minerals, forests and water as well as some of the most fervently contested contemporary issues regarding phenomena like the 'greenhouse' effect, and the depletion of the ozone layer. Regardless of personal views, they have become issues for the strategic marketing planner. We have witnessed adapted aerosol products that are now 'ozone friendly', and increasingly, products and technologies are designed to be energy efficient; degradable plastic packaging is now widely available as is recyclable packing, and car manufacturers are working towards completely recyclable vehicles.

ENVIRONMENTAL SCANNING

Discussion has concentrated on reviewing the significance of environmental factors as well as a format for classifying different levels and factors associated with each level. These may impact on different industries in different ways and to a different extent. Environmental trends or changes may affect an organization and its strategic marketing planning in different ways from other organizations. Trends and changes in the environment give rise to marketing opportunities and threats. These observations suggest the requirement for an effective **environmental scanning** system: effective, in the sense of improving the process of strategic marketing planning. These requirements are:

1   an ability to identify environmental forces and factors at any point in time that are of significance to the organization, i.e. which environmental forces are likely to pose the most significant opportunities and threats to the company;
2   an ability both to monitor and forecast future trends and changes in these factors;
3   the ability to interpret the significance of these environmental trends and changes i.e. their implications for future marketing strategies;
4   the ability to develop and implement marketing strategies to respond to environmental trends and changes.

The last of these requirements is not only a requirement of an effective environmental scanning system, but also part of a broader set of issues involving the ability of the organization to cope with environmental change, encompassing organizational resources, flexibility and the quality of management. This final element is included because it illustrates the point that the sole purpose of a system of environmental scanning is that is should improve strategic marketing plans in the sense of improving the opportunity for organizational success. We now focus on requirements for an effective environmental scanning system.

Organizational practice and environmental scanning

One of the earliest studies on environmental scanning in organizations was that conducted by Francis Aguilar[2] and published in 1967. Based on a sample of selected chemical companies in Europe and America, Aguilar identified four basic patterns for scanning information about the environment:

1 *undirected viewing* representing the most unsystematic approach to environmental scanning, composed of 'exposure without a specific purpose';
2 *conditioned viewing* adopted by companies who are aware of some key factors and trends in their environment, but do not undertake active search;
3 *informed search* where companies actively collect information on their environment for specific planning and decision-making processes, but do so in an informal and ad hoc manner;
4 *formal search* representing the most highly developed environmental scanning practices. Aguilar found that some companies had a structured process for the collection of specific information for a specific purpose.

Aguilar's study showed there was a lack of a systematic approach to environmental scanning in the companies he studied, with few conducting formal searches.

Over time, more and more companies have come to develop formal scanning systems. By the mid-1980s, a study by Jain[3] suggested that although still evolving, more and more companies were beginning to develop formalized environmental scanning procedures. Jain identified four distinct phases in this evolution, namely:

Phase 1: Primitive where information is noted with no purpose and effort to scanning and little discrimination used to distinguish between strategic and non-strategic information;
Phase 2: Ad hoc where there is no formally planned scanning, but increased sensitivity to information on certain issues or events which may be explored further;
Phase 3: Reactive where scanning is still unstructured and random, but often specific information is collected with a view to making appropriate responses to markets and competition;
Phase 4: Proactive where scanning is structured and deliberate using pre-established methodologies with a view to predicting the environment for a desired future.

Perhaps the overriding reason for the slow development of formal environmental scanning and appraisal systems is that it is difficult to achieve. However, modern companies have developed skills in this area. In addition, although it was once a neglected area in the planning literature, Johnson *et al.*[4] illustrate how environmental appraisal is now the subject of more research as its importance to strategic planning has become appreciated. The development of more 'proactive' appraisal systems requires the establishment of systematic procedures designed specifically to input into strategic marketing decisions. We now consider one such system.

A framework for appraisal

A number of frameworks for environmental appraisal have been developed. In our view, one of the most useful of these is that proposed by Jain[5] and shown in Figure 13.2.

The six key steps are as follows:

1   Seek to maintain an awareness of broad trends in each of the key environmental factors outlined earlier. At this stage, scanning need not be detailed so long as trends are monitored.

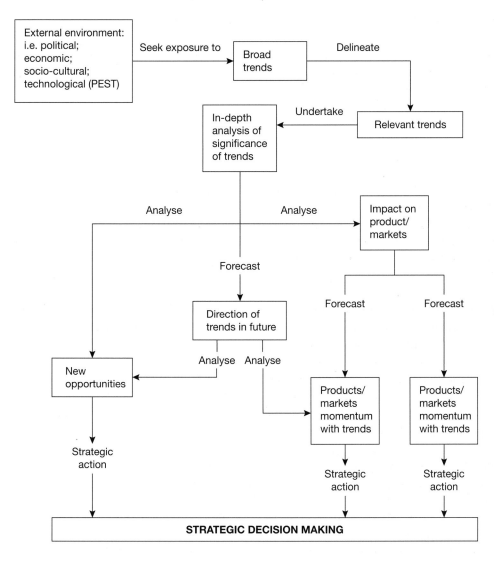

FIGURE 13.2 Environment appraisal and strategic planning

2 Delineate those trends which are deemed most relevant – i.e. to have potential significance to the company – for further more detailed investigation.

3 Undertake an in-depth analysis on the possible impact of these selected trends on the company's current product or markets. In particular, this analysis should delineate the extent to which the trend is an opportunity or a threat and the potential magnitude of its impact. In addition, an analysis should be made of the extent to which the trends isolated open up new opportunities.

4 Forecast the future direction of the trends isolated.

5 Further analyse possible effects of the forecasted trends on future product or market momentum: (a) on the assumption of no action, (b) on the assumption that trends are responded to.

6 The final step is to assess the implication of the preceding analysis for overall strategic decision making.

This framework for environmental appraisal represents a structured and logical approach to this procedure. Moreover, it fulfils many of the requirements outlined earlier for an effective appraisal system. However, there are still practical problems in this appraisal process which we need to consider further.

STRATEGIC DECISION MAKING

We have seen that by definition the 'environment' encompasses all events and trends outside the boundaries of the marketing function. A key problem in environmental appraisal is the identification of the most significant of these trends for further analysis. Jain suggests there are no 'hard and fast rules' for distinguishing between what is relevant and irrelevant. A useful approach to identifying what to scan and which environmental trends and changes are relevant is the business definition for a strategic business unit.

For example, imagine that a strategic business unit of a large insurance company has defined its part of the business as being 'the provision of peace of mind insurance solutions to the private motor car owner'. The following might be some of the more important environmental trends and changes for the strategic business unit to monitor:

- trends and changes in levels and types of private car ownership together with the factors affecting these;
- trends and changes in car usage levels and patterns together with the factors affecting these;
- strategies of major competitors;
- potential new entrants to the market;
- changes in legislation that might affect the types of insurance cover legally required;
- technological developments which might affect the way in which, say, customers purchase private car insurance.

These are examples but they illustrate the potential range and complexity required in environmental scanning.

Although business definition provides the key to isolating relevant trends (any one of the environmental factors just described would give rise to major environmental opportunities and threats) identifying relevant areas requires a considerable degree of creativity and foresightedness. Some trends or changes are obviously significant, e.g. the emergence of a new and potentially strong competitor, but the environmental scanning process also requires judgement and experience in spotting opportunities and threats. Often a seemingly unrelated trend or change can be highly significant in the long run.[6]

Who would have thought that one of the most significant threats to the publishers and distributors of books would have come from the Internet? After all, traditionally the book-buying public has selected and purchased books by browsing through them on the booksellers' shelves. From nothing in this market, the Internet bookseller Amazon has taken a substantial market share in next to no time. Initially, probably considered as simply an upstart in the industry by the large publishing and book distributing organizations, Amazon has, through its success, forced these more traditional companies in the market to consider them as a powerful competitive force.

This example not only shows the need for constant vigilance in environmental scanning, but in addition illustrates the need to think creatively about what is relevant.

FORECASTING THE FUTURE

Strategic market planning is concerned with plotting the future of a company. It is not enough to wait until a major environmental threat has emerged before taking action. The company requires not only the identification of environmental trends, but the forecasting of both the magnitude and direction of these trends. However, forecasting the future, especially with regard to complex and often inter-related trends in the environment, is complicated and may require specialist techniques and personnel.

We have examined some of these specialist techniques of technological forecasting in Chapter 11, and the strategic market planner needs to make estimates of likely sources of future opportunities and threats.

ASSESSING THE IMPACT OF ENVIRONMENTAL TRENDS

In addition to this, the strategic market planner must assess their likely impact on the organization for after all, there is no other reason for appraising the environment. Kotler and Keller[7] suggests that the planner can begin to make this assessment using opportunity and threat matrices, as illustrated in Figures 13.3 and 13.4.

The opportunity matrix is based on the planner assessing the relative attractiveness of an environmental opportunity and the probability of success should the company decide to act upon it. In turn, this assessment requires an assessment of the strengths and weaknesses of the company, which we look at later in this chapter. In the same way, the planner should assess the likely impact of any possible threats to which trends in the environment give rise. Here we need to assess both the probability of the threat occurring and its seriousness for the activities of the organization.

Clearly, these matrices are an oversimplification of the analysis required to assess the impact of environmental changes on an organization. Not uncommonly, two or more trends, each of which on its own would not represent significant opportunities or threats, can, in combination, be highly significant. This means that several trends may need to be evaluated together to assess their cross-impact.

Despite the problems of determining the impact of trends it is essential that this is done. One of the benefits is the fact that even if the precise effects are difficult to predict, the very process of assessment and the necessary cross-functional discussion to which this gives rise can help the company to become prepared for the future.

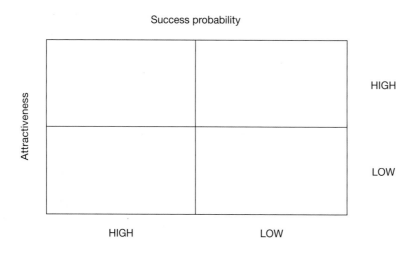

FIGURE 13.3 Opportunity matrix

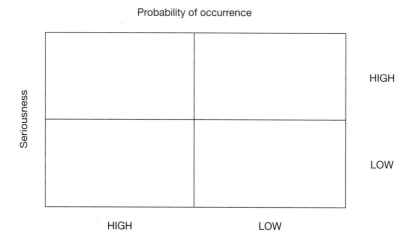

FIGURE 13.4 Threat matrix

TRADITIONAL VIEW OF COMPETITIVE INDUSTRY STRUCTURES

Figure 13.5 shows the traditional view of competitive industry structures preferred by economists. Different types of industry structure are based on the two key dimensions of 'number of sellers' (competitors) and the degree of product differentiation in the market. This results in five distinct types of competitive industry structure, ranging from 'monopoly', which is characterized by there being only one supplier and hence no competition, to 'perfect competition', this market structure being characterized by many sellers (competitors) and undifferentiated products.

Both the number of competitors and degree of product differentiation are important facts of competitive industry structure. Useful though this framework is it is generally recognized that it yields only a partial view of competitive forces at work in an industry so planners need to look to some of the more comprehensive frameworks of industry analysis.

The Porter framework of competitive industry structure

One of the most useful frameworks for analysing competitive structure is that developed by Michael E. Porter[8] who suggests that competition in an industry is rooted in its underlying economic structure and goes beyond the behaviour of current competitors. The state of competition depends on five basic competitive forces, shown in Figure 13.6. Together, these factors determine the ultimate profit potential in an industry where profit potential is measured in terms of long-run return on invested capital. Not all industries have the same potential. Forces range from intense, e.g. tyres, paper, steel with no spectacular returns available; to mild, e.g. cosmetics, toiletries, soft drinks with high returns being common.

The goal of competitive strategy is to find a position in the industry where the company can best defend itself against these forces, or can influence them in its favour. Knowledge of these underlying

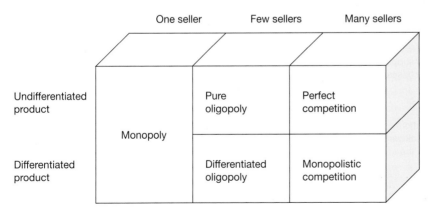

FIGURE 13.5 Traditional view of competitive industry structure

pressures highlights critical strengths and weaknesses of the company, shows the position in the industry, clarifies areas where strategy changes yield the greatest pay-off and highlights areas where industry trends hold greatest significance as opportunities or threats. Structure analysis is fundamental for formulating competitive strategy.

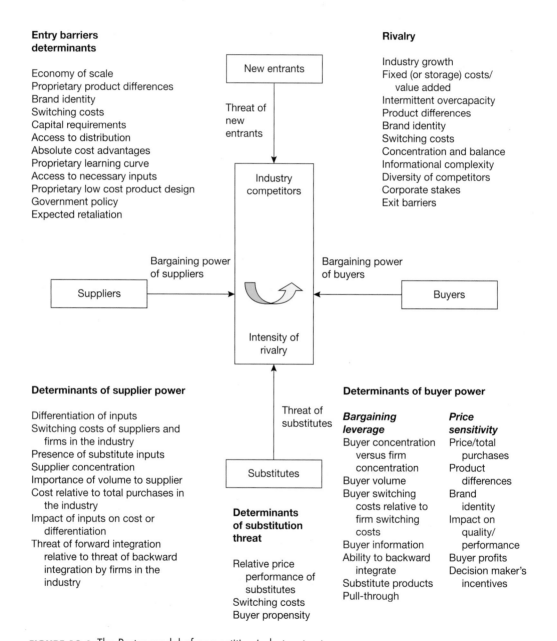

Entry barriers determinants

Economy of scale
Proprietary product differences
Brand identity
Switching costs
Capital requirements
Access to distribution
Absolute cost advantages
Proprietary learning curve
Access to necessary inputs
Proprietary low cost product design
Government policy
Expected retaliation

Rivalry

Industry growth
Fixed (or storage) costs/
    value added
Intermittent overcapacity
Product differences
Brand identity
Switching costs
Concentration and balance
Informational complexity
Diversity of competitors
Corporate stakes
Exit barriers

New entrants

Threat of new entrants

Industry competitors

Bargaining power of suppliers

Bargaining power of buyers

Suppliers

Buyers

Intensity of rivalry

Determinants of supplier power

Differentiation of inputs
Switching costs of suppliers and
    firms in the industry
Presence of substitute inputs
Supplier concentration
Importance of volume to supplier
Cost relative to total purchases in
    the industry
Impact of inputs on cost or
    differentiation
Threat of forward integration
    relative to threat of backward
    integration by firms in the
    industry

Threat of substitutes

Substitutes

Determinants of substitution threat

Relative price
    performance of
    substitutes
Switching costs
Buyer propensity

Determinants of buyer power

Bargaining leverage	**Price sensitivity**
Buyer concentration versus firm concentration	Price/total purchases
Buyer volume	Product differences
Buyer switching costs relative to firm switching costs	Brand identity
Buyer information	Impact on quality/ performance
Ability to backward integrate	Buyer profits
Substitute products Pull-through	Decision maker's incentives

FIGURE 13.6 The Porter model of competitive industry structure

The five competitive forces in Porter's model

As suggested earlier, the five competitive forces suggested by Porter jointly determine the intensity of industry competition and hence profitability. As Figure 13.6 shows, each of the five major forces in turn comprises a number of elements which together combine to determine the strength of each factor and hence its effect on competitiveness. Some of these are outlined here.

1   *New entrants* can potentially serve to increase the degree of competition in an industry. In turn, threat of new entrants is largely a function of the extent to which barriers to entry exist in the market. Some of the key factors affecting these entry barriers include:

   ■   economies of scale;
   ■   product differentiation and brand identity;
   ■   capital requirements;
   ■   switching costs;
   ■   government policy;
   ■   access to distribution.

   Because high barriers to entry can make even a potentially lucrative market unattractive (or even impossible) to enter for new competitors, the marketing planner should not take a passive approach but should actively pursue ways of raising barriers to new competitors.

2   *Suppliers* Bargaining power of suppliers is greater when, for example:

   ■   supply is dominated by a few companies and they are more concentrated than the industry they sell to;
   ■   their products are unique or differentiated, or if they have built up switching costs;
   ■   they are not obliged to contend with other products for sale to the industry;
   ■   they pose a credible threat of integrating forward into the industry's business;
   ■   the industry is not an important customer to the supplier group.

3   *Buyers* Bargaining power of buyers is greater when, for example:

   ■   they are concentrated or purchase in large volumes;
   ■   the products they purchase are standard or undifferentiated;
   ■   the products they purchase from the industry form a component of the product and represent a significant fraction of the cost;
   ■   they earn low profits which create a great incentive to lower purchasing cost;
   ■   the industry's product is unimportant to the quality of the buyer's products;
   ■   the industry's product does not save the buyer money;
   ■   the buyers pose a credible threat of integrating backwards to manufacture the industry's product.

   A company can improve its strategic posture by finding suppliers or buyers who possess the least power to influence it adversely.

4   *Substitute products* can limit the potential of an industry by placing a ceiling on prices it can charge. If the industry is successful and earning high profits then it is more likely that competitors

will enter the market via substitute products in order to obtain a share of the potential profits available.

5 *Industry competitors* Intensity of rivalry between industry competitors depends upon:

- the concentration of the industry (numerous competitors of equal size will lead to more intense rivalry);
- rate of industry growth (slow growth will tend towards greater rivalry);
- value of fixed costs (high fixed costs might be a temptation to cut prices);
- whether the product is a commodity dependent upon price and service;
- the similarity of competitor strategies (if they have different ideas of how to compete they will run into each other continuously);
- whether the firm has high stakes in achieving success;
- whether the industry exhibits high exit barriers (if yes, firms will tend to remain in the industry even if they are making low or negative returns).

The Porter framework has added considerably to our knowledge of how to appraise the elements of competitive industry structure. Another approach is the concept of **strategic group analysis**.

STRATEGIC GROUP ANALYSIS

This idea is based on the notion that groups of companies with similar strategic characteristics within an industry are in more direct competition with one another than other groups of companies in the same industry with dissimilar strategic characteristics. The strategic characteristics appropriate to form strategic groupings differ from industry to industry, but Johnson et al.[9] include the following:

- extent of geographic coverage;
- distribution channels used;
- size of organization;
- number of market segments served;
- pricing policy;
- marketing mix;
- cost position;
- utilization of capacity.

An example of strategic groupings for the UK brewing industry produced by Johnson and Thomas[10] is shown in Figure 13.7 to illustrate how this concept works. The figure shows that there were four distinct strategic groupings in the UK brewing industry when this analysis was conducted. In this example, the strategic groupings (which show companies with similar strategic characteristics and/or following similar strategies and/or competing on a similar basis) have been arrived at on the basis of the extent to which the companies are national or local, and the extent to which they have diversified into non-brewing activities. Unsurprisingly, these two characteristics also appear to be linked to the size of the organization, with smaller companies being less diversified and more local.

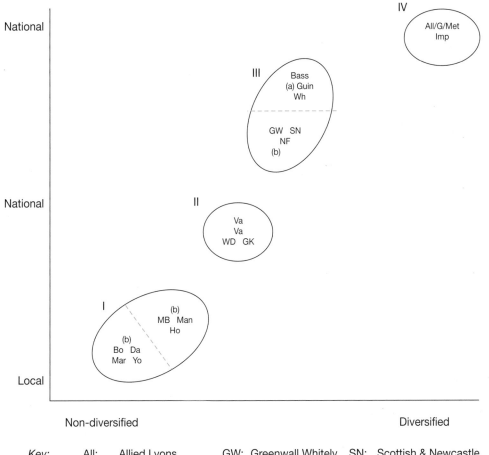

Key:

All:	Allied Lyons	GW:	Greenwall Whitely	SN:	Scottish & Newcastle
Bass:	Bass	Ho:	Home	Va:	Vaux
Bo:	Boddingtons	Imp:	Imperial Foods	WD:	Wolvs. & Dudley
Da:	Davenports	Man:	Mansfield	Wh:	Whitbread
GK:	Greet King	Mar:	Marstons	Yo:	Youngs
G.Met:	Grand Metropolitan	MB:	Matthew Brown	NF:	Northern Foods
Guin:	Guinness				

Group 1: Local brewers concentrating on single business brewing. However (b) are rather more diversified, particularly in terms of soft drinks production and distribution

Group 2: More geographically extended regional brewers

Group 3: (a) National or (b) semi-national brewers who have grown and diversified from a brewing base

Group 4: Diversified conglomerates with interest in brewing

FIGURE 13.7 Strategic groups in the UK brewing industry

Source: Johnson, G. and Thomas, H. (1988), 'Research in the brewing industry', in Johnson, G. and Scholes, K. (eds), *Exploring Corporate Strategy*, 2nd edn, Upper Saddle River, NJ: Prentice-Hall, p. 74.

Competitors' objectives and strategies

As the strategic group analysis approach to analysing competitive industry structure indicates, in addition to structural characteristics of an industry, it is also important to assess how a company's competitors compete (their strategies) and to what purpose (their objectives).

If a company was contemplating entering a new market in which there were existing competitors, it would be important to analyse how these competitors compete. For example, competition might be based primarily on price; it might alternatively be on delivery and quality. Whatever the basis, it is important to assess the extent to which the company can compete successfully on the same basis, or whether competing on a different basis might be more appropriate.

In markets where competitors compete on a similar basis i.e. where their competitive strategies are similar, competition tends to be fiercer. Markets where there are a variety of strategies for competing tend to offer more scope for establishing a competitive advantage for a company and are usually more attractive.

Competitor objectives should also be considered in this part of the appraisal. In many organizations the overall objective may be to maximize profits, but objectives are rarely as simple as this. In any event, many companies that operate in the non-profit-making business arena still have fierce competition.

As an example of the importance of establishing competitor objectives, consider the case where a company establishes that its major competitor has objective of increasing market share with a long-term view to securing market leadership. Knowing this would not only indicate what the major thrusts of this competitor are likely to be, but in addition, the company would also begin to delineate what its defensive reaction should be. Similarly, if competitors are part of larger companies it is useful to know how they feature in the overall operation and plans of these parent companies.

Competitors' strengths and weaknesses

Having identified competitors, assessed the competitive structure of the industry and assessed competitors' present and future objectives and strategies, the next stage is to assess their relative strengths and weaknesses.

It is not too difficult to appreciate the importance of this part of competitive analysis. A soccer team manager assesses the relative strengths and weaknesses of opponents before deciding how to take them on. If major competitors are aggressive, cash rich and have lower operating costs than we have, it would not make sense to attack them on price. Similarly, if competitors are much larger than ourselves (and consequently more powerful) it would make more sense to avoid head-on confrontation and instead pursue flanking or niche strategies in the market. We examine the range of competitive strategies in subsequent chapters, but at this stage we need to consider the sort of factors that should be included in an analysis of their strengths and weaknesses.

Financial
- liquidity ratio;
- profits;
- turnover;
- breakeven points;
- return on investment.

Human resources
- labour supply;
- qualifications;
- experience;
- aggressiveness;
- style.

Production
- capacity;
- size of plant;
- productivity;
- plant location;
- quality control.

Market
- market share;
- customer service;
- price competitiveness;
- distribution channels.

Clearly, there are many factors against which we might assess the relative strengths and weaknesses of identified competitors. In addition, some of them would not be easy to assess. In order to help in this process of assessment it helps to proceed in a systematic and objective way using rating scales. One possible approach is as follows:

1 *Identify **key factors for success (KFS)** in the industry*
   For example, if product quality, price and delivery are essential to competitive success in the industry, it makes sense to appraise your own company and competitors against these factors.
2 *Rank both your own company and competitors against these factors using an appropriate rating scale*
   For example, you might assign a score to your own company and competitors against each criterion on the following basis:

Score	Evaluation
0	Very poor/dismal
1	Poor
2	Below average
3	Average
4	Above average
5	Good
6	Excellent

Better still, where appropriate get your customers to make the evaluation; after all it is their perceptions which count.

3   *Assess implications for future competitive strategies*
    Having completed the evaluation, a company is then in a position to assess what its future
    competitive strategies need to be so that account can be taken of the relative strengths and
    weaknesses identified.

You will note that we have included in this assessment the assessing of the company itself; this is
important as we are assessing *relative* strengths and weaknesses. The fact that competition is strong,
but you are stronger, would result in a very different competitive strategy from one where the
assessment shows that you are strong, but your competitors are stronger. Similarly, an assessment which
showed your competitors to be weak, but your company weaker would result in different strategies
from one where the assessment showed your company to be weak but your competitors weaker. This
sort of analysis can be useful in determining which competitors to attack (if any) and which to avoid.

It is impossible to be definitive about the criteria for assessment. After all, the key factors for
success will vary from industry to industry and even from one customer group to another. Certainly,
financial and market strengths and weaknesses are likely to figure in most assessments, but it is for
the marketing planner to determine the assessment criteria most appropriate to the circumstances.

Owing to the importance of assessing 'relative' strengths and weaknesses we return to this important
aspect later in the chapter when we look at the assessment of internal strengths and weaknesses.

Assessing and anticipating competitors' reactions

A crucial stage in competitor analysis is to try to gauge how competitors will react in the marketplace,
and in particular to assess how they might respond to your own competitive moves. In a sense this
is similar to an army general trying to assess how his counterpart might respond in battle.

Studying competitors can tell us a lot about their likely moves and reactions to such things as
promotional campaigns, price cuts or new product launches. However, different competitors will
react in different ways to different forms of competition. Kotler[11] outlined four common 'reaction
profiles' among competitors in 1997:

- the *laid-back competitor:* little or no response to competitive moves;
- the *selective competitor:* sensitive to some strategies (e.g. price cutting) but not to others;
- the *tiger competitor:* responds quickly and aggressively to any competitor move;
- the *stochastic competitor:* responds in an unpredictable manner.

Likely competitor actions are perhaps the most difficult aspect of behaviour to assess. Even the most
predictable of competitors can sometimes act or react unpredictably.

Competitor intelligence: collecting information on competitors

Competitor analysis requires an efficient and effective competitor intelligence system. One of the
problems here is that competitors are not knowingly willing to volunteer information required for
the analysis we have just covered. Indeed this information can be amongst the most difficult and

sensitive of market information to obtain. Some sort of competitor intelligence-gathering goes on in most organizations. A competitor intelligence system should address the following:

1 nature and type of information required;
2 frequency of information gathering and reporting;
3 responsibility for information gathering
4 methods of data collection and sources;
5 information analysis and dissemination procedures.

There is a fine dividing line between what could properly be termed 'legitimate' intelligence-gathering activities on competitors and what might be termed 'snooping'. At the extreme, of course, some intelligence-gathering activities fall into the category of industrial espionage, which may bring with it legal ramifications. Having said this, competitor intelligence-gathering is becoming more and more intense. The lengths to which some companies will now go in order to collect this information is evidenced by Flax[12] who lists at least 20 techniques for 'snooping' on competitors.

In addition to the more conventional sources, such as competitors' publications, balance sheets and past employees, Flax also includes more radical approaches such as 'collecting competitors' garbage' and aerial photography.

Data for analysing the environment

The scope and complexity of environmental analysis means that the marketer can be involved in extensive data collection. As we have seen, not all this data is readily available. Moreover, the amount of data that can be required for environmental analysis means the marketer must be careful to avoid the problem of information overload. The marketer must discriminate between essential and non-essential data for the analysis. Data can come from a variety of sources: internal data, for example, can come from sales, accounts, customer service and research and development, whereas external data can come from secondary sources such as government publications and industry statistics, and from primary sources such as customer questionnaires and focus groups.

Much information for environmental analysis is collected online and analysed via computer-based information systems. We have seen the growth of databases which allow constant and instant access to up-to-date information on a company's environment. These and other aspects of information provision for marketing analysis and decision making have already been considered in the previous chapter.

Problems and issues in assessing strengths and weaknesses

The assessment of strengths and weaknesses is central to the development of strategic marketing plans. In many case-based marketing courses and texts, this analysis is often suggested as being the starting point for students. Resource analysis, and interpreting what this implies in terms of strengths and weaknesses, is often misunderstood and performed poorly by academic analysts and marketing practitioners. Underpinning this misunderstanding are two basic factors.

First, assessment of strengths and weaknesses is complex and multifaceted and there is a need to exercise creativity, judgement and managerial expertise in the assessment process. Appraisal of strengths and weaknesses involves more than a 'mechanical' listing of organizational resources, although such a 'listing' commonly occurs in practice.

Second, development of conceptual frameworks and methods to help marketing planners assess strengths and weaknesses have been poor. There is a need to recognize and deal with the practical problems and issues which confront the strategic marketing planner in this area. Specifically, it is essential to address the following questions:

■   What attributes and activities should be included in a strengths and weaknesses appraisal?
■   How can we evaluate what are 'strengths' and what are 'weaknesses'?
■   How should we organize and conduct the appraisal procedure?
■   How can we interpret and use the output of a strengths and weaknesses appraisal?

We now turn our attention to each of these questions.

What attributes and activities should be included in the appraisal?

The first step in conducting an appraisal of strengths and weaknesses is to determine the attributes to assess, i.e. what activities and resources should form the basis of the analysis? According to what we assess in our strengths and weaknesses analysis, we will arrive at different conclusions and thus very different strategy formulations. Determination of the 'right' attributes to measure is not easy and requires considerable analysis and creativity.

The most common approach to analysing strengths and weaknesses is to use a checklist for the delineation of resources and/or activities to be assessed. For example, it is suggested that one should start by listing all the functional areas in the organization and then proceed to produce a list of all the attributes in each functional area which might conceivably be assessed for strengths and weaknesses. An example of this type of approach is:

Marketing
■   brand names;
■   corporate image;
■   distribution;
■   product range;
■   prices;
■   sales force;
■   marketing systems.

Financial
■   cost of capital;
■   liquidity;
■   profitability;

■ asset structure;

■ price/earnings ratio.

Manufacturing

■ capacity usage;

■ age profile of plant;

■ manufacturing systems;

■ quality control;

■ flexibility;

■ economies of scale.

Human resource

■ skill levels;

■ adaptability;

■ manpower planning;

■ industrial relations;

■ working conditions.

Checklists are helpful in enabling the market planner to think more broadly about the range of factors which might usefully be assessed. However, there are three problems with the use of checklists:

1   *Number of attributes*

There are many possible attributes which could conceivably be appraised. Analysis of all of them is extremely time consuming and costly. More importantly not all company resources and activities are strategically significant. This brings us to the second problem associated with using 'standardized' checklists.

2   *Which attributes?*

A particular company's resources and activities are strategically important. Which ones are vital to assess from a 'strengths' and 'weaknesses' perspective, are specific to that company and the product/market combinations in which it operates. It is crucial to asses the resources and activities which are what Ohmae[13] first referred to as key factors for success (KFS) in the markets in which the company competes. KFSs are resources and activities that underpin the key factors that should be assessed. This point is strongly emphasized. This, in turn, means that each company must establish its own list of attributes for assessment according to its existing or proposed market strategy.

If a company does not know what these critical success factors are, it must establish them. It is important that the process of establishing these key attributes be carried out as systematically and objectively as possible and not based on guesswork of what management 'feels' the key attributes should be.

In most industries and companies the critical attributes against which to assess strengths and weaknesses will be 'known' to experienced marketing managers. For example, in the confectionery industry, both brand reputation and strong distribution are critical factors to competitive success and these will need to be appraised in any analysis of strengths and weaknesses. Similarly, for most companies, assessment of, say, financial strengths and weaknesses will be critical in delineating and selecting between alternative marketing strategies. It is often the case that relatively few factors will be critical to success or failure in a market.

The key factors for success in the UK fashion jeans market are:

■   strong and effective branding;
■   distribution effectiveness;
■   quality;
■   innovation and new product development.

A company that has all of these attributes and remains a leader in this market, despite extensive competition, is the Levi Strauss Company. Building on its strong brand presence in this market, combined with a reputation for quality, Levi Strauss continues to innovate. The 'Engineered' range proved to be very popular. Levis focused on the quality end of the market with this product and its strong distribution channels gave it a competitive edge in the market.

A key attribute for strengths and weaknesses assessment is how and why customers choose, and in particular what they consider to be of value. Customer needs assessment is crucial in answering the question, namely: 'How can we evaluate what are strengths and what are weaknesses?' A customer-oriented focus is vital. Before we consider this question we must consider the third problem in the checklist approach to assessing strengths and weaknesses.

3   *Interrelationships between attributes, synergy and balance*
    Even after identifying key attributes for the strengths and weaknesses assessment, it is important to recognize that invariably individual attributes will be interlinked. A simple checklist approach, even if this is based on an objective, customer-based assessment of key attributes, fails to recognize this. For example, a company may be only moderately strong in, say, selling and sales management, branding and promotion, and product range when these are assessed independently. Looked at in combination, 'moderate strengths' may be such that it will render the company very competitive in the marketplace. This concept of the combined effect of parts being greater than the sum of their individual effects as the concept of synergy was first popularized in planning by Ansoff.[14] Synergy can be either positive or negative in its effect. The checklist approach tends to underestimate the importance of assessing the extent to which various activities and resources of an organization complement, or do not complement, each other. Very often it is the balance of organizational resources and activities which is crucial. Although this makes the assessment of strengths and weaknesses more problematical, it is a vital consideration. The question of 'balance' is increasingly being recognized as an important facet of a strengths and weaknesses appraisal and some of the more recent techniques and tasks of strategic appraisal such as portfolio analysis, which we shall consider in Chapter 14, are particularly useful in this respect.

How can we evaluate what are strengths and what are weaknesses?

Our second practical problem for the strategic marketing planner relates to the seemingly straightforward issue of what constitutes a strength or a weakness, i.e. what is involved in their evaluation. This is not straightforward. To illustrate this issue we consider first the question of what a strength is and the significance of **distinctive competencies.** Second, we look at customer needs and the notion of **value chains.** Third, we examine once more the importance of evaluating competition. Finally, we look at the use of profiles in assessing strengths and weaknesses.

To illustrate some of these key issues in evaluating organizational strengths, let us imagine a company has recently completed an analysis of its strengths and weaknesses and that this analysis suggests that the company has the following strengths:

- a reputation for high quality;
- good after-sales service;
- distinctive brands and packaging;
- efficient production;
- spare capacity;
- a well trained and effective sales force.

Certainly, any company which possessed these attributes would seem to have a number of significant strengths. The key question for this hypothetical company is the extent to which these are truly strengths, and how the company arrived at this conclusion. Here are some of the important considerations in answering these questions.

First, how strong is 'strong'? One of the considerations for the company is to assess precisely how strong the company is in each of the areas listed above. For example, the company feels it has a strength in the areas of after-sales service, but does this mean it is 'very strong' in this area, or is it only 'moderately strong', or is it simply 'not weak'? At first glance, these distinctions may appear to be pedantic. Nevertheless, in strategic terms the degree of strength is crucial. Being 'satisfactory' or even 'moderately strong' along some dimension is very different from having a major strength. Where a company has a major strength with respect to some factor, we refer to it as having a distinctive competence.

Hamel and Prahalad[15] clarify the importance of being distinctively competent as opposed to merely competent: 'Differentiation must be unique. If every company in the industry has the skill, then it is not a basis for differentiation unless the organization's skills in the area are really special.' There are plenty of examples of companies going out of business because they have failed to identify real strengths, i.e. their distinctive competence as opposed to what they merely 'can do'. Similarly, many companies fail to capitalize on marketing opportunities to which an identification of their true strengths might give rise.

Next, are these the factors which are relevant to competitive success? A second consideration in assessing a company's strengths is to relate distinctive competence to customer needs. Let us assume that after-sales service in the company is a distinctive competence. We must then ask whether or not after-sales service is an important factor to its customers. Put another way, the company has to determine the extent to which after-sales service is important in business success. The point here is that a company can be extremely strong in areas which are unrelated to business success, either in existing, or future/envisaged business areas. Such 'strengths' are not strengths at all and they can in fact constitute a major source of weakness if a company attempts to use these to compete strategically.

You will recognize that this consideration is related to the first problem of which attributes to include in the assessment of strengths and weaknesses. You will recall that it was suggested that the key attributes for a strengths and weaknesses assessment are those which underpin customer choice and in particular what they consider to be of value. It was also suggested that most experienced marketing managers in an industry will have a good 'feel' for what these key success factors are for their own product/market combinations and that often there are relatively few key factors. Nevertheless, both in the selection of attributes for assessment and in the assessment process itself it is vital to ensure that we understand what the customer considers value to be and the activities of the company which either add to or detract from this value. A useful concept in this respect is the concept of 'value chains'.

THE CONCEPT OF VALUE CHAINS

Developed by Porter,[16] **value chain analysis** is aimed at identifying potential competitive advantages. Porter suggested that the activities of a company can be broken down into nine 'value activities', five being primary and four secondary. These value activities collectively comprise those activities involved in designing, manufacturing, marketing and delivering the organization's products and services. Figure 13.8 illustrates the nine major groupings of activities in the value chain.

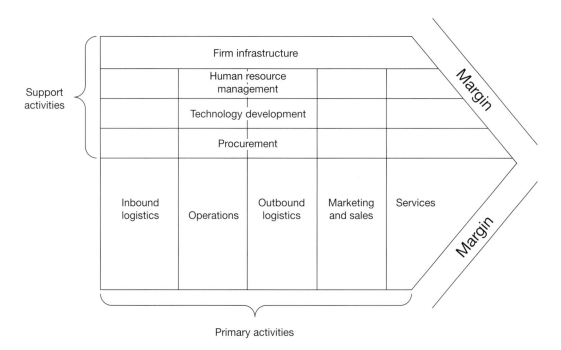

FIGURE 13.8 The value chain

Source: Porter, M.E. (1985), *Competitive Advantage: Creating and Sustaining Superior Performance*, New York: Free Press, p. 37.

Primary activities comprise activities associated with the input, throughput and output of goods and services in the organization, and include the following:

1   inbound logistics: e.g. materials handling, stock control and delivery inwards;
2   operations: e.g. packaging, assembly, equipment maintenance and testing;
3   outbound logistics: e.g. finished goods warehousing, materials handling, order processing and delivery outwards;
4   marketing and sales: e.g. advertising, promotion, sales force, pricing and channels;
5   service: e.g. installations, repairs and parts supply.

Support activities comprise those activities which facilitate primary activities in the physical creation of the product and its sales and transfer to buyer and including:

6   procurement: refers to the function of purchasing inputs used in the organization's value chain, and not to the purchased inputs themselves. Examples include purchasing procedures, techniques of vendor analysis and information systems. In addition, procurement activities may also include the procurement of more than simply raw materials and components. An organization also 'procures' market research or accountancy expertise; hence activities concerned with procuring these services would also be included.
7   technology development: support activities that improve the product and the process. The areas of support activities here are those which are carried out in the research and development function, but they also include technology support activities, office automation, communicating with customers, measuring quality, etc.
8   human resource management: includes recruitment, selection, training and development.
9   firm infrastructure: support activities here include systems of quality control, financial systems and marketing planning.

   Although the broad categories of value activities, both primary and secondary, are common to most organizations, individual components of value activities will tend to be company specific. The basic idea of the value chain concept is that each activity can be categorized and analysed with a view to securing competitive advantage. Specifically, a company should analyse all its activities with a view to determining how these contribute to the value the customer receives. They should also be analysed with respect to cost and competitor margins. Figure 13.8 shows the difference between total value and the cost of performing all the value activities. In simple terms by looking at both value activities and the cost of performing them compared to the competition, it is suggested that an organization can seek competitive advantage either by cutting the cost of performing the value activities while simultaneously maintaining the value, or by increasing the value of the activities to the customer. Two further points about value chain analysis are worthy of note.

1   First, value chains extend outside the organization itself to include suppliers and distributors. For example, a supplier may, through its own quality control activities, enhance inbound logistics and operations activities of its customers, thereby adding value to its customers' customers. Similarly, distributors can influence value. For example, a distributor may undertake to offer

after-sales service for the manufacturers' brands it supplies, thereby potentially adding value to these brands for the customer. Porter refers to these as '**vertical linkages**'.

2   Second, it is important to recognize that the value chain is not a set of independent activities. Each of the primary and secondary activities is interdependent. These are what Porter calls '**horizontal linkages**' and it is often these linkages which form the basis of competitive advantage. For example, improved quality management (a 'firm infrastructure' activity) can enhance both manufacturing (an 'operations' activity) and marketing and service activities. In other words, all the value activity areas must be looked at together to achieve optimization and co-ordination.

This is a brief introduction to the concept of value chains. In fact, the uses of value chain analyses are complex and multifaceted. Porter has developed the concept and techniques of value chain analysis to enable the company to look for ways of securing competitive advantage. In the context of assessing strengths and weaknesses, value chain analysis has four distinct benefits:

1   It provides a framework for addressing an earlier problem of which attributes (or activities) to assess in strengths and weaknesses analyses.
2   By using the concept of 'value' it forces the analysis of strengths and weaknesses to relate better both to how the customer views them and to competition. Johnson et al.[17] have captured this use of the value chain:

> Value chain analysis describes the activities within and around an organization and relates them to an analysis of the competitive strengths of the organization or its ability to provide 'value for money' products or services.

> Analysis of value chain activities enables us to assess what are truly 'strengths' and what are truly 'weaknesses'.

3   The concept of horizontal linkages in value chain analysis reinforces the earlier point about the importance of looking at interrelationships between resources and the related concept of synergy and balance.
4   Finally, the concept of vertical linkages in value chain analysis forces us to think more broadly of possible strengths and weaknesses that derive from linkages with suppliers and distributors and which, in turn, stem from their strengths and weaknesses in relation to ours.

From its highly successful American base, the US retailer Walmart then expanded into Europe. The company acquired the ASDA group of supermarkets in the UK and has overtaken Sainsbury's to become the second most powerful retailer in the UK after Tesco. Walmart built its strategy for success around offering good value products with low prices, while maintaining good quality. This strategy is built upon effective value chain management and in particular the efficient use of vertical links with suppliers. Walmart has been able to reduce its costs throughout the supply chain, thereby being able to pass these cost savings onto its customers. To compete successfully against this, Walmart's competitors have had to better secure and manage their own vertical links in the value chain as effectively and efficiently as Walmart have done.

Next, are our competitors stronger or weaker than ourselves? This consideration in evaluating strengths and weaknesses takes us back to the importance of competitor analysis. Once we have identified what are key strengths and weaknesses, and where our distinctive competences lie, we need also to assess the extent to which we have a competitive advantage with respect to these competences.

In the same way that we cannot evaluate what constitutes a 'strength' or a 'weakness' without assessing the extent to which customers value these competences, so too we should not proceed to develop marketing strategies and plans based on these without also assessing how strong or weak our competitors are in these areas. The perspective that needs to be taken is from the market to the company, and not from the company to the market, which is, after all, the essence of marketing orientation.

The importance of assessing strengths and weaknesses in relation to competition, as well as to needs of customers, stems from the fact that a key reason for assessment of strengths and weaknesses is, as we have seen, to help in the delineation and selection of competitive marketing strategies. For example, the company might have distinctive strengths in the areas of quality and after-sales service, and these might be strengths which the customer values, and hence are key factors for success in these areas. Stronger, weaker or equal; it simply does not make sense to evaluate our strengths and weaknesses without comparing ourselves to the competition.

We can see from our discussion that the issues which arise in the process of evaluating strengths and weaknesses are complex. It might be said that weaknesses are easier to understand than strengths. Essentially weaknesses are constraints, but as with strengths we need to assess them in the context of customer and market needs and of the competition. A weakness in terms of after-sales service would matter less if this factor were unimportant to business success and if our competitors were even weaker. Again, as with strengths, we also need to assess if our weaknesses are major or minor.

A useful approach to the evaluation of both strengths and weaknesses relative to the competition is the use of a strengths and weaknesses profile.

PROFILING SYSTEMS IN EVALUATING STRENGTHS AND WEAKNESSES

The first two issues in appraising resources for strategic marketing planning relate to the important areas of attribute selection and the evaluation of those attributes as true strengths or weaknesses. The second of these, i.e. the evaluation of strengths and weaknesses, involves both the identification of distinctive competences and assessment of competitor strengths and weaknesses in the same areas. Simple profiling systems may be used to address both these issues and are now described.

Having identified key resources or attributes for our strengths and weaknesses evaluation, we can then score our company with respect to these key attributes or resources using a simple numerical scale, as shown in Figure 13.9. Once this is completed for each attribute we can then repeat the process for each of our key competitors. Admittedly, this second part of the process is not easy, but it is extremely useful. In this way we can build up a series of 'profiles' of our own and competitor strengths and weaknesses, as shown in Table 13.1, which in turn can be used to delineate and select future strategies. Although such profiling enables a systematic approach to be made when evaluating strengths and weaknesses, inevitably the resultant profiles will depend on who is carrying out the evaluation. For example, the marketing manager may have a very different view of, say, product quality from that of the production manager. This brings us to the question of how we might organize and conduct the appraisal procedure.

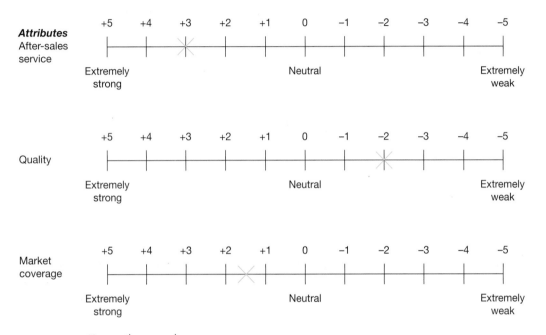

FIGURE 13.9 Key attributes scale

TABLE 13.1 Strengths and weaknesses: company and competitor profiles

	Assessment of relative strengths			
Attributes	Own company	Competitor A	Competitor B	Competitor C
Range of products	+5	−1	+5	+2
Terms of trade	+3	+2	+4	−1
Low cost production	−2	+2	+3	−1
After-sales service	+4	+2	−1	−3
Quality of products	+5	−3	+4	+1
Market coverage	+3	+5	+5	+1

How should we organize and conduct the appraisal?

Even though a company's approach to evaluating strengths and weaknesses may be systematic, it may not always be objective. Perhaps inevitably the evaluation is likely to be subjective, especially when it is carried out by managers of that company. After all, most people find it difficult to be objectively self-critical. For this reason it is preferable to use an inter-functional team approach to internally based assessment systems. Where a company can call in external consultants to make the assessment, this is better. Not only are customers likely to be more objective and thorough, but it is customers' perceptions of our strengths and weaknesses which are critical. The customer will not necessarily be in a position to make a full assessment (e.g. on finance and production), but is capable of appraising perceived marketing strengths and weaknesses.

A related problem with company staff being involved in strengths and weaknesses assessment is that the process is often seen as being threatening; a fact that can severely detract from the objectivity of the exercise. Properly administered, the effective use of a SWOT analysis delivers key benefits over and above its obvious input to the marketing plan. In particular, SWOT analysis helps foster collaboration and information exchange between different functional areas of the business. In turn, this can help create an environment of creativity and innovation. In order to achieve this benefit, the SWOT analysis process should be approached positively. In particular, it must not be used to criticize functions or individuals in the organization whenever weaknesses are identified.

How can we interpret and use the outcome of strengths and weaknesses assessment?

The assessment of a company's strengths and weaknesses is not an end in itself. This assessment should feed into, and affect, the process of strategic market planning. Some of the major uses of the outcome of a strengths and weaknesses assessment, together with major strategic planning concepts which accompany this use are now described.

Matching strengths and weaknesses to opportunities and threats: the concept of 'strategic fit'

Environmental monitoring is important to assess opportunities and threats which might face an organization. Only when a company has assessed its own strengths and weaknesses, is it in an objective position to evaluate what constitutes a company marketing opportunity or threat. By carefully matching environmental trends and changes to its own particular blend of distinctive competences the strategic marketing planner is able to devise strategies which build on the company's strengths, while at the same time minimizing its weaknesses. By so doing, the planner aims to achieve a **'strategic fit'**.

Responding to environmental changes and trends: the concept of 'strategic windows'

A key feature of the environment is that it is constantly changing. Because of this, both the opportunities and threats assessment and the assessment of company strengths and weaknesses (SWOT analysis) should be carried out at regular intervals. If a company does not do this, then over time it is likely to find that a previously good 'strategic fit' has changed. In a changing environment there are often only limited periods when the fit between the distinctive competences of a company and the opportunities presented by the environment are at optimum positions. Abell[18] has referred to such periods as **'strategic windows'**; unless the organization acts quickly (which requires an effective system of SWOT analysis) then these windows will close. He suggests that the 'strategic window' concept can be used both by companies already in a market and by would-be entrants. For incumbents, the concept enables the assessment of future strategies to take account of changes in the environment, and in particular to assess the allocation of resources to existing activities. For the new entrant, the concept provides a framework for assessing possible diversification and new market entry opportunities based on matching these to organizational strengths.

The 1990s witnessed a large increase in the number of people living alone. This group comprises several segments including, for example, young people leaving home for the first time, newly divorced individuals and new widows and widowers. It is primarily the first two of these groups which account for the increase in the demand for small, one-person dwellings that are easily managed and affordable. The builder and developer, Barratt, were one of the first companies to spot this trend and develop homes and marketing programmes to fill this need. Barratt developed a competitive edge by being amongst the first to spot this strategic window of opportunity.

RELATIONSHIP TO OTHER AREAS OF STRATEGIC MARKETING PLANNING

We have seen that the assessment of an organization's strengths and weaknesses, together with the analysis of environmental trends and changes, is a key input to the identification of strategic windows and the development of a strategic fit. It is important to recognize that in achieving this, appraisal of strengths and weaknesses is an essential input to the whole of the strategic marketing process, including for example:

- business definition and objective setting;
- the selection of appropriate target markets;
- the formulation and implementation of marketing mix strategies.

In particular, we must remember that a strengths and weaknesses assessment enables the planner to determine what might be wanted or needed to change the company's profile of strengths and weaknesses. In contrast to environmental opportunities and threats, over which the company may have little or no control, with strengths and weaknesses it can implement action programmes to alter its profile.

For example, if an assessment indicates areas of relative weakness that are important to competitive success in the markets in which a company operates, then steps can be taken to correct these weaknesses. Similarly, a company need not limit itself to future strategies and opportunities which make use only of its existing strengths. If the opportunity is potentially substantial then a company can seek to develop or acquire the strengths required to take advantage of the situation.

Assessing core competencies

Closely related to the notion of distinctive competencies and key factors for success discussed earlier, Prahalad and Hamel[19] suggested that a sustainable competitive advantage for a company is often based on a set of central strengths which together form what they term a '**core competence**'. This is what can be used to develop successful strategies against competitors, e.g. it is suggested that 3M's core competence is based on their knowledge and applications of sticky-tape technology. Canon, on the other hand, has core competencies in precision mechanics, optical technologies and micro-electronics. The Black and Decker Company's core competencies are in the design and manufacture of small motors. Central to the notion of core competencies is the fact that they underpin the company as a whole and can be used to support a number of different markets and businesses in the organization. For this reason core competencies are likened to the root system of a tree which supports the rest of the structure; core products of the company stem from the core competencies represented by the trunk of a tree and its major limbs, whereas the smaller branches are business units and the leaves and flowers are specific end products. A company must identify the core competencies around which its current and possibly future success will be built and seek to ensure that these are nurtured, protected and enhanced. As with all strengths, core competencies will only develop a sustainable competitive advantage where they can be used to generate customer value and where they are defendable and superior to competitors.

The notion of marketing assets

First used by Davidson[20-22] in a series of three articles in *Marketing* magazine, the notion of **marketing assets** is a valuable contribution to our knowledge of how to utilize an internal appraisal of strengths and weaknesses in competitive marketing. Essentially, Davidson contends that marketing assets are strengths that can be used to advantage in the marketplace (which is after all the reason for assessing a company's strengths and weaknesses in the first place). He contrasts asset-based marketing with more traditional market-based marketing. Market-based marketing is the notion of identifying customer needs and seeking ways to satisfy these needs profitably. Asset-based marketing, somewhat controversially, starts with a company and its assets and asks how the company can use these assets more effectively in the marketplace. It involves considering, for example, how any identified skills and resources from an internal appraisal can be converted into better value for the customer. In practice there needs to be a combination of both market-based and asset-based marketing. This makes sense because strategic market plans essentially match company resources and strengths to the needs of the environment and the marketplace.

The starting point of developing an asset-based approach to marketing is essentially the same as in a conventional strengths and weaknesses assessment, inasmuch as it commences with the identification and appraisal of all the resources, skills and assets of a company. Davidson suggests a checklist to identify key areas of assets. This checklist encompasses the following examples of asset types: people; working capital; capital equipment; customer franchises e.g. brand names, unique products or processes, patents, superior service skills; access to third-party resources such as joint ventures or agreements; sales distribution and service networks and scale advantages due to market share and size.

Having established an inventory of assets, the marketing manager should then establish key exploitable assets for future strategy. This involves asking a number of key questions about identified assets such as: 'How can the brand name be exploited further, and how far can the brand be stretched without weakening the franchise?' Overall, we are seeking to establish how the assets of the company can be exploited more effectively in marketing terms. It is important to note that throughout the exercise, assets are examined from a marketer's point of view and not from an accountant's stance. An example of how this can lead to more effective marketing, which exemplifies this notion of asset-based marketing, is the strategy of brand extension. Davidson gives the example of Johnson & Johnson's baby shampoo which until the early 1970s was positioned exclusively for babies. Research showed that it was also being used by mothers and the company decided that by repositioning the brand to extend product usage, much more effective use could be made of the powerful asset of the brand name. A similar example is the move by many of the food companies to extend their brand franchises, e.g. when Mars extended the brand to include ice cream and food products.

Marketing assets has proved to be a useful perspective on the assessment and uses of an analysis of strengths and weaknesses. However, both market brand and asset-based marketing are necessary to achieve a balance between satisfying consumers and the effective utilization of a company's resources.

SUMMARY

Environmental analysis is important in strategic market planning. This appraisal is crucial because it is from trends and changes in the environment that marketing opportunities and threats arise. This means it is important for the planner to appraise or 'scan' the environment. We have seen the development of formal systematic scanning systems, but this has not perhaps kept pace with the development of strategic approaches to planning. The 'environment' of the marketing planner and its organization includes all those factors outside the marketing management function of the firm; it encompasses the intra-firm environment, the micro-environment and the macro-environment.

Effective environmental appraisal requires the use of a systematic framework in an organization, although such frameworks are rare. Even using a systematic framework, environmental appraisal is made more difficult by the problems of identifying 'relevant' trends, forecasting the future and assessing the impact of environmental trends and changes. It is important to remember that the prime purpose of the assessment of environmental factors is to identify marketing opportunities and threats.

A key element of environmental appraisal for planning purposes is the analysis of the competitive environment. The marketing planner must identify competitors in existing and proposed markets and in particular should understand the competitive structure of relevant industries. In addition to this the strategic marketing planner must appraise and understand competitor objectives and strategies; their relative strengths and weaknesses; and their likely reactions to competitive moves. All of this requires an effective system of competitor intelligence-gathering activities.

The extent of competition in many markets has prompted considerable research regarding the relationship between a company's competitive position in an industry and the choice of strategies. We have seen that strategies differ according to a company's competitive market position. On the one hand a company's competitive position may be designated along a continuum ranging between 'dominant' to 'untenable'. An alternative perspective on competitive position is that of market leadership, challenger, follower or nicher. Both perspectives provide useful insight into possible marketing strategies. With respect to the competitor element of the environment, we have increasingly seen that marketers are drawing upon the concepts and principles developed by the military for the battlefield in developing suitable marketing strategies.

The assessment of an organization's strengths and weaknesses is the second key strand in the process of conducting a SWOT analysis. At first sight this seems straightforward. In fact, the analysis of strengths and weaknesses is complex and multifaceted. In particular, we have seen that the planner must think beyond simply listing resources, although the use of checklists can be helpful. It is important to establish the attributes to be assessed, with the key ones deriving from the key factors for competitive success in an industry which, in turn, are linked to how customers choose and what they consider to be 'good value'. Related to this, it is important to understand precisely what constitutes a 'strength' or a 'weakness', to establish the magnitude of these in the organization and assess these in relation to competition.

There are advantages to having consultants conduct a strengths and weaknesses assessment, although through cross-functional teamwork the problems of using company personnel to perform the analysis can be minimized. Valuable insights into organizational strengths and weaknesses can be gleaned from customers' perceptions of a company and its competitors and the use of profiling systems.

The SWOT analysis is an essential but preliminary step in the delineation and selection of marketing strategies. A strengths and weaknesses assessment provides a key input into defining the business, objective setting and strategy selection and implementation. Finally, we examined the notions of relating the analysis of strengths and weaknesses to the concept of 'core competencies' and 'marketing assets'.

KEY TERMS

CASE STUDY

Pathological Investigations Ltd

Bob Scott has just received the latest figures from his market research agency regarding last year's overall market position. He is pleased as this is the third year that the company in which he is marketing director, has come out leader in terms of market share.

The company, Pathological Investigations Ltd, was formed ten years ago and supplies specialist measuring and testing machinery for use primarily in pathological laboratories. From nothing, the company has grown by overtaking competitors in the market based on innovative new products, aggressive pricing and high levels of after-sales service and technical advice. When the company started, the present incumbents in the market were well established with stable market positions and traditional ways of trading. In fact Bob Scott's competitors had become complacent over the years. Although these competitors were well established and much larger than the new entrant, perhaps because of these characteristics, some of their products and technologies were outdated. For example, they did not include the most recent developments in pharmaceutical measuring and testing machinery from America. Technology had moved on and Scott's company spotted the opportunity of applying this new technology to a new range of products for the industry.

In addition to changes in technology, the market had also changed. Government initia-

tives had forced hospital administrators and purchasing officers to become more effective and efficient in their supplier choice for equipment and consumables. New systems of tendering were introduced which made existing supplier relationships, often developed over many years, less important as more and more emphasis in supplier choice was placed on value for money. Scott and his colleagues spotted these trends and decided there was an opportunity for a new competitor in the market.

Ten years on, Scott quite rightly could feel a degree of satisfaction in how things had gone. They had moved from being a market nicher, to being a market challenger, and eventually market leader in the short space of ten years.

Scott has a forthcoming meeting with his fellow directors in research and development, finance, personnel and production. He is worried that their now established position as market leader is beginning to lead to an air of complacency in the company. It seems to him that new product development has slowed, and there is not as much enthusiasm to secure new business. He is also worried that two more small new companies have entered the market with exceptionally good products and very cost-effective pricing policies.

He feels that at the forthcoming meeting he needs to impress upon his fellow directors the fact that history appears to be repeating itself.

CASE STUDY QUESTION

What elements of the marketing environment should Bob Scott and his marketing team analyse and assess with regard to developing future marketing plans, and how can the company attempt to protect its position as the market leader?

REFERENCES

1 Carson, R. (1962), *Silent Spring*, New York: Houghton Mifflin.

2 Aguilar, F.J. (1967), *Scanning the Business Environment*, Basingstoke: Macmillan.

3 Jain, S.C. (1984), 'Environmental scanning; how the best companies do it', *Journal of Long Range Planning*, April: 117–28.

4 Johnson, G., Scholes, K. and Whittington, R. (2008), *Exploring Corporate Strategy*, 8th edn, London: Prentice-Hall, p. 505.

5 Jain, S.C. (2004), *Marketing Planning and Strategy*, 7th edn, Cincinnati: South Western Publishing Co.

6 Tversky, A. and Kahnemann, D. (1995), 'Judgements under uncertainty, heuristics and biases', *Science*, 185: 1124–31.

7 Kotler, P. and Keller, K.L. (2009), *Marketing Management*, 13th edn, Upper Saddle River, NJ: Prentice-Hall, p. 91.

8 Porter, M.E. (1985), *Competitive Advantage: Creating and Sustaining Superior Performance*, New York: Free Press, p. 32.

9 Johnson, G., Scholes, K. and Whittington, op. cit. (4).

10 Johnson, G. and Thomas, H. (2008), 'Research in the brewing industry', in G. Johnson, K. Scholes and R. Whittington, *Exploring Corporate Strategy*, 8th edn, London: Prentice-Hall, pp. 88–91.

11 Kotler, P. (1997), *Marketing Management: Analysis, Planning, Implementation and Control*, 9th edn, Upper Saddle River, NJ: Prentice-Hall, p. 239.

12 Flax, S., 'How to snoop on your competition', *Fortune*, 14 May 1984, 29–33.

13 Ohmae, K. (2008), *The End of the Nation State: The Rise of Regional Economies*, London: HarperCollins, Chapter 2.

14 Ansoff, H.I. (2007), *Strategic Management*, New York: McGraw-Hill.

15 Hamel, G. and Prahalad, C.K. (1989), 'Strategic intent', *Harvard Business Review*, 67(3): 63–76.

16 Porter, M.E. (1985), *Competitive Advantage: Creating and Sustaining Superior Performance*, New York: Free Press.

17 Johnson, G., Scholes, K. and Whittington R., op. cit. (4), p. 110.

18 Abell, D.F. (1978), 'Strategic windows', *Journal of Marketing*, July.

19 Prahalad, C.K., and Hamel, G. (1990), 'The core competence of the corporation', *Harvard Business Review*, May–June: 79–91.

20 Davidson, H. (1983), 'Putting assets first', *Marketing*, Haymarket Business Publications, 17 November.

21 Davidson, H. (1983), 'Building on a winner', *Marketing*, Haymarket Business Publications, 24 November: 32–6.

22 Davidson, H. (1983), 'Making an entrance', *Marketing*, Haymarket Business Publications, 1 December: 38–41.

Evaluating and controlling strategic marketing

LEARNING OBJECTIVES

By the end of this chapter you will:

- understand the importance of evaluation and controlling strategic marketing activities
- be aware of the elements of the control process and how these apply to the key areas for control in marketing
- understand the distinctions and relationships between profit control, efficiency control and strategic control in marketing

INTRODUCTION

In this chapter we assess the efficiency and effectiveness of strategic marketing efforts. The evaluation and control of marketing probably represents one of the weakest areas of marketing practice in many companies. There are a number of reasons for this. First, there is no such thing as a 'standard' system of control for marketing. Other functional areas of management have well established techniques and systems of control in, for example, production planning and control, financial planning and control and quality control. With the exception of annual sales and profit control, marketing theory and practice has no universally accepted system of evaluation and control procedures. Second, and perhaps related to this, there is no doubt that evaluation and control of marketing presents complex problems for the designer of control systems. For example, in large companies several marketing areas, each with different specialists, will need to be controlled. The efforts of sales managers, marketing researchers, advertising personnel, brand managers, etc., need to be closely co-ordinated if the control and evaluation process is to be successful.

Finally, and more controversially, marketing management has resisted notions of control that are widely accepted and indeed welcomed in other functional areas. This resistance has been, and still is, justified on the basis that much marketing activity does not lend itself to traditional control concerns, and indeed can detract from more 'creative' approaches to marketing. This argument is rejected here. Certainly, control of marketing, with its myriad of complex interrelationships, is difficult. Control of marketing presents distinct measurement problems, as we saw with, for example, the evaluation of the effectiveness of advertising. We should be careful not to over-constrain marketing management with control, but such control and evaluation of marketing effort are essential, even if it is only part of 'good housekeeping'.

Sponsorship spend is a good example of how some areas of marketing have been difficult to evaluate and control. Few marketers have known exactly what they were getting from substantial spends in this area. To some extent, marketers have colluded in this failure to measure the effectiveness of sponsorship spending as it has enabled them to have more discretion over how much and where a major part of the promotional budget was spent. This is now changing. Sponsors are now demanding to know what they are getting for their money. Recent large sponsorship deals have involved clauses in the contract which allow the sponsor to withdraw if pre-specified promotional objectives and results are not achieved.

For this reason, a good understanding of the nature of control is needed, not only by designers of the control system, but also by those being controlled.

THE ESSENTIALS OF THE CONTROL PROCESS

The essentials of the control process for any management function are shown in Figure 14.1. We can see that it contains four essential elements, namely:

- setting specific performance standards;
- locating responsibility for achieving these standards;
- evaluating performance against standards;
- taking corrective action.

In addition, we can see that performance standards should stem from and reflect the objectives, strategies and tactics of the planning process. The corrective action then feeds back to, and potentially affects, the planning process itself, performance standards, and those responsible for achieving these standards.

Building on this overview of the control process, designing an effective system of control requires consideration of the following:

Information

In Chapter 12 we considered the importance and design of the marketing information system. The control process is reliant upon timely, accurate and up-to-date information. In designing the control systems for marketing strategy, the information element should be based on establishing minimum rather than maximum information needs. This will mean improved, not reduced, performance. When designing a control system, if we are not careful, marketing personnel can spend

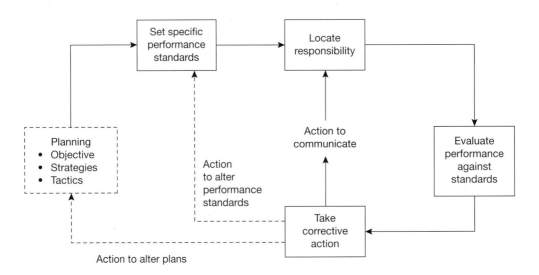

FIGURE 14.1 An overview of the control process

more time accounting for their activities than performing them. In addition, information costs money. The control system, of which information is a part, should not cost more than the costs that would be incurred if there were no controls. Finally, information needs to be analysed and presented in a way that is understandable to those who require it.

Communication and 'noise' in the system

As shown in Figure 14.1, communication is essential for effective control. Managers need to be made aware of standards of performance against which their activities and those of their own subordinates are to be judged. In addition, rapid feedback of results is important so that differences between required and actual standards of performance can be corrected. Direct communication between manager and subordinates, rather than passing information down a potentially long chain of command, is preferred as this minimizes the **'noise'** in the control system which can occur when information is distorted by having it passed down an extended scalar chain of command.

Human aspects of control

'Control' can be viewed negatively if individuals fear that the control process will be used not only to judge their performance, but as a basis for punishment. Another reason for this negative view is the fact that the process of collecting information for control is often seen as detracting from 'real' work. Salespeople, in particular, often see control in this way – they often resent having to fill in visit report forms which contain essential control information because they feel it leaves less time for selling.

To be successful, people involved and affected by the control process should be consulted in both the design and implementation stages of marketing control and need to be convinced that the purpose of control is to improve their personal levels of success and that of the company. Subordinates need to be involved in setting and agreeing their own standards of performance, preferably through a system of **management by objectives**.

THE CONTROL PROCESS IN ACTION

The strategic control process should enable management to accomplish the following:

1   to allow problems, i.e. deviations from plans and budgets to be identified at an early stage on a continuous basis as the plan is being implemented;
2   to assess causes of deviations from standards of performance so corrective action can be taken;
3   to provide an input to the process of identifying and analysing opportunities and threats;
4   to provide a positive incentive to staff to improve their performance.

Figure 14.2 shows how the concept of a control process can be translated into action. In the context of a marketing control system, each of the steps involves the following.

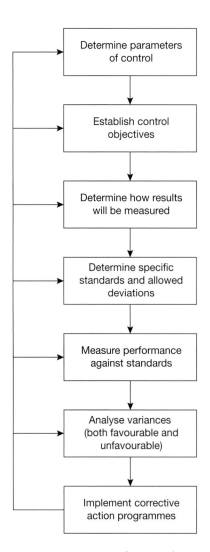

FIGURE 14.2 Steps in the control process

Determining control parameters

Determining what to **control** (the **parameters**) is the start point of the control process. Overall, sales, costs and profits are the major parameters, but marketing control involves more than just these key areas. The company may have other key objectives which relate to, for example, social responsibility or technological reputation. In addition, each of the marketing functions will also involve objectives, and hence parameters, which will need to be controlled. The parameters of marketing control must include those for controlling the marketing objectives and strategies themselves in order to assess whether or not they are still relevant to the marketing environment.

The objectives of control

When we have decided what to control, control objectives can be set. These will encompass functional and financial performance in addition to more qualitative objectives. If planning objectives have been clearly set, the control process can build on these. Each objective must be achieved within a given budget, so budgetary control is essential. Broad control objectives need to be broken down into sub-objectives for each area of marketing activity. Having done this we can then establish specific standards of performance, together with the degree of deviation, if any, which will be tolerated in the system.

Establishing specific standards of performance and allowed deviations

The next step in the control process is to establish specific performance standards that will need to be achieved for each area of activity if overall and sub-objectives are to be achieved. For example, to achieve a specified sales objective, a target of performance for each sales area may be required. In turn, this may require a specific standard of performance from each of the salespeople in the region with respect to, for example, number of calls, conversion rates and order value.

Like each standard of performance, we must also try to determine what are allowable deviations for both under- and over-performance. When these allowable deviations are exceeded, then this would initiate some sort of corrective action. Such limits are useful for initiating ongoing control.

Measuring performance

Clearly, standards mean that we must measure performance against them. In addition to determining appropriate techniques of measurement we have to determine such things as frequency of measurement, e.g. daily, weekly, monthly or annually and the responsibility for measurement, i.e. who should do it. More frequent and more detailed measurement usually means more cost. We need to be careful to ensure that the costs of measurement and the control process itself do not exceed the value of such measurements and do not overly interfere with the activities of those being measured.

Analysing results

Analysis and interpretation of results prior to taking any action is one of the most important and yet most difficult steps in the control process. Because marketing is a complex process there is potential for misinterpreting the causes of variances from standards and hence compounding the problem by taking the wrong corrective action. The system of marketing control, therefore, requires an information system which is based on disaggregative data so that variances can be broken down into their constituent causes. The system should also allow responsibilities for these variances to be pinpointed so that corrective action can be communicated. The analysis system should also allow sufficient time for detailed analysis to be made to avoid taking precipitous actions.

Taking corrective action

The final step in the control process is implementation of action programmes designed to correct any deviations from standard. There is a temptation to assume that corrective action only needs to be taken when results are less than those required or when budgets and costs are being exceeded. In fact, both 'negative' (underachievement) and 'positive' (overachievement) deviations may require corrective action. For example, failure to spend the amount budgeted for, say, sales force expenses may indicate either that the initial sum allocated was excessive and needs to be reassessed, and/or that the sales force was not as 'active' as they might be. Similarly, overachievement on, say, market share or profitability may mean that overall marketing objectives in these areas need to be looked at again. This relates back to the analysis stage of the control sequence, but it shows that *all* significant deviations from standards should be looked at with a view to taking corrective action.

Another question which arises *vis-à-vis* corrective action (and indeed the whole process of control) is timing: how quickly should corrective action be implemented? This will vary according to the area of control and the nature and extent of deviations from standards. For example, a sudden fall in sales and profits will probably require immediate action. In broader terms, some elements of control will effectively be continuous; for example, the control of sales calls and expenses, which may be carried out on a monthly, weekly or even daily basis. Other areas of control will relate more to the annual planning sequence and will include sales and market share analysis. Finally, we may have control processes which relate to the totality of marketing activities and systems, i.e. a comprehensive examination of the marketing function itself within the organization. In effect, this is a **marketing audit** which is an essential part of the strategic control process.

KEY AREAS FOR CONTROL IN MARKETING

Kotler and Keller[1] distinguish four types of marketing control, involving different approaches, different purposes and a different allocation of responsibilities as illustrated in Table 14.1.

Annual plan control

The purpose of annual plan control is to determine the extent to which marketing efforts over the year have been successful. Annual plan control activities are the responsibility of senior and middle management. Analysis and control will centre on measuring and evaluating sales in relation to sales goals, market share analysis, expense analysis and financial analysis.

Sales analysis

Sales performance is understandably a key indicator of marketing effectiveness, and hence an essential element of annual plan control. The marketing budget will specify objectives for sales, and according to the individual company these will be broken down into sales targets for individual parts of the business, customer groups, individual products and/or brands and ultimately individual

TABLE 14.1 Types of marketing control

Type of control	Prime responsibility	Purpose of control	Examples of techniques/approaches
Annual plan control	Top management Middle management	To examine whether planned results are being achieved	▪ Sales analysis ▪ Market share analysis ▪ Sales to expense ratios ▪ Financial analysis ▪ Customer tracking
Profit control	Marketing controller	To examine where the company is making and losing money	Profitability by: ▪ Product ▪ Territory ▪ Customer ▪ Segment ▪ Trade channel ▪ Order size
Efficiency control	Line and staff management Marketing controller	To evaluate and improve the spending efficiency and impact of marketing expenditures	Efficiency of: ▪ Sales force ▪ Advertising ▪ Sales promotion ▪ Distribution
Stragetic control	Top management Marketing auditor	To examine whether company is pursuing its best opportunities with respect to markets, products and channels	▪ Marketing effectiveness ratings ▪ Marketing audit ▪ Marketing excellence review ▪ Company ethical and social responsibility review

salespeople. In other words, sales analysis and control is likely to comprise a hierarchy of standards and control levels, each of which are interlinked, as shown in Figure 14.3.

We can see that analysis and control of sales may involve considerable time and effort. Any variance in achieving sales targets at the corporate level are ultimately a result of variances in the performance of individual salespeople. At every level of sales analysis and control, variances must be investigated with a view to determining their causes. For example, at the broadest level, variances may be due to one or a combination of volume or price. Put simply, sales revenue may be down on target because the company has not sold enough or because volume has been achieved only on the bias of price cutting. A more detailed analysis of the reasons for volume variances might, in turn, be refined to volume variances by individual members of the sales force due to, say, poor motivation or bad journey planning.

From this example, it can be seen that throughout the control process we may need to provide disaggregated control information so that broad measures of evaluation and control can be

Total corporate sales targets

Frequency of
evaluation
and control

Divisional/SBU sales targets

Product line sales targets

Individual product/brand sales targets

Sales targets by, e.g.

Increasing

- Customer group/individual customer
- Distribution channel
- Sales territories/sales manager
- Individual salesperson

FIGURE 14.3 The hierarchy of sales analysis and control

investigated in sufficient detail to pinpoint causes of possible variances, both favourable and unfavourable, to take the necessary corrective action.

Market share analysis

Portfolio techniques of planning are detailed in Chapter 15 and these are underpinned by the relationship between market share and cash flow and profits. In addition, in the context of marketing control, marketing objectives, both short and long term, are set for market share.

The principal reason for measuring and evaluating market share performance is because it allows a company to assess how well it is doing compared with the overall market and competition. A company might find that while sales volume has declined over the year its market share has increased. Clearly, declining sales volume would still represent a cause for concern. Nevertheless, an increase in market share would indicate that a company is faring better than competitors in a market which has declined overall. This observation suggests a very different course of action on the part of marketing management than that suggested by a simple analysis of sales.

As the last millennium came to a close, Marks & Spencer were struggling to maintain the sales and profits they had enjoyed in previous years. Most worrying for Marks & Spencer was their fall in market share. Like most companies, the company realized that even small drops in market share can have a tremendous impact, not only on profitability but also on the market standing and image of a company. Marks & Spencer started the new millennium therefore with a determined effort to recapture lost market share. This has involved substantial restructuring of the company and the introduction of major new lines, the sale of non-M&S branded merchandise and store developments, which the company hopes will restore their standing in the market.

As with sales analysis, measurement of market share alone is not sufficient to determine the action(s) to be taken. The evaluation process requires that marketing management determines the reasons for observed levels of company market share and any significant differences and trends. On the basis of this, the marketing manager must then determine the actions required and by whom. Results and conclusions of the evaluation of the annual marketing plan must be discussed with those responsible and a future plan of action agreed.

It is important to recognize that in interpreting market share results, several bases of measuring market share might be needed to provide useful control information for further decision making. For example, Figures 14.4(a)–(d) show how various measures of market share for the same product might produce different pictures of the position of the product in the marketplace. The example shows four possible market share percentages for a hypothetical marketer of car tyres. Figures 14.4(a) and (b) represent this manufacturer's percentage market share by volume and value respectively of the total UK car tyre market. We see straight away that very different pictures of market share are obtained using these different measures and they may in themselves provide insights into this company's market position compared to competitors.

Figure 14.4(c) represents this company's market share of the replacement (rather than original equipment) UK tyre market. Again we can see that a very different picture of market share is obtained than when using the total UK tyre market as a basis. This simply illustrates that we need to be quite

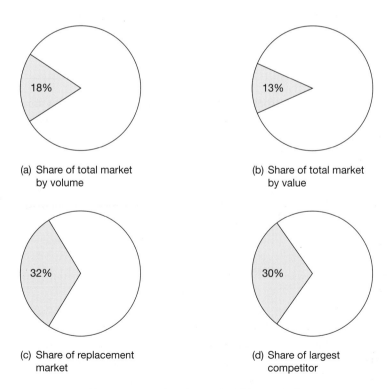

(a) Share of total market
    by volume

(b) Share of total market
    by value

(c) Share of replacement
    market

(d) Share of largest
    competitor

FIGURE 14.4 Measuring market share: the UK tyre market

clear about which 'market' we are talking about when we set objectives for market share and how we interpret our performance in this respect.

Figure 14.4(d) uses a measure of market share based on this company's share relative to its largest competitor. As we shall see in Chapter 15, relative market share is a key input to many of the 'portfolio techniques' of strategic market planning.

Marketing expenses to sales ratios

An important element of the marketing budget is the planned expenditures on the elements of marketing activity designed to achieve budgeted levels of sales. Precisely what these elements comprise, and how they are to be grouped together for the purpose of control and evaluation, will vary from company to company, but common expense areas for marketing would include:

- sales force expenses;
- promotional expenses;
- distribution expenses;
- market research expenses.

As indicated, each of these groups of expense will comprise a series of activities, each of which may have its own budgeted expense level for the year e.g. promotional expenses may comprise:

- advertising expenses;
- sales promotion expenses;
- public relations expenses.

Finally, budgeted expenses for each activity may comprise expenses for each product, sales area, customer group and so on. For example, sales force expenses might be broken down into budget expenses as shown in Figure 14.5.

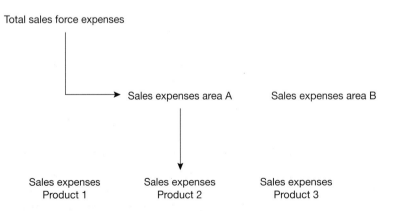

FIGURE 14.5 Breaking down sales force expenses

As we have seen throughout the discussion of control, the evaluation process, in the case of marketing expenses to sales ratios, usually starts with broad measures e.g. we should first measure and control the ratio of total marketing expenses to sales. We start by determining the standards for marketing expenses to sales together with upper and lower limits between which we are prepared to allow these expenses to deviate. Ideally, total marketing expenses to sales should be evaluated on a continuous basis throughout the planning year, normally each month. Where total expenses deviate outside the control limits the reasons should be investigated and corrective action taken. At this stage the broad measure of total marketing expenses to sales will need to be broken down into the previously defined expense areas of sales, promotion, distribution, market research etc. In turn, each of the expense areas can then be further disaggregated in order to pinpoint the precise reasons for deviations from standards. If all this appears to imply a detailed and comprehensive system of marketing expenses control – it does. Provided that the costs of control do not exceed the benefits derived from it, and provided that these benefits are perceived and accepted by those being controlled, then the control system should be as detailed as possible.

Customer tracking

The control elements we have discussed in the context of the annual marketing plan involve quantitative elements of marketing control. Equally important to the control process are the more qualitative elements of marketing control, in particular **customer tracking**, or the assessment and evaluation of customer feedback and attitudes. Effective marketing control should include systematic and regular tracking of factors that indicate how customers feel about the company's marketing activities and in particular should highlight any potential problems before they become serious. Examples of information and procedures which form this part of the control system include:

- consumer panel information;
- returns and complaints;
- customer surveys;
- sales force reports.

This last element, sales force reports, is a valuable source of information on customer attitudes and can highlight early signs of problems. Unfortunately, this element of reporting is often resented by salespersons who view it as a chore and a distraction from what they see as their main task of selling. In addition, it might be regarded with some suspicion by salespeople as to how such information might be used for control purposes, so care should be taken to ensure that they understand the purpose and accept the value of providing such information.

Customer tracking can be carried out typically on a monthly basis for such matters as customer complaints, panel data and sales force reports, backed up by customer surveys on a biannual or annual basis. Although most qualitative control will relate to customers, other important publics, such as the local community, watchdog bodies and shareholders, might also usefully be included as part of the qualitative control system.

Profit control: the marketing budget

In addition to the previously discussed control elements of the annual marketing plan, organizations should be concerned with **profit control.** We have seen that key areas of marketing control, such as sales analysis and marketing expense analysis, are evaluated against pre-set standards for both sales and costs. These standards for sales and costs derive from the marketing budget. When we combine the notion of profit control with sales and costs we have the basis of a complete system of budgetary control for marketing.

However, when it comes to the analysis of profits in the budgetary control process, a number of complex and controversial issues arise, not only with respect to the control of profits, but also with respect to the compilation of budgets. We can illustrate these contentions by examining the essence of profitability control.

The focus of profitability control begins with the company evaluating the profitability of different marketing entities. Precisely what these entities will be will vary according to the particular company, and how its profit and cost centres are organized. In addition, the entities may also vary according to the precise purpose of the profitability analysis, but examples of marketing entities would include products, channels of distribution, customer groups and so on, with the objective of discovering where the firm is making profits or losses in various parts of its business; e.g. consider a one-product company selling to three distinct customer groups:

- Customer Group 1: industrial buyers;
- Customer Group 2: institutional buyers;
- Customer Group 3: domestic buyers.

A profitability analysis of these marketing entities (i.e. customer groups) would allow marketing management to assess the differences, if any, in profitability between these customer groups and hence the extent to which future strategies and tactics might be designed to reflect this. In order to assess the profitability of these three customer groups we need to be able to associate both costs and revenues with each of them. A simple example serves to illustrate the problems that can arise when we try to do this for this hypothetical company.

First of all, let us assume that the overall profit and loss statement for the company is as shown in Table 14.2. As mentioned earlier, if we now want to know the profitability by customer group we have to be able to associate the revenues and costs associated with each. For some elements of the overall profit and loss account, this is relatively straightforward. For example, variable costs, and some elements of marketing expenses, such as sales force costs and marketing research, may be directly attributed to each customer group. This still leaves us, however, with *fixed costs* and some of the marketing expenses, such as administration and elements of the promotional expenses, which must be in some way *allocated* to each customer group. In practice it can be difficult to identify some aspects of marketing costs. Certainly, it is possible to devise a way of allocating these remaining costs to the three customer groups, but often, and particularly with fixed costs, the allocation is arbitrary. We may end up with a 'profitability' analysis that is possibly misleading for evaluation and decision making with respect to marketing entities. Related to this, though perhaps more fundamental to the issue of profitability control, is the question of what constitutes an appropriate

TABLE 14.2 The conventional profit and loss statement

	£	£
Sales		100,000
Cost of goods:		
Fixed costs	30,000	
Variable costs	20,000	
Total costs		50,000
Gross margin		50,000
Marketing expenses:		
Advertising	10,000	
Sales force cost	15,000	
Administration	5,000	
Distribution	5,000	
Market research	5,000	
Total marketing expense		40,000
Net profit		**10,000**

measure of profitability for marketing entities and marketing effort. Specifically, what we are talking about is the issue of which costs to deduct from revenues for the purpose of marketing profitability control.

In the example, the net profit figure for the company requires the deduction of all costs. Similarly, if we require a net profit figure for each of our customer groups, as we have seen, the total costs associated with each customer group must be deducted from the revenues derived from that group. For purposes of control, evaluation and decision making, perhaps a more useful and relevant measure of marketing profitability is *contribution to profit* rather than net profit.

Although there are some differences between the suggested approaches to using these contribution-based control mechanisms for marketing profitability, the idea is illustrated in Table 14.3 for one of our hypothetical customer groups. The controllable margin represents the contribution to profits of customer group one, taking into account only those revenues and costs that can be directly attributed to this customer group.

Clearly this is not to deny the importance of net profit to the organization, nor the fact that in the long run all costs need to be covered. However, the contribution approach to marketing budgeting and profitability control recognizes the fact that non-traceable fixed costs lie outside the control of the marketing manager and that to allocate them to marketing entities potentially distorts the picture of the true profitability of these entities, which, after all, is what we are seeking to establish. Needless to say, a distorted picture also leads to ineffective decision making.

TABLE 14.3 The contribution approach to measuring marketing profitability

		£
Minus:	Variable production costs: customer group 1	_____
	Manufacturing contribution: customer group 1	_____
Minus:	Attributable marketing costs for customer group 1	_____
	Contribution margin: customer group 1	_____
	Less the non-variable costs incurred specifically for customer group 1	_____
	Controllable margin: customer group 1	_____

A further broader, but inevitable, issue which the marketing contribution approach raises is whether or not net profits should be included in marketing objectives and budgets, and hence form part of the responsibilities of the marketing department. Many believe they should not, in that so many other factors affect net profits that are clearly outside the direct control of marketing. The view taken here is that the contribution method in fact offers a sounder approach to planning and controlling the profitability element of marketing.

Finally, it is important to stress that profitability control requires a carefully designed, pre-determined information and control system. In particular, the accountancy system needs to be designed to provide information on costs that can be easily translated into profit performance by the marketing entities of most relevance to the particular organization. Budgeting can be difficult, but its implementation is facilitated by the use of computer models.

Efficiency control

As the term suggests, **efficiency control** is concerned with ensuring that each element of the marketing mix, together with their sub-elements, is being utilized as efficiently as possible. Examination of the efficiency of marketing activities may derive from other parts of the control system. For example, we may instigate an examination of efficiency as a result of, say, adverse profitability results for a marketing entity. However, efficiency controls should be built into the marketing planning and control systems so as to make them part of a dynamic system. As an example of how efficiency control might be applied, we can take the example of personal selling.

Personal selling can be evaluated at two levels – first, at the level of the individual salesperson, and second, as we have seen, by looking at the total selling effort. The individual salesperson will be evaluated on how well he or she has met performance targets such as:

- number of sales calls per day (number of orders);
- strike rate (number of quotations);
- average order value;

- prospective success ratio;
- expense targets.

In addition to these quantitative aspects of efficiency, we should also include some qualitative aspects such as:

- sales skills;
- customer relationships;
- co-operation and attitudes.

The evaluation of total selling effort is basically derived from the sum of the contributions of all sales personnel. Evaluation of individual sales personnel and the total selling function is often viewed as a negative device for the control of salespeople, which is too narrow a view. A more comprehensive view is that the evaluation process, in addition to providing information about performance, can also be used to motivate and encourage sales personnel to plan their sales campaigns more efficiently and effectively. Hence evaluation brings considerable benefits both to the organization as a whole and to the individual salesperson.

This sort of detailed evaluation and control of marketing efficiency should be applied to each element of marketing mix activity, including advertising, sales promotion and distribution.

Strategic control

The **strategic control** of marketing planning process pertains to the control of the strategic planning process itself. Two tools are available to marketing management for this process: the marketing effectiveness rating review and the marketing audit.

Control of marketing effectiveness

Control of marketing effectiveness is essentially aimed at evaluating:

- the extent to which the company is customer oriented;
- the extent to which the different functions are integrated with the marketing function, and the extent to which the marketing functions themselves are co-ordinated one with another;
- the effectiveness of the marketing information system;
- the extent to which there is a strategic perspective to marketing planning, the quality of current strategies and the efficacy of contingency planning;
- the extent to which marketing plans are communicated to lower levels, the speed of response to marketing developments and the use of marketing resources.

As we can see, control of marketing effectiveness is wide ranging, complex and requires considerable management judgement and skill. A questionnaire approach can be used, with marketing effectiveness being scored against a prepared checklist of questions. Total scores are obtained and the organization scored on a scale of marketing effectiveness ranging from poor to superior.

THE MARKETING AUDIT

Even more wide ranging than a marketing effectiveness rating is a full marketing audit. The major purpose of a marketing audit is to examine and evaluate periodically, in the light of current circumstances, the marketing objectives and policies that have been guiding the company. A marketing audit is essentially a systematic, critical and impartial review and appraisal of the total marketing operation – of the basic objectives and policies of the operation and the assumptions which underlie them, as well as of the procedures, personnel and organization employed to implement these policies and achieve the objectives.

The audit should also include a careful analysis of the company's marketing environment. Recommendations for improving marketing performance should be a major outcome from the audit process.

Any company carrying out an audit will be faced with two kinds of variable. First, there are variables over which the company has not direct control. These usually take the form of *environmental variables*. Second, there are variables over which the company has complete control that are called *operational variables*.

The process of auditing is usually associated with the financial side of the business and is conducted according to a defined set of accounting standards, which are well documented and easily understood. The total business, moreover, can also be audited, although this process is more complicated and demands considerable powers of judgement. A marketing audit is part of this larger audit and is concerned with the collection and analysis of information and data essential to effective problem solving. As Lancaster and Massingham[2] point out, the marketing audit should be concerned not only with marketing performance, but with the overall marketing philosophy in the company. For it to be beneficial an audit should be carried out on a regular basis and the company should not wait until things start to go wrong.

Carrying out the audit

We have now come full circle in the marketing planning process. The text began by discussing the importance of analysing the environment, followed by an internal appraisal of the company itself. We stressed the importance of both customers and competitors and can now remind ourselves of some of these factors by looking at how they form part of the marketing audit.

Auditing the environment

Three distinct elements of the environment are relevant to the marketing audit:

1   business/economic and market factors;
2   competitors;
3   customer needs and wants.

In the context of the marketing audit, we describe some of the factors that will need to be assessed under each category of environmental factors.

Business/economic and market factors

The following elements should be examined during a marketing audit:

■ Demographic trends are important, since it is people who make up markets. A change in size of the population, its age distribution or its regional distribution may have implications for the type of industry the company is in.

■ Markets require purchasing power as well as people. The company should audit the main economic trends. For example, high inflationary pressure may lead to a change in customer expenditure patterns, or an impending shortage of raw materials vital to the firm's business may result in the firm increasing its costs.

■ One of the most dramatic forces shaping business destiny is technology. Each new technology creates major long-run consequences. The marketer should audit changes occurring in product or process technology that can affect the company.

■ Any changes in the political/legal environment should also be audited. This environment is made up of laws, government agencies and pressure groups that may influence and constrain organizations and/or individuals. There is a substantial amount of legislation regulating businesses, which protects companies from each other, protects the larger interest of society against unbridled business behaviour and protects customers from unfair business practices.

■ The society that people grow up in shapes their basic beliefs, values and norms. The major cultural vales of the population are expressed in people's relationships to themselves, others, institutions and society. Companies need to anticipate cultural shifts to identify threats, e.g. people vary in their attitudes towards corporations, government agencies and other institutions. Most people accept these institutions, but there may be a point when they become critical of them and less trusting. A company finding itself in such a position needs to find new ways to win back confidence, perhaps by reviewing advertising communications.

■ In addition to these major forces, an examination of trends in the markets the company serves is necessary to reveal what is happening to the market size. It may be increasing or declining, with major segments behaving differently.

Competitors

As a first step in auditing its competitive environment, a company must find out who are its direct and indirect competitors, their objectives, strengths and weaknesses. The industry structure, its growth and the number of competitors in the industry help determine the degree of rivalry between the different firms. The determination of a threat of entry of new firms and the threat of substitute products provides a basis for analysing indirect and possible future competition. However, barriers such as economies of scale tend to deter new entrants. The bargaining power of suppliers refers to the ability of the industry's raw material suppliers to demand higher prices or better terms, and the bargaining power of buyers refers to the ability of the industry's customers to effect price reductions using their combined strength. These are important factors that can instigate competition. The interaction of these forces determines the intensity of competition within the industry, and should be audited on a regular basis.

Customer needs and wants

In Chapter 2, we emphasized that to achieve a profitable and durable penetration of a market, a company must base its marketing strategy upon a thorough understanding of customer needs and wants. It must also make itself familiar with the buying processes utilized by the customer and factors that influence customer choice. This requirement holds for all companies no matter what their products or the markets to which their efforts are directed. We should remember that industrial or organizational customers will not be buying on their own behalf, but on behalf of an organization, and will respond to a different set of circumstances from an individual. It is always the needs of the ultimate user that must be recognized and satisfied with the product/service. Monitoring of needs in an attempt to identify opportunities and any unsatisfied needs is also required.

The internal audit

The internal part of the marketing audit should be a comprehensive and detailed look at how effectively marketing is currently responding to the environment and its potential to do so in the future. The audit should encompass:

■ marketing objective and strategies;
■ the organizational structure for marketing, including interfaces with other functions;
■ marketing systems and procedures, including those for marketing information and control;
■ marketing mix elements, i.e. how effective are product, price, place and promotion?
■ sales, market share and profitability analysis.

There is no definitive checklist for a marketing audit. Each company must determine for itself what constitutes the detail of an appropriate audit. However, to illustrate in more detail the scope of an audit, we give an illustrative checklist for a marketing audit.

1   *Business and economic environment*

Economic	Inflation
	Unemployment
	Energy prices
	Price volatility
Political/fiscal/legal	Availability of materials, etc.
	Nationalization
	Privatization
	Trade unions
	Taxation
	Duties/levies
	Regulatory constraints, e.g. labelling, quality, safety

Social/cultural	Demographic issues, e.g. age distribution
	Changes in consumer lifestyle
	Environmental issues, e.g. pollution
	Education
	Immigration/emigration
	Religion etc.
Technological	New technology/processes
	Energy saving techniques
	New materials/substitutes
	New equipment
	New products

2 *The market*

Total market	Size (value/volume)
	Growth (value/volume)
	Trends (value/volume)
Characteristics	Developments, etc.
Products	Principal products bought
	How they are used
	Where they are used
	Packaging
	Accessories
Prices	Price levels/range
	Terms and conditions of sale
	Trade practices
	Special discounts
	Official regulations
Physical distribution	Principal methods
	Batch sizes
	Mechanical handling
	Protection
Distribution channels	Principal channels
	Purchasing patterns
	Geographical disposition
	Stocks
	Turnover
	Incentives
	Purchasing ability
	Needs
	Tastes

	Profits
	Prices paid
Communications	Principal methods
	Sales force
	Advertising
	Exhibitions
	Public relations
	Promotions
	New developments
Industry practices	Inter-firm comparisons
	Trade associations
	Trade regulations/practices
	Links with government
	Historical attitudes
	Image

3 *Competition*

Industry structure	Companies in the industry
	Their make-up
	Their market standing/reputation
	Their capacity to produce, market, distribute
	Their diversification
	Their origins and ownership
	New entrants
	Mergers and acquisitions
	Bankruptcies
	International links
	Strengths/weaknesses
Industry profitability	Historical data
	Current performance
	Relative performance of competitors
	Structure of operating costs
	Level on investment
	Return on investment
	Pricing/volume
	Sources of funding

4 *Internal audit*

Sales	Total (value/volume)
	By geographical location
	By industry/market segment

| | By customer |
| | By product |

Markets	Market share
	Profit margins
	Marketing procedures
	Organization structure
	Sales/marketing control data

Marketing mix variables	Market research
	Product development
	Product range
	Product quality
	Unit of sale
	Stock levels
	Distribution
	Dealer support
	Pricing/discounts/credit
	Packaging
	Samples
	Exhibitions
	Selling
	Sales aids
	Point of sale
	Advertising
	Sales promotion
	Public relations
	After-sales service
	Training and development

Systems and procedures	Marketing planning system, i.e. is it effective?
	Marketing objectives; are they clear and consistent with corporate objectives?
	Marketing strategy; are they appropriate for objectives?
	Structure, i.e. are duties and responsibilities clear?
	Information, i.e. adequacy of marketing intelligence and its presentation?
	Control, e.g. suitable mechanisms?
	Communication, e.g. its effectiveness? In all areas?
	Interfunction efficiency between functions/departments?
	Profitability, e.g. regular monitoring and analysis?
	Cost effectiveness, e.g. are functions/products continually reviewed in attempts to reduce excess cost?

We can see from this list that the marketing audit is far reaching and potentially complex. It encompasses not only marketing performance but also the underpinning objectives and strategies of the company. It is important to ensure that the elements of the audit match the elements of the marketing strategies that underpin it. The implication here is that the precise nature of the marketing audit and the elements contained therein should be company specific, reflecting the individual strategy of the company. We must be careful though in the application of audit 'checklists' which are useful but should be used with care and discretion in selecting those elements that are appropriate to a particular company and its situation.

SUMMARY

The final, but often neglected stage of strategic market planning is the control process. Not only is control important to evaluate how we have performed, but it completes the circle of planning in that it provides the feedback necessary for the start of the next planning cycle.

Control is often viewed with suspicion by those whose activities are being controlled and it needs to be implemented with some sensitivity by senior management. In particular, it is important to involve people in the setting of standards and in the process of determining and agreeing corrective action.

Every element of marketing should be controlled using both quantitative and qualitative standards for performance. The most obvious areas of control relate to the control of the annual marketing plan and include sales control, control of market share, control of expenses and customer tracking. In addition, profitability control is an essential element of marketing control, preferably using a contribution rather than net profit basis.

Control of marketing efficiency involves potentially detailed analysis of each and every element of the marketing mix. Again, although some of these are difficult to evaluate, e.g. the effectiveness of advertising spend, it is possible provided clear objectives and standards of performance, that are essential stages in the control process, are established.

The control process should stretch to the evaluation of the effectiveness of the marketing process itself in the organization. The marketing audit represents the most comprehensive process of marketing control and seeks to assess the entirety of a company's marketing system with a view to establishing what future strategies and actions will be required to match an ever changing and turbulent marketing environment.

KEY TERMS

CASE STUDY

Helensgate Glass Ltd

John Heady is worried about the latest sales figures for his company. As marketing manager of Helensgate Glass Ltd, he is concerned that over a twelve month period sales have dropped by some 10 per cent. However, more than this, he knows that he will have to present and explain these figures to the main board at the company's annual review of results.

He knows that understandably, the directors will want answers as to why sales have dropped. After all, in the previous five years that the company has been trading, sales have increased every year. The problem is that John simply does not know why sales have dropped, nor what this means in the context of the market as a whole.

For the past two years, he has been arguing that the control and evaluation systems in the company, particularly with respect to marketing activities, have been neglected. In arguing for more resources and effort in this area, however, the directors have always been able to point to the fact that there was no need to put more effort into this area of evaluation and control because sales were constantly rising. John now feels caught in a trap in the sense that he is going to have to explain the reasons for a drop in sales, but without having had the support of the necessary control and evaluation techniques required to provide this information.

He is determined to use the situation to reinforce his case for improved control and evaluation techniques, including the resources necessary to implement these. At the moment, the company only has a system of profit control in operation that can be used to examine profitability by product and customer group. In addition, there is a relatively crude system of sales analysis. There is no market share analysis, no systems of customer tracking, no efficiency controls and no systems of strategic control in the company. John is determined to make this case for implementing some of thee key areas of marketing control in the company at the forthcoming meeting.

CASE STUDY QUESTION

Prepare John's case for the types of controls he feels are necessary.

REFERENCES

1   Kotler, P. and Keller, K.L. (2009), *Marketing Management*, 13th edn, Upper Saddle River, NJ: Prentice-Hall, p. 689.

2   Lancaster, G. and Massingham, L. (2002), *Essentials of Marketing*, 4th edn, Maidenhead: McGraw-Hill, pp. 373–4.

Chapter 15

Strategic marketing planning tools

LEARNING OBJECTIVES

After reading this chapter you will:

- appreciate the evolution and uses of strategic marketing planning tools
- understand how these tools have become increasingly sophisticated and complex
- be familiar with the applications and limitations of the most frequently used strategic marketing planning tools
- appreciate the ways in which our knowledge of these tools of planning is constantly evolving and improving

INTRODUCTION

In Chapter 4 we examined issues relating to the actual product or service and discussed the basic theories of product life cycle and how this can be applied strategically. We also looked at new product development and specifically examined issues related to service marketing and the notion of the three Ps (people, process and physical evidence).

The chapter also detailed work by Booz, Allen and Hamilton in terms of developing and launching new products. Finally, the chapter concluded with a discussion and explanation of the work of Everett Rogers and the notion of the diffusion of innovations.

In this chapter we take the discussion to a more strategic level in terms of examining the notion of **'portfolio analysis'** along with other marketing planning tools. These tools allow us to more scientifically plan marketing strategy, and the first of the ideas that we examine relates to what is regarded as the classic work of Michael Porter.

PORTER'S MODEL OF INDUSTRY/MARKET EVOLUTION

Porter[1] distinguishes between the following three broad stages in the evolution of an industry/market:

- emerging industry;
- transition to maturity;
- decline.

Each of these stages has its own particular characteristics, some of the more important of which are shown for each stage.

Emerging industry:

uncertainty among buyers over:

product performance;
potential applications;
likelihood of obsolescence.

uncertainty among sellers over:

> customer needs;
> demand levels;
> technological developments.

Transition to maturity

> falling industry profits;
> slowdown in growth;
> customers knowledgeable about products and competitive offerings;
> less product innovation;
> competition in non-product aspects.

Decline

> competition from substitutes;
> changing customer needs;
> demographic and other macro-environmental forces and factors affecting markets.

Porter then uses the characteristics of each stage to suggest the following strategies as being appropriate to each:

Emerging industry:

Strategies developed to take account of industry competitive structure characteristics i.e.:

- threat of entry;
- rivalry among competitors;
- pressure of substitutes;
- bargaining power of buyers and suppliers.

Transition to maturity:

Strategies focused on:

- developing new market segments;
- focusing strategies for specific segments;
- more efficient organizations.

Decline

- seek pockets of enduring demand;

or

- divest.

Stage of industry development

	Growth	Maturity	Decline
Leader	• Keep ahead of the field	• Cost leadership • Raise barriers • Deter competitors	• Redefine scope • Divest peripherals • Encourage departures
Follower	• Imitation at lower cost	• Differentiation • Focus	• Differentiation • New opportunities

FIGURE 15.1 Industry life cycle and strategic position

Source: Porter, M.E. (1995), *Competitive Advantage: Creating and Sustaining Superior Performance*, New York: Free Press, p. 192.

Clearly this approach is similar to the conventional concept of product life cycle analysis in identifying the stage, specifying the characteristics of each stage, and suggesting appropriate strategies for the stages. Porter has developed the notion of industry life cycle further by linking it to the 'strategic position' of the individual organization. Strategic position is categorized in terms of whether the individual organization is a leader or a follower. This approach is shown in Figure 15.1.

Genetic engineering and biotechnology are examples of what Porter would classify as 'emerging' industries. At the moment in these industries there is substantial jockeying for position amongst the incumbents. Some organizations, however, are already emerging as leaders. For example, in genetic engineering, particularly in the area of food production, Monsanto is probably ahead of the field.

A good example of an industry in Porter's stage of 'transition to maturity' is the market for cars in the West, which has seen companies such as Mercedes and Volkswagen paying more attention to developing new market segments.

It is not difficult to find examples of industries in Porter's 'decline' stage. The textile industry in the UK is probably a good example of this. Coates Viyella, a once major employer in the UK textile industry has recently pursued strategies of divestment while at the same time seeking pockets of enduring demand – just as Porter suggests.

ARTHUR D. LITTLE'S INDUSTRY MATURITY/ COMPETITIVE POSITION MATRIX

A similar approach to that developed by Porter is that used by the business consultants, Arthur D. Little.[2] A summary of this approach is shown in Figure 15.2. The two axes of the matrix comprise 'stage of industry maturity' on the horizontal axis and 'competitive position' on the vertical axis. Stage of industry maturity is broken into four categories: embryonic, growth, maturity and ageing. A classification of which of these four the industry is in, is determined by assessing eight key descriptions:

Company's competitive position	Stage of industry maturity			
	Embryonic	Growth	Maturity	Ageing
Dominant				
Strong				
Favourable				
Tentative				
Weak				

FIGURE 15.2 The A.D. Little competitive position/industry maturity matrix

■ rate of market growth;
■ industry potential;
■ product line;
■ number of competitors;
■ market share stability;
■ purchasing patterns;
■ ease of entry;
■ technology.

A 'mature' industry, for instance, is characterized by slow or negligible rates of growth; little or no further growth potential; few changes in breadth of product line; stable or declining numbers of competitors; stable market share positions; established buying patterns; high barriers to entry; and process and materials innovations in technology.

In both Porter's and the Arthur D. Little approach we see a strong flavour of their intellectual forebear, the basic product life cycle. This, in itself, is a measure of the enduring impact which the PLC concept continues to have in strategic market planning.

We now turn our attention to another early tool of strategic marketing planning, namely, the 'experience curve' effect.

THE EXPERIENCE CURVE EFFECT IN STRATEGIC MARKETING PLANNING

In 1925, the commander of the Wright Patterson Air Force Base in the USA observed that the number of direct labour hours required to build an aeroplane decreased as the number of aircraft previously assembled increased. Eventually this phenomenon was explored across a wide range of industries and was found to be present in most of them. The phenomenon came to be termed the '**experience curve**'. It has significant implications for the determination of marketing objectives and strategy.

Basis and definition

The basis and meaning of the experience curve effect are relatively easy to understand, and are encapsulated in the name of the phenomenon itself. Put simply, experience curve effects are derived from the fact that the more times we repeat an activity, the more proficient we become: in other words 'practice makes perfect'. In the case of the Wright Patterson Air Force Base, the commander noticed that this led to a reduction in the time it took to assemble an aircraft as cumulative production increased. The assembly workers simply became more adept at assembling an aircraft because over time they had assembled increasing numbers.

In the 1960s, the Boston Consulting Group,[3] whose work we look at in more detail later in this chapter, observed that the experience curve effect was not confined to assembly operations, or even simply to direct labour costs, but encompassed almost all cost areas of a business.

> The experience curve effect is observed to encompass all costs – capital, administrative, research and marketing – and to have transferred impact from technological displacements and product evolution.
>
> (Boston Consulting Group: 1970)

Furthermore, not only was the experience curve effect found to encompass more than just production, even more importantly, the effect was found to be predictable (Abell and Hammond).[4]

> Personnel from the Boston Consulting Group and others showed that each time cumulative volume of a product doubled, total value-added costs . . . fell by a constant and predictable percentage.
>
> (Abell and Hammond: 1986)

It is this predictable relationship between costs and experience that constitutes the experience curve effect.

Specific sources of experience curve effects

We have observed that experience curve effects are based on the old adage 'practice makes perfect'. We can now isolate five specific major sources:

1   increased labour efficiency, e.g. learning short cuts, improved dexterity and greater familiarity with systems/procedures;
2   greater specialization/redesign of working methods;
3   process and production improvements, e.g. design of more effective plant and increased automation;
4   changes in the resources mix, e.g. substitution of initially highly qualified labour by less qualified personnel;
5   product standardization and product redesign.

The important point to note about these sources of experience curve effects is that many of them are not 'automatic', i.e. in order to achieve experience curve effects management must undertake the necessary steps and exercise initiative.

Experience effects provide the opportunities to lower costs, but appropriate strategies are required to grasp them.

Calculating experience curve effects

Understandably experience curve effects differ between industries and between companies. The basic formula for the experience curve is:

$$Cq = Cn \left(\frac{q}{n}\right) - b$$

Where:

q = the experience (cumulative production) to date
n = the experience (cumulative production) at an earlier date
Cq = the cost of a unit q (adjusted for inflation)
Cn = the cost of a unit n (adjusted for inflation)
b = a constant depending on the learning rate.

Experience curves are normally expressed in percentage terms, e.g. an '85 per cent' experience curve or a '70 per cent' experience curve. Expressing the experience curve in this way tells us the expected reduction in costs for each doubling of cumulative production. An '85 per cent' curve means that the unit cost of producing (say) 2,000 cumulative units of production will be only 85 per cent of the unit cost when cumulative production had reached only 1,000 units. It is important to note

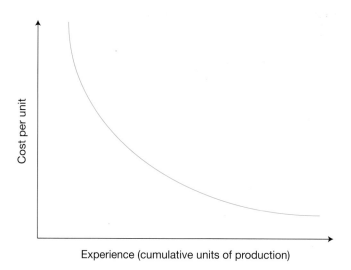

FIGURE 15.3 A typical experience curve

that evidence shows that this percentage impact in costs is the same across the whole range of cumulative experience i.e. doubling experience from four million to eight million units results in exactly the same percentage cost reduction as doubling experience from 100 to 200 units in the company. This too, has important strategic implications.

A typical experience curve is shown in Figure 15.3. Note how the curve shows that the higher the level of cumulative production the lower the cost per unit will be.

Strategic implications of the experience curve effect

In industries where curve effects are present (and this is in most industries) and particularly where these are substantial, a significant competitive edge can be gained by adopting a strategy aimed at moving down the experience curve more rapidly than competitors.

In effect, this means being the dominant firm in an industry, with strategies aimed at being the early leader and capturing market share. Remember that the experience curve effect is based on cumulative production and not scale of production. This means that in the early stages it is simple to, for example, double market share at relatively low volumes. Early leadership can thus ensure that the leaders' costs can be reduced relatively quickly and often before competitors have time to enter the market. By the time these competitors are able to do this the early market leader has established an unassailable cost advantage and competes on price leadership. Owing to the experience curve effect, high market share undoubtedly becomes a prime objective in marketing strategies. When considering this strategy the following points need to be borne in mind:

- Achieving high market shares can be expensive. In the short term we need to consider if we can finance the capture of market share.

■ Market share – and hence cumulative volume – is easier to achieve in high growth markets where experience can be gained by taking a disproportionate share of new sales.

■ The pursuit of market share in order to lower costs – and hence competing through price leadership – assumes that the market is price sensitive. Not all markets are; it often makes more sense to compete on superior products or service rather than price.

Experience curve effects are much greater and therefore more relevant in industries such as Aerospace than they are in many service product industries. This explains why the European Consortium which has produced the 'Eurofighter' aeroplane was reliant on securing market share. Only major orders from the defence departments of different governments enabled the venture to succeed.

In short, the pursuit of competitive advantage based on experience curves is not a certain solution for success in an industry. The experience curve concept is a useful adjunct to the strategic market planner's portfolio of ideas and is particularly useful for market share and pricing decisions. Like the product life cycle concept, it has in part provided the impetus to the development of more comprehensive planning tools. The first of these is the Boston Consulting Group's growth/share matrix, but before this we need to consider the nature of these modern tools of strategic marketing planning.

COMPREHENSIVE TOOLS OF STRATEGIC MARKETING PLANNING

In Chapter 4 and the earlier part of this chapter we looked at some of the earlier tools of analysis available to the marketing planner for analysing strategic alternatives and choices. We have seen that although they are useful, they represent only a partial framework for analysis and decision making. In recent years progress has been made in developing more comprehensive tools of strategic analysis. Different though the various tools may be, they are all primarily directed towards two essential activities:

1   diagnosis of the current position of the company;
2   prescription of strategies for the future aimed at maintaining, or improving, performance.

A particular problem for the marketing planner in the large multi-product/multi-market company is that decisions must be made as to what priority to place on each of several business areas, each competing for scarce resources. For future success in business, it is vital that these conflicting demands for resources are balanced so as to offer the greater chance of meeting overall corporate objectives. The partial perspectives offered by the tools of analysis examined earlier are particularly inappropriate for this need, hence the development of more comprehensive approaches.

Before we look at these more comprehensive tools of strategic market planning, we must emphasize that none of the tools provides a fail-safe panacea for diagnosis and decision. Each requires managerial judgement and experience in its application and interpretation. If we think of them as being aids to marketing management rather than a replacement for judgement, we have gone some way towards using these more powerful tools wisely.

Some tools of strategic market analysis fall into the category of 'portfolio analysis models'. Referred to as 'product market grids', these models are based on positioning each business unit, or specific product market on a grid according to the attractiveness of the market and the company's competitive position.

One of the earliest and most influential of the product/market portfolio techniques is that developed by the Boston Consulting Group. We now examine this strategic tool in detail, and examine its uses and limitations.

THE BOSTON CONSULTING GROUP'S (BCG) GROWTH/SHARE MATRIX

In the mid 1960s the Boston Consulting Group (BCG) was founded to provide advice to strategic marketing planners. Building on previous work and evidence relating to the experience curve effect BCG developed a simple, but potentially powerful, framework for analysing an organization's business with a view to providing strategic guidelines. The essentials of **BCG's growth/share matrix** are illustrated in Figure 15.4.

Compiling the BCG matrix

The completion of the matrix is straightforward. The four steps are:

1 For each strategic business unit (SBU) or product determine annual growth rate in the market.
2 According to this growth rate, next determine the extent to which the growth rate is 'high' or 'low'. Normally, growth rates of 10 per cent or more are considered 'high'.

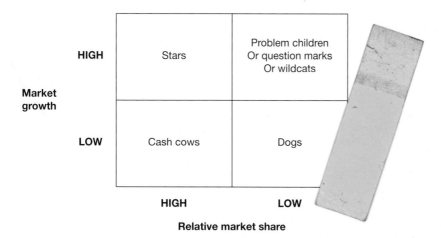

FIGURE 15.4 BCG's growth/share matrix

3   For each SBU or product determine relative market share. Normally this is calculated on the basis of market share compared to that of the largest competitor.

4   According to relative market share, determine the extent to which this is 'high' or 'low'. Normally a relative market share of 10 per cent is required to fall into the 'high' category.

We now have all the information we need to position our SBUs or products in the matrix. We can also calculate the value of the turnover of each SBU or product and denote this by using circles, where the area of the circle is proportionate to its turnover.

Interpreting and using the matrix

An illustration of a completed growth/share matrix is shown in Figure 15.5. Having completed the growth/share matrix, each SBU may be classified as follows:

■   *Low growth/high share: 'cash cows'*
    As the term implies, these products or SBUs generate more cash than they use and can be used for funding other products or SBUs.

■   *Low growth/low share: 'dogs'*
    These products or SBUs tend to be loss makers, but might provide small amounts of cash; long term their potential is usually weak. When a 'dog' produces a small profit it is termed a 'cash dog', and where it produces a loss it is termed a 'true dog'.

■   *High growth/low share: 'problem children' (sometimes called 'question marks' or 'wildcats')*
    These are products with possible long-term potential, but they tend to use large amounts of cash. This is so if they are to increase their market share, as they must do if they are to survive in the long run.

■   *High growth/high share: 'stars'*
    Managed well, these SBUs or products have the potential to become cash cows of the future. This means that the company must maintain their market share, usually in the face of strong competition, until market growth subsides. This means that these products or SBUs tend to be heavy users of cash arising from high promotional expenditures in growth markets.

The concept of building a balanced portfolio

Once strategic business units have been analysed in this way, a key feature of the BCG approach is its emphasis on the need to build a balanced portfolio of businesses or products. This notion is captured in the following quote from Lancaster and Massingham:[5]

A balanced portfolio would ideally contain few or no dogs, some problem children, some stars and some cash cows. The balance between problem children, stars and cash cows

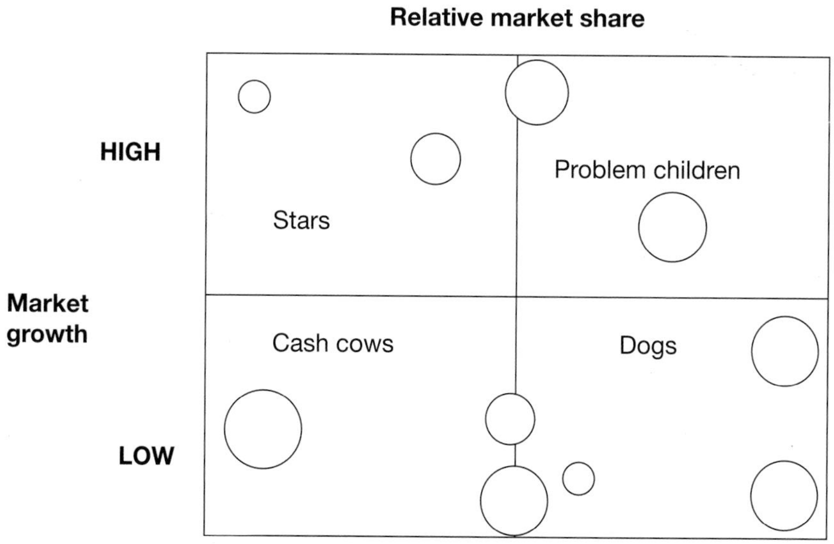

Relative market share

FIGURE 15.5 Example of a completed BCG matrix

should be such as to ensure that the company has sufficient net positive cash flow from its cash cows to fund its stars and turn them eventually into cash cows. Funds from cash cows are also used to turn products which are currently problem children . . . into stars. Not all problem children can be moved in this way and eventually some of them will . . . become dogs. In the long run all dogs are potential candidates for elimination from the product range.

A balanced portfolio is thus intended to ensure sufficient positive net cash flow to guarantee long-run success for the company as a whole. In order to achieve this, each SBU or product must be analysed and a decision made as to which of the following strategies is to be applied in order to maintain the balanced portfolio:

- *Build*: As the term implies, this means increasing the product or SBU's market share, usually implying a net input of cash or resources.
- *Hold*: This strategy is aimed at maintaining market share and is therefore appropriate for strong cash cows.
- *Harvest*: Here a decision is made to generate as much short-term cash flow from the SBU or product as is possible and it is appropriate to weak cash cows.
- *Divest*: A divest strategy means either selling or liquidating the SBU. This strategy is appropriate for weaker problem children and for most dogs. It should be noted that sometimes dogs may be retained for other strategic reasons such as maintaining a full product portfolio.

The BCG approach offers a simple method of analysing and evaluating current businesses, and is a relatively straightforward way of arriving at future strategies for them. There are, however, a number of problems with the use of the BCG growth/share matrix.

Criticisms and limitations of the BCG approach

Among the major criticisms and limitations of this portfolio technique we include:

- *Over-simplification*: The matrix uses only the factors of market growth and relative market share to assign products or SBUs to its various cells. This is based on strong empirical evidence showing that cash flow is related to these two factors. There are usually many more factors that can, and do, affect net cash flow in a company.
- *Cash flow as the performance criterion*: Some doubt the use of cash flow as being the most appropriate objective in a company, arguing instead that return on investment is more appropriate.
- *Ambiguity in classifications*: The analysis in BCG's product portfolio matrix can be undertaken either at the SBU level, or for each product/market. It is, however, often difficult in practice to separate these. There is also controversy over what constitutes a 'high' versus a 'low' market growth rate and what constitutes a 'high' versus 'low' market share.
- The technique does not deal with issues surrounding new products, or in markets with negative rates of growth.

Partly because of these criticisms, a number of other techniques have been developed which go some way to countering these problems. The techniques we now examine are some of the better known examples of these, i.e. the McKinsey/General Electric business screen, the Shell International directional policy matrix, and the product life cycle portfolio matrix. We commence with the McKinsey/General Electric model.

THE MCKINSEY/GENERAL ELECTRIC BUSINESS SCREEN

The BCG growth share matrix is criticized for is its reliance on only two factors to position strategic business units in the matrix. A number of strategic planning portfolio techniques have been developed which use several factors to analyse strategic business units, instead of only two in BCG's approach. Working in conjunction with McKinsey & Co. (management consultants) General Electric (GE) have developed one of the more popular of these **multi-factor portfolio matrices**.

In the GE matrix, SBUs are evaluated using the dimensions of 'market attractiveness' and 'business position'. In contrast to the BCG approach, each of these two dimensions is, in turn, further analysed into a number of factors which underpin each dimension. In order to use this technique,

TABLE 15.1 Cravens' factor analysis

Attractiveness of market	Status position of business
Market factors	
■ Size (volume/value both)	■ Market share
■ Growth rate per year	■ Company's annual growth rate
■ Sensitivity to price	■ Your influence on market
■ Cyclicality, etc.	■ Lags or leads in sales
Competition	
■ Types of competitor	■ Comparison in terms of products, markets, capabilities.
■ Degree of concentration	■ Relative share change
■ Changes in share	■ Company's level of integration
■ Degrees and types of integration	
Financial and economic factors	
■ Contribution margins	■ Company's margins
■ Barriers to entry/exit	■ Barriers to company's entry or exit
■ Capacity utilization	■ Company's capacity utilization
Technical factors	
■ Maturity and volatility	■ Company's ability to cope with change
■ Patents and copyright	■ Degree of patent protection
■ Complexity	■ Depth of company skills

the strategic planner must first determine these various factors contributing to market attractiveness and business position.

Cravens[6] gives good examples of factors associated with market attractiveness and business position, and the relationship between them. Table 15.1 lists some of these.

GE's product/market attractiveness factors

The original GE matrix used certain factors to assess product/market attractiveness:

- size;
- growth rates;
- competitive diversity and structure;
- profitability;
- technological impacts;
- social impacts;

- environmental impacts;
- legal impacts;
- human impacts.

GE's business strength factors

For assessing business strength, the GE matrix uses ten factors:

- size;
- growth rate;
- market share;
- profitability;
- margins;
- technology position;
- strengths and weaknesses;
- image;
- environmental impact;
- management.

GE believes that these are the key factors for their business, which taken together influence return on investment (note that the BCG approach uses cash flow). This list of GE factors can be modified for each company according to its own particular circumstances, and indeed many of the alternative multiple factor matrices simply use a different checklist of attributes.

Constructing the GE matrix

The five steps in compiling the GE matrix are:

1 identify strategic business units;
2 determine factors contributing to market attractiveness;
3 determine factors contributing to business position;
4 establish ways of measuring market attractiveness and business position;
5 rank each SBU according to whether it is:

- high, medium or low on business strength;
- high, medium or low on market attractiveness.

The final two factors (measuring and ranking) require that some numerical rating be given to both the relative importance of each factor used to assess market attractiveness (assuming they are not all equally important) and business strength. Multiplying these together and totalling them for each strategic business unit then gives an overall composite score which, in turn, enables the compilation of the matrix. In addition, the total market size for each SBU can be represented by the area of a circle, with the share of the company's SBUs in each product market being indicated by a segment in the circle.

The approach typically results in a portfolio similar to the one shown in Figure 15.6. As with BCG's matrix, its visual presentation enables a considerable amount of complex information to be presented in an easily digestible form.

Interpreting and using the GE matrix

Having completed the matrix, as with the BCG approach, the marketing planner can then assess the balance of SBUs in the organization and determine appropriate future strategies for each.

Strategy guidelines Of itself, the GE matrix does not purport to establish detailed strategies for each SBU. This is a task for company management and will require consideration of many factors. However, according to an SBU's position in the matrix we can distinguish between three broad strategic guidelines. These are indicated in Figure 15.7.

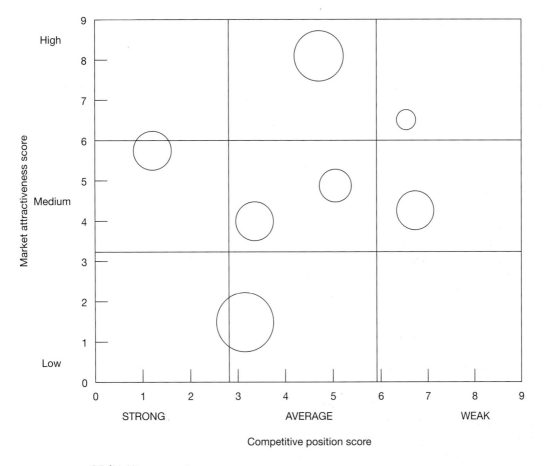

FIGURE 15.6 GE/McKinsey matrix

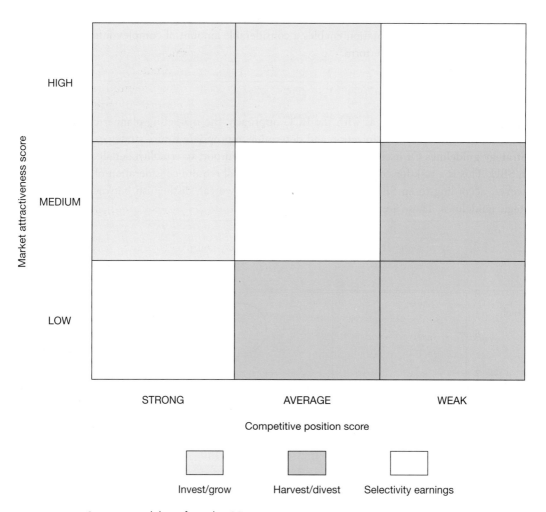

FIGURE 15.7 Strategy guidelines from the GE matrix

Strategy guidelines in action

Clearly, those SBUs which score high/strong or medium/strong or average/high on competitive position and market attractiveness are the ones where a company should seek at least to maintain investment and preferably grow. SBUs which score a combination of low/weak or low/average or medium/weak or competitive position and market attractiveness are candidates for which, at the very least, no more investment can be warranted. Wherever possible as much cash should be harvested from them as is feasible. SBUs scoring either high/weak or medium/average or low/strong combinations on competitive position/market market attractiveness should be examined to see whether some degree of selective investment to maintain or increase earnings would be appropriate.

Criticisms and limitations of the GE matrix

Wind and Mahajam[7] criticized obtaining composite scores on position and attractiveness. They pointed out that identical scores can hide key differences between products, and suggest there are limitations to the simple weighting system that is used. They preferred more custom-built approaches. Each cell will contain several SBUs, so it is argued that because a number of different criteria have placed each SBU in the cell, that a simple singular investment strategy is insufficient.

Abell and Hammond[8] suggested three distinct problems in making assessments of either industry attractiveness or business position:

1   the relevant list of contributing factors in any given situation has to be identified;
2   the direction and form of the relationships have to be determined;
3   each of the contributing factors has to be weighted in any composite measure of 'attractiveness' or 'position', depending on its relative importance.

Company position/industry attractiveness is less easily measured than the growth/share approach as this requires subjective judgements about where a particular business unit should be placed. This is more likely to be open to misjudgement. The value of the GE matrix much depends on having access to comparative information regarding competitors and such access is not always readily or easily available.

We see that the GE matrix is not without its limitations and problems. Nevertheless, we should not discount the fact that this particular matrix was instrumental in spawning several later multi-factor matrices for strategic market planning. One of these is Shell's directional policy matrix.

THE SHELL DIRECTIONAL POLICY MATRIX

A somewhat similar approach to the GE business screen is the Shell directional policy matrix.[9] This approach also has two dimensions: company's competitive capabilities (vertical axis) and prospects for sector profitability (horizontal axis) as shown in Figure 15.8. The firm's SBUs or products are plotted into one of the nine cells in Figure 15.8 and subsequently there is a suggested strategy for each of the nine cells. The cells represent, starting at the bottom right hand corner:

- **Leader** where major resources are focused on the SBU.
- **Try harder** might be vulnerable over longer periods of time, but OK now.
- **Double or quit** gamble on potential SBUs for the future.
- **Growth** grow the market by focusing some resources here.
- **Custodial** like a cash cow, milk it and do not commit more resources.
- **Cash generation** milk for expansion elsewhere.
- **Phased withdrawal** move cash to SBUs with greater potential.
- **Divest** liquidate or move these assets on as fast as possible.

Prospects for sector profitability

	UNATTRACTIVE	AVERAGE	ATTRACTIVE
WEAK	Disinvest	Phased withdrawal	Double or quit
AVERAGE	Phased withdrawal	Custodial	Try harder
STRONG	Cash generation	Growth	Leader

(Vertical axis label: Company's competitive capability)

FIGURE 15.8 The Shell directional policy matrix

There follows a description of how to complete the matrix and what each of the horizontal and vertical axes in the model mean.

The horizontal axis: prospects for sector profitability

This includes criteria of market growth rate, market quality, industry situation and environmental considerations. On each of these factors an SBU or product is given from one to five stars. For instance, the factor of 'market quality' might be judged on the basis of several criteria such as pricing behaviour, past stability or profitability of that sector. The qualitative or quantitative evaluation of market quality is then converted into a rating from nought to four. The same procedure is followed for each of the other three factors, so the overall score on sector profitability is the total of the ratings on all four factors.

The vertical axis: company's competitive capability

The same approach is used here, except that the company's capabilities are assessed on the basis of market position, product research and development and production capability. These are further divided into sub-factors applicable to any particular industry.

Shell emphasize that whatever strategy is eventually selected, the aim is that is should be 'resilient', i.e. viable in a diverse range of potential futures. Hence, each strategy ideally should be evaluated against all future possible scenarios.

Limitations of the Shell directional policy matrix

The Shell directional policy matrix has been criticized on the grounds that, like the BCG approach, it assumes that the same set of factors is universally applicable for assessing the prospects of any product or business. Critics believe that the relevant factors and their relative importance will vary both according to the firm's products and the individual characteristics of each company. In addition, the matrix does not provide any guidelines on how to implement the strategies suggested in each cell of the matrix.

THE PRODUCT LIFE CYCLE PORTFOLIO MATRIX

Developed by Barksdale and Harris,[10] the **product life cycle portfolio matrix** is specifically designed to deal with the criticisms that the BCG matrix ignores products that are new, and that it overlooks markets with a negative growth rate, i.e. markets that are in decline. Because of this, the product life cycle portfolio matrix includes a specific focus on the growth and maturity stages of the product life cycle in developing the portfolio technique. However, the same assumptions that underlie both the conventional product life cycle experience curves and the BCG growth/share matrix are also built into this model. These assumptions, which we have already witnessed, are repeated:

- Products have finite life spans. They enter the market, pass through a period of growth, reach a stage of maturity, subsequently move into a period of decline and finally disappear.
- Strategic objectives and marketing strategy should match the market growth rate changes to take advantage of the challenges and opportunities as the product goes through the different stages.
- For most mass-produced products, costs of production are closely linked to experience (volume). Hence, for most types of products, the unit cost goes down as volume increases.
- Expenditures – investment in plant and equipment and marketing expenses are directly related to rate of growth. Consequently, products in growth markets will use more resources than products in mature markets.
- Margins and the cash generated are positively related to share of the market. Products with high relative share of the market will be more profitable than products with low shares.
- When the maturity stage is reached, products with high market share generate a stream of cash greater than that needed to support them in the market. This cash is available for investment in other products or in research and development to create new products.

Building on these assumptions, Barksdale and Harris also highlight the additional issues which arise out of pioneering new products, which they label *infants*, and products in declining markets which they label as either *warhorses* (high share products in declining markets) or *dodos* (low share products in declining markets). The result is combined PLC/product portfolio model as shown in Figure 15.9. This approach is based on the notions that both the initial and decline stages of the life cycle are important and, more specifically, recognizes that product innovations as well as products with negative growth rates are important and should not be ignored in strategic analysis. The result is an expanded (2 × 4) portfolio matrix, as shown in Figure 15.10. The seven-cell matrix is composed of the usual four BCG categories plus the new categories as outlined.

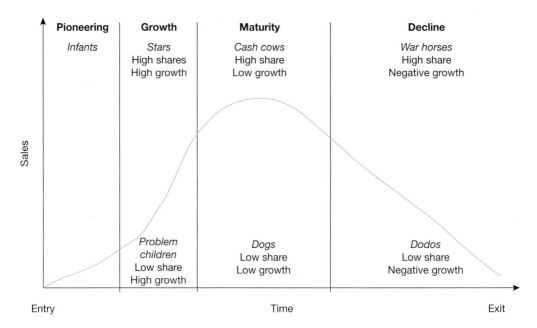

Warhorses

When a market begins to exhibit negative growth, cash cows become warhorses. These products still have high market share and hence can still be substantial cash generators. This might require reduced marketing expenditure or it may take the form of selective withdrawal from market segments or elimination of certain models.

Dodos

These are products that have low shares of declining markets with little opportunity for growth or cash generation. The appropriate strategy is to remove them from the portfolio, but if competitors have already removed themselves from the market it may still be marginally profitable to remain. Timing is thus crucial.

Infants

These are pioneering products that possess a high degree of risk. They do not immediately earn profits and consume substantial cash resources. The length of the innovation can vary from a short time with consumer packaged goods to an extended period with a product that is innovative enough to require a shift in buying habits.

LOW	INFANTS Negative cash flow	
HIGH	STARS Modest positive or negative cash flow	PROBLEM CHILDREN Large negative cash flow
LOW	CASH COWS Large positive cash flow	DOGS Modest positive or negative cash flow
NEGATIVE	WAR HORSES Positive cash flow	DODOS Negative cash flow

FIGURE 15.10 Product life cycle portfolio matrix

Uses and limitations of the product life cycle portfolio matrix

The developers of the matrix claim that it is comprehensive. Regardless of the level of analysis – corporate, business division or product/market categories – they suggest that the expanded model provides an improved system for classifying and analysing the full range of market situations. Classification of products according to this expanded model is meant to reveal the relative competitive position of products, indicate the rate of market growth and enable the configuration of strategic alternatives in a general sense if not in specific terms.

The key here is that it is only 'general'. Barksdale and Harris admit that the new matrix does not eliminate the problems involved in defining, say, products and markets, or rates of growth. As with the other strategic planning tools, the benefits a company can achieve are only as good as the inputs upon which they are based.

It is claimed that it provides an improved framework that identifies the cash flow potential and the investment opportunity for every product offered by an organization. In addition, it helps conceptualize the strategic alternatives of all product/market categories of an organization.

PROFIT IMPACT OF MARKETING STRATEGY (PIMS)

In the mid-1960s, Sidney Schoeffler and his colleagues at the Strategic Planning Institute in Cambridge, Massachusetts, began to collect and analyse data from a large number of companies, covering literally hundreds of different product markets. The intention was to provide participating companies with advice, based on empirical evidence about the most suitable strategies to pursue in search of increased profitability. Essentially the analysis focused on comparing the effect of various business strategies on net cash flow and profitability and this came to be termed the **'profit impact of marketing strategy'** (PIMS).

The full PIMS service is available to subscribing companies (i.e. clients). Each client is asked to subscribe more than 100 data items for each 'business', which is defined as an operating unit that:

- sells a distinct set of products or services;
- sells to an identifiable set of customers;
- is in competition with a well-defined set of competitors.

Using a special data form, the client answers questions on factors such as:

- the market environment;
- the state of competition;
- strategy pursued by the business;
- operating results;
- assumptions as to the future in terms of prices, sales, etc.

Information reports

Using the evidence built up in the database, the subscribing company then receives both diagnostic and prescriptive information contained in four main reports:

- *The 'Par' Report*: specifying what return on investment is normal (or 'par') for that particular type of business;
- *The Strategy Analysis Report*: the likely outcome (on profit, sales, cash flow, etc.) of several possible 'broad' strategic moves based on evidence of similar moves by similar businesses;
- *The Optimum Strategy Report*: nominates the combination of strategic moves likely to give the client optimal results for the business;
- *Report on 'Look alikes' (ROLA)*: provides information on likely successful tactics based on analysing the successful moves of strategically similar businesses.

The information is thus client- and business-specific, but in addition, the extensive analyses made by the Strategic Planning Institute have provided a number of general guidelines to strategy selection and implementation.

Thirty-seven basic strategic influences on profitability and cash flow have been identified by the Institute. Taken together, the Institute suggests that these account for 80 per cent of the determination of business success or failure. Of primary importance are the following:

- *Investment intensity*: Higher investment intensity is associated with lower rates of return and cash flow.
- *Productivity*: High value is added for each employee in the businesses, making the company generally more profitable.
- *Market position*: Higher share of served markets leads to higher profits and cash flow.
- *Growth of served market*: 'Favourable to cash' measures of profit; no effect on percentage measures of profit; negative effect on cash flow.
- *Quality of products or services*: Favourable impact on all measures of financial performance.
- *Innovation/differentiation*: Usually has positive effect on financial performance, but only if company has strong initial market position.
- *Vertical integration*: Positive effect in stable markets, negative in unstable ones.
- *Cost push*: Increases in salaries, raw material prices etc., have complex effects on performance according to specific nature of business or company.
- *Current strategic effort*: The existing direction of change of any of the preceding factors often affects financial performance in an inverse manner, e.g. having strong market share increases cash flow; achieving strong market share reduces it.

These and other profit impact marketing strategies (PIMS) findings provide useful insights for the process of strategy development and implementation. A company can use PIMS data in a variety of ways to help in strategic market planning. Clearly, for the subscriber company the information provided is detailed and wide-ranging; in particular, PIMS data can be used for:

- analysing business performance;
- formulating and selecting future strategies;
- analysing and focusing on problems and opportunities;
- assessing competitor performance.

Criticisms and limitations of PIMS

Although PIMS is useful, there is some criticism. The findings are given as conclusions from empirical research, but many of them are self-evident. O'Shaughnessy[11] believes that 'the findings cannot distinguish between causal factors and factors in a state of mere co-existence'. He goes on to say: 'without supporting explanations and appropriate tests, the findings can be misleading in tempting management to deal with symptoms rather than causes'.

Day[12] to some extent agrees with O'Shaughnessy when he states three basic limitations of PIMS:

1 Interpreting and utilizing PIMS findings: PIMS has been used to predict profitability. This should not be so because the model does not tell us about causality.
2 Specification problems: i.e. whether the regression models have omitted important variables and have been properly structured.
3 Measurement error: this happens because of eliminating outliners, standardized inputs etc.

Research by Doyle,[13] although not specifically aimed at criticizing the PIMS system, has shown that perhaps the database does not give sufficient importance to certain facets of marketing strategy.

In particular, Doyle's research illustrates that there is significant potential impact of the brand and its management on company profitability; an aspect which the PIMS data tends to understate.

GREEN PORTFOLIO ANALYSIS

Despite criticisms of portfolio analysis, the techniques and applications of these of analyses have continued to develop. One recent development which illustrates how these tools are continuously evolving to meet the needs of the contemporary marketer is the combination of portfolio analysis and the issue of 'green' marketing. Developed by Ilinitch and Schaltegger,[14] this notion of a 'green' business portfolio is shown in Figure 15.11. The basic notion in this three-dimensional matrix is suggested as involving quantifying the environment impacts of business activities and comparing them with economic aspects of examined business.

The horizontal plane of the matrix consists of the traditional BCG matrix of growth against profitability with the quadrants retaining their respective metaphors. The size of the circle represents the size of the product or firm, in economic or environmental terms. The third, vertical dimension measures environmental impact. Recent developments in accounting mean this can be quantified at plant, SBU, or firm level. The pollution units are calculated by multiplying toxic discharges by regulation standards weighting coefficients. Products deemed to be ecologically sound are called *'green'* and their counterparts are called *'dirty'*. Thus we see the quaint notion of *'green cash cows'* and *'dirty dogs'*.

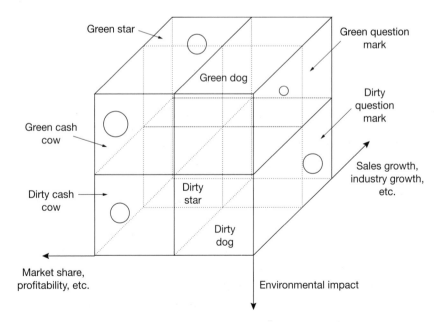

FIGURE 15.11 The 'green' business portfolio

The authors suggest that 'dirty cash cows' are usually old, declining industries that are in the short term very profitable to firms and communities. However, in the long term, the negative publicity and financial penalties ultimately make such industries risky. Alternatively, although the 'green dog' is financially unprofitable, the authors argue that the strategic challenge is to make it viable. This, they suggest, can be done by creating a market for the product and/or capturing market share. Creating a market may in turn involve changing customer values and behaviour, whereas capturing market share may involve lowering production costs.

Battery powered vehicles probably represent an example of 'green dogs'. Many of these vehicles are at the stage where technologically they represent a substitute for conventional petrol and diesel-engine alternatives. Technically proficient as such vehicles may be, the strategic challenge facing their marketers is, as the green business portfolio suggests, that of creating a market. Quite simply, still not enough customers value the undoubtedly green benefits which electric vehicles offer. The marketers of such vehicles face the task of changing customer values and behaviour, although recent initiatives by Government should boost their popularity.

We have included this 'green' portfolio technique not because there is any evidence of it being potentially more valuable to the development of strategic marketing than some of the other recent ideas on portfolio analysis, but rather it illustrates that portfolio techniques are being constantly improved and have changed substantially since the early days of the original BCG portfolio. Indeed the 'green' portfolio notion reflects current concerns in relation to global warming.

Portfolio analysis provides a limited solution to the issue of the allocation of resources and the creation of more appropriate strategies as a result of the analysis required when applying such procedures to businesses. After all, it is more 'scientific' than simply guesswork and intuition in making decision. Such techniques should be regarded as supporting decision-making processes and not as a substitute for them.

SUMMARY

The contemporary marketing planner needs the right tools if marketing strategies are to be effectively developed and implemented. Recent years have seen significant developments in analytical concepts and frameworks of marketing analyses and decision making. Through only partial tools of analysis, and often criticized, some of the earlier frameworks of marketing planning are useful concepts.

More recently, more comprehensive tools of analysis and planning, including portfolio planning tools, have been developed, ranging from the two-dimensional growth/share matrix to the multi-factor matrices of which the GE and Shell Directional Policy matrix are examples.

We have seen the emergence of empirically based comprehensive planning tools, of which PIMS is perhaps the best known. These are aimed at helping the strategic planner delineate and select between alternative strategies for achieving the highest return on investment.

We have also examined some of the recent developments in portfolio analysis and in particular stressed the fact that these tools are continually being improved and updated as empirical knowledge and experience regarding their uses and limitations develop. In addition, we have seen that the tools are evolving to meet the needs of the contemporary marketing environment.

The tools selected and discussed represent only some of the planning tools now available to the strategic marketer. None of these tools was designed or is able to replace management judgement: nor should they. As we have seen, each of the approaches and tools discussed has its own advantages and limitations. Ideally, these planning tools are best used in combination when developing marketing strategies.

KEY TERMS

CASE STUDY

Breakwater Products plc

Breakwater Products plc produces a range of leisure products for the UK market. Originally, the company was set up to produce rubber airbeds and swimming rings in the 1950s as swimming boomed as a leisure pursuit. From these humble beginnings the company now produces over 150 products, all in some way connected with leisure pursuits.

The company is organized into four strategic business units (SBUs). This organization is based on the fact that the different business units supply different end-use markets and/or customers and in doing so are responsible for different product ranges. So we have the following strategic business units together with their latest market share and market growth rates for the previous year:

. . . continued

CASE STUDY ... *continued*

SBU1 Inflatable products: including the original airbeds and swimming rings (now in plastic) but also including fun items and inflatable dingys, etc.
Market share for this SBU 55% (UK market)
Market growth rate 5%

SBU2 Wheeled products: including skateboards, mountain bikes and scooters, including the most recent fashionable city scooters, etc.
Market share for this SBU 20%
Market growth rate 15%

SBU3 Outdoor products: including tents, climbing boots and clothing, accessories etc.
Market share for this SBU 5%
Market growth rate 3%

SBU4 Fitness products: including fitness wear, rowing machines, exercise bikes, cross trainers, etc.
Market share for this SBU 8%
Market growth rate 15%

CASE STUDY QUESTIONS

1 How can Portfolio Analysis be used by Breakwater Products PLC?
2 What information would be required in order to conduct a BCG Analysis?

REFERENCES

1 Porter, M.E. (1985), *Competitive Advantage: Creating and Sustaining Superior Performance*, New York: Free Press.

2 Arthur D. Little (2000–2010), *Concepts of Market/Industry*, series of booklets published by consultants Arthur D. Little, New York.

3 The Boston Consulting Group (1970), *Perspectives on Experience*, Boston.

4 Abell, D.F. and Hammond, J.S. (1986), *Strategic Market Planning*, Upper Saddle River, NJ: Prentice-Hall.

5 Lancaster, G. and Massingham, L.C. (2002), *Essentials of Marketing*, 4th edn, Maidenhead: McGraw-Hill, p. 383.

6 Cravens, D.W. (1982), *Strategic Marketing*, Homewood, IL: Irwin.

7 Wind, Y. and Mahajam, V. (1981), 'Designing product and business portfolios', *Harvard Business Review*, Jan.–Feb.: 37–63.

8 Abell, D.F. and Hammond, J.S. op. cit. (4) pp. 112–13.

9 Shell Chemicals UK, *The Directional Policy Matrix: A New Aid to Corporate Planning*, November 1975.

10 Barksdale, H.C. and Harris, C.E. (1982), 'Portfolio analysis and the product life cycle', *Journal of Long Range Planning*, 15(6): 35–64.

11 O'Shaughnessy, J. (1988), *Competitive Marketing: A Strategic Approach*, 2nd edn, London: Unwin Hyman, p. 44.

12 Day, G. (1981), 'Analytical approaches to strategic market planning', *Review of Marketing*, Fall: 89–95.

13 Doyle, P. (1999), 'Branding', in Baker, M.J. (ed.), *The Marketing Book*, 4th edn, Oxford: Butterworth-Heinemann.

14 Ilinitch, A.Y. and Schaltegger, S.C. (1995), 'Developing a green business portfolio', *Journal of Long Range Planning*, 28(2): 29–58.

Chapter 16

Global marketing

LEARNING OBJECTIVES

By the end of this chapter you will:

- understand the importance of international and global aspects of marketing to the modern marketer
- appreciate some of the key factors which have given rise to the growth of international marketing
- be familiar with the different possible levels of involvement in international marketing
- understand some of the key differences and additional complexities encountered when developing marketing strategies for international markets
- comprehend the key decision areas in planning international marketing strategies
- appreciate the importance of, and difficulties associated with, researching and appraising international markets

INTRODUCTION

International and global marketing activities continue to grow to the extent that virtually every marketing manager in today's competitive environment is involved in, or is affected by international and global issues. For this reason, the contemporary marketing manager who does not understand the nature and significance of international marketing and how to plan strategically for these markets, is deficient in the skills required of a modern professional marketing manager.

This chapter seeks to address some of these key issues and skills required when managing marketing programmes in international markets. It is important to stress that this chapter only gives an overview of the issues and skills associated with international marketing management. As such, we are focused on what we believe to be some of the key contemporary issues in international marketing and some of the key decision areas and considerations when developing marketing strategies in these markets. Students and managers who are interested in acquiring a more detailed knowledge in this area are advised to consult one of the specialist texts in this increasingly complex region of marketing. We start by examining some of the background to the growth in international trade and marketing and some of the reasons put forward as to why companies and nations become involved in such activities.

THE GROWTH OF INTERNATIONAL/GLOBAL MARKETING

One of the most striking business trends of the past 40 years has been the increase in internationalization; that is, the growing number of firms that participate in international trade. Of course international trade is not new; after all, nations have traded ever since the start of commerce. However, the 1990s was really the first decade when companies around the world started to think globally. It was during the 1990s that time and distance, dimensions which have been shrinking for centuries between countries, began to become really compressed. The advent of ever faster transport and communication systems which in turn have led to vastly increased travel and more cosmopolitan consumers, have served to 'shrink' the world even further, so much so that writers now refer to the so-called 'global village'. Needless to say, in this millennium this shrinking will continue, aided principally by the Internet.

Although companies such as Nestlé, IBM, Shell, Toshiba and others have been conducting international marketing for decades, global competition has now intensified to the extent that even purely 'domestic companies' that have hitherto never thought about international marketing are affected in their marketing by global competitors.

In addition, the importance of international trade to governments and their economies has meant that more and more firms are being urged to internationalize thereby selling more of their products abroad and as a consequence adding positively to balance of payments. This 'urging' has resulted in many governments offering material encouragement to companies to become involved more in international marketing through, for example, grants and loans and offers of expert advice. Finally, global markets themselves have changed, and are changing with developments such as the enlarged and more co-ordinated European Union, with the majority of the member states having adopted a single currency. The development of the so-called 'tiger economies' of the Pacific rim, and the collapse of Communism and ensuing growth of more liberal economies in Eastern Europe, many now having joined the EU, have given rise to significant new opportunities for companies that have been willing and able to take advantage of them and threats for those who have not. These and other developments largely explain the increased activity and importance of international marketing, but do not, of themselves, explain basic reasons and motives for companies becoming involved in international markets. It is useful in our understanding of international markets management to identify some of these key underpinning reasons and motives.

The prime motive for a company becoming involved in international trade and marketing is essentially profit. This is a very simplistic view and we shall return to some of the added complexities and considerations in making this decision later in this chapter. However, related to the profitability issue, economists have long known some of the prime reasons for international trade.

Adam Smith was the first major writer on international trade. He produced the theory of **'absolute advantage'** in which a country exported products over which it had an absolute cost advantage compared to foreign competition, and imported products over which it had an absolute cost disadvantage. This, he argued was not only common sense, but through specialization in production and trade which it gave rise to, would actually increase the wealth and wellbeing of each participating nation. Other economists developed Adam Smith's basic thesis to include considerations of comparative rather than absolute costs, or the notion that trade was largely explained by relative factor endowments such as land, labour, capital and entrepreneurial skills possessed by a nation. These legacies concerning the notions of absolute, comparative, and factor endowment considerations to explain international trade are still to be found in more recent explanations of international marketing and trade. The major conclusions of these theories are that an examination of price, cost structures and factor endowments between countries will indicate which products and services they are likely to export and import.

Other contributors have amended these economic theories. Some, for example, have highlighted the fact that many of the more traditional economists' theories of trade are essentially only 'supply side' theories. They point out that demand patterns may reverse or at least affect trading flows that we might otherwise predict on the basis of classical economics alone. For example, we may find that the demand for a product in a country may be so high that despite the country possessing a comparative advantage, demand exceeds supply. Instead of being a net exporter, the country then becomes a net importer, often from higher cost foreign suppliers. Similarly, we know as marketers that markets are not homogeneous as the classical economists assumed. They are often segmented, which means a nation can be both an exporter and importer within the same product group. Brand image reinforces this phenomenon. For example, the UK exports cars, but imports more than it exports. Much of this trading flow results from the plant location strategies of US, Far Eastern, and

European multinational vehicle manufacturers, complicating the more simplistic notions to explain production and trade suggested by the classical economists. Another example is Sweden which has a comparative advantage in luxury cars such as Volvo and Saab, but has a comparative disadvantage in small, medium and budget cars.

Perhaps one of the most interesting alternative trade theories to explain international trade and marketing is that developed by Wells.[1] He suggested that international trading in products and services follows a pattern that was broadly similar in nature to that of the product life cycle with which we are already so familiar. Essentially he suggested that many products and services follow a pattern that can be divided into four stages as follows:

1   *Innovation and exporting*: New products and innovations are developed in the most 'advanced' economies essentially for domestic consumption. However, these countries will quickly begin to export these new products and services to other 'less developed' economies.
2   *Start of foreign production*: As the market for the new product or service begins to grow in the importing countries, companies in these countries begin to start their own production to take account of local demand.
3   *Foreign production becomes more competitive in domestic markets*: As production and demand in the previously importing country grows, factors such as economies of scale and experience curve effects begin to make domestic production much more cost competitive compared to imports.
4   *Foreign production becomes competitive in export markets*: In this final stage the previously importing countries become competitive in export markets to the extent that their products begin to substitute for the original innovators'/exporters' products in their own markets. In effect we have come full circle with the early producers and exporters becoming net importers.

Wells further suggests that this pattern of trade is repeated over time with successively less developed and therefore lower cost economies becoming in turn the foreign producers and eventually net exporters to countries from which they previously imported.

Many empirical studies have in fact confirmed this 'pecking order' over time. Lancaster and Wesenlund[2] have modified and extended Wells's basic theory to suggest that as the cycle of trade from one group of countries to another progresses, sales of the product or service in question gradually increase. However, Lancaster and Wesenlund's evidence still supports the basic notion of a product life cycle at work for international trade.

Notwithstanding the insights which these various theories of international trade provide about the reasons and motives for international marketing, as mentioned earlier, the prime motive for the individual company to become involved in this area of marketing is the potential for increased profits. It is this potential which largely explains why a company might move from purely domestic marketing to some involvement in international markets. However, the term 'international marketing' can mean very different levels of involvement in international markets and very different issues for the participating company with regard to, for example, strategic marketing planning. Before we consider these issues in more detail, and to continue the development of our understanding as to the reasons and motives for international marketing, we need to explore further this notion of different levels of involvement in international marketing.

INTERNATIONAL MARKETING DEFINITIONS: LEVELS OF INVOLVEMENT IN INTERNATIONAL MARKETING

The simple notion that international marketing involves marketing across national boundaries belies the potential complexities of defining precisely what international marketing is and what it involves. On the one hand marketing across national boundaries may simply involve a company passively responding to an unsolicited foreign order received from, say, an independent broker. The company involved in this transaction simply sells its product or service to the broker with little effort, additional considerations or long-term commitment. On the other hand, marketing across national boundaries may involve a company devoting most of its resources to foreign market activities with substantial commitment to markets across the globe and with production or marketing in many countries. Clearly, the term 'international marketing' can encompass a wide range of different activities and commitments even though products and services are still essentially being sold across national boundaries. Different levels of involvement allow us to explore and categorize distinct types of activities and commitments encompassed when marketing across national boundaries:

1   *Casual or accidental exporting* This type of international business entails the lowest levels of commitment and involvement by a company. It essentially consists of a company responding to largely unsolicited foreign orders and there is not real commitment to international marketing.

2   *Active exporting* is where a company makes a positive commitment to its international marketing with an ensuing higher degree of involvement. Not only is there an active recognition that foreign markets exist and represent possible marketing opportunities, but because of this, attempts are made to cultivate sales across national boundaries in a proactive manner. However, even this type of export marketing tends still simply to apply marketing principles to exporting a product which the firm is already selling in its domestic market. Because of this, overall corporate strategy does not really reflect foreign market importance and activities although minor adjustments may be made to the company's strategy to accommodate these.

3   *Committed international marketing* This level of commitment to international marketing entails the greatest degree of involvement on the part of the company. Markets across national boundaries are a key consideration in the marketing strategy of the company. International marketing activities are an integral part of the overall marketing programme. Organizational systems, structures and procedures may be developed specifically for the purpose of enhancing international marketing operations and profitability.

A committed international marketer is the Coca-Cola Company. International marketing activities form the centre of the company's overall marketing programme. All of the company's organizational systems, structures and procedures are purposely designed to enhance international marketing operations and profitability.

The level of involvement and commitment by a company to 'marketing across national boundaries' can vary considerably which means that no single simple definition of what constitutes international marketing can adequately encompass the possible range and scope of activities involved. Related to this notion of different levels of involvement and types of international marketing, is the notion of different types of company perspectives and approaches to organizational structure and systems with regard to its non-domestic marketing.

The export marketing company, as suggested in our earlier discussion of levels of involvement, is a company which simply sells its products overseas. This company may or may not have a separate export marketing division, but essentially uses the same marketing strategies in both its domestic and export markets.

The **international company** is one whose headquarters are located in one country and where ownership is dominated by the nationals of that one country. However, this sort of company views international marketing in a much more positive manner and sees it as being more central to their overall strategy and profits. Marketing strategy tends to emanate from the company headquarters, although they may possess marketing operations in other countries which, in turn, may reflect the particular requirements of each of the foreign markets and customers.

The **multinational company (MNC)** is generally agreed to have the following characteristics:

- They treat the various national markets in which they operate as if they were one. In other words they do not see a distinction between domestic and global marketing opportunities.
- They have a single management strategy that guides all their various operating companies throughout the world.
- They think and operate in what Wind *et al.*[3] term a 'geocentric' manner. This means that they are essentially world oriented in their approach to their marketing and planning. We return to this notion when we consider alternative organizational systems and structures for international marketing later in this chapter, but essentially the multinational company which will predominantly have a geocentric perspective will be concerned to achieve complete integration of its marketing strategies throughout the world. Lascu[4] refers to this as the most extreme type of international involvement. Increasingly, multinational corporations are practising global marketing. A global marketing company views the world as a whole as its market and develops a global marketing strategy.

Both the level of involvement and commitment by a company to its international markets, and associated perspectives regarding these markets, constitute key decisions by a company regarding its international marketing strategy. Simply stated, a company must decide whether it is going to be either a passive exporter or a fully fledged global marketing operator, or of course any number of levels of involvement and commitment in between. However, while this is obviously a crucial determinant of virtually every other aspect of a company's international marketing operations and strategies, we know that the decision to 'go international' is often not a rational 'searching after business' opportunity, but rather the result of a series of chance decisions and many companies go through a process of gradually evolving their international marketing operations. For example, in the first stage a company begins by filling unsolicited orders, but does not actively seek to export. In the next stage the company may actively seek out export markets, but exporting still remains a small part of its business. If the exporting is successful, the company becomes established in one or more export markets and exporting becomes a major activity. The company may then begin to invest in production and other facilities in overseas markets and eventually the company move towards becoming a fully fledged global marketer.

Progression through the stages of involvement to international marketing is by no means an automatic one. Marks & Spencer, for example, despite early forays into overseas expansion including the opening of stores in France, North America and the Far East, have never really developed into a full-blown international retailer. IKEA on the other hand have progressed through successful expansion of their international operations.

Although this gradual evolution of international marketing is how many companies develop their global marketing activities, it is better if the organization plans a systematic development of its activities into the international arena. A firm may enter into marketing across national boundaries passively, due to problems in their domestic market, or actively, by seeking attractive opportunities abroad. We consider some of the reasons for deciding to 'go international' shortly, together with some of the factors that should affect this choice if it is to be planned, as suggested, systematically as part of the overall strategic planning process for international marketing. Before we do this, it is useful to consider what, if anything is different or 'special' about the management of international marketing compared to pure domestic marketing. We now consider these differences.

INTERNATIONAL MARKETING MANAGEMENT: DIFFERENCES AND SPECIAL ISSUES

The main concepts and techniques of marketing management apply both in domestic and international markets. Many of the steps in strategic marketing planning – analysing strengths, weaknesses, opportunities and threats, research and appraising markets and customers, segmentation and targeting, the management of the marketing mix – apply in both situations. Even though the principles of marketing management are the same, there are some additional important issues that arise once a company begins to extend its marketing operations beyond its national boundaries. The areas of marketing management and planning where there are inherent differences between domestic and international marketing management are now considered in Table 16.1. We can see that there are differences between domestic and international marketing management. Many of these differences and additional complexities stem simply from operating in markets with a different environment to that encountered in the domestic market. Of particular significance in this respect are the differences which arise from the cultural and social elements of the environment. Because of this importance we now consider these factors in more detail.

CULTURAL AND SOCIAL FORCES IN INTERNATIONAL MARKETING

Many of the additional complexities and problems faced by international marketers stem from differences in the cultural and social environment which the marketer faces when marketing internationally. Influences of cultural differences when marketing across national boundaries take on a heightened importance.

We know how people consume, their needs and wants, and the ways in which these wants are satisfied are determined by culture. Culture is the human-made part of environment that includes

TABLE 16.1 Comparison between domestic and international marketing

Domestic	International
1 Single language and nationality	1 Multi-lingual/multi-national/multicultural
2 Relatively homogeneous market	2 Fragmented and diverse markets
3 Data usually accurate and easily available	3 Data collection a formidable task requiring significantly higher budget and personnel allocation
4 Political factors relatively unimportant	4 Political factors frequently vital
5 Relative freedom from government and interference	5 Involvement in national economic plans Government influences company plans
6 Individual company has little effect on environment	6 'Gravitational' distortion by large companies in small countries
7 Chauvinism helps	7 Chauvinism hinders
8 Relatively stable business environment	8 Multiple environments, many of which are unstable, but may be highly profitable
9 Uniform financial climate	9 Variety of financial climates ranging from over conservative to wildly inflationary
10 Single currency	10 Currencies differing in real value and stability
11 Business 'rules of the game' understood	11 Rules diverse, changeable and unclear
12 Management generally accustomed to sharing responsibilities and using financial controls	12 Management sometimes autonomous and unfamiliar with budgets and controls

knowledge, beliefs, morals, laws, customs and other elements acquired by humans in society. Because cultures are so different between countries, cultural forces and factors take on a particular significance for the international marketer. We highlight some of the possible areas or aspects of culture where there may be important differences when marketing in foreign markets:

- social organization;
- norms and values;
- religion;
- language;
- education;
- arts and aesthetics.

Sometimes seemingly relatively small and subtle differences in cultural habits and practices can be important in marketing products in different cultures. For example, attitudes towards body hair differ between even relatively geographically proximate European countries. In the UK for instance, most women shave their under-arm hair, whereas most German women do not. A company like Gillette takes this difference into account in preparing its marketing plans for the different European countries.

The marketer must understand the implications of these different elements of culture for developing marketing strategies e.g. there may be very different norms and values pertaining to say gender roles, or the use of sex in advertising when marketing in a foreign country. Similarly, religious beliefs may have a significant impact on what is acceptable marketing practice.

It is important to recognize that within any national culture there are often a number of sub-sets of culture. In the UK there is a distinct cultural difference between the north and south, which affects purchasing behaviour – in direct and observable ways, but sometimes in quite subtle ways. In addition to geographical sub-cultures, cultural sub-sets will often be created by, for example, different racial groups within a country, such as the Chinese in Malaysia and Mexicans in the USA.

Sub-cultures within countries have become prime targets for many marketers. In the European Union, the Asian sub-culture, once a neglected area of the market, now represents a major market segment. Such sub-cultures have their own particular marketing needs and represent substantial opportunities for the marketer willing and able to cater for these.

There are a number of key concepts relating to culture that become especially important when marketing across national boundaries:

1 **Self reference criterion** (SRC). This notion emphasizes the fact that it is all too easy to use all one's own cultural experience and values when developing and implementing marketing plans in another country. When confronted with a situation or set of facts we assess this situation or facts on the basis of our own knowledge and experiences, usually relating to the culture in which we were raised and with which we are most familiar. This can give rise to unconscious but disastrous mistakes in international marketing strategies.

A simple example is the word 'pet'. In many societies this word is used in an affectionate manner to describe domestic animals or even, in some societies, loved ones. In France however, the word 'pet' means, in certain circumstances, flatulence. Simple cultural differences like this can be significant in developing marketing branding programmes. It is important to isolate differences in cultural values between one's own culture and the new culture. Inevitably we use our own criterion and culture frameworks to assess markets, but these may not always be appropriate.

There are many examples of 'misnamed' products or unfortunate advertising slogans including:

'Nova' – Vauxhall's small car which in Spanish means literally 'no go';

'Pschitt' – a French soft drink brand which needs no explanation;

The 'Come alive with Pepsi' campaign slogan was translated in some countries to 'Pepsi will bring your relatives back from the grave'.

2 **High and low context culture.** Cultures and societies differ in terms of certain aspects of their development. Differences between high and low context cultures have implications for various

facets of their cultural elements. An example is in the use of language. Chee and Harris[5] suggest that language is a major factor in distinguishing one culture from another. It is not only the formal written and oral structure of the language to which we refer, but also symbolic communication that is termed 'silent language'. These are ways of communicating in a culture other than through verbal communication. Silent language includes aspects such as time, e.g. the use of deadlines and scheduling appointments and space, e.g. conversation differences in communication. Much communication in high context cultures takes place through silent rather than spoken language. For example, in some cultures arriving late for a meeting is a sign of respect; in others it is a sign of power. Self-reference criteria create more difficulty with silent languages than with spoken ones. Spoken languages are more obvious in their differences, whereas silent languages are much less obvious and yet can significantly impact on marketing.

3   **Cultural sensitivity**. Culture is potentially important to all products and services, and hence to marketing plans, but some products are more 'culturally sensitive' than others. Food usage, preparation and consumption and overall attitudes towards food in general can differ significantly between cultures and subcultures. For example, attitudes to drinking coffee in Italy and France are still very different to those in the UK. Some products are taboo for social or religious reasons in some cultures. Consumer products are more culturally sensitive than business-to-business products, but even in business-to-business markets there are rules of social and business etiquette that marketers need to appreciate and adhere to when conducting business in other countries. Cultural differences represent one of the most important areas of increased complexity compared to purely domestic marketing. As we have seen, there are other differences and complexities, but as already suggested, the overall concepts and principles of marketing remain the same. However, some of the decision areas involved in planning international marketing also differ from purely domestic ones, and it is to the key steps and decision areas in developing international marketing plans that we now turn our attention.

INTERNATIONAL MARKETING STRATEGIES AND DECISIONS

As in domestic marketing, international marketing strategies must be systematically planned and implemented. The following represents the key steps and decisions in planning and implementing international marketing programmes.

1   *The extent of involvement and commitment to international markets*, i.e. does the company wish to become involved in international markets, and if so, to what extent, e.g. does it intend to be simply at the one extreme a passive exporter, or at the other extreme, a global marketing company.

2   *Foreign market selection* where the company must decide which markets it wishes to enter. The company must determine not only which specific markets offer the best opportunities, but how many markets it wishes and is able to enter.

3   *The method of market entry* involves determining how the foreign market is to be developed.

4   *Marketing mix strategies*: As in domestic markets, this involves decisions regarding the 4Ps and for service products, the 7Ps of the marketing mix.

5   *Marketing organization and implementation for developing international markets*: Here the company must decide factors such as organizational systems and procedures including its orientation towards international markets.

These are the key decision areas which we now consider in more detail. In addition to these five key areas, as in purely domestic markets, these decisions need to be based on a careful appraisal of markets including: market size, customer needs and competitors. In short, they need to be based on accurate and up-to-date marketing research and information. We therefore also consider a sixth key area, namely the process of *planning and collecting marketing information for international marketing decisions*.

THE EXTENT OF INVOLVEMENT AND COMMITMENT TO INTERNATIONAL MARKETS

We have discussed the notion of different levels of involvement and commitment to international markets. It was suggested that although this is often the result of a process of evolution, in many companies it is a well planned, systematic and considered decision area and indeed the first one in planning international marketing strategies.

Many factors influence and determine the extent to which a company wishes to become involved and committed to international markets. It is therefore not possible to be specific about what constitutes an appropriate degree of involvement as it varies from company to company and even within a company. A company should decide in a rational manner the extent of its current and planned future involvement and commitment to international markets, and where this commitment is planned to increase over time, this should be done in a systematic and ordered manner. Amongst factors that will affect these decisions are:

- situation in domestic market regarding sales and profits;
- opportunities afforded through international expansion;
- corporate objectives and plans;
- company resources and skills;
- attitudes towards risk;
- outside influences e.g. government incentives and changes in trading blocks.

What is most important is that international marketing plans should be developed from, and be consistent with overall corporate objectives and plans.

Foreign market selection

Having determined how committed and involved a company is to be to international markets, the company must then select specific foreign markets it intends to target. In many ways this is an issue of market segmentation and targeting which were considered in Chapter 3. Overall, it is a question of matching company strengths and resources against potential market opportunities after considering aspects such as competition, market size and growth. Of particular importance, especially for inexperienced international marketing companies, is the need to resist the temptation to attack too many markets, thereby spreading effort and resources too thinly to be successful. Often, initial efforts should be directed at a single market and this can be later extended to other markets.

Market selection can be based on a number of criteria:

1 *Market potential*: e.g. market size and trends, location of competition and their marketing mixes, customer profiles, needs and wants and channels of distribution.
2 *Market similarity*: often a company will select markets which are similar to their own domestic markets. 'Psychological' proximity is often more important than geographical proximity in international markets. While it is understandable that companies would prefer markets similar to their own domestic markets in which they have experience, there is a danger that a company may be tempted to take too much for granted and ignore subtle but critical environmental differences.
3 *Accessibility*: encompasses both geographical distance and logistics, but also for example, political distance which involves legal and technical import controls, political constraints on business and exchange controls.

The selection of which markets to enter, and how many (i.e. coverage) is a crucial strategic decision. Overall we are looking for those markets which offer the greatest potential for the company to achieve its overall objectives for its international markets.

METHODS OF MARKET ENTRY

There are a number of ways in which a company can become involved in foreign markets depending on its level of commitment and involvement. Related to this, and having decided this degree of involvement and commitment, and determined which foreign markets are to be targeted, the company must determine how it will most appropriately enter these markets. There are two broad alternative methods as shown in Table 16.2. Each of these methods of entry has its own advantages and disadvantages and must be assessed against a number of criteria. Examples of criteria which may be used to assess the alternative methods of entry are:

Company-specific factors
- corporate goals;
- size of company, resources.

General factors
- number of markets;
- penetration within markets;
- competition.

Political factors
- government restrictions/incentives;
- political risk, stability.

TABLE 16.2 Alternative methods of entry

A. Home based production

Indirect export	Direct export
Trading company	Overseas agents
Export management company	Overseas distributor
Piggy-back operation	Overseas marketing subsidiary

B. Foreign production sources

Assembly
Contract manufacturer
Licensing
Joint venture
100% ownership

Control

- more direct involvement affords greater control.

Incremental costs/investment requirements

- marketing outlay varies directly with method of entry as do investment requirements.

Profit and sales potential

- long-term sales and profit potential associated with each method of entry need to be considered.

Administrative requirements

- documentation, red tape, management and legal time.

Personnel requirements

- the more direct the method of entry, the greater the skills required.

Risk

- political as well as commercial.

Flexibility

- an optimal choice at one point in time may change over time and long-term involvement may require initial flexibility.

THE MARKETING MIX STRATEGIES TO BE USED

Although there are differences in detail, management of the marketing mix elements in international marketing involves the same 'ingredients', i.e. the basic 4Ps or 7Ps in the case of services, and the same general principles for their management as in domestic markets. There are some differences, for example, the 'place' element of the marketing mix for international markets is more likely to include more specialized intermediaries in the channels of distribution such as agents or overseas distributors. Similarly, logistics, because of sheer distance, is likely to be more complex to plan. In the area of pricing, the marketing manager has to consider exchange rates when quoting prices and matters such as currency regulations and provision for export credit guarantees. Nonetheless, despite these and other added considerations and complexities when marketing abroad, as already mentioned the basic concepts and techniques for managing the marketing mix remain the same. However, there is one major aspect of managing marketing mix elements in international marketing which broadly is not an issue when marketing on a solely domestic basis. This aspect, which is central to managing the marketing mix in international marketing, concerns the extent to which the elements of the marketing mix, and indeed the marketing mix as an overall package, need to be modified or adapted to each of the foreign markets in which a company is involved. On the other hand, it can be applied in a standardized manner across all the markets in which the company operates. This is an issue of 'standardization' and can often be the major issue when considering managing the marketing mix in international markets. We therefore concentrate in our discussion on the management of the international marketing mix on this area.

When a company operates in one or more international markets a decision must be made as to the extent to which it is appropriate and/or possible to use a standardized versus a non-standardized approach to its marketing mix in these markets. Keegan[6] proposed five strategies for international marketing as shown in Table 16.3. Examples of strategies and products and services that fall under each of the above categories are:

1   straight extension e.g. famous cola brands;
2   product adaptation e.g. famous petrol brands using international logos and advertising themes, but adapted in terms of the product being slightly different for different climatic conditions;
3   communications adaptation e.g. bicycles promoted as a leisure item in advanced economies, but as a prime means of transport in less well developed countries;
4   dual adaptation e.g. clothing where fashion might be the principal motivator in some countries, but in others it might be functionality;

TABLE 16.3 Keegan's five strategies for international marketing

Strategy	Promotion	Product
1	Same	Same
2	Same	Different
3	Different	Same
4	Different	Different
5	(Re)invention	

5   product invention or re-invention to meet customer needs at affordable prices a standard item might have to be simplified e.g. a hand-cranked washing machine or sewing machine.

It is appropriate here to use Buzzell's[7] interpretation to define the meaning of standardization and non-standardization in international markets:

> In a literal sense, multinational standardization would mean the offering of identical product lines, at identical prices, through identical distribution systems, supported by identical promotional programmes, in several different countries. At the other extreme, completely and 'localized' marketing strategies would contain no common elements whosoever.

It is not always an either/or decision to standardize or not. Very often it is a question of deciding the degree of standardization for the mix as a whole and for each of the individual elements of the mix in particular.

On the one hand supporters of standardization argue that for any given product consumers' interests everywhere are basically the same and therefore standardization is possible. Increasingly the world is becoming a global marketplace where, mainly because of improvements in communication and transportation, there has been a trend towards a more homogeneous world market. The marketing manager must determine the appropriate level of standardization given the particular circumstances and the nature of the markets for his or her company. The potential benefits of standardization are:

1   *Cost savings*: With standardization a company can achieve larger production runs, spread the cost of marketing and research and development and thus reduce total unit costs.
2   *A uniform global image*: Standardization enables the development of a uniform image throughout the world, a consistency in product design, brand name and packaging, in sales and customer service and generally in the image projected to customers which can become a powerful competitive weapon.
3   *Improved planning and control*: A strategy of global standardization helps facilitate improved planning and control within a company. If all major decisions are made at company headquarters and implemented throughout all worldwide divisions and subsidiaries there is less potential for conflicting policies being pursued.

Despite the potential advantages to be gained from a standardized marketing mix, there are several factors which render this strategy less suitable and on occasions may make it impossible to standardize certain elements of the mix. For example, there may be legal restrictions which prevent standardizing elements of the marketing mix. Similarly, geographical or climatic conditions may prevent standardization. Economic factors, such as standards of living and disposable income may make it less effective to standardize marketing mix elements. Cultural factors may make standardization difficult.

The extent of standardization can only be determined for each particular company at a particular point in time in its overall strategic planning, but it is one of the key decisions regarding the management of the marketing mix elements in international marketing. Even a company like

McDonald's, who have standardized as much of their international marketing as possible, have to vary the marketing mix to meet local needs. For example, there is a non-beef product for the Hindu segment of the Indian market. Their New York outlets cater for lunch-time workers whereas in Holland they are geared up to family groups. In parts of the Far East they cater for the needs of the teenage market, and in the UK they are strongly positioned in the children's birthday party segment.

MARKETING ORGANIZATION AND IMPLEMENTATION FOR DEVELOPING INTERNATIONAL MARKETS

The final element in the strategic management of international marketing is the important area of organization and implementation of international marketing programmes. A highly centralized structure is likely to develop a more standardized approach. A more decentralized structure is likely to lead to less standardization. Majaro[8] has identified three alternative types of organizational structure for international marketing:

1 The **'Macropyramid' structure** – This type of structure is characterized by a strong central 'nerve centre'. All strategic planning is centralized and subsidiaries operate primarily at the management and operational levels. Marketing effort is directed towards a maximum standardization of its mix with strong control procedures from the centre and centralized determination of policy.

   This approach obviously encourages standardization, but may be characterized by a degree of inflexibility and a lack of empathy and sensitivity for dealing effectively with local and national business. Local managers may feel hindered by having to operate within rigid standards of performance.

2 The **'Umbrella' structure** – Here, the nerve centre lays down a broad set of objectives in terms of profits, growth and return on investment, but local management has freedom to interpret these objectives and adapt them to local needs and conditions. This organizational structure is based on the recognition that markets and countries differ and that a degree of local independence and freedom of action is more effective than totally centralized control and standardization.

   Although the Umbrella organization is responsive to local needs, it may give rise to increased costs through the need for more adaptations to the elements of the marketing mix and can lead to over-fragmentation.

3 The **'Interconglomerate' structure** – In this type of organization central control and planning is exercised almost exclusively with regard to financial matters. Funds are manipulated on a transnational basis with a view to maximizing returns from factors such as exchange disparities. There is strong communication between the centre and subsidiaries, but only as regards financial planning and control and marketing tends to be non-standardized.

Many factors will affect choice of appropriate structures for implementing international marketing programmes such as: company size, number of markets and their geographical spread, management attitudes and culture. However, one of the most important determinants of organization, and indeed the overall approach to developing and implementing strategic international marketing plans, is the level of involvement and commitment to international markets. You will recall that Wind *et al.*[9] suggested that the company that is totally committed to and involved in international marketing, i.e. the global marketer, will tend to have what they term a 'geocentric' approach to its marketing. This is in fact part of these authors' EPRG schema.

The authors contend that firms can be classified as having an ethnocentric, polycentric, regio-centric or geocentric orientation (EPRG) according to the level of involvement and commitment to international markets by the organization. The **ethnocentric orientation** is one that is essentially characterized by a company concentrating primarily on its home markets i.e. with little or no commitment to international markets. The **polycentric orientation** company organizes its international marketing around each host country and has little central control and standardization. The **regio-centric orientation** company, as the term implies, organizes its marketing strategies and systems around specific regions, often geographical, but often political or economic, such as the European Union. As we have seen, the geocentric company looks at the world and its markets in a global context. Such a **geocentric orientation** global marketing strategy will extend to have more standardized global marketing programmes. Even the global marketer needs to be sensitive to different environments.

INTERNATIONAL MARKETING RESEARCH AND INFORMATION SYSTEMS

As with all marketing plans, international marketing decisions must be based on accurate and up-to-date information and intelligence. The approaches to marketing research and information systems are the same internationally as domestically. However, at an international level market research and information gathering are more complex, have wider dimensions and are generally more difficult to plan and control. Some of the operational problems of conducting international marketing research are caused by differences in language and literacy, different cultural values and unreliable or unobtainable secondary data.

Information requirements for international marketing depend upon the decisions to be taken on the basis of that information, but each of the elements of international marketing strategy outlined here will require marketing research and intelligence. Examples of the information required for some of the key decision areas in developing international marketing plans are illustrated in Table 16.4.

A systematic approach to marketing research and information gathering activities is even more important when conducting an international marketing research programme. Problem definition, and the design of the research brief, need to be done as precisely as possible so there is less room for misinterpretation. In developing the research plan, the timing and scheduling of events needs thorough planning to enable data to be collected, analysed, interpreted and reported upon in a common language and in the most efficient manner. Specification of the analysis and method of interpretation must be standardized to enable international comparisons and a meaningful report to be produced. Obtaining information on international markets can be done through secondary information supplied by governments, Chambers of Commerce, banks, and organizations like the United Nations. The availability of such secondary data differs by country, but major developed economies have substantial amounts of secondary information available for marketing research.

TABLE 16.4 Information requirements for key international marketing decisions

Marketing decision	Information/Intelligence needed
1 Degree of involvement/commitment in international marketing	Assessment of global market demand and firm's potential share in view of local and international competition and compared to domestic opportunities.
2 Market selection	A ranking of potential markets based on e.g. market size and growth, political, cultural and economic factors and extent of local competition.
3 Market entry method	Size of market, trade barriers, transport costs, intermediary availability, local competition, government requirements and political stability.
4 Marketing mix strategies	For each market: buyer behaviour, competitive practice, distributors and channels, promotional media and practice, economic factors.

SUMMARY

Many of the principles and practices of marketing management that are used in purely domestic marketing apply when marketing across international boundaries. However, there are some additional considerations and decision areas when marketing internationally and such considerations are key ones when making decisions in areas of planning international marketing operations.

KEY TERMS

Absolute advantage	486	High and low content culture	492
Casual exporting	488	Cultural sensitivity	493
Active exporting	488	Macropyramid structure	499
Committed international marketing	488	Umbrella structure	499
		Interconglomerate structure	499
International company	489	Ethnocentric orientation	500
Multinational company (MNC)	489	Polycentric orientation	500
		Regio-centric orientation	500
Self reference criterion	492	Geocentric orientation	500

CASE STUDY

Fashionista Mode

Tina Stead is pondering a major decision for her UK-based company, Fashionista Mode. Twelve months ago, Tina received an unsolicited enquiry from a customer in France. From what was essentially a tentative enquiry regarding simply the possibility of supplying some of the company's products to this customer, this export customer now accounts for some 12 per cent of the company's total sales. Quite simply, this largely passive exporting activity has become very important to Tina's company.

On the basis of this success Tina has to decide whether or not to become more actively involved in other export markets. However, apart from the French market, the company has little or no experience of international marketing and markets. Partly due to feedback from her large French customer, Tina is sure that there is more potential for the firm to develop its international operations.

She is therefore actively researching other markets in Europe both within and outside European Union countries.

At this stage, she wants to assess which markets to target for future international expansion. She also has to decide the degree of commitment she is prepared to make on behalf of the company to international marketing. She is also aware that once she commits beyond the passive exporting stage she will have to consider appropriate methods of market entry for the countries she selects as the next target markets. Finally, she will have to consider the marketing mix strategies to be used, and in particular the degree of standardization with regard to the marketing mix.

With little experience in these areas, Tina has sought the advice of an external consultant in international marketing. She is awaiting an initial outline report from the consultant summarising the main considerations in making the decisions she is currently pondering.

CASE STUDY QUESTION

Prepare the summary report for Tina.

REFERENCES

1 Wells, L.T. (1968), 'A product lifecycle for international trade', *Journal of Marketing*, 32: 1–6.
2 Lancaster, G.A. and Wesenlund, I. (1984), 'A product life cycle theory for international trade: an empirical investigation', *European Journal of Marketing*, 18(6/7): 72–89.
3 Wind, Y., Douglas, S.P. and Perlmutter, H.V. (1973), 'Guidelines for developing international marketing strategy', *Journal of Marketing*, April: 14–23.
4 Lascu, D. (1996), 'International marketing planning and practice', *Journal of Global Marketing*, 9(3).
5 Chee, H. and Harris, R. (1998), 'Global marketing strategies', *Financial Times*, London: 144–5.
6 Keegan, W.J. (2002), *Global Marketing Management*, 7th edn, Englewood Cliffs, NJ: Prentice Hall.
7 Buzzell, R.D. (2000), *International Marketing*, 6th edn, Englewood Cliffs, NJ: Prentice Hall.
8 Majaro, S. (1997), *International Marketing: A Strategic Approach to World Markets*, Oxford: Butterworth Heinemann.
9 Wind, Y. *et al.*, op. cit. (3).

Chapter 17

Services marketing and not-for-profit marketing

LEARNING OBJECTIVES

By the end of this chapter you will:

■ appreciate the nature and scope of services marketing
■ be aware of special issues to which the marketing of service products gives rise
■ understand the practical applications of the marketing mix in not-for-profit organizations

INTRODUCTION

Several times we have touched on what are probably two of the most significant developments to affect marketing managers in recent years. The first is the continued growth in importance of service industries with an attendant rise in services marketing, while the second is the shift towards a relationship approach to marketing. Each of these developments has had major implications for marketing theory and practice.

In this chapter we expand on the nature and meaning of services marketing, as customer relationship marketing has already been covered in Chapter 9.

SERVICES MARKETING

In Chapter 9 we mentioned the growth of service industries, pointing out that in some economies, service sectors now predominate. In the future, more and more developed economies will move towards a preponderance of service industries and products and many future marketing managers will be involved in service marketing. As noted in Chapter 9, although many of the basic principles involved in marketing service products are the same as for their physical product counterparts, service products have a number of characteristics which set them aside from physical products and give rise to additional issues with regard to their marketing and in particular to the elements of the marketing mix. We now discuss some of these differences and their implications in more detail, and first consider what is meant by a service product.

SERVICE PRODUCT CHARACTERISTICS: INTANGIBILITY AND NON-OWNERSHIP

The term **'service product'** encompasses a myriad of different types of services. The definition proposed by Berry[1] is still one of the most effective in capturing the key distinguishing characteristics of different types of service products: 'A service is an intangible product involving a deed, a performance, or an effort that cannot be physically possessed.'

There is little doubt that both intangibility and non-ownership are key characteristics of service products, although other characteristics are important. Staying with Berry's definition, if we can see that the product is essentially intangible then the customer does not take physical possession. There are, however, tangible elements to the product of a flight: the aeroplane itself, the seat we occupy, the meals and drinks we are served are tangible aspects of the air travel product. In addition, we do take 'physical possession' of certain elements of the product, e.g. the seat, the meals and drinks. However, the core benefit that the customer is purchasing is essentially intangible.

This example shows that most products have a mixture of both tangible and intangible components. If we think of tangibility as a continuum, service products are those where the intangible element is predominant. This idea of a continuum of intangibility is frequently encountered in texts on services marketing and is a useful way of evaluating whether the customer is buying what is essentially a tangible product or a service. An example for business products/services adapted from Shostack[2] is shown in Figure 17.1. A list of examples of where the intangible element is dominant, and hence examples of what we define as service products, includes:

- fast food;
- hotels;
- holidays;
- travel;
- insurance and banking;
- education;
- health care;
- public transport;
- legal/financial advice;
- consultancy;
- personal health and beauty.

There are numerous different service products. An important fact to note is that although they are usually relatively easy for the marketer to classify as being service or non-service products, ultimately it is the customer who decides whether or not a product or service is being purchased, and hence marketed, according to the relative importance attached to the tangible versus intangible elements.

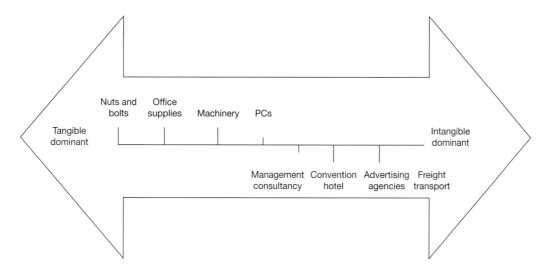

FIGURE 17.1 A continuum of tangibility and intangibility: business/product service classifications

Intangibility is certainly one of the key characteristics that distinguishes service products from tangible products. What about the notion of 'non-possession' referred to in Berry's definition, and what are the other distinguishing or special characteristics of service products? These other suggested special characteristics of service products, including the aspect of non-possession, or non-ownership, are now outlined. As with the characteristic of tangibility these so-called 'special characteristics' are a matter of degree and best thought of as a continuum. For each of these characteristics we have outlined the marketing implications and issues to which these characteristics give rise.

Non-ownership

As explained in the air travel example a characteristic of many services is that they are used rather than owned. Another example is a holiday where we simply use the services of the holiday provider as opposed to taking physical possession of a product.

Non-ownership can sometimes make it difficult for a customer to assess and appreciate the advantages of purchasing the service. The marketer therefore needs to pay particular attention in emphasizing benefits of non-ownership, such as no long-term commitment and inexpensive maintenance in promotional programmes.

At one time few private car buyers in the UK would have considered leasing a car on a long-term basis as opposed to purchasing one either outright or on credit. However, partly as a way to help customers finance the use of a car, over the last ten years the majority of the major car manufacturers have introduced what effectively are leasing schemes albeit often under other names. An increasing number of customers not only find this a more convenient way of covering the costs of having access to a new car, but also find there are many benefits to not actually taking ownership of a vehicle.

INSEPARABILITY

Unlike the majority of physical products, services are often consumed at the same point and at the same time as they are produced e.g. a visit to the hairdresser's where the hairdresser 'produces' the service while we are at the salon: production and consumption are simultaneous and producer and consumer are inseparable. In such a situation the person providing the service becomes important and in effect becomes the service product. This inseparability of consumer and service provider means that both provider and customer affect the 'quality' of the relationship.

Inseparability places emphasis on the selection and training of the service provider's personnel. The service provider must also be careful to examine the circumstances and processes that can affect the quality of the relationship between provider and consumer, especially in the hairdresser example as it is a service that the provider wants the customer to return to on a regular basis.

PERISHABILITY

Generally, service products cannot be stored. For example, if a restaurant has empty tables, if a hotel room is not booked, or if an aeroplane flies with empty seats, then these services i.e. the tables, rooms or seats that the provider was hoping to fill cannot be 'stored' and sold later. The revenue that would otherwise have accrued has been lost for ever. The fact that service products have this high degree of perishability makes effective matching of demand and supply of service products particularly important. This is especially relevant with service products where there are time periods of excess demand and supply. The marketer therefore needs to manage the balance between demand and supply and may adopt devices such as differential pricing, the development of complementary services, effective pre-booking systems and the use of part-time staff to facilitate effective matching of demand and supply.

VARIABILITY

Because service products have high 'people' content i.e. a significant human element in their provision, the quality of the service product is potentially more variable than with a physical product. What the service provider must seek to minimize is customers experiencing poor service as a result of people variability. Staff selection and training become very important, as does customer care.

We have also indicated some of the implications for the marketer associated with service characteristics. A major implication of these characteristics is the notion of an extended marketing mix for service products, which was introduced in Chapter 9 and to which we now return.

THE MARKETING MIX FOR SERVICES

Characteristics of service products mean they must be marketed in a different way from other products. The three additional 'Ps' were introduced in Chapter 4 as 'People', 'Process' and 'Physical Evidence'. We now expand these elements.

People

The characteristics of inseparability and variability associated with service products in particular mean that people are an extremely important element of the marketing mix in services marketing. The nature of services means that their production and consumption often must take place at the same time and in the same place, often on the supplier's premises. This is the characteristic of 'inseparability'. This almost inevitably means that service providers' personnel and the customer come into direct contact during the provision and consumption of the service. It means that the service 'product' is potentially more variable than in physical product marketing. With a physical product, what the customer gets and experiences can be much more tightly planned and controlled than in services marketing. In services marketing, the product is affected by the people element of the service provider and is potentially much more variable. For example, in dealing with customers, some of the service provider's staff might be feeling unwell, or have family problems, or simply be feeling argumentative and might not be attentive to customer needs on a particular day.

In services marketing, the customer participates in and potentially adds to or subtracts from the process of value creation. This adds to the potential for variability in the service product. For example if a customer arrives late at a restaurant for a pre-booked reservation this may end up detracting from the customer experience because the table originally booked is no longer available and the customer has to be allocated another less satisfactory one at which to eat their meal. Similarly, using the same example, a restaurant customer may detract from the overall service experience because they have had a bad day at the office and turn up determined to take this out on the restaurant by being rude to staff. Person-to-person contact with provider and customer in services marketing means that the 'people' element of the exchange process becomes very important and is a key part of customer experience and levels of satisfaction or dissatisfaction with the service provider. In turn, this means the services marketer must pay particular attention to ensuring that the people element is planned and managed as an integral part of the marketing process. There are a number of key implications of this importance of the people element in services marketing:

Selection and training of customer contact employees

Effective selection and training of all types of staff is important to all marketing, but the interactive nature of service exchanges means that careful selection and training of staff who come into direct contact with customers is particularly important and entails a number of special considerations not encountered when considering the training of staff who do not have this direct contact with customers. Any staff customers come into contact with during the service provision process form an important part of customer perceptions and evaluation of the service experience and hence the perception and evaluation of the service provider itself.

With regard to the selection of such staff, the services marketer must ensure that as part of the selection process, care is taken to evaluate the extent to which customer contact employees have the necessary skills, characteristics and attitudes to interact with customers effectively. For example, service employees must be able to relate to, and empathise with, customers effectively. Aggressive or abrasive personalities are unlikely to function effectively in customer-facing functions. Service marketer personnel must want to deliver good service, be empathetic and above all be interested in, and open to, other people.

If selection is one part of the effective management of the people element in services marketing, another is training and development. Both new and existing services marketing personnel need to be effectively trained to perform their customer-facing functions. For example, staff should be trained in how to interact with customers. All customers are potentially different so dealing with them can be difficult. Services marketing staff need, for example, to learn how to identify and assess individual customer requirements. They also need to be able to deal with sometimes angry or rude customers. They also need to be trained in company policies and procedures with respect to dealing with customers and the required levels of customer service and care. In services marketing in particular, it is vital that staff should be aware of the levels of customer service they are expected to meet. When staff are not fully trained, or are inadequately informed of these required levels of service, they may fail to deliver required service levels. Local improvisation will cause inconsistencies, and variations in the quality of service delivered to customers.

Compared to non-services marketing, services marketing staff need to have effective behavioural skills including for example: listening skills, the use of body language, dealing with conflict, and skills in co-operating with customers. In addition, the services marketer must anticipate and train service provision staff in coping with the variability of service products due to customer involvement and the co-creation of customer value

Overall, the inseparability of service products puts a premium on 'interaction' skills on the part of services marketing personnel. This is because perceived service quality and overall levels of customer satisfaction depend not only on the technical quality of the service delivery, e.g. quality of the equipment in a fitness centre, but also on the quality of the service delivery. In the case of a fitness centre, this would include the care and concern of the fitness training staff. Services marketers often refer to these interactions between customers and service provider staff as 'moments of truth'.

Leadership and motivation

In addition to selection and training, two more important areas of managing the people element in services marketing are leadership and motivation.

With regard to leadership, effective management of the people element of the services marketing mix needs to originate from, and be supported by, top echelons of management in the organization. In effect, they should lead the way for all levels of customer service staff in the organization and should lead by example. One practical way of doing this is by creating a culture of commitment to customer service in the organization. For example, expected standards of customer service should be enshrined in company mission and value statements which in turn should be translated into corporate policies, objectives, strategies and standards.

With regard to motivation, services marketing staff need to be motivated to provide desired levels of customer service. All too often there is little or no incentive for staff to provide good customer service. The services marketer must determine required levels of customer service, but also ensure that staff are encouraged, and preferably rewarded, for achieving these. Often, services marketing staff may perceive that the organization rewards other, perhaps short-term, goals and results, such as for example meeting a sales target, rather than rewarding the provision of a good customer service experience.

Another aspect of encouraging staff to take a more positive and proactive approach to improving the service product is allowing them more discretion to use their initiative and judgement in dealing with customers and especially customer complaints. For example, staff can be empowered to deal with minor customer complaints as they occur rather than having to refer them to a senior manager or head office before action is taken. Many companies encourage this by allowing their front-line personnel to refund customers where necessary or provide additional services.

The characteristics of inseparability and variability associated with service products in particular mean that the service provider's staff, i.e. people, are an extremely important element of the marketing mix for services. As already indicated, this means that the selection and training of service staff is an important part of the overall marketing effort of the service provider, but in addition it is important that service staff interact positively with customers and are adequately motivated and rewarded. In particular front-line employees who have direct contact with customers should exhibit enthusiastic, positive and caring attitudes.

Many of the fast-food retailers such as Pizza Express and McDonald's empower their restaurant staff to deal immediately with customers' complaints. For example, if a customer is unhappy about the quality or even quantity of a meal, front-line staff have the discretion to offer either a full refund, a replacement meal or additional portions.

Internal marketing

The development of a marketing culture and, in particular, the training and motivation of all the individuals in an organization to achieve this is termed internal marketing. The importance and value of internal marketing in services marketing in particular has increasingly been recognized by organizations. All employees and not just those with a direct contact with customers need to be committed to delivering customer satisfaction. In turn, achieving this commitment requires senior management to communicate the need for all employees to adopt a customer orientation. Internal marketing starts by identifying how customer orientation relates to the needs of all employees in an organization and how non-marketing employees can contribute to providing customer satisfaction. At its most basic, by helping meet customer needs an employee derives the benefit of helping the company to stay in business. Internal marketing goes further than this by convincing service company employees that by helping generate customer satisfaction, job satisfaction and motivation can be improved. Another facet of internal marketing is the use of the tools of marketing within the organization such as segmentation and targeting. For example internal marketing recognize that different employee groups or functional areas of the business will have different needs and requirements, so when marketing internally, these should be identified. In addition, internal marketing is achieved through the application of an internal 'marketing mix' including, for example, the use of staff training; the provision of systems and technology to help employees provide customer satisfaction through their work activities; linking reward and remuneration structures to customer satisfaction and so on.

Although internal marketing is important for all organizations, for the reasons discussed, it has proved particularly popular in services marketing organizations, for example banks, hotels, and so on, where a wide range of staff are in direct contact with customers and the people element is of paramount important.

Process

In Chapter 9 we indicated that **'process'** relates to how the service is provided. The 'inseparability' and 'intangibility' characteristics of service products are important characteristics underpinning this 'P' of the service marketing mix, but the characteristic of 'variability' also underpins the importance and planning of process. The process element of the services marketing mix relates to procedures for dealing with service customers before, during, and after the process of service product consumption.

Elements of process differ according to, for example, the particular service product, the needs and wants of customers and competitor and cost considerations. Process decisions involve determining the processes and procedures to be used in service product delivery, including systems and technologies which will be used to support these.

For example, in a fast-food outlet, process elements of the marketing mix might include:

- ordering systems;
- customer queuing systems;

- food delivery systems;
- food and table clearing systems;
- booking and reservation systems;
- complaints systems.

The process element should be planned and run to ensure consistency in service delivery in line with pre-determined levels of customer service. Again, the reduction of service quality variability is a key objective, but this must be balanced against the flexibility and potential advantage of being responsive to individual customer needs and requirements.

In planning the process elements of service it is important to consider the whole chain of interrelated elements of the service product delivery and these should be planned, managed and controlled as a total integrated system. For example, improvements in the ordering part of the system may lead to problems of production and delivery. Increasingly, technology is being used in designing, administering and controlling the process elements of services marketing.

Microsoft have recently introduced the 'Microsoft Surface', an interactive table top which allows customers in restaurants and cafes to view the products available from the table and the screen incorporated into the table top and then place the order direct with the kitchen.

The services marketer often has to balance the advantages of standardizing the processes of preparing and delivering their products, such as speed of production and lower costs, against the merits of meeting the different tastes and preference of individual customers.

The highly successful sandwich retailer Subway have a standard menu but within this, individual customers can to some extent personalize their sandwich by being able to select from a choice of fillings at the 'production' stage.

The process element of the service mix is a major way of differentiating the service provider from its competition. Successful process systems and services markets are frequently easy to copy which means that services marketers must constantly search for new service process innovations.

Physical evidence

This element of the marketing mix for services includes decisions regarding those marketing tools that pertain to the physical attributes of the service marketer's offer. With non-service product the customer can feel, touch, see and sometimes smell the product in evaluating whether or not it will meet their needs. However, owing to the 'intangiblity' characteristic of many service products, this physical evaluation of the product itself is not possible. Particularly with a new service product or with a customer who has not used the service provider before, the customer will use other physical signals as 'evidence' in evaluating the service provider's offering. For example, say we were new to a town and wanted to register with a dentist, we might use 'evidence' of the appearance and facilities of the dentist's surgery waiting room to decide whether or not the services of the dentist would be likely come up to our expectations. Banks, building societies, hairdressers, airlines, hotels and management consultants are examples of service marketers who make use of the mix elements of physical evidence. Examples of tools in this area of the mix include:

- building facilities: office/shop frontage, reception and waiting areas;
- production facilities/areas;

- staff appearance/uniforms;
- company livery, vehicles and logos.

Primarily because of the intangible nature of services, it can often be difficult for consumers to evaluate service offerings, particularly aspects such as quality and value for money, prior to purchase. In the same way, this intangibility can also make it difficult for the marketer to position new service product offerings. Because of this, the marketer often needs to 'tangibilize' the service offering by managing the 'physical evidence' that accompanies service examples listed above.

Most service marketers are aware of the importance of physical evidence and the use by the potential customer of such evidence to gauge elements like service quality. Many service marketers place great emphasis on the appearance of their employees, often spending large amounts of their marketing budgets on aspects such as staff grooming and uniforms. In addition, the service marketer must pay particular attention to achieving consistency throughout the promotional mix with regard to things like the use of company colours and logos.

Airlines in particular appreciate the importance of physical evidence when it comes to a customer choosing an airline. This is reflected in the attention given to the appearance and demeanour of cabin staff. Airlines insist on certain standards of personal grooming for their cabin staff and require staff to wear uniforms. In this market we also find that the appearance of the staff and the style of uniforms selected are designed to reflect the overall corporate image and positioning the airline wishes to portray to its target customers.

IMPLICATIONS FOR MARKETING OF SERVICE PRODUCTS

Services characteristics mean they must be marketed somewhat differently from other products. Table 17.1 attempts to summarize these implications for marketing. These are some of the major distinguishing or special characteristics of service products together with some of the major additional marketing issues and complexities which they give rise to. We emphasize that most of the other elements of effective marketing management and strategy, e.g. the need for effective segmentation and targeting, adequate market research and information systems, are no different for services than they are for physical products. In addition, both types of marketing are being impacted by the second major development in marketing thought and practice discussed in Chapter 9, namely, the growth of relationship marketing.

Service quality in services marketing: the SERVQUAL model

The importance of adequate levels of service quality, the notions of effective customer care and relationship marketing apply to all marketers and products whether physical or service products and markets. However, some of the special characteristics of service products mean that sometimes what constitutes service quality, the areas that are important in service quality and how to measure and evaluate levels of service quality can be more difficult than for the tangible physical product marketer.

TABLE 17.1 Service characteristics and implications for marketing

Characteristic	Major effect/issues	Marketing implications
Intangibility	Difficult for consumers to evaluate service offerings, e.g. quality. Positioning is difficult to achieve or signal.	'Tangibalize' the service offering by managing the 'physical evidence' that accompanies the service, e.g. staff appearance, buildings/facilities, promotional material.
Inseparability	Direct contact with service provider. Both provider and client affect quality of relationship. Market may be limited by time constraints on provider.	Selection and training of service provider's personnel is essential. Franchise/train other service providers. Develop systems and procedures for increasing customer throughput.
Variability	Difficult to ensure that service quality levels are maintained. Customer may have 'bad' experiences.	Ensure strict quality control. Staff training essential. Develop customer care programmes and systems.
Perishability	Periods of excess demand: periods of excess supply.	Manage demand and supply, e.g. differential pricing; develop complementary services; effective pre-booking systems; use part-time personnel.

For example, with a physical product it is relatively easy to objectively measure its functional performance. With an intangible service product, however, this can be more difficult. Recognizing this, several models have been proposed with regard to the criteria for assessing service quality and the sorts of data which would need to be collected and interpreted in order to make this assessment. One of the most influential of the models in this area is that developed by Parasuraman, Zeithaml and Berry and referred to as the 'SERVQUAL' model.[3]

The main ideas and elements of this model are that it proposes that most customers take five main factors into account when assessing the quality of a service they have received. These five main factors are easily remembered by the initials *RATER* which respectively stand for:

- *Reliability* – the extent to which the service is delivered to the standards expected and promised. In essence it represents the customer getting what they feel they have paid for. Needless to say any shortcomings by the service provider in this respect are likely to be major causes of customer dissatisfaction.
- *Assurance* – the degree of trust and confidence the customer feels that the service provider is competent to supply the service. Mostly this stems from the degree of confidence that the customer has in the service provider's staff. The customer will not be satisfied if he/she does not feel assured about the competence of the service provider.
- *Tangibles* – a key characteristic of service products is their intangibility. Because of this, the services customer often looks to any tangible signs which may be used as indicators of the quality

of the service provision. Remember we have previously referred to this as the 'physical evidence' element of the services marketing mix. For example the customer will assess the premises of the service provider; or perhaps the appearance of the service provider's staff.

- *Empathy* – services customers often have expectations with regard to the extent to which the service provider appears to understand and is concerned about their individual needs and wants. The more the service provider can see things from the customer's point of view the better. We refer to this ability on the part of the service provider as 'empathy'.

- *Responsiveness* – this refers to the willingness and ability of the service provider to meet and adapt to customers needs, For example, a service provider may be willing to deliver outside of normal delivery times, and perhaps may have systems for responding to customer complaints on the same day.

The SERVQUAL model provides a comprehensive framework for identifying what are key criteria from the customer's perspective when evaluating and assessing the quality of services provision. In turn, it suggests the key areas where a service provider has to perform effectively. Finally, and related to these first two aspects, the SERVQUAL model guides the implementation of quality programmes for services marketers together with systems of evaluation and control.

The SERVQUAL model stresses that a company has service quality problems where there is a gap between what consumers expect and what they perceive they receive with regard to services quality. There are possible bases for such gaps and therefore strategies for filling them:

1 *Customer intelligence gaps* – First of all, a gap can exist because a company simply does not understand what customers want, and in particular what represents the key service attributes and levels of performance. They simply do not understand their customers' needs.

2 *Design gaps* – Even if the service marketer understands the service need and requirements of customers, service levels may still be decided which we know do not meet these. This may be because of resource constraints on the part of the service provider or perhaps because the customers desired service levels are deemed to be too costly to provide and hence unprofitable.

3 *Production gaps* – Even if the marketer understands and proposes to meet customers' service needs and requirements the process may simply fail to deliver these. Often such gaps are due to unrealistic targets for service levels and especially where these unrealistic levels are promised to customers so that the customer now expects them. Sometimes, this type of gap stems from lack of resources, training or systems devoted to achieving the standards set.

   When Virgin Trains was first established, Virgin made several promises about the service standards customers could expect from the Virgin Train Service. These related to areas such as punctuality, reliability, cleanliness, safety and so on. As much as anything, some of the problems that Virgin Trains have experienced with regard to customer complaints about the service stem from the initial expectations which these promises encouraged on the part of customers. In some respects, at least in the short term, some of them were probably unachievable. www.manchesteronline.co.uk/news.

4 *Perceptual gaps* – This type of gap stems from the customer simply not recognizing that their service requirements and expectations have in fact been met. For some reason the marketer has failed to persuade or convince the customer about this.

NOT-FOR-PROFIT MARKETING

Marketing is increasingly being used outside the profit making/commercial sectors. A particular growth area for the application of marketing concepts and techniques has been the area of not-for-profit organizations. Before we consider specifically the applications of the marketing tools in such organizations it is useful to consider the background to the application of marketing in these organizations, and whether they really need marketing at all.

Whether such organizations are inside or outside of the mainstream of the public service, they are frequently the subject of criticism for having a top-heavy bureaucratic structure, an apathetic attitude to their customers and poor and wasteful management, characterized by a reluctance to innovate. Such criticisms infer unresponsiveness and lack of communication. These are classic marketing problems, and it is not unreasonable to assume that marketing can contribute to their solution. This view can be supported if we examine some of the marketing issues in what constitutes a large proportion of not-for-profit organizations, namely in the public sector.

Due to the fact that many public services are virtual monopolies and funded by government, it is not possible to draw significant parallels between such systems and the commercial sector, other than to recognize that both have marketing problems. The essential difference is that for many public sector organizations the principle of consumer sovereignty has a reduced significance. For the most part it has not been possible for consumers to exercise the ultimate sanction: the withdrawal of patronage. This is not to say that all public bodies have failed to respond effectively to their consumers. It is, however, true that where such failure has taken place, had the rules of the commercial sector been applicable, the guilty organizations would probably have been forced to change or go out of existence.

Since the period immediately after the Second World War, the UK has witnessed dramatic growth in the number of not-for-profit organizations dedicated to the service of the public. At the outset, the level of altruism and the immediate job in hand were probably such that a conscious marketing effort was not thought necessary. Over time the same trends that have necessitated changes in commercial marketing have also affected the public sector. Changes in lifestyle, levels of affluence and the economy have altered attitudes to institutions which were once considered to be major social benefits. These changes have not been restricted to amenities such as libraries and other public recreational facilities, but have extended to charities, the police force and the health service. It could be argued that the public has little choice but to accept the public services with which they are provided. To accede to such a proposition would, however, be to deny the fundamentals of the marketing concept. While a city library may lose custom because it is not a pleasant place to visit, the only equivalent to such a sanction with respect to more immediately essential services is an unresponsiveness which engenders apathy and eventually hostility. When such a situation occurs, an organization becomes inefficient, not only from an internal viewpoint, but from the viewpoint of consumer satisfaction.

The missing element in organizations that have had experiences as described above is 'communication'. Quite simply, the organization has lost touch with its consumers. During the last decade not-for-profit organizations have begun to adopt a 'marketing orientation' which is designed to remedy this, not only in what is physically being offered, but also in terms of image and customer impressions. Like the business sector, there has been a transitional period during which organizations have moved from a 'selling' to a 'marketing' orientation. The providers of public amenities, for example, have recognized that it is not sufficient merely to offer short-term incentives and promotional campaigns; rather they have come to terms with deciding 'what business they are in'. Libraries or public swimming baths are more than what they seem to be if one considers them as satisfying the 'leisure' needs of the community, rather than providing a lending service or a pool of water in which to swim.

That not-for-profit organizations can have marketing problems has not always been recognized. This recognition is the principal step of readjustment to the changing needs of society and to better serving those needs that have always existed. The next step is to adopt a marketing approach to management. This can be achieved by viewing the not-for-profit organization as the marketer views the firm and its markets.

The principles of marketing are no different for not-for-profit organizations than they are for any commercial enterprise. The concept of the marketing mix has equal application: just as different companies employ a mix that is appropriate to their markets, the optimum marketing mix for public bodies will depend on the type of organization and the market conditions that prevail.

Applying marketing to not-for-profit organizations is made easier by regarding their marketing structures first, as one would regard that of any commercial enterprise. Not-for-profit organizations are made up of the following components:

1   *Production* This may seem unusual at first sight, but it makes sense if one considers production as an input/output system, whatever the 'product' might be. Input may simply involve the generation of ideas or the acquisition of the means to produce a service. However, this should be subject to the same degree of impetus and control that is applied to any production line of physical goods.

2   *Personnel* The labour force is an integral part of the total marketing system; the appointment, training and reward structure should be implemented with this 'total' system in mind.

3   *Purchasing* Just as in business, this should be conducted with cost and the finished product in mind.

4   *Marketing* Marketing is responsible for thinking in terms of the 'product', whether this be for goods or a service. Marketing's role should also concern image, the environment and the optimization of the individual components that make up the organization. A marketing director is an increasingly evident feature of progressive organizations.

5   *Consumers* Whatever the degree of choice that consumers have in their use of an organization, it should be uppermost in the minds of managers that, although customers may not be lost by inefficiency and poor communication (as can be the case for a hospital) these defects imply that the marketing concept is not being successfully implemented. All the factors listed should, therefore, be focused on consumers.

Although there may need to be some modification to their application, most of the central concepts and techniques of marketing discussed in earlier chapters, such as target marketing, market research and forecasting and analysing consumers are equally relevant and useful to the not-for-profit organization. Just as in the profit-oriented organization, the basic aim of not-for-profit organizations is to obtain a desired response from a target market. The desired response may be, for example, a visit to a health centre or increased support for a police force, rather than the exchange of money for products and services, but the principles of marketing remain the same. As regards the application and combination of the marketing mix, in many ways not-for-profit organizations, but more specifically their 'products', are similar to service products. For example, they are often intangible in nature and variability. The additional elements of the marketing mix for services, therefore, come into play together with some of the variations in the application of the conventional four Ps with regard to service products already discussed.

SUMMARY

There are special issues associated with the marketing of service products. The special characteristics of services compared to their physical product counterparts give rise to additional considerations in their marketing. In particular, service marketing requires us to consider an additional '3Ps' in an extended marketing mix to encompass People, Process, and Physical evidence considerations.

Not-for-profit sectors have traditionally tended to be production-oriented. Such organizations are now more publicly accountable as evidenced by the fact that the marketing concept is being increasingly acknowledged in such situations. The view is taken that the application of marketing principles are essential and appropriate in such situations.

KEY TERMS

Service product	504	Physical evidence	511
Process	510		

CASE STUDY

Marine Services Ltd

Don Horne has recently joined Marine Services Ltd, a specialist consultancy company providing technical advice and services to marine exploration companies. Don's background, somewhat unusually in this industry, is entirely in consumer services marketing. The company has employed him for this expertise and experience, believing that the marine exploration industry is lacking in its knowledge and application of up-to-date marketing ideas and techniques being used so successfully in other industries. Marketing in the past in this company has been dominated by people with technical backgrounds and an in-depth knowledge of marine biology, marine engineering and marine exploration.

. . . continued

CASE STUDY ... *continued*

The idea of introducing a marketing specialist to the company came from the managing director of the company who recent attended two marketing seminars. The first of these was on services marketing and although not exclusively concerned with technical and consultancy services, the course had provided what the managing director felt were useful insights into some of the additional considerations in marketing service products, including the notion of an extended marketing mix to include People, Processes and Physical Evidence. The managing director realized that these were just as potentially important in the competitive world of marine exploration as they appeared to be in the fast food and other consumer service industries. Certainly, he felt there was food for thought as to how some of the ideas from these service industries could be applied to the company and its markets.

The second course he attended focused on the concept of relationship marketing. The course leaders had stressed the move towards relationship marketing in many industries and the way that relationship marketing tools and techniques could be used to help build customer loyalty and retain customers.

This was of particular interest to the managing director as current relationships with customers in the industry seemed to be characterized by antagonism and lack of co-operation between the companies in the industry and their customers, including Marine Services Ltd. Again, he felt there was potential to apply some of the ideas about relationship marketing to the company and its markets.

Having appointed Don Horne with the specific job remit to develop and apply service and relationship marketing concepts and techniques to the company and its marketing, the managing director has asked Don as his first task in the company to produce a brief written and verbal report outlining how these concepts and techniques could be of value in the company's future marketing. He has informed Don that he would be presenting this report to a meeting of the company directors and senior managers at the next monthly meeting. He has also warned Don that he could expect some reservations and even antagonism regarding the use of some of the more recent marketing ideas in what is after all a very traditional and conservative company.

CASE STUDY QUESTION

Prepare the outline report that Don will present to the board and senior management.

REFERENCES

1   Berry, L.L. (1980), 'Services marketing is different', *Business Horizons*, May–June: 24–9.
2   Schostack, G.L. (1977), 'Breaking free from product marketing', *Journal of Marketing*, 41(April): 177.
3   Parasuraman, A., Zeithaml, V.A. and Berry, L.L. (1988), 'SERVQUAL: A multiple item scale for measuring customer perceptions of service quality', *Journal of Retailing*, 64(January): 12–24.

Index

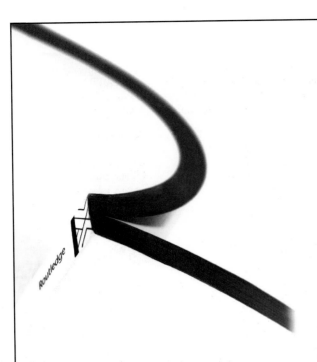